An Introduction to Management Science

Third Edition

An Introduction to Management Science

Quantitative Approaches to Decision Making

David R. Anderson
University of Cincinnati
Dennis J. Sweeney
University of Cincinnati
Thomas A. Williams
Rochester Institute of Technology

West Publishing Company
St Paul   New York   Los Angeles   San Francisco

A study guide has been developed to assist you in mastering concepts presented in this text. The study guide reinforces concepts by presenting them in condensed concise form. Additional illustrations and examples are also included. The study guide is available from your local bookstore under the title, *Study Guide to Accompany An Introduction to Management Science: Quantitative Approaches to Decision Making,* third edition, prepared by John A. Lawrence, Jr. and Barry Alan Pasternack.

COPYRIGHT © 1976, 1979, 1982 by WEST PUBLISHING CO.
50 West Kellogg Boulevard
P.O. Box 3526
St. Paul, Minnesota 55165

Printed in the United States of America

Library of Congress Cataloging in Publication Data

Anderson, David Ray, 1941–
    An introduction to management science.
    Bibliography: p. 690
    Includes index.
    1. Management—Mathematical models.   2. Linear
programming.   3. Operations research.   I. Sweeney,
Dennis J.   II. Williams, Thomas Arthur, 1944–
III. Title
HD30.25.A53   1982   658.4'03   81-16234
ISBN 0-314-63149-6   AACR2
    2nd Reprint—1983

INTL. ED. ISBN 0-314-68188-4

To Our Parents

Contents

Preface

As with the previous editions, the purpose of this text is to provide students, primarily in the fields of administration and economics, with a sound conceptual understanding of the role management science plays in the decision-making process. Specifically, the text is concerned with that part of management science referred to as quantitative approaches to decision making. Emphasis is placed not only on how the quantitative approaches work but also on how they can be applied and interpreted by the decision maker.

We have written this book with the needs of the nonmathematician in mind; it is applications oriented. In each chapter, a problem situation is described in conjunction with the quantitative procedure being introduced. The development of the quantitative technique or model includes applying it to the problem situation in order to generate a solution or recommended decision. We believe that this approach helps to motivate the student by demonstrating not only how the procedure works, but also how it can be applied and how it contributes to the decision-making process.

We have been pleased with the positive response and wide usage of the previous editions of our text. In preparing this third edition, we have been careful to maintain the format and approach of the previous edition while making selected additions and changes designed to enhance the content and readability of the text. The new features in this edition are:

1. To further emphasize the applications of management science, nine cases supplied by practitioners from business and industry have been added at the end of selected chapters. Each case describes an actual company and its current usage of the management science technique introduced in the chapter. Cases appear at the end of the following chapters: Introduction, Linear Programming Applications, Assignment Problem, Integer Linear Programming, PERT/CPM, Inventory Models, Simulation, Waiting Line Models, and Management Science and Decision Support Systems.
2. The material on linear programming has been repackaged so that all topics involving graphical methods are treated in Chapter 2. Chapter 2 now includes a new section on graphical sensitivity analysis as well as a discussion of infeasibility and unboundedness. The discussion of the Simplex method, including sensitivity analysis and duality, is contained in Chapters 3 and 4. Instructors wishing to cover only the graphical method may cover Chapter 2 and then move on to the linear programming applications of Chapter 5.

3. A new section has been added in order to amplify the important role the computer plays in solving linear programming problems. The computer software package discussed is IBM's MPSX/370 system, which is one of the most widely used linear programming packages available today. Whether or not the instructor chooses to use a linear programming computer package as part of the course, this new section (Section 4.6) will give the student an understanding of the valuable information computer packages can provide. The section is written so that instructors choosing to skip treatment of the Simplex method may cover it after Chapter 2.

4. The simulation chapter (Chapter 14) has been substantially revised and now includes simulation applications for both waiting line and inventory systems. The waiting line application is used to introduce the simulation methodology. However, the waiting line example is developed in such a fashion that the instructor can introduce simulation and waiting lines simultaneously without first treating analytical waiting line or queueing models (i.e., it is not necessary to cover the chapter on waiting lines prior to simulation).

5. A new concluding chapter has been written in order to provide an overview of the interaction between management science models and decision support systems.

6. Answers to the even-numbered problems are now included at the back of the text.

We have also refined and modified other sections of the text in order to enhance the readability and pedagogical effectiveness of the material. These changes include new surveys cited in Chapter 1 in order to reflect current usage of the various quantitative techniques and the incorporation of higher inventory costs to reflect inflationary trends. Finally, approximately 100 new and/or revised problems have been included in this edition.

The problems at the end of each chapter have been expanded and continue to be an important part of the book. In addition to reinforcing the material in the chapters, the problems are suggestive of the types of situations in which the methods can be applied. A good number of the examples are actually scaled down versions of problems that have been encountered in practice.

The mathematical prerequisite for this text is a course in college algebra. However, an introductory knowledge of probability and statistics should precede a study of the chapter on decision theory. Such a background would be desirable, but not necessary, for Chapters 9, 13, 14, 15, and 17. Only Chapter 18, which discusses calculus-based solution procedures, requires mathematical skills beyond college algebra and basic probability; this chapter, which we consider optional, requires a knowledge of differential calculus.

Throughout the text we have utilized notation that is generally accepted for the topic being covered. In this regard students that pursue study beyond the level of this text will find the difficulties of reading more advanced material minimized. To assist in further study, we have included a bibliography at the end of the text.

The text has been designed such that the instructor has substantial flexibility in terms of selecting topics to meet specific course needs. While many variations are possible, the following one-quarter and one-semester courses are illustrative of the options available.

Possible Course Outlines

One-Quarter	One-Semester
Introduction (Chapter 1)	Introduction (Chapter 1)
Introduction to Linear Programming and Selected Applications (Chapter 2, Section 4.6 and Chapter 5)	Linear Programming and Selected Applications (Chapters 2–5)
Assignment Problems (Sections 6.1–6.3)	Assignment Problem (Sections 6.1–6.3)
Transportation Problem (Chapter 7)	Transportation Problem (Chapter 7)
PERT/CPM (Chapter 9)	Integer Linear Programming (Sections 8.1–8.3)
Inventory Models (Sections 12.1 and 12.2)	PERT/CPM (Chapter 9)
Computer Simulation (Chapter 14)	Inventory Models (Sections 12.1–12.2)
	Computer Simulation (Chapter 14)
	Waiting Line Models (Chapter 15)

Many other possibilities exist for such a course, dependent upon the time available and the background of the students. However, it is probably not possible to cover all the material in a one-term course, unless some of the topics have been previously studied.

Accompanying the text is a complete package of support materials, including a statement of learning objectives for each chapter, solutions for all problems, and a revised student study guide with self-correcting exercises. The study guide was coauthored by John Lawrence and Barry Pasternack (California State University at Fullerton). In addition, adopters will be provided with a new bank of questions and problems specifically designed for examination purposes. The test bank was prepared by Fabienna Godlewski at the University of Cincinnati. We believe that the applications orientation of the text combined with this package of support materials provides an ideal basis for introducing students to management science.

We would again like to express our appreciation to individuals who made significant contributions to the earlier edition of our text including Stanley A. Brooking (University of Southern Mississippi), John L. Eatman (University of North Carolina at Greensboro), Ronald Ebert (University of Missouri at Columbia), Lawrence P. Ettkin (University of Tennessee at Chattanooga), Jack Goodwin, Raymond Jackson (Southeastern Massachusetts University), Phillip E. Lowery, Richard R. McCready, Patrick McKeown (University of Georgia), Richard E. Rosenthal (University of Tennessee at Knoxville), William Truscott (McMaster University) and Ed Winkofsky (Mead Corporation).

In addition, we would like to express our appreciation to the practitioners from business and industry who provided the application cases for this edition. These individuals are: Jerry T. Ranney and Keith R. Weiss (Marathon Oil), James R. Evans (American League), John Tomlin (Ketron, Inc.), Lee Mairose and Debbie Schoening (Seasongood & Mayer), Walt Fenske (Goodyear Tire &

Rubber Company), Carol Hays (Informatics, Inc.), Bill Griggs and Walter Foody (Champion International), and Richard Murphy (Optimal Decision Systems).

We are also indebted to Norman Baker (University of Cincinnati) for providing suggestions for the revision of the simulation chapter and to our editor, Mary Schiller, and others at West Publishing Company for their editorial counsel and support during the preparation of this text. Finally, we would again like to express our appreciation to Linda Leininger and Phyllis Trosper for their continued typing support.

David R. Anderson
Dennis J. Sweeney
Thomas A. Williams

February 1982

An Introduction to Management Science

Chapter 1

Introduction

Management science is a broad discipline which includes all rational approaches to managerial decision making that are based upon an application of scientific methodology. The management science function considers organizational objectives and resources and, by using a scientific problem-solving approach, attempts to establish long- and/or short-range policies and decisions that are in the best interest of the organization. A management science problem may be as specific as improving the efficiency of a production line or as broad as establishing a long-range corporate strategy involving a combination of financial, marketing, and manufacturing considerations.

Disciplines such as operations research, decision sciences, information sciences, behavioral sciences, and some aspects of systems analysis are often included under the broad heading of management science. While a precise definition of each of these specific disciplines is not necessary for our purposes, it is important to realize that studies, projects, or analyses employing methodology from one or more of the above scientific disciplines could correctly be called a management science activity.

This book is concerned primarily with the portion of management science dealing with quantitative approaches to decision making. In recent years, many new and important quantitative techniques have been developed as aids to the decision-making process. The emphasis of this book is not on the techniques per se, but rather on showing how the techniques can be used to contribute to a better decision-making process. Our approach is to describe decision-making situations in which quantitative techniques have been successfully applied and then show how the appropriate quantitative analysis can be used to help the manager make better decisions.

While a variety of names exist for the body of knowledge and methodology involving quantitative approaches to decision making, one of the most widely known and accepted names is *operations research* (OR). Actually operations research may be more broadly defined to include a multidisciplinary scientific approach to decision making. Under this definition, many use the terms "operations research" and "management science" almost interchangeably. In practice, operations research studies are frequently conducted by an operations research team which might consist of a quantitative specialist, an engineer, an accountant, a behavioral scientist, and an expert from the particular problem area being studied. While the analysis of a problem situation almost always includes some qualitative considerations, significant portions of most operations research studies are based upon quantitative decision-making techniques.

1.1   Dominance of the Problem

A central theme in the management science/operations research (MS/OR) approach to decision making is a problem orientation. Nearly all MS/OR projects begin with the recognition of a problem situation which does not have an obvious solution. Quantitative analysts may then be asked to assist in identifying the "best" decision or solution for the problem. Reasons why a quantitative approach might be used in the decision-making process include the following:

1. The problem is complex, and the manager cannot develop a good solution without the aid of quantitative specialists.
2. The problem is very important (for example, a great deal of money is involved), and the manager desires a thorough analysis before attempting to make a decision.
3. The problem is new, and the manager has no previous experience to draw upon.
4. The problem is repetitive, and the manager saves time and effort by relying upon quantitative procedures to make the routine decision recommendations.

A survey of corporate-level OR activities by Turban[1] identified the following typical problem areas where quantitative techniques have been successfully applied:

1. Distribution systems design (such as transportation networks, plant and warehouse location, etc.);
2. Inventory ordering and stocking decisions;
3. Resource allocation for corporate activities;
4. Capital investment analysis;
5. Portfolio selection;
6. Information systems design;
7. Product mix and production decisions;
8. New product analysis.

Another survey of MS/OR activities by Gaither[2] reported a variety of manufacturing-related applications which have utilized quantitative techniques. The three problem areas most frequently cited were production planning and control, project planning and control, and inventory analysis.

The problem areas mentioned in both the Turban and Gaither surveys by no means comprise a complete list of the applications where managers have found quantitative methodology to be beneficial. However, they do indicate the wide variety of problems in which quantitative procedures have been successfully applied.

1.2 Quantitative Analysis and the Decision-Making Process

The role of quantitative analysis in the managerial decision-making process is perhaps best understood by considering the flowchart in Figure 1.1. Note that the process is initiated by the appearance of a problem. The manager

[1]Turban, E., "A Sample Survey of Operations-Research Activities at the Corporate Level," *Operations Research,* vol. 20, pp. 708–721, 1972.
[2]Gaither, N., "The Adoption of Operations Research Techniques by Manufacturing Organizations," *Decision Sciences,* vol. 6, no. 4, pp. 797–813, 1975.

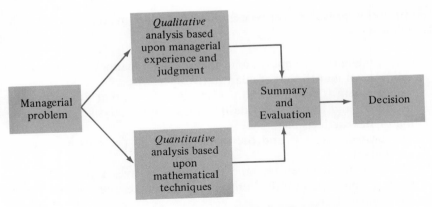

Figure 1.1   The Decision-Making Process

responsible for making a decision or selecting a course of action will probably make an analysis of the problem which includes a statement of the specific goals or objectives, an identification of all constraints, an evaluation of alternative decisions, and a selection of the apparent "best" decision or solution for the problem.

The analysis process employed by the manager may take two basic forms: qualitative and quantitative. The qualitative analysis is based primarily upon the manager's judgment and experience. This type of analysis includes the manager's intuitive "feel" for the problem and is more an art than a science. If the manager has had experience with similar problems or if the problem is relatively simple, heavy emphasis may be placed upon a qualitative analysis and the final decision made accordingly. However, if the manager has had little experience with similar problems or if the decision problem is sufficiently important and complex, then a quantitative analysis of the problem can be a very important consideration in the manager's final decision. In the quantitative approach to the problem, an analyst will concentrate on the quantitative facts or data associated with the problem and develop mathematical expressions that describe the objectives, constraints, and relationships that exist in the problem. Then, by using one or more quantitative techniques, the analyst will provide a decision recommendation based upon the quantitative aspects of the problem.

Both the qualitative and the quantitative analyses of a problem provide important information for the manager or decision maker. In many cases a manager will draw upon both sources and, through a comparison and evaluation of the information, make a final decision.

While skills in the qualitative approach are inherent in the manager and usually increase with experience, the skills of the quantitative approach can be learned only by study of the assumptions and methods of quantitative analysis. A manager can increase decision-making effectiveness by learning more about quantitative methodology and by better understanding its contribution to the decision-making process. The manager who is knowledgeable in quantitative decision-making procedures is in a much better

Table 1.1   Quantitative Techniques Most Frequently Used

Techniques	Frequency of Use (percent)
Statistical analysis*	29
Simulation	25
Linear programming	19
Inventory theory	6
PERT/CPM	6
Dynamic programming	4
Nonlinear programming	3
Queueing	1
Heuristic programming	1
Miscellaneous	6
Total	100

*Includes probability theory, regression analysis, exponential smoothing, statistical sampling, and tests of hypotheses.

position to compare and evaluate the qualitative and quantitative sources of decision recommendations and ultimately combine the two sources in order to make the best possible decision.

The section of Figure 1.1 entitled "Quantitative analysis based upon mathematical techniques" encompasses most of the subject matter of this text. We will consider a managerial problem, introduce the appropriate quantitative methodology, and then develop and evaluate the recommended decision.

There are several important tools, or techniques, that have been found useful in the quantitative analysis phase of the decision-making process. One of your objectives in studying this book should be to develop an understanding of what these techniques are, how they are used, and, most importantly, how they can assist the manager in making better decisions. The most frequently used quantitative techniques as determined by the Turban study are those listed in Table 1.1. A survey by Ledbetter and Cox[3] lends support to the Turban study findings by ranking regression (statistical analysis), linear programming, simulation, network models (PERT/CPM), queueing, dynamic programming, and game theory in order of usage.

The Gaither study of applications in manufacturing firms also supports the high frequency of utilization for statistical analysis, simulation, and linear programming. However, PERT/CPM is identified as the technique most frequently used in the manufacturing firms surveyed. The manufacturing firms also report a higher than average usage of queueing theory, nonlinear programming, and integer programming.

Recently, a survey of OR practitioners in government, industry, and

[3]Ledbetter, W., and J. Cox, "Are OR Techniques Being Used?" *Industrial Engineering,* vol. 9, no. 2, pp. 19–21, 1977.

Table 1.2   Familiarity with and Use of Various Quantitative Techniques by Operations Research Practitioners

Technique	Familiarity Rank	Usage (percent)
Linear programming	1	83.8
Simulation	2	80.3
Network analysis	3	58.1
Queueing theory	4	54.7
Decision trees	5	54.7
Integer programming	6	38.5
Dynamic programming	7	32.5
Nonlinear programming	8	30.7
Markov processes	9	31.6
Replacement analysis	10	38.5
Game theory	11	13.7
Goal programming	12	20.5

academia was conducted by Shannon, Long, and Buckles.[4] The authors of this study asked practitioners to indicate whether or not they were familiar with the various quantitative techniques and whether or not they had actually used the techniques in specific applications. The results of this study are shown in Table 1.2.

Since nearly every student takes a separate course in statistical analysis, we have not included topics from this area in the text. However, we do describe and present applications for the other major quantitative techniques most frequently used in decision making.

Before proceeding with the study of the specific quantitative techniques, let us look more closely at the general steps that are involved in carrying out the quantitative analysis of a managerial problem.

1.3   The Quantitative Analysis Process

We begin our study of quantitative approaches to decision making by considering a five-step procedure: (1) problem definition, (2) model development, (3) data preparation, (4) model solution, and (5) report generation.

Problem Definition

The problem definition step is the most critical phase of the quantitative analysis process. It usually takes imagination, teamwork, and considerable effort to transform a rather general problem description into a well-defined problem that can be approached quantitatively. For example, a broadly

[4]Shannon, R. E., Long, S. S., and B. P. Buckles, "Operations Research Methodologies in Industrial Engineering: A Survey," *AIIE Transactions*, vol. 12, no. 4, pp. 364–367, 1980.

described "excessive inventory" problem must be clearly defined in terms of specific objectives and operating constraints before an analyst can proceed to the next step in the quantitative analysis process.

Model Development

Models are representations of real objects or situations. These representations, or models, can be presented in various forms. For example, a scale model of an airplane is a representation of a real airplane. Similarly, a child's toy truck is a model of a real truck. The model airplane and toy truck are examples of models that are physical replicas of real objects. In modeling terminology, physical replicas are referred to as *iconic* models.

A second classification of models includes those that are physical in form but do not have the same physical appearance as the object being modeled. Such models are referred to as *analog* models. The speedometer of an automobile is an analog model in that the position of the needle on the dial represents the speed of the automobile. A thermometer is an analog model representing temperature.

A third classification of models—the primary type of model we will be studying—includes those that represent the real situation by a system of symbols and mathematical relationships or expressions. Such models are referred to as *mathematical* models and are a critical part of any quantitative approach to decision making. For example, the total profit from the sale of a product can be determined by multiplying the profit per unit by the quantity sold. If we let x represent the number of units sold and P the total profit, then, with a profit of \$10 per unit, the following mathematical model defines the total profit earned by selling x units:

$$P = 10x. \tag{1.1}$$

The purpose, or value, of any model is that it enables us to draw conclusions about the real situation by studying and analyzing the model. For example, an airplane designer might test an iconic model of a new airplane in a wind tunnel in order to learn about the potential flying characteristics of the full-size airplane. Similarly, a mathematical model may be used to draw conclusions about how much profit will be earned if a specified quantity of a particular product is sold. According to the mathematical model of equation (1.1), we would expect to obtain a \$30 profit by selling three units of the product. With both the airplane model and the production examples, an analyst would be able to test and experiment with the model in order to learn about the real situation.

In general, experimenting with models requires less time and is less expensive than experimenting with the real object or situation. Certainly, a model airplane is quicker and less expensive to build and study than the full-size airplane. Similarly, the mathematical model allows a quick identification of profit expectations without requiring the manager to wait and see what the profit is after actually producing and selling x units. In addition, models also have the advantage of reducing the risk associated with the real situation. In particular, bad designs or bad decisions that cause the model airplane to crash or the mathematical model to project a $10,000 loss can be avoided in the real situation.

The accuracy of the conclusions and decisions based on a model are dependent upon how well the model represents the real situation. The more closely the model of the airplane represents the real airplane, the more accurate the conclusions and predictions about the airplane's flight characteristics will be. Similarly, the closer the mathematical model represents the company's true profit-volume relationship, the more accurate the profit projections will be.

Since this text deals with mathematical models, let us look more closely at the mathematical modeling process. When initially considering a managerial problem, we usually find that the problem definition phase leads to a specific objective, such as maximization of profits or minimization of costs, and possibly a set of restrictions or constraints, such as production capacities. The success of the mathematical model and quantitative approach will depend heavily upon how accurately the objective and constraints can be expressed in terms of mathematical equations or relationships.

A mathematical expression that describes the problem's objective is referred to as the *objective function*. For example, the profit equation $P = 10x$ would be an objective function for a firm attempting to maximize profit. A production capacity constraint would be necessary if five hours of labor are required to produce each unit and there are only 40 hours of production time available per week. Let x indicate the number of units produced each week. The production time constraint is given by

$$5x \leq 40. \tag{1.2}$$

The value of $5x$ is the total production time required to produce the x units; the symbol $\leq$ indicates that the production time required must be less than or equal to the 40 hours available.

The question or decision problem is the following: How many units of the product should be scheduled each week in order to maximize profit? A complete mathematical model for this simple production problem is

maximize $\qquad P = 10x \qquad$ objective function

subject to (s.t.)

$$\left. \begin{array}{c} 5x \leq 40 \\ x \geq 0 \end{array} \right\} \quad \text{constraints.}$$

The $x \geq 0$ constraint requires the production quantity x to be greater than or equal to zero, which simply recognizes the fact that it is not possible to manufacture a negative number of units. The optimal solution to this model can be easily calculated and is given by $x = 8$, with an associated profit of $80. This model is an example of a linear programming model. In subsequent chapters we will discuss more complicated mathematical models and learn how to solve them in situations where the answers are not nearly so obvious.

In the above mathematical model the profit per unit ($10), the production time per unit (5 hours), and the production capacity (40 hours) are environmental factors that are not under the control of the manager or decision maker. Such environmental factors, which can affect both the objective function and the constraints, are referred to as the *uncontrollable inputs* to the model. The inputs which are controlled or determined by the decision maker are referred to as the *controllable inputs* to the model. In the above example the production quantity x is the controllable input to the model. The controllable inputs are the decision alternatives specified by the manager and thus are also referred to as the *decision variables* of the model.

Once all controllable and uncontrollable inputs are specified, the objective function and constraints can be evaluated and the output of the model determined. In this sense, the output of the model is simply the projection of what would happen if those particular environmental factors and decisions occurred in the real situation. A flowchart of how controllable and uncontrollable inputs are transformed by the mathematical model into output is shown in Figure 1.2. A similar flowchart showing the specific details of the production model is shown in Figure 1.3.

As stated earlier, the uncontrollable inputs are those which the decision maker cannot influence. The specific controllable and uncontrollable inputs of a model depend upon the particular problem or decision-making situation. In the production problem the number of hours of labor available, 40, was an uncontrollable input. However, if it were possible to hire more employees or use overtime, the number of hours of labor would become a controllable input and therefore a decision variable in the model.

Uncontrollable inputs either can be known exactly or can be uncertain and subject to variation. If all uncontrollable inputs to a model are known and cannot vary, the model is referred to as a *deterministic* model. Corporate income tax rates are not under the influence of the manager and thus constitute an uncontrollable input in many decision models. Since these rates are known and fixed (at least in the short run), a mathematical model with corporate income tax rates as the only uncontrollable input would be a deterministic model. The distinguishing feature of a deterministic model is that the uncontrollable input values are known in advance.

If any of the uncontrollable inputs are uncertain and subject to

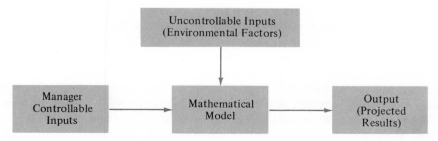

Figure 1.2   Flowchart of the Process of Transforming Model Inputs into Output

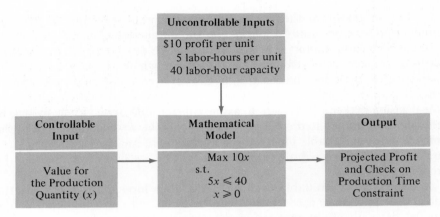

Figure 1.3   Flowchart for the Production Model

variation, the model is referred to as a *stochastic* model. An uncontrollable input to many production planning models is demand for the product. Since future demand may be any of a range of values, a mathematical model which treats demand with uncertainty would be called a stochastic model. In the production model the number of hours of labor required per unit, the total hours available, and the unit profit were all uncontrollable inputs. Since the uncontrollable inputs were all known to take on fixed values, the model was deterministic. If, however, the number of hours of labor required per unit of production could vary from 3 to 6 hours depending upon the quality of the raw material, the model would have been stochastic. The distinguishing feature of a stochastic model is that the value of the output cannot be determined even if the value of the controllable input is known because the specific values of the uncontrollable inputs are unknown. In this respect, stochastic models are often more difficult to analyze.

Data Preparation

The third step in the process of quantitative analysis is the preparation of the data required by the model. Data in this sense refers to the values of the uncontrollable inputs to the model. All uncontrollable inputs or data must be specified before we can analyze the model and select a recommended decision or solution for the problem.

In the production model the values of the uncontrollable inputs or data were $10 per unit for profit, 5 hours per unit for production time, and 40 hours for production capacity. In the development of the model these data values were known and were incorporated into the model as it was being developed. If the model is relatively small and the uncontrollable input values or data required are few, the quantitative analyst will probably combine model development and data preparation into one step. That is, in these situations the data values are inserted as the equations of the mathematical model are developed.

However, in most mathematical modeling situations the data, or uncontrollable input values, are not readily available. In these situations the quantitative analyst may know that the model will need profit per unit, production time, and production capacity data, but the values are not known until the accounting, production, and engineering departments can be consulted. Rather than attempting to collect the required data as the model is being developed, the analyst will usually adopt a general notation for the model development step and then perform a separate data preparation step to obtain the uncontrollable input values required by the model.

Using the general notation of

p = profit per unit

t = production time in hours per unit

c = production capacity in hours,

the model development step of our production model would have resulted in the following general model:

$$\text{max} \quad px$$

$$\text{s.t.}$$

$$tx \leq c$$

$$x \geq 0.$$

Then a separate data preparation step to identify the values for p, t, and c would be necessary in order to complete the model.

Many inexperienced quantitative analysts assume that once the problem has been defined and a general model developed, the problem is essentially solved. These individuals tend to believe that data preparation is a trivial step in the process and can be easily handled by clerical staff. Actually, especially with large-scale models having numerous data input values, this assumption could not be further from the truth. For example, a moderate-size linear programming model with 50 decision variables and 25 constraints will have over 1300 data elements that must be identified in the data preparation step. The time required to prepare these data and the possibility of data collection errors will make the data preparation step a critical part of the quantitative analysis process.

Model Solution

Once the model development and data preparation steps have been completed, we can proceed to the model solution step. In this step the analyst will attempt to identify the values of the decision variables that provide the "best" output for the model. The specific decision-variable value or values providing the "best" output will be referred to as the optimal solution for the model. For the production problem the model solution step involves finding the value of the production quantity decision variable x that maximizes profit while not causing a violation of the production capacity constraint.

One procedure that might be used in the model solution step involves a trial-and-error approach, where the model is used to test and evaluate various decision alternatives. In the production model this would mean testing and evaluating the model under various production quantities or values of x. Referring to Figure 1.3, note that we could input trial values for x and check the corresponding output for projected profit and satisfaction of the production capacity constraint. If a particular decision alternative does not satisfy one or more of the model constraints, the decision alternative is rejected as being *infeasible,* regardless of the objective function value. If all constraints are satisfied, the decision alternative is *feasible* and is a candidate for the "best" solution or recommended decision. Through this trial-and-error process of evaluating selected decision alternatives a decision maker can identify a good—and possibly the best—feasible solution to the problem. This solution would then be the recommended decision for the problem under study.

Table 1.3 shows the results of a trial-and-error approach to solving the production model of Figure 1.3. The recommended decision is a production quantity of 8, since the feasible solution with the highest projected profit occurs at $x = 8$.

While the trial-and-error solution process is often acceptable and can provide valuable information for the manager, it has the drawbacks of not necessarily providing the best solution and of being inefficient in terms of requiring numerous calculations if many decision alternatives are tried. Thus quantitative analysts have developed special solution procedures for many models that are much more efficient than the trial-and-error approach. Throughout this text you will be introduced to solution procedures that are applicable to the specific mathematical models that will be formulated. While some relatively small models or problems can be solved by hand computations, many of the solution procedures will require the use of a computer.

It is important to realize that the model development and model solution steps are not completely separable. While an analyst will want to develop an accurate model or representation of the actual problem situation,

Table 1.3   Trial-and-Error Solution for the Production Model of Figure 1.3.

Decision Alternative (Production Quantity) x	Projected Profit	Total Hours of Production	Feasible Solution? (Capacity = 40)
0	0	0	Yes
2	20	10	Yes
4	40	20	Yes
6	60	30	Yes
8	80	40	Yes
10	100	50	No
12	120	60	No

the analyst also wants to be able to find a solution to the problem. If we approach the model development step by attempting to find the most accurate and realistic mathematical model, we may find the model so large and complex that it is impossible to obtain a solution. In this case a simpler and perhaps more easily understood model with a readily available solution procedure is preferred, even if the recommended solution is only a rough approximation of the best decision. As you learn more about the quantitative solution procedures available, you will have a better idea of the types of mathematical models that can be developed and solved.

After a model solution has been obtained, both the quantitative analyst and the manager will be interested in determining how good the solution really is. While the analyst has undoubtedly taken many precautions to develop a realistic model, often the goodness or accuracy of the model cannot be assessed until model solutions are generated. Model testing and validation are frequently conducted with relatively small "test" problems which have known or at least expected solutions. If the model generates the expected solutions and if other output information appears correct, the go-ahead may be given to the use of the model on the full-scale problem. However, if the model test and validation identifies potential problems or inaccuracies inherent in the model, corrective action such as model modification and/or collection of more accurate input data may be taken. Whatever the corrective action, the model solution will not be used in practice until the model has satisfactorily passed testing and validation.

Report Generation

The final step in the quantitative analysis process is the preparation of managerial reports based upon the model's solution. Referring to Figure 1.1, we see that the solution based upon the quantitative analysis of a problem is one of the inputs that is considered by the manager before making a final decision. Thus it is essential that the results of the model appear in a managerial report which can be easily understood by the decision maker. The report will include the recommended decision and other pertinent information about the model results that may be helpful to the decision maker. Figure 1.4 summarizes the five-step quantitative analysis process.

The generation of a managerial report is the final step in the quantitative analysis process, but the use and implementation of the information contained in the report is a final action that remains to be taken by the manager or decision maker. As discussed in Section 1.2, it is the responsibility of the manager to integrate the quantitative solution with qualitative considerations in order to make the best possible decision. After doing this, the manager must oversee the implementation and followup evaluation of the decision. During the implementation and followup the manager should continue to monitor the contribution of the model. At times this process may lead to requests for model expansion or refinement which will cause the analyst to return to one of the earlier steps of the quantitative analysis process.

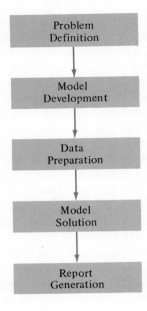

Summary

This is a book about how quantitative approaches to decision problems may be used to help managers make better decisions. The focus of the text is on the decision-making process and on the role of quantitative analysis in that process. We have discussed the problem orientation of this process and in an overview have shown how mathematical models can be used in this type of analysis.

The difference between the model and the situation or managerial problem it represents is an important point. Mathematical models are abstractions of real-world situations and, as such, cannot capture all of the aspects of the real situation. However, if a model can capture the major relevant aspects of the problem and provide a solution recommendation, it can be a valuable aid to decision making.

One of the characteristics of quantitative analysis that will become increasingly apparent as we proceed through the text is the search for a best solution to the problem. In carrying out the quantitative analysis, we shall be attempting to develop procedures for finding the "best" or optimal solutions.

Glossary

1. *Model*—Representation of a real object or situation.
2. *Iconic model*—Physical replica or representation of a real object.

3.   *Analog model*—While physical in form, a model that does not have a physical appearance similar to the real object or situation it represents.

4.   *Mathematical model*—Mathematical symbols and expressions used to represent a real situation.

5.   *Objective function*—A mathematical expression used to identify the objective of a problem.

6.   *Constraints*—Restrictions or limitations imposed on the problem.

7.   *Controllable input*—The decision alternatives or inputs that can be specified by the decision maker.

8.   *Uncontrollable input*—The environmental factors or inputs that cannot be specified by the decision maker.

9.   *Deterministic model*—A model where all uncontrollable inputs are known and cannot vary.

10. *Stochastic model*—A model where at least one uncontrollable input is uncertain and subject to variation.

11. *Feasible solution*—A decision alternative or solution that satisfies all constraints.

12. *Infeasible solution*—A decision alternative or solution that violates one or more constraints.

Problems

1.   Define the terms "management science" and "operations research."
2.   Discuss the different roles played by the qualitative and quantitative approaches to managerial decision making. Why is it important for a manager or decision maker to have a good understanding of both of these approaches to decision making?
3.   A firm has just completed a new plant which will produce over 500 different products using over 50 different production lines and machines. The product scheduling decisions are critical in that sales will be lost if customer demands are not met on time. If no one in the firm has had experience with this production operation and if new production schedules must be generated each week, why should the firm consider a quantitative approach to the production scheduling problem?
4.   List and discuss the five steps of the quantitative approach to decision making.
5.   List and give an example of the three types of model discussed in this chapter.
6.   What are the advantages of analyzing and experimenting with a model of a real object or situation?
7.   Recall the production model from Figure 1.3:

$$\max \quad 10x$$
$$\text{s.t.}$$
$$5x \leq 40$$
$$x \geq 0.$$

Suppose the firm in this example considers a second product which has a unit profit of $5 and requires 2 hours of labor for each unit produced. Use y as the number of units of product 2 produced.

a.   Show the mathematical model when both products are considered simultaneously.

    b.   Identify the controllable and uncontrollable inputs for this model.

    c.   Draw the flowchart of the input-output process for this model (see Figure 1.3).

    d.   What are the optimal solution values of x and y?

8. Is the model developed in Problem 7 a deterministic or a stochastic model? Explain.

9. Suppose we modify the model in Figure 1.3 to obtain the following mathematical model:

$$\max \quad 10x$$

$$\text{s.t.}$$

$$ax \le 40$$

$$x \ge 0,$$

where a is the number of hours of labor required for each unit produced. With $a = 5$ we saw that the optimal solution was $x = 8$. If we have a stochastic model with $a = 3$, $a = 4$, $a = 5$, or $a = 6$ as the possible values for the number of hours required per unit, what is the optimal value for x? What problems does this stochastic model cause?

10. A retail store in Des Moines, Iowa, receives shipments of a particular product from Kansas City and Minneapolis. Let

    x = units of product received from Kansas City in one month,

    y = units of product received from Minneapolis in one month.

    a.   Develop the mathematical model for the total units of product received by the retail store in Des Moines in one month.

    b.   Shipments from Kansas City cost $.20 per unit, and shipments from Minneapolis cost $.25 per unit. Develop an objective function representing the total cost of shipments to Des Moines in one month.

    c.   If the monthly demand at the retail store is 5000 units, develop a constraint that requires 5000 units to be shipped to Des Moines.

    d.   No more than 4000 units can be shipped from Kansas City and no more than 3000 units can be shipped from Minneapolis in a month. Develop constraints to model this situation.

    e.   Of course negative amounts cannot be shipped. Combine the objective function and constraints developed to state a mathematical model for satisfying the demand at the Des Moines retail store at minimum cost.

11. Suppose you are going on a weekend trip to a city that is d miles away. Develop a model that determines your roundtrip gasoline costs. What assumptions or approximations do you have to make in order to treat this model as a deterministic model? Are these assumptions or approximations acceptable to you as a decision maker?

12. For most products higher prices result in a decreased demand while lower product prices result in an increased demand.

    d = annual demand for a product in units,

    p = price per unit.

Assume that a firm accepts the following price-demand relationship as being realistic:

$$d = 800 - 10p,$$

where the price p must be between $20 and $70.

a. How many units can the firm sell at the $20 per-unit price? At the $70-per-unit price?

b. Show the mathematical model for the total revenue (TR), which is the annual demand multiplied by the unit price.

c. Based on other considerations, the firm's management will only consider price alternatives of $30, $40, and $50. Use your model from part b to determine the price alternative that will maximize the total revenue.

d. What are the expected annual demand and total revenue according to your recommended price?

13. Suppose that a manager has a choice between the following two mathematical models of a given situation: (a) a relatively simple model that is a reasonable approximation of the real situation, and (b) a thorough and complex model that is the most accurate mathematical representation of the real situation possible. Why might the model described in (a) be preferred by the manager?

14. The O'Neill Shoe Manufacturing Company will produce a special style shoe if the order size is large enough to provide a reasonable profit. For each special style order the company incurs a fixed cost of $1000 for the production setup. The variable cost is $10 per pair, and each pair sells for $15.

a. Let x indicate the number of pairs of shoes produced. Develop a mathematical model for the total cost of producing x pairs of shoes.

b. Let P indicate the total profit. Develop a mathematical model for the total profit realized from an order for x pairs of shoes.

c. How large must the shoe order be before O'Neill will break even?

15. Financial Analysts, Inc. is an investment firm that manages stock portfolios for a number of clients. A new client has just requested that the firm handle an $80,000 portfolio. As an initial investment strategy the client would like to restrict the portfolio to a mix of the following two stocks:

Stock	Price/ Share	Estimated Annual Return/Share	Maximum Possible Investment
Oil Alaska	$50	$6	$50,000
Southwest Petroleum	$30	$4	$45,000

Let

x = number of shares of Oil Alaska,

y = number of shares of Southwest Petroleum.

a. Develop the objective function, assuming that the client desires to maximize the total annual return.

b. Show the mathematical expression for each of the following three constraints:
   1. Total investment funds available $80,000.
   2. Maximum Oil Alaska investment $50,000.
   3. Maximum Southwest Petroleum investment $45,000.

Note: Adding the $x \geq 0$ and $y \geq 0$ constraints provides a linear programming model for the investment problem. Solution procedures for the model will be discussed in Chapters 2 and 3.

Introduction to Chapter Ending Applications

At the end of nine chapters, interspersed throughout the text, applications writeups prepared by management science professionals are presented. We feel these provide a meaningful extension to the text material. The purpose of these application writeups is to provide the reader with a better appreciation for the types of companies which use management science and the types of problems these companies are able to solve.

Each application writeup begins with a description of the company involved and continues with a discussion of the areas where the company has successfully applied management science. The remainder of the writeup deals with an application that is closely related to the preceding chapter and/or part of the book. An effort has been made to avoid unnecessary technical detail and to focus on the managerial aspects and the value of the results to the company.

Since Chapter 1 is designed to provide an introduction to management science, we have not emphasized any particular solution methodology. Similarly, we have placed the International Paper application at the end of this first chapter because it provides an overview of the many areas in which management science can be used effectively. It is evidence of the impact management science is having at some companies.

Application

International Paper Company*
New York, New York

International Paper Company (IPCo) is the world's largest manufacturer of pulp, paper, and paper products and a major producer of lumber and plywood. The company owns over 8.4 million acres of timberland and has rights over another 11.6 million acres. To generate higher future returns from these renewable assets, the company is consolidating its land base through sales, acquisitions, swaps, and donations and is growing genetically superior trees which produce more wood fiber per acre and which grow more quickly. The company relies heavily on the quantitative techniques of management science and biometrics to evaluate timberland sites and to plan and budget forest prescriptions to be used in planting, managing, harvesting, and regenerating the timberlands.

IPCo operates an extensive manufacturing system consisting of two dozen paper mills and more than 100 plants worldwide. The company is the world's largest supplier of paper and packaging used in books, magazines, newspapers, labels, and cartons. Sales of paper packaging, used principally in food packaging and the distribution of industrial and agricultural products, exceed the next nearest competitor's by several hundred million dollars.

Most of IPCo's products are commodity items, where price is determined by the market. Thus IPCo's relative profitability is chiefly a function of its manufacturing efficiency. The company emphasizes process controls, technological innovation, improvements in operating strategies, research and development in tree genetics and environmental protection, and investments in energy efficiency in order to keep its mills and plants competitive. Management science plays a key role in developing and implementing strategies aimed at increasing manufacturing efficiency and cost containment.

Historical Growth of Management Science

Management science applications started at IPCo in the early 1970s. Typically, the applications were the product of isolated efforts resulting from

*Based in part on the following: "Practical Modeling for Resource Management" by Paul S. Bender, William D. Northup, and Jeremy F. Shapiro, *Harvard Business Review*, March–April 1981. Application Brief: Logistic Modeling System Using IBM's MPSX/370 at International Paper Company, IBM Publication GK20-1341-0, April 1980. International Paper Company Annual Report 1980.

the need of a particular group within the company. In 1977 IPCo organized a Resource Allocation System group, now referred to as the Corporate Operations Research (COR) group. COR was mandated to address and resolve problems of logistics on a company wide basis. To the greatest extent possible, management science tools were to be devised to form an integrated logistics system to optimize the use of company resources and to support the centralized decision-making process at corporate headquarters.

The result of this effort is a modular, hierarchical, and fully integrated logistics manufacturing system (see Figure A-1). This system makes possible the systematic allocation of key company resources such as land, facilities, equipment, and materials. It also provides management with a consistent and systematic way of evaluating the impact of given strategic, tactical, and operational plans on the manufacturing and distribution operation.

Principally the management science applications of the logistics manufacturing system are in the areas of resource allocation, purchasing and inventory, and transportation and distribution management. In the remainder of this presentation, discussion focuses on the management science applications that are performed by the individual modules of the logistics manufacturing system.

MARKETING ORIENTED MANUFACTURING SYSTEM

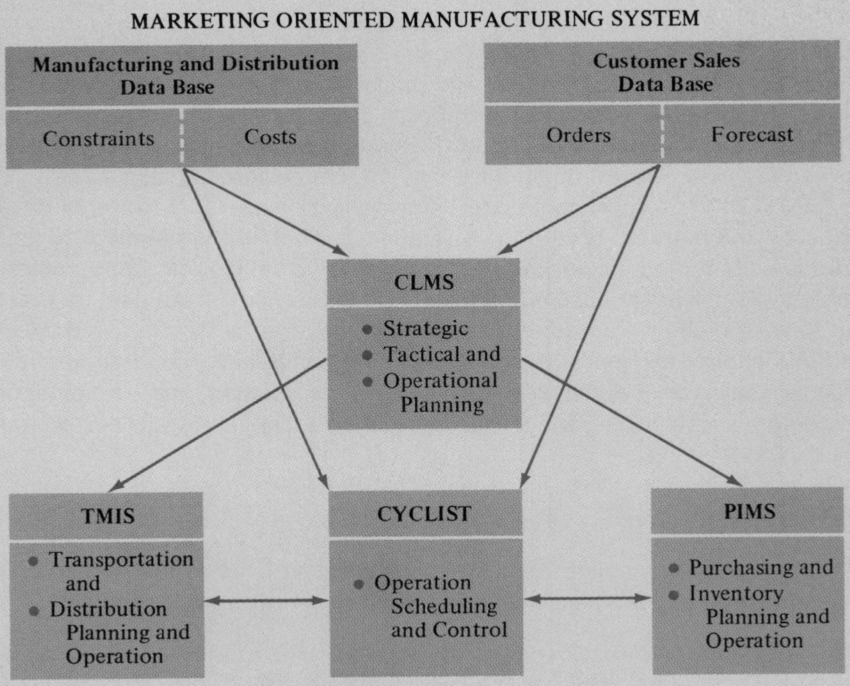

Figure A.1   Logistics Manufacturing System

Corporate Logistics Modeling System

At IPCo the optimal allocation of resources is supported by the corporate logistic modeling system (CLMS). This system is based on a generalized network modeling capability that can be applied to the flow of raw materials from company woodlands and suppliers through woodyards, sawmills, paper mills, converting operations, and warehouses to satisfy market demand. CLMS incorporates an innovative mathematical modeling system which consists of (1) a simple yet complete language that enables users to input the description of the planning model in operational terms; (2) an automatic generation of models representing various network configurations; (3) efficient and dependable model optimization via IBM's linear programming software package MPSX/370; and (4) concise, user-oriented reports generated from optimization results. CLMS is itself a large-scale mathematical model usually involving over 20,000 variables and 5000 constraints. Often as many as two or three thousand of the variables will be required to be integer valued.

CLMS has become the central tool for analyzing IPCo's planning problems. The system has been applied to strategic, tactical, and operational planning. Strategically, outputs of CLMS are used to determine optimal marketing, production, and financial strategies, which are translated into land, facilities, equipment, and materials plans. At the tactical level, the production plan provides the input to a bill-of-materials explosion system that calculates the materials required at each location to support the annual plan. This in turn is used by CLMS to select vendors at minimum landed costs of materials at each location. The same production plan also serves as input to a distribution and transportation system in order to ensure that the proper equipment is available to support the annual plan. Operationally, the system is used to determine the allocation of customer orders to paper mills in order to meet demand.

Production Scheduling System

The allocation of customer orders from CLMS is input to an interactive production scheduling system (CYCLIST) which assists operations planning managers in the preparation of short-term pulp mill and paper machine production schedules. CYCLIST gives operations planning managers the capability to quickly evaluate production schedules before they are implemented; to prepare new schedules on regular and emergency bases as a function of manufacturing, purchasing, and transportation constraints; and to develop various reports.

Purchasing and Inventory Management

Applications in this area are supported in part by a purchasing and inventory management system (PIMS). PIMS is a state-of-the-art on-line distributed data processing system. It is installed on IBM computers at the paper mills, with a central data base residing in one of the company's computers. PIMS permits central control over $1.0 billion in expenditures by generating on-line systemwide vendor, buyer, price, purchasing, and inventory analyses. This system is expected to generate annually nine times more savings than the annual operating cost of the system.

PIMS has a number of management science subroutines to perform, including purchasing and storeroom simulation, and statistical trending of item requirements, expenditures, and prices. Automated interfaces also exist with the CLMS and CYCLIST systems discussed above. The interface with the CLMS system enables the use of mathematical programming techniques for vendor selection. The interface with the CYCLIST system ensures that items are procured on a timely basis to support a given production schedule (see Figure A.1).

Distribution and Transportation Management

Management science applications in this area are supported by a transportation management information system (TMIS). TMIS is an automated information system for planning, documenting, operating, and controlling transportation operations companywide; for providing transportation data to be shared with other components of the logistics manufacturing system; and for interchanging data electronically with carriers, customers, and suppliers. TMIS keeps records of inbound, intracompany, and outbound freight activities using rail, truck, barge, and ocean transportation. Altogether, it keeps track of freight costs exceeding $500 million annually.

TMIS is routinely used to document transportation activities and their costs by commodity, origin, and destination; carrier activities by shipment destination and route; and car activities by facility. Also, it can perform functions such as cost variance reporting; car control; rates; route and transit analysis; and monitoring and controlling of private trucking. Electronic data interchange enables all parties involved with a shipment to be simultaneously notified, shipment data to be entered only once, and communication to take place in a standardized fashion.

The logistics manufacturing system represents a major effort on the part of the International Paper Company to integrate its strategic, tactical, and operational planning activities. It is evidence of the substantial commitment the company is making to management science in planning for the future.

Chapter 2

Linear Programming: The Graphical Method

Linear programming is a mathematical technique that has been developed to help managers make decisions. Instead of presenting a formal definition of a linear program at this time, let us begin our discussion by presenting some typical problems in which linear programming can be used:

1. A manufacturer wants to develop a production schedule and an inventory policy that will satisfy sales demand in future periods. Ideally the schedule and policy will enable the company to satisfy demand and at the same time *minimize* the total production and inventory costs.

2. A financial analyst must select an investment portfolio from a variety of stock and bond investment alternatives. The analyst would like to establish the portfolio that *maximizes* the return on investment.

3. A marketing manager wants to determine how to best allocate a fixed advertising budget among alternative advertising media such as radio, television, newspaper, and magazine. The manager would like to determine the media mix that *maximizes* the advertising effectiveness.

4. A company has warehouses in a number of locations throughout the United States. Given a set of customer demands for its products, the company would like to determine which warehouse should ship how much product to which customers so that the total transportation costs are *minimized*.

Although these are but a few of the possible applications where linear programming has been used successfully, the examples do point out the broad nature of the types of problems that can be tackled using linear programming. Even though the applications are diverse, a close scrutiny points out one basic property that all of these problems have in common. That is, in each sample problem we were concerned with *maximizing* or *minimizing* some quantity. In example 1 we wanted to minimize costs; in example 2 we wanted to maximize return on investment; in example 3 we wanted to maximize total advertising effectiveness; and in example 4 we wanted to minimize total transportation costs. In linear programming terminology the maximization or minimization of a quantity is referred to as the *objective* of the problem. Thus the objective of all linear programs is to maximize or minimize some quantity.

A second property common to all linear programming problems is that there are restrictions or *constraints* that limit the degree to which the objective can be pursued. In example 1 the manufacturer is restricted by the constraints requiring product demand to be satisfied and by the constraints indicating limited production capacities. The financial analyst's portfolio problem is constrained by the total amount of investment funds available and the maximum amounts that can be invested in each stock or bond. The marketing manager's media selection decision is constrained by a fixed advertising budget and the availability of the various media. In the transportation problem the minimum cost shipping schedule is constrained by the supply of product available at each warehouse. Thus constraints are another general feature of every linear programming problem.

2.1 A Simple Maximization Problem

Let us consider the problem currently being analyzed by the management of Par, Inc., a small manufacturer of golf equipment and supplies. Par has been convinced by its distributor that there is an existing market for both a medium- and a high-priced golf bag. In fact, the distributor is so confident of the market that if Par can make the bags at a competitive price, the distributor has agreed to purchase everything Par can manufacture over the next three months.

After a thorough investigation of the steps involved in manufacturing a golf bag, Par has determined that each golf bag produced will require the following operations:

1. Cutting and dyeing of material;
2. Sewing;
3. Finishing (such as inserting umbrella holder, club separators, etc.);
4. Inspection and packaging.

The director of manufacturing has analyzed each of the operations and has concluded that if the company produces a medium-priced, standard model, each bag produced will require $7/10$ hour in the cutting and dyeing department, $1/2$ hour in the sewing department, 1 hour in the finishing department, and $1/10$ hour in the inspection and packaging department. The more expensive deluxe model will require 1 hour of cutting and dyeing time, $5/6$ hour of sewing time, $2/3$ hour of finishing time, and $1/4$ hour of inspection and packaging time. This production information is summarized in Table 2.1.

The accounting department has analyzed these production figures, assigned all relevant variable costs, and arrived at prices for both bags that will result in a profit of $10 for every standard bag and $9 for every deluxe bag produced.

In addition, after studying departmental workload projections, the director of manufacturing estimates 630 hours of cutting and dyeing time, 600 hours of sewing time, 708 hours of finishing time, and 135 hours of inspection and packaging time will be available for production of golf bags during the next three months. Par's problem is to determine how many standard and how many deluxe bags should be produced in order to

Table 2.1   Production Operations and Production Requirements Per Bag

Product	Production Time (hours)			
	Cutting and Dyeing	Sewing	Finishing	Inspection and Packaging
Standard bag	$7/10$	$1/2$	1	$1/10$
Deluxe bag	1	$5/6$	$2/3$	$1/4$

maximize profit. If you were in charge of production scheduling for Par, Inc., what decision would you make? That is, how many standard and how many deluxe bags would you produce in the next three months? Write your decision below. Later you can check and see how well you did.

Number of Standard Bags	Number of Deluxe Bags	Total Profit

2.2   The Objective Function

As pointed out earlier, every linear programming problem has a specific objective. For the Par problem the objective is to maximize profit. We can write this objective in a more specific form with the introduction of some simple notation. Let

x_1 = the number of standard bags Par, Inc. produces

x_2 = the number of deluxe bags Par, Inc. produces.

Par's profit will come from two sources: (1) the profit made by producing x_1 standard bags and (2) the profit made by producing x_2 deluxe bags. Since Par makes \$10 for every standard bag produced, the company will make \$10x_1 if x_1 standard bags are produced. Also, since Par makes \$9 for every deluxe bag produced, the company will make \$9x_2 if x_2 deluxe bags are produced. Denoting the total profit by z, we have

$$\text{total profit} = z = \$10x_1 + \$9x_2.$$

From now on we will assume that the profit is measured in dollars and write the total profit expression without the dollar signs. That is,

$$\text{total profit} = z = 10x_1 + 9x_2. \tag{2.1}$$

The solution to Par's problem is the *decision* that will maximize total profit. That is, Par, Inc. must determine the values of the variables x_1 and x_2 that will yield the highest possible value of z. In linear programming terminology we refer to x_1 and x_2 as the *decision variables*. Since the objective—maximize total profit—is a *function* of these decision variables, we refer to $10x_1 + 9x_2$ as the *objective function*. Thus in linear programming terminology we say that Par's goal or objective is to maximize the value of its objective function. Using max as an abbreviation for maximize, the objective is written as follows:

$$\max z = \max 10x_1 + 9x_2. \tag{2.2}$$

Suppose Par decided to make 400 standard bags and 200 deluxe bags. According to equation (2.2) the corresponding profit would be

$$z = 10(400) + 9(200)$$
$$= 4000 + 1800$$
$$= 5800.$$

What if Par decided upon a different production combination, such as producing 800 standard bags and no deluxe bags? In this case Par's profit would be

$$z = 10(800) + 9(0)$$
$$= 8000.$$

Certainly the latter production combination is better for Par, Inc. in terms of the stated objective of maximizing profit. However, it may not be possible for Par, Inc. to manufacture 800 standard bags and no deluxe bags. Let us look at the number of hours that will be required for each of the four operations if we consider this particular production combination. Using the data in Table 2.1, we see that this particular product combination would require 560 hours of cutting and dyeing time, 400 hours of sewing time, 800 hours of finishing time, and 80 hours of inspection and packaging time. Can Par, Inc. produce 800 standard bags? The answer is no, since one department—the finishing department—does not have a sufficient number of hours available. Because of the constraints on the number of hours available, Par, Inc. is not able to consider 800 standard bags and no deluxe bags as an acceptable production alternative. In fact, Par, Inc. can consider only the production alternatives that have total hour requirements less than or equal to the maximum hours available for each of the four operations.

In the Par, Inc. problem any particular production combination of standard and deluxe bags is referred to as a *solution* to the problem. However, only those solutions which satisfy *all* the constraints are referred to as *feasible solutions*. The particular feasible production combination or feasible solution that results in the largest profit will be referred to as the *optimal* production combination or, equivalently, the *optimal solution*. At this point, however, we have no idea what the optimal solution will be because we have not developed a procedure for identifying feasible solutions. The procedure for determining the feasible solutions requires us to first identify all the constraints of the problem.

2.3 The Constraints

Every standard and deluxe bag produced has to go through the four manufacturing operations. Since there is a limited amount of production time available for each of these operations, we can expect that four restrictions or constraints will limit the total number of golf bags Par can produce. Hence the next step in the linear programming approach will be to specify clearly all the constraints associated with the problem.

From the production information (see Table 2.1) we know that every standard bag Par manufactures will use $7/10$ hour of cutting and dyeing time. Hence the total number of hours of cutting and dyeing time used in the manufacture of x_1 standard bags will be $7/10x_1$. On the other hand, every deluxe bag Par produces will use 1 hour of cutting and dyeing time; thus x_2 deluxe bags will use $1x_2$ hours of cutting and dyeing time. The total cutting and dyeing time required for the production of x_1 standard bags and x_2 deluxe bags is given by

$$\text{total cutting and dyeing time required} = 7/10x_1 + 1x_2.$$

Since the director of manufacturing has stated that Par has at most 630 hours of cutting and dyeing time available, it follows that the product combination we select must satisfy the requirement

$$7/10x_1 + 1x_2 \leq 630 \tag{2.3}$$

where the symbol $\leq$ means *less than or equal to*. Relationship (2.3) is referred to as an inequality and denotes the fact that the total number of hours used for the cutting and dyeing operation in the production of x_1 standard bags and x_2 deluxe bags must be less than or equal to the maximum amount of cutting and dyeing time Par, Inc. has available. Inequality (2.3) then represents the cutting and dyeing constraint for Par, Inc.

From Table 2.1 we also see that every standard bag manufactured will require $1/2$ hour of sewing time and that every deluxe bag manufactured will require $5/6$ hour of sewing time. Since there are 600 hours of sewing time available, it follows that

$$1/2x_1 + 5/6x_2 \leq 600. \tag{2.4}$$

Inequality (2.4) is the mathematical representation of the sewing constraint. Verify for yourself that the constraint for finishing capacity is

$$1x_1 + 2/3x_2 \leq 708 \tag{2.5}$$

and that the constraint for inspection and packaging capacity is

$$1/10x_1 + 1/4x_2 \leq 135. \tag{2.6}$$

We now have specified the mathematical relationships for the constraints associated with the four production operations. Are there any other constraints we have forgotten? Can Par produce a negative number of standard or deluxe bags? Clearly, the answer is no. Thus in order to prevent the decision variables x_1 and x_2 from having negative values two constraints

$$x_1 \geq 0 \quad \text{and} \quad x_2 \geq 0 \tag{2.7}$$

must be added. The symbol $\geq$ means *greater than or equal to*. These constraints ensure that the solution to our problem will contain nonnegative values for the decision variables and are thus referred to as the *nonnegativity constraints*. Nonnegativity constraints are a general feature of all linear programming problems and will be written in the following abbreviated form:

$$x_1, x_2 \geq 0.$$

2.4 The Mathematical Statement of the Par, Inc. Problem

The mathematical statement or mathematical formulation of the Par, Inc. problem is now complete. We have succeeded in translating the objective and constraints of the "real-world" problem into a set of mathematical relationships referred to as a *mathematical model*. The complete mathematical model for the Par problem is as follows:

$$\max 10x_1 + 9x_2$$

subject to (s.t.)

$\frac{7}{10}x_1 + 1x_2 \leq 630$	cutting and dyeing
$\frac{1}{2}x_1 + \frac{5}{6}x_2 \leq 600$	sewing
$1x_1 + \frac{2}{3}x_2 \leq 708$	finishing
$\frac{1}{10}x_1 + \frac{1}{4}x_2 \leq 135$	inspection and packaging

$$x_1, x_2 \geq 0.$$

Our job now is to find the product mix (that is, the combination of x_1 and x_2) which satisfies all the constraints and, at the same time, yields a value for the objective function that is greater than or equal to the value given by any other feasible solution. Once this is done, we will have found the optimal solution to the problem.

The above mathematical model of the Par problem is a *linear program*. The problem has the objective and constraints that we said earlier were common properties of all linear programs. But what is the special feature of this mathematical model that makes it a linear program? The special feature that makes it a linear program is that the objective function and all constraint functions (the left-hand sides of the constraint inequalities) are linear functions of the decision variables.

Mathematically speaking, functions where each of the variables appears in a separate term and is raised to the first power are called *linear functions*. The objective function $(10x_1 + 9x_2)$ is linear since each decision variable appears in a separate term and has an exponent of 1. If the objective function had appeared as $(10x_1^2 + 9\sqrt{x_2})$, it would not have been a linear function and we would not have had a linear program. The amount of production time required in the cutting and dyeing department $(\frac{7}{10}x_1 + 1x_2)$ is also a linear function of the decision variables for the same reasons. Similarly, the functions on the left-hand side of all the constraining inequalities (the constraint functions) are linear functions. Thus the mathematical formulation of the Par problem is referred to as a linear program.

2.5   The Graphical Solution Approach

An easy way to solve a linear programming problem having only two decision variables is the graphical solution procedure. Although the graphical method is awkward in solving three-variable problems, and cannot be used for larger problems, the insight gained from studying this method will be invaluable as an aid to understanding some of the more advanced concepts to be discussed later in the book. In addition, the graphical method provides an intuitive basis for more practical solution methods such as the Simplex method, which will be discussed in Chapter 3.

Let us begin our graphical solution procedure by developing a graph that can be used to display the possible solutions (x_1 and x_2 values) for the Par problem. The graph (Figure 2.1) will have values of x_1 on the horizontal axis and values of x_2 on the vertical axis. Any point on the graph can be identified by the x_1 and x_2 values, which indicate the position of the point along the x_1 and x_2 axes, respectively. Since every point (x_1, x_2) corresponds to a possible solution, every point on the graph is called a *solution point*. The solution point where $x_1 = 0$ and $x_2 = 0$ is referred to as the origin.

The next step is to show which of the possible combinations of x_1 and x_2, that is, solution points, correspond to feasible solutions for the linear program. Since both x_1 and x_2 must be nonnegative, we need only consider

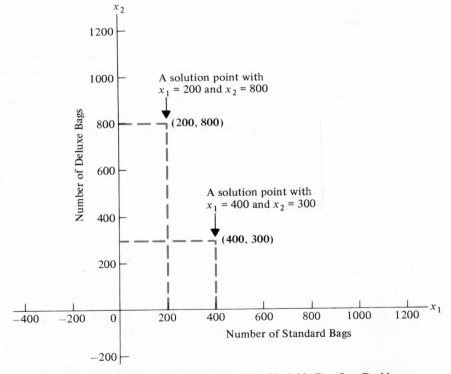

FIGURE 2.1   Graph of Solution Points for the Two-Variable Par, Inc. Problem

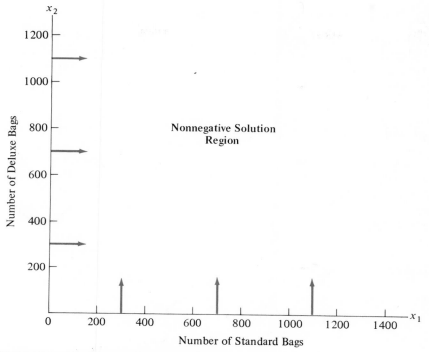

FIGURE 2.2   The Nonnegativity Constraints

points where $x_1 \geq 0$ and $x_2 \geq 0$. This is indicated in Figure 2.2 by arrows pointing in the direction of production combinations that will satisfy the nonnegativity constraints. In all future graphs we will assume that the nonnegativity relationships hold and only draw the portion of the graph corresponding to nonnegative x_1 and x_2 values.

Earlier we saw that the inequality representing the cutting and dyeing constraint was of the form

$$\tfrac{7}{10}x_1 + 1x_2 \leq 630.$$

To show all solution points that satisfy this relationship, we start by graphing the line corresponding to the equation

$$\tfrac{7}{10}x_1 + 1x_2 = 630.$$

The graph of this equation is found by identifying two points that lie on the line and then drawing a line through the points. Setting $x_1 = 0$ and solving for x_2, we see that the point ($x_1 = 0$, $x_2 = 630$) satisfies the above equation. To find a second point satisfying this equation, we set $x_2 = 0$ and solve for x_1. By doing this we obtain $\tfrac{7}{10}x_1 + 1(0) = 630$, or $x_1 = 900$. Thus a second point satisfying the equation is ($x_1 = 900$, $x_2 = 0$). Given these two points we can now graph the line corresponding to the equation

$$\tfrac{7}{10}x_1 + 1x_2 = 630.$$

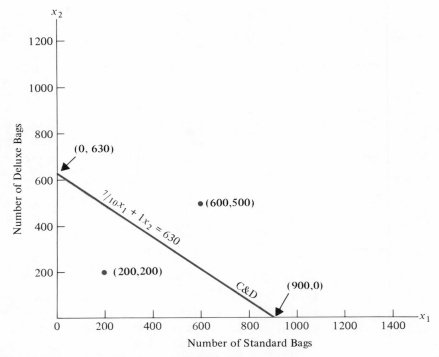

FIGURE 2.3   The Cutting and Dyeing Constraint Line

This line, which will be called the cutting and dyeing *constraint line,* is shown in Figure 2.3. For purposes of identification we label this line "C & D" to indicate that it represents the cutting and dyeing constraint.

Recall that the inequality representing the cutting and dyeing constraint is

$$\tfrac{7}{10}x_1 + 1x_2 \leq 630.$$

Can you identify all of the solution points that satisfy this constraint? Well, since we have the line where $\tfrac{7}{10}x_1 + 1x_2 = 630$, we know any point on this line must satisfy the constraint. But where are the solution points satisfying $\tfrac{7}{10}x_1 + 1x_2 < 630$? Consider two solution points ($x_1 = 200$, $x_2 = 200$) and ($x_1 = 600$, $x_2 = 500$). You can see from Figure 2.3 that the first solution point is below the constraint line and the second is above the constraint line. Which of these solutions will satisfy the cutting and dyeing constraint? For the point ($x_1 = 200$, $x_2 = 200$) we see that

$$\tfrac{7}{10}x_1 + 1x_2 = \tfrac{7}{10}(200) + 1(200) = 340.$$

Since the 340 hours is less than the 630 hours available, the $x_1 = 200$, $x_2 = 200$ production combination, or solution point, satisfies the constraint. For $x_1 = 600$, $x_2 = 500$ we have

$$\tfrac{7}{10}x_1 + 1x_2 = \tfrac{7}{10}(600) + 1(500) = 920.$$

Since the 920 hours is greater than the 630 hours available, the $x_1 = 600$, $x_2 = 500$ solution point does not satisfy the constraint and is thus an unacceptable production alternative.

Are you ready to identify the solution points that satisfy the cutting and dyeing constraint? You should be satisfied that any point *below* the cutting and dyeing constraint line satisfies the constraint. You may want to prove this to yourself by selecting additional solution points above and below the constraint line and checking to see if the solutions satisfy the constraint. You will see that for this $\leq$ constraint only solution points on or below the line satisfy the constraint. In Figure 2.4 we indicate all such points by shading the region of the graph corresponding to the solution points that satisfy the cutting and dyeing constraint.

Next let us identify all solution points that satisfy the sewing constraint

$$\tfrac{1}{2}x_1 + \tfrac{5}{6}x_2 \leq 600.$$

We start by drawing the constraint line corresponding to the equation

$$\tfrac{1}{2}x_1 + \tfrac{5}{6}x_2 = 600.$$

As before, the graphing of a line is most easily done by finding two points on the line and then connecting them. Thus we first set x_1 equal to zero and solve for x_2, which yields the point ($x_1 = 0$, $x_2 = 720$). Next we set x_2 equal to zero and solve for x_1, which gives the second point ($x_1 = 1200$, $x_2 = 0$). In

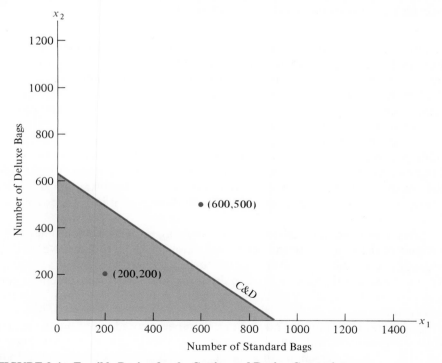

FIGURE 2.4   Feasible Region for the Cutting and Dyeing Constraint

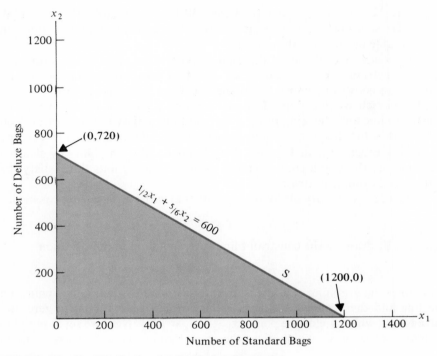

FIGURE 2.5 **Feasible Region for the Sewing Constraint**

Figure 2.5 we have drawn the line corresponding to the sewing constraint. For identification purposes we label this line S. Using the same approach as for the cutting and dyeing constraint, we realize that only points on or below the line will satisfy the sewing time constraint. Thus in Figure 2.5 the shaded region corresponds to all feasible production combinations or feasible solution points for the sewing operation.

In a similar manner, we can determine the set of all feasible production combinations for each of the remaining constraints. The results are shown in Figures 2.6 and 2.7. For practice, try to graph the feasible solution region for the finishing (F) constraint and the inspection and packaging (I & P) constraint and see if your results agree with those shown in Figures 2.6 and 2.7.

We now have four separate graphs showing the feasible solution points for each of the four constraints. In a linear programming problem we need to identify the solution points that satisfy *all* the constraints *simultaneously*. To find these solution points, we can draw our four constraints on one graph and observe the region containing the points that do in fact satisfy all the constraints.

The graphs in Figures 2.4–2.7 can be superimposed to obtain one graph with all four constraints. This combined-constraint graph is shown in Figure 2.8. The shaded region in this figure includes every solution point that satisfies all the constraints. Since solutions that satisfy all the constraints are

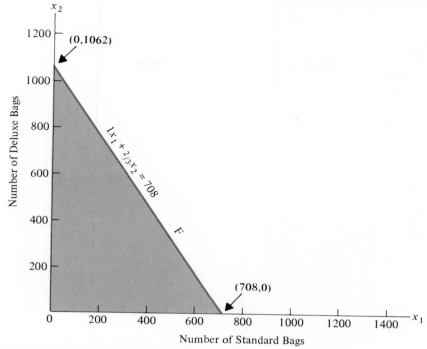

FIGURE 2.6   Feasible Region for the Finishing Constraint

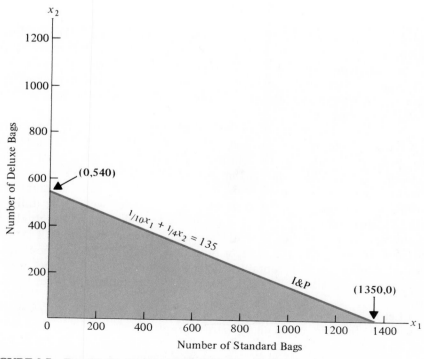

FIGURE 2.7   Feasible Region for the Inspection and Packaging Constraint

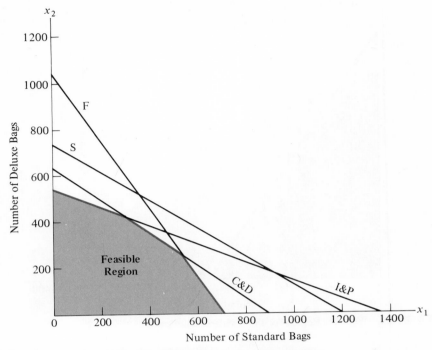

FIGURE 2.8   Feasible Solution Region for the Par, Inc. Problem

termed *feasible solutions,* the shaded region is called the feasible solution region, or simply the *feasible region.* Any point on the boundary of the feasible region or within the feasible region is a *feasible solution point.* You may want to check points outside the feasible region to prove to yourself that these solution points violate one or more of the constraints and are thus infeasible or unacceptable.

Now that we have identified the feasible region we are ready to proceed with the graphical solution method and find the optimal solution to the Par, Inc. problem. Recall that the optimal solution for a linear programming problem is the feasible solution that provides the best possible value of the objective function. We could arbitrarily select feasible solution points (x_1, x_2) and compute the associated profit $10x_1 + 9x_2$. However, the difficulty with this approach is that there are too many feasible solutions (actually an infinite number), and thus it would not be possible to evaluate all feasible solutions. Hence this trial-and-error procedure would not guarantee that the optimal solution could be obtained. What we would like is a better way of identifying the feasible solution that does in fact maximize the profit for Par, Inc.

Let us start the optimizing step of the graphical solution procedure by drawing the feasible region on a separate graph. This is shown in Figure 2.9.

Rather than selecting an arbitrary feasible solution and computing the associated profit, let us select an arbitrary profit and identify all of the

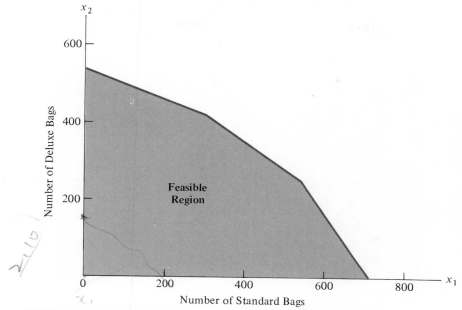

FIGURE 2.9 **Feasible Solution Region for the Par, Inc. Problem**

feasible solution points (x_1, x_2) that yield the selected profit. For example, what feasible solution points provide a profit of $1800? That is, we wish to find the values of x_1 and x_2 in the feasible region that will make the objective function

$$10x_1 + 9x_2 = 1800.$$

The above expression is simply the equation of a line. Thus all feasible solution points (x_1, x_2) yielding a profit of $1800 must be on the line. We learned earlier in this section how to graph a constraint line. The procedure for graphing the profit or objective function line is the same. Letting $x_1 = 0$, we see that x_2 must be 200; thus the solution point $(x_1 = 0, x_2 = 200)$ is on the line. Similarly, by letting $x_2 = 0$ we see that the solution point $(x_1 = 180, x_2 = 0)$ is also on the line. Drawing the line through these two points identifies all the solutions that have a profit of $1800. A graph of this profit line is presented in Figure 2.10. From this graph you can see that there are an infinite number of feasible production combinations that will provide an $1800 profit.

Since the objective is one of finding the feasible solution point that has the highest profit, let us proceed by selecting higher profit values and finding the solution points that yield the stated profits. For example, what solution points provide a $3600 profit? What solution points provide a $5400 profit? To answer these questions we must find the x_1 and x_2 values that are on the following lines:

$$10x_1 + 9x_2 = 3600$$

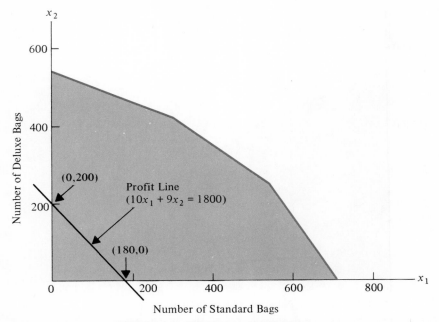

FIGURE 2.10   **$1800 Profit Line for the Par, Inc. Problem**

and

$$10x_1 + 9x_2 = 5400.$$

Using the previous procedure for graphing profit and constraint lines, we have drawn the $3600 and $5400 profit lines on the graph in Figure 2.11. While not all solution points on the $5400 profit line are in the feasible region, at least some points on the line are, and thus it is possible to obtain a feasible production combination that provides a $5400 profit.

Can we find a feasible solution yielding even higher profits? Look at Figure 2.11 and see what general observations you can make about the profit lines. You should be able to identify the following properties: (1) the profit lines are *parallel* to each other, and (2) higher profit lines occur as we move farther from the origin. This can also be seen algebraically. Let z represent total profit. The objective function is

$$z = 10x_1 + 9x_2.$$

Solving for x_2 in terms of x_1 and z, we obtain

$$9x_2 = -10x_1 + z,$$
$$x_2 = -\tfrac{10}{9}x_1 + \tfrac{1}{9}z. \qquad (2.8)$$

Equation (2.8) is the *slope-intercept form* of the linear equation relating x_1 and x_2. The coefficient of x_1, $-\tfrac{10}{9}$, is the slope of the line, and the term $\tfrac{1}{9}z$ is the x_2 intercept (that is, the value of x_2 where the graph of equation (2.8) crosses the x_2 axis). Substituting the profit values of $z = 1800$, $z = 3600$, and

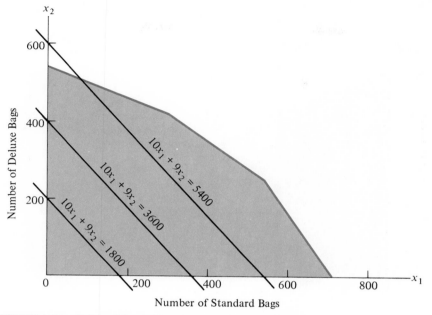

FIGURE 2.11   **Selected Profit Lines for the Par, Inc. Problem**

$z = 5400$ into equation (2.8) yields the following slope-intercept equations for the profit lines shown in Figure 2.11:

For profit $z = 1800$,

$$x_2 = -\tfrac{10}{9}x_1 + 200.$$

For profit $z = 3600$,

$$x_2 = -\tfrac{10}{9}x_1 + 400.$$

For profit $z = 5400$,

$$x_2 = -\tfrac{10}{9}x_1 + 600.$$

Since the slope $(-\tfrac{10}{9})$ is the same for each profit line, the profit lines are parallel. Further, we see that the x_2 intercept increases with larger values of profit. Thus higher profit lines are farther from the origin.

Because the profit lines are parallel and higher profit lines are farther from the origin, we can obtain solution points that yield increasingly higher values for the objective function by continuing to move the profit line farther from the origin in such a fashion that it remains parallel to the other profit lines. However, at some point we will find that any further outward movement will place the profit line outside the feasible region. Since points outside the feasible region are unacceptable, the point in the feasible region which lies on the highest profit line is the optimal solution to our linear program.

You should now be able to identify the optimal solution point for the Par, Inc. problem. Use a ruler or the edge of a piece of paper and move the

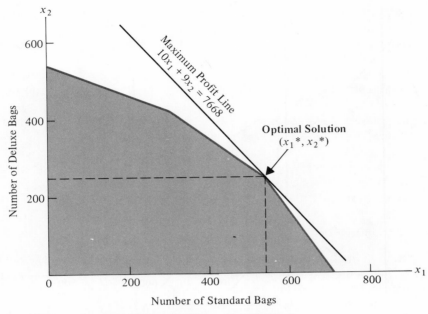

FIGURE 2.12   Optimal Solution for the Par, Inc. Problem

profit line as far from the origin as you can. What is the last point in the feasible region that you reach? This point, which is the optimal solution, is shown graphically in Figure 2.12.

The optimal values of the decision variables x_1 and x_2 are the x_1 and x_2 values at the optimal solution. Depending upon the accuracy of your graph, you may or may not be able to read the *exact* x_1 and x_2 values from the graph. The best we can do with respect to the optimal solution in Figure 2.12 is to conclude that the optimal production combination consists of approximately 550 standard bags (x_1) and 250 deluxe bags (x_2). As you will see in Section 2.6 the actual x_1 and x_2 values at the optimal solution are $x_1 = 540$ and $x_2 = 252$. The optimal solution of 540 standard bags and 252 deluxe bags yields a profit of $10(540) + 9(252) = \$7668$.

Summary of the Graphical Solution Procedure for Maximization Problems

As you have seen, the graphical solution procedure is one method of solving two-variable linear programming problems such as the Par, Inc. problem. The steps of the graphical solution procedure for a maximization problem are outlined below.

1. Prepare a graph of the feasible solution points for each of the constraints.

2. Determine the feasible region by identifying the solution points that satisfy all the constraints simultaneously.
3. Draw a profit line showing all values of the x_1 and x_2 variables that yield a specified value of the objective function.
4. Move parallel profit lines toward higher profits (usually away from the origin) until further movement would take the profit line completely outside the feasible region.
5. The feasible point that lies on the highest profit line is the optimal solution.
6. Determine, at least approximately, the optimal values of the decision variables by estimating the x_1 and x_2 values at the optimal solution directly from the graph.

Slack Variables

In addition to the optimal solution and the expected profit, the management of Par, Inc. will probably want information about the production time requirements for each production operation. We can determine this information by substituting the optimal x_1 and x_2 values into the constraints of our linear program. For the Par, Inc. problem the production time requirements, are as follows:

$$7/10(540) + 1(252) = 630 \text{ hours of cutting and dyeing time,}$$
$$1/2(540) + 5/6(252) = 480 \text{ hours of sewing time,}$$
$$1(540) + 2/3(252) = 708 \text{ hours of finishing time,}$$
$$1/10(540) + 1/4(252) = 117 \text{ hours of inspection and packaging time.}$$

The complete solution tells management that the production of 540 standard bags and 252 deluxe bags will require all available cutting and dyeing time (630 hours) and all available finishing time (708 hours), while 120 hours of sewing time $(600 - 480)$ and 18 hours of inspection and packaging time $(135 - 117)$ will remain idle. The 120 hours of unused sewing time and 18 hours of unused inspection and packaging time are referred to as *slack* for the two departments. In linear programming terminology, any unused or idle capacity for a $\leq$ constraint is referred to as the *slack* associated with the constraint.

Often variables are added to the formulation of a linear programming problem to represent the slack, or idle capacity. Such variables are called *slack variables,* and since the unused capacity makes no contribution to profit, they have coefficients of zero in the objective function. More generally, slack variables can be thought of as representing the difference between the right-hand side and the left-hand side of a $\leq$ constraint. After addition of slack variables to the mathematical statement of the Par, Inc. problem, the mathematical model appears as follows:

$$\max \quad 10x_1 + 9x_2 + 0s_1 + 0s_2 + 0s_3 + 0s_4$$

s.t.

$$
\begin{aligned}
\tfrac{7}{10}x_1 + 1x_2 + 1s_1 &&&&&= 630 \\
\tfrac{1}{2}x_1 + \tfrac{5}{6}x_2 &+ 1s_2 &&&&= 408 \\
1x_1 + \tfrac{2}{3}x_2 &&+ 1s_3 &&&= 708 \\
\tfrac{1}{10}x_1 + \tfrac{1}{4}x_2 &&&+ 1s_4 &&= 135
\end{aligned}
$$

$$x_1, x_2, s_1, s_2, s_3, s_4 \geq 0.$$

Whenever a linear program is written in a form with all constraints expressed as equalities, it is said to be written in *Standard form*.

At the optimal solution, $x_1 = 540$ and $x_2 = 252$, the values for the slack variables are as follows:

Constraint	Value of Slack Variable
Cutting and Dyeing	$s_1 = 0$
Sewing	$s_2 = 120$
Finishing	$s_3 = 0$
Inspection and Packaging	$s_4 = 18$

Could we have used the graphical analysis to provide some of this information? The answer is yes. By finding the optimal solution point on Figure 2.8, we can see that the cutting and dyeing and the finishing constraints restrict, or *bind,* the feasible region at this point. Thus this solution requires the use of all available time for these two operations. In other words, the cutting and dyeing and the finishing departments will have zero slack. On the other hand, since the sewing and the inspection and packaging constraints are not binding the feasible region at the optimal solution, we can expect some unused time or slack for these two operations.

As a final comment on the graphical analysis of the Par, Inc. problem, we call your attention to the sewing capacity constraint as shown in Figure 2.8. Note, in particular, that this constraint did not affect the feasible region. That is, the feasible region would be the same whether the sewing capacity constraint was included or not. This tells us that there is enough sewing time available to accommodate any production level that can be achieved by the other three departments. Since the sewing constraint does not affect the feasible region and thus cannot affect the optimal solution, it is called a *redundant* constraint. Redundant constraints can be dropped from the problem without having any effect upon the optimal solution.[1]

---

[1] We point out here that in most linear programming problems redundant constraints are not discarded because these constraints are often not immediately recognizable as being redundant.

2.6   Extreme Points and the Optimal Solution

Suppose that the profit for the Par, Inc. standard bag is reduced from \$10 to \$5 per bag while the profit for the deluxe bag and all the constraints remain unchanged. The complete linear programming model of this new problem is identical to the mathematical model in Section 2.4, except for the revised objective function:

$$\max z = 5x_1 + 9x_2.$$

How does this change in the objective function affect the optimal solution to our Par, Inc. problem? Figure 2.13 shows the graphical solution of the Par, Inc. problem with the revised objective function. Note that since the constraints have not changed, the feasible region has not changed. However, the profit lines have been altered to reflect the new objective function.

By moving the profit line in a parallel manner away from the origin, we find the optimal solution as shown in Figure 2.13. The values of the decision variables at this point are $x_1 = 300$ and $x_2 = 420$. The reduced profit for the standard bags has caused a change in the optimal solution. In fact, as you may have suspected, we are cutting back the production of the lower-profit standard bags and increasing the production of the higher-profit deluxe bags.

What have you noticed about the location of the optimal solutions in the

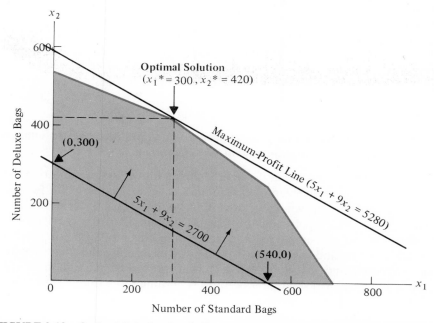

FIGURE 2.13   Optimal Solution for the Par, Inc. Problem with an Objective Function of $5x_1 + 9x_2$

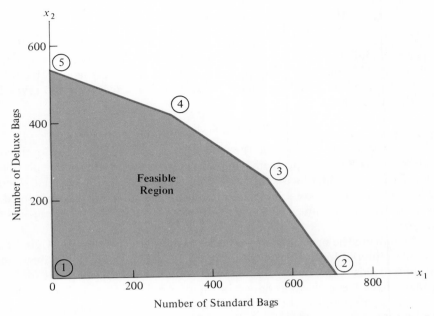

FIGURE 2.14   The Five Extreme Points of the Feasible Region for the Par, Inc. Problem

two linear programming problems that we have solved thus far? Look closely at the graphical solutions in Figures 2.12 and 2.13. An important observation that you should be able to make is that the optimal solutions occur at one of the vertices or "corners" of the feasible region. In linear programming terminology these vertices are referred to as the *extreme points* of the feasible region. Thus the Par, Inc. problem has five vertices or five extreme points for its feasible region (see Figure 2.14). We can now state our observation about the location of optimal solutions as follows:[2]

The optimal solution to a linear programming problem can be found at an extreme point of the feasible region for the problem.

This property means that if you are looking for the optimal solution to a linear programming problem, you do not have to evaluate all feasible solution points. In fact, you have to consider *only* the feasible solutions that occur at the extreme points of the feasible region. Thus for the Par, Inc. problem, instead of computing and comparing the profit for all feasible solutions, we can find the optimal solution by evaluating the five extreme-point solutions and selecting the one that provides the highest profit. Actually the graphical solution procedure is nothing more than a convenient way of identifying an optimal extreme point for two-variable problems.

[2]We will see in Section 2.8 that there are two special cases (infeasibility and unboundedness) in linear programming where there is no optimal solution. Thus the above statement does not apply to these cases.

To help convince yourself that the optimal solution to a linear program always occurs at an extreme point, select several different objective functions for the Par, Inc. problem and graphically find the optimal solution for each case. You will see that as you move the profit lines away from the origin, the last feasible solution point—the optimal solution—is always one of the extreme points.

Alternate Optimal Solutions

What happens if the highest profit line coincides with one of the constraint lines on the boundary of the feasible region? This case is shown for a $6.3x_1 + 9x_2$ objective function in Figure 2.15. Does an optimal solution still occur at an extreme point? The answer is yes. In fact, in this case an optimal solution occurs at extreme point ③, extreme point ④, and any point on the line segment joining these two points. This is the special case of alternate optimal solutions, or *alternate optima*. As you can see, whenever alternate optima occur there will be an infinite number of optimal solutions lying on the line segment joining two extreme points. A linear programming

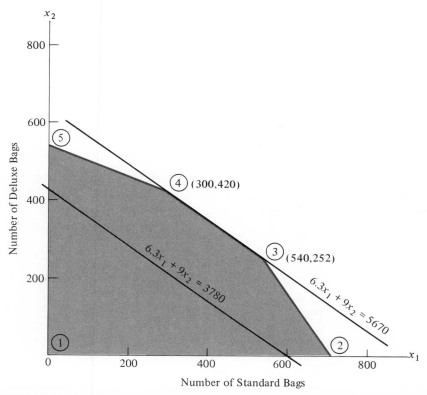

FIGURE 2.15   Par, Inc. Problem with an Objective Function of $6.3x_1 + 9x_2$ (Alternate Optima)

problem having alternate optima is a good situation for the manager attempting to implement the solution. It means that many combinations of the variables are optimal and that the manager can select the specific solution that is most appropriate.

Finding the Exact Location of Graphical Solution Extreme Points

Let us consider extreme point ③ of the Par problem, as shown in Figure 2.16. In the graphical solution procedure of Section 2.5 extreme point ③ was identified as the optimal solution to the original Par problem. However, we had difficulty reading the exact values of x_1 and x_2 at extreme point ③ directly from the graph. Actually, the best we could do was to arrive at approximate values for the decision variables.

Refer to Figure 2.16. Note the constraint lines that determine the exact location of extreme point ③. The cutting and dyeing constraint line and the finishing constraint line intersect at this extreme point. That is, extreme point ③ is on both the cutting and the dyeing constraint line

$$\tfrac{7}{10}x_1 + 1x_2 = 630 \tag{2.9}$$

and the finishing constraint line

$$1x_1 + \tfrac{2}{3}x_2 = 708. \tag{2.10}$$

Thus the values of the decision variables x_1 and x_2 at extreme point ③ must satisfy both equations (2.9) and (2.10) simultaneously. Using equation (2.9) and solving for x_1 gives

$$\tfrac{7}{10}x_1 = 630 - 1x_2$$

or

$$x_1 = 900 - \tfrac{10}{7}x_2. \tag{2.11}$$

Substituting this expression for x_1 into equation (2.10) and solving for x_2 provides the following:

$$
\begin{aligned}
1(900 - \tfrac{10}{7}x_2) + \tfrac{2}{3}x_2 &= 708 \\
900 - \tfrac{10}{7}x_2 + \tfrac{2}{3}x_2 &= 708 \\
900 - \tfrac{30}{21}x_2 + \tfrac{14}{21}x_2 &= 708 \\
- \tfrac{16}{21}x_2 &= -192 \\
x_2 = \frac{192}{\tfrac{16}{21}} &= 252.
\end{aligned}
$$

Using $x_2 = 252$ in equation (2.11) and solving for x_1 provides

$$
\begin{aligned}
x_1 &= 900 - \tfrac{10}{7}(252) \\
&= 900 - 360 = 540.
\end{aligned}
$$

Thus the exact location of extreme point ③ is $x_1 = 540$ and $x_2 = 252$. Since we have previously observed that the optimal solution occurs at this extreme

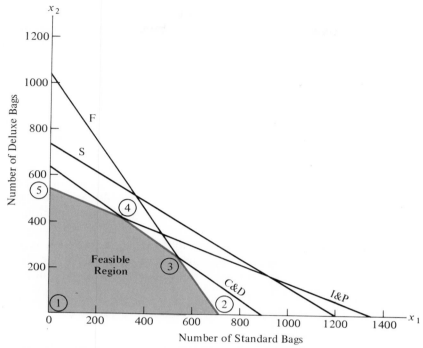

FIGURE 2.16   Feasible Solution Region for the Par, Inc. Problem

point, we now know the optimal production quantities for Par are 540 standard bags and 252 deluxe bags.

In any graphical solution of a two decision variable linear programming problem the exact values of the decision variables at the optimal solution can be determined by first using the graphical procedure to identify the optimal extreme point and then solving the two simultaneous equations associated with the optimal extreme point.

2.7   A Simple Minimization Problem

While the Par problem involves maximization, many linear programming problems are more naturally formulated as minimization problems. For example, consider the case of a manufacturer who has contracted to sell a certain number of units of a product to various buyers. The manufacturer is no longer concerned with how many units to produce; the problem is one of minimizing the total cost of production subject to the constraints of satisfying demand. As an illustration of how a minimization problem might occur, consider the problem encountered by Photo Chemicals, Inc.

Photo Chemicals produces two types of photograph-developing fluids. Both products cost Photo Chemicals $1 per gallon to produce. Based upon an analysis of current inventory levels and outstanding orders for the next month, Photo Chemicals' management has specified that at least 30 gallons of product 1 and at least 20 gallons of product 2 must be produced during the next two weeks. Management has also stated that an existing inventory of highly perishable raw material required in the production of both fluids must be used within the next two weeks. The current inventory of the perishable raw material is 80 pounds. While more of this raw material can be ordered if necessary, any of the current inventory that is not used within the next two weeks will spoil; hence the management requirement that at least 80 pounds be used in the next two weeks. Furthermore, it is known that product 1 requires one pound of this perishable raw material per gallon and product 2 requires two pounds of the raw material per gallon. Since Photo Chemicals' objective is to keep its production costs at the minimum possible level, the firm's management is looking for a minimum cost production plan that uses all the 80 pounds of perishable raw material and provides at least 30 gallons of product 1 and at least 20 gallons of product 2. What is the minimum cost solution?

To answer this question, let us attempt to write the problem as a linear program. Following a procedure similar to the one used for the Par, Inc. problem, we first define the decision variables and the objective function for the problem. Let

$$x_1 = \text{the number of gallons of product 1 produced,}$$
$$x_2 = \text{the number of gallons of product 2 produced.}$$

Since the production costs for Photo Chemicals, Inc. are \$1 for each gallon of product 1 and \$1 for each gallon of product 2 produced, the objective function representing total cost is

$$1x_1 + 1x_2.$$

Using the z notation for the value of the objective function, the minimum cost objective can be written as

$$\min z = 1x_1 + 1x_2.$$

Next consider the constraints placed on the Photo Chemicals problem. For the perishable raw material constraint, product 1 uses one pound of raw material and product 2 uses two pounds of raw material. Thus the total number of pounds of raw material required to produce x_1 units of product 1 and x_2 units of product 2 is

$$1x_1 + 2x_2.$$

Since the constraint is to use *at least* 80 pounds of the perishable raw material, the raw material constraint becomes

$$1x_1 + 2x_2 \geq 80.$$

With the constraints of producing at least 30 gallons of product 1 ($x_1 \geq 30$), at least 20 gallons of product 2 ($x_2 \geq 20$) and the nonnegativity constraints ($x_1, x_2 \geq 0$), we have the following linear programming formulation of the Photo Chemicals problem:

$$\min \quad 1x_1 + 1x_2$$

s.t.

$$
\begin{array}{lll}
1x_1 + 2x_2 & \geq 80 & \text{raw material} \\
1x_1 & \geq 30 & \text{product 1} \\
1x_2 & \geq 20 & \text{product 2} \\
x_1, x_2 \geq 0. &
\end{array}
$$

Since the linear programming model has only two decision variables, the graphical solution procedure can be used to find the optimal production quantities. The graphical method for this problem, just as in the Par problem, requires us first to graph all constraint lines in order to find the feasible solution points. Note that in the Photo Chemicals problem the greater-than-or-equal-to constraints will cause the feasible solution points to be above the constraint lines. The constraint lines and the feasible region are shown in Figure 2.17.

In order to determine the minimum value of the cost $(1x_1 + 1x_2)$, we

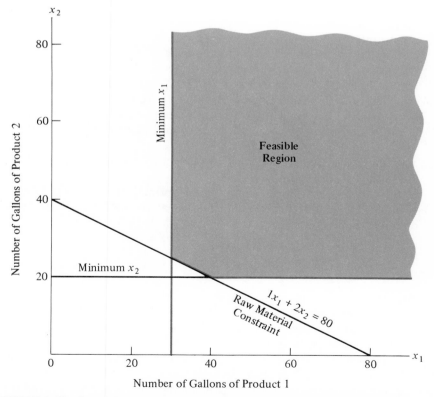

FIGURE 2.17   Set of Feasible Solutions for the Photo Chemicals, Inc. Problem

first draw the cost line corresponding to a particular value of $z = 1x_1 + 1x_2$. For example, we might start by drawing the line $1x_1 + 1x_2 = 80$. Figure 2.18 shows the graph of this line. Clearly, there are many points in the feasible region yielding this cost value (for example, $x_1 = x_2 = 40$).

To find the values of x_1 and x_2 which yield the minimum cost solution we move the cost line in a lower left direction until, if we moved it any further, it would be entirely outside the feasible region. Note that the line $1x_1 + 1x_2 = 55$ intersects the feasible region at the point ($x_1 = 30$, $x_2 = 25$). Thus the optimal solution to the problem is $x_1 = 30$, $x_2 = 25$, with a corresponding objective function value of 55. Also in Figure 2.18 we can see that the raw material constraint and the minimum x_1 constraint are binding and that, just as in the Par maximization problem, the optimal solution occurs at an extreme point of the feasible region.

Summary of the Graphical Solution Procedure for Minimization Problems

The steps of the graphical solution procedure for a minimization problem are outlined below:

1. Prepare a graph of the feasible solution points for each of the constraints.
2. Determine the feasible solution region by identifying the solution points that satisfy all the constraints simultaneously.
3. Draw a cost line showing all values of the x_1 and x_2 variables that yield a specified value of the objective function.
4. Move parallel cost lines toward lower costs (usually toward the origin) until further movement would take the cost line completely outside the feasible region.
5. The feasible extreme point that is touched by the lowest possible cost line is the optimal solution.
6. Determine, at least approximately, the optimal values of the decision variables by reading the x_1 and x_2 values at the optimal solution point directly from the graph.

Surplus Variables

A complete analysis of the optimal solution to the Photo Chemicals problem shows that a total of $1x_1 + 2x_2 = 1(30) + 2(25) = 80$ pounds of raw material will be used in the production process. In addition, product 1 will be at its minimum acceptable production level of 30 units, while the production of product 2 will exceed by 5 units its minimum level of 20 units. The excess production for product 2 is referred to as *surplus*. In linear programming terminology, any excess quantity corresponding to a $\geq$ constraint is referred to as the surplus associated with the constraint.

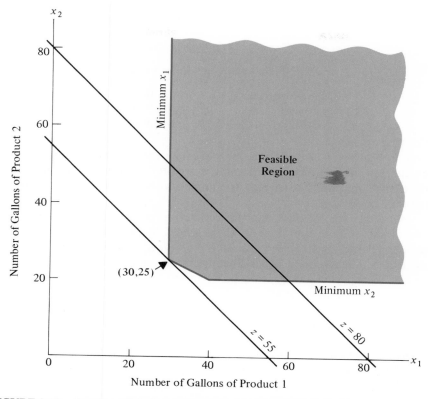

FIGURE 2.18   Graphical Solution for the Photo Chemicals, Inc. Problem

Recall that with $\leq$ constraints, slack variables could be added to the formulation to represent the difference between the right-hand and left-hand sides of the constraint. With a $\geq$ constraint a *surplus variable* can be subtracted from the left-hand side to convert the constraint to equality form. Just as with slack variables, the surplus variables are given a coefficient of zero in the objective function because they have no effect on its value. After including surplus variables, the mathematical model of the Photo Chemicals problem would appear as follows:

$$\min \quad 1x_1 + 1x_2 + 0s_1 + 0s_2 + 0s_3$$

s.t.

$$1x_1 + 2x_2 - 1s_1 \qquad\qquad = 80$$
$$1x_1 \qquad\qquad - 1s_2 \qquad = 30$$
$$1x_2 \qquad\qquad - 1s_3 = 20$$
$$x_1, x_2, s_1, s_2, s_3 \geq 0$$

All the constraints are now equalities. Hence this is the Standard form representation of the Photo Chemicals problem. At the optimal solution

$(x_1 = 30$ and $x_2 = 25)$ the values for the surplus variables are as follows:

Constraint	Values of Surplus Variables
Raw material	$s_1 = 0$
Product 1	$s_2 = 0$
Product 2	$s_3 = 5$

Refer to Figures 2.17 and 2.18 and note how the graphical solution shows that the raw material constraint and the product 1 constraint are binding at the optimal solution. The surplus of 5 units is associated with the nonbinding product 2 constraint.

Note that in the Par, Inc. maximization problem all the constraints were of the $\leq$ type and that in the Photo Chemicals, Inc. minimization problem all the constraints were of the $\geq$ type. Although this pattern of constraints may occur in other linear programming problems, we caution you *not* to expect maximization problems to have only $\leq$ constraints and minimization problems to have only $\geq$ constraints. In fact, linear programming problems that are either maximization or minimization may have some $\leq$ constraints, some $\geq$ constraints, and some equality $(=)$ constraints. The equality constraints mean that the optimal solution must satisfy the constraint conditions exactly as defined by the constraint lines.

An example of a linear program with the three possible constraint forms is given below (Problem 21 at the end of the chapter will ask you to solve this problem using the graphical procedure):

$$\min \quad 2x_1 + 2x_2$$
$$\text{s.t.}$$
$$1x_1 + 3x_2 \leq 12$$
$$3x_1 + 1x_2 \geq 13$$
$$1x_1 - 1x_2 = 3$$
$$x_1, x_2 \geq 0$$

The Standard form representation of this problem is

$$\min \quad 2x_1 + 2x_2 + 0s_1 + 0s_2$$
$$\text{s.t.}$$
$$1x_1 + 3x_2 + 1s_1 \qquad = 12$$
$$3x_1 + 1x_2 \qquad - 1s_2 = 13$$
$$1x_1 - 1x_2 \qquad = 3$$
$$x_1, x_2, s_1, s_2 \geq 0.$$

This formulation requires a slack variable for the $\leq$ constraint and a surplus variable for the $\geq$ constraint. However, a slack or a surplus variable is not required for the third constraint, since it is already in equality form.

The graphical solution method is a convenient way to find optimal extreme point solutions for two-variable linear programming problems. When solving linear programs graphically it is not necessary to write the problem in its standard form. Nevertheless, we should be able to compute the values of the slack and surplus variables and understand what they mean. In Chapter 3 we will introduce an algebraic solution procedure, the Simplex method, which can be used to find optimal extreme-point solutions for linear programming problems having as many as several thousand decision variables. The mathematical steps of the Simplex method involve solving simultaneous equations which represent the constraints of the linear program. Thus in setting up a linear program for solution by the Simplex method we must have one linear equation for each constraint in the problem; therefore the problem must be in its standard form.

As a final point, it is important to realize that the standard form of the linear programming problem is equivalent to the original formulation of the problem. That is, the optimal solution to any linear programming problem is the same as the optimal solution to the standard form of the problem. The standard form has not changed the basic problem; it has only changed how we write the constraints for the problem.

2.8 Infeasibility and Unboundedness

In this section we discuss two special situations that can arise when we attempt to solve linear programming problems.

Infeasibility

Infeasibility comes about when there is no solution to the linear programming problem which satisfies all the constraints, including the nonnegativity conditions $x_1, x_2 \geq 0$. Graphically, infeasibility means that a feasible region does not exist; that is, there are no points which satisfy all the constraining equations and the nonnegativity conditions simultaneously. To illustrate this situation, let us look again at the problem faced by Par, Inc.

Suppose that management had specified that at least 500 of the standard bags and 360 of the deluxe bags must be manufactured. The graph of our solution region may now be constructed to reflect these requirements (see Figure 2.19). The shaded area in the lower left-hand portion of the graph depicts those points satisfying the departmental constraints on the availability of time. The shaded area in the upper right-hand portion depicts those points satisfying the minimum production requirements of 500 standard and 360 deluxe bags. But there are no points satisfying both sets of constraints. Thus we see that if management imposes these minimum production requirements, there will be no feasible solution to the linear programming model.

How should we interpret this infeasibility in terms of our current problem? First we should tell management that given the resources available

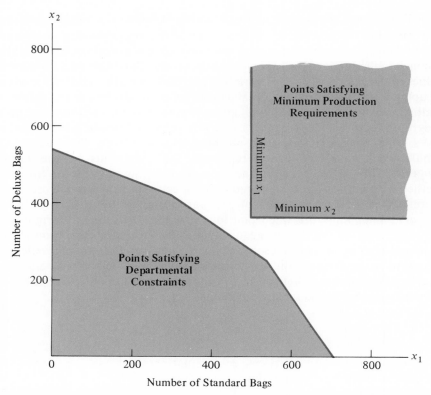

FIGURE 2.19   No Feasible Region for the Par, Inc. Problem with Production Requirements of 500 Standard and 360 Deluxe Bags

(that is, cutting and dyeing time, sewing time, finishing time, and inspection and packaging time) it is not possible to make 500 standard bags and 360 deluxe bags. Moreover, we can tell management exactly how much of each resource must be expended in order to make it possible to manufacture 500 standard and 360 deluxe bags. The following minimum amounts of resources must be available:

Operation	Minimum Required Resources (hours)	Available Resources (hours)
Cutting and dyeing	$7/10(500) + 1(360) = 710$	630
Sewing	$1/2(500) + 5/6(360) = 550$	600
Finishing	$1(500) + 2/3(360) = 740$	708
Inspection and packaging	$1/10(500) + 1/4(360) = 140$	135

Thus we need 80 more hours of cutting and dyeing time, 32 more hours of finishing time, and 5 more hours of inspection and packaging time in order to meet management's production requirements.

If after seeing our report management still wants to manufacture 500 standard and 360 deluxe bags, it must somehow provide additional resources. Perhaps this will mean hiring another person to work in the cutting and dyeing department, transferring a person from elsewhere in the plant to work part time in the finishing department, or having the sewing people help out periodically with the inspection and packaging. As you can see, there are many possibilities for corrective management action, once we discover that there is no feasible solution. The important thing for us to realize is that linear programming analysis can help us determine whether or not management's plans are feasible. By analyzing the problem using linear programming, we are often able to point out infeasible conditions and initiate corrective action.

Unboundedness

A solution to a linear programming problem is *unbounded* if the value of the solution may be made infinitely large without violating any of the constraints. This condition might be termed "managerial utopia." If this condition were to occur in a profit maximization problem, it would be true that the manager could achieve an unlimited profit.

In linear programming models of real-world problems the occurrence of an unbounded solution means that the problem has been improperly formulated. For example, we know that it is not possible to increase profits indefinitely. Therefore we must conclude that if a profit maximization problem results in an unbounded solution, the mathematical model is not a sufficiently accurate representation of the real-world problem. Usually what has happened is that a constraint has been inadvertently omitted in the problem formulation.

Graphically speaking, if a linear programming problem has an unbounded solution, the feasible region extends to infinity in some direction. As an illustration, consider the simple numerical example

$$\max \quad 2x_1 + 1x_2$$

s.t.

$$1x_1 \qquad \geq 2$$
$$1x_2 \leq 5$$
$$x_1, x_2 \geq 0.$$

In Figure 2.20 we have graphed the feasible region associated with this problem. Note that we can only indicate part of the feasible region, since the feasible region extends indefinitely in the direction of the x_1 axis. Looking at the profit lines in Figure 2.20, we see that the solution to this problem may be made as large as we desire. That is, no matter what solution we pick, there will always be some feasible solution with a larger value. Thus we say that the solution to this linear program is *unbounded*.

2.9 Graphical Sensitivity Analysis

In linear programming problems we may want to consider what happens to the optimal solution if changes occur in some of the coefficients of the

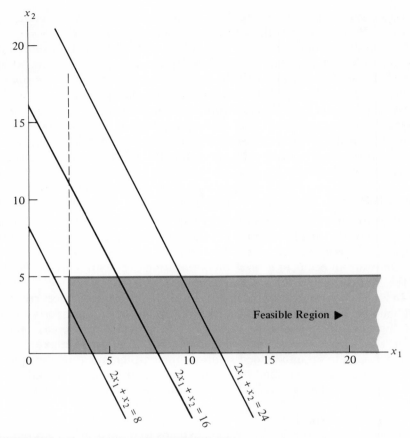

FIGURE 2.20   Example of an Unbounded Problem

original problem. To be specific, let us return to a consideration of the Par, Inc. problem. New pricing and/or cost information could change the profit coefficients for the standard or the deluxe bags in the objective function. The hiring of new employees, layoffs, and/or the use of overtime could lead to changes in the labor hours available in one or more of the four departments. The study of the effect changes such as these have on the optimal solution to the linear program is called *sensitivity analysis*.

In this section we show how graphical solution methods can be used to perform sensitivity analysis on the objective function coefficients and on the right-hand side values for the constraints.

Objective Function Coefficients

Let us first consider how changes in the objective function coefficients might affect the number of standard bags and the number of deluxe bags that Par, Inc. should produce. For example, the profit associated with one standard bag is $10. Suppose that an increase in raw material cost reduces the profit for standard bags to $9.50 per bag, while the profit for the deluxe bags and all the constraints remain unchanged. Such a small change in the profitability of the standard bag may have no effect on the optimal solution, and Par Inc. may still maximize its profit by manufacturing 540 standard bags and 252 deluxe bags. However, if the profitability of the standard bags were reduced further, it might be advisable for Par to reduce the number of standard bags produced and increase production of the more profitable deluxe bags. For example, in Section 2.6 we saw that when the profit for standard bags was reduced to $5 per bag a new optimal solution consisting of 300 standard bags and 420 deluxe bags was obtained (see Figure 2.13).

Sensitivity analysis of the objective function coefficients involves computing the range of values for the objective function coefficients that will not cause a change in the optimal solution to the problem. That is, what range of values for the profit of standard bags can exist without causing Par, Inc. to change from the solution of 540 standard bags and 252 deluxe bags? Such a range of values is called the *range of optimality* for the objective function coefficient.

Figure 2.21 shows the graphical solution to the Par, Inc. problem. A careful inspection of this graph shows that as long as the slope of the objective function is between the slope of line A (which coincides with the

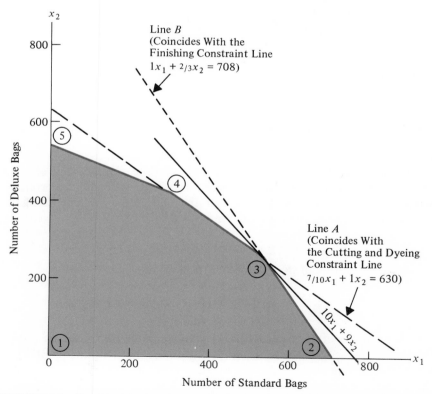

FIGURE 2.21   Graphical Solution of Par, Inc. Problem With Slope of Objective Function Between Slopes of Line A and Line B. Extreme Point ③ Is Optimal

cutting and dyeing constraint line) and the slope of line B (which coincides with the finishing constraint line), extreme point ③ with $x_1 = 540$ and $x_2 = 252$ will be optimal. Rotating the objective function line counterclockwise (increasing the slope) we find an upper limit on the slope. When the slope of the objective function coincides with that of line A, we obtain alternate optima between the extreme points ③ and ④. Rotating the objective function line clockwise (decreasing the slope) we find a lower limit. In this case, when the slope of the objective function coincides with that of line B, we obtain alternate optima between extreme points ③ and ②.

The equation of line A in Figure 2.21 is

$$\tfrac{7}{10}x_1 + 1x_2 = 630.$$

Writing this equation in slope-intercept form we obtain

$$x_2 = -\tfrac{7}{10}x_1 + 630.$$

Thus the slope of line A is $-\tfrac{7}{10}$.

The equation for line B is

$$1x_1 + \tfrac{2}{3}x_2 = 708.$$

Writing this equation in slope-intercept form, we have

$$x_2 = -\tfrac{3}{2}x_1 + 1062.$$

Thus the slope of line B is $-\tfrac{3}{2}$.

Now that the slopes of line A and line B have been computed, we can identify the interval within which the slope of the objective function must lie in order for extreme point ③ with $x_1 = 540$ and $x_2 = 252$ to remain optimal. That is, we must have

$$-\tfrac{3}{2} \leq \quad \text{the slope of the objective function} \quad \leq -\tfrac{7}{10} \qquad (2.12)$$

in order for there to be no change in the optimal solution.

Let us now consider the general form of the slope of the objective function. Let c_1 denote the profit of a standard bag, c_2 denote the profit of a deluxe bag, and z denote the value of the objective function. Using this notation, the objective function can be written as

$$z = c_1 x_1 + c_2 x_2.$$

Writing this equation in slope-intercept form we obtain

$$x_2 = -\frac{c_1}{c_2}x_1 + \frac{z}{c_2}.$$

Thus we see that the slope of the objective function is given by $-c_1/c_2$. Substituting $-c_1/c_2$ into expression (2.12), we see that extreme point ③ will be optimal as long as the following expression is satisfied:

$$-\tfrac{3}{2} \leq -\frac{c_1}{c_2} \leq -\tfrac{7}{10}. \qquad (2.13)$$

When $c_2 = 0$ the slope is undefined and the objective function line is vertical. We consider this case later in the subsection.

Now suppose that the profit coefficient for the deluxe bag stays fixed at $c_2 = 9$. We can compute the range of optimality for the profit coefficient of the standard bag by using expression (2.13) as follows:

$$-\tfrac{3}{2} \leq -c_1/9 \leq -\tfrac{7}{10}.$$

Working with the left-hand inequality, we have

$$-\tfrac{3}{2} \leq -c_1/9,$$
$$c_1 \leq \tfrac{27}{2} = 13.5.$$

Working with the right-hand inequality we have

$$-c_1/9 \leq -\tfrac{7}{10},$$
$$c_1 \geq \tfrac{63}{10} = 6.3.$$

Therefore we see that the range of optimality for the profit coefficient of the standard bag is given by

$$6.3 \leq c_1 \leq 13.5.$$

We can conclude that for a deluxe bag profit of $9 per unit the profit of standard bags can be between $6.30 and $13.50 per unit, and the solution $x_1 = 540$ and $x_2 = 252$ will remain optimal.

Setting $c_1 = 10$ in expression (2.13) and performing some algebraic simplification we obtain a range of optimality for c_2.

$$6\tfrac{2}{3} \leq c_2 \leq 14\tfrac{2}{7}.$$

Thus for a standard bag profit of $10.00 per unit the profit on deluxe bags can range from $6.67 to $14.29 per bag and the solution $x_1 = 540$ and $x_2 = 252$ will remain optimal.

We caution the reader that in some cases it may not be possible to compute either the upper or lower limit on the slope of the objective function. Suppose the objective function for the Par, Inc. problem had been such that extreme point ② was optimal. Rotating counterclockwise we find the upper limit on the slope $(-\tfrac{3}{2})$ to be when the objective function line coincides with the finishing constraint line (extreme points ② and ③ are alternate optima). Rotating clockwise, as the objective function line approaches a vertical line its slope approaches minus infinity $(-\infty)$ and we cannot obtain a lower limit to use in (2.13). Further analysis in this case shows there is no lower limit on c_2 and no upper limit on c_1.

In summary, to compute the range of optimality for objective function coefficients we must first determine the interval within which the slope of the objective function must lie to maintain optimality. With the limits expressed in the form of expression (2.13) we solve for the objective function coefficients one at a time to compute the appropriate range of optimality. In cases where either the upper or lower limit is undefined (eg. extreme point ②) further analysis is necessary.

Right-Hand Sides

Let us now consider how a change in the right-hand-side value for a constraint may affect the feasible region and perhaps cause a change in the optimal solution to the problem. For example, let us consider what happens if an additional 10 hours of production time are made available in the cutting and dyeing department. The right-hand side of the cutting and dyeing constraint is changed from 630 to 640, and the constraint is written

$$\tfrac{7}{10}x_1 + x_2 \leq 640.$$

By obtaining an additional 10 hours of cutting and dyeing time we have expanded the feasible region for the problem, as shown in Figure 2.22. Since the feasible region has been enlarged, we want to determine whether or not one of the new feasible solutions provides an improvement in the value of the objective function. Applying the graphical solution procedure to the problem with the enlarged feasible region shows that the extreme point at $x_1 = 527.5$ and $x_2 = 270.75$ now provides the optimal solution. The new value for the objective function is $10(527.5) + 9(270.75) = \$7711.75$; this provides an

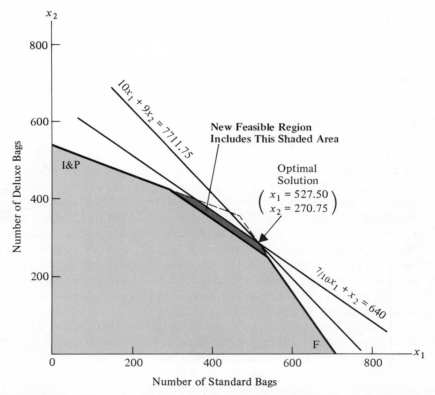

FIGURE 2.22   Effect of a 10-unit Change in the Right-Hand-Side of the Cutting and Dyeing Constraint

increase in profit of $7711.75 − 7668.00 = $43.75. Thus the increased profit occurs at a rate of $43.75/10 = $4.375 per hour added.

The change in the value of the objective function resulting from a one-unit increase in the value of the right-hand side is called the *shadow price*. The shadow price of a particular constraint is considered important because it may be possible to purchase or obtain additional units of the resource. The value of the shadow price represents the maximum a manager should be willing to pay to obtain an additional unit of the resource. In the Par, Inc. problem, if it is possible to obtain additional hours of cutting and dyeing time, we should be willing to pay up to $4.375 per hour for it.

We caution here that the value of the shadow price may be applicable only for small changes in the right-hand-side value. As more and more resources are obtained and the right-hand-side value continues to increase, other constraints will become binding and limit the change in the value of the objective function. For example, in the Par, Inc. problem at some point enough hours can be added to the cutting and dyeing department so that the constraint will no longer be binding. The optimal solution will then be found at the intersection of the inspection and packaging constraint line and the finishing constraint line. At this point, additional hours for the cutting and dyeing department will have no effect on the value of the objective function. The topic of how much one can change a resource or right-hand-side value before it is no longer desirable to do so will be discussed further in Chapter 4.

We close this section on sensitivity analysis by noting that the value of the shadow price associated with a nonbinding constraint is always zero. The reason for this is that a nonbinding constraint will have a positive value for its corresponding slack or surplus variable. Therefore a small change in the value of the right-hand side for the constraint will merely change the amount of slack or surplus in the final solution and will not affect the value of the objective function. Thus the shadow price for the corresponding resource will be zero.

Summary

Two problems, the Par, Inc. and Photo Chemicals, Inc., were formulated as linear programs and solved by a graphical procedure. In studying the graphical solution procedure we noted that if an optimal solution to a linear programming problem exists, it occurs at one of the extreme points of the feasible region.

In the process of formulating a mathematical model of these problems the following general definition of a linear program was developed.

A linear program is a mathematical model which has the following properties:

1. A linear objective function which is to be maximized or minimized;
2. A set of linear constraints;
3. Variables which are all restricted to nonnegative values.

We have seen how slack variables can be used to write less-than-or-equal-to constraints in equality form and how surplus variables can be used to write greater-than-or-equal-to constraints in equality form. The value of a slack variable can usually be interpreted as the amount of unused resource, while the value of a surplus variable indicates the amount over and above some stated minimum requirement. We stated that when all constraints have been written as equalities, the linear program has been written in its Standard form. In special cases of infeasibility and unboundedness, we showed that there was no optimal solution to the problem. In the case of infeasibility there are no feasible solutions, while in the case of unboundedness the objective function can be made infinitely large for a maximization problem and infinitely small for a minimization problem. In addition, a third special case, alternate optima, was discussed. In this case we have two optimal extreme points, and all the points on the line segment connecting them are also optimal. Finally, we concluded the chapter by discussing sensitivity analysis for the objective function coefficients and the right-hand-side values. In doing so we presented the important concept of the shadow price, which shows the value of an additional unit of a particular resource.

Glossary

1. *Objective function*—All linear programs have a linear objective function that is either to be maximized or minimized. In most linear programming problems the objective function will be used to measure the profit or cost of a particular solution.

2. *Constraint*—An equation or inequality which rules out certain combinations of variables as feasible solutions.

3. *Constraint function*—The left-hand side of a constraint relationship (that is, the portion of the constraint containing the variables).

4. *Solution*—Any set of values for the variables.

5. *Optimal solution*—A feasible solution that maximizes or minimizes the value of the objective function.

6. *Nonnegativity constraints*—A set of constraints that requires all variables to be nonnegative.

7. *Mathematical model*—A representation of a problem where the objective and all constraint conditions are described by mathematical expressions.

8. *Linear program*—A mathematical model with a linear objective function, a set of linear constraints, and nonnegative variables.

9. *Linear equations or functions*—Mathematical expressions in which the variables appear in separate terms and are raised to the first power.

10. *Feasible solution*—A solution which satisfies all the constraints.

11. *Feasible region*—The set of all possible feasible solutions.

12. *Redundant constraint*—A constraint which does not affect the feasible region. If a constraint is redundant, it could be removed from the problem without affecting the feasible region.

13.   *Extreme point*—Graphically speaking, extreme points are the feasible solution points occurring at the vertices or "corners" of the feasible region. With two variables, extreme points are determined by the intersection of the constraint lines.

14.   *Slack variable*—A variable added to the left-hand side of a less-than-or-equal-to constraint to convert the constraint into an equality. The value of this variable can usually be interpreted as the amount of unused resource.

15.   *Surplus variable*—A variable subtracted from the left-hand side of a greater-than-or-equal-to constraint to convert the constraint into an equality. The value of this variable can usually be interpreted as the amount over and above the required minimum level.

16.   *Standard form*—A linear program in which all of the constraints are written as equalities. The optimal solution of the Standard form of a linear program is the same as the optimal solution of the original formulation of the linear program.

17.   *Alternate optima*—The situation when a linear program has two or more optimal solutions.

18.   *Infeasibility*—The situation in which there is no solution to the linear programming problem which satisfies all the constraints.

19.   *Unbounded*—A maximization linear programming problem is said to be unbounded if the value of the solution may be made infinitely large without violating any of the constraints.

20.   *Range of optimality*—The range of values over which the objective function coefficient for a variable may change without changing the optimal solution.

21.   *Shadow price*—The change in the value of the objective function resulting from adding one unit to the right-hand side of a linear programming constraint.

Problems

1.   Consider the following linear programming problem:

$$\max \quad 4x_1 + 8x_2$$
$$\text{s.t.}$$
$$1x_1 + 4x_2 \le 8$$
$$1x_1 + 1x_2 \le 5$$
$$x_1, x_2 \ge 0.$$

Find the optimal solution. What is the value of the objective function at the optimal solution?

2.   Consider the following linear programming problem:

$$\max \quad 3x_1 + 3x_2$$
$$\text{s.t.}$$
$$2x_1 + 4x_2 \le 12$$
$$6x_1 + 4x_2 \le 24$$
$$x_1, x_2 \ge 0.$$

    a. Find the optimal solution.

    b. If the objective function were changed to $2x_1 + 6x_2$, what would the optimal solution be?

    c. How many extreme points are there? What are the values of x_1 and x_2 at each extreme point?

3. Consider the following linear programming problem:

$$\max \quad 3x_1 + 2x_2$$

$$\text{s.t.}$$

$$2x_1 + 2x_2 \le 8$$
$$3x_1 + 2x_2 \le 12$$
$$1x_1 + .5x_2 \le 3$$
$$x_1, x_2 \ge 0.$$

    a. Find the optimal solution. What is the value of the objective function?

    b. Does this problem have a redundant constraint? If so, what is it? Does the solution change if the redundant constraint is removed from the problem? Explain.

4. Suppose that the management of Par, Inc. encounters each of the following situations:

    a. The accounting department revises its profit estimate on the deluxe bags to $18 per bag.

    b. A new low-cost material is available for the standard bag, and the profit per standard bag can be increased to $20 per bag. (Assume the profit of the deluxe bag is the original $9 value.)

    c. New sewing equipment is available and would increase the sewing operation capacity to 750 hours. (Assume $10x_1 + 9x_2$ is the appropriate objective function.)

If each of the above conditions is encountered separately, what is the optimal solution and profit for each situation?

5. Which of the following mathematical relationships could be found in a linear programming model and which could not? For the relationships that are unacceptable for linear programs, state your reasons.

    a. $-1x_1 + 2x_2 - 1x_3 \le 70.$

    b. $2x_1 - 2x_3 = 50.$

    c. $1x_1 - 2x_2^2 + 4x_3 \le 10.$

    d. $3\sqrt{x_1} + 2x_2 - 1x_3 \ge 15.$

    e. $1x_1 + 1x_2 + 1x_3 = 6.$

    f. $2x_1 + 5x_2 + 1x_1x_2 \le 25.$

6. Kelson Sporting Equipment, Inc. makes two different types of baseball gloves: a regular model and a catcher's model. The firm has 900 hours of production time available in its cutting and sewing department, 300 hours of production time available in its finishing department, and 100 hours of production time available in its packaging and shipping department. The production time requirements and the profit per glove are given below:

Model	Production Time (hours)			
	Cutting and Sewing	Finishing	Packaging and Shipping	Profit/Glove
Regular model	1	1/2	1/8	$5
Catcher's model	3/2	1/3	1/4	$8

a. Assuming that the company wants to maximize profit, how many gloves of each model should Kelson manufacture?
b. What is the profit Kelson can earn with the above production quantities?
c. How many hours of production time will be scheduled in each department?
d. What is the slack time in each department?

7. The Erlanger Manufacturing Company makes two products. The profit estimates are $25 for each unit of product 1 sold and $30 for each unit of product 2 sold. The labor-hour requirements for the products in each of three production departments are summarized below:

	Product 1	Product 2
Department A	1.50	3.00
Department B	2.00	1.00
Department C	.25	.25

The production supervisors in the departments have estimated the following number of labor-hours available during the next month: 450 hours in department A, 350 hours in department B, and 50 hours in department C. Assuming that the company is interested in maximizing profits, answer the following:
a. What is the linear programming model for this problem?
b. Find the optimal solution. How much of each product should be produced, and what is the projected profit?
c. What is the scheduled production time and slack time in each department?

8. Yard Care, Inc. manufactures a variety of lawn care products, including two well-known lawn fertilizers. Each fertilizer product is a blend of two raw materials known as K40 and K50. During the current production period, 900 pounds of K40 and 400 pounds of K50 are available. Each pound of the product known as "Green Lawn" uses 3/5 pound of K40 and 2/5 pound of K50. Each pound of the product known as "Lawn Care" uses 3/4 pound of K40 and 1/4 pound of K50. In addition, a current limit on the availability of packaging materials restricts the production of Lawn Care to a maximum of 500 pounds.
a. If the profit contribution for both products is $3 per pound, how many pounds of each product should the company manufacture?
b. Should it be a concern to the company that the availability of packaging materials is restricting the production of Lawn Care? What would happen to the production quantities and the projected profit if the firm were able to remove the restriction on the amount of Lawn Care that could be produced?

9. Special K Candy Company has a limited supply of a chocolate ingredient that is used in the production of two of its candy bar products. The company's "Chocolate Wonder Bar" uses .5 ounce of the chocolate ingredient per bar. The company's "Big Crunch Bar" uses .3 ounce per bar. During the coming month the company has a maximum of 250 pounds of chocolate available for use in these two products. In addition, the marketing department reports that the maximum quantities that the company can sell are 5000 bars of Chocolate Wonder and 7500 bars of Big Crunch. If the company can make a profit of 12 cents for each Chocolate Wonder Bar and 8 cents for each Big Crunch Bar, what mix of these two products will maximize the firm's profits?

10. What constraint lines combine to form extreme point ④ of the Par, Inc. problem (see Figure 2.16)? Solve the simultaneous linear equations to show that the exact values of x_1 and x_2 at this extreme point are $x_1 = 300$ and $x_2 = 420$.

11. Investment Advisors, Inc. is a brokerage firm that manages stock portfolios for a number of clients. A new client has requested that the firm handle an $80,000 investment portfolio. As an initial investment strategy the client would like to restrict the portfolio to a mix of the following stocks:

Stock	Price/ Share	Estimated Annual Return/Share	Risk Index/Share
US Oil	$25	$3	.50
Hub Properties	$50	$5	.25

The risk index for the stock is a rating of the relative risk of the two investment alternatives. For the data given, US Oil is judged to be the more risky investment. By constraining the total risk for the portfolio, the investment firm avoids placing excessive amounts of the portfolio in potentially high-return but also high-risk investments. For the current portfolio an upper limit of 700 has been set for the total risk index of all investments. In addition, the firm has set an upper limit of 1000 shares for the more risky US Oil stock. How many shares of each stock should be purchased in order to maximize the total annual return?

12. Consider the following linear program:

$$\min \quad 3x_1 + 4x_2$$

s.t.

$$1x_1 + 3x_2 \geq 6$$
$$1x_1 + 1x_2 \geq 4$$
$$x_1, x_2 \geq 0.$$

Identify the feasible region and find the optimal solution. What is the value of the objective function?

13. Greentree Kennels, Inc., provides overnight lodging for a variety of pets. A particular feature at Greentree's is the quality of care the pets receive, including excellent food. The kennel's dog food is made by mixing two brand-name dog food products to obtain what the kennel calls the "well-balanced dog diet." The data for the two dog foods are as follows:

Dog Food	Cost/ Ounce	Protein (percent)	Fat (percent)
Bark Bits	$.06	30	15
Canine Chow	$.05	20	30

If Greentree wants to be sure that the dogs receive at least 5 ounces of protein and at least 3 ounces of fat per day, what is the minimum cost mix of the two dog food products?

14. Jack Kammer has been trying to figure out the correct amount of fertilizer that should be applied to his lawn. After getting his soil analyzed at the local agricultural agency, he was advised to put at least 60 pounds of nitrogen, 24 pounds of phosphorus compounds, and 40 pounds of potassium compounds on the lawn this season. One third of the mixture is to be applied in May, one third in July, and one

third in late September. After checking the local discount stores, Jack finds that one store is currently having a sale on packaged fertilizer. One type on sale is the 20–5–20 mixture consisting of 20% nitrogen, 5% phosphorus compounds, and 20% potassium compounds, and selling at $4 for a 20 pound bag. The other type on sale is a 10–10–5 mixture selling for $5 for a 40 pound bag. Jack would like to know how many bags of each type he should purchase so he can combine the ingredients to form a mixture that will meet the minimum agricultural agency requirements. Like all homeowners plagued by large lawns, Jack would like to spend as little as possible to keep his lawn healthy. What should Jack do?

15. Write the following linear program in Standard form:

$$\max \quad 5x_1 + 2x_2 + 8x_3$$

s.t.

$$1x_1 - 2x_2 + \tfrac{1}{2}x_3 \le 420$$
$$2x_1 + 3x_2 - 1x_3 \le 610$$
$$6x_1 - 1x_2 + 3x_3 \le 125$$
$$x_1, x_2, x_3 \ge 0.$$

16. For the linear program

$$\max \quad 4x_1 + 1x_2$$

s.t.

$$10x_1 + 2x_2 \le 30$$
$$3x_1 + 2x_2 \le 12$$
$$2x_1 + 2x_2 \le 10$$
$$x_1, x_2 \ge 0$$

a. Write this problem in its Standard form.
b. Solve the problem.
c. What are the values of the three slack variables at the optimal solution?

17. Given the linear program

$$\max \quad 3x_1 + 4x_2$$

s.t.

$$-1x_1 + 2x_2 \le 8$$
$$1x_1 + 2x_2 \le 12$$
$$2x_1 + 1x_2 \le 16$$
$$x_1, x_2 \ge 0$$

a. Write the problem in its Standard form.
b. Solve the problem.
c. What are the values of the three slack variables at the optimal solution?

18. For the linear program

$$\min \quad 6x_1 + 4x_2$$

s.t.

$$2x_1 + 1x_2 \ge 12$$
$$1x_1 + 1x_2 \ge 10$$
$$1x_2 \le 4$$
$$x_1, x_2 \ge 0$$

a. Write the problem in its Standard form.
b. Solve the problem using the graphical procedure.
c. What are the values of the slack and surplus variables?

19. Consider the following linear program:

$$\max \quad 1x_1 + 2x_2$$

s.t.

$$1x_1 \qquad \leq \ 5$$
$$1x_2 \leq \ 4$$
$$2x_1 + 2x_2 = 12$$
$$x_1, x_2 \geq 0.$$

a. Graphically show the feasible region.
b. What are the extreme points of the feasible region?
c. Find the optimal solution by the graphical procedure.

20. Consider the following linear program:

$$\min \quad 2x_1 + 2x_2$$

s.t.

$$1x_1 + 3x_2 \leq 12$$
$$3x_1 + 1x_2 \geq 13$$
$$1x_1 - 1x_2 = \ 3$$
$$x_1, x_2 \geq 0.$$

a. Graphically show the feasible region.
b. What are the extreme points of the feasible region?
c. Find the optimal solution by the graphical procedure.

21. Bryant's Pizza, Inc. is a producer of frozen pizza products. The company makes a profit of $1.00 for each regular pizza it produces and $1.50 for each deluxe pizza produced. Each pizza includes a combination of dough mix and topping mix. Currently the firm has 150 pounds of dough mix and 50 pounds of topping mix. Each regular pizza uses 1 pound of dough mix and 4 ounces of topping mix. Each deluxe pizza uses 1 pound of dough mix and 8 ounces of topping mix. Based on past demand Bryant can sell at least 50 regular pizzas and at least 25 deluxe pizzas. How many regular and deluxe pizzas should the company make in order to maximize profits?
a. Show the above problem in Standard form.
b. What are the values and interpretations of all slack and surplus variables?
c. Which constraints are binding the optimal solution?

22. Wilkinson Motors, Inc. sells standard automobiles and station wagons. The firm makes $400 profit for each automobile it sells and $500 profit for each station wagon it sells. The company is planning next quarter's order, which the manufacturer says cannot exceed 300 automobiles and 150 station wagons. Dealer preparation time requires 2 hours for each automobile and 3 hours for each station wagon. Next quarter the company has 900 hours of shop time available for new car preparation. How many automobiles and station wagons should be ordered so that profit is maximized?
a. Show the linear programming model of the above problem.
b. Show the Standard form and identify the slack variables.
c. Identify the extreme points of the feasible region.

   d. Solve.

   e. Which constraints are binding the optimal solution?

23. Ryland Farms in northwestern Indiana grows soybeans and corn on its 500 acres of land. An acre of soybeans brings a $100 profit and an acre of corn brings a $200 profit. Because of government regulations no more than 200 acres may be planted in soybeans. During the planting season 1200 hours of planting time will be available. Each acre of soybeans requires 2 hours, while each acre of corn requires 6 hours. How many acres of soybeans and how many acres of corn should be planted in order to maximize profits?

   a. Show the linear programming model of the above problem.

   b. Show the Standard form and identify all slack variables.

   c. Solve.

   d. Identify all the extreme points of the feasible region.

   e. If the farm could get either more hours of labor for planting or additional land, which should it attempt to obtain? Why?

24. The marketing department of KT Company is interested in finding out how to get the greatest audience exposure from its current advertising budget. The company would like to determine how much of its advertising budget should be spent on each of three media: radio, television, and newspaper.

     Each dollar spent on radio advertising is worth 6 exposure points to the company. Similarly, KT believes it will get 5 and 8 exposure points, respectively, for every dollar spent on television and newspaper advertising.

     KT's total advertising budget consists of $10,000. However, because of an agreement with a local television station, KT may not spend more than half as much on radio advertising as it does on television. In addition, the combined expenditure on television and newspaper advertising may not exceed 80% of the total advertising expenditure.

     Assuming that KT is interested in maximizing its exposure points, formulate this problem as a linear program. (Hint: Let x_1 = dollars spent on radio, x_2 = dollars spent on television, and x_3 = dollars spent on newspaper.) Set up the Standard form for this problem and interpret all slack variables. (Do not attempt to solve this problem.)

25. Does the following linear program involve infeasibility, unboundedness, and/or alternate optimal solutions? Explain.

$$\max \quad 4x_1 + 8x_2$$

$$\text{s.t.}$$

$$2x_1 + 2x_2 \le 10$$
$$-1x_1 + 1x_2 \ge 8$$
$$x_1, x_2 \ge 0.$$

26. Does the following linear program involve infeasibility, unboundedness, and/or alternate optimal solutions? Explain.

$$\max \quad 1x_1 + 1x_2$$

$$\text{s.t.}$$

$$8x_1 + 6x_2 \ge 24$$
$$4x_1 + 6x_2 \ge -12$$
$$2x_2 \ge 4$$
$$x_1, x_2 \ge 0.$$

27. Consider the following linear program:

$$\max \quad 1x_1 + 1x_2$$

$$\text{s.t.}$$

$$5x_1 + 3x_2 \leq 15$$
$$3x_1 + 5x_2 \leq 15$$
$$x_1, x_2 \geq 0.$$

   a. What is the optimal solution for this problem?
   b. Suppose that the objective function is changed to $1x_1 + 2x_2$. Find the new optimal solution.
   c. By adjusting the coefficient of x_2 in the objective function, develop a new objective function that will make the solutions found in parts a and b above alternate optimal solutions.

28. Consider the following linear program:

$$\max \quad 1x_1 - 2x_2$$

$$\text{s.t.}$$

$$-4x_1 + 3x_2 \leq 3$$
$$1x_1 - 1x_2 \leq 3$$
$$x_1, x_2 \geq 0.$$

   a. Graph the feasible region for the problem.
   b. Is the feasible region unbounded? Explain.
   c. Find the optimal solution.
   d. Does an unbounded feasible region imply that the optimal solution to the linear program will be unbounded?

29. Given below are three objective functions for linear programming problems:

$$z = 7x_1 + 10x_2,$$
$$z = 6x_1 + 4x_2,$$
$$z = -4x_1 + 7x_2.$$

   Find the slope of the objective function in each case. Show the graph of each of the three objective functions.

30. Reconsider the Kelson Sporting Equipment, Inc. production example (Problem 6). Discuss the concepts of infeasibility, unboundedness, and alternate optima as they occur in each of the following situations:
   a. Management has requested that the production of baseball gloves (regular model plus catcher's model) be such that the total number of gloves produced is at least 750. That is, $1x_1 + 1x_2 \geq 750$.
   b. The original problem has to be solved again because the profit for the regular model is adjusted downward to $4 per glove.
   c. What would have to happen for this problem to be unbounded?

31. Compute the range of optimality for the objective function coefficients in the Kelson Sporting Equipment, Inc. example presented in Problem 6. What is your interpretation of the ranges you have found?

32. Reconsider the Investment Advisors portfolio decision from Problem 11.
   a. What range of the return per share of US Oil could exist before it would be desirable to consider modifying the portfolio?
   b. What range of the return per share of Hub Properties could exist before it would be desirable to consider modifying the portfolio?

c. Just before the stock purchases were to be made a financial analyst's report projected a return of $5 per share for US Oil. Should the firm consider modifying the original portfolio decision? Explain. If you decided to modify the decision, what is the revised decision?

33. Perform sensitivity analysis on the coefficients of the objective function for the Wilkinson Motors, Inc. example in Problem 22. What range of values can the profits for automobiles and station wagons take on before it would be desirable for Wilkinson to change its order decision of 300 automobiles and 100 station wagons?

34. With regard to Wilkinson Motors, Inc. (Problem 22)
    a. What are the binding constraints?
    b. Would it be desirable for Wilkinson to consider providing additional hours of dealer preparation time? Use the shadow price concept to determine the value of one additional hour of dealer preparation time.
    c. If the overtime cost of obtaining additional hours of preparation time is $20.00 per hour, should the company consider the use of overtime? Explain.
    d. What happens if the company attempts to add more than 150 hours of overtime?

35. What are the shadow prices associated with the three production departments for Kelson Sporting Equipment, Inc. (Problem 6)? What is your interpretation of these values?

36. The shadow price of the cutting and dyeing department time in the Par, Inc. problem was shown to be $4.375 per hour. What are the shadow prices associated with the other three Par production departments? What is your interpretation of these values? If Par would consider additional hours of production time, which department should be the first priority? Explain.

37. In order to satisfy the production and raw material usage constraints for the Photo Chemicals, Inc. problem of Section 2.7, the solution called for $x_1 = 30$ and $x_2 = 25$, with a total cost of 55. Management is considering relaxing the raw material constraint such that less than the full 80 pounds of raw material must be used. What is the shadow price or value per unit associated with relaxing the raw material usage constraint? If it is economically desirable to reduce the raw material constraint, what is the maximum amount that poundage can be reduced? Explain.

Chapter 3

Linear Programming: The Simplex Method

In Chapter 2 we saw how to find the optimal solution for two-variable linear programming problems using the graphical procedure. However, most real-world problems contain more than two decision variables and are thus too large for this solution technique. An algebraic solution procedure, the Simplex method, will have to be used to solve these larger linear programming problems. Computer programs of the Simplex method are used routinely to solve linear programming problems having as many as several thousand variables and constraints.

In this chapter we first present the Simplex method in a step-by-step fashion using the Par, Inc. maximization problem of Chapter 2. We will then use the Photo Chemicals, Inc. example of Chapter 2 to show how the Simplex method can be used to solve minimization problems. After the method has been developed for these particular problems, we will set forth the general Simplex procedure which can be used to solve any linear program.

3.1   An Algebraic Overview of the Simplex Method

Let us return to the Par, Inc. problem, which is written below in its Standard form:

$$\max \quad 10x_1 + 9x_2 + 0s_1 + 0s_2 + 0s_3 + 0s_4 \tag{3.1}$$

s.t.

$$\tfrac{7}{10}x_1 + 1x_2 + 1s_1 \qquad\qquad\qquad = 630 \tag{3.2}$$

$$\tfrac{1}{2}x_1 + \tfrac{5}{6}x_2 \qquad + 1s_2 \qquad\qquad = 600 \tag{3.3}$$

$$1x_1 + \tfrac{2}{3}x_2 \qquad\qquad + 1s_3 \qquad = 708 \tag{3.4}$$

$$\tfrac{1}{10}x_1 + \tfrac{1}{4}x_2 \qquad\qquad\qquad + 1s_4 = 135 \tag{3.5}$$

$$x_1, x_2, s_1, s_2, s_3, s_4 \geq 0. \tag{3.6}$$

What is involved in finding the optimal solution to this problem algebraically? First note that equations (3.2)–(3.5), the constraint equations, form a system of four simultaneous linear equations in six variables. In order to satisfy the constraints of the Par, Inc. problem, the optimal solution must be a solution to this set of linear equations. Whenever a set of simultaneous equations has more variables than constraints, we can expect an infinite number of solutions. Thus any algebraic procedure for solving linear programs must be capable of finding solutions to systems of simultaneous equations involving more variables than equations.

Second, note that not every solution to equations (3.2)–(3.5) is a feasible solution to the linear program. That is, we cannot expect every solution to equations (3.2)–(3.5) to satisfy also the nonnegativity conditions $(x_1, x_2, s_1, s_2, s_3, s_4 \geq 0)$. Thus we see that an algebraic procedure for solving linear programming problems should be capable of eliminating from consideration those solutions to equations (3.2)–(3.5) which do not also satisfy the nonnegativity requirement.

Finally, an algebraic procedure for solving linear programs must be capable of picking one of these feasible solutions as the one which maximizes the objective function. The *Simplex method* is an algebraic procedure with all three of the capabilities outlined above.

Since the Par, Inc. constraint equations (3.2)–(3.5) have more variables (six) than equations (four), the Simplex method finds solutions for these equations by assigning zero values for two of the variables and then solving for the values of the remaining four variables. For example, suppose we set $x_2 = 0$ and $s_1 = 0$. Our system of equations then becomes

$$\tfrac{7}{10} x_1 \qquad\qquad\qquad = 630 \qquad\qquad (3.7)$$

$$\tfrac{1}{2} x_1 + 1 s_2 \qquad\qquad = 600 \qquad\qquad (3.8)$$

$$1 x_1 \qquad + 1 s_3 \qquad = 708 \qquad\qquad (3.9)$$

$$\tfrac{1}{10} x_1 \qquad\qquad + 1 s_4 = 135. \qquad\qquad (3.10)$$

By setting $x_2 = 0$ and $s_1 = 0$ we have in effect reduced our system of linear equations to four variables and four equations.

Using equation (3.7) to solve for x_1, we have

$$\tfrac{7}{10} x_1 = 630$$

$$x_1 = \tfrac{10}{7} (630) = 900.$$

Substituting this value of x_1 in the remaining equations provides the following values for s_2, s_3, and s_4.

$$s_2 = 600 - \tfrac{1}{2}(900) = 150$$

$$s_3 = 708 - 1(900) = -192$$

$$s_4 = 135 - \tfrac{1}{10}(900) = 45.$$

Thus we have found the following solution to the four-equation, six-variable set of linear equations determined by the Par, Inc. constraints:

$$\begin{bmatrix} x_1 \\ x_2 \\ s_1 \\ s_2 \\ s_3 \\ s_4 \end{bmatrix} = \begin{bmatrix} 900 \\ 0 \\ 0 \\ 150 \\ -192 \\ 45 \end{bmatrix}$$

The above solution is referred to as a *basic solution* for the linear programming problem. In general, if we have a Standard form linear programming problem consisting of n variables and m equations, where n is greater than m, a basic solution can be obtained by setting $n - m$ of the variables equal to zero and solving the m constraint equations for the remaining m variables.[1] In terms of our Par, Inc. problem, a basic solution

---

[1]There are cases where a unique solution cannot be found for the resulting system of m equations in m variables. However, these cases are exceptions to the rule and will never be encountered when using the Simplex method.

can be obtained by setting *any* two variables equal to zero and then solving the system of four equations for the remaining four variables. We shall refer to the $n - m$ variables set equal to zero as the *nonbasic* variables and the remaining m variables (usually nonzero) as the *basic* variables. Thus in the example above, x_2 and s_1 are the nonbasic variables and x_1, s_2, s_3, and s_4 are the basic variables.

Using Elementary Row Operations to Find Basic Solutions

The computational procedure that the Simplex method uses to find basic solutions is based upon the use of *elementary row operations*. Actually elementary row operations can be used to solve any system of simultaneous linear equations. However, here we are only interested in solving linear programs, so we will restrict our attention to using elementary row operations for finding basic solutions to linear programs.

The elementary row operations that will be used are as follows:

1. Multiplication of any row (equation) by a nonzero number.
2. Replacing any row (equation) by the result of adding or subtracting a multiple of another row (equation) to it.

The application of these elementary row operations to a system of simultaneous linear equations will not change the solution to the system of equations; however, the row operations will change the coefficients of the variables and the values of the right-hand sides.

The system of simultaneous equations that must be solved when using the Simplex method is the set of constraint equations in the Standard form representation of the problem. By applying a sequence of elementary row operations to these constraint equations, the Simplex method changes the coefficients of the constraint equations in such a fashion that the value of the basic solution desired is given by the values on the right-hand sides of the constraint equations.

Previously in this section we showed that a basic solution for the Par, Inc. linear program is $x_1 = 900$, $x_2 = 0$, $s_1 = 0$, $s_2 = 150$, $s_3 = -192$, and $s_4 = 45$. Let us now illustrate how elementary row operations can be used to obtain the same basic solution. The constraint equations in the Standard form representation of the Par, Inc. problem are rewritten below:

$$\tfrac{7}{10}x_1 + 1x_2 + 1s_1 \qquad\qquad = 630 \qquad (3.2)$$
$$\tfrac{1}{2}x_1 + \tfrac{5}{6}x_2 \quad + 1s_2 \qquad\qquad = 600 \qquad (3.3)$$
$$1x_1 + \tfrac{2}{3}x_2 \qquad\qquad + 1s_3 \quad = 708 \qquad (3.4)$$
$$\tfrac{1}{10}x_1 + \tfrac{1}{4}x_2 \qquad\qquad\qquad + 1s_4 = 135. \qquad (3.5)$$

Using row operation 1, we multiply (3.2) by the nonzero number $\tfrac{10}{7}$ to obtain (3.2′) as follows:

$$\tfrac{10}{7}\left(\tfrac{7}{10}x_1 + 1x_2 + 1s_1 = 630\right)$$

or

$$1x_1 + \tfrac{10}{7}x_2 + \tfrac{10}{7}s_1 = 900. \qquad (3.2′)$$

We next apply row operation 2 by multiplying (3.2′) by $-\frac{1}{2}$ and adding the result to (3.3). Thus the second row becomes (3.3′), as shown below:

$$-\tfrac{1}{2}(1x_1 + {}^{10}\!/_{7}x_2 + {}^{10}\!/_{7}s_1 = 900)$$

$$\longrightarrow -\tfrac{1}{2}x_1 - \tfrac{5}{7}x_2 - \tfrac{5}{7}s_1 \qquad\qquad = -450$$

$$\text{added to (3.3)} \qquad \tfrac{1}{2}x_1 + \tfrac{5}{6}x_2 \qquad\qquad + 1s_2 = \quad 600$$

$$\tfrac{5}{4}x_2 - \tfrac{5}{7}s_1 + 1s_2 = \quad 150. \qquad (3.3')$$

Row operation 2 is again applied by multiplying (3.2′) by -1 and adding the result to (3.4). Thus we obtain (3.4) as shown below:

$$-1(1x_1 + {}^{10}\!/_{7}x_2 + {}^{10}\!/_{7}s_1 = 900)$$

$$\longrightarrow -1x_1 - {}^{10}\!/_{7}x_2 - {}^{10}\!/_{7}s_1 \qquad\qquad = -900$$

$$\text{added to (3.4)} \qquad 1x_1 + \tfrac{2}{3}x_2 \qquad\qquad + 1s_3 = \quad 708$$

$$-{}^{16}\!/_{21}x_2 - {}^{10}\!/_{7}s_1 + 1s_3 = -192. \qquad (3.4')$$

Finally, row operation 2 is again applied by multiplying (3.2′) by $-\frac{1}{10}$ and adding the result to (3.5). This provides (3.5′), as shown below:

$$-\tfrac{1}{10}(1x_1 + {}^{10}\!/_{7}x_2 + {}^{10}\!/_{7}s_1 = 900)$$

$$\longrightarrow -\tfrac{1}{10}x_1 - \tfrac{1}{7}x_2 - \tfrac{1}{7}s_1 \qquad\qquad = -\ 90$$

$$\text{added to (3.5)} \qquad \tfrac{1}{10}x_1 + \tfrac{1}{4}x_2 \qquad\qquad + 1s_4 = \quad 135$$

$$\tfrac{3}{28}x_2 - \tfrac{1}{7}s_1 + 1s_4 = \quad 45. \qquad (3.5')$$

Thus after applying row operation 1 one time and row operation 2 three times we have transformed the system of linear equations (3.2)–(3.5) into the system of linear equations (3.2′)–(3.5′). This new system of equations is shown below:

$$1x_1 + {}^{10}\!/_{7}x_2 + {}^{10}\!/_{7}s_1 \qquad\qquad\qquad = \quad 900 \qquad (3.2')$$

$$\tfrac{5}{42}x_2 - \tfrac{5}{7}s_1 + 1s_2 \qquad\qquad = \quad 150 \qquad (3.3')$$

$$-{}^{16}\!/_{21}x_2 - {}^{10}\!/_{7}s_1 \qquad + 1s_3 \quad = -192 \qquad (3.4')$$

$$\tfrac{3}{28}x_2 - \tfrac{1}{7}s_1 \qquad\qquad + 1s_4 = \quad 45. \qquad (3.5')$$

As previously stated, elementary row operations can be expected to alter the coefficients of the variables in the equations. However, the solution to the system of equations remains the same; that is, the values of x_1, x_2, s_1, and so on that solve (3.2)–(3.5) also solve (3.2′)–(3.5′). Let us use (3.2′)–(3.5′) to find a basic solution for the Par, Inc. problem.

Recall that a basic solution for the Par, Inc. problem requires two variables to be set equal to zero. Letting $x_2 = 0$ and $s_1 = 0$ allows us to write equations (3.2′)–(3.5′) as follows:

$$1x_1 \qquad\qquad = \quad 900$$

$$1s_2 \qquad\qquad = \quad 150$$

$$1s_3 \qquad = -192$$

$$1s_4 = \quad 45.$$

Thus elementary row operations provide the basic solution $x_1 = 900$, $x_2 = 0$, $s_1 = 0$, $s_2 = 150$, $s_3 = -192$, and $s_4 = 45$. Note that this is the same basic solution we obtained earlier in this section.

The Simplex method employs computations using elementary row operations as demonstrated above. The specific row operations used depend upon the problem. However, as demonstrated above, the goal of the elementary row operations is to transform the original system of constraint equations such that the *values of the basic variables appear in the right-hand side of the system of equations*. The use of elementary row operations appears to have expanded the work necessary to obtain the basic solution, but we shall see later that this extra work is necessary in applying the Simplex method.

Basic Feasible Solutions

Certainly the basic solution identified above is not feasible, since the nonnegativity conditions are not satisfied (that is, s_3 is less than zero). Thus we see that a basic solution does *not* have to be a feasible solution. However, when a basic solution is also feasible, we refer to it as a *basic feasible solution*. For example, setting $x_1 = 0$ and $x_2 = 0$ and solving for s_1, s_2, s_3, and s_4 provides the following result:

$$s_1 \quad = 630$$

$$s_2 \quad = 600$$

$$s_3 \quad = 708$$

$$s_4 = 135.$$

Thus the complete solution corresponding to $x_1 = 0$ and $x_2 = 0$ is

$$\begin{bmatrix} x_1 \\ x_2 \\ s_1 \\ s_2 \\ s_3 \\ s_4 \end{bmatrix} = \begin{bmatrix} 0 \\ 0 \\ 630 \\ 600 \\ 708 \\ 135 \end{bmatrix}$$

Clearly, this solution is a basic solution, since it was obtained by setting two of the variables equal to zero and solving for the other four. Moreover, it is a basic feasible solution, since each of the variables is greater than or equal to zero. Referring to Figure 3.1, we see that this basic feasible solution corresponds to extreme point ① of the feasible region ($x_1 = 0$ and $x_2 = 0$). Thus in this case a basic feasible solution corresponds to an extreme point. This is not just a coincidence, but an important property of all basic feasible solutions. That is, basic feasible solutions always occur at the extreme points

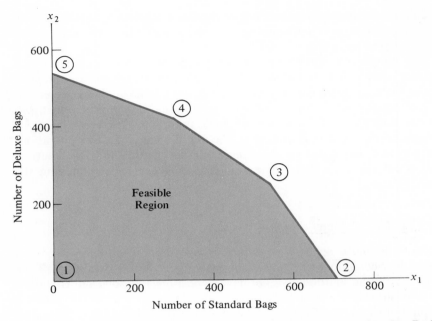

FIGURE 3.1   The Five Extreme Points of the Feasible Region for the Par, Inc. Problem

of the feasible region. In other words, *a basic feasible solution and an extreme point solution are one and the same.*

A basic feasible solution to the system of m constraint equations and n variables is required as a starting point for the Simplex method. When all constraints are of the $\leq$ type, such a solution can be easily found by setting all the decision variables equal to zero. This corresponds to selecting the origin (extreme point ① in the Par, Inc. problem) as the initial basic feasible solution for the Simplex procedure. From this starting point, the Simplex method successively generates basic feasible solutions to our system of equations, making sure that the objective function increases for each new solution. Since, as we saw in Chapter 2, an optimal solution to a linear programming problem always occurs at an extreme point, and since a basic feasible solution and an extreme-point solution are synonymous, the Simplex method must eventually locate an optimal solution to the problem. Thus the Simplex method can be described as an iterative procedure for moving from one basic feasible solution (extreme point) to another until the optimal solution is reached. The way in which this iterative procedure is carried out is the subject of the remainder of this chapter.

3.2   Tableau Form

As discussed in Section 3.1, the Simplex method always begins with a basic feasible solution and then moves from one basic feasible solution to another until the optimal basic feasible solution (extreme point) is reached. Thus prior to beginning the Simplex method, we must find an initial basic feasible solution for the system of constraint equations. Recall that for the Par, Inc. problem the Standard form was

$$\max \quad 10x_1 + 9x_2 + 0s_1 + 0s_2 + 0s_3 + 0s_4$$

s.t.

$$\begin{aligned}
\tfrac{7}{10}x_1 + 1x_2 + 1s_1 &&&&= 630 \\
\tfrac{1}{2}x_1 + \tfrac{5}{6}x_2 &+ 1s_2 &&&= 600 \\
1x_1 + \tfrac{2}{3}x_2 &&+ 1s_3 &&= 708 \\
\tfrac{1}{10}x_1 + \tfrac{1}{4}x_2 &&&+ 1s_4 &= 135
\end{aligned}$$

$$x_1, x_2, s_1, s_2, s_3, s_4 \geq 0.$$

We saw in Section 3.1 that it was easy to find an initial basic feasible solution for this problem by setting $x_1 = 0$, $x_2 = 0$, and solving for s_1, s_2, s_3, and s_4. This procedure resulted in the solution $x_1 = 0$, $x_2 = 0$, $s_1 = 630$, $s_2 = 600$, $s_3 = 708$, and $s_4 = 135$. This basic feasible solution was so easy to find because as soon as x_1 and x_2 had been set equal to zero, the values for the remaining variables could simply be read from the right-hand side of the constraint equations. If we study this particular system of equations closely, we can identify two properties that make it possible to easily find a basic feasible solution.

The first property enables us to find a basic solution. Loosely stated, this property says that m of the variables ($m = 4$ in this case) must each have both a coefficient of one in exactly one equation and appear with a zero coefficient in all other equations. Then if these m variables are made basic by setting the other $n - m$ variables equal to zero, the values of the basic variables can be read from the right-hand side of the constraint equations. In the example the variables s_1, s_2, s_3, and s_4 satisfy this first property.

The second property enables us to easily find a basic feasible solution for a linear program. This property requires that the values on the right-hand side of the constraint equations be nonnegative. In our example we see that this property is also satisfied.

If we can write our linear programming problem in a form which satisfies the first property, then the values of the basic variables are given by the right-hand sides of the constraint equations. If, in addition, the second property is satisfied, the values of the variables will be nonnegative and the basic solution will also be feasible.

If a linear programming problem satisfies both of the above properties, it is said to be in *Tableau form*. Note that the Standard form representation of the Par, Inc. problem is already in Tableau form. In fact, the Standard form and the Tableau form representations of linear programs that have all less-than-or-equal-to constraints and nonnegative right-hand-side values are the same. However, as we shall see later in this chapter, there are many linear programming problems for which Standard form and Tableau form are not the same.

Let us pause for a moment and reflect on the reason for introducing the notion of Tableau form. Since the Simplex method always begins with a basic feasible solution and since the Tableau form provides an easy way of obtaining an initial basic feasible solution, putting a linear programming problem into Tableau form is an important step in preparing the problem for solution by the Simplex method. The following three steps are necessary in order to prepare a linear programming problem for solution using the Simplex method:

Step 1:   Formulate the problem.
Step 2:   Set up the Standard form representation of the problem.
Step 3:   Set up the Tableau form representation of the problem.

3.3   Setting up the Initial Simplex Tableau

After a linear programming problem has been converted to Tableau form, we have an initial basic feasible solution which can be used to begin the Simplex method. The next step is to set up the initial *Simplex tableau*. The Simplex tableau provides a convenient means for keeping track of and performing the calculations necessary during the Simplex solution procedure.

Part of the initial Simplex tableau is simply a table containing all the information shown in the Tableau form representation of a linear program. If we adopt the general notation

$$c_j = \text{objective function coefficient for variable } j,$$

$$b_i = \text{right-hand-side value for constraint } i,$$

$$a_{ij} = \text{coefficient associated with variable } j \text{ in constraint } i,$$

we can show a portion of the Simplex tableau as follows:

$$
\begin{array}{cccc|c}
c_1 & c_2 & \cdots & c_n & \\
\hline
a_{11} & a_{12} & \cdots & a_{1n} & b_1 \\
a_{21} & a_{22} & \cdots & a_{2n} & b_2 \\
\cdot & \cdot & \cdots & \cdot & \cdot \\
\cdot & \cdot & \cdots & \cdot & \cdot \\
\cdot & \cdot & \cdots & \cdot & \cdot \\
a_{m1} & a_{m2} & \cdots & a_{mn} & b_m \\
\end{array}
$$

In the above partial tableau, the horizontal and vertical lines are used to separate the different parts of the Tableau form representation of a linear program. The upper horizontal line separates the coefficients of the variables in the objective function from the coefficients of the variables in the constraint equations. The vertical line can be interpreted as an equality line; the values to the left of this line are the coefficients of the variables in the constraint equations, and those to the right of the line are the right-hand-side values of the constraint equations.

Later we may want to refer to all the objective function coefficients, all the right-hand-side values, or all the coefficients in the constraints. To do this we will find the following general notation helpful:

c row   = row of objective function coefficients,

b column = column of right-hand-side values of the constraint equations,

A matrix   = m rows and n columns of coefficients of the variables in the constraint equations.

Using this notation, we can show the above portion of the Simplex tableau as follows:

$$
\begin{array}{c|c}
c \text{ row} & \\
\hline
A \text{ matrix} & \begin{array}{c} b \\ \text{column} \end{array}
\end{array}
$$

Before we can apply the Simplex method, two more rows and two more columns will have to be added to our tableau. However, before defining these new rows and columns, let us set up the partial Simplex tableau for our Par, Inc. problem. The Tableau form (the same as Standard form in this case) for the Par, Inc. problem is

$$\max \quad 10x_1 + 9x_2 + 0s_1 + 0s_2 + 0s_3 + 0s_4$$

s.t.

$$\begin{aligned}
\tfrac{7}{10}x_1 + 1x_2 + 1s_1 \quad\quad\quad\quad\quad &= 630 \\
\tfrac{1}{2}x_1 + \tfrac{5}{6}x_2 \quad\quad + 1s_2 \quad\quad\quad &= 600 \\
1x_1 + \tfrac{2}{3}s_2 \quad\quad\quad + 1s_3 \quad &= 708 \\
\tfrac{1}{10}x_1 + \tfrac{1}{4}s_2 \quad\quad\quad\quad\quad + 1s_4 &= 135 \\
x_1, x_2, s_1, s_2, s_3, s_4 &\geq 0.
\end{aligned}$$

A partial Simplex tableau can then be written as

10	9	0	0	0	0	
7/10	1	1	0	0	0	630
1/2	5/6	0	1	0	0	600
1	2/3	0	0	1	0	708
1/10	1/4	0	0	0	1	135

Note that the row above the first horizontal line contains the coefficients of the objective function for our Par, Inc. problem in Tableau form. The elements appearing between the horizontal lines and to the left of the vertical line are simply the coefficients of the constraint equations, whereas the elements to the right of the vertical line are the right-hand-side values of the constraint equations. It may be easier to recall that each of the rows contains the coefficients of one constraint equation if we note that each of the columns is associated with one of the variables. For example, x_1 corresponds to the first column, x_2 the second, s_1 the third, and so on. To help us keep this in mind, we will write the variable associated with each column directly above the column. Doing this, we get

x_1	x_2	s_1	s_2	s_3	s_4	
10	9	0	0	0	0	
7/10	1	1	0	0	0	630
1/2	5/6	0	1	0	0	600
1	2/3	0	0	1	0	708
1/10	1/4	0	0	0	1	135

Can you write the constraint equations contained in the partial Simplex tableau of a different linear program? Try it:

x_1	x_2	s_1	s_2	
6	8	0	0	
2	5	1	0	11
4	1	0	1	14

Did you get the following:

$$2x_1 + 5x_2 + 1s_1 + 0s_2 = 11,$$
$$4x_1 + 1x_2 + 0s_1 + 1s_2 = 14.$$

We can also see that the objective function for this problem is $6x_1 + 8x_2 + 0s_1 + 0s_2$.

We stated earlier that the Simplex method must be started with a basic feasible solution. Certainly, one basic feasible solution for the Par, Inc. problem is the one found by setting $x_1 = 0$ and $x_2 = 0$ in the Tableau form of our problem. This solution corresponds to a product combination of zero standard bags and zero deluxe bags and is represented by the solution

$$\begin{bmatrix} x_1 \\ x_2 \\ s_1 \\ s_2 \\ s_3 \\ s_4 \end{bmatrix} = \begin{bmatrix} 0 \\ 0 \\ 630 \\ 600 \\ 708 \\ 135 \end{bmatrix}$$

The initial Simplex tableau contains the Tableau form of the problem, and thus it is easy to find the above basic feasible solution from the initial Simplex tableau. As you can see, a column in the Simplex tableau which has a 1 in the only nonzero position is associated with each basic variable. Such columns are known as *unit columns* or *unit vectors*. Also, a row of the tableau is associated with each basic variable. This row can be identified by the fact that it contains the 1 in the unit column. The value of each basic variable is then given by b_i in the row associated with the basic variable. For example, s_3 has a 1 in row 3; therefore the value of this basic variable is given by $s_3 = b_3 = 708$. This procedure for determining the value of a basic variable is shown in Table 3.1.

At this point we have seen how to go about finding an initial basic feasible solution and setting up a partial Simplex tableau. The Simplex method now proceeds from one basic feasible solution to another until the optimal basic feasible solution is reached. In the next section we discuss how the Simplex method moves from an initial basic feasible solution to a better solution.

3.4 Improving the Solution

In order to improve the solution, we will need to generate a new basic feasible solution (extreme point) that yields a larger profit. To do this we will have to change the set of basic variables; that is, we will have to select one of the current nonbasic variables to bring into solution and one of the current basic variables to leave the solution in such a fashion that the new basic feasible solution yields a larger value for the objective function. The Simplex method provides us with an easy way to carry out this change in the basic feasible solution.

For convenience we will add two new columns to the present form of the Simplex tableau in order to keep track of the basic variables and the profit

TABLE 3.1 Illustration of Procedure for Finding Values of Basic Variables from the Simplex Tableau

	x_1	x_2	s_1	s_2	s_3	s_4	
	10	9	0	0	0	0	
	7/10	1	1	0	0	0	630
	1/2	5/6	0	1	0	0	600
	1	2/3	0	0	1	0	708
	1/10	1/4	0	0	0	1	135

Row associated with s_3　　　　　　　　　　　　　　　　value of s_3

associated with these variables. One column will be labeled *Basis* and the other c_j. Under the column labeled *Basis* we shall list the names of the current basic variables, and under the column labeled c_j we shall list the profit corresponding to each of these basic variables. For the Par, Inc. problem this results in the following initial Simplex tableau:

Basis	c_j	x_1	x_2	s_1	s_2	s_3	s_4	
		10	9	0	0	0	0	
s_1	0	7/10	1	1	0	0	0	630
s_2	0	1/2	5/6	0	1	0	0	600
s_3	0	1	2/3	0	0	1	0	708
s_4	0	1/10	1/4	0	0	0	1	135

We note in the *Basis* column that s_1 is listed first, since its value is given by b_1, s_2 second, since its value is given by b_2, and so on.

Can we improve upon the present basic feasible solution? To help find out if this is possible, we introduce two additional rows for the tableau. The first row, labeled z_j, will represent the *decrease* in the value of the objective function that will result if one unit of the variable corresponding to the jth column of the A matrix is brought into solution. For example, z_1 will represent the decrease in profit that will result if one unit of x_1 is brought into solution.

Let us see why a decrease in profit might result if we bring x_1 into solution. If one unit of x_1 is produced, we will have to change the value of some of the current basic variables in order to satisfy our constraint equations. In the first constraint equation we have

$$\tfrac{7}{10}x_1 + 1x_2 + 1s_1 = 630.$$

If we are considering making x_1 some positive value, we will have to reduce x_2 and/or s_1 in order to satisfy this constraint. Since x_2 is already zero (x_2 is a nonbasic variable), it cannot be reduced any further. Thus the value of s_1 will be reduced if x_1 is made positive. This reduction in the value of a basic variable may result in a reduction in the value of the objective function. The amount of the reduction depends of course upon the coefficient of s_1 in the objective function. In this case, since s_1 is a slack variable, its coefficient is zero; thus reducing s_1 will not decrease the value of the objective function.

On the other hand, every unit of x_1 introduced will improve the value of the objective function by the amount c_1, which in our Par, Inc. problem is the $10 profit associated with each standard bag produced. Since the value of the objective function will decrease by z_1 for each unit of x_1 produced, the net change in the value of the objective function that results due to one unit of x_1 being introduced is given by $c_1 - z_1$. The next row we introduce into our tableau, which we refer to as the *net evaluation row,* will contain the value of $c_j - z_j$ for every variable (column) in the tableau. In terms of position in the tableau, the z_j and $c_j - z_j$ rows will be placed directly under the A matrix in the existing tableau. Now let us get back to the original question of which variable we should make basic by calculating the entries in the net evaluation row for the Par, Inc. problem.

If we were to bring one unit of x_1 into the solution, we see from analyzing the constraint equations that we would have to give up $7/10$ hour of cutting and dyeing time, $1/2$ hour of sewing time, 1 hour of finishing time, and $1/10$ hour of inspection and packaging time. Thus we note that the coefficients in each row of the x_1 column indicate how many units of the basic variable in that row will be driven out of solution when one unit of x_1 is brought in. In general, all the column coefficients can be interpreted this way. Thus if we were to bring one unit of x_2 into solution, we would have to give up 1 unit of s_1, $5/6$ unit of s_2, $2/3$ unit of s_3, and $1/4$ unit of s_4.

To calculate how much the objective function will decrease when one unit of a nonbasic variable is brought into solution, we must know the value of the objective function coefficients for the basic variables. These values are given in the c_j column of our tableau. Hence *the values in the z_j row can be calculated by multiplying the elements in the c_j column by the corresponding elements in the columns of the A matrix and summing them.* Thus we get

$$
\begin{aligned}
z_1 &= 0(7/10) + 0(1/2) + 0(1)\ + 0(1/10) = 0 \\
z_2 &= 0(1)\ \ \ + 0(5/6) + 0(2/3) + 0(1/4)\ = 0 \\
z_3 &= 0(1)\ \ \ + 0(0)\ \ \ + 0(0)\ \ \ + 0(0)\ \ \ = 0 \\
z_4 &= 0(0)\ \ \ + 0(1)\ \ \ + 0(0)\ \ \ + 0(0)\ \ \ = 0 \\
z_5 &= 0(0)\ \ \ + 0(0)\ \ \ + 0(1)\ \ \ + 0(0)\ \ \ = 0 \\
z_6 &= 0(0)\ \ \ + 0(0)\ \ \ + 0(0)\ \ \ + 0(1)\ \ \ = 0.
\end{aligned}
$$

Since the initial basic feasible solution consists entirely of slack variables and since the c_j values for these variables are all zero, reducing the value of these slack variables when a nonbasic variable is introduced into solution causes no decrease in profit.

The objective function coefficient for x_1 is 10; thus the value of $c_1 - z_1$ is $10 - 0 = 10$. This indicates that the net result of bringing a unit of x_1 into the *current solution* will be an increase in profit of $10. Hence in the net evaluation row corresponding to x_1 we enter the value of 10.

In the same manner we can calculate the corresponding z_j and $c_j - z_j$ values for the remaining variables. The result is the following complete initial Simplex tableau:

Basis	c_j	x_1 10	x_2 9	s_1 0	s_2 0	s_3 0	s_4 0	
s_1	0	7/10	1	1	0	0	0	630
s_2	0	1/2	5/6	0	1	0	0	600
s_3	0	1	2/3	0	0	1	0	708
s_4	0	1/10	1/4	0	0	0	1	135
z_j		0	0	0	0	0	0	0
$c_j - z_j$		10	9	0	0	0	0	

PROFIT

In this tableau we also see a 0 in the z_j row in the last column. This zero represents the profit associated with the current basic solution. This value was obtained by multiplying the values of the basic variables, which are given in the last column, by their corresponding contributon to profit as given in the c_j column.

By looking at the net evaluation row, we see that every standard bag Par produces will increase the value of the objective function by $10, and every deluxe bag will increase the value of the objective function by $9. Given only this information it would make sense to produce as many standard bags as possible. We know that every standard bag produced uses $7/10$ hour of cutting and dyeing time. Therefore if we produce x_1 standard bags, we will use $7/10\,x_1$ hours of cutting and dyeing time. Since we only have 630 hours of cutting and dyeing time available, the maximum possible value of x_1, considering the cutting and dyeing constraint, can be calculated by solving the equation

$$7/10\,x_1 = 630.$$

Thus there is only enough time available in the cutting and dyeing department to manufacture a maximum of 900 standard bags.

In a similar manner, every standard bag produced uses $1/2$ hour of the available 600 hours of sewing time; therefore the maximum number of standard bags we can produce and still satisfy the sewing constraint is given by

$$1/2\,x_1 = 600.$$

This indicates that x_1 could be at most 1200. But we know that it is impossible to produce 1200 standard bags, since we do not have enough cutting and dyeing time available. In fact, we saw that we only have enough capacity in the cutting and dyeing department to make 900 standard bags.

Considering these constraints simultaneously, the cutting and dyeing time is more restrictive.

From the finishing constraint we see that x_1 standard bags would use $1x_1$ of the available 708 hours of finishing time. Solving the equation

$$1x_1 = 708$$

shows that in terms of the three constraints considered so far we can produce at most 708 standard bags.

In the inspection and packaging department every standard bag produced uses $1/10$ hour of inspection and packaging time. Since only 135 hours are available we can solve

$$1/10 x_1 = 135$$

to find that the largest number of standard bags that can be processed by the inspection and packaging department is 1350. When we consider all the constraints together, we see that the most restrictive constraint in terms of the maximum number of standard bags we can produce is the finishing constraint. That is, making 708 standard bags will use all the finishing capacity available. Hence if x_1 is introduced into solution at its maximum value, we will produce 708 standard bags ($x_1 = 708$), and there will be no slack time in the finishing department ($s_3 = 0$).

In making the decision to produce as many standard bags as possible, we have changed the set of variables in the basic feasible solution. The previous nonbasic variable x_1 is now a basic variable with $x_1 = 708$, while the previous basic variable s_3 is now a nonbasic variable with $s_3 = 0$. This interchange of roles between two variables is the essence of the Simplex method. That is, the way the Simplex method moves from one basic feasible solution to another is by selecting a nonbasic variable to replace one of the current basic variables. This process of moving from one basic feasible solution to another is called *iteration*.

Before presenting general rules for carrying out the steps of the Simplex method, let us consider the following constraint equation which might appear in the Tableau form of a linear program:

$$-2/3 x_1 + 0x_3 + 1s_2 = 500.$$

Suppose that s_2 is a basic variable and that x_1 and x_3 are nonbasic variables. Since the coefficient of x_1 is negative ($-2/3$), every unit of x_1 introduced into solution would require the basic variable s_2 to increase by $2/3$ of a unit in order to maintain the constraint equation. Thus no matter how large we make x_1, the basic variable s_2 will also become larger and hence will never be driven out of the basic solution (that is, forced to zero). Similarly, since the coefficient of x_3 is zero, making x_3 basic would not affect the value of s_2. No matter how large we make x_3, the basic variable s_2 would remain unchanged and could never be driven out of solution. Thus if the coefficient of a nonbasic variable is less than or equal to zero in some constraint, then that constraint can never limit the number of units of the nonbasic variable that can be brought into solution. Hence the basic variable associated with that constraint can never be driven out of solution. Therefore in determining which variable should leave the current basis we only need to consider rows of our tableau in which the coefficient of the incoming nonbasic variable is *strictly positive*. With this additional consideration in mind, we now present the general Simplex rules for selecting a nonbasic variable to enter the basis and a current basic variable to leave the basis.

Criterion for Entering a New Variable into the Basis

Look at the net evaluation row and select as the variable to enter the basis that variable which will cause the largest per unit increase in the objective function. Let us say that this variable corresponds to column j in the A portion of the tableau.

Criterion for Removing a Variable from the Current Basis

For each row i compute the ratio b_i/a_{ij} for every a_{ij} greater than zero. This ratio tells us the maximum amount of the variable x_j that can be brought into solution and still satisfy the constraint equation represented by that row. The minimum of these ratios tells us which constraint will be most restrictive if x_j is introduced into the solution. Hence we get the following rule for selecting the variable to remove from the current basis: For all the ratios b_i/a_{ij} where $a_{ij} > 0$ select the basic variable corresponding to the minimum of these ratios as the variable to leave the basis.

Let us illustrate the above procedure by applying it to our Par, Inc. problem. For illustration purposes we have added an extra column showing the b_i/a_{ij} ratios for the initial Simplex tableau associated with the Par, Inc. problem:

Basis	c_j	x_1	x_2	s_1	s_2	s_3	s_4		$\dfrac{b_i}{a_{i1}}$	
		10	9	0	0	0	0			
s_1	0	7/10	1	1	0	0	0	630	$\dfrac{630}{7/10} =$	900
s_2	0	1/2	5/6	0	1	0	0	600	$\dfrac{600}{1/2} =$	1200
s_3	0	①	2/3	0	0	1	0	708	$\dfrac{708}{1} =$	708
s_4	0	1/10	1/4	0	0	0	1	135	$\dfrac{135}{1/10} =$	1350
	z_j	0	0	0	0	0	0	0		
	$c_j - z_j$	10	9	0	0	0	0			

Note that $c_1 - z_1 = 10$ is the largest positive value in the $c_j - z_j$ row. Hence x_1 is selected to become the new basic variable. Checking the ratios b_i/a_{i1} for $a_{i1} > 0$, we see that $b_3/a_{31} = 708$ is the minimum of these ratios. Thus the current basic variable associated with row 3 (s_3) is the variable selected to leave the basis. In our tableau we have circled a_{31}, ①, to indicate that the variable corresponding to the first column is to enter the basis and to indicate that the basic variable corresponding to the third row is to leave the basis. Adopting the usual linear programming terminology, we refer to this circled element as the *pivot element*.

In order to improve the current solution of $x_1 = 0$, $x_2 = 0$, $s_1 = 630$, $s_2 = 600$, $s_3 = 708$, and $s_4 = 135$, we should increase x_1 to 708. This would call for the production of 708 standard bags at a corresponding profit of $\$10 \times 708$ units $= \$7080$. In doing so, we will use all the available finishing capacity, and thus s_3 will be reduced to zero. Hence x_1 will become the new basic variable, replacing s_3 in the old basis.

3.5 Calculating the Next Tableau

We saw in the previous section that the initial basic feasible solution could be improved by introducing x_1 into the basis to replace s_3. Before we can determine if this new basic feasible solution can be improved upon, it will be necessary to develop the corresponding Simplex tableau.

Recall that the initial Simplex tableau is simply a table containing the coefficients of the Tableau form for the linear programming problem. Because of the special properties of the Tableau form representation, the initial Simplex tableau contained a unit column corresponding to each of the basic variables. Thus the value of the basic variable with a 1 in row i could be found simply by reading the ith element of the last column in the Simplex tableau, b_i.

Now we will formulate a new tableau in such a fashion that all the columns associated with the new basic variables are unit columns, such that the value of the basic variable in row i is given by b_i. Thus we would like to make the column in the new tableau corresponding to x_1 look just like the column corresponding to s_3 in our original tableau. Hence our goal is to get the column in our A matrix corresponding to x_1 to appear as

$$0$$
$$0$$
$$1$$
$$0.$$

The way in which we transform the Simplex tableau so that it still represents an equivalent system of constraint equations with the above properties is to employ the elementary row operations discussed in Section 3.1. You will recall that there were two row operations that we could perform on a system of equations and still retain an equivalent system: (1) we could multiply any row by a nonzero number, and (2) we could multiply any row by a nonzero number and add it to another row. By performing these row operations, we will be able to change the column for the variable entering the basis to a unit column and, at the same time, change the last column of the tableau so that it contains the values of the new basic variables. We emphasize that performing these operations will in no way affect the solution to our problem, since the feasible solutions to the constraint equations are not changed by these elementary row operations.

Clearly, many of the numerical values in the new Simplex tableau are going to change as the result of performing these row operations. However, we know that after the row operations are performed, the new Simplex tableau will still represent an equivalent system of equations. Nonetheless, because the elements in the new Simplex tableau will usually change as the result of the required row operations, the present method of referring to elements in the Simplex tableau may lead to confusion. Let us see why this is so.

Up to now we have made no distinction between the A matrix and b column for the Tableau form and the corresponding portions of the Simplex tableau. Indeed, we showed that the initial Simplex tableau was formed by properly placing the a_{ij}, c_j, and b_i elements as given in the Tableau form into the Simplex tableau. From now on we will refer to the portion of the Simplex tableau that initially contained the a_{ij} values with the symbols $\bar{A}$, and the portion of the tableau that initially contained the b_i values with the symbol $\bar{b}$. In terms of the Simplex tableau, elements in $\bar{A}$ will be denoted by $\bar{a}_{ij}$ and elements in $\bar{b}$ will be denoted by $\bar{b}_i$. We recognize that using this notation we will have $\bar{A} = A$ and $\bar{b} = b$ in the initial Simplex tableau. However, in subsequent Simplex tableaus this relationship will usually not hold. This notation will avoid any possible confusion when we wish to distinguish between the original constraint coefficient values a_{ij} and right-hand-side values b_i of the Tableau form, and the Simplex tableau elements $\bar{a}_{ij}$ and $\bar{b}_i$.

Now let us illustrate the procedure for calculating the next tableau by returning to the Par, Inc. problem. Recall that our goal is to get the column in the $\bar{A}$ portion of the tableau corresponding to x_1 to appear as

$$\begin{bmatrix} \bar{a}_{11} \\ \bar{a}_{21} \\ \bar{a}_{31} \\ \bar{a}_{41} \end{bmatrix} = \begin{bmatrix} 0 \\ 0 \\ 1 \\ 0 \end{bmatrix}$$

Since we already have $\bar{a}_{31} = 1$ in the initial Simplex tableau, no row operations need to be performed on the third row of the tableau.

In order to set $\bar{a}_{11} = 0$, we multiply the *pivot row* (the row corresponding to the finishing constraint) by $-\frac{7}{10}$ to obtain the equivalent equation

$$-\tfrac{7}{10}(x_1 + \tfrac{2}{3}x_2 + 0s_1 + 0s_2 + 1s_3 + 0s_4) = -\tfrac{7}{10}(708)$$

or

$$-\tfrac{7}{10}x_1 - \tfrac{14}{30}x_2 - 0s_1 - 0s_2 - \tfrac{7}{10}s_3 - 0s_4 = -495.6. \qquad (3.11)$$

Now let us consider the cutting and dyeing constraint equation, which is

$$\tfrac{7}{10}x_1 + 1x_2 + 1s_1 + 0s_2 + 0s_3 + 0s_4 = 630. \qquad (3.12)$$

Now add equation (3.11) to the cutting and dyeing constraint equation (3.12). Dropping the terms with zero coefficients and performing this addition, we have

$$(\tfrac{7}{10}x_1 + 1x_2 + 1s_1) + (-\tfrac{7}{10}x_1 - \tfrac{14}{30}x_2 - \tfrac{7}{10}s_3) = 630 - 495.6$$

or

$$0x_1 + \tfrac{16}{30}x_2 + 1s_1 - \tfrac{7}{10}s_3 = 134.4. \qquad (3.13)$$

Since this is just a simple row operation, we will have an equivalent system of equations if equation (3.12) is replaced by equation (3.13). Making this substitution in the original tableau, we see that we have obtained a zero in the first position in the x_1 column (that is, $\bar{a}_{11} = 0$).

Basis	c_j	x_1	x_2	s_1	s_2	s_3	s_4	
		10	9	0	0	0	0	
		0	16/30	1	0	-7/10	0	134.4
		1/2	5/6	0	1	0	0	600
		1	2/3	0	0	1	0	708
		1/10	1/4	0	0	0	1	135
z_j								
$c_j - z_j$								

We still need to set the elements in the second row and the fourth row of the x_1 column equal to zero. Can you find a way to do this? Recall that we accomplished this result for row 1 by multiplying the pivot row by a nonzero constant $(-\tfrac{7}{10})$ and then adding the result to the first row. Note that the constant in this case was just the negative of the coefficient in the first row and x_1 column. Thus to set the element in the second constraint corresponding to the x_1 column equal to zero, we multiply the pivot row by $-\tfrac{1}{2}$ and add this result to the second constraint. This gives the result

$$(\tfrac{1}{2}x_1 + \tfrac{5}{6}x_2 + 1s_2) + (-\tfrac{1}{2}x_1 - \tfrac{1}{3}x_2 - \tfrac{1}{2}s_3) = 600 - 354,$$

which is equivalent to

$$0x_1 + \tfrac{1}{2}x_2 + 0s_1 + 1s_2 - \tfrac{1}{2}s_3 + 0s_4 = 246.$$

This becomes the new representation of the second constraint equation in the Simplex tableau.

To obtain a zero in the $\bar{a}_{41}$ position, we just multiply the pivot row by $-\frac{1}{10}$ and then add the result to the last row. The resulting constraint equation is

$$0x_1 + \frac{22}{120}x_2 + 0s_1 + 0s_2 - \frac{1}{10}s_3 + 1s_4 = 64.2.$$

Placing these last two equations into the new tableau gives us the following Simplex tableau:

Basis	c_j	x_1 10	x_2 9	s_1 0	s_2 0	s_3 0	s_4 0	
s_1	0	0	16/30	1	0	−7/10	0	134.4
s_2	0	0	1/2	0	1	−1/2	0	246
x_1	10	1	2/3	0	0	1	0	708
s_4	0	0	22/120	0	0	−1/10	1	64.2
z_j								7080
$c_j - z_j$								

Since s_1, s_2, x_1, and s_4 are the basic variables in this tableau, x_2 and s_3 are set equal to 0. We can now read the solution for s_1, s_2, x_1, and s_4 directly from the tableau:

$$s_1 = 134.4$$
$$s_2 = 246$$
$$x_1 = 708$$
$$s_4 = 64.2.$$

The profit corresponding to this solution is $7080. Note that this value for profit was obtained by multiplying the solution values for the basic variables in the $\bar{b}$ column by their corresponding objective function coefficients as given in the c_j column—that is, $0(134.4) + 0(246) + 10(708) + 0(64.2) = 7080$. We still have not calculated any entries in the z_j and $c_j - z_j$ rows. Before doing so, let us reflect for a moment on the present solution.

Interpreting the Results of an Iteration

Starting with one Simplex tableau, changing the basic variables, and finding a new Simplex tableau is referred to as an iteration of the Simplex method.

In our example the initial basic feasible solution was

$$
\begin{bmatrix} x_1 \\ x_2 \\ s_1 \\ s_2 \\ s_3 \\ s_4 \end{bmatrix} = \begin{bmatrix} 0 \\ 0 \\ 630 \\ 600 \\ 708 \\ 135 \end{bmatrix}
$$

with a corresponding profit of $0. One iteration of the Simplex method moved us to another basic feasible solution where the value of the objective function was $7080. This new basic feasible solution was

$$
\begin{bmatrix} x_1 \\ x_2 \\ s_1 \\ s_2 \\ s_3 \\ s_4 \end{bmatrix} = \begin{bmatrix} 708 \\ 0 \\ 134.4 \\ 246 \\ 0 \\ 64.2 \end{bmatrix}
$$

Graphically this iteration moved us from one extreme point to another extreme point along the edge of our feasible region. In Figure 3.2 we see that the initial basic feasible solution corresponded to extreme point ①. The first iteration moved us in the direction of the greatest increase per unit in profit, that is, along the x_1 axis. We moved away from extreme point ① in the x_1 direction until we could move no further without violating one of the constraints. The tableau we calculated after one iteration represents the basic feasible solution corresponding to extreme point ②.

We know that the slack variables represent the unused capacity associated with each constraint. Noting the value of s_1 in our Simplex tableau, we see that the unused cutting and dyeing capacity is 134.4 hours. Does this seem reasonable? Since the solution indicated that we should make 708 standard bags, and since each standard bag requires $7/10$ hour of cutting and dyeing time, the total number of hours used in producing the 708 standard bags is $7/10(708) = 495.6$. We started with 630 hours; thus we now have 134.4 hours of unused time available. Similarly, since every standard bag produced requires $1/2$ hour of sewing time, the total amount of sewing time used in producing 708 standard bags is 354 hours. We started with 600 hours of sewing time; therefore 246 hours remain. Every standard bag requires 1 hour of finishing time. Thus since 708 hours of finishing time are available, we will use all the finishing time by producing 708 standard bags. This is the reason, you see, that the finishing constraint is binding at extreme point ②. Producing 708 standard bags will use $1/10(708) = 70.8$ hours of

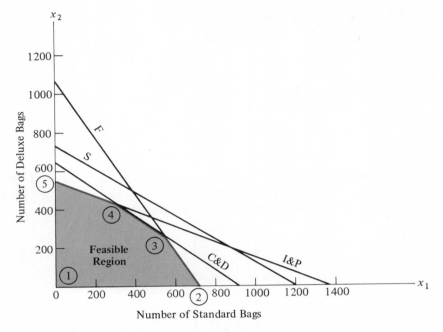

FIGURE 3.2   Feasible Solution Region for the Par, Inc. Problem

inspection and packaging time, leaving a slack of 64.2 hours in this department.

Moving Toward a Better Solution

We are ready to start things all over again. The next question we must ask ourselves is, can we find a new basic feasible solution (extreme point) that will increase the value of the objective function any further? To answer this, we need to calculate the z_j and $c_j - z_j$ rows for the current Simplex tableau.

Recall that the elements in the z_j row can be calculated by multiplying the elements in the c_j column of the Simplex tableau by the corresponding elements in the columns of the $\bar{A}$ matrix and summing. Thus we get

$$
\begin{aligned}
z_1 &= 0(0) &&+ 0(0) &&+ 10(1) &+ 0(0) &&= 10 \\
z_2 &= 0(^{16}\!/_{30}) &&+ 0(\tfrac{1}{2}) &&+ 10(\tfrac{2}{3}) &+ 0(^{22}\!/_{120}) &&= {}^{20}\!/_{3} \\
z_3 &= 0(1) &&+ 0(0) &&+ 10(0) &+ 0(0) &&= 0 \\
z_4 &= 0(0) &&+ 0(1) &&+ 10(0) &+ 0(0) &&= 0 \\
z_5 &= 0(-^{7}\!/_{10}) &&+ 0(-\tfrac{1}{2}) &&+ 10(1) &+ 0(-^{1}\!/_{10}) &&= 10 \\
z_6 &= 0(0) &&+ 0(0) &&+ 10(0) &+ 0(1) &&= 0.
\end{aligned}
$$

Subtracting z_j from c_j to obtain the net evaluation row, we get the complete Simplex tableau:

Basis	c_j	x_1	x_2	s_1	s_2	s_3	s_4	
		10	9	0	0	0	0	
s_1	0	0	16/30	1	0	$-7/10$	0	134.4
s_2	0	0	1/2	0	1	$-1/2$	0	246
x_1	10	1	2/3	0	0	1	0	708
s_4	0	0	22/120	0	0	$-1/10$	1	64.2
z_j		10	20/3	0	0	10	0	7080
$c_j - z_j$		0	7/3	0	0	-10	0	

Before considering the question of changing the basis and moving on to an even better basic feasible solution, let us see if we can interpret some of the numerical values appearing in the above Simplex tableau in terms of the original Par, Inc. problem.

We know that the elements in the x_2 column indicate how much each of the four basic variables will have to change in order to produce one unit of x_2 and still satisfy all the constraint relationships. Using the *Basis* column to identify the basic variable corresponding to each element in the x_2 column, we can see that introducing one unit of x_2 will force us to decrease s_1 by $^{16}/_{30}$ of a unit, s_2 by $^1/_2$ of a unit, x_1 by $^2/_3$ of a unit, and s_4 by $^{22}/_{120}$ of a unit.

Why does producing one deluxe bag require us to decrease the production of standard bags by $^2/_3$ of a unit? Note that when we decided to produce 708 standard bags we used all the finishing time available. Since every unit of x_2 we produce requires $^2/_3$ hour of finishing time ($\bar{a}_{32} = ^2/_3$), and every unit of x_1 requires 1 full hour, we see that in order to produce a unit of x_2 we will have to cut back $^2/_3$ of a unit of x_1 in order to free up enough finishing time. Thus $\bar{a}_{32} = ^2/_3$ does indeed indicate correctly how many units of the basic variable x_1 must be given up if one unit of x_2 is introduced.

In the original tableau (*look back and check this*) we saw that each deluxe bag required 1 hour of cutting and dyeing time. Why, then, is $\bar{a}_{12} = ^{16}/_{30}$? Once again, each deluxe bag we produce will kick out $^2/_3$ of a standard bag from the solution and hence free up $^2/_3$ of the cutting and dyeing time required for one standard bag. Since each standard bag requires $^7/_{10}$ hour, we see that $^2/_3 (^7/_{10}) = ^{14}/_{30}$ hour would be made available because $^2/_3$ of a standard bag leaves the solution. Since each deluxe bag requires 1 hour of cutting and dyeing time, the net effect of producing one deluxe bag is to really only use up an additional $(1 - ^{14}/_{30}) = ^{16}/_{30}$ hour of cutting and dyeing time. The remaining coefficients in the x_2 column can be interpreted in the same manner.

To see why $c_2 - z_2 = ^7/_3$ we note that since the basic variables s_1, s_2, and s_4 are slack variables and have zero objective function coefficients, their reduction when one unit of x_2 is brought into solution does not decrease total profit. However, since the profit associated with each unit of x_1 is \$10, the $2/3$ reduction will cost \$$20/3$. On the other hand, every unit of x_2 we bring into solution will increase profit by \$9, or \$$27/3$. Thus the net increase in the value of the objective function resulting from a one unit increase in x_2 will be given by \$$27/3 - 20/3 = $7/3$.

Note that for all the basic variables s_1, s_2, x_1, and s_4 the value of $c_j - z_j$ is equal to zero. Since each of these variables is associated with a unit column in our Simplex tableau, we can interpret this as meaning that bringing one unit of a basic variable into solution would force us to remove one unit of the same basic variable. The result obviously is no net change in the value of the objective function.

In summary we note that at each iteration of the Simplex method

1. The value of the current basic feasible solution can be found in the $\bar{b}$ column of the Simplex tableau;
2. The value of $c_j - z_j$ for each of the basic variables is equal to zero;
3. The coefficients in a particular column of the $\bar{A}$ portion of the Simplex tableau indicate how much the current basic solution will change if one unit of the variable associated with that column is introduced.

Let us now analyze the net evaluation row to see if we can introduce a new variable into the basis and continue to improve the objective function. Using the rule for determining which variable should enter the basis next, we select x_2, since it has the highest positive coefficient in the net evaluation row.

In order to determine which variable will be removed from the basis when x_2 enters, we must compute for each row i the ratio $\bar{b}_i/\bar{a}_{i2}$ (remember, though, that we compute this ratio only if $\bar{a}_{i2}$ is greater than zero) and then select the variable corresponding to the minimum ratio as the variable to leave the basis. As before, we will show these ratios in an extra column of the Simplex tableau. Thus the tableau becomes

Basis	c_j	x_1 10	x_2 9	s_1 0	s_2 0	s_3 0	s_4 0		$\dfrac{\bar{b}_i}{\bar{a}_{i2}}$	
s_1	0	0	(16/30)	1	0	$-7/10$	0	134.4	$\dfrac{134.4}{16/30}$	$= 252$
s_2	0	0	$1/2$	0	1	$-1/2$	0	246	$\dfrac{246}{1/2}$	$= 492$
x_1	10	1	$2/3$	0	0	1	0	708	$\dfrac{708}{2/3}$	$= 1062$
s_4	0	0	$22/120$	0	0	$-1/10$	1	64.2	$\dfrac{64.2}{22/120}$	$= 350.18$
	z_j	10	$20/3$	0	0	10	0	7080		
	$c_j - z_j$	0	$7/3$	0	0	-10	0			

Since 252 is the minimum ratio, s_1 will be the variable that will leave the basis. The pivot element will be $\bar{a}_{12} = {}^{16}\!/_{30}$, which is circled in the above tableau. The variable x_2 must now be made a basic variable. This means that we must perform the row operations necessary to convert the x_2 column into a unit column; that is, we will have to transform the second column in the tableau to the form

$$\begin{bmatrix} 1 \\ 0 \\ 0 \\ 0 \end{bmatrix}$$

We can do this by performing row operations according to the following

Step 1: Multiply every element in row 1 by ${}^{30}\!/_{16}$. Note that this will get us a 1 in position $\bar{a}_{12}$.

Step 2: Multiply the new row 1 by $(-\frac{1}{2})$ and add the result to row 2. This will set $\bar{a}_{22} = 0$.

Step 3: Multiply the new row 1 by $(-\frac{2}{3})$ and add the result to row 3. This will set $\bar{a}_{32} = 0$.

Step 4: Multiply the new row 1 by $(-{}^{22}\!/_{120})$ and add the result to row 4. This will set $\bar{a}_{42} = 0$.

The above elementary row operations again change the appearance of our Simplex tableau, but do not alter the solutions to the system of equations contained in the tableau. The only difference is that now we have $x_2, s_2, x_1,$ and s_4 as the basic variables, and s_1 and s_3 as the nonbasic variables. The new tableau resulting from these row operations is presented below:

Basis	c_j	x_1	x_2	s_1	s_2	s_3	s_4	
		10	9	0	0	0	0	
x_2	9	0	1	30/16	0	$-21/16$	0	252
s_2	0	0	0	$-15/16$	1	5/32	0	120
x_1	10	1	0	$-20/16$	0	30/16	0	540
s_4	0	0	0	$-11/32$	0	9/64	1	18
	z_j							7668
	$c_j - z_j$							

Note that the profit corresponding to this basic feasible solution is $252(9) + 120(0) + 540(10) + 18(0) = 7668$, and that the basic variables are $x_2 = 252, s_2 = 120, x_1 = 540,$ and $s_4 = 18$.

This basic feasible solution corresponds to extreme point ③ in Figure 3.2. As you may recall from the graphical solution in Chapter 2, this is the optimal solution to the Par, Inc. problem. However, the Simplex method has not yet identified this solution as optimal. Thus we must continue to investigate whether or not it makes sense to bring any other variable into the basis and move to another basic feasible solution. As we saw before, this involves calculating the z_j and $c_j - z_j$ rows and then selecting the variable to enter the basis that corresponds to the highest positive value in the net evaluation row.

After performing the z_j and $c_j - z_j$ calculations for the current solution, we obtain the following complete Simplex tableau:

Basis	c_j	x_1 10	x_2 9	s_1 0	s_2 0	s_3 0	s_4 0	
x_2	9	0	1	30/16	0	−21/16	0	252
s_2	0	0	0	−15/16	1	5/32	0	120
x_1	10	1	0	−20/16	0	30/16	0	540
s_4	0	0	0	−11/32	0	9/64	1	18
z_j		10	9	70/16	0	111/16	0	7668
$c_j - z_j$		0	0	−70/16	0	−111/16	0	

Looking at the net evaluation row we see that every element is zero or negative. Since $c_j - z_j$ is less than or equal to zero for both of our nonbasic variables s_1 and s_3, an attempt to bring a nonbasic variable into the basis at this point will result in lowering the current value of the objective function. Hence the above tableau represents the optimal solution to our linear programming problem.

Stopping Criterion

The optimal solution to a linear programming problem has been reached when there are no positive values in the net evaluation row of the Simplex tableau. If all entries in the net evaluation row are zero or negative, we stop the calculations. The optimal solution is given by the current Simplex tableau.

Interpreting the Optimal Solution

We see that in the final solution to the Par, Inc. problem the basic variables are x_2, s_2, x_1, and s_4. The complete optimal solution to the Par, Inc. problem is thus

$$\begin{bmatrix} x_1 \\ x_2 \\ s_1 \\ s_2 \\ s_3 \\ s_4 \end{bmatrix} = \begin{bmatrix} 540 \\ 252 \\ 0 \\ 120 \\ 0 \\ 18 \end{bmatrix}$$

That is, our optimal solution is $x_1 = 540$, $x_2 = 252$, $s_1 = -0$, $s_2 = 120$, $s_3 = 0$, and $s_4 = 18$, with a corresponding value of the objective function of $7668. Thus if the management of Par, Inc. wants to maximize profit, they should produce 540 standard bags and 252 deluxe bags. In addition, management should note that there will be 120 hours of idle time in the sewing department and 18 hours of idle time in the inspection and packaging department. If it is possible to make alternate use of these additional resources, management should plan to do so.

We can also see that with $s_1 = 0$ and $s_3 = 0$ there is no slack time available in the cutting and dyeing and the finishing departments. The constraints for these operations are both binding in the optimal solution (see Figure 3.2). If it is possible to obtain additional hours for these two departments, management should consider doing so.

3.6   Solution of a Sample Problem

In this section we will carry out the complete solution of a numerical example using the Simplex method. This is to provide you with an opportunity to check your understanding of the previous sections. You should attempt to solve the problem yourself before studying the solution presented here.

Solve the following linear program using the Simplex method:

$$\begin{aligned} \max \quad & 4x_1 + 6x_2 + 3x_3 + 1x_4 \\ \text{s.t.} \quad & \\ & \tfrac{3}{2}x_1 + 2x_2 + 4x_3 + 3x_4 \le 550 \\ & 4x_1 + 1x_2 + 2x_3 + 1x_4 \le 700 \\ & 2x_1 + 3x_2 + 1x_3 + 2x_4 \le 200 \\ & x_1, x_2, x_3, x_4 \ge 0. \end{aligned}$$

First we add slack variables to convert the problem to Standard form:

$$\begin{aligned} \max \quad & 4x_1 + 6x_2 + 3x_3 + 1x_4 + 0s_1 + 0s_2 + 0s_3 \\ \text{s.t.} \quad & \\ & \tfrac{3}{2}x_1 + 2x_2 + 4x_3 + 3x_4 + 1s_1 \qquad\qquad\quad = 550 \\ & 4x_1 + 1x_2 + 2x_3 + 1x_4 \qquad\; + 1s_2 \qquad = 700 \\ & 2x_1 + 3x_2 + 1x_3 + 2x_4 \qquad\qquad\quad + 1s_3 = 200 \\ & x_1, x_2, x_3, x_4, s_1, s_2, s_3 \ge 0. \end{aligned}$$

The next step is to write the problem in Tableau form. But since all the constraints are of the less-than-or-equal-to type and since the right-hand-side values are all nonnegative, Standard form and Tableau form are the same. From this Tableau form we can set up the initial Simplex tableau:

Basis	c_j	x_1 4	x_2 6	x_3 3	x_4 1	s_1 0	s_2 0	s_3 0		$\bar{b}_i$ $\bar{a}_{i2}$	
s_1	0	3/2	2	4	3	1	0	0	550	550/2 =	225
s_2	0	4	1	2	1	0	1	0	700	700/1 =	700
s_3	0	2	③	1	2	0	0	1	200	200/3 =	66⅔
	z_j	0	0	0	0	0	0	0	0		
	$c_j - z_j$	4	6	3	1	0	0	0			

Two iterations of the Simplex method are required to reach the optimal solution.

Result of iteration 1:

Basis	c_j	x_1 4	x_2 6	x_3 3	x_4 1	s_1 0	s_2 0	s_3 0		$\bar{b}_i$ $\bar{a}_{i3}$	
s_1	0	1/6	0	(10/3)	5/3	1	0	−2/3	416⅔	125	
s_2	0	10/3	0	5/3	1/3	0	1	−1/3	633⅓	380	
x_2	6	2/3	1	1/3	2/3	0	0	1/3	66⅔	200	
	z_j	12/3	6	6/3	12/3	0	0	6/3	400		
	$c_j - z_j$	0	0	3/3	−9/3	0	0	−6/3			

Result of iteration 2:

Basis	c_j	x_1 4	x_2 6	x_3 3	x_4 1	s_1 0	s_2 0	s_3 0	
x_3	3	3/60	0	1	5/10	3/10	0	−2/10	125
s_2	0	39/12	0	0	−15/30	−5/10	1	0	425
x_2	6	39/60	1	0	15/30	−1/10	0	12/30	25
	z_j	81/20	6	3	9/2	3/10	0	54/30	525
	$c_j - z_j$	−1/20	0	0	−7/2	−3/10	0	−54/30	

All the $c_j - z_j$ elements are less than or equal to zero. Hence there is no variable which we can introduce into the solution and obtain an increase in the objective function. Therefore the current solution is optimal. The basic variables are x_3, s_2, and x_2, and the complete optimal solution is given by

$$
\begin{bmatrix} x_1 \\ x_2 \\ x_3 \\ x_4 \\ s_1 \\ s_2 \\ s_3 \end{bmatrix} = \begin{bmatrix} 0 \\ 25 \\ 125 \\ 0 \\ 0 \\ 425 \\ 0 \end{bmatrix}
$$

The value of the objective function for this solution is 525.

3.7 Tableau Form—The General Case

In Section 3.2 we pointed out how setting up the Tableau form of a linear programming problem is a necessary step in preparation for the Simplex solution procedure. You may recall that the Tableau form had two important properties: (1) the b column values (right-hand-side values) were nonnegative, and (2) with m constraints, m columns of the A matrix were unit columns with the 1's of the unit columns all in different rows.

The purpose of the Tableau form is to make it easy to identify an initial basic feasible (extreme point) solution in order to start the Simplex procedure.

When we formulated the Par, Inc. problem we found that the right-hand-side values were all nonnegative [property (1) satisfied], and that the Standard form of the four less-than-or-equal-to constraints provided four unit columns for the slack variables associated with the constraints [property (2) satisfied]. Thus we were lucky in this particular case in that the Standard form of the Par, Inc. problem was also the Tableau form. However, when we encounter negative right-hand-side values, greater-than-or-equal-to constraints, and/or equality constraints we will have to take additional steps in order to convert a linear program into its Tableau form. The necessary steps are outlined in this section.

Negative Right-Hand Sides

What if one or more of the values on the right-hand side of our constraints are *negative?* For example, suppose that management of Par, Inc. had specified that the number of standard bags produced had to be less than or equal to the number of deluxe bags after 25 deluxe bags had been saved for display purposes. We could formulate this constraint as

$$1x_1 \le 1x_2 - 25. \tag{3.14}$$

Subtracting x_2 from both sides of the inequality allows us to place all the variables on the left-hand side of the constraint and the constant on the right-hand side. Thus we have

$$1x_1 - 1x_2 \leq -25. \tag{3.15}$$

The procedure of adding a slack variable ($x_1 - x_2 + s_1 = -25$) to obtain the Tableau form is unacceptable, since the constraint would not satisfy the Tableau form requirement of nonnegative right-hand sides. Thus we must look for ways to remove the negative right-hand-side values before we can set up the Tableau form representation of the problem. This is relatively easy to do. There are three separate cases to consider. We must consider whether the constraint in question is an equality, greater-than-or-equal-to, or less-than-or-equal-to constraint.

Case 1: Equality constraint   For example,

$$6x_1 + 3x_2 - 4x_3 = -20.$$

We need only multiply both sides of the equation by -1 in order to obtain

$$-6x_1 - 3x_2 + 4x_3 = 20$$

which has an acceptable right-hand-side value for the Tableau form.

Case 2: Greater-than-or-equal-to constraint   For example,

$$6x_1 + 3x_2 - 4x_3 \geq -20.$$

What would happen if we multiplied both sides by -1? The rule is that if you multiply both sides of an inequality by a negative number, the sign of the inequality changes direction. For example, the inequality $1 \geq -2$ is certainly true. However, if we multiply both sides by -1 we must change the direction of the inequality in order to have the correct relationship $-1 \leq 2$. Similarly, multiplying the above constraint by -1 and changing the direction of the inequality yields

$$-6x_1 - 3x_2 + 4x_3 \leq 20.$$

This constraint can now be treated the same as any ordinary less-than-or-equal-to constraint by adding a slack variable to the left-hand side.

Case 3: Less-than-or-equal-to constraint   For example,

$$6x_1 + 3x_2 - 4x_3 \leq -20.$$

We multiply both sides by -1 and change the direction of the inequality to get

$$-6x_1 - 3x_2 + 4x_3 \geq 20.$$

Using this method, the Par, Inc. constraint (3.15) could be rewritten as

$$-1x_1 + 1x_2 \geq 25. \tag{3.16}$$

Now we have the usual situation for a greater-than-or-equal-to constraint. That is, all we need to do now to obtain the Standard form is to subtract a surplus variable from the left-hand side.

Summarizing, we see that any time the original formulation of a linear program contains a negative right-hand side we should perform the preliminary operations outlined above before adding slack and surplus variables.

Greater-Than-or-Equal-to Constraints

Suppose that in the Par, Inc. problem, management wanted to ensure that at least one hundred bags of each model were produced. We could incorporate these new restrictions by adding a constraint that ensures that x_1 will be greater than or equal to one hundred bags, and adding another constraint that ensures that x_2 will be greater than or equal to one hundred bags; that is, we can add the constraints

$$1x_1 \geq 100 \tag{3.17}$$

$$1x_2 \geq 100. \tag{3.18}$$

With these two additions our modified problem can now be written as

$$
\begin{aligned}
\max \quad & 10x_1 + 9x_2 \\
\text{s.t.} \quad & \\
& \tfrac{7}{10}x_1 + 1x_2 \leq 630 \\
& \tfrac{1}{2}x_1 + \tfrac{5}{6}x_2 \leq 600 \\
& 1x_1 + \tfrac{2}{3}x_2 \leq 708 \\
& \tfrac{1}{10}x_1 + \tfrac{1}{4}x_2 \leq 135 \\
& 1x_1 \qquad\quad \geq 100 \\
& \qquad 1x_2 \geq 100 \\
& x_1, x_2 \geq 0.
\end{aligned}
$$

The graphical solution to this problem is shown in Figure 3.3 and is the same as the solution to the original Par, Inc. problem. However, if we are going to use the Simplex method for solving this problem, we need to know how to put the greater-than-or-equal-to constraints into the Tableau form.

We can first use slack and surplus variables to write this Par, Inc. program in the following Standard form:

$$
\begin{aligned}
\max \quad & 10x_1 + 9x_2 + 0s_1 + 0s_2 + 0s_3 + 0s_4 + 0s_5 + 0s_6 \\
\text{s.t.} \quad &
\end{aligned}
$$

$$
\begin{aligned}
\tfrac{7}{10}x_1 + 1x_2 + 1s_1 \qquad\qquad\qquad\qquad\qquad\qquad &= 630 \tag{3.19} \\
\tfrac{1}{2}x_1 + \tfrac{5}{6}x_2 \qquad + 1s_2 \qquad\qquad\qquad\qquad\qquad &= 600 \tag{3.20} \\
1x_1 + \tfrac{2}{3}x_2 \qquad\qquad + 1s_3 \qquad\qquad\qquad\qquad &= 708 \tag{3.21} \\
\tfrac{1}{10}x_1 + \tfrac{1}{4}x_2 \qquad\qquad\qquad + 1s_4 \qquad\qquad\qquad &= 135 \tag{3.22} \\
1x_1 \qquad\qquad\qquad\qquad\qquad\qquad - 1s_5 \qquad\qquad &= 100 \tag{3.23} \\
+ 1x_2 \qquad\qquad\qquad\qquad\qquad\qquad - 1s_6 &= 100 \tag{3.24} \\
x_1, x_2, s_1, s_2, s_3, s_4, s_5, s_6 \geq 0. &
\end{aligned}
$$

Now let us reconsider the way we generated an initial basic feasible solution to get the Simplex method started. We set $x_1 = 0$, $x_2 = 0$, and selected the slack variables as our initial basic variables. Extension of this notion to our current problem would suggest setting $x_1 = 0$, $x_2 = 0$, and selecting as initial basic variables the slack and surplus variables. However, looking at the graphical representation of this problem (Figure 3.3) we see that the solution corresponding to the origin is no longer feasible. The inclusion of the two greater-than-or-equal-to constraints $x_1 \geq 100$ and $x_2 \geq 100$ has made the basic solution with $x_1 = x_2 = 0$ infeasible.

To see this another way, look at equations (3.23) and (3.24) in the Standard form representation of the problem. When x_1 and x_2 are set equal to zero, equations (3.23) and (3.24) reduce to

$$-1s_5 = 100$$

and

$$-1s_6 = 100.$$

Thus setting x_1 and x_2 equal to zero gives us the basic solution

$$\begin{bmatrix} s_1 \\ s_2 \\ s_3 \\ s_4 \\ s_5 \\ s_6 \end{bmatrix} = \begin{bmatrix} 630 \\ 600 \\ 708 \\ 135 \\ -100 \\ -100 \end{bmatrix}$$

Clearly this is not a basic feasible solution, since s_5 and s_6 violate the nonnegativity requirements. Thus our former method of creating an initial basic feasible solution by setting each of the decision variables to zero will not work. The difficulty here is that the Standard form and the Tableau form are equivalent only for problems with less-than-or-equal-to constraints.

In order to set up the Tableau form for this problem, we shall resort to a mathematical "trick" that will enable us to find an initial basic feasible solution in terms of the slack variables s_1, s_2, s_3, and s_4 and two new variables we shall denote a_1 and a_2. These two new variables constitute the mathematical "trick." Variables a_1 and a_2 really have nothing to do with the Par, Inc. problem; they merely serve to enable us to set up the Tableau form and thus obtain an initial basic feasible solution. Since these new variables have been artificially created in order to just get things going, we will refer to such variables as *artificial variables*. We caution the student to avoid confusing

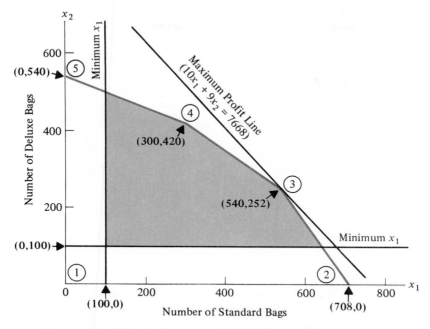

FIGURE 3.3   Graphical Solution to the Modified Par, Inc. Problem

the notation for artificial variables with that used for elements of the A matrix. Elements of the A matrix always have two subscripts, whereas artificial variables have only one.

With the addition of two artificial variables, we can convert the Standard form representation of the modified Par, Inc. problem into the Tableau form. We add artificial variable a_1 to equation (3.23) and artificial variable a_2 to equation (3.24) to obtain the following representation of the system of equations in Tableau form:

$$
\begin{aligned}
\tfrac{7}{10}x_1 + 1x_2 + 1s_1 &&&&&&&= 630 \\
\tfrac{1}{2}x_1 + \tfrac{5}{6}x_2 &+ 1s_2 &&&&&&= 600 \\
1x_1 + \tfrac{2}{3}x_2 &&+ 1s_3 &&&&&= 708 \\
\tfrac{1}{10}x_1 + \tfrac{1}{4}x_2 &&&+ 1s_4 &&&&= 135 \\
1x_1 &&&&- 1s_5 &+ 1a_1 &&= 100 \\
1x_2 &&&&&- 1s_6 &+ 1a_2 &= 100
\end{aligned}
$$

$$x_1, x_2, s_1, s_2, s_3, s_4, s_5, s_6, a_1, a_2 \geq 0.$$

Since the variables s_1, s_2, s_3, s_4, a_1, and a_2 each appear only once with a coefficient of 1, and since the right-hand sides are nonnegative, both requirements of the Tableau form have been satisfied.

We can now obtain an initial basic feasible solution to the system of equations in the Tableau form by setting $x_1 = x_2 = s_5 = s_6 = 0$. This complete solution is

$$
\begin{bmatrix}
x_1 \\
x_2 \\
s_1 \\
s_2 \\
s_3 \\
s_4 \\
s_5 \\
s_6 \\
a_1 \\
a_2
\end{bmatrix}
=
\begin{bmatrix}
0 \\
0 \\
630 \\
600 \\
708 \\
135 \\
0 \\
0 \\
100 \\
100
\end{bmatrix}
$$

Is this solution feasible in terms of our real-world problem? No. It does not satisfy the requirements that we produce at least one hundred each of standard and deluxe bags. Thus we must make an important distinction between a basic feasible solution for the Tableau form of our problem and a basic feasible solution for the real-world problem. A basic feasible solution for the Tableau form of a linear programming problem is not always a basic feasible solution to the real-world problem. This is because of the appearance of the artificial variables in the Tableau form of the problem. However, since the Standard form representation of the problem does not include any of these artificial variables, a basic feasible solution for the Standard form representation will be feasible for the real-world problem. We see, then, that the Standard form representation is equivalent to the original problem, whereas whenever we have to add artificial variables the Tableau form representation is not.

As we saw earlier in this chapter, the reason for creating the Tableau form was to obtain an initial basic feasible solution to get the Simplex method started. Thus we see that whenever it is necessary to introduce artificial variables the initial Simplex solution will not in general be feasible for the real-world problem. This situation is not as difficult as it might seem, however, since the only time we *must* have a feasible solution is at the *last* iteration of the Simplex method (that is, the optimal solution must be feasible). Thus if we could devise some means to guarantee that the artificial variables would be driven out of the basis before the optimal solution was reached, there would be no difficulty.

The way in which we guarantee that these artificial variables will be driven out before the optimal solution is reached is to assign a very large cost to each of these variables in the objective function. For example, in the problem we are currently considering, we assign a very large negative number as the profit coefficient of each artificial variable in the objective function of the Tableau form. Hence if these variables are in the solution, they will necessarily be substantially reducing profits. As a result, these variables will be eliminated from the basis as soon as possible, and this is precisely what we want to happen.

As an alternative to picking a large negative number like $-100,000$ for the profit coefficient, we will denote the profit coefficient of each artificial variable by $-M$. Here it is assumed that $-M$ represents some very large negative number. This notation will make it easier for us to keep track of the elements of the Simplex tableau which depend on the profit coefficients of the artificial variables. Using $-M$ as the profit coefficient for the artificial variables, we can now write the objective function for the Tableau form of our problem:

$$\max z = 10x_1 + 9x_2 + 0s_1 + 0s_2 + 0s_3 + 0s_4 + 0s_5 + 0s_6 - Ma_1 - Ma_2.$$

In terms of our new artificial variables a_1 and a_2, we can now write the following initial Simplex tableau:

Basis	c_j	x_1	x_2	s_1	s_2	s_3	s_4	s_5	s_6	a_1	a_2	
		10	9	0	0	0	0	0	0	$-M$	$-M$	
s_1	0	7/10	1	1	0	0	0	0	0	0	0	630
s_2	0	1/2	5/6	0	1	0	0	0	0	0	0	600
s_3	0	1	2/3	0	0	1	0	0	0	0	0	708
s_4	0	1/10	1/4	0	0	0	1	0	0	0	0	135
a_1	$-M$	①	0	0	0	0	0	-1	0	1	0	100
a_2	$-M$	0	1	0	0	0	0	0	-1	0	1	100
	z_j	$-M$	$-M$	0	0	0	0	M	M	$-M$	$-M$	$-200M$
	$c_j - z_j$	$10+M$	$9+M$	0	0	0	0	$-M$	$-M$	0	0	

The above tableau corresponds to the solution $s_1 = 630$, $s_2 = 600$, $s_3 = 708$, $s_4 = 135$, $a_1 = 100$, $a_2 = 100$, and $x_1 = x_2 = s_5 = s_6 = 0$. In terms of our tableau this is a basic feasible solution, since all the variables are greater than or equal to zero and $n - m$ of the variables are equal to zero. However, in terms of our modified Par, Inc. problem, $x_1 = x_2 = 0$ is clearly not feasible. This difficulty is caused by the fact that the artificial variables are in our current basic solution at positive values. Let us complete the Simplex solution to this problem and see if the artificial variables are driven out of solution as we hope they will be.

We see that at the first iteration x_1 will be brought into the basis and a_1 will be driven out. The Simplex tableau after this iteration is presented below.

Result of iteration 1:

Basis	c_j	x_1 10	x_2 9	s_1 0	s_2 0	s_3 0	s_4 0	s_5 0	s_6 0	a_1 $-M$	a_2 $-M$	
s_1	0	0	1	1	0	0	0	7/10	0	$-7/10$	0	560
s_2	0	0	5/6	0	1	0	0	1/2	0	$-1/2$	0	550
s_3	0	0	2/3	0	0	1	0	1	0	-1	0	608
s_4	0	0	1/4	0	0	0	1	1/10	0	$-1/10$	0	125
x_1	10	1	0	0	0	0	0	-1	0	1	0	100
a_2	$-M$	0	①	0	0	0	0	0	-1	0	1	100
	z_j	10	$-M$	0	0	0	0	-10	M	10	$-M$	$1000-100M$
	$c_j - z_j$	0	$9+M$	0	0	0	0	10	$-M$	$-M-10$	0	

The current solution is still not feasible, since artificial variable a_2 is in the basis at a positive value. It does not satisfy the $x_2 \geq 100$ requirement. Graphically we see in Figure 3.4 that this iteration has moved us from the origin (labeled Ⓐ) to point Ⓑ, which is still not in the feasible region.

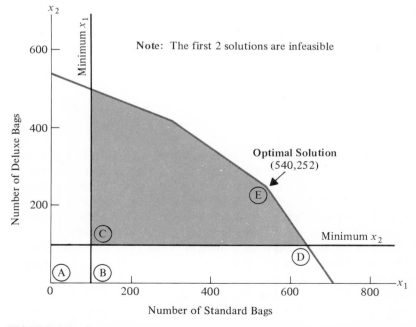

FIGURE 3.4   Sequence of Simplex Solutions to the Modified Par, Inc. Problem

At the next iteration x_2 will be brought into solution and a_2 will be driven out. The Simplex tableau after this iteration is presented below:

Result of iteration 2:

Basis	c_j	x_1 10	x_2 9	s_1 0	s_2 0	s_3 0	s_4 0	s_5 0	s_6 0	a_1 $-M$	a_2 $-M$	
s_1	0	0	0	1	0	0	0	7/10	1	$-7/10$	-1	460
s_2	0	0	0	0	1	0	0	1/2	5/6	$-1/2$	$-5/6$	466⅔
s_3	0	0	0	0	0	1	0	①	2/3	-1	$-2/3$	541⅓
s_4	0	0	0	0	0	0	1	1/10	1/4	$-1/10$	$-1/4$	100
x_1	10	1	0	0	0	0	0	-1	0	1	0	100
x_2	9	0	1	0	0	0	0	0	-1	0	1	100
z_j		10	9	0	0	0	0	-10	-9	10	9	1900
$c_j - z_j$		0	0	0	0	0	0	10	9	-10	-9	

The current solution is now feasible, since all the artificial variables have been driven out of solution. We now have the situation where the basic feasible solution contained in the Simplex tableau is also a basic feasible solution to the real-world problem. As you can see from Figure 3.4 the current solution corresponds to point Ⓒ on the corner of the feasible region.

The next two iterations of the Simplex method move us from point Ⓒ to Ⓓ and from Ⓓ to Ⓔ on our graph. The resulting Simplex tableaus are given below:

Result of iteration 3:

Basis	c_j	x_1 10	x_2 9	s_1 0	s_2 0	s_3 0	s_4 0	s_5 0	s_6 0	a_1 $-M$	a_2 $-M$	
s_1	0	0	0	1	0	$-7/10$	0	0	(16/30)	0	$-16/30$	2432/30
s_2	0	0	0	0	1	$-1/2$	0	0	3/6	0	$-3/6$	588/3
s_5	0	0	0	0	0	1	0	1	2/3	-1	$-2/3$	1624/3
s_4	0	0	0	0	0	$-1/10$	1	0	11/60	0	$-11/60$	1376/30
x_1	10	1	0	0	0	1	0	0	2/3	0	$-2/3$	1924/3
x_2	9	0	1	0	0	0	0	0	-1	0	1	100
z_j		10	9	0	0	10	0	0	$-7/3$	0	7/3	7313⅓
$c_j - z_j$		0	0	0	0	-10	0	0	7/3	$-M$	$-M-7/3$	

Result of iteration 4:

Basis	c_j	x_1	x_2	s_1	s_2	s_3	s_4	s_5	s_6	a_1	a_2	
		10	9	0	0	0	0	0	0	$-M$	$-M$	
s_6	0	0	0	30/16	0	$-210/160$	0	0	1	0	-1	152
s_2	0	0	0	$-15/16$	1	25/160	0	0	0	0	0	120
s_5	0	0	0	$-20/16$	0	300/160	0	1	0	-1	0	440
s_4	0	0	0	$-11/32$	0	45/320	1	0	0	0	0	18
x_1	10	1	0	$-20/16$	0	300/160	0	0	0	0	0	540
x_2	9	0	1	30/16	0	$-210/160$	0	0	0	0	0	252
z_j		10	9	70/16	0	111/16	0	0	0	0	0	7668
$c_j - z_j$		0	0	$-70/16$	0	$-111/16$	0	0	0	$-M$	$-M$	

Just as with the graphical approach, we see that the addition of the two greater-than-or-equal-to constraints has not changed our optimal solution. However, it has taken us more iterations to get to this point. This is because it took us two iterations to eliminate the artificial variables and hence obtain a basic feasible solution for the real-world problem.

Fortunately, once we obtain the initial Simplex tableau using artificial variables, we need not concern ourselves with worrying about whether the basic solution at a particular iteration is feasible for the real-world problem. We need only follow all the rules for the Simplex method. If we reach the stopping criterion (that is, all $c_j - z_j \leq 0$) and all the artificial variables have been eliminated from the solution, then we have found the optimal solution to our linear program. On the other hand, if we reach the stopping criterion and one or more of the artificial variables remains in solution at a positive value, then there is no feasible solution to the real-world problem. This special case will be discussed in more detail in Section 3.9.

Equality Constraints

When an equality constraint occurs in a linear programming problem, we need only add an artificial variable to get an initial basic feasible solution for the Simplex tableau. For example, if we had the equality constraint

$$6x_1 + 4x_2 - 5x_3 = 30$$

we would simply add an artificial variable, say a_1, to enable us to create an initial basic feasible solution in the tableau. The above equation would then become

$$6x_1 + 4x_2 - 5x_3 + 1a_1 = 30.$$

Once we have created the Tableau form by adding artificial variables to all the equality constraints, the Simplex method proceeds exactly as in the case for the greater-than-or-equal-to constraint situation.

Summary of the Steps to Create the Tableau Form

1. If the original formulation of the linear program contains one or more negative right-hand-side values, multiply the corresponding constraint(s) by -1 and change the direction of the inequalities. This will provide an equivalent linear program with nonnegative right-hand-side values. We can then follow steps 2–4 below to obtain the Tableau form and an initial basic feasible solution.

2. For $\leq$ constraints, simply add a slack variable to each less-than-or-equal-to constraint to obtain an equality. The coefficient of the slack variable in the objective function is assigned a value of zero. This gives us the Tableau form, and the slack variable becomes one of the variables in our initial basic feasible solution.

3. For equality constraints, add an artificial variable to each equality constraint to obtain the Tableau form. The coefficient of this artificial variable in the objective function is assigned a value of $-M$. This artificial variable becomes part of our initial basic feasible solution.

4. For $\geq$ constraints, subtract a surplus variable to obtain an equality. Then add an artificial variable to get the Tableau form of the problem. This artificial variable becomes part of the initial basic feasible solution. The coefficient of the artificial variable in the objective function is $-M$.

To get some practice applying the above principles, let us now convert the following numerical example into Tableau form and set up the initial Simplex tableau:

$$\begin{aligned}
\max \quad & 6x_1 + 3x_2 + 4x_3 + 1x_4 \\
\text{s.t.} \quad & \\
& -2x_1 - \tfrac{1}{2}x_2 + 1x_3 - 6x_4 = -60 \\
& 1x_1 \qquad\quad + 1x_3 + \tfrac{2}{3}x_4 \leq 20 \\
& \qquad - 1x_2 - 5x_3 \qquad\quad \leq -50 \\
& x_1, x_2, x_3, x_4 \geq 0.
\end{aligned}$$

In order to handle the negative right-hand-side values in constraints 1 and 3, we multiply both constraints by -1 and reverse the direction of the inequality to obtain the following linear program:

$$\max \quad 6x_1 + 3x_2 + 4x_3 + 1x_4$$
$$\text{s.t.}$$
$$2x_1 + \tfrac{1}{2}x_2 - 1x_3 + 6x_4 = 60$$
$$1x_1 \qquad + 1x_3 + \tfrac{2}{3}x_4 \le 20$$
$$1x_2 + 5x_3 \qquad \ge 50$$
$$x_1, x_2, x_3, x_4 \ge 0.$$

By using slack and surplus variables where appropriate, we obtain the following Standard form representation:

$$\max \quad 6x_1 + 3x_2 + 4x_3 + 1x_4 + 0s_1 + 0s_2$$
$$\text{s.t.}$$
$$2x_1 + \tfrac{1}{2}x_2 - 1x_3 + 6x_4 \qquad\qquad = 60 \qquad (3.25)$$
$$1x_1 \qquad + 1x_3 + \tfrac{2}{3}x_4 + 1s_1 \qquad = 20 \qquad (3.26)$$
$$1x_2 + 5x_3 \qquad\qquad - 1s_2 = 50 \qquad (3.27)$$
$$x_1, x_2, x_3, x_4, s_1, s_2 \ge 0.$$

In order to obtain the Tableau form, we must add an artificial variable to equations (3.25) and (3.27). Adding artificial variable a_1 to equation (3.25) and artificial variable a_2 to equation (3.27), we get

$$\max \quad 6x_1 + 3x_2 + 4x_3 + 1x_4 + 0s_1 + 0s_2 - Ma_1 - Ma_2$$
$$\text{s.t.}$$
$$2x_1 + \tfrac{1}{2}x_2 - 1x_3 + 6x_4 \qquad\qquad + 1a_1 \qquad = 60$$
$$1x_1 \qquad + 1x_3 + \tfrac{2}{3}x_4 + 1s_1 \qquad\qquad = 20$$
$$1x_2 + 5x_3 \qquad\qquad - 1s_2 \qquad + 1a_2 = 50$$
$$x_1, x_2, x_3, x_4, s_1, s_2, a_1, a_2 \ge 0.$$

The initial Simplex tableau corresponding to this Tableau form is

Basis	c_j	x_1	x_2	x_3	x_4	s_1	s_2	a_1	a_2	
		6	3	4	1	0	0	$-M$	$-M$	
a_1	$-M$	2	$1/2$	-1	6	0	0	1	0	60
s_1	0	1	0	1	$2/3$	1	0	0	0	20
a_2	$-M$	0	1	5	0	0	-1	0	1	50
	z_j	$-2M$	$\tfrac{3}{2}M$	$-4M$	$-6M$	0	M	$-M$	$-M$	$-110M$
	$c_j - z_j$	$2M+6$	$\tfrac{3}{2}M+3$	$4M+4$	$6M+1$	0	$-M$	0	0	

3.8 Solving the Minimization Problem Using the Simplex Method

There are two ways in which we can solve a minimization problem using the Simplex method. The first requires that we change the rule used to introduce a variable into solution. Recall that in the maximization case, we selected the

Table 3.2   Comparison of Feasible Solutions to Show that the min z Solution Is the max $(-z)$ Solution

Selected Feasible Solutions		$z = 1x_1 + 1x_2$	$-z = -1x_1 - 1x_2$
$x_1 = 40$	$x_2 = 40$	80	-80
$x_1 = 40$	$x_2 = 30$	70	-70
$x_1 = 40$	$x_2 = 20$	60	-60
$x_1 = 30$	$x_2 = 40$	70	-70
$x_1 = 30$	$x_2 = 30$	60	-60
$x_1 = 30$	$x_2 = 25$	55 [min value of z]	-55 [max value of $(-z)$]

variable with the largest positive $c_j - z_j$ as the variable to introduce next into the basis. This was because the value of $c_j - z_j$ told us the amount the objective function would increase if one unit of the variable in column j was brought into the basis. To solve the minimization problem we can simply reverse this rule. That is, we can select the variable with the most negative $c_j - z_j$ as the one to introduce next. Of course, this means our stopping rule will also have to be changed. In the minimization case we stop when every value in the net evaluation row is nonnegative. When this condition occurs, we have an optimal solution to the minimization problem.

Let us now look at the second way in which we can solve a minimization problem using the Simplex method. This second approach is the one we shall use in the remainder of the book whenever we are required to solve a minimization problem. The approach relies on a well-known mathematical "trick" often employed in optimization problems. It turns out that if one wishes to solve the problem minimize z subject to a set of constraints (linear or otherwise),[2] an equivalent problem is maximize $-z$ subject to the same constraints. These problems are equivalent in the sense that the same solution which minimizes z also maximizes $-z$. The only difference is that the value of the solution to one is the negative of the value of the solution to the other. That is,

$$\min z = -\max (-z).$$

Consider the data in Table 3.2, which shows the values of the objective function z and $-z$ for selected feasible solutions to the Photo Chemicals, Inc. problem introduced in Section 2.7. As you can see, the values of x_1 and x_2 that minimize z are also the values of x_1 and x_2 that maximize $-z$. Moreover, we see that the value of the solution that minimizes $z = 1x_1 + 1x_2$, that is, $z = 55$, is the negative of the value of the solution that maximizes $-z = -1x_1 - 1x_2$. Thus we see that if we want to solve min $(1x_1 + 1x_2)$, we need only solve the problem max $(-1x_1 - 1x_2)$ and multiply the value of the solution to max $(-1x_1 - 1x_2)$ by -1. This relationship will always hold true, and will be the method we shall use to solve minimization problems.

Employing the max $(-z)$ approach to solving the minimization problem

---

[2] z is being used to indicate the value of the objective function.

means that we can follow exactly the same Simplex solution procedure that was outlined for the maximization problem earlier. The only change necessary is that we multiply the objective function by -1 before setting up the Standard form representation. Let us see how this procedure works for the Photo Chemicals problem that we solved graphically in Section 2.7.

We previously saw that the Photo Chemicals problem could be formulated as

$$\begin{aligned} \min \quad & 1x_1 + 1x_2 \\ \text{s.t.} \quad & \\ & 1x_1 \qquad\quad \geq 30 \\ & \qquad 1x_2 \geq 20 \\ & 1x_1 + 2x_2 \geq 80 \\ & x_1, x_2 \geq 0. \end{aligned}$$

To solve the problem using our maximization Simplex procedure, we first multiply the objective function by -1 in order to convert the minimization problem into the following equivalent maximization problem:

$$\begin{aligned} \max \quad & -1x_1 \quad - 1x_2 \\ \text{s.t.} \quad & \\ & 1x_1 \qquad\quad \geq 30 \\ & \qquad 1x_2 \geq 20 \\ & 1x_1 \quad + 2x_2 \geq 80 \\ & x_1, x_2 \geq 0. \end{aligned}$$

After subtracting surplus variables, we obtain the following Standard form representation for the problem:

$$\begin{aligned} \max \quad & -1x_1 - 1x_2 + 0s_1 + 0s_2 + 0s_3 \\ \text{s.t.} \quad & \\ & 1x_1 \qquad\quad - 1s_1 \qquad\qquad = 30 \\ & \qquad 1x_2 \qquad - 1s_2 \qquad = 20 \\ & 1x_1 + 2x_2 \qquad\qquad - 1s_3 = 80 \\ & x_1, x_2, s_1, s_2, s_3 \geq 0. \end{aligned}$$

Since the problem is one involving $\geq$ constraints, we must add artificial variables to obtain the Tableau form. After adding artificial variables to each of the constraints, we get the following Tableau form for the Photo Chemicals problem:

$$\begin{aligned} \max \quad & -1x_1 - 1x_2 + 0s_1 \quad + 0s_2 + 0s_3 - Ma_1 - Ma_2 - Ma_3 \\ \text{s.t.} \quad & \\ & 1x_1 \qquad - 1s_1 \qquad\qquad + 1a_1 \qquad\qquad = 30 \\ & \qquad 1x_2 \qquad - 1s_2 \qquad\qquad + 1a_2 \qquad = 20 \\ & 1x_1 + 2x_2 \qquad\qquad - 1s_3 \qquad\qquad + 1a_3 = 80 \\ & x_1, x_2, s_1, s_2, s_3, a_1, a_2, a_3 \geq 0. \end{aligned}$$

The initial Simplex tableau becomes

Basis	c_j	x_1 -1	x_2 -1	s_1 0	s_2 0	s_3 0	a_1 $-M$	a_2 $-M$	a_3 $-M$	
a_1	$-M$	1	0	-1	0	0	1	0	0	30
a_2	$-M$	0	①	0	-1	0	0	1	0	20
a_3	$-M$	1	2	0	0	-1	0	0	1	80
	z_j	$-2M$	$-3M$	M	M	M	$-M$	$-M$	$-M$	$-130M$
	$c_j - z_j$	$-1+2M$	$-1+3M$	$-M$	$-M$	$-M$	0	0	0	

Three iterations of the Simplex method are required to reach an optimal solution to this problem. The results of each iteration are summarized on page 116.

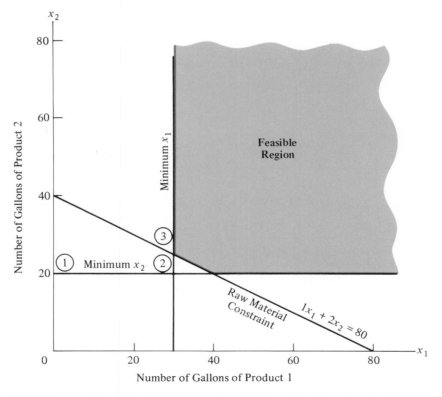

FIGURE 3.5   Set of Feasible Solutions for the Photo Chemicals, Inc. Problem. Circled Numbers Show the Sequence of Simplex Iterations

Result of iteration 1:

Basis	c_j	x_1	x_2	s_1	s_2	s_3	a_1	a_2	a_3	
		-1	-1	0	0	0	$-M$	$-M$	$-M$	
a_1	$-M$	①	0	-1	0	0	1	0	0	30
x_2	-1	0	1	0	-1	0	0	1	0	20
a_3	$-M$	1	0	0	2	-1	0	-2	1	40
	z_j	$-2M$	-1	M	$-2M+1$	M	$-M$	$-1+2M$	$-M$	$-70M-20$
	$c_j - z_j$	$-1+2M$	0	$-M$	$-1+2M$	$-M$	0	$-3M+1$	0	

Result of iteration 2:

Basis	c_j	x_1	x_2	s_1	s_2	s_3	a_1	a_2	a_3	
		-1	-1	0	0	0	$-M$	$-M$	$-M$	
x_1	-1	1	0	-1	0	0	1	0	0	30
x_2	-1	0	1	0	-1	0	0	1	0	20
a_3	$-M$	0	0	1	②	-1	-1	-2	1	10
	z_j	-1	-1	$-M+1$	$-2M+1$	M	$-1+M$	$-1+2M$	$-M$	$-10M-50$
	$c_j - z_j$	0	0	$-1+M$	$-1+2M$	$-M$	$-2M+1$	$-3M+1$	0	

Result of iteration 3:

Basis	c_j	x_1	x_2	s_1	s_2	s_3	a_1	a_2	a_3	
		-1	-1	0	0	0	$-M$	$-M$	$-M$	
x_1	-1	1	0	-1	0	0	1	0	0	30
x_2	-1	0	1	$1/2$	0	$-1/2$	$-1/2$	0	$1/2$	25
s_2	0	0	0	$1/2$	1	$-1/2$	$-1/2$	-1	$1/2$	5
	z_j	-1	-1	$1/2$	0	$1/2$	$1/2$	0	$-1/2$	-55
	$c_j - z_j$	0	0	$-1/2$	0	$-1/2$	$-M-1/2$	$-M$	$-M+1/2$	

It turns out that the third iteration provides the optimal solution (all $c_j - z_j$ values are ≤ 0). Looking back to the solution obtained using the graphical procedure, we see that this is indeed the same solution.

Now refer to Figure 3.5. Look at the path we followed in going from the origin to the optimal solution. We started at the origin ($x_1 = 0$, $x_2 = 0$) with our initial Simplex tableau. The first iteration took us from the origin to the point ($x_1 = 0$, $x_2 = 20$). Note that at this point we were still in the infeasible region. The second iteration took us to the point ($x_1 = 30$, $x_2 = 20$) as x_1 was introduced into solution. However, we still did not have a feasible solution to our real-world problem. Finally, the last iteration took us to ($x_1 = 30$, $x_2 =$

25). This is a feasible solution, as we can easily verify from the graph. Indeed, it is also the optimal solution to the problem. Note that the optimal solution from the tableau shows that we produce 30 units of product 1 and 25 units of product 2 and that with $s_2 = 5$ we will have a surplus of 5 units of product 2 over what was required.

Now we are able to solve minimization problems as well as maximization problems. Actually we had this ability all along. We just did not recognize until now that any minimization problem could be converted to an equivalent maximization problem by simply multiplying the objective function by -1. In the next section we shall concentrate on discussing some important special cases that may occur when trying to solve any linear programming problem. We will only consider the case for maximization problems, recognizing that all minimization problems may be placed into this form.

3.9 Special Cases

In the previous chapter we discussed how infeasibility, unboundedness, and alternate optima could occur during attempts to solve linear programming problems using the graphical solution procedure. These special cases can also arise when one is attempting to solve a linear program using the Simplex method. One additional special case, degeneracy, can "theoretically" cause difficulties when the Simplex solution procedure is employed. In this section we show how these special cases can be recognized when the Simplex method is being used.

Infeasibility

Infeasibility occurs when there is no solution to the linear program which satisfies all the constraints, including the nonnegativity conditions (x_1, $x_2, \ldots, x_n \geq 0$). In Chapter 2 we saw that graphically this meant that the feasible region was empty. Let us now see how infeasibility is recognized in the Simplex tableau.

We mentioned in Section 3.7, when discussing artificial variables, that infeasibility could be recognized when the stopping criterion indicated an optimal solution and one or more of the artificial variables remained in the solution at a positive value. As an illustration of this phenomenon, let us consider the modification of the Par, Inc. problem which called for producing at least 500 standard bags and at least 360 deluxe bags. (We saw in Section 2.8 that there was no feasible solution to this problem.) The formulation of the Par, Inc. problem that incorporates these changes is restated at the top of page 118.

The Simplex solution follows the problem statement (note that two artificial variables were added to the last two rows in order to obtain a basic feasible solution in the initial Simplex tableau).

$$\text{max} \quad 10x_1 + 9x_2$$
$$\text{s.t.}$$
$$\tfrac{7}{10}x_1 + 1x_2 \leq 630$$
$$\tfrac{1}{2}x_1 + \tfrac{5}{6}x_2 \leq 600$$
$$1x_1 + \tfrac{2}{3}x_2 \leq 708$$
$$\tfrac{1}{10}x_1 + \tfrac{1}{4}x_2 \leq 135$$
$$1x_1 \qquad\ \geq 500$$
$$1x_2 \geq 360$$
$$x_1, x_2 \geq 0.$$

Initial tableau:

Basis	c_j	x_1 10	x_2 9	s_1 0	s_2 0	s_3 0	s_4 0	s_5 0	s_6 0	a_1 $-M$	a_2 $-M$	
s_1	0	7/10	1	1	0	0	0	0	0	0	0	630
s_2	0	1/2	5/6	0	1	0	0	0	0	0	0	600
s_3	0	1	2/3	0	0	1	0	0	0	0	0	708
s_4	0	1/10	1/4	0	0	0	1	0	0	0	0	135
a_1	$-M$	①	0	0	0	0	0	-1	0	1	0	500
a_2	$-M$	0	1	0	0	0	0	0	-1	0	1	360
	z_j	$-M$	$-M$	0	0	0	0	M	M	$-M$	$-M$	$-860M$
	c_j-z_j	$M+10$	$M+9$	0	0	0	0	$-M$	$-M$	0	0	

Second tableau:

Basis	c_j	x_1 10	x_2 9	s_1 0	s_2 0	s_3 0	s_4 0	s_5 0	s_6 0	a_1 $-M$	a_2 $-M$	
s_1	0	0	①	1	0	0	0	7/10	0	$-7/10$	0	280
s_2	0	0	5/6	0	1	0	0	1/2	0	$-1/2$	0	350
s_3	0	0	2/3	0	0	1	0	1	0	-1	0	208
s_4	0	0	1/4	0	0	0	1	1/10	0	$-1/10$	0	85
x_1	10	1	0	0	0	0	0	-1	0	1	0	500
a_2	$-M$	0	1	0	0	0	0	0	-1	0	1	360
	z_j	10	$-M$	0	0	0	0	-10	M	10	$-M$	$5000-360M$
	c_j-z_j	0	$M+9$	0	0	0	0	10	$-M$	$-M-10$	0	

Final tableau:

Basis	c_j	x_1 10	x_2 9	s_1 0	s_2 0	s_3 0	s_4 0	s_5 0	s_6 0	a_1 $-M$	a_2 $-M$	
x_2	9	0	1	1	0	0	0	7/10	0	$-7/10$	0	280
s_2	0	0	0	$-5/6$	1	0	0	$-1/12$	0	$1/12$	0	$116\frac{2}{3}$
s_3	0	0	0	$-2/3$	0	1	0	$16/30$	0	$-16/30$	0	$21\frac{1}{3}$
s_4	0	0	0	$1/4$	0	0	1	$-9/120$	0	$9/120$	0	15
x_1	10	1	0	0	0	0	0	-1	0	1	0	500
a_2	$-M$	0	0	-1	0	0	0	$-7/10$	-1	$7/10$	1	80
z_j		10	9	$9+M$	0	0	0	$\dfrac{-37+7M}{10}$	M	$\dfrac{37-7M}{10}$	$-M$	$7520-80M$
c_j-z_j		0	0	$-9-M$	0	0	0	$\dfrac{37-7M}{10}$	$-M$	$\dfrac{-37-8M}{10}$	0	

Just as you might have expected, one of the artificial variables, a_2, is in the final solution. Note that $c_j - z_j \le 0$ for all the variables; therefore according to the rules we established earlier this should be the optimal solution. But this solution is not feasible for our real-world problem, since it has $x_1 = 500$ and $x_2 = 280$. (Recall that we had to make at least 360 deluxe bags.) The fact that artificial variable a_2 is in the solution at a value of 80 tells us that the final solution violates the sixth constraint ($x_2 \ge 360$) by 80 units.

If we are interested in knowing which constraints are preventing us from getting a feasible solution, we can obtain at least a partial answer to this from our final Simplex tableau. Notice that $s_2 = 116\frac{2}{3}$, $s_3 = 21\frac{1}{3}$, and $s_4 = 15$. Since s_1 is not in the solution, it has a value of zero. This tells us that the current solution uses all the cutting and dyeing time available but does not use $116\frac{2}{3}$ hours of sewing time, $21\frac{1}{3}$ hours of finishing time, and 15 hours of inspection and packaging time. Thus what has actually happened is that the cutting and dyeing operation is causing a bottleneck. Since there is not enough cutting and dyeing time available, we cannot obtain the necessary x_1 and x_2 volumes. This occurs even though idle time exists in other departments.

The management implications here are that additional cutting and dyeing time should be made available in order to eliminate the bottleneck. After eliminating the problem in the cutting and dyeing department, it may still turn out that we cannot obtain a feasible solution. (This will obviously be the case for Par, Inc., since not enough finishing or inspection and packaging time is available to make the required number of bags.) Unless management decides to relax the requirement that 500 standard bags and 360 deluxe bags be manufactured, it will have to continue allocating resources to bottleneck departments until the linear programming problem has a feasible solution.

In summary, a linear program is infeasible if there is no solution which satisfies all the constraints and nonnegativity conditions simultaneously. Graphically, we recognize this situation as the case where there is no feasible region. In terms of the Simplex solution procedure, we know that if one or more of the artificial variables remains in the final solution at a positive value, there is no feasible solution to the real-world problem.

In closing, we note that for linear programming problems with only $\leq$ constraints and nonnegative right-hand sides there will always be a feasible solution. Since it is not necessary to introduce artificial variables to set up the initial Simplex tableau, there could not possibly be an artificial variable in the final solution.

Unboundedness

For maximization problems we say that a linear program is unbounded if the value of the solution may be made infinitely large without violating any constraints. We mentioned, while discussing unboundedness from a graphical point of view in Section 2.8, that unbounded profit maximization problems do not occur in practice. Thus when this case occurs we can generally look for an error in our formulation.

The Simplex method will automatically uncover any unboundedness that exists before the final tableau is reached. What will happen is that the rule for determining the variable to be removed from the solution will not work. Recall that we calculated the ratio $\bar{b}_i / \bar{a}_{ij}$ for each of the elements of column j which were *positive*. Then we picked the smallest ratio to tell us which variable to remove from the current basic feasible solution.

The coefficients in a particular column of $\bar{A}$ indicate how much each of the current basic variables will decrease if one unit of the variable associated with that particular column is brought into solution. Suppose, then, that for a particular linear program we found that $c_2 - z_2 = 5 > 0$, and that all the $\bar{a}_{i2}$ in column 2 were ≤ 0. This would mean that each unit of x_2 brought into solution would increase the objective function by five units. Furthermore, since $\bar{a}_{i2} \leq 0$ for all i, this would mean that none of the current basic variables would be driven to zero, no matter how many units of x_2 we introduced. Thus we could introduce an infinite amount of x_2 into solution and still maintain feasibility. Since each unit of x_2 increases the objective function by five, you can see that we would have an unbounded solution in this case. Hence *the way we recognize the unbounded situation is that all the $\bar{a}_{ij}$ are ≤ 0 in column j, and the Simplex method indicates that variable x_j is to be introduced into solution.*

To illustrate this concept let us consider the example of an unbounded problem which we introduced in Section 2.8:

$$\max \quad 2x_1 + 1x_2$$
$$\text{s.t.}$$
$$1x_1 \qquad \geq 2$$
$$1x_2 \leq 5$$
$$x_1, x_2 \geq 0.$$

We first subtract a surplus variable, s_1, from the first constraint equation and add a slack variable, s_2, to the second constraint equation to obtain the Standard form. We then add an artificial variable, a_1, to the first constraint equation in order to obtain the Tableau form and set up the initial Simplex tableau in terms of the basic variables a_1 and s_2. After bringing in x_1 at the first iteration, our Simplex tableau is as follows:

Basis	c_j	x_1	x_2	s_1	a_1	s_2	
		2	1	0	$-M$	0	
x_1	2	1	0	-1	1	0	2
s_2	0	0	1	0	0	1	5
	z_j	2	0	-2	2	0	4
	$c_j - z_j$	0	1	2	$-M-2$	0	

Since s_1 has the largest positive $c_j - z_j$, we know we can increase the value of the objective function most rapidly by bringing s_1 into the basis. But $\bar{a}_{13} = -1$ and $\bar{a}_{23} = 0$; hence we cannot form the ratio $\bar{b}_i / \bar{a}_{i3}$ for positive $\bar{a}_{i3}$, since there are none. This is our indication that the solution to the linear program is unbounded. We interpret this condition below.

Each unit of s_1 that we bring into the basis drives zero units of s_2 out of solution and "gives" us an extra unit of x_1, since $\bar{a}_{13} = -1$. This is because s_1 is a surplus variable and can be interpreted as the amount of product 1 we produce over the minimum amount required; that is, $x_1 \geq 2$. Since our Simplex tableau has indicated that we can introduce as much of s_1 as we desire without violating any constraints, this tells us that we can make as much as we want above the minimum amount of x_1 required. Thus there will be no upper bound on the value of the objective function, since the objective function coefficient associated with x_1 is positive.

In summary, a maximization linear program is unbounded if it is possible to make the value of the optimal solution as large as desired without violating any of the constraints. We can recognize this condition graphically as the case where the feasible region extends to infinity in some direction. When employing the Simplex solution procedure, an unbounded linear program is easy to recognize. If at some iteration the Simplex method tells us to introduce x_j into solution and all the $\bar{a}_{ij}$ are less than or equal to zero in the jth column, we recognize that we have a linear program with an unbounded solution.

We emphasize that the case of an unbounded solution will never occur in real-world cost minimization or profit maximization problems because it is not possible to reduce costs to minus infinity or to increase profits to plus infinity. Thus if we encounter this situation when solving a linear programming model in practice, we should go back and examine carefully our formulation of the problem to determine if we have made an error, or if the linear programming model is inappropriate.

Alternate Optimal Solutions

A linear program with two or more optimal solutions is said to have alternate optima. In Section 2.6 we saw that alternate optima could be recognized whenever the objective function line was parallel to one of the binding constraints. When using the Simplex method of solution, one will probably not recognize that a linear program has alternate optima until the final Simplex tableau. Then if the program has alternate optima, $c_j - z_j$ will equal zero for one or more of the variables not in solution.

To illustrate the occurrence of alternate optima when the Simplex method is being used, consider the following modification of the Par, Inc. problem (the objective function has been changed from $10x_1 + 9x_2$ to $7x_1 + 10x_2$):

$$\begin{aligned}
\max \quad & 7x_1 + 10x_2 \\
\text{s.t.} \quad & \\
& \tfrac{7}{10}x_1 + 1x_2 \leq 630 \\
& \tfrac{1}{2}x_1 + \tfrac{5}{6}x_2 \leq 600 \\
& 1x_1 + \tfrac{2}{3}x_2 \leq 708 \\
& \tfrac{1}{10}x_1 + \tfrac{1}{4}x_2 \leq 135 \\
& x_1, x_2 \geq 0.
\end{aligned}$$

The graphical solution to this problem is shown in Figure 3.6.

The final Simplex tableau for this problem is shown below:

Basis	c_j	x_1 7	x_2 10	s_1 0	s_2 0	s_3 0	s_4 0	
x_1	7	1	0	10/3	0	0	−40/3	300
s_2	0	0	0	−10/18	1	0	−20/18	100
s_3	0	0	0	−22/9	0	1	64/9	128
x_2	10	0	1	−4/3	0	0	28/3	420
z_j		7	10	10	0	0	0	6300
$c_j - z_j$		0	0	−10	0	0	0	

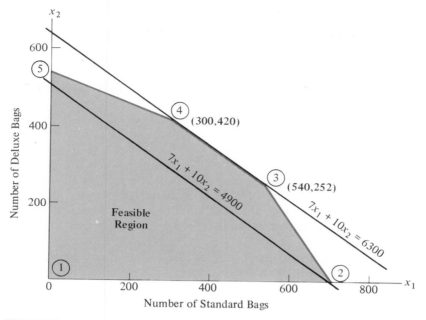

FIGURE 3.6   Par, Inc. Problem with a Modified Objective Function (Alternate Optima)

All values in the net evaluation row are less than or equal to zero, indicating that we have reached the optimal solution. This solution yields $x_1 = 300$, $x_2 = 420$, $s_2 = 100$, and $s_3 = 128$. Note, however, that the entry in the net evaluation row for the nonbasic variable s_4 is equal to zero. This indicates that the linear program has alternate optima. That is, since the $c_j - z_j$ value corresponding to s_4 is equal to zero, we could introduce s_4 into the solution without changing the value of the optimal solution. The tableau, after introducing s_4, is

Basis	c_j	x_1 7	x_2 10	s_1 0	s_2 0	s_3 0	s_4 0	
x_1	7	1	0	$-5/4$	0	120/64	0	540
s_2	0	0	0	$-30/32$	1	10/64	0	120
s_4	0	0	0	$-22/64$	0	9/64	1	18
x_2	10	0	1	15/8	0	$-84/64$	0	252
	z_j	7	10	10	0	0	0	6300
	$c_j - z_j$	0	0	-10	0	0	0	

After introducing s_4 we have a different solution: $x_1 = 540$, $x_2 = 252$, $s_2 = 120$, and $s_4 = 18$. However, this solution is still optimal ($c_j - z_j \leq 0$ for all j). Another way to confirm that this solution is still optimal is to note that the value of the objective function has remained at 6300.

In summary, we can recognize that a linear program has alternate optima by observing graphically that the objective function is parallel to one of the binding constraints. When using the Simplex method, we can recognize alternate optima if $c_j - z_j$ equals zero for one of the variables not in solution.

Degeneracy

A linear program is said to be *degenerate* if one or more of the variables in the basic solution has a value of zero. Degeneracy does not cause any particular difficulties for the graphical solution procedure; however, degeneracy can cause some difficulties when the Simplex method is used to solve a linear program.

To see how a degenerate linear program may come about, consider the following modification of the Par, Inc. problem:

$$\max \quad 10x_1 + 9\,x_2$$
s.t.
$$\tfrac{7}{10}\,x_1 + 1\,x_2 \le 630$$
$$\tfrac{1}{2}\,x_1 + \tfrac{5}{6}\,x_2 \le 480 \qquad \text{sewing capacity reduced to 480}$$
$$1\,x_1 + \tfrac{2}{3}\,x_2 \le 708$$
$$\tfrac{1}{10}\,x_1 + \tfrac{1}{4}\,x_2 \le 135$$
$$x_1, x_2 \ge 0.$$

Let us solve this new Par, Inc. problem using the Simplex method. The tableau after the first iteration is presented below:

		x_1	x_2	s_1	s_2	s_3	s_4	
Basis	c_j	10	9	0	0	0	0	
s_1	0	0	16/30	1	0	−7/10	0	134.4
s_2	0	0	1/2	0	1	−1/2	0	126
x_1	10	1	2/3	0	0	1	0	708
s_4	0	0	22/120	0	0	−1/10	1	64.2
	z_j	10	20/3	0	0	10	0	7080
	$c_j - z_j$	0	7/3	0	0	−10	0	

The entries in the net evaluation row indicate that we should introduce variable x_2 into solution. Calculating the appropriate ratios to determine the pivot element, we get

$$\frac{\bar{b}_1}{\bar{a}_{12}} = \frac{134.4}{16/30} = 252$$

$$\frac{\bar{b}_2}{\bar{a}_{22}} = \frac{126}{1/2} = 252$$

$$\frac{\bar{b}_3}{\bar{a}_{32}} = \frac{708}{2/3} = 1062$$

$$\frac{\bar{b}_4}{\bar{a}_{42}} = \frac{64.2}{22/120} = 350.2.$$

We see that there is a tie between the first and second *rows*. This is an indication that we will have a degenerate linear program at the next iteration. To see why, let us arbitrarily select row one and perform the necessary row operations. The Simplex tableau after this iteration is as follows:

Basis	c_j	x_1	x_2	s_1	s_2	s_3	s_4	
		10	9	0	0	0	0	
x_2	9	0	1	30/16	0	−210/160	0	252
s_2	0	0	0	−15/16	1	25/160	0	0
x_1	10	1	0	−20/16	0	300/160	0	540
s_4	0	0	0	−11/32	0	45/320	1	18
	z_j	10	9	70/16	0	111/16	0	7668
	$c_j - z_j$	0	0	−70/16	0	−111/16	0	

Do you see anything unusual about this tableau? When we performed our iteration and introduced 252 units of x_2 into the basis, we not only drove s_1 out of solution, setting s_1 equal to zero, but we also drove s_2 to zero. Hence we have a solution where one of the basic variables is equal to zero. Whenever we have a tie in the $\bar{b}_i/\bar{a}_{ij}$ ratios, there will always be a basic variable equal to zero in the next tableau. Since we are at the optimal solution in this case, we do not care that s_2 is in solution at a zero value. However, if this condition occurs at some iteration prior to reaching the optimal solution, it is theoretically possible for the Simplex algorithm to cycle; that is, the algorithm could possibly alternate between the same set of nonoptimal points at each iteration and never reach the optimal solution. Cycling has not proved to be a significant difficulty in practice. Therefore we do not recommend introducing any special machinery into the Simplex algorithm to eliminate the possibility of degeneracy occurring. If while performing the iterations of the Simplex algorithm a tie occurs for the minimum $\bar{b}_i/\bar{a}_{ij}$ ratio, then we recommend simply selecting the upper row as the pivot row.

Summary

In Chapter 2 we saw how small linear programs could be solved using a graphical approach. In Chapter 3 the Simplex method was developed as a procedure for solving larger linear programs. Actually the Simplex method is also an easy way to solve small linear programs by hand calculations. However, as problems get larger, even the Simplex method becomes too cumbersome for efficient hand computation. As a result, we must utilize a computer if we want a solution to larger linear programs in any reasonable length of time. At the end of Chapter 4, we show how the computer is used to solve linear programs.

We described how developing the Tableau form of a linear program was a necessary step in the Simplex solution procedure. In addition, we have shown in this chapter how to convert greater-than-or-equal-to constraints, equality constraints, and constraints with negative right-hand-side values into the form required for writing a linear program in Tableau form. Doing this required noteing that when both sides of an inequality are multiplied by -1 the direction of the inequality changes and that for linear programs with greater-than-or-equal-to constraints and/or equality constraints it is necessary to introduce artificial variables in order to go from Standard to Tableau form. We assigned an objective function coefficient of $-M$, where M is a very large number, to these variables. Thus if there was a feasible solution to the real-world linear program, these artificial variables would be driven out of solution before the Simplex method reached its stopping criterion.

We then presented two techniques for solving minimization problems. The first involved changing the Simplex rules for introducing a variable into solution and changing the stopping criterion. The second approach enabled us to solve any minimization problem using the same rules as for a maximization problem. That is, we showed that minimizing z was equivalent to maximizing $-z$. The only difference was that the value of the solution to max $(-z)$ was the negative of the value of the solution to min z. Thus to solve a minimization problem using our maximization Simplex rules, we multiply each decision variable coefficient in the objective function by -1 and then apply the maximization procedure. When we get the optimal solution to this problem, we multiply the value of the optimal solution by -1 to get the value of the optimal solution for our original minimization problem.

As a review of the material in this chapter we present here a detailed step-by-step procedure for solving linear programs using the Simplex method:

Step 1:   Formulate a linear programming model of the real-world problem. This is to obtain a mathematical representation of the problem.

Step 2: Define an equivalent linear program by

    a. multiplying negative right-hand-side constraints by -1 and changing the direction of the inequalities;

    b. if it is a min z problem, change to max $(-z)$.

Step 3: Set up the Standard form representation of the linear program. This is to make every constraint an equality and is the first step in preparing the problem for solution using the Simplex method.

Step 4: Set up the Tableau form representation of the linear program. This is necessary in order to obtain an initial basic feasible solution. All linear programs must be put in this form before the initial Simplex tableau can be set up.

Step 5: Set up the Simplex tableau. This is used to keep track of the calculations made as we carry out the Simplex method. The solution corresponding to the initial Simplex tableau is always the origin. That is, in the initial solution all the decision variables are equal to zero.

Step 6: Choose the variable with the largest $c_j - z_j$ to introduce into solution. The value of $c_j - z_j$ tells us the amount by which the value of the objective function will increase for every unit of x_j introduced into the solution.

Step 7: Choose as the pivot row that row with the smallest ratio of $\bar{b}_i/\bar{a}_{ij}$, $\bar{a}_{ij} > 0$. This determines which variable will leave the basis when x_j enters. This also tells us how many units of x_j can be introduced into solution before the basic variable in the ith row equals zero.

Step 8: Perform the necessary row operations to convert column j to a unit column:

    a. multiply the pivot row by the constant necessary to make the pivot element a 1.

    b. obtain zeros in all the other rows by multiplying the new pivot row by an appropriate constant and adding it to the appropriate row.

Once these row operations have been performed, we can read the values of our basic variables from the $\bar{b}$ column of our tableau.

Step 9: Test for optimality. If $c_j - z_j \leq 0$ for all columns, we have the optimal solution. If not, return to Step 6. If $c_j - z_j \leq 0$ for all variables, there is no variable that we can introduce which will cause the objective function to increase. Hence we have the optimal solution.

In Section 3.9 we discussed how the special cases of infeasibility, unboundedness, alternate optima, and degeneracy are handled when solving problems using the Simplex method.

Some additional notation was introduced in this chapter. We use $\bar{A}$ and $\bar{a}_{ij}$ to denote the positions in the Simplex tableau corresponding to the A

matrix in the Tableau form representation of our linear program. Similarly, we used $\bar{b}$ and $\bar{b}_i$ to denote the positions in the Simplex tableau corresponding to the b column in our Tableau form representation.

Glossary

1. *Simplex method*—An algebraic procedure for solving linear programs. It moves from one basic feasible solution (extreme point) to another, making sure that the objective function increases at each iteration until the optimal solution is reached.

2. *Basic solution*—For a general linear program with n variables and m constraints in standard form a basic solution may be found by setting $n - m$ of the variables equal to zero and solving the constraint equations for the values of the other m variables. If a unique solution exists, it is a basic solution.

3. *Elementary row operations*—Operations that may be performed on a system of simultaneous equations without changing the solution to the system of equations. They are used to find basic solutions in the Simplex method.

4. *Basic feasible solution*—A basic solution which is also in the feasible region (that is, it satisfies the nonnegativity requirement). A basic feasible solution corresponds to an extreme point.

5. *Tableau form*—The form in which a linear program must be written prior to setting up the initial Simplex tableau. When a linear program is written in this form, its A matrix contains m unit columns corresponding to basic variables, and the values of these basic variables are given by the b column. A further requirement is that the entries in the b column be greater than or equal to zero. This requirement provides us with a basic feasible solution.

6. *Simplex tableau*—A table used to keep track of the calculations made when the Simplex solution method is employed.

7. *Unit vector or unit column*—A vector or column of a matrix, which has a zero in every position except one. In the nonzero position there is a 1.

8. *Net evaluation row*—The row in the Simplex tableau that contains the value of $c_j - z_j$ for every variable (column).

9. *Current solution*—When carrying out the Simplex method, the current solution refers to the current basic feasible solution (extreme point).

10. *Basis*—The set of variables which are not restricted to equal zero in the current basic solution. The variables which make up the basis are termed basic variables, and the remaining variables are called nonbasic variables.

11. *Iteration*—An iteration of the Simplex method consists of the sequence of steps performed in moving from one basic feasible solution to another.

12. *Pivot element*—The element of the Simplex tableau that is in both the pivot row and the pivot column.

13. *Pivot column*—The column corresponding to the nonbasic variable that is about to be introduced into the basic feasible solution.

14. *Pivot row*—The row in the Simplex tableau corresponding to the basic variable that will leave the solution as the algorithm iterates from one basic feasible solution to another.

15. *Artificial variable*—A variable that has no physical meaning in terms of the original linear programming problem, but serves merely to enable a basic feasible solution to be created for starting the Simplex method. Artificial variables are assigned an objective function coefficient of $-M$, where M is a very large number.

16. *Degeneracy*—When one or more of the variables in the basic feasible solution to a linear program has a value of zero.

Problems

1. Use elementary row operations to solve the following system of linear equations (that is, what values of x_1 and x_2 satisfy both equations?):

$$6x_1 + 3x_2 = 33$$
$$10x_1 - 2x_2 = 6$$

2. Use elementary row operations to solve the following system of linear equations (that is, what values of x_1, x_2, and x_3 satisfy all three equations?):

$$1x_1 + 3x_2 - 1x_3 = 4$$
$$2x_1 + 4x_2 + 2x_3 = 22$$
$$5x_1 - 2x_2 + 1x_3 = 27$$

3. Start with the Par, Inc. constraint equations (3.2–3.5).
    a. Use elementary row operations to solve for the basic solution when s_1 and s_3 are set equal to zero.
    b. Repeat part a for the basic solution when x_1 and s_4 are set equal to zero.
    c. Are your solutions for part a and/or b basic feasible solutions for the Par, Inc. problem? Explain.
    d. Are your solutions for part a and/or b extreme-point solutions for the Par, Inc. problem? Explain. Using Figure 3.1, what extreme points, if any, have you found?

4. Consider the following linear program:

$$\max \quad 5x_1 + 9x_2$$
$$\text{s.t.}$$
$$\tfrac{1}{2}x_1 + 1x_2 \le 8$$
$$1x_1 + 1x_2 \ge 10$$
$$\tfrac{1}{4}x_1 + \tfrac{3}{2}x_2 \ge 6$$
$$x_1, x_2 \ge 0.$$

    a. Write the problem in standard form.
    b. How many variables will be set equal to zero in a basic solution for this problem? Explain.
    c. Use elementary row operations to find the basic solution that corresponds to s_1 and s_2 equal to zero.

    d. Use elementary row operations to find the basic solution that corresponds to x_1 and s_3 equal to zero.

    e. Are your solutions for part c and/or d basic feasible solutions? Extreme-point solutions? Explain.

    f. Use the graphical approach to determine the solutions found in parts c and d. Do the graphical results agree with your answer to part e? Explain.

5. The following partial initial Simplex tableau is given:

Basis	c_j	x_1	x_2	x_3	s_1	s_2	s_3	
		5	20	25	0	0	0	
	2	1	0	1	0	0	40	
	0	2	1	0	1	0	30	
	3	0	$-1/2$	0	0	1	15	
z_j								
$c_j - z_j$								

    a. Complete the initial tableau.

    b. Write the problem in its Tableau form.

    c. What is the initial basis? Does this correspond to the origin? Explain.

    d. What is the value of the objective function at this initial solution?

    e. For the next iteration, what variable should enter the basis and what variable should leave the basis?

    f. How many units of the entering variable will be in the next solution? Before making this first iteration, what should be the value of the objective function after the first iteration?

    g. Find the optimal solution using the Simplex method.

6. Solve the following linear program using the graphical approach:

$$\begin{aligned} \max \quad & 4x_1 + 5x_2 \\ \text{s.t.} \quad & \\ & 2x_1 + 2x_2 \le 20 \\ & 3x_1 + 7x_2 \le 42 \\ & x_1, x_2 \ge 0. \end{aligned}$$

Now put the linear program in Tabular form and solve using the Simplex method. Show the sequence of extreme points generated by the Simplex method.

7. Explain in your own words why the Tableau form and the Standard form are the same for problems with less-than-or-equal-to constraints and nonnegative b_i's.

8. Solve the Ryland Farm problem (2.23) using the Simplex method. Compare each iteration to the graphical solution procedure.

9. Solve the Wilkinson Motor, Inc. problem (2.22), using the Simplex method. Compare each iteration to the graphical solution procedure.

10. Solve the following linear program:

$$\max\ 2.5x_1 +\ 5x_2 +\ 1x_3 +\ 1x_4$$
$$\text{s.t.}$$
$$1x_1 + 1.4x_2 + 0.2x_3 + 0.8x_4 \le 1600$$
$$2x_1 +\ 2x_2 + 1.6x_3 +\ 1x_4 \le 1300$$
$$1.2x_1 +\ 1x_2 +\ 1x_3 + 1.2x_4 \le\ 960$$
$$x_1, x_2, x_3, x_4 \ge 0.$$

11. Solve the following linear program using both the graphical and the Simplex methods:

$$\max\ 2x_1 + 8x_2$$
$$\text{s.t.}$$
$$3x_1 + 9x_2 \le 45$$
$$2x_1 + 1x_2 \ge 12$$
$$x_1, x_2 \ge 0 .$$

Show graphically how the Simplex method moves from one basic feasible solution to another. Find the coordinates of all extreme points of the feasible region.

12. How many basic solutions are there to a linear program which has seven variables and four constraints when written in Standard form?

13. Explain in your own words why, when we are trying to determine which basic variable to eliminate at a particular iteration, we consider only the $\bar{a}_{ij}$ which are strictly greater than zero.

14. Suppose that instead of introducing x_1 into the solution at the first iteration of the Simplex method for the Par, Inc. problem, you had mistakenly introduced x_2.
   a. Conduct the Simplex calculations for the Par, Inc. problem and introduce x_2 into the basis at the first iteration. Then continue with the Simplex method until an optimal solution has been reached.
   b. Do we always have to introduce the variable into the solution that has the largest $c_j - z_j$ value?
   c. Why does the criterion for introducing the variable into the solution use the largest $c_j - z_j$ value?

15. Suppose that we did not remove the basic variable with the smallest ratio of $\bar{b}_i/\bar{a}_{ij}$ at a particular iteration. What effect would this have on the Simplex tableau for our next solution?

16. Suppose a company manufactures three products from two raw materials where

	Product A	Product B	Product C
Raw material I	7 lb	6 lb	3 lb
Raw material II	5 lb	4 lb	2 lb

If the company has available 100 pounds of material I and 200 pounds of material II, and if the profits for the three products are $20, $20, and $15, how much of each product should be produced in order to maximize profits?

17. Liva's Lumber, Inc. manufactures three types of plywood. The data below summarize the production hours per unit in each of three production operations and other

data for the problem:

Plywood	Operations (hours) I	Operations (hours) II	Operations (hours) III	Profit/ Unit
Grade A	2	2	4	$40
Grade B	5	5	2	$30
Grade X	10	3	2	$20
Maximum time available	900	400	600	

How many units of each grade of lumber should be produced?

18. Ye Olde Cording Winery in Peoria, Illinois makes three kinds of authentic German wine: Heidelberg Sweet, Heidelberg Regular, and Deutschland Extra Dry. The raw materials, labor, and profit for a gallon of each of these wines is summarized below:

Wine	Grapes Grade A (bushels)	Grapes Grade B (bushels)	Sugar (pounds)	Labor (hours)	Profit/ Gallon
Heidelberg Sweet	1	1	2	2	$1.00
Heidelberg Regular	2	0	1	3	$1.20
Deutschland Extra Dry	0	2	0	1	$2.00

If the Winery has 150 bushels of grade A grapes, 150 bushels of grade B grapes, 80 pounds of sugar, and 225 labor-hours available during the next week, what product mix of wines will maximize the company's profit?
a.   Solve by the Simplex method.
b.   Interpret all slack variables.
c.   An increase in what resources could improve the company's profit?

19. Set up the Tableau form for the following linear program (do not attempt to solve):

$$\max \quad 4x_1 + 2x_2 - 3x_3 + 5x_4$$
$$\text{s.t.}$$
$$2x_1 - 1x_2 + 1x_3 + 2x_4 \geq 50$$
$$3x_1 \qquad - 1x_3 + 2x_4 \leq 80$$
$$1x_1 + 1x_2 \qquad + 1x_4 = 60$$
$$x_1, x_2, x_3, x_4 \geq 0.$$

20. Set up the Tableau form for the following linear program (do not attempt to solve):

$$\min \quad 4x_1 + 5x_2 + 3x_3$$
$$\text{s.t.}$$
$$4x_1 \qquad + 2x_3 \geq 20$$
$$1x_2 - 1x_3 \leq -8$$
$$1x_1 - 2x_2 \qquad = -5$$
$$2x_1 + 1x_2 + 1x_3 \leq 12$$
$$x_1, x_2, x_3 \geq 0.$$

21. Solve the following linear program:

$$\min \quad 3x_1 + 4x_2 + 8x_3$$
$$\text{s.t.}$$
$$4x_1 + 2x_2 \qquad \geq 12$$
$$4x_2 + 8x_3 \geq 16$$
$$x_1, x_2, x_3 \geq 0.$$

22. Solve the following linear program:

$$\min \quad 4x_1 + 2x_2 + 3x_3$$
$$\text{s.t.}$$
$$1x_1 + 3x_2 \qquad \geq 15$$
$$1x_1 \qquad + 2x_3 \geq 10$$
$$2x_1 + 1x_2 \qquad \geq 20$$
$$x_1, x_2, x_3 \geq 0.$$

23. Captain John's Yachts, Inc., located in Fort Lauderdale, Florida, rents three types of ocean-going boats: sailboats, cabin cruisers, and Captain John's favorite, the luxury yachts. Captain John advertises his boats with his famous "you rent—we pilot" slogan, which means that the company supplies the captain and crew for each rented boat. Each rented boat, of course, has one captain, but the crew sizes (that is, deck hands, galley, and so on) differ. The crew requirements, in addition to a captain, are 1 for sailboats, 2 for cabin cruisers, and 3 for yachts. Ten employees are captains, and an additional 18 employees qualify for the crew positions. Currently Captain John has rental requests for all of his boats: 4 sailboats, 8 cabin cruisers, and 3 luxury yachts. If Captain John's daily profit is $50 for sailboats, $70 for cruisers, and $100 for luxury yachts, how many boats of each type should he rent?

24. The Our-Bags-Don't-Break (OBDB) plastic bag company manufactures three plastic refuse bags for home use: a 20-gallon garbage bag, a 30-gallon garbage bag, and a 33-gallon leaf and grass bag. Using purchased plastic material, three operations are required to produce each end product: cutting, sealing, and packaging. The production time required to process each type of bag in every operation, as well as the maximum production time available for each operation, are shown below (note that the production time figures in this table are per box of each type of bag):

Type of Bag	Production Time (seconds/box)		
	Cutting	Sealing	Packaging
20 gallons	2	2	3
30 gallons	3	2	4
33 gallons	3	3	5
Time available	2 hours	3 hours	4 hours

If OBDB makes a profit of $0.10 for each box of 20-gallon bags produced, $0.15 for each box of 30-gallon bags, and $0.20 for each box of 33-gallon bags, what is the optimal product mix?

25. Kirkman Brothers ice cream parlors sell three different flavors of Dairy Sweet ice milk: chocolate, vanilla, and banana. Due to extremely hot weather and a high demand for its products, Kirkman has run short of its supply of ingredients: milk, sugar, and cream. Hence Kirkman will not be able to fill all the orders received from

its retail outlets, the ice cream parlors. Due to these circumstances, Kirkman has decided to make the best amounts of the three flavors given the constraints on supply of the basic ingredients. The company will then ration the ice milk to the retail outlets.

Kirkman has collected the following data on profitability of the various flavors, availability of supplies, and amounts required for each flavor.

Flavor	Profit/ Gallon	Milk (gallons)	Usage/Gallon Sugar (pounds)	Cream (gallons)
Chocolate	$1.00	0.45	0.50	0.10
Vanilla	$0.90	0.50	0.40	0.15
Banana	$0.95	0.40	0.40	0.20
Maximum available		200	150	60

Determine the optimal product mix for Kirkman Brothers. What additional resources should be used?

26. Uforia Corporation sells two different brands of perfume: Incentive and Temptation No. 1. Uforia sells exclusively through department stores and employs a three-person sales staff to call on its customers.

The amount of sales time necessary for each sales representative to sell one case of each product varies with experience and ability. Data on the average time for each of Uforia's three sales reps is presented below:

Salesperson	Average Sales Time per Case (minutes) Incentive	Temptation No. 1
John	10	15
Brenda	15	10
Red	12	6

Each sales representative spends approximately 80 hours per month in the actual selling of these two products. Cases of Incentive and Temptation No. 1 sell at profits of $30 and $25, respectively. How many cases of each perfume should each person sell during the next month in order to maximize the firm's profits?
(Hint: Let x_1 = number of cases of Incentive sold by Red, x_2 = number of cases of Temptation No. 1 sold by John, x_3 = number of cases of Incentive sold by Brenda, and so on.)

27. The Our-Paint-Dries-Quickest (OPDQ) paint company produces two interior enamels: Quick-Dry and Super-Speedie. Both enamels are manufactured from premix silicate base and linseed oil solutions, which OPDQ purchases from a number of different suppliers. Currently only two types of premix solutions are available. Type A contains 60% silicates and 40% linseed oil, whereas type B contains 30% silicates and 70% linseed oil. Type A costs $0.50 per gallon and type B costs $0.75 per gallon. If each gallon of Quick-Dry requires at least 25% silicates and 50% linseed oil, and each gallon of Super-Speedie requires at least 20% silicates but at most 50% linseed oil, how many gallons of each premix should OPDQ

purchase in order to produce exactly 100 gallons of Quick-Dry and 100 gallons of Super-Speedie?

28. Suppose the management at Par, Inc. learned that the accounting department made a mistake and that the profit on the deluxe bag was really $18 per bag. Shown below is a partial Simplex tableau corresponding to the optimal basic feasible solution with $c_1 = 10$ and $c_2 = 9$ (the only difference is that we have changed c_2 to 18):

Basis	c_j	x_1 10	x_2 18	s_1 0	s_2 0	s_3 0	s_4 0	
x_2	18	0	1	30/16	0	$-21/16$	0	252
s_2	0	0	0	$-15/16$	1	25/160	0	120
x_1	10	1	0	$-20/16$	0	300/160	0	540
s_4	0	0	0	$-11/32$	0	45/320	1	18
z_j								
$c_j - z_j$								

a. Calculate the remainder of the Simplex tableau and show that the Simplex method indicates that the current solution is not optimal.

b. Find the optimal solution with $c_2 = 18$. What new variable enters the basis? What variable leaves?

c. Refer to the original graphical solution of the Par, Inc. problem. What extreme point is now optimal? What constraints are now binding?

29. Catalina Yachts, Inc. is a builder of cruising sailboats. They manufacture three models of sailboats: the C-32, the C-40, and the C-48. The company, because of its excellent reputation, is in the position of being able to sell all the boats it manufactures. Catalina is currently in the process of taking orders for the coming year. How many orders for each model should be accepted in order to maximize profits?

The manufacture of each model requires different amounts of time spent on each of three operations: molding, carpentry, and finishing. The number of days required to perform each of these activities on the three models is given below:

	Production Time (person–days)		
Model	Molding	Carpentry	Finishing
C-32	3	5	4
C-40	5	12	5
C-48	10	18	8

Based on past experience, management expects the profit per boat to be $5000 on the C-32, $10,000 on the C-40, and $20,000 on the C-48.

Catalina currently has 40 people employed in manufacturing these sailboats: 10 in molding, 20 in carpentry, and 10 in finishing. On the average each employee works 240 days per year. The only other constraint is a management-imposed restriction on the number of C-48 models that may be sold. Because Catalina does not want the C-48 to become commonplace, it will not take orders for more than 20 of this model.

30. The World-Wide Grocery Store Company, in preparation for the upcoming holiday season, has just purchased the following quantities of nuts:

Type of Nut	Amount (pounds)
Almonds	6000
Brazil	7500
Filberts	7500
Pecans	4000
Walnuts	7500

They would like to package these nuts in one-pound bags and are presently considering producing a regular mix (consisting of 10% pecans, 15% almonds, 25% filberts, 25% Brazil, 25% walnuts), a deluxe mix (20% of each type of nut), and individual bags of each type of nut. The profit figures for each bag they produce are as follows:

Type of Bag	Profit/Bag
Regular mix	$0.20
Deluxe mix	$0.25
Almonds	$0.05
Brazil	$0.10
Filberts	$0.10
Pecans	$0.05
Walnuts	$0.15

Formulate a linear program that World-Wide could use to determine how many bags of each type should be produced in order to maximize profits. What is the optimal solution?

31. In Section 3.7 we defined a modified Par, Inc. problem where the minimum production levels for each golf bag were given by

$$x_1 \geq 100$$
$$x_2 \geq 100.$$

It was perfectly acceptable to use these constraints in the Simplex procedure, but consider the following variation. Since we know x_1 and x_2 will both be at least 100, let us define new decision variables x_1' and x_2', where

x_1' = production of standard bags above the 100-unit minimum,

x_2' = production of deluxe bags above the 100-unit minimum.

Thus if we know the values of x_1' and x_2', we can find our total production x_1 and x_2 by

$$x_1 = 100 + x_1'$$
$$x_2 = 100 + x_2'.$$

Return to the Par, Inc. problem in Section 3.1 and substitute the expression $x_1 = 100 + x_1'$ and $x_2 = 100 + x_2'$ in the linear program. State the linear program in terms of the x_1' and x_2' decision variables.

What is the primary advantage of this procedure? Solve the linear program for the optimal value of the x_1' and x_2' variables. Do you obtain the same optimal production plan?

Note: In problems 32–37, we provide examples of linear programs that result in one or more of the following situations:

1.   Optimal solution;
2.   Infeasible solution;
3.   Unbounded solution;
4.   Alternate optimal solution;
5.   Degenerate solution.

For each linear program, determine the solution situaton that exists and indicate how you identified each situation using the Simplex method. For the problems with alternate optimal solutions, calculate at least two optimal solutions.

32.   max $4x_1 + 8x_2$
   s.t.
$$2x_1 + 2x_2 \le 10$$
$$-1x_1 + 1x_2 \ge 8$$
$$x_1, x_2 \ge 0.$$

33.   min $3x_1 + 3x_2$
   s.t.
$$2x_1 + 0.5x_2 \ge 10$$
$$2x_1 \qquad \ge 4$$
$$4x_1 + 4x_2 \ge 32$$
$$x_1, x_2 \ge 0.$$

34.   max $1x_1 + 1x_2$
   s.t.
$$8x_1 + 6x_2 \ge 24$$
$$4x_1 + 6x_2 \ge -12$$
$$2x_2 \ge 4$$
$$x_1, x_2 \ge 0.$$

35.   max $2x_1 + 1x_2 + 1x_3$
   s.t.
$$4x_1 + 2x_2 + 2x_3 \ge 4$$
$$2x_1 + 4x_2 \qquad \le 20$$
$$4x_1 + 8x_2 + 2x_3 \le 16$$
$$x_1, x_2, x_3 \ge 0.$$

36.   max $2x_1 + 4x_2$
   s.t.
$$1x_1 + \tfrac{1}{2}x_2 \le 10$$
$$1x_1 + 1x_2 = 12$$
$$1x_1 + \tfrac{3}{2}x_2 \le 18$$
$$x_1, x_2 \ge 0.$$

37. min $\quad -4x_1 + 5x_2 + 5x_3$
    s.t.
    $$-1x_2 + 1x_3 \geq \quad 2$$
    $$-1x_1 + 1x_2 + 1x_3 \geq \quad 1$$
    $$1x_3 \leq -1$$
    $$x_1, x_2, x_3 \geq 0.$$

38. In addition to its line of bicycles, Hot Wheels, Inc. manufactures three types of kiddie tricycles: a model known as the Fat Wheel, a model called the Toad, and their ever-popular model, the Ridge Runner. Hot Wheels manufactures these tricycle models on special order or whenever slack time is available during the bicycle production. Hot Wheels currently has slack time available and would like to determine the optimal number of each type of tricycle to produce in order to maximize the total number of tricycles produced. Because of the popularity of the Ridge Runner model, Hot Wheels would like the number of Ridge Runners to be at least twice the number of Fat Wheels. In addition, the number of Ridge Runners should also be at least twice the number of Toads. In terms of manufacturing time each Fat Wheel and each Toad tricycle requires 10 minutes, whereas each Ridge Runner tricycle requires 4 minutes. In addition, Fat Wheels require 8 minutes of assembly time, Toads require 6 minutes, and Ridge Runners require 4 minutes. There are 40 hours of manufacturing time and 20 hours of assembly time available. The warehouse has capacity to store a maximum of 150 tricycles. What should Hot Wheels do? Consider the possibility of alternate optimal solutions. What flexibility does this provide for Hot Wheels?

39. The menu planner at Happy Harry's Lakeside Resort has a problem. In addition to knowing how to prepare just three different dishes, he has been told by Happy Harry to use the ingredients on hand to make up meals having the highest possible nutritional value (so Harry can advertise that his resort is not only a fun place but also a healthy place). The menu planner currently has 40 pounds of ingredient A, 30 pounds of ingredient B, and 60 pounds of ingredient C. Each unit of recipe 1 calls for 1 pound of A, ½ pound of B, and 1 pound of C. Each unit of recipe 2 requires 2 pounds of B and 1 pound of C. Each unit of recipe 3 requires 1 pound of both A and B and 2 pounds of C. If one unit of recipe 1 contains 15 nutritional units, one unit of recipe 2 contains 30 nutritional units, and one unit of recipe 3 contains 25 nutritional units, how many units of each recipe should be made in order to maximize the nutritional value of the meals?

40. Supersport Footballs, Inc. manufactures three kinds of football: an All-Pro model, a College model, and a High-School model. All three footballs require operations in the following departments: cutting and dyeing, sewing, and inspection and packaging. The production times and maximum production availabilities are shown below:

| | Production Time (minutes) | | |
Model	Cutting and Dyeing	Sewing	Inspection and Packaging
All-Pro	12	15	3
College	10	15	4
High-School	8	12	2
Time available	300 hours	200 hours	100 hours

Current orders indicate that at least 1000 All-Pro footballs must be manufactured.

a. If Supersport realizes a profit of $3 for each All-Pro model, $5 for each College model, and $4 for each High-School model, how many footballs of each type should be produced? What occurs in the solution of this problem? Why?

b. If Supersport can increase sewing time to 300 hours and inspection and packaging time to 150 hours by using overtime, what is your recommendation?

Chapter 4

Linear Programming: Sensitivity Analysis, Duality, And Computer Solution

Sensitivity analysis for linear programming was introduced and treated graphically in Chapter 2. In the graphical sensitivity analysis we restricted our analysis to two-variable problems. In this chapter we extend and generalize sensitivity analysis, taking advantage of the knowledge developed in using the Simplex method to solve linear programs. Following sensitivity analysis we discuss duality, and then we close the chapter with a demonstration of how linear programs are solved using a commercially available computer package.

4.1   Sensitivity Analysis

Sensitivity analysis is the study of how the optimal solution and the value of the optimal solution to a linear program change, given changes in the various coefficients of the problem. That is, we are interested in answering questions such as the following: (1) What effect will a change in the coefficients in the objective function (c_j) have? (2) What effect will a change in the right-hand-side values (b_i) have? (3) What effect will a change in the coefficients in the constraining equations (a_{ij}) have? Since sensitivity analysis is concerned with how these changes affect the optimal solution, the analysis begins only after the optimal solution to the original linear programming problem has been obtained. Hence sensitivity analysis can be referred to as postoptimality analysis.

There are several reasons why sensitivity analysis is considered so important from a managerial point of view. First, consider the fact that businesses operate in a dynamic environment. Prices of raw materials change over time, companies purchase new machinery to replace old, stock prices fluctuate, employee turnovers occur, and so on. If a linear programming model has been used in a decision-making situation and later we find that changes in the situation cause changes in some of the coefficients associated with the initial linear programming formulation, we would like to determine how these changes affect the optimal solution to our original linear programming problem. Sensitivity analysis provides us with this information without requiring us to completely solve a new linear program. For example, if the profit for the Par, Inc. standard bags were reduced from $10 to $7 per bag, sensitivity analysis could tell the manager whether the production schedule of 540 standard bags and 252 deluxe bags is still the best decision or not. If it is, we will not have to solve a revised linear program with $7x_1 + 9x_2$ as the objective function.

Sensitivity analysis can also be used to determine how critical estimates of coefficients are in the solution to a linear programming problem. For example, suppose the management of Par, Inc. realizes that the $10 profit coefficient for standard bags is a good, but rough, estimate of the profit the bags will actually provide. If sensitivity analysis shows that Par, Inc. should produce 540 standard bags and 252 deluxe bags as long as the actual profit for standard bags remains between $6 and $14, management can feel comfortable that the recommended production quantities are optimal. However, if the range for the profit of Standard bags is $9.90 to $12, management may want to reevaluate the accuracy of the $10 profit estimate. Management would especially want to consider what revisions would have to be made in the optimal production quantities if the profit for standard bags dropped below the $9.90 limit.

As another phase of postoptimality analysis, management may want to investigate the possibility of adding resources to relax the binding constraints. In the Par, Inc. problem, management would possibly like to consider providing additional hours (such as overtime) for the cutting and dyeing and finishing operations. Sensitivity analysis can help answer the important questions of how much each added hour will be worth in terms of increasing profits, and what is the maximum number of hours that can be added before a different basic solution becomes optimal.

Thus you can see that through sensitivity analysis we will be able to provide additional valuable information for the decision maker. We begin our study of sensitivity analysis with the coefficients of the objective function.

4.2 Sensitivity Analysis—The Coefficients of the Objective Function

In this phase of sensitivity analysis we will be interested in placing ranges on the values of the objective function coefficients such that as long as the actual value of the coefficient is within this range, the optimal solution will remain unchanged. As stated in the previous section, this information will tell us if we have to alter the optimal solution when a coefficient actually changes and will provide us with an indication of how critical the estimates of the coefficients are in arriving at the optimal solution.

In the following sensitivity analysis procedures we will be assuming that only one coefficient changes at a time and that all other objective function coefficients remain at the values defined in the initial linear programming model. To illustrate the analysis for the coefficients of the objective function, let us again consider the final Simplex tableau for the Par, Inc. problem:

		x_1	x_2	s_1	s_2	s_3	s_4	
Basis	c_j	10	9	0	0	0	0	
x_2	9	0	1	30/16	0	−21/16	0	252
s_2	0	0	0	−15/16	1	5/32	0	120
x_1	10	1	0	−20/16	0	30/16	0	540
s_4	0	0	0	−11/32	0	9/64	1	18
	z_j	10	9	70/16	0	111/16	0	7668
	$c_j - z_j$	0	0	−70/16	0	−111/16	0	

Coefficients of the Nonbasic Variables

The sensitivity analysis procedure for coefficients of the objective function depends upon whether we are considering the coefficient of a basic or a nonbasic variable. For now, let us consider only the case of nonbasic variables.

Since the nonbasic variables are not in the solution, we are interested in the question of how much the objective function coefficient would have to change before it would be profitable to bring the associated variable into solution. Recall that it is only profitable to bring a variable into solution if its $c_j - z_j$ entry in the net evaluation row is greater than or equal to zero.

Let us denote a change in the objective function coefficient of variable x_j by Δc_j. Thus

$$\Delta c_j = c_j' - c_j, \tag{4.1}$$

where

c_j = the value of the coefficient of x_j in the original linear program,
c_j' = the new value of the coefficient of x_j.

Using this notation, we can write the new objective function coefficient as

$$c_j' = c_j + \Delta c_j. \tag{4.2}$$

It will be desirable to bring the nonbasic variable x_j into solution if the new objective function coefficient is such that $c_j' - z_j > 0$ (that is, if it will increase the value of the objective function). On the other hand, we will not want to bring the variable x_j into solution and thus will not change our current optimal solution as long as $c_j' - z_j \le 0$. Our goal in this phase of sensitivity analysis is to determine the range of values that c_j' can take on without affecting the optimal solution.

Recall that z_j is computed by multiplying the coefficients of the *basic variables* (c_j column of the Simplex tableau) by the corresponding elements in the jth column of the $\bar{A}$ portion of the tableau. Thus a change in the objective function coefficient for a nonbasic variable cannot affect the value of the z_j. The values of c_j' that do not require us to change the optimal solution are given by

$$c_j' - z_j \le 0.$$

Since z_j will be known in the final Simplex tableau, any new coefficient c_j' for a nonbasic variable such that

$$c_j' \le z_j$$

will not cause a change in the current optimal solution.

Note that there is no lower limit on the new coefficient c_j'. This is certainly as expected, since we have a maximization objective function and thus lower and lower c_j' values will make the nonbasic variables even less desirable.

Thus for nonbasic variables we can now establish a range of c_j' values which will not affect the current optimal solution. We call this range the *range of insignificance* for the nonbasic variables. It is given by

$$-\infty < c_j' \leq z_j.$$

As long as the objective function coefficients for nonbasic variables remain within their respective ranges of insignificance, the nonbasic variables will remain at a zero value in the optimal solution. Thus the current optimal solution and the value of the objective function at the optimal solution will not change.

Coefficients of the Basic Variables

Let us start by asking the question of how much the objective function coefficient of a basic variable would have to change before it would be profitable to change the current optimal solution. Again, realize that we will only change the current optimal solution if one or more of the net evaluation row values $(c_j - z_j)$ becomes greater than zero.

Let us consider a change in the objective function coefficient for the basic variable x_1 in the Par, Inc. problem. Let the new coefficient value be c_1'. Using equation (4.2), we can write $c_1' = c_1 + \Delta c_1$, where c_1 is the original coefficient 10 and Δc_1 is the change in the coefficient. Thus

$$c_1' = 10 + \Delta c_1. \tag{4.3}$$

Let us now see what happens to the final Simplex tableau of the Par, Inc. problem when the objective function coefficient for x_1 becomes $10 + \Delta c_1$. This tableau is given below.

Basis	c_j	x_1 $10 + \Delta c_1$	x_2 9	s_1 0	s_2 0	s_3 0	s_4 0	
x_2	9	0	1	$30/16$	0	$-21/16$	0	252
s_2	0	0	0	$-15/16$	1	$5/32$	0	120
x_1	$10+\Delta c_1$	1	0	$-20/16$	0	$30/16$	0	540
s_4	0	0	0	$-11/32$	0	$9/64$	1	18
z_j		$10 + \Delta c_1$	9	$70/16 - 20/16\Delta c_1$	0	$111/16 + 30/16\Delta c_1$	0	$7668+540\Delta c_1$
$c_j - z_j$		0	0	$-70/16+20/16\Delta c_1$	0	$-111/16-30/16\Delta c_1$	0	

How does the change of Δc_1 affect our final tableau? First, note that since x_1 is a basic variable, the new objective function coefficient $c_1' = 10 + \Delta c_1$ appears in the c_j column of the Simplex tableau. This means that the $10 + \Delta c_1$, value will affect the z_j values for several of the variables. By looking at the z_j row you can see that the new coefficient affects the z_j values of the basic variable x_1, both nonbasic variables (s_1 and s_3), and the objective function.

Recall that a decision to change the current optimal solution must be based on values in the net evaluation row. What variables have experienced a change in the $c_j - z_j$ values because of the change Δc_j? As you can see, the change in objective function coefficient for basic variable x_1 has caused changes in the $c_j - z_j$ values for both of the nonbasic variables. The $c_j - z_j$ values for all the basic variables remained unchanged; $c_j - z_j = 0$.

We have just identified the primary difference between the objective function sensitivity analysis procedures for basic and nonbasic variables. That is, a change in the objective function coefficient for a nonbasic variable affects only the $c_j - z_j$ value for that variable. However, a change in the objective function coefficient for a basic variable can affect the $c_j - z_j$ values for *all* nonbasic variables.

Returning to the Par, Inc. problem with the coefficient for x_1 changed to $10 + \Delta c_1$, we know that our current solution will remain optimal as long as all $c_j - z_j \leq 0$. Since the basic variables all still have $c_j - z_j = 0$, we will have to determine what range of values for Δc_1 will keep the $c_j - z_j$ values for all nonbasic variables less than or equal to zero.

For nonbasic variables s_1 we must have

$$-\tfrac{70}{16} + \tfrac{20}{16}\Delta c_1 \leq 0. \tag{4.4}$$

Solving for Δc_1, we see that it will not be profitable to introduce s_1 as long as

$$\tfrac{20}{16}\Delta c_1 \leq \tfrac{70}{16}$$
$$\Delta c_1 \leq \tfrac{16}{20}\left(\tfrac{70}{16}\right) = \tfrac{7}{2}$$
$$\Delta c_1 \leq 3.5.$$

For nonbasic variable s_3 we must have

$$-\tfrac{111}{16} - \tfrac{30}{16}\Delta c_1 \leq 0. \tag{4.5}$$

Solving for Δc_1, we see that it will not be profitable to introduce s_3 as long as

$$-\tfrac{30}{16}\Delta c_1 \leq \tfrac{111}{16}$$
$$\tfrac{30}{16}\Delta c_1 \geq -\tfrac{111}{16}$$
$$\Delta c_1 \geq \tfrac{16}{30}\left(-\tfrac{111}{16}\right) = -\tfrac{111}{30}$$
$$\Delta c_1 \geq -3.7.$$

Thus in order to keep the net evaluation row values of the nonbasic variables less than or equal to zero, and keep the current solution optimal, changes in c_1 cannot exceed a 3.5 increase ($\Delta c_1 \leq 3.5$) or a 3.7 decrease ($\Delta c_1 \geq -3.7$). Hence our current solution will remain optimal as long as

$$-3.7 \leq \Delta c_1 \leq 3.5. \tag{4.6}$$

From equation (4.3) we know that $\Delta c_1 = c_1' - 10$, where c_1' is the new value of the coefficient for x_1 in the objective function. Thus we can use equation (4.6) to define a range for the coefficient values of x_1 that will not cause a change in the optimal solution. This is done as follows:

$$-3.7 \le (c_1' - 10) \le 3.5.$$

Therefore

$$6.3 \le c_1' \le 13.5.$$

The above result indicates to the decision maker that as long as the profit for one standard bag is between $6.30 and $13.50, the current production quantities of 540 standard bags and 252 deluxe bags will be optimal. We refer to the above range of values for the objective function coefficient of x_1 as the *range of optimality for* c_1.

This is the same range of optimality that we obtained using the graphical method of Section 2.9. However, the methods employed here are more general and can be applied to problems with any number of variables.

To see how the management of Par, Inc. can make use of the above sensitivity analysis information, suppose that because of an increase in raw material prices the profit of the standard bag is reduced to $7 per unit. The range of optimality for c_1 indicates that the current solution $x_1 = 540$, $x_2 = 252$, $s_1 = 0$, $s_2 = 120$, $s_3 = 0$, and $s_4 = 18$ will still be optimal. To see the effect of this change, let us calculate the final Simplex tableau for the Par, Inc. problem after c_1 has been reduced to $7:

Basis	c_j	x_1 7	x_2 9	s_1 0	s_2 0	s_3 0	s_4 0	
x_2	9	0	1	30/16	0	$-21/16$	0	252
s_2	0	0	0	$-15/16$	1	5/32	0	120
x_1	7	1	0	$-20/16$	0	30/16	0	540
s_4	0	0	0	$-11/32$	0	9/64	1	18
z_j		7	9	130/16	0	21/16	0	6048
$c_j - z_j$		0	0	$-130/16$	0	$-21/16$	0	

All the $c_j - z_j$ values are less than or equal to zero, indicating the solution is optimal. As you can see, this solution is the same as our previous optimal solution. Note, however, that because of the decrease in profit for the standard bags, the total profit has been reduced to $7668 + 540\Delta c_1 = 7668 + 540 (-3) = \$6048$.

What would happen if the profit per standard bag were reduced to $5? Again, we refer to the range of optimality for c_1. Since $c_1 = 5$ is outside the range, we know that a change this large will cause a new solution to be optimal. Consider the following Simplex tableau containing the same basic feasible solution but with the value of $c_1 = 5$:

		x_1	x_2	s_1	s_2	s_3	s_4	
Basis	c_j	5	9	0	0	0	0	
x_2	9	0	1	30/16	0	$-21/16$	0	252
s_2	0	0	0	$-15/16$	1	5/32	0	120
x_1	5	1	0	$-20/16$	0	30/16	0	540
s_4	0	0	0	$-11/32$	0	9/64	1	18
	z_j	5	9	170/16	0	$-39/16$	0	4968
	$c_j - z_j$	0	0	$-170/16$	0	39/16	0	

As expected, the solution $x_1 = 540$, $x_2 = 252$, $s_1 = 0$, $s_2 = 120$, $s_3 = 0$, and $s_4 = 18$ is no longer optimal. The coefficient for s_3 in the net evaluation row is now greater than zero. This implies that at least one more iteration must be performed to reach the optimal solution. Check for yourself to see that the new optimal solution will require production of 300 standard bags and 420 deluxe bags.

We now see how the range of optimality can be used to quickly determine whether or not a change in the objective function coefficient of a basic variable will cause a change in the optimal solution. Note that by using the range of optimality to determine whether or not the change in a profit coefficient for a basic variable is large enough to cause a change in the optimal solution, we can avoid the time-consuming process of reformulating and resolving the entire linear programming problem.

The general procedure for determining the range of optimality for the basic variable associated with column j and row i of the Simplex tableau is to first find the range of values for Δc_j that satisfy

$$(c_k' - z_k) - \bar{a}_{ik}\Delta c_j \le 0 \tag{4.7}$$

for each nonbasic variable. In this process we will obtain a limit on Δc_j for each nonbasic variable. The most restrictive upper and lower limits on Δc_j will be used to define the range of optimality. For example, if one of these inequalities requires $\Delta c_j \le 3$ and another requires $\Delta c_j \le 1$, the $\Delta c_j \le 1$ is the most restrictive limit and will be the upper limit for Δc_j.

After considering every nonbasic variable, we will have found upper and lower limits on Δc_j in the following form:

$$\alpha \le \Delta c_j \le \beta,$$

where

$$\alpha = \text{lower limit,}$$
$$\beta = \text{upper limit.}[1]$$

---

[1] α is $-\infty$ if inequalities (4.7) do not provide a lower limit on Δc_j, and β is $+\infty$ if inequalities (4.7) do not provide an upper limit.

Using the relationship $\Delta c_j = c_j' - c_j$, the range of optimality is then given by

$$\alpha \leq (c_j' - c_j) \leq \beta$$

or

$$c_j + \alpha \leq c_j' \leq c_j + \beta. \tag{4.8}$$

Applying the above procedure to the objective function coefficient c_2 in our Par, Inc. problem (the profit per unit for deluxe bags), we see that in order to satisfy inequalities (4.7), Δc_2 must satisfy

$$-{}^{70}\!/_{16} - ({}^{30}\!/_{16})\Delta c_2 \leq 0 \tag{4.9}$$

and

$$-{}^{111}\!/_{16} - (-{}^{21}\!/_{16})\Delta c_2 \leq 0. \tag{4.10}$$

From equation (4.9) we get

$$\Delta c_2 \geq -{}^{7}\!/_{3}$$

and from equation (4.10) we get

$$\Delta c_2 \leq {}^{111}\!/_{21}.$$

Thus we have

$$-{}^{7}\!/_{3} \leq \Delta c_2 \leq {}^{111}\!/_{21}.$$

Using equation (4.8) and our original profit coefficient of $c_2 = 9$, we have the following range of optimality for c_2:

$$9 - {}^{7}\!/_{3} \leq c_2' \leq 9 + {}^{111}\!/_{21}$$

or

$$6.67 \leq c_2' \leq 14.29.$$

Thus we see that as long as the profit for deluxe bags is between $6.67 per unit and $14.29 per unit, the production quantities of 540 standard bags and 252 deluxe bags will remain optimal.

Again, this is the same range of optimality that we obtained in Section 2.9. In Section 4.6 we will see how this range of optimality information, as well as other sensitivity analysis information, is provided routinely by the computer solution of a linear program.

As a summary, we present the following managerial interpretation of sensitivity analysis for the objective function coefficients. Think of the basic variables as corresponding to our current product line and the nonbasic variables as representing other products we might produce. Within bounds, changes in the profit associated with one of the products in our current product line would not cause us to change our product mix or the amounts produced, but the changes would have an effect on our total profit. Of course, if the profit associated with one of our products changed drastically, we would change our product line (that is, move to a different basic solution). For products we are not currently producing (nonbasic variables) it is obvious that a decrease in per unit profit would not make us want to produce them. However, if the per unit profit for one of these products became large enough, we would want to consider adding it to our product line.

4.3 Sensitivity Analysis—The Right-Hand Sides

A very important phase of sensitivity analysis, both from a theoretical and a practical point of view, is the study of the effect of changes of the right-hand sides on the optimal solution and the value of the optimal solution. By changes of the right-hand sides we mean simply changing the values of one of the elements in the *b* column of a linear program.

Quite often in linear programming problems we can interpret the b_i's as the resources available. For example, in the Par, Inc. problem the right-hand-side values represented the number of hours of labor available in each of four departments. Thus valuable management information could be provided if we knew how much it would be worth to the company if one or more of these production time resources were increased. Sensitivity analysis of the right-hand sides can help provide this information.

Shadow Prices

The final Simplex tableau for the original Par, Inc. problem is shown below; let us concentrate on the net evaluation row, or $c_j - z_j$ values:

Basis	c_j	x_1 10	x_2 9	s_1 0	s_2 0	s_3 0	s_4 0	
x_2	9	0	1	30/16	0	−21/16	0	252
s_2	0	0	0	−15/16	1	5/32	0	120
x_1	10	1	0	−20/16	0	30/16	0	540
s_4	0	0	0	−11/32	0	9/64	1	18
z_j		10	9	70/16	0	111/16	0	7668
$c_j - z_j$		0	0	−70/16	0	−111/16	0	

What information is contained in the net evaluation row? As we developed the Simplex method, we learned that the $c_j - z_j$ values tell us how much the objective function changes as one unit of a variable is introduced into the solution. Thus when all $c_j - z_j \leq 0$, we know we cannot increase the value of the objective function and thus the optimal solution has been reached.

We want to see now how the $c_j - z_j$ values can also be used to determine how much the additional resources are worth. For the Par, Inc. problem we have the following $c_j - z_j$ values for the slack variables:

Resource Constraint	Associated Slack Variable	Value of $c_j - z_j$ at Optimum
Cutting and dyeing	s_1	$-70/16$
Sewing	s_2	0
Finishing	s_3	$-111/16$
Inspection and packaging	s_4	0

An important property of the net evaluation row is that the *negative* of the $c_j - z_j$ values for a slack variable associated with a constraint tells us how much the objective function will increase if one additional unit above the initial amount of the resource corresponding to the constraint is made available. Using this important property we could conclude that additional resources for Par, Inc. have the following values:

Resource	Value of an Additional Hour
Cutting and dyeing	$70/16 = \$4.375$
Sewing	0
Finishing	$111/16 = \$6.9375$
Inspection and packaging	0

The above values can be interpreted as the maximum value or price we would be willing to pay to obtain one additional unit of the resource. Because of this interpretation, the value of one additional unit of a resource is often called the *shadow price* of the resource.

The shadow price of \$4.375 for the cutting and dyeing constraint is the same value we computed using graphical sensitivity analysis in Section 2.9. Unfortunately, in order to compute this value graphically we had to solve the problem a second time with a new cutting and dyeing constraint. We now see that when the Simplex solution procedure is used the values of the shadow prices for all the constraints can be obtained directly from the final Simplex tableau.

Let us look more closely at these resource shadow prices to see if we can intuitively see why the negative of the $c_j - z_j$ values does in fact indicate the value of an additional unit of resource.

How much would you be willing to pay for additional resources in the sewing and the inspection and packaging departments? Since slack time exists in these departments ($s_2 = 120$ and $s_4 = 18$), we already have excess capacity. Thus an additional unit of resources in either of these departments would simply increase the slack time. Clearly this is of no value to the company. In general, if a slack variable is a basic variable, in the optimal solution the shadow price of the corresponding resource is zero.

The slack variables associated with the cutting and dyeing and finishing departments are nonbasic variables in the optimal solution and are thus zero ($s_1 = s_3 = 0$). This indicates that all resources in these departments have been used. Thus the resource constraints corresponding to these two departments are the binding constraints. If Par, Inc. had additional resources available, it would obviously make sense to add production time in the cutting and dyeing and the finishing departments.

To see why we place a $70/16$ value on an additional unit of cutting and dyeing time, consider the following question: What happens if we bring one unit of s_1 into solution? We know that $c_j - z_j = -70/16$ tells us that profit will decrease by $70/16$ for each unit of s_1 brought into solution. Having $s_1 = 1$ means we would be using only 629 hours in the cutting and dyeing department (that is, one hour of the 630 is slack time). Thus we see that decreasing our resource usage by one unit to 629 hours changes the profit by $-70/16$. Hence we conclude that the value of an additional unit of this resource is equal to $70/16$. As a result, if we increase our resource usage by one unit to 631 hours, we should expect the profit to increase by $70/16$. Thus $70/16$, or $4.375, is the value of an additional unit of cutting and dyeing time.

Shown below is the final Simplex tableau we would obtain if Par, Inc. had 631 hours of cutting and dyeing time available. As you can see, the profit has increased by $7672 6/16 - 7668 = \$4.375$, which is the shadow price of this resource.

Basis	c_j	x_1 10	x_2 9	s_1 0	s_2 0	s_3 0	s_4 0	
x_2	9	0	1	$30/16$	0	$-21/16$	0	$253^{14}/_{16}$
s_2	0	0	0	$-15/16$	1	$5/32$	0	$119^{1}/_{16}$
x_1	10	1	0	$-20/16$	0	$30/16$	0	$538^{12}/_{16}$
s_4	0	0	0	$-11/32$	0	$9/64$	1	$17^{21}/_{32}$
	z_j	10	9	$70/16$	0	$111/16$	0	$7672^{6}/_{16}$
	$c_j - z_j$	0	0	$-70/16$	0	$-111/16$	0	

You are probably wondering how this final tableau was computed. Certainly, we did not go through all of the Simplex iterations again after changing b_1 from 630 to 631. You can see that the only changes in the tableau are the differences in the values of the basic variables (that is, the last column). The entries in this last column of the Simplex tableau have been obtained by merely adding the first five entries in the third column to the last column in the previous tableau; that is,

$$
\begin{bmatrix} 30/16 \\ -15/16 \\ -20/16 \\ -11/32 \\ 70/16 \end{bmatrix} + \begin{bmatrix} 252 \\ 120 \\ 540 \\ 18 \\ 7668 \end{bmatrix} = \begin{bmatrix} 253^{14}/_{16} \\ 119^{1}/_{16} \\ 538^{12}/_{16} \\ 17^{21}/_{32} \\ 7672^{6}/_{16} \end{bmatrix}
$$

The reason for this is as follows: The entries in column s_1 tell us how many units of the basic variables will be driven out of solution if one unit of variable s_1 is introduced into solution. Increasing b_1 by one unit has just the reverse effect; that is, it is just the same as decreasing s_1 by one unit. If b_1 is increased by one unit, then the entries in the s_1 column tell us how many units of each of the basic variables may be added to the solution for every unit of b_1 added. The increase in the value of the objective function corresponding to adding one unit of b_1 is equal to the negative of $c_3 - z_3$.

Range of Feasibility for the Right-Hand-Side Values

The negative of the $c_j - z_j$ row can be used to predict the change in the value of the objective function corresponding to a unit change in one of the b_i. But here is the "catch": This interpretation can be used only as long as the change in the b_i is not large enough to make the current basis infeasible.

Thus we will be interested in determining how much a particular b_i can be changed without causing a change in the current optimal basis. In effect, we will do this by calculating a range of values over which a particular b_i can vary without any of the current basic variables becoming infeasible (i.e., less than zero). This range of values will be referred to as the *range of feasibility*.

To demonstrate the effect of increasing a resource by several units, consider increasing the available cutting and dyeing time for the Par, Inc. problem by 10 hours. Will the new basic solution be feasible? If so, we can expect an increase in the objective function of $10(^{70}/_{16}) = \$43.75$. As before, we can calculate the new values of the basic variables by adding to the old values the change in b_1 times the coefficients in the s_1 column; that is,

$$
\begin{bmatrix} 252 \\ 120 \\ 540 \\ 18 \end{bmatrix} + 10 \begin{bmatrix} ^{30}/_{16} \\ -^{15}/_{16} \\ -^{20}/_{16} \\ -^{11}/_{32} \end{bmatrix} = \begin{bmatrix} 270^{12}/_{16} \\ 110^{10}/_{16} \\ 527^{8}/_{16} \\ 14^{9}/_{16} \end{bmatrix}
$$

Since the new solution is still feasible (that is, all the basic variables are ≥ 0), the prediction made by the shadow price of a \$43.75 change in the objective function resulting from a 10-unit increase in b_1 is correct.

How do we know when a change in b_1 is so large that the current basis will become infeasible? We shall first answer this question specifically for the Par, Inc. problem. But you should realize that the following procedure applies only for the less-than-or-equal-to constraints of a linear program. The procedures for the cases of greater-than-or-equal-to and equality constraints will be discussed later in this section.

We begin by showing how to calculate upper and lower bounds for the maximum amount that b_1 can be changed before the current basis becomes infeasible. Given a change in b_1 of Δb_1, the new basic solution is given by

$$\begin{bmatrix} x_2 \\ s_2 \\ x_1 \\ s_4 \end{bmatrix} = \begin{bmatrix} 252 \\ 120 \\ 540 \\ 18 \end{bmatrix} + \Delta b_1 \begin{bmatrix} 30/16 \\ -15/16 \\ -20/16 \\ -11/32 \end{bmatrix} = \begin{bmatrix} 252 + 30/16\Delta b_1 \\ 120 - 15/16\Delta b_1 \\ 540 - 20/16\Delta b_1 \\ 18 - 11/32\Delta b_1 \end{bmatrix} \qquad (4.11)$$

As long as the value of each variable in the new basic solution remains nonnegative, the new basic solution will remain feasible and therefore optimal. We can keep the variables nonnegative by limiting the change in b_1 (that is, Δb_1) so that we satisfy each of the following conditions:

$$252 + 30/16\Delta b_1 \geq 0 \qquad (4.12)$$
$$120 - 15/16\Delta b_1 \geq 0 \qquad (4.13)$$
$$540 - 20/16\Delta b_1 \geq 0 \qquad (4.14)$$
$$18 - 11/32\Delta b_1 \geq 0. \qquad (4.15)$$

Note that the left-hand sides of the above inequalities represent the values of the basic variables after b_1 has been changed by Δb_1.

Working algebraically with the four inequalities (4.12)–(4.15) we get

$$\Delta b_1 \geq \quad (16/30)(-252) = -134.4$$
$$\Delta b_1 \leq (-16/15)(-120) = \quad 128$$
$$\Delta b_1 \leq (-16/20)(-540) = \quad 432$$
$$\Delta b_1 \leq (-32/11)(-18) \quad = \quad 52 4/11.$$

Since we must satisfy all four inequalities, the most restrictive limits on Δb_1 must be used. Therefore we have

$$-134.4 \leq \Delta b_1 \leq 52 4/11.$$

Using $\Delta b_1 = b'_1 - b_1$, where b'_1 is the new number of hours available in the cutting and dyeing department and b_1 is the original number of hours available ($b_1 = 630$), we have the following:

$$-134.4 \leq (b'_1 - 630) \leq 52 4/11$$

or

$$495.6 \leq b'_1 \leq 682 4/11.$$

The above range of values for b_1' indicates that as long as the time available in the cutting and dyeing department is between 495.6 and $682\frac{4}{11}$ hours, the current basis will remain feasible and optimal. Thus this is the range of feasibility for the right-hand-side value of the cutting and dyeing constraint.

Since $c_3 - z_3 = -\frac{70}{16}$, we know that we can improve the profit by $\frac{70}{16}$ for an additional hour of cutting and dyeing time. Suppose we increase b_1 by $52\frac{4}{11}$ hours to the upper limit of its range of feasibility, $682\frac{4}{11}$. The new profit with this change will be $7668 + (\frac{70}{16})(52\frac{4}{11}) = \$7897\frac{1}{11}$, and the new optimal solution using equation (4.11) is

$$x_2 = 252 + \tfrac{30}{16}(52\tfrac{4}{11}) = 350\tfrac{2}{11}$$
$$s_2 = 120 - \tfrac{15}{16}(52\tfrac{4}{11}) = 70\tfrac{10}{11}$$
$$x_1 = 540 - \tfrac{20}{16}(52\tfrac{4}{11}) = 474\tfrac{6}{11}$$
$$s_4 = 18 - \tfrac{11}{32}(52\tfrac{4}{11}) = 0$$

with the nonbasic variables s_1 and s_3 still equal to zero.

What has happened to our solution in the above process? You can see that the increased cutting and dyeing time has caused us to revise the production plan so that Par will produce a greater number of deluxe bags and a slightly smaller number of standard bags. Overall, the profit will be increased by $(\frac{70}{16})(52\frac{4}{11}) = \$229\frac{1}{11}$.

Problem 8 at the end of the chapter will ask you to show what happens in the Simplex method as we increase the cutting and dyeing time resource to its upper limit of $682\frac{4}{11}$ hours.

Our procedure for determining the range of feasibility has involved only the cutting and dyeing constraint. The procedure for calculating the range of feasibility for the right-hand-side value of any less-than-or-equal-to constraint is the same. The first step [paralleling equation (4.11)] for a general constraint i is to calculate the range of values for Δb_i that satisfy the conditions shown below:

$$\begin{bmatrix} \bar{b}_1 \\ \bar{b}_2 \\ . \\ . \\ . \\ \bar{b}_m \end{bmatrix} + \Delta b_i \begin{bmatrix} \bar{a}_{1j} \\ \bar{a}_{2j} \\ . \\ . \\ . \\ \bar{a}_{mj} \end{bmatrix} \geq \begin{bmatrix} 0 \\ 0 \\ . \\ . \\ . \\ 0 \end{bmatrix} \qquad (4.16)$$

current solution (last column of the final Simplex tableau)

column of the final Simplex tableau corresponding to the *slack* variable associated with constraint i

This determines a lower and an upper limit on Δb_i. The range of feasibility can then be established.

Similar arguments to the ones presented in this section can be used to develop a procedure for determining the range of feasibility for the right-hand-side value of a greater-than-or-equal-to constraint. Essentially the procedure is the same with the column corresponding to the surplus variable associated with the constraint playing the central role. For a general greater-than-or-equal-to constraint i we first calculate the range of values for Δb_i that satisfy the conditions shown in equation (4.17).

$$
\begin{bmatrix} \bar{b}_1 \\ \bar{b}_2 \\ \cdot \\ \cdot \\ \cdot \\ \bar{b}_m \end{bmatrix} - \Delta b_i \begin{bmatrix} \bar{a}_{1j} \\ \bar{a}_{2j} \\ \cdot \\ \cdot \\ \cdot \\ \bar{a}_{mj} \end{bmatrix} \geq \begin{bmatrix} 0 \\ 0 \\ \cdot \\ \cdot \\ \cdot \\ 0 \end{bmatrix} \tag{4.17}
$$

current solution   column of the final Simplex tableau corresponding to the *surplus* variable associated with constraint i

Once again, these conditions establish a lower and an upper limit on Δb_i. Given these limits, the range of feasibility is easily determined.

To calculate the range of feasibility for the right-hand-side value of an equality constraint, we use the column of the Simplex tableau corresponding to the artificial variable associated with that constraint. The limits of Δb_i are given by the Δb_i values satisfying equation (4.18):

$$
\begin{bmatrix} \bar{b}_1 \\ \bar{b}_2 \\ \cdot \\ \cdot \\ \cdot \\ \bar{b}_m \end{bmatrix} + \Delta b_i \begin{bmatrix} \bar{a}_{1j} \\ \bar{a}_{2j} \\ \cdot \\ \cdot \\ \cdot \\ \bar{a}_{mj} \end{bmatrix} \geq \begin{bmatrix} 0 \\ 0 \\ \cdot \\ \cdot \\ \cdot \\ 0 \end{bmatrix} \tag{4.18}
$$

current solution   column of the final Simplex tableau corresponding to the *artificial* variable associated with constraint i

As long as the change in a b_i is such that the value of b_i' stays within its range of feasibility, the same basis will remain feasible and optimal. Changes that force b_i' outside its range of feasibility will force us to perform additional Simplex iterations to find the new optimal basic feasible solution. More advanced linear programming texts show how this can be done without completely resolving the problem. In any case, the calculation of the range of feasibility for each of the b_i is valuable management information and should be included as part of the management report on any linear programming project. As we shall see in Section 4.6, the range of feasibility can be made available as part of the computer solution to the problem.

Note that the procedure for determining the range of feasibility for the right-hand-side values has involved changing only *one* value at a time (that is, only one Δb_i). Multiple changes are more difficult to analyze and in practice usually require the complete generation of a new final Simplex tableau.

4.4   Sensitivity Analysis—The Coefficients of the Constraints

A change in one of the coefficients of the constraints can have a significant effect on the optimal solution to a linear programming problem. A complete discussion of the ramifications of making changes in the coefficients is beyond the scope of this text. However, we can make a few remarks based on an analysis of the graphical solution of the example problem shown below:

$$\max \quad 2x_1 + 3x_2$$
$$\text{s.t.}$$
$$1x_1 + 2x_2 \le 8$$
$$3x_1 + 2x_2 \le 12$$
$$x_1, x_2 \ge 0.$$

The graphical solution to this problem is shown in Figure 4.1.

Suppose we make a change in the first constraint such that the coefficient associated with x_2 is 3. The problem now becomes

$$\max \quad 2x_1 + 3x_2$$
$$\text{s.t.}$$
$$1x_1 + 3x_2 \le 8$$
$$3x_1 + 2x_2 \le 12$$
$$x_1, x_2 \ge 0.$$

The graphical solution to this problem is shown in Figure 4.2.

The optimal solution of $x_1 = 2$, $x_2 = 3$, and $z = 13$ for the original example has been revised to $x_1 = {}^{20}\!/_7$, $x_2 = {}^{12}\!/_7$, and $z = {}^{76}\!/_7$ as a result of this change. Thus the effect was to reduce the amount of x_2 in the optimal solution and to increase the amount of x_1. Graphically, we see that the slope and the x_2 intercept of the first constraint have changed. As a consequence, this has altered the feasible region and has caused a decrease in the value of the optimal solution.

The way to analyze qualitatively the effects of a change in a_{ij} for basic variable x_j is to think about the effect this change has on a constraint equation. Let us assume for the moment that all our constraints are of the less-than-or-equal-to type. Then if a_{ij} is increased and constraint i is binding, the value of the objective function will decrease, and the amount of x_j in the optimal solution will also decrease (assuming $x_j > 0$ — that is, no degenera-

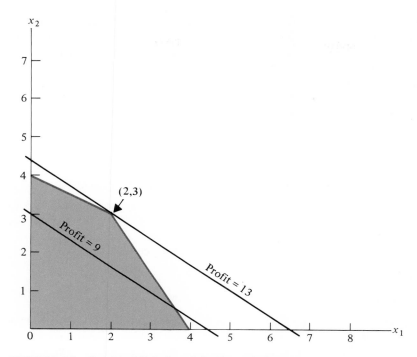

FIGURE 4.1   Graphical Solution of the Example Problem

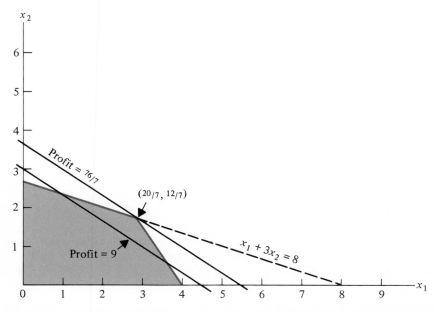

FIGURE 4.2   Graphical Solution of the Example Problem after Changing a_{12} from 2 to 3

cy). If a_{ij} is decreased and constraint i is binding, then the value of the optimal solution will increase, and the amount of x_j will increase in the optimal solution. The converse of the above is true if our constraints are of the greater-than-or-equal-to type. For the case of equality constraints, additional analysis is necessary to determine the effect on the optimal solution. If one of the a_{ij} should change for a nonbinding constraint, this will have no effect on the optimal solution unless the change is large enough to make a new basis optimal. In addition, if one of the a_{ij} change for a nonbasic variable, the change will have no effect on the optimal solution unless the change is large enough to cause the $c_j - z_j$ for that variable to become greater than or equal to zero.

A range can be computed for any a_{ij} such that values within the range do not require a new basis for the optimal solution. However, the calculations are much more complicated than they were for the coefficients of the objective function and for the right-hand sides. Thus a detailed analysis of changes in the constraint coefficients is beyond the scope of this text.

4.5 Duality

In this section we shall see that every linear programming problem has an associated linear programming problem called the *dual*. Referring to the original formulation of the linear programming problem as the *primal*, we will see how the primal can be converted into its corresponding dual. Then we will solve the dual linear programming problem and interpret the results. A fundamental property of the primal-dual relationship is that the solution to either the primal or the dual problem also provides the solution to the other. In cases where the primal and the dual problems differ in terms of computational difficulty, we can choose the easier form to solve.

Let us return to the Par, Inc. problem. The original formulation—the primal—is as follows:

$$\max \quad 10x_1 + 9x_2$$
$$\text{s.t.}$$
$$\tfrac{7}{10}x_1 + 1x_2 \leq 630$$
$$\tfrac{1}{2}x_1 + \tfrac{5}{6}x_2 \leq 600$$
$$1x_1 + \tfrac{2}{3}x_2 \leq 708$$
$$\tfrac{1}{10}x_1 + \tfrac{1}{4}x_2 \leq 135$$
$$x_1, x_2 \geq 0.$$

A maximization problem with all less-than-or-equal-to constraints and nonnegativity requirements for the decision variables is said to be in *canonical form*.[2] For a maximization problem in canonical form, such as

[2]See, for example, Bazarra, M. S., and J. J. Jarvis, *Linear Programming and Network Flows,* New York, John Wiley & Sons, 1977.

Par, Inc., the conversion to the associated dual linear program is relatively easy. Let us state the dual form for the Par, Inc. problem and then identify the steps taken to make the primal-dual conversion. The Par, Inc. dual problem is as follows:

$$\min \quad 630u_1 + 600u_2 + 708u_3 + 135u_4$$
$$\text{s.t.}$$
$$\tfrac{7}{10}u_1 + \tfrac{1}{2}u_2 + 1u_3 + \tfrac{1}{10}u_4 \geq 10$$
$$1u_1 + \tfrac{5}{6}u_2 + \tfrac{2}{3}u_3 + \tfrac{1}{4}u_4 \geq 9$$
$$u_1, u_2, u_3, u_4 \geq 0.$$

The variables u_1, u_2, u_3, and u_4 are referred to as *dual variables*.

With the above example in mind, we make the following general statements about the dual of a maximization problem in canonical form:

1. The dual is a minimization problem.
2. The dual has all greater-than-or-equal-to constraints.
3. When the primal has n decision variables ($n = 2$ in the Par, Inc. problem), the dual will have n constraints. The first constraint of the dual is associated with variable x_1 in the primal, the second constraint in the dual is associated with variable x_2 in the primal, and so on.
4. When the primal has m constraints ($m = 4$ in the Par, Inc. problem), the dual will have m decision variables. Dual variable u_1 is associated with the first primal constraint, dual variable u_2 is associated with the second primal constraint, and so on.
5. The right-hand-side values of the primal become the objective function coefficients in the dual.
6. The objective function coefficients of the primal become the right-hand-side values in the dual.
7. The constraint coefficients of the ith primal variable become the coefficients in the ith constraint of the dual.
8. Both the primal and the dual have nonnegativity restrictions for the variables.

The above eight statements are the general requirements that must be satisfied when converting a maximization problem in canonical form to its associated dual. While these requirements may seem cumbersome at first, practice with a few simple problems will show that this primal-dual conversion process is relatively easy to implement.

Since we have formulated the Par, Inc. dual linear programming problem, let us now proceed to solve it. With four variables in the dual, we will need to use the Simplex method. By multiplying the objective function by -1 to convert to a maximization problem, subtracting surplus variables s_1 and s_2 to obtain Standard form, and then adding artificial variables a_1 and a_2 to obtain Tableau form, we can develop the following initial Simplex tableau:

Basis	c_j	u_1 -630	u_2 -600	u_3 -708	u_4 -135	s_1 0	s_2 0	a_1 $-M$	a_2 $-M$	
a_1	$-M$	$7/10$	$1/2$	1	$1/10$	-1	0	1	0	10
a_2	$-M$	①	$5/6$	$2/3$	$1/4$	0	-1	0	1	9
	z_j	$-\dfrac{17M}{10}$	$-\dfrac{4M}{3}$	$-\dfrac{5M}{3}$	$-\dfrac{42M}{120}$	M	M	$-M$	$-M$	$-19M$
	$c_j - z_j$	$-630+\dfrac{17M}{10}$	$-600+\dfrac{4M}{3}$	$-708+\dfrac{5M}{3}$	$-135+\dfrac{42M}{120}$	$-M$	$-M$	0	0	

By introducing variable u_1 at the first iteration, we drive out a_2. Performing the usual Simplex operations, the second tableau becomes

Basis	c_j	u_1 -630	u_2 -600	u_3 -708	u_4 -135	s_1 0	s_2 0	a_1 $-M$	a_2 $-M$	
a_1	$-M$	0	$-1/12$	$8/15$	$-9/120$	-1	⑦⁄₁₀	1	$-7/10$	$37/20$
u_1	-630	1	$5/6$	$2/3$	$1/4$	0	-1	0	1	9
	z_j	-630	$-525+\dfrac{M}{12}$	$-420-\dfrac{8M}{15}$	$-157\tfrac{1}{2}+\dfrac{9M}{120}$	M	$630-\dfrac{7M}{10}$	$-M$	$\dfrac{7M}{10}-630$	$-\dfrac{37M}{10}-5670$
	$c_j - z_j$	0	$-75-\dfrac{M}{12}$	$-288+\dfrac{8M}{15}$	$22\tfrac{1}{2}-\dfrac{9M}{120}$	$-M$	$\dfrac{7M}{10}-630$	0	$630-\dfrac{17M}{10}$	

At the second iteration we introduce s_2, and a_1 is driven out of the solution. After performing the Simplex operations, the third tableau becomes

Basis	c_j	u_1 -630	u_2 -600	u_3 -708	u_4 -135	s_1 0	s_2 0	a_1 $-M$	a_2 $-M$	
s_2	0	0	$-10/84$	⑯⁄₂₁	$-9/84$	$-10/7$	1	$10/7$	-1	$37/7$
u_1	-630	1	$60/84$	$30/21$	$12/84$	$-10/7$	0	$10/7$	0	$100/7$
	z_j	-630	-450	-900	-90	900	⓪	-900	0	-9000
	$c_j - z_j$	0	-150	192	-45	-900	0	$900-M$	$-M$	

Note that all of the artificial variables have now been driven out and that we have a basic feasible solution to the dual (i.e., $s_2 = {}^{37}\!/_7$ and $u_1 = {}^{100}\!/_7$). At the third iteration, we introduce u_3, and s_2 is driven out of solution. After performing the Simplex operations, the fourth tableau becomes:

Basis	c_j	u_1 -630	u_2 -600	u_3 -708	u_4 -135	s_1 0	s_2 0	a_1 $-M$	a_2 $-M$	
u_3	-708	0	$-5/32$	1	$-9/64$	$-15/8$	$21/16$	$15/8$	$-21/16$	$111/16$
u_1	-630	1	$15/16$	0	$11/32$	$5/4$	$-15/8$	$-5/4$	$15/8$	$70/16$
	z_j	-630	-480	-708	-117	540	252	-540	-252	-7668
	$c_j - z_j$	0	-120	0	-18	-540	-252	$540-M$	$252-M$	

Since all the $c_j - z_j$ values in the net evaluation row are ≤ 0, this iteration provides the optimal solution:

$$u_1 = {}^{70}\!/_{16}, \qquad u_2 = 0, \qquad u_3 = {}^{111}\!/_{16}, \qquad u_4 = 0,$$
$$s_1 = 0, \qquad s_2 = 0, \qquad a_1 = 0, \quad \text{and} \quad a_2 = 0.$$

Since we have been maximizing the negative of the dual objective function, the value of the objective function for the dual solution must be $-(-7668)$, or 7668.

Shown below is the final Simplex tableau for the primal form of the Par, Inc. problem:

Basis	c_j	x_1 10	x_2 9	s_1 0	s_2 0	s_3 0	s_4 0	
x_2	9	0	1	30/16	0	$-21/16$	0	252
s_2	0	0	0	$-15/16$	1	5/32	0	120
x_1	10	1	0	$-20/16$	0	30/16	0	540
s_4	0	0	0	$-11/32$	0	9/64	1	18
z_j		10	9	70/16	0	111/16	0	7668
$c_j - z_j$		0	0	$-70/16$	0	$-111/16$	0	

The optimal solution for the primal problem is $x_1 = 540$, $x_2 = 252$, $s_1 = 0$, $s_2 = 120$, $s_3 = 0$, and $s_4 = 18$.

The optimal value of the objective function is 7668.

What observation can we make about the relationship between the value of the objective function in the primal and dual of the Par, Inc. problem? The optimal value of the objective function is the same (7668) for both. This is true for all primal and dual linear programming problems and is stated as property 1 below.

Property 1. If the dual problem has an optimal solution, the primal problem has an optimal solution and vice versa. Furthermore, the values of the optimal solutions to the dual and primal problems are equal.

This property tells us that if we had solved only the dual problem, we would have known that Par, Inc. could make a maximum of $7668 from the production of standard and deluxe golf bags.

Economic Interpretation of the Dual Variables

Before making further observations about the relationship between the primal and the dual solutions, let us consider the meaning or interpretation of the dual variables u_1, u_2, u_3, and u_4. Remember that in setting up the dual problem, each dual variable is associated with one of the constraints in the primal. Specifically, u_1 is associated with the cutting and dyeing constraint, u_2 with the sewing constraint, u_3 with the finishing constraint, and u_4 with the inspection and packaging constraint. The Simplex method provided the following solution values for the dual variables:

$$u_1 = {}^{70}/_{16}, \qquad u_2 = 0, \qquad u_3 = {}^{111}/_{16}, \qquad u_4 = 0.$$

In order to better understand and interpret these dual variables, let us return to property 1 of the primal-dual relationship, which stated that the objective function values for the primal and dual problems must be equal. At the optimal solution, the primal objective function shows

$$10x_1 + 9x_2 = 7668, \tag{4.19}$$

while the dual objective function shows

$$630u_1 + 600u_2 + 708u_3 + 135u_4 = 7668. \tag{4.20}$$

Using equation (4.19), let us restrict our interest to the physical interpretation of each term. Since the objective function coefficients, 10 and 9, are dollar values per unit of the product and since x_1 and x_2 are units of products 1 and 2 respectively, we have

$$\left(\frac{\$ \text{ value}}{\text{unit of product 1}}\right)\left(\begin{array}{c}\text{units of}\\\text{product 1}\end{array}\right) + \left(\frac{\$ \text{ value}}{\text{unit of product 2}}\right)\left(\begin{array}{c}\text{units of}\\\text{product 2}\end{array}\right)$$

= total dollars.

Performing a similar physical interpretation of the dual objective function, equation (4.20), we see that since the coefficients 630, 600, 708, and 135 are units of each resource available, we must have

(units of resource 1)u_1 + (units of resource 2)u_2
+ (units of resource 3)u_3 + (units of resource 4)u_4 = total dollars.

In order to be consistent in our units and noting that the total dollar values of the objective functions are equal, we see the dual variables must carry the physical interpretation of being the price (or \$ value) per unit of resource. Thus for the Par, Inc. problem,

u_1 = \$ value per hour of cutting and dyeing time,

u_2 = \$ value per hour of sewing time,

u_3 = \$ value per hour of finishing time, and

u_4 = \$ value per hour of inspection and packaging time.

Have we ever attempted to identify the value of the resources previously? Recall that in Section 4.3, when we considered sensitivity analysis of the right-hand sides, we identified the value of an additional unit of each resource. These values were called shadow prices and were helpful to the decision maker in determining whether or not additional units of the resources should be made available. Our analysis in Section 4.3 led to the following shadow prices for the resources in the Par, Inc. problem:

Resource	Value per Additional Hour (Shadow Price)
Cutting and dyeing	$4.375
Sewing	0
Finishing	$6.9375
Inspection and packaging	0

Let us now return to the optimal solution for the Par, Inc. dual problem. The values of the dual variables at the optimal solution were $u_1 = {}^{70}/_{16} = 4.375$, $u_2 = 0$, $u_3 = {}^{111}/_{16} = 6.9375$, and $u_4 = 0$. This observation leads to the important economic interpretation that *the value of the dual variable and the value of the shadow price are one and the same.* Thus the optimal values of the dual variables identify the per unit value of each additional resource or input unit at the optimal solution.

In light of the above discussion, the following interpretation of the primal and dual problems can be made:

The primal problem: Given a value per unit of each product or output unit, determine how much of each output should be produced in order to maximize the value of the total output. Constraining conditions involve requiring the amount of each resource used to be less than or equal to the maximum available.

The dual problem: Given the availability of each resource or input, determine the value assigned to each unit of input such that the value of the total input is minimized. Constraining conditions involve requiring the total resource value per unit of output to be greater than or equal to the value of each unit of output.

Using the Dual to Identify the Primal Solution

When we started this section we mentioned that an important feature of the primal-dual relationship was that the solution of either would also provide the solution to the other. We have seen that when an optimal solution is reached, the primal and dual carry the same value for the objective function. However, the question remaining is the following: If we solve only the dual, how do we identify the optimal values for the primal variables?

Recall that in Section 4.3 we showed that when a primal problem is solved by the Simplex method the optimal values of the primal variables appear in the right-hand column of the final tableau, while the shadow prices (values of the dual variables) are found in the $c_j - z_j$ row. Since the final Simplex tableau of the dual problem provides the optimal values of the dual variables in the right-hand column, you might expect the values of the primal variables to be found in the $c_j - z_j$ row. This is in fact the case and is formally stated as property 2.

Property 2. The optimal values of the primal decision variables are given by the negative of the $c_j - z_j$ entries for the surplus variables in the Simplex tableau corresponding to the optimal dual solution. Furthermore, the optimal values of the primal slack variables are given by the negative of the $c_j - z_j$ entries for the u_j variables in the Simplex tableau corresponding to the optimal dual solution.

The above property enables us to use the final Simplex tableau for the Par, Inc. dual problem to determine the optimal primal solution of $x_1 = 540$ standard bags and $x_2 = 252$ deluxe bags. These values of x_1 and x_2, as well as the values for all primal slack variables, are given in the $c_j - z_j$ row of the final Simplex tableau of the dual problem shown below.

Basis	c_j	u_1 -630	u_2 -600	u_3 -708	u_4 -135	s_1 0	s_2 0	a_1 $-M$	a_2 $-M$	
u_3	-708	0	$-5/32$	1	$-9/4$	$-15/8$	$21/16$	$15/8$	$-21/16$	$111/16$
u_1	-630	1	$15/16$	0	$11/32$	$5/4$	$-15/8$	$-5/4$	$15/8$	$70/16$
	z_j	-630	-480	-708	-117	540	252	-540	-252	-7668
	$c_j - z_j$	0	-120	0	-18	-540	-252	$540-M$	$252-M$	

Primal
Solution $s_1=0$ $s_2=120$ $s_3=0$ $s_4=18$ $x_1=540$ $x_2=252$ profit=$7668

Finding the Dual of Any Primal Problem

The Par, Inc. primal problem was a nice problem to use in the initial demonstration of duality, since it was formulated as a maximization problem in canonical form. For this form of primal problem we have seen that conversion to the dual problem is rather easily accomplished. However, what if the primal is a minimization problem and/or what if at least some of the constraints are not of the $\leq$ form? While we could state a special set of rules for converting each variety of primal problem into its associated dual, we tend to believe it is easier to first write any primal problem as a maximization problem in canonical form. Once this has been accomplished we can find the dual problem by following the procedure used to convert the Par, Inc. primal problem into its dual.

We will show the steps necessary for converting any primal linear program into a maximization problem in canonical form by considering the following primal linear programming problem:

$$\begin{align}
\min \quad & 2x_1 - 3x_2 \\
\text{s.t.} \quad & \\
& 1x_1 + 2x_2 \leq 12 \\
& 4x_1 - 2x_2 \geq 3 \\
& 6x_1 - 1x_2 = 10 \\
& x_1, x_2 \geq 0.
\end{align}$$

The appropriate steps are stated first in general and then applied to the example problem.

1. If the objective function requires minimization, convert to maximization by multiplying by -1.

Thus the objective function for our example becomes

$$\max \quad -2x_1 + 3x_2.$$

2. For a $\geq$ constraint, convert to a $\leq$ form by multiplying by -1.

Thus constraint 2 for our example becomes

$$-4x_1 + 2x_2 \leq -3.$$

3. For an equality constraint, form two inequality constraints, one with a $\leq$ form and one with a $\geq$ form. Then use rule 2 above to convert the $\geq$ constraint to a $\leq$ form.

Thus constraint 3 for our example is rewritten as two inequality constraints:

$$6x_1 - 1x_2 \leq 10$$
$$6x_1 - 1x_2 \geq 10.$$

Using rule 2 these can be written as

$$6x_1 - 1x_2 \leq 10$$
$$-6x_1 + 1x_2 \leq -10.$$

Thus the initial primal problem has been restated in the following equivalent form:

$$\max \quad -2x_1 + 3x_2$$
$$\text{s.t.}$$
$$1x_1 + 2x_2 \leq 12$$
$$-4x_1 + 2x_2 \leq -3$$
$$6x_1 - 1x_2 \leq 10$$
$$-6x_1 + 1x_2 \leq -10$$
$$x_1, x_2 \geq 0.$$

With the primal in canonical form for a maximization problem, we can easily convert to the dual linear programming problem by the primal-dual procedure presented earlier in this section. The dual becomes[3]

$$\min \quad 12u_1 - 3u_2 + 10u'_3 - 10u''_3$$
$$\text{s.t.}$$
$$1u_1 - 4u_2 + 6u'_3 - 6u''_3 \geq -2$$
$$2u_1 + 2u_2 - 1u'_3 + 1u''_3 \geq 3$$
$$u_1, u_2, u'_3, u''_3 \geq 0.$$

---

[3]Note that the right-hand side of the first constraint is negative. Thus one must multiply through by -1 to obtain a positive value for the right-hand side prior to attempting to solve the problem with the Simplex method.

Since the equality primal constraint required two $\leq$ constraints, we denoted the dual variables associated with these constraints as u'_3 and u''_3. This reminds us that u'_3 and u''_3 both refer to the third constraint in the initial primal problem. Since there are two dual variables associated with an equality constraint, the interpretation of the dual variable as the shadow price of the right-hand-side resource must be modified slightly. The shadow price is given by the difference between the two dual variables. Thus the shadow price for the equality constraint $6x_1 - x_2 = 10$ is given by the value of $u'_3 - u''_3$ in the optimal solution to the dual. Hence the shadow price for an equality constraint could actually be negative.

Computational Considerations

We have shown that solving either the primal or the dual problem provides the solution to the other as well. Thus whenever computation time and effort are important considerations in solving linear programs, practitioners have the option of solving either the primal or the dual, depending upon which is easier to solve.

Recall that if the primal problem has m constraints and n variables, the dual problem will have n constraints and m variables. Also recall that the basic solution identified at each iteration of the Simplex method contains as many basic variables as constraints in the problem. For computer procedures designed for large-scale linear programming problems, the number of computations performed at each iteration and the total number of iterations are proportional to the number of basic variables in the problem. Thus, in general, we expect linear programs with a larger number of constraints, and therefore a larger number of basic variables, to require greater computational time and effort. As a result, when there is a substantial difference in the number of constraints in the primal and the dual problems, practitioners often recommend solving the form of the problem (primal or dual) with fewer constraints.

4.6   Computer Solution of Linear Programming Problems

Computer programs especially designed to solve linear programming problems are now widely available. Most large companies as well as most universities have access to these computer programs. The developmental effort for these so-called "software packages" has come primarily from computer manufacturers and/or software service companies such as IBM, Control Data, Ketron, and others. These software packages are available for sale or lease. Companies that sell computer time and/or services often make linear programming packages available to subscribers as an added feature. Usually after a short period of familiarization with the specific features of the package, users can solve linear programming problems with few difficulties. Problems having thousands of variables and thousands of constraints can now be solved routinely through the use of computer packages. Most large linear programs can be solved with just a few minutes of computer time; small linear programs may require only a few seconds.

In this section we will illustrate the use of a computer package to solve linear programming problems by focusing our attention on IBM's MPSX/ 370 (Mathematical Programming System Extended). MPSX/370 uses the Simplex method—with a few special features—to solve linear programming problems. Specifically, we will show how this package can be used to solve the Par, Inc. problem.

User-Specified Input Information

The user of virtually any linear programming computer package will be required to prepare two types of input information:

1. Data describing the specific linear programming problem to be solved;
2. A control program which provides instructions to the computer describing what solution procedures and options are to be employed in solving the current problem.

Although the above input information may be entered through a computer terminal, we will describe the process as it would be done with punched cards.

Every linear programming application involves a unique mathematical formulation of the problem. Before a computer package can be employed to solve the problem, data describing the specific characteristics of the problem must be input to the computer. That is, information about the number of constraints, the number of variables, the coefficients in the objective function and constraints, and the right-hand-side values of the constraints must be prepared in an acceptable computer format. The data deck used to provide this information for the Par, Inc. problem is shown in Figure 4.3. This data deck includes the information necessary to describe the specific characteristics of the Par, Inc. problem.

Each line of Figure 4.3 shows the information contained on a single data card. The first line or card provides the name of the data deck, "PAR-INC." The second line or card, "ROWS," signals the computer that the next section of input data will contain information about the rows in the linear programming problem. The next five cards, one for the objective function and one for each constraint, identify the type of the row or constraint and the name assigned to it. Specifically, "N" is used to identify the objective function row, which for identification purposes is named "PROFIT." The letter "L" indicates that the corresponding constraint is a less-than-or-equal-to ($\leq$) constraint. In other linear programming problems "G" or "E" could appear for some constraints indicating greater-than-or-equal to ($\geq$) or equal-to ($=$) constraints, respectively. The row names "CUT," "SEW," and

Card no.

1	NAME		PAR-INC			
2	ROWS					
3	N	PROFIT				
4	L	CUT				
5	L	SEW				
6	L	FINISH				
7	L	INSPECT				
8	COLUMNS					
9		STD-BAG	PROFIT	10.00000	CUT	.70000
10		STD-BAG	SEW	.50000	FINISH	1.00000
11		STD-BAG	INSPECT	.10000		
12		DEL-BAG	PROFIT	9.00000	CUT	1.00000
13		DEL-BAG	SEW	.83333	FINISH	.66667
14		DEL-BAG	INSPECT	.25000		
15	RHS					
16		HRS-AVL	CUT	630.00000	SEW	600.00000
17		HRS-AVL	FINISH	708.00000	INSPECT	135.00000
18	ENDATA					

FIGURE 4.3   Data Deck for Computer Solution of the Par, Inc. Problem Using MPSX/370

so on are simply the abbreviated names for the constraint rows corresponding to the cutting and dyeing department, sewing department and so on.

The eighth card, "COLUMNS," indicates that the following section of input data will contain information about the variables or columns of the linear programming problem. "STD-BAG" is used as the abbreviated name for variable x_1, the number of standard bags produced. The corresponding data values for x_1 are shown as 10 for the "PROFIT" row or objective function, .70 for the "CUT" constraint row, .50 for the "SEW" constraint row, and so on. Column data for variable x_2, the number of deluxe bags produced, are shown in a similar format on the cards labeled "DEL-BAG." The computer package provides any necessary slack and/or surplus variables automatically. Thus the "COLUMNS" section of the data deck shows only the information needed for variables x_1 and x_2.

Note that the coefficient for the "DEL-BAG" in the "SEW" constraint row appears as .83333 rather than the $\frac{5}{6}$ we used in the original formulation of the problem; the computer input data must be in decimal form rather than fractional form. As a result, .83333 is used as the closest five-place decimal value to the fraction $\frac{5}{6}$. A similar rounding occurs for the "DEL-BAG" in constraint row "FINISH," where the decimal .66667 is used as the closest five-place decimal value to the fraction $\frac{2}{3}$. When this rounding of the input data is required we may expect the computer solution to be slightly different than the hand-calculated solution based on the exact fraction values. However, as you will see, the two solutions are extremely close, and the slight rounding of the input data causes no serious problem.

The last section of the input data deck contains the right-hand-side values for the constraints and is identified by the data card "RHS." The

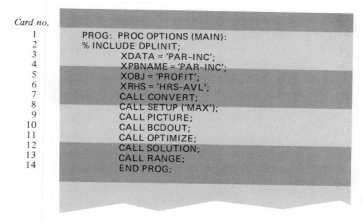

Card no.

```
 1     PROG:  PROC OPTIONS (MAIN):
 2        % INCLUDE DPLINIT;
 3              XDATA = 'PAR-INC';
 4              XPBNAME = 'PAR-INC';
 5              XOBJ = 'PROFIT';
 6              XRHS = 'HRS-AVL';
 7              CALL CONVERT;
 8              CALL SETUP ('MAX');
 9              CALL PICTURE;
10              CALL BCDOUT;
11              CALL OPTIMIZE;
12              CALL SOLUTION;
13              CALL RANGE;
14              END PROG;
```

FIGURE 4.4   MPSX/370 Control Program for Solving the Par, Inc. Problem

right-hand-side values appear in the column named "HRS-AVL," with the row names used again to indicate the right-hand-side value for the specific constraints. The final card, "ENDATA," signals the end of the data deck.

The input data deck for the Par, Inc. problem is rather small (18 cards). In extremely large linear programs the data deck can become so large that it is impractical to punch all the data cards. In these cases a special computer program, called a *matrix generator,* is prepared by the user for the sole purpose of creating the data deck. While the data deck format is as shown in Figure 4.3, the "data deck" is usually retained in computer disk storage rather than on punched cards.

In addition to the data deck, the user must supply instructions to the computer that inform the computer to solve the Par, Inc. problem. These instructions are provided through the control program shown in Figure 4.4. Cards 1 through 10 of the control program provide information for reading the data deck, setting up the problem in the computer, and printing some preliminary information concerning the problem. Card 11 contains the command that causes the computer to employ the Simplex method to solve the problem. Card 12 instructs the computer to print out the solution to the problem. Card 13 instructs the computer to provide the sensitivity-analysis ranges we discussed earlier in this chapter. Finally, Card 14 simply ends the program.

Computer Output and Interpretation

Figure 4.5 shows a portion of the computer printout generated from the computer solution of the Par, Inc. problem. Let us try to relate the computer results to what we have previously studied about linear programming.

The section of the output entitled "SECTION 1 — ROWS" provides information concerning the value of the optimal solution and the number of

```
SECTION 1 — ROWS

NUMBER... ROW ... ACTIVITY ... SLACK ACTIVITY .. UPPER LIMIT .. DUAL ACTIVITY
      1  PROFIT    7667.99417
      2  CUT        630.00000          .             630.00000       4.37496—
      3  SEW        479.99929      120.00071          600.00000           .
      4  FINISH     708.00000          .             708.00000       6.93753—
      5  INSPECT    117.00012       17.99988          135.00000           .


SECTION 2 — COLUMNS

NUMBER . COLUMNS .. ACTIVITY ... .. INPUT COST ... REDUCED COST .
      6  STD-BAG     539.99842       10.00000            .
      7  DEL-BAG     252.00110        9.00000            .

ROWS AT LIMIT LEVEL

... ROW ..... ACTIVITY ...   SLACK ACTIVITY     LOWER ACTIVITY
                                                UPPER ACTIVITY
CUT          630.00000            .             495.60001
                                                682.36316

FINISH       708.00000            .             580.00139
                                                899.99998


COLUMNS AT INTERMEDIATE LEVEL

. COLUMN .  AT  ... ACTIVITY .... INPUT COST ... LOWER COST ..
                                                .. UPPER COST ..
STD-BAG    BS    539.99829        10.00000       6.30000
                                                 13.49993
DEL-BAG    BS    252.00110         9.00000       6.66670
                                                 14.28571
```

FIGURE 4.5   **Computer Solution to the Par, Inc. Problem**

labor hours used in each department. In the "ACTIVITY" column the value of the optimal solution ("PROFIT" row) is given as 7667.99417. Our previous solution of the Par, Inc. problem provided an objective function value of 7668. This slight difference between computer and hand-calculated results is due in part to the slight rounding of the input data we discussed previously. The other entries in the "ACTIVITY" column show the amounts of resources or labor hours used in each of the four departments in order to obtain the $7668 profit.

The "SLACK ACTIVITY" column shows the amount of slack time in each of the four departments. As we have seen previously, there is no slack in the departments providing the binding constraints. That is, the cutting and dyeing ("CUT") and finishing ("FINISH") departments show no slack time (a "." on the computer output indicates a zero value). However, the sewing department and the inspection and packaging department show slack, or unused, capacity. The "UPPER LIMIT" column simply contains the original capacities or right-hand-side values for the problem.

The "DUAL ACTIVITY" column shows values of 4.37496— and

6.93753−. The "−" following the numerical values is the MPSX/370 convention for indicating a negative number. Thus the "DUAL ACTIVITY" column actual values are −4.37496 and −6.93753. The shadow prices for the various resources are given by the negative of the numbers appearing in the "DUAL ACTIVITY" column. We see that an additional hour of cutting and dyeing time is worth $4.37 and an additional hour of finishing time is worth $6.94. The zero values for the sewing and inspection and the packaging constraints indicate that these departments still have unused or slack time available.

The section of the output entitled "SECTION 2 — COLUMNS" provides the values of the decision variables at the optimal solution. In the "ACTIVITY" column we see that the optimal solution calls for the production of 539.99842, or 540, standard bags and 252.00110, or 252, deluxe bags. Once again there are slight differences resulting in part from the rounding of the input data. The "INPUT COST" column provides the coefficients of the corresponding variables as they appear in the objective function. The "REDUCED COST" column provides the corresponding entries in the net evaluation row of the optimal Simplex tableau. Since x_1 ("STD-BAG") and x_2 ("DEL-BAG") are both basic variables, both entries in the "REDUCED COST" column are zero.

The "ROWS AT LIMIT LEVEL" section provides the range of feasibility for the right-hand-side values of the binding constraints. The "ACTIVITY" and "SLACK ACTIVITY" columns show that all the resources are utilized in the cutting and dyeing and the finishing departments. The "LOWER ACTIVITY/UPPER ACTIVITY" column shows the range of feasibility for these two constraints. For example, we see that the range of feasibility for the capacity of the cutting and dyeing department is 495.60001 to 682.36316. This agrees with the range of feasibility calculated by hand in Section 4.3.

The last section of the printout, entitled "COLUMNS AT INTERMEDIATE LEVEL," provides further sensitivity analysis information. In addition to showing the optimal values of x_1 and x_2 and the original objective function coefficients for these variables, this section contains a "LOWER COST/UPPER COST" column which provides the range of optimality for the objective function coefficients. In particular, note that the range $6.3 \leq c_1 \leq 13.49993$ for the standard bags agrees with the range of optimality computed in Section 4.2.

In closing this section, we note that one of the primary reasons for the widespread use of linear programming today is the availability of computer packages such as MPSX/370. Most packages are fairly easy to use. Persons who have a knowledge of linear programming as provided in this text can use these packages for straightforward applications of linear programming. One particular advantage of the computer solution procedure is the wealth of information provided in the solution report. Specifically, we saw how the sensitivity analysis information discussed in this chapter is provided routinely as part of the MPSX/370 solution.

Summary

In this chapter we showed how sensitivity analysis can provide the decision maker with valuable information as to how the optimal solution and value of that solution could be expected to change, given a change in one of the coefficients of the problem. For the objective function we calculated a range of optimality over which the coefficients of the basic variables could range with no resultant change in the optimal solution. Similarly, a range of insignificance was calculated for the objective function coefficients of the nonbasic variables. For the right-hand-side values we computed a range of feasibility over which the b_i could vary without causing the current basis to become infeasible. With respect to the A matrix, our remarks were qualitative, since calculating a range of feasibility for the a_{ij} is outside the scope of this text.

The calculations and the resulting conclusions we obtained from sensitivity analysis were based on the assumption that *only one* coefficient was being changed at a time and that all other coefficients remained fixed. It is possible through sensitivity analysis to study the effects of multiple changes in the problem coefficients, but the calculations are more complicated.

In studying duality, we saw how an original linear programming problem, called the primal, could be converted to its associated dual linear programming problem. Solving either the primal or the dual provided the solution to the other. In some cases, the dual possesses computational advantages, particularly when the primal has relatively few variables but many constraints. The value of the dual variable (shadow price) identified the economic contribution or value of additional resources in the primal problem.

We closed the chapter with an overview of how the computer is used to solve linear programs. Computer software packages are widely available, which explains some of the popularity of linear programming as a problem-solving technique.

Glossary

1. *Range of insignificance*—The range of values over which c_j associated with a nonbasic variable may vary without causing any change in the optimal solution or the value of the objective function.

2. *Range of optimality*—The range of values over which a c_j associated with a basic variable may vary without causing any change in the optimal solution (that is, the values of all the variables will remain the same, but the value of the objective function will change).

3. *Shadow price*—The change in the value of the objective function resulting from adding one unit to the right-hand side of a linear programming constraint.

4. *Range of feasibility*—The range of values over which a b_i may vary without causing the current basic solution to become infeasible. The values of the variables in solution will change, but the same variables will remain basic.

5. *Primal problem*—The original formulation of a linear programming problem.

6. *Canonical form for a maximization problem*—A maximization problem with all less-than-or-equal-to constraints and nonnegativity requirements for the decision variables.

7. *Dual problem*—A linear programming problem associated with the primal problem. Solution of the dual also provides the solution to the primal.

8. *Dual variable*—The variable in a dual linear programming problem. Its value can be interpreted as the shadow price for the associated primal resource.

Problems

1. Consider the linear program

$$\max \quad 7.5x_1 + 15x_2 + 10x_3$$
$$\text{s.t.}$$
$$2x_1 \qquad\quad + \; 2x_3 \le 8$$
$$\tfrac{1}{2}x_1 + \; 2x_2 + \; 1x_3 \le 3$$
$$1x_1 + \; 1x_2 + \; 2x_3 \le 6$$
$$x_1, x_2, x_3 \ge 0.$$

    a. Find the optimal solution.

    b. Calculate the range of optimality or range of insignificance (whichever is appropriate) for c_1.

    c. What would be the effect of a 2.5-unit increase in c_1 (from 7.5 to 10) on the optimal solution and the value of that solution?

    d. Calculate the range of optimality or range of insignificance (whichever is appropriate) for c_3.

    e. What would be the effect of a five-unit increase in c_3 (from 10 to 15) on the optimal solution and the value of that solution?

2. Consider again the linear programming problem presented in Problem 1. Use your knowledge of shadow prices to answer the following:

    a. How much will the value of the objective function change if b_1 is increased from 8 to 9?

    b. How much will the value of the objective function change if b_2 is increased from 3 to 4?

    c. How much will the value of the objective function change if b_3 is increased from 6 to 7?

3. Consider the following linear program:

$$\max \quad 3x_1 + 1x_2 + 5x_3 + 3x_4$$
$$\text{s.t.}$$
$$3x_1 + 1x_2 + 2x_3 \qquad = 30$$
$$-2x_1 + 1x_2 + 3x_3 + 1x_4 \geq 15$$
$$2x_2 \qquad + 3x_4 \leq 25$$
$$x_1, x_2, x_3, x_4 \geq 0.$$

a. Find the optimal solution.
b. Calculate the range of optimality or range of insignificance (whichever is appropriate) for c_3.
c. What would be the effect of a four-unit decrease in c_3 (from 5 to 1) on the optimal solution and the value of that solution?
d. Calculate the range of optimality or range of insignificance (whichever is appropriate) for c_2.
e. What would be the effect of a three-unit increase in c_2 (from 1 to 4) on the optimal solution and the value of that solution?

4. Consider the Par, Inc. problem formulated below:

$$\max \quad 10x_1 + 9x_2$$
$$\text{s.t.}$$

$$\begin{array}{lll} \tfrac{7}{10}x_1 + 1x_2 \leq 630 & \quad \text{cutting and dyeing} \\ \tfrac{1}{2}x_1 + \tfrac{5}{6}x_2 \leq 600 & \quad \text{sewing} \\ 1x_1 + \tfrac{2}{3}x_2 \leq 708 & \quad \text{finishing} \\ \tfrac{1}{10}x_1 + \tfrac{1}{4}x_2 \leq 135 & \quad \text{inspection and packaging} \\ x_1, x_2 \geq 0. \end{array}$$

The final tableau is

		x_1	x_2	s_1	s_2	s_3	s_4	
Basis	c_j	10	9	0	0	0	0	
x_2	9	0	1	30/16	0	−21/16	0	252
s_2	0	0	0	−15/16	1	5/32	0	120
x_1	10	1	0	−20/16	0	30/16	0	540
s_4	0	0	0	−11/32	0	9/64	1	18
	z_j	10	9	70/16	0	111/16	0	7668
	$c_j - z_j$	0	0	−70/16	0	−111/16	0	

a. Calculate the range of optimality for the profit contribution c_2 of the deluxe bag.
b. If the profit per deluxe bag drops to $7 per unit, how will the optimal solution be affected?

c. What unit profit would the deluxe bag have to have before Par would consider changing its current production plan?

d. If the profit of the deluxe bags can be increased to $15 per unit, what is the optimal production plan? State what you think will happen before you compute the new optimal solution.

5. The final Simplex tableau for the Photo Chemicals problem is shown below:

Basis	c_j	x_1	x_2	s_1	s_2	s_3	a_1	a_2	a_3	
		-1	-1	0	0	0	$-M$	$-M$	$-M$	
x_1	-1	1	0	-1	0	0	1	0	0	30
x_2	-1	0	1	$1/2$	0	$-1/2$	$-1/2$	0	$1/2$	25
s_2	0	0	0	$1/2$	1	$-1/2$	$-1/2$	-1	$1/2$	5
z_j		-1	-1	$1/2$	0	$1/2$	$1/2$	0	$-1/2$	-55
$c_j - z_j$		0	0	$-1/2$	0	$-1/2$	$-M-1/2$	$-M$	$-M+1/2$	

Compute the range of optimality for both c_1 (cost per unit of product 1) and c_2 (cost per unit of product 2). What is your interpretation of these ranges?

6. In Section 4.3 we found the range of feasibility for the right-hand side of the Par, Inc. cutting and dyeing constraint to be $495.6 \le b_1' \le 682\frac{4}{11}$. Using the graphical procedure,

a. Show what happens as the number of available hours of cutting and dyeing time is changed from the original 630 hours. Specifically, show the feasible region with 650 hours and then 550 hours.

b. What are the optimal solutions and profits for the two cases in part a?

c. Describe graphically and verbally what happens when the cutting and dyeing time extends beyond its upper or its lower limit.

7. For the Par, Inc. problem,

a. Calculate the range of feasibility for b_2 (sewing capacity).

b. Calculate the range of feasibility for b_3 (finishing capacity).

c. Calculate the range of feasibility for b_4 (inspection and packaging capacity).

d. Which of these three departments are you interested in scheduling for overtime? Explain.

e. Management can schedule overtime in the finishing department for a premium of $4.50 per hour over the current rate. Does it make sense to schedule this overtime? If so, how much overtime can be used? What is the new optimal solution and profit after this overtime is used?

f. What happens when the range of feasibility for the finishing capacity is exceeded?

8. a. Calculate the final Simplex tableau for the Par, Inc. problem after increasing b_1 from 630 to $682\frac{4}{11}$.

b. Would the current basis be optimal if b_1 were increased further? If not, what would be the new optimal basis?

9. Also for the Par, Inc. problem,
   a. How much would profit increase if an additional 30 hours became available in the cutting and dyeing department (that is, b_1 were increased from 630 to 660)?
   b. How much would profit decrease if 40 hours were removed from the sewing department and used elsewhere (say, in making saddles)?
   c. How much would profit decrease if because of an employee accident there were only 570 hours instead of 630 available in the cutting and dyeing department?

10. Below are additional conditions encountered by Par, Inc.
   a. Suppose because of some new machinery Par, Inc. was able to make a small reduction in the amount of time it took to do the cutting and dyeing (constraint 1) for a standard bag. What effect would this have on the objective function?
   b. Management believes that by buying a new sewing machine the sewing time for standard bags can be reduced from $\frac{1}{2}$ hour to $\frac{1}{3}$ hour. Do you think this machine would be a good investment? Why?

11. Consider the final Simplex tableau shown below:

Basis	c_j	x_1	x_2	x_3	x_4	s_1	s_2	s_3	
		4	6	3	1	0	0	0	
x_3	3	3/60	0	1	1/2	3/10	0	-2/10	125
s_2	0	39/12	0	0	-1/2	-5/10	1	-1	425
x_2	6	39/60	1	0	1/2	-1/10	0	12/30	25
	z_j	81/20	6	3	9/2	3/10	0	54/30	525
	$c_j - z_j$	-1/20	0	0	-7/2	-3/10	0	-54/30	

The original right-hand-side values were $b_1 = 550$, $b_2 = 700$, and $b_3 = 200$.
   a. Calculate the range of feasibility for b_1.
   b. Calculate the range of feasibility for b_2.
   c. Calculate the range of feasibility for b_3.

12. Consider the following final Simplex tableau:

Basis	c_j	x_1	x_2	x_3	x_4	a_1	s_1	a_2	s_2	
		3	1	5	3	$-M$	0	$-M$	0	
s_1	0	5/2	7/6	0	0	3/2	1	-1	1/3	115/3
x_3	5	3/2	1/2	1	0	1/2	0	0	0	15
x_4	3	0	2/3	0	1	0	0	0	1/3	25/3
	z_j	15/2	9/2	5	3	5/2	0	0	1	100
	$c_j - z_j$	-9/2	-7/2	0	0	$-5/2-M$	0	$-M$	-1	

The original right-hand-side values were $b_1 = 30$, $b_2 = 15$, and $b_3 = 25$; s_2 is a slack variable for constraint 3.

  a. Calculate the range of feasibility for b_1.

  b. Calculate the range of feasibility for b_2.

  c. Calculate the range of feasibility for b_3.

13. Suppose that in a product-mix problem x_1, x_2, x_3, and x_4 indicate the units of product 1, 2, 3, and 4, respectively, and we have

$$\max \quad 4x_1 + 6x_2 + 3x_3 + 1x_4$$

s.t.

$$
\begin{aligned}
1.5x_1 + 2x_2 + 4x_3 + 3x_4 &\leq 550 \quad &\text{(machine A hours)} \\
4x_1 + 1x_2 + 2x_3 + 1x_4 &\leq 700 \quad &\text{(machine B hours)} \\
2x_1 + 3x_2 + 1x_3 + 2x_4 &\leq 200 \quad &\text{(machine C hours).} \\
x_1, x_2, x_3 &\geq 0.
\end{aligned}
$$

  a. Formulate the dual to this problem.

  b. Solve the dual. Use the dual solution to show that the profit-maximizing product mix is $x_1 = 0$, $x_2 = 25$, $x_3 = 125$, and $x_4 = 0$.

  c. Use the dual variables to identify the machine or machines that are producing at maximum capacity. If the manager can select one machine for additional production capacity, which machine should have priority? Why?

14. Find the dual problem for the linear program given below:

$$\max \quad 10x_1 + 9x_2 + 4x_3 + 6x_4$$

s.t.

$$
\begin{aligned}
3x_1 + 2x_2 + 4x_3 + 2x_4 &\leq 70 \\
5x_1 + 5x_2 + 1x_3 + 3x_4 &\leq 60 \\
5x_1 + 6x_2 + 3x_3 + 1x_4 &\leq 25 \\
x_1, x_2, x_3, x_4 &\geq 0.
\end{aligned}
$$

15. Write the following primal linear program in canonical form:

$$\max \quad 5x_1 + 1x_2 + 3x_3$$

s.t.

$$
\begin{aligned}
1x_1 + 1x_2 \quad\quad &\geq 40 \\
2x_1 + 3x_2 + 1x_3 &\leq 50 \\
3x_1 + 2x_2 + 2x_3 &\leq 25 \\
1x_2 + 1x_3 &\geq 10 \\
x_1, x_2, x_3 &\geq 0.
\end{aligned}
$$

From a computational point of view, would you rather solve the above linear programming problem or its dual?

16. Write the following primal problem in canonical form:

$$\max \quad 3x_1 + 1x_2 + 5x_3 + 3x_4$$

s.t.

$$
\begin{aligned}
3x_1 + 1x_2 + 2x_3 \quad\quad &= 30 \\
2x_1 + 1x_2 + 3x_3 + 1x_4 &\geq 15 \\
2x_2 \quad\quad + 3x_4 &\leq 25 \\
x_1, x_2, x_3, x_4 &\geq 0.
\end{aligned}
$$

17. Write the dual of Problem 16.

18. Consider the following linear program:

$$\max \quad 2x_1 + 3x_2$$
$$\text{s.t.}$$
$$1x_1 + 2x_2 \leq 8$$
$$3x_1 + 2x_2 \leq 12$$
$$x_1, x_2 \geq 0.$$

a. Write the dual of this problem.
b. Solve both the primal and the dual problems using the graphical procedure.
c. Solve both the primal and the dual problems using the Simplex method.
d. Using your results from parts b and c, identify where and how you can observe properties 1 and 2 of the primal-dual relationship.

19. The Photo Chemicals problem asked you to determine the minimum cost production plan for two of its products. The formulation was as follows:

$$\min \quad 1x_1 + 1x_2$$
$$\text{s.t.}$$
$$1x_1 \qquad \geq 30 \qquad \text{minimum product 1}$$
$$1x_2 \geq 20 \qquad \text{minimum product 2}$$
$$1x_1 + 2x_2 \geq 80 \qquad \text{minimum raw material}$$
$$x_1, x_2 \geq 0.$$

d. Write this primal linear program in canonical form for a maximization problem.
b. Show the dual problem.
c. Solve the dual problem, and show that the optimal production plan is $x_1 = 30$ and $x_2 = 25$.
d. Recall that the third constraint involved a management request that the current 80 pounds of a perishable raw material be used as soon as possible. However, after learning that the optimal solution calls for an excess production of five units of product 2, management is reconsidering the raw material requirement. Specifically, you have been asked to identify the cost effect if this constraint were relaxed. Use the dual variable to indicate the change in the cost if only 79 pounds of raw material had to be used.

20. Write the dual problem for the following linear program:

$$\min \quad 3x_1 + 1x_2 + 2x_3$$
$$\text{s.t.}$$
$$2x_1 + 1x_2 + 3x_3 = 5$$
$$4x_1 + 1x_2 + 1x_3 = 4$$
$$2x_1 \qquad + 1x_3 \geq 7$$
$$1x_1 + 2x_2 \qquad \geq 4$$
$$x_1, x_2, x_3 \geq 0.$$

21. Find the dual problem for the following linear programming problem:

$$\min \quad 4x_1 + 3x_2 + 6x_3$$
$$\text{s.t.}$$
$$1x_1 + 0.5x_2 + 1x_3 \geq 15$$
$$2x_2 + 1x_3 \geq 30$$
$$1x_1 + 1x_2 + 2x_3 \geq 20$$
$$x_1, x_2, x_3 \geq 0.$$

22. A sales representative who sells two products is trying to determine the number of calls that should be made during the next month to promote each product. Based on past experience, there is an average $10 commission for every call for product 1 and a $5 commission for every call for product 2. The company requires at least 20 calls per month for each product and not more than 100 calls per month on any one product. In addition, the sales representative spends about 3 hours for each call for product 1 and 1 hour for each call for product 2. If there are a total of 175 selling hours available next month, how many calls should be made for each of the two products in order to maximize the commission?
    a. Formulate the primal linear programming problem.
    b. We have five constraints and only two variables; solve the dual problem.
    c. Use the final Simplex tableau for the dual to determine the optimal number of calls for the products. What is the maximum commission?
    d. Interpret the values of the dual variables.

23. Consider the linear program

$$\max \quad 3x_1 + 2x_2$$
$$\text{s.t.}$$
$$1x_1 + 2x_2 \leq 8$$
$$2x_1 + 1x_2 \leq 10$$
$$x_1, x_2 \geq 0.$$

    a. Solve this problem using the Simplex method. Keep a record of the value of the objective function at each extreme point.
    b. Formulate and solve the dual of this problem using the graphical procedure.
    c. Compute the value of the dual objective function for each extreme-point solution of the dual problem.
    d. Compare the values of the objective functions for each primal and dual extreme-point solution.
    e. Can a dual feasible solution yield a value less than a primal feasible solution? Can you state a result concerning bounds on the value of the primal solution provided by any feasible solution to the dual problem?

24. Consider the following linear program:

$$\max \quad 15x_1 + 30x_2 + 20x_3$$
$$\text{s.t.}$$
$$1x_1 \quad\quad + 1x_3 \leq 4$$
$$0.5x_1 + 2x_2 + 1x_3 \leq 3$$
$$1x_1 + 1x_2 + 2x_3 \leq 6$$
$$x_1, x_2, x_3 \geq 0.$$

    The MPSX/370 computer solution to this problem is shown at the top of page 180.

    Using the computer output information answer the following questions:
    a. What is the optimal solution?
    b. What is the value of the objective function?
    c. Which constraints are the binding constraints?
    d. How much slack is available in the nonbinding constraints?
    e. What are the shadow prices associated with the three constraints? Which right-hand-side value would have the greatest effect on the value of the objective function if it could be changed?
    f. Develop the appropriate ranges for the coefficients of the objective function. What is your interpretation of these ranges?
    g. Develop and interpret the ranges of feasibility for the right-hand-side values.

```
SECTION 1 — ROWS

NUMBER.. ROW.... ACTIVITY.. SLACK ACTIVITY   .. UPPER LIMIT. DUAL ACTIVITY.
      1 OBJ2      75.00000
      2 ROW1       4.00000          .                4.00000      7.50000—
      3 ROW2       3.00000          .                3.00000     15.00000—
      4 ROW 3      4.50000       1.50000             6.00000          .

SECTION 2 — COLUMN

NUMBER   .COLUMNS   ...ACTIVITY...  ..INPUT COST..  .REDUCED COST.
      5 X1             4.00000        15.00000             .
      6 X2              .50000        30.00000
      7 X3                 .          20.00000         2.50000

ROWS AT LIMIT LEVEL

...ROW..  ...ACTIVITY...  SLACK ACTIVITY   LOWER ACTIVITY
                                           UPPER ACTIVITY
                                                 .
ROW1         4.00000            .           6.00000

ROW2         3.00000            .           2.00000
                                            6.00000

COLUMNS AT INTERMEDIATE LEVEL

.COLUMN.   AT   ...ACTIVITY....  ..INPUT COST..   ..LOWER COST..
                                                  ..UPPER COST..

X1         BS       4.00000         15.00000         12.50000
                                                     INFINITY

X2         BS        .50000         30.00000         20.00000
                                                     60.00000
```

25. The computer printout for the Photo Chemicals, Inc. problem is shown at the top of page 181.

$$x_1 = \text{units of product 1 produced}$$
$$x_2 = \text{units of product 2 produced}$$

RAW-MAT = name of the raw material constraint

PROD1 = name of the minimum production of product 1 constraint

PROD2 = name of the minimum production of product 2 constraint

Using the computer information answer the following questions:

a. What is the optimal solution in terms of the amounts of both products that must be produced to obtain minimum cost?

b. What is the value of the objective function?

c. What is your interpretation of the −5 in the "SLACK ACTIVITY" column associated with the product 2 constraint?

d. The raw material usage was restricted to 80 pounds. The firm might be willing to consider relaxing this constraint such that fewer pounds need be used; comment on the effect of this decision upon the total cost.

e. If it appears desirable to relax the raw-material-usage constraint, what is the limit to which it can be relaxed and still maintain feasibility? What happens if it is relaxed by more than this amount?

f. Develop and interpret the ranges of optimality for the cost coefficients in the objective function. What would you expect to happen if the cost of product 2 went up to $2.25? Explain.

SECTION 1 — ROWS

NUMBER	ROW	ACTIVITY	SLACK ACTIVITY	LOWER LIMIT	DUAL ACTIVITY
1	COST	55.00000			
2	RAW-MAT	80.00000	.	80.00000	.50000—
3	PROD1	30.00000	.	30.00000	.50000—
4	PROD2	25.00000	5.00000—	20.00000	.

SECTION 2 — COLUMNS

NUMBER	COLUMNS	ACTIVITY	INPUT COST	REDUCED COST
5	X1	30.00000	1.00000	.
6	X2	25.00000	1.00000	.

ROWS AT LIMIT LEVEL

ROW	ACTIVITY	SLACK ACTIVITY	LOWER ACTIVITY UPPER ACTIVITY
RAW-MAT	80.00000	.	70.00000 INFINITY
PROD1	30.00000	.	40.00000

COLUMNS AT INTERMEDIATE LEVEL

COLUMN	AT	ACTIVITY	INPUT COST	UPPER COST LOWER COST
X1	BS	30.00000	1.00000	INFINITY .50000
X2	BS	25.00000	1.00000	2.00000 .

26. Supersport Footballs, Inc. (Problem 40, Chapter 3) had the problem of determining the best number of All-Pro (x_1), College (x_2), and High School (x_3) models of footballs to produce in order to maximize profits. Constraints included production capacity limitations in each of three departments (cutting and dyeing, sewing, and inspection and packaging) as well as the constraint for at least 1000 All-Pro footballs. The linear program in part b was written as follows:

$$\max \quad 3x_1 + 5x_2 + 4x_3 \quad \text{(time in minutes)}$$

$$\text{s.t.}$$

$$12x_1 + 10x_2 + 8x_3 \leq 18{,}000 \quad \text{(cutting and dyeing)}$$

$$15x_1 + 15x_2 + 4x_3 \leq 18{,}000 \quad \text{(sewing)}$$

$$3x_1 + 4x_2 + 2x_3 \leq 9{,}000 \quad \text{(inspection and packaging)}$$

$$1x_1 \qquad\qquad\quad \geq 1{,}000 \quad \text{(All-Pro model)}$$

$$x_1, x_2, x_3 \geq 0$$

The computer printout of the MPSX/370 solution to the Supersport problem is shown at the top of page 182.

Using the computer information, answer the following questions:
a. What is the production mix of the three models of football that will maximize profits for Supersport Footballs, Inc.?
b. What is the profit associated with this decision?
c. Which production department(s) is causing the restriction of the optimal solution?

SECTION 1 – ROWS

NUMBER	ROW	ACTIVITY	SLACK ACTIVITY	UPPER LIMIT	DUAL ACTIVITY
1	OBJ1	4000.00000			
2	CD	14000.00000	4000.00000	18000.00000	.
3	SEW	18000.00000	.	18000.00000	.33333
4	IP	3800.00000	5200.00000	9000.00000	.
5	PROD1	10000.00000	.	NONE	2.00000

SECTION 2 – COLUMNS

NUMBER	COLUMNS	ACTIVITY	INPUT COST	REDUCED COST
6	X1	1000.00000	3.00000	.
7	X2	200.00000	5.00000	.
8	X3	.	4.00000	.

ROWS AT LIMIT LEVEL

ROW	ACTIVITY	SLACK ACTIVITY	LOWER ACTIVITY UPPER ACTIVITY
SEW	18000.00000	.	15000.00024 24000.00000
PROD1	1000.00000	.	. 1199.99998

COLUMNS AT INTERMEDIATE LEVEL

COLUMN	AT	ACTIVITY	INPUT COST	LOWER COST UPPER COST
X1	BS	1000.00000	3.00000	INFINITY– 5.00000
X2	BS	199.99998	5.00000	5.00000 INFINITY

d. How much slack time is available in each of the three production departments?

e. Overtime rates in the sewing department show an added cost of $12.00 per hour. Would you recommend the company consider using overtime in the sewing department? Explain.

f. What is the maximum amount of overtime that you would consider adding in the sewing department?

g. Using the "DUAL ACTIVITY" value for the "PROD1" row, what observations and/or recommendations would you make about the requirement of producing at least 1000 units of the All-Pro model?

h. If the profit associated with the College model were reduced to $4.50, would you anticipate a change in the recommended production quantities? Explain.

i. Note that variable x_3 has a value of zero in the "REDUCED COST" column. What is your interpretation of this result?

Chapter 5

Linear Programming Applications

Our study thus far has been directed toward obtaining an understanding of linear programming methodology. This background is essential for knowing when linear programming is an appropriate problem-solving tool and for interpreting the results of a linear programming solution to a problem. However, the benefits of this study will be realized only by learning how this methodology can be used to solve real-world decision-making problems. The purpose of this chapter is to show how selected real-world decision-making problems can be formulated and solved using linear programming.

There are two ways in which one may develop skills in model building. (In this chapter model building should be taken to mean formulating a linear program that is a "model" of the real-world decision-making problem for which a solution is desired.) The first way is by on-the-job experience. This is essentially a trial-and-error approach and obviously could not be attempted in a textbook. The second way in which one may develop these skills is by studying how others have developed successful models. Thus in this chapter we attempt to develop your skills along these lines by presenting several reasonably detailed examples of successful linear programming applications. Relatively small problems will be used in the examples, but the principles being developed are applicable to much larger problem sizes.

In practice, linear programming has proven to be one of the most successful quantitative aids for managerial decision making. Numerous applications have been reported in the chemical, airline, steel, paper, petroleum, and other industries. The specific problems studied have included production scheduling, capital budgeting, plant location, transportation, media selection, and many others.

As the variety of the applications mentioned would suggest, linear programming is a flexible problem-solving tool with applications in many disciplines. In this chapter we present introductory applications from the areas of finance, marketing, accounting, and management, as well as the standard linear programming applications in blending and diet problems. In addition, goal programming and an application involving environmental protection are presented.

An understanding of the material presented in this chapter should give the reader an appreciation of the broad range of practical linear programming applications and provide a basis for the reader to further develop modeling skills by creating similar and possibly new linear programming applications in her/his own field of interest.

5.1   Financial Applications

Portfolio Selection

Portfolio selection problems are financial management situations in which a manager must select specific investments—for example, stocks, bonds—from a variety of investment alternatives. This type of problem is frequently encountered by managers of mutual funds, credit unions, insurance compa-

TABLE 5.1 Investment Opportunities for
Welte Mutual Funds

Investment	Projected Rate of Return (percent)
Atlantic Oil	7.3
Pacific Oil	10.3
Midwest Steel	6.4
Huber Steel	7.5
Government bonds	4.5

nies, and banks. The objective function for these problems is usually maximization of expected return or minimization of risk. The constraints usually take the form of restrictions on the type of permissible investments, state laws, company policy, maximum permissible risk, and so on.

Problems of this type have been formulated and solved using a variety of mathematical programming techniques. However, if in a particular portfolio selection problem it is possible to formulate a linear objective function and linear constraints, then linear programming can be used to solve the problem. In this section we show how a simplified portfolio selection problem can be formulated and solved as a linear program.[1]

Consider the case of Welte Mutual Funds, Inc., located in New York City. Welte has just obtained $100,000 by converting industrial bonds to cash and is now looking for other investment opportunities for these funds. Considering Welte's current investments, the firm's top financial analyst recommends that all new investments should be made in the oil industry, steel industry, or government bonds. Specifically, the analyst has identified five investment opportunities and projected their annual rates of return. The investments and rate of return are shown in Table 5.1.

Management of Welte has imposed the following investment guidelines:

1. Neither industry should receive more than 50% of the total new investment.
2. Government bonds should be at least 25% of the steel industry investments.
3. The investment in Pacific Oil, the high-return but high-risk investment, cannot be more than 60% of the total oil industry investment.

What portfolio recommendations—investments and amounts—should be made for the available $100,000? Given the objective of maximizing projected return subject to the budgetary and managerially imposed

---

[1] For a discussion of some other approaches to portfolio selection, see Markowitz, H., *Portfolio Selection* (Cowles Foundation Monograph No. 16), New York, John Wiley & Sons, 1959.

constraints, we can answer this question by formulating a linear programming model of the problem. The solution to this linear programming model will then provide investment recommendations for the management of Welte Mutual Funds.

Let

$$x_1 = \text{dollars invested in Atlantic Oil,}$$
$$x_2 = \text{dollars invested in Pacific Oil,}$$
$$x_3 = \text{dollars invested in Midwest Steel,}$$
$$x_4 = \text{dollars invested in Huber Steel,}$$
$$x_5 = \text{dollars invested in Government bonds.}$$

The complete linear programming model is as follows:

max $\quad 0.073x_1 + 0.103x_2 + 0.064x_3 + 0.075x_4 + 0.045x_5$
s.t.

$$
\begin{array}{llllll}
x_1 + & x_2 + & x_3 + & x_4 + x_5 = 100{,}000 & \text{available funds} \\
x_1 + & x_2 & & \leq \ 50{,}000 & \text{oil industry} \\
& & & & \text{maximum} \\
& & x_3 + & x_4 \quad \leq \ 50{,}000 & \text{steel industry} \\
& & & & \text{maximum} \\
& -0.25x_3 & -0.25x_4 + x_5 \geq & 0 & \text{government bonds} \\
& & & & \text{minimum} \\
-0.6x_1 + 0.4x_2 & & \leq & 0 & \text{Pacific Oil} \\
& & & & \text{restriction}
\end{array}
$$

$$x_1, x_2, x_3, x_4, x_5 \geq 0.$$

The solution to this linear programming model is shown in Table 5.2.

We note that the optimal solution indicates that the portfolio should be diversified among all the investment opportunities except Midwest Steel. The projected expected annual return for this portfolio is 8%.

One shortcoming of the linear programming approach to the portfolio selection problem is that we may not be able to invest the exact amount

TABLE 5.2   Optimal Portfolio Selection for Welte Mutual Funds

Investment	Amount	Expected Annual Return
Atlantic Oil	$ 20,000	$1460
Pacific Oil	30,000	3090
Huber Steel	40,000	3000
Government bonds	10,000	450
	$100,000	$8000
Expected annual return of $8000 = 8%		

specified in each of the securities. For example, if Atlantic Oil sold for $75 a share, we would have to purchase exactly 266⅔ shares in order to spend exactly the recommended $20,000. The approach usually taken to avoid this difficulty is to purchase the largest possible whole number of shares with the amount of funds recommended (for example, 266 shares of Atlantic Oil). Hence we guarantee that our budget constraint will not be violated. This, of course, introduces the possibility that our solution will no longer be optimal, but the danger is slight if large numbers of securities are involved.

Financial Mix Strategy

Financial-mix strategies involve the selection of means for financing company projects, inventories, production operations, and various other activities. In this section we illustrate how linear programming can be used to solve problems of this type by formulating and solving a problem involving the financing of production operations. In this particular application a financial decision must be made with regard to how much production is to be supported by internally generated funds and how much is to be supported by external funds.

The Jefferson Adding Machine Company will begin production of two new models of electronic adding machines during the next three months. Since this new line requires an expansion of the current production operation, the company will need operating funds to cover material, labor, and selling expenses during this initial production period. Revenue from this initial production run will not be available until after the end of the period. Thus the company must arrange financing for these operating expenses before production can begin.

Jefferson has set aside $3000 in internal funds available to cover expenses of this operation. If additional funds are needed, they will have to be generated externally. A local bank has offered a line of short-term credit in an amount not to exceed $10,000. The interest rate over the life of the loan will be 12% per year on the average amount borrowed. One stipulation set by the bank requires that the remainder of the company cash set aside for this operation plus the accounts receivable for this product line be at least twice as great as the outstanding loan plus interest at the end of the initial production period.

In addition to the financial restrictions placed on this operation, labor capacity is also a factor for Jefferson to consider. Specifically, only 2500 hours of assembly time and 150 hours of packaging and shipping time are available for the new product line during the initial three-month production period. Relevant cost, price, and production time requirements for the two models are shown in Table 5.3.

Additional restrictions have been imposed by company management in order to guarantee that the market reaction to both products can be tested; that is, at least 50 units of model Y and at least 25 units of model Z must be produced in this first production period.

Since the cost of units produced on borrowed funds will in effect experience an interest charge, the profit margins for the units of models Y

TABLE 5.3   Cost, Price, and Labor Data for the Jefferson Adding Machine Company

Model	Unit Cost (Materials and Other Variable Expenses)	Selling Price	Profit Margin	Labor Hours Required Assembly	Packaging and Shipping
Y	$ 50	$ 58	$ 8	12	1
Z	$100	$120	$20	25	2

and Z produced on borrowed funds will be reduced. Hence we adopt the following notation for the decision variables in our problem:

x_1 = units of model Y produced with company funds,

x_2 = units of model Y produced with borrowed funds,

x_3 = units of model Z produced with company funds,

x_4 = units of model Z produced with borrowed funds.

How much will the profit margin be reduced for units produced on borrowed funds? To answer this question, one must know for how long the loan will be outstanding. We assume that all units of each model are sold as they are produced to independent distributors and that the average rate of turnover of accounts receivable is three months. Since company management has specified that the loan is to be repaid by funds generated by the units produced on borrowed funds, the funds borrowed to produce one unit of model Y or Z will be repaid approximately three months later. Hence the profit margin for each unit of model Y produced on borrowed funds is reduced from $8.00 to $8.00 − ($50 × 0.12 × ¼ yr) = $6.50, and the profit margin for each unit of model Z produced on borrowed funds is reduced from $20.00 to $20.00 − ($100 × 0.12 × ¼ yr) = $17.00. With this information we can now formulate the objective function for Jefferson's financial mix problem:

$$\max 8x_1 + 6.5x_2 + 20x_3 + 17x_4.$$

We can also specify the following constraints for the model:

$$
\begin{aligned}
12x_1 + 12x_2 + 25x_3 + 25x_4 &\le 2500 && \text{assembly} \\
x_1 + x_2 + 2x_3 + 2x_4 &\le 150 && \text{packaging and shipping} \\
50x_1 + 100x_3 &\le 3000 && \text{internal funds} \\
50x_2 + 100x_4 &\le 10{,}000 && \text{external funds} \\
x_1 + x_2 &\ge 50 && \text{model Y requirement} \\
x_3 + x_4 &\ge 25 && \text{model Z requirement}
\end{aligned}
$$

In addition, the following constraint must be included to satisfy the bank loan requirement:

$$\text{cash} + \text{accounts receivable} \geq 2(\text{loan} + \text{interest}).$$

This restriction must be satisfied at the end of the period. Recalling that accounts receivable are outstanding for an average of three months, the following relationships can be used to derive a mathematical expression for the above inequality at the end of the period:

$$\text{cash} = 3000 - 50x_1 - 100x_3,$$
$$\text{accounts receivable} = 58x_1 + 58x_2 + 120x_3 + 120x_4,$$
$$\text{loan} = 50x_2 + 100x_4,$$
$$\text{interest} = (0.12 \times \tfrac{1}{4} \text{ yr})(50x_2 + 100x_4) = 1.5x_2 + 3x_4.$$

Therefore the constraint resulting from the bank restriction can be written as

$$3000 - 50x_1 - 100x_3 + 58x_1 + 58x_2 + 120x_3 + 120x_4$$
$$\geq 2(51.5x_2 + 103x_4)$$

or

$$-8x_1 + 45x_2 - 20x_3 + 86x_4 \leq 3000.$$

The complete linear programming model for our problem can now be stated:

$$
\begin{aligned}
\max \quad & 8x_1 + 6.5x_2 + 20x_3 + 17x_4 \\
\text{s.t.} \quad & \\
& 12x_1 + 12x_2 + 25x_3 + 25x_4 \leq 2500 \\
& x_1 + x_2 + 2x_3 + 2x_4 \leq 150 \\
& 50x_1 + 100x_3 \leq 3000 \\
& 50x_2 + 100x_4 \leq 10{,}000 \\
& x_1 + x_2 \geq 50 \\
& x_3 + x_4 \geq 25 \\
& -8x_1 + 45x_2 - 20x_3 + 86x_4 \leq 3000 \\
& x_1, x_2, x_3, x_4 \geq 0.
\end{aligned}
$$

The solution to this four-variable, seven-constraint financial mix problem is shown in Table 5.4. The optimal financial mix requires the company to use all its internal funds ($3000) but only slightly over $4000 of the available $10,000 line of credit.

5.2 Marketing Applications

Media Selection

Media selection applications of linear programming are aimed at helping marketing managers allocate a fixed advertising budget across various media. Potential advertising media include newspapers, magazines, radio

TABLE 5.4   Optimal Financial Mix for the Production of Jefferson Adding Machines

	Units	Expected Profit
Model Y		
Borrowed funds (x_2)	50	$ 325
Model Z		
Company funds (x_3)	30	$ 600
Borrowed funds (x_4)	15.7	$ 267
	Total	$1192

commercials, television commercials, direct mailings, and others. In most of these applications the objective is taken to be the maximization of audience exposure. Restrictions on the allowable allocation usually arise through considerations such as company policy, contract requirements, and availability of media. In the application which follows we illustrate how a simple media selection problem might be formulated and solved using a linear programming model.

Consider the case of the Relax-and-Enjoy Lake Development Corporation. Relax-and-Enjoy is developing a lakeside community at a privately owned lake and is in the business of selling property for vacation and/or retreat cottages. The primary market for these lakeside lots includes all middle and upper income families within approximately one hundred miles of the development. Relax-and-Enjoy has employed the advertising firm of Boone Phillips and Jackson to design the promotional campaign for the project.

After considering possible advertising media and the market to be covered, Boone has made the preliminary recommendation to restrict the first month's advertising to five sources. At the end of this month, Boone will then reevaluate its strategy based upon the month's results. Boone has collected data on the number of potential purchase families reached, the cost per advertisement, the maximum number of times each medium is available, and the expected exposure for each of the five media. The expected exposure is measured in terms of an exposure unit, a management judgment measure of the relative value of one advertisement in each of the media. These measures, based on Boone's experience in the advertising business, take into account such factors as audience profile (age, income, and education of the audience reached), image presented, and quality of the advertisement. The information collected to date is presented in Table 5.5

Relax-and-Enjoy has provided Boone with an advertising budget of $30,000 for the first month's campaign. In addition, Relax-and-Enjoy has imposed the following restrictions on how Boone may allocate these funds: At least ten television commercials must be used, and at least 50,000 potential purchasers must be reached during the month. In addition, no more than $18,000 may be spent on television advertisements. What advertising media selection plan should the advertising firm recommend?

TABLE 5.5 Advertising Media Alternatives for the Relax-and-Enjoy
Lake Development Corporation

Advertising Media	Number of Potential Purchase Families Reached	Cost per Advertise- ment	Maximum Times Available per Month*	Expected Exposure Units
1. Daytime TV (1 min), station WKLA	1000	$1500	15	65
2. Evening TV (30 sec), station WKLA	2000	$3000	10	90
3. Daily newspaper (full page), *The Morning Journal*	1500	$400	25	40
4. Sunday newspaper magazine (½ page color), *The Sunday Press*	2500	$1000	4	60
5. Radio, 8:00 A.M. or 5:00 P.M. news (30 sec), station KNOP	300	$100	30	20

*The maximum number of times the medium is available is either the maximum number of times the advertising medium occurs (that is, four Sundays for medium 4) or the maximum number of times Boone will allow the medium to be used.

The first step in formulating a linear programming model of this problem is the definition of variables. We let

x_1 = number of times daytime TV is used,

x_2 = number of times evening TV is used,

x_3 = number of times daily newspaper is used,

x_4 = number of times Sunday newspaper is used,

x_5 = number of times radio is used.

With the overall goal of maximizing the expected exposure, the objective function becomes

$$\max 65x_1 + 90x_2 + 40x_3 + 60x_4 + 20x_5.$$

The constraints for our model can now be formulated from the information given:

$$
\begin{array}{rcll}
x_1 & & \le & 15 \\
x_2 & & \le & 10 \\
x_3 & & \le & 25 \\
x_4 & & \le & 4 \\
x_5 & \le & 30
\end{array}
\left.\begin{array}{c}\\\\\\\\\\\end{array}\right\} \begin{array}{l}\text{availability} \\ \text{of media}\end{array}
$$

$$1500x_1 + 3000x_2 + 400x_3 + 1000x_4 + 100x_5 \leq 30,000 \quad \text{budget}$$

$$\left. \begin{array}{r} x_1 + x_2 \geq 10 \\ 1500x_1 + 3000x_2 \leq 18,000 \end{array} \right\} \begin{array}{l} \text{television} \\ \text{restrictions} \end{array}$$

$$1000x_1 + 2000x_2 + 1500x_3 + 2500x_4 + 300x_5 \geq 50,000 \quad \begin{array}{l} \text{audience} \\ \text{coverage} \end{array}$$

$$x_1, x_2, x_3, x_4, x_5 \geq 0.$$

The solution to this five-variable, nine-constraint linear programming model is presented in Table 5.6.

We point out that the above media selection model, probably more than most other linear programming models, requires crucial subjective evaluations as input. The most critical of these inputs is the expected exposure rating measure. While marketing managers may have substantial data concerning expected advertising exposure, the final coefficient that includes image and quality considerations is based primarily on managerial judgment. However, judgment input is a very acceptable way of obtaining necessary data for a linear programming model.

Another shortcoming of this model is that even if the expected exposure measure was not subject to error, there is no guarantee that maximization of total expected exposure will lead to a maximization of profit or of sales (a common surrogate for profit). However, this is not a shortcoming of linear programming; rather it is a shortcoming of the use of exposure as a criterion. Certainly if we were able to measure directly the effect of an advertisement on profit we would use total profit as our objective to be maximized.

In addition, you should be aware that the media selection model as formulated in this section does not include considerations such as the following:

1. Reduced exposure value for repeat media usage;
2. Cost discounts for repeat media usage;
3. Audience overlap by different media;
4. Timing recommendation for the advertisement.

TABLE 5.6   Advertising Plan for the Relax-and-Enjoy Lake Development Corporation

Media	Frequency	Budget
Daytime TV	10	$15,000
Daily newspaper	25	10,000
Sunday newspaper	2	2,000
Radio	30	3,000
		$30,000

Total audience contacted = 61,500
Expected exposure = 2,370

A more complex formulation—more variables and constraints—can often be used to overcome some of these limitations, but it will not always be possible to overcome all of them with a linear programming model. However, even in these cases a linear programming model can often be used to arrive at a rough approximation to the best decision. Management evaluation combined with the linear programming solution should then make possible the selection of an overall effective advertising strategy.

Marketing Strategy

One particular marketing strategy decision involves the optimal allocation of sales force and advertising effort. As we discussed in the previous section on media selection problems, one would like to make this decision in such a fashion as to maximize profit or sales. Unfortunately, one seldom has enough information to specify the relationship between the allocation of sales force and advertising effort and the ultimate criterion of profit or sales. We illustrate in this section a case where the company has been able to specify this relationship. Thus the marketing strategy decision can be made with the objective of maximizing profit.

Electronic Communications, Inc. manufactures portable radio systems that can be used for two-way communications. The company's new product, which has a range of up to 25 miles, is particularly suitable for use in a variety of applications such as mobile unit–home office systems, marina sales and service systems, and others. In these applications the two-way communication system enables an office to easily contact field sales personnel, repair personnel, and so on. The primary distribution channel for the product will be through industrial communications equipment distributors. However, the firm is also considering distribution through a national chain of discount stores and a marine equipment distributor. These latter two distribution channels have the advantage of allowing the product to reach individuals interested in radio-oriented hobbies and individuals desiring boat communication systems.

Because of differing distribution and promotional costs, the profitability of the product varies with the distribution alternative selected. In addition, the company's estimate of the advertising cost and sales time per unit sold will vary with the different distribution channels. Since the company only produces these units on order, the number of units produced and the number of units sold are the same.

Table 5.7 summarizes the data prepared by Electronic Communications with respect to profit, expected advertising effort per unit sold, and estimated sales force effort per unit sold. The advertising and sales force estimates are based upon past experience with similar radio equipment.

Company management has specified that at least 100 units must be distributed through the discount stores during the next three months. The firm has set the advertising budget at $5000 and stated that a maximum of 1200 hours of sales force time will be available during the current planning period. In addition, production capacity is 600 units.

TABLE 5.7   Profit, Cost, and Time Data for Electronic Communications, Inc.

Distributor	Profit per Unit Sold	Estimated Average Advertising Effort per Unit Sold	Estimated Sales Force Effort per Unit Sold (hours)
Industrial	$90	$10	2.5
Discount stores	$70	$18	3.0
Marine	$84	$ 8	3.0

The company is now faced with the task of establishing a profitable marketing strategy. Specifically, decisions need to be made on the following:

1. How many units should be produced, and how should they be allocated to the three market segments? *~u~y*
2. How much advertising should be devoted to the three market segments?
3. How should the sales force effort be allocated among the three market segments?

Proceeding to a linear programming formulation of this problem, we introduce the following notation:

$$x_1 = \text{units produced for the industrial market,}$$
$$x_2 = \text{units produced for the discount store market,}$$
$$x_3 = \text{units produced for the marine market.}$$

In terms of this notation, the objective function and the constraints can be written as follows:

max $90x_1 + 70x_2 + 84x_3$

s.t.

$10x_1 + 18x_2 + 8x_3 \leq 5000$	advertising budget
$2.5x_1 + 3x_2 + 3x_3 \leq 1200$	sales force availability
$x_1 + x_2 + x_3 \leq 600$	production capacity
$x_2 \geq 100$	minimum discount store volume

$x_1, x_2, x_3 \geq 0.$

The solution to this linear programming model is given in Table 5.8.

Sensitivity analysis techniques may provide the marketing manager with some additional valuable information. Specifically, the shadow prices for the first three resources are 6, 12, and 0. Recall from Chapter 4 that a shadow price of zero for a slack variable indicated that an increase in the value of the right-hand side for the corresponding constraint would have no effect on profit. Therefore we can conclude in this case that the production

TABLE 5.8   Profit Maximizing Marketing Strategy for
Electronic Communications, Inc.

Market Segment	Volume	Advertising Allocation	Sales Force Allocation (hours)
Industrial	240	$2400	600
Discount store	100	1800	300
Marine	100	800	300
Total	440	$5000	1200
	Profit projection = $37,000		

capacity (constraint 3) is not restricting our profit. In fact, the slack variable associated with this constraint shows the excess production capacity to be 160 units.

Recall that the nonzero shadow prices mean that the corresponding constraints are binding. Therefore we know that we are using the maximum available advertising and sales force resources. The results in Table 5.8 confirm this analysis. The values of these shadow prices give the marginal value of additional advertising budget and sales force effort. Specifically, an additional advertising dollar has a potential of increasing the profit by $6, while an additional hour of sales force effort has a potential value of $12. Thus the manager should consider the possibility of obtaining these additional resources as long as the cost of the addition is less than the potential benefits. Recall, however, that we saw in Chapter 4 that we cannot expect additional resources to increase profit without limit. In this case we might consider increasing the advertising budget and using part-time sales assistance. However, as we continue to increase these resources, sales will increase and production capacity will become binding, causing any additional advertising and sales efforts to be of no value.

5.3   Management Applications

Production Scheduling

One of the richest areas of linear programming applications is production scheduling. The solution to a production scheduling problem enables the manager to establish an efficient low-cost production schedule for one or more products over several time periods, such as, weeks, months, and so on. Essentially, a production scheduling problem can be viewed as a product mix problem for each of several periods in the future. The manager must determine the production levels that will allow the company to meet product demand requirements, given limitations on production capacity, labor capacity, and storage space. At the same time it is desired to minimize the total cost of carrying out this task.

One major reason for the widespread application of linear programming to production scheduling problems is that these problems are of a recurring nature. A production schedule must be established for the current month, then again for the next month, the month after that, and so on. When the production manager looks at the problem each month, he will find that while demands for the products have changed, production times, production capacities, storage space limitations, and so on, are roughly the same. Thus the production manager is basically resolving the same problem handled in previous months. Hence a general linear programming model of the production scheduling procedure may be frequently applied. Once the model has been formulated, the manager can simply supply the data—demands, capacities, and so on—for the given production period, and the linear programming model can then be used to develop the production schedule. Thus one linear programming formulation may have many repeat applications.

Let us consider the case of the Bollinger Electronics Company, which produces two different electronic components for a major airplane engine manufacturer. The airplane engine manufacturer notifies the Bollinger sales office each quarter as to what the monthly requirements for components will be during each of the next three months. The monthly demands for the components may vary considerably depending upon the type of engine the airplane engine manufacturer is producing. The order shown in Table 5.9 has just been received for the next three-month period.

After the order is processed, a demand statement is sent to the production control department. The production control department must then develop a three-month production plan for the components. Knowing the preference of the production department manager for constant demand levels (such as balanced workload, constant machine and labor utilization), the production scheduler might consider the alternative of producing at a constant rate for all three months. This would set monthly production quotas at 3000 units per month for component 322A and 1500 units per month for component 802B. Why not adopt this schedule?

While this schedule would obviously be quite appealing to the production department, it may be undesirable from a total-cost point of view. In particular, this schedule ignores inventory costs. Consider the projected inventory levels that would result from this schedule calling for constant production (Figure 5.1).

Thus we see that this production schedule would lead to high inventory

TABLE 5.9   Three-Month Demand Schedule for Bollinger Electronics Company

	April	May	June
Component 322A	1000	3000	5000
Component 802B	1000	500	3000

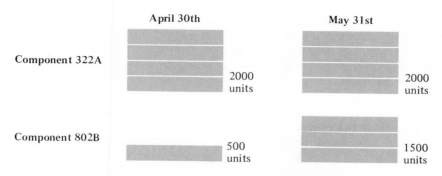

FIGURE 5.1   Projected Inventory Levels Under a Constant-Rate Production Schedule

levels. When we consider the cost of tied up capital and storage space, a schedule that provides lower inventory levels might be economically more desirable.

At the other extreme of the constant rate production schedule is the produce-to-meet-demand approach. While this schedule eliminates the inventory holding cost problem, the wide monthly production level fluctuation may cause some serious production problems and costs. For example, production capacity would have to be available to meet the total 8000-unit peak demand in June. Unless other components could be scheduled on the same production equipment in April and May, there would be significant unused capacity and thus low machine utilization in those months. In addition, the large production variations will require substantial labor adjustments; employee turnover or training problems may be encountered. Thus it appears that the best production schedule will be one that compromises between the constant rate–high inventory and the variable rate–low utilization extremes.

The production scheduler will therefore want to identify and consider the following costs:

1.   Production costs,
2.   Storage costs,
3.   Change-in-production-level costs.

In the remainder of this section we show how a linear programming model of the production process for Bollinger Electronics can be formulated to account for these costs in such a fashion that the total system cost is minimized.

In order to develop our model we introduce a double subscript notation for the decision variables in the problem. We let the first subscript indicate the product number and the second subscript the month. Thus in general we let x_{im} denote the production volume in units for product i in month m. Here $i = 1,2$ and $m = 1,2,3$; $i = 1$ refers to component 322A, $i = 2$ refers to component 802B. The purpose of the double subscript is to provide a more descriptive notation. We could simply use x_6 to represent the number of units of product 2 produced in month 3, but x_{23} is more descriptive in that we know directly the product and month the variable represents.

If component 322A costs \$20 per unit produced and component 802B costs \$10 per unit produced, the production cost part of the objective function becomes

Production cost $= 20x_{11} + 20x_{12} + 20x_{13} + 10x_{21} + 10x_{22} + 10x_{23}.$

You should note that in this particular problem the production cost per unit is the same each month, and thus we need not include production costs in our objective function; that is, no matter what production schedule is selected, the total production costs will remain the same. In cases where the cost per unit is expected to change each month, these variable production costs per unit per month must be included in the objective function. For the Bollinger Electronics problem we have elected to include them. This means that the value of the linear programming objective function will include all the costs associated with the problem.

To incorporate the inventory costs into our model, we introduce the following double subscripted decision variable to indicate the number of units of inventory for each product for each month. We let s_{im} be the inventory level for product i at the end of month m.

Bollinger has determined that on a monthly basis, inventory holding costs are 1.5% of the value of the product—that is, \$0.30 per unit for component 322A and \$0.15 per unit for component 802B. A common assumption made in linear programming approaches to the production scheduling problem is now invoked. We assume that monthly ending inventories are an acceptable approximation to the average inventory levels throughout the month. Given this assumption, the inventory holding cost portion of the objective function can be written as follows:

inventory holding cost $= 0.30s_{11} + 0.30s_{12} + 0.30s_{13} + 0.15s_{21}$
$$+ 0.15s_{22} + 0.15s_{23}.$$

In order to incorporate the costs due to fluctuations in production levels, we need to define the following additional decision variables:

$I_m =$ increase in the production hours during month m,

$D_m =$ decrease in the production hours during month m.

After estimating the effect of employee layoffs, turnovers, reassignment training costs, and other costs associated with fluctuating manpower requirements, Bollinger estimated that the cost associated with an increase in labor was \$10 per hour, while the cost associated with a decrease was only \$2.50 per hour. Thus the third portion of our objective function can now be written

Production fluctuation costs $= 10I_1 + 10I_2 + 10I_3$
$$+ 2.5D_1 + 2.5D_2 + 2.5D_3.$$

You should note that Bollinger has elected to measure the cost associated with production fluctuations as a function of the change in hours of labor required. In other production scheduling problems such costs might be measured in terms of machine hours or in terms of total units produced.

Combining all three costs, our complete objective function becomes

$$\text{objective function} = 20x_{11} + 20x_{12} + 20x_{13} + 10x_{21} + 10x_{22}$$
$$+ 10x_{23} + 0.30s_{11} + 0.30s_{12} + 0.30s_{13} + 0.15s_{21} + 0.15s_{22}$$
$$+ 0.15s_{23} + 10I_1 + 10I_2 + 10I_3 + 2.5D_1 + 2.5D_2 + 2.5D_3.$$

Now let us consider the constraints. First we must guarantee that our schedule meets customer demand. Since the units shipped can come from the current month's production or from inventory carried over from previous periods, we have the following basic requirements:

$$\begin{pmatrix} \text{ending} \\ \text{inventory} \\ \text{from previous} \\ \text{month} \end{pmatrix} + \begin{pmatrix} \text{current} \\ \text{production} \end{pmatrix} \geq \begin{pmatrix} \text{this month's} \\ \text{demand} \end{pmatrix}$$

In fact, the difference in the left-hand side and the right-hand side will be the amount of ending inventory at the end of this month. Thus the demand requirement takes the form

$$\begin{pmatrix} \text{ending} \\ \text{inventory} \\ \text{from previous} \\ \text{month} \end{pmatrix} + \begin{pmatrix} \text{current} \\ \text{production} \end{pmatrix} - \begin{pmatrix} \text{ending} \\ \text{inventory} \\ \text{for this} \\ \text{month} \end{pmatrix} = \begin{pmatrix} \text{this} \\ \text{month's} \\ \text{demand} \end{pmatrix}$$

Suppose that the inventories at the beginning of our three-month scheduling period were 500 units for component 322A and 200 units for component 802B. Recalling that the demand for both products in the first month (April) was 1000 units, the constraints for meeting demand in the first month become

$$500 + x_{11} - s_{11} = 1000$$
$$200 + x_{21} - s_{21} = 1000.$$

Moving the constants to the right-hand side, we have

$$x_{11} - s_{11} = 500$$
$$x_{21} - s_{21} = 800.$$

Similarly, we need demand constraints for both products in the second and third months. These can be written as follows:

Month 2: $s_{11} + x_{12} - s_{12} = 3000$
$$s_{21} + x_{22} - s_{22} = 500.$$

Month 3: $s_{12} + x_{13} - s_{13} = 5000$
$$s_{22} + x_{23} - s_{23} = 3000.$$

TABLE 5.10   Machine, Labor, and Storage Capacities for
Bollinger Electronics

	Machine Capacity (hours)	Labor Capacity (hours)	Storage Capacity (square feet)
April	400	300	10,000
May	500	300	10,000
June	600	300	10,000

If the company specifies a minimum inventory level at the end of the three-month period of at least 400 units of component 322A and at least 200 units of component 802B, we can add the constraints

$$s_{13} \geq 400$$
$$s_{23} \geq 200.$$

Let us suppose that we have the additional information available on production, labor, and storage capacity given in Table 5.10. Machine, labor, and storage space requirements are given in Table 5.11. To reflect these limitations, the following constraints are necessary:

Machine capacity:

$$0.10x_{11} + 0.08x_{21} \leq 400 \qquad \text{month 1}$$
$$0.10x_{12} + 0.08x_{22} \leq 500 \qquad \text{month 2}$$
$$0.10x_{13} + 0.08x_{23} \leq 600 \qquad \text{month 3}$$

Labor capacity:

$$0.05x_{11} + 0.07x_{21} \leq 300 \qquad \text{month 1}$$
$$0.05x_{12} + 0.07x_{22} \leq 300 \qquad \text{month 2}$$
$$0.05x_{13} + 0.07x_{23} \leq 300 \qquad \text{month 3}$$

Storage capacity:

$$2s_{11} + 3s_{21} \leq 10,000 \qquad \text{month 1}$$
$$2s_{12} + 3s_{22} \leq 10,000 \qquad \text{month 2}$$
$$2s_{13} + 3s_{23} \leq 10,000 \qquad \text{month 3.}$$

One final set of constraints must be added. These are necessary in order to guarantee that I_m and D_m will reflect the increase or decrease in the number of hours of labor used for production in month m. Suppose that the number of hours of labor used for production of the two components in March, the month before the start of our planning period, had been 225. We can find the amount of the change in the labor level for April from the

TABLE 5.11   Machine, Labor, and Storage Requirements for
Components 322A and 802B

	Requirements		
	Machine (hours/unit)	Labor (hours/unit)	Storage (sq. ft./unit)
Component 322A	0.10	0.05	2
Component 802B	0.08	0.07	3

relationship

$$\text{April usage} \quad - \text{ March usage} = \text{change}$$
$$(0.05x_{11} + 0.07x_{21}) - \quad 225 \quad = \text{change}.$$

Note that the change can be positive or negative. A positive change reflects an increase in the labor level, and a negative change reflects a decrease. Using this relationship, we can now specify the following constraint for the change in the number of hours used in April:

$$(0.05x_{11} + 0.07x_{21}) - 225 = I_1 - D_1.$$

Of course we cannot have an increase and a decrease in the same period; thus either I_1 or D_1 will be zero. If April requires 245 hours, $I_1 = 20$ and $D_1 = 0$. If April requires only 175 hours, $I_1 = 0$ and $-D_1 = -50$ (therefore $D_1 = 50$). This technique of denoting the change in hour requirements as the difference of two variables (I_m and D_m) means that even though these variables will both be forced to assume nonnegative values by our linear programming model, we can represent both positive and negative fluctuations. Using the same approach in the following months (always subtracting the previous month's labor usage from the current month's), we have the following constraints for the second and third months:

$$(0.05x_{12} + 0.07x_{22}) - (0.05x_{11} + 0.07x_{21}) = I_2 - D_2$$
$$(0.05x_{13} + 0.07x_{23}) - (0.05x_{12} + 0.07x_{22}) = I_3 - D_3.$$

Placing the variables on the left-hand side and the constants on the right-hand side, the complete set of labor smoothing constraints can be written as

$$0.05x_{11} + 0.07x_{21} \qquad\qquad\qquad\qquad\qquad\qquad - I_1 + D_1 = 225$$
$$-0.05x_{11} - 0.07x_{21} + 0.05x_{12} + 0.07x_{22} \qquad\qquad\qquad - I_2 + D_2 = 0$$
$$- 0.05x_{12} - 0.07x_{22} + 0.05x_{13} + 0.07x_{23} - I_3 + D_3 = 0$$

Our initially rather small, two-product, three-month scheduling problem has now developed into an 18-variable, 20-constraint linear programming problem. Note that in our problem we were concerned only with one type of machine process, one type of labor and one type of storage area. In actual production scheduling problems you may encounter several machine types, several labor grades, and/or several storage areas. Thus you are probably beginning to realize how large-scale linear programs of production systems come about. A typical application might involve developing a production schedule for 100 products over a 12-month horizon. Such a problem would have over 1000 variables and constraints.

The complete solution to the Bollinger Electronics Company production scheduling problem is shown in Table 5.12.

At first glance the variation in the production schedule may look rather strange. But let us examine the logic of the recommended solution. Recall that the inventory cost for component 802B is one half the inventory cost for component 322A. Therefore, as might be expected, component 802B tends to be carried in inventory, while the more expensive component 322A tends to be produced when demanded.

Why do we recommend producing over 2800 units of 802B in April when at least some of the units cannot be shipped until June? The answer to this is also logical. Recall that a labor level of 225 hours was used in March. The low demand in April tends to dictate a labor cutback; however, as you can see from the May and June demands, the firm would then have to rehire or add labor resources in later months. The model is in effect smoothing the labor requirements. Rather than recommending expensive labor fluctuations, the linear programming model indicates that it is cheaper to maintain a relatively high April production, even though it means a higher inventory cost for component 802B. Keeping the April labor force at 225 hours means that the only labor force change will be a 42.5 hour increase in May. This level will be maintained during the month of June.

We have seen in this illustration that a linear programming application of a relatively small two-product system (18 variables and 20 constraints) has provided some valuable information in terms of identifying a minimum-cost production schedule. In larger systems, where the number of variables and constraints are too numerous to humanly track, linear programming models often provide significant cost savings for the firm.

TABLE 5.12   Optimal Production, Labor, and Inventory
Policy for Bollinger Electronics Company

Schedule	April	May	June
Production			
Component 322A	500	3050	5350
Component 802B	2858	1642	—
Labor Hours	225	267.5	267.5
Inventory			
Component 322A	—	50	400
Component 802B	2058	3200	200

Total cost (including production, inventory, and labor smoothing costs) = $224,378

Labor Planning

Labor planning or scheduling problems frequently occur when managers must make decisions involving departmental staffing requirements for a given period of time. This is particularly true when labor assignments have some flexibility and at least some labor effort can be assigned to more than one department or work center. This is often the case when employees have been cross-trained on two or more jobs. In the following example we present a product mix problem similar to the Par, Inc. problem and show how linear programming can be used to determine not only an optimal product mix but also an optimal labor allocation for the various departments.

McCarthy's Everyday Glass Company is planning to produce two styles of drinking glasses during the next month. The glasses are processed in four separate departments. Excess equipment capacity is available and will not be a constraining factor. However, the company's labor resources are limited and will probably constrain the production volume for the two products. The labor requirements per case produced (one dozen glasses) are shown in Table 5.13.

The company makes a profit of $1.00 per case of product 1 and $0.90 per case of product 2. If the number of hours available in each department is fixed, we can formulate McCarthy's problem as a standard product mix linear program. We use the usual notation:

x_1 = cases of product 1 manufactured,

x_2 = cases of product 2 manufactured,

b_i = hours of labor available in department i, $i = 1,2,3,4$.

The linear program can be written as

$$\max \quad 1.00x_1 + 0.90x_2$$
$$\text{s.t.}$$

$$0.070x_1 + 0.100x_2 \leq b_1$$
$$0.050x_1 + 0.084x_2 \leq b_2$$
$$0.100x_1 + 0.067x_2 \leq b_3$$
$$0.010x_1 + 0.025x_2 \leq b_4$$
$$x_1, x_2 \geq 0.$$

TABLE 5.13   **Hours of Labor per Case of Product**

Department	Product 1	Product 2
1	0.070	0.100
2	0.050	0.084
3	0.100	0.067
4	0.010	0.025

To solve the normal product mix problem we would ask the production manager to specify the hours available in each department (b_1, b_2, b_3, and b_4); then we could solve for the profit maximizing product mix. However, in this case we assume that the manager has some flexibility in allocating labor resources, and we would like to make a recommendation for this allocation as well as determining the optimal product mix.

Suppose that after consideration of the training and experience qualifications of the workers, we find this additional information:

Possible Labor Assignments	Hours of Labor Available
Department 1 only	430
Department 2 only	400
Department 3 only	500
Department 4 only	135
Departments 1 or 2	570
Departments 3 or 4	300
Total	2335

Of the 2335 hours available for the month's production, we see that 870 hours can be allocated with some management discretion. The constraints for the hours available per department are as follows:

$$b_1 \leq 430 + 570 = 1000$$
$$b_2 \leq 400 + 570 = 970$$
$$b_3 \leq 500 + 300 = 800$$
$$b_4 \leq 135 + 300 = 435.$$

Since the 570 hours that have a flexible assignment between departments 1 and 2 cannot be assigned to both departments simultaneously, we need the following additional constraint:

$$b_1 + b_2 \leq 430 + 400 + 570 = 1400.$$

Similarly, for the 300 hours that can be allocated between departments 3 and 4, we need the constraint

$$b_3 + b_4 \leq 500 + 135 + 300 = 935.$$

In this formulation we are now treating the labor assignments to departments as variables. The objective function coefficients for these variables will be zero, since the b_i variables do not directly affect profit. Thus placing all variables on the left-hand side of the constraints, we have the following complete formulation.

max $1.00x_1 + 0.90x_2 + 0b_1 + 0b_2 + 0b_3 + 0b_4$
s.t.

$$0.070x_1 + 0.100x_2 - b_1 \qquad\qquad \le \quad 0$$
$$0.050x_1 + 0.084x_2 \qquad - b_2 \qquad\qquad \le \quad 0$$
$$0.100x_1 + 0.067x_2 \qquad\qquad - b_3 \qquad \le \quad 0$$
$$0.010x_1 + 0.025x_2 \qquad\qquad\qquad - b_4 \le \quad 0$$
$$b_1 \qquad\qquad \le 1000$$
$$b_2 \qquad\qquad \le \; 970$$
$$b_3 \qquad \le \; 800$$
$$b_4 \le \; 435$$
$$b_1 + \; b_2 \qquad\qquad \le 1400$$
$$b_3 + \; b_4 \le \; 935$$
$$x_1, x_2, b_1, b_2, b_3, b_4 \ge 0.$$

This linear programming model will actually solve two problems: (1) it will find the optimal product mix for the planning period, and (2) it will allocate the total labor resource to the departments in such a fashion that profits will be maximized. The solution to this six-variable, ten-constraint model is shown in Table 5.14.

Note that the optimal labor plan utilizes all 2335 hours of labor by making the most profitable allocations. In this particular solution there is no idle time in any of the departments. This will not always be the case in problems of this type; however, if the manager does have the freedom to assign certain employees to different departments, the effect will probably be a reduction in the overall idle time. The linear programming model automatically assigns such employees to the departments in the most profitable manner. If the manager had used judgment to allocate the hours to the departments, and we had then solved the product mix problem with fixed b_i, we would in all probability have found slack in some departments

TABLE 5.14. **Optimal Production Plan and Labor Allocation for McCarthy's Everyday Glass Company**

Production plan:	
Product 1 (x_1) = 4700 cases	
Product 2 (x_2) = 4543 cases	
Labor allocation:	
Department 1	783 hours
Department 2	617 hours
Department 3	774 hours
Department 4	161 hours
Total	2335 hours
Profit = $8789	

while other departments represented b̲o̲t̲t̲l̲e̲n̲e̲c̲k̲s̲ because of insufficient resources.

Variations in the basic formulation of this section might be used in situations such as allocating raw material resources to products, allocating machine time to products, and allocating sales force time to product lines or sales territories.

5.4   Accounting Applications

Audit Staff Assignments

A problem common to large and small CPA firms alike is the effective utilization of manpower resources. For many firms it is difficult to keep all employees engaged in productive (billable) assignments at certain times of the year. At other times—and this is more often the case—there is more work to be done than there are people to do it.

Especially at the busy or peak periods it is essential that the firm develop an efficient auditor-client schedule for its staff. In the following example we consider an audit staff assignment problem involving the assignment of senior accountants to manage audits so that all audits are completed with a minimum expenditure of staff hours.

The certified public accounting firm of Scott and Warner has three new clients who have just requested an audit by the firm. While the current auditing staff is overloaded, Scott and Warner would like to accommodate these new clients. After reviewing current audit progress reports, the manager in charge has identified four senior accountants who could possibly be assigned to supervise the audits for the new clients. However, all four senior accountants are busy, and therefore each could handle at the most one of the new clients. O̲v̲e̲r̲a̲l̲l̲ staff utilization is critical, and the firm wants to be sure that the new client assignments are made in the most efficient manner (that is, minimum total hour requirement).

The differences in experience and ability among the senior accountants will cause the estimated audit completion times to differ for the various auditor-client assignments. After considering all possible assignments, the manager has made estimates of the audit completion times for each possible assignment. These data are summarized in Table 5.15. It is estimated, for example, that Kirkman would require 170 hours to complete the Cincinnati Drug audit, while Warren would take 150 hours for this audit.

Let us attempt to formulate this auditor assignment problem as a linear programming problem. Once again we use double subscript notation for the decision variables:

$$x_{ij} = \begin{cases} 1 \text{ if senior accountant } i \text{ is assigned to client } j; \\ \quad i = 1,2,3,4; \ j = 1,2,3 \\ 0 \text{ otherwise.} \end{cases}$$

TABLE 5.15. Estimated Audit Completion Time (hours) for the Scott and Warner Accounting Firm

Senior Accountant	Cincinnati Drug	Client Pruitt Trucking	Strom Foods
Warren	**150**	**210**	**270**
Kirkman	170	230	220
Howard	180	230	225
Phipps	160	240	230

Wait a minute, you say. How can these variables be appropriate linear programming decision variables when they can only take on the values of zero or one? Technically you are correct; they cannot be. Actually, the problem we are solving is a zero–one integer programming problem. However, this problem has a very nice feature that makes it possible for us to treat it as a linear programming problem; that is, the values of all the basic variables will be either zero or one at the extreme points of the feasible region, and since the optimal solution to a linear program lies at an extreme point, we will satisfy the requirement that $x_{ij} = 0$ or 1.

Using the above decision variables, the objective function calling for a minimization of total hours can be written as

$$\min \quad 150x_{11} + 210x_{12} + 270x_{13}$$
$$+ 170x_{21} + 230x_{22} + 220x_{23}$$
$$+ 180x_{31} + 230x_{32} + 225x_{33}$$
$$+ 160x_{41} + 240x_{42} + 230x_{43}.$$

Constraints affecting this problem are that all three clients must be assigned exactly one senior accountant. These conditions are satisfied by the following constraints:

$$x_{11} + x_{21} + x_{31} + x_{41} = 1$$
$$x_{12} + x_{22} + x_{32} + x_{42} = 1$$
$$x_{13} + x_{23} + x_{33} + x_{43} = 1.$$

The fact that the firm will not allow any of the four senior accountants to take more than one additional assignment leads to the following set of constraints:

$$x_{11} + x_{12} + x_{13} \le 1 \quad \text{Warren}$$
$$x_{21} + x_{22} + x_{23} \le 1 \quad \text{Kirkman}$$
$$x_{31} + x_{32} + x_{33} \le 1 \quad \text{Howard}$$
$$x_{41} + x_{42} + x_{43} \le 1 \quad \text{Phipps.}$$

TABLE 5.16   Audit Staff Assignments for Scott and Warner

Client	Senior Accountant		Estimated Labor Hours
Cincinnati Drug	Phipps		160
Pruitt Trucking	Warren		210
Strom Foods	Kirkman		220
		Total	590
	Unassigned: Howard		

In addition, the nonnegativity constraints for all variables are included as usual.

The solution to this twelve-variable, seven-constraint linear programming model ($x_{12} = 1$, $x_{23} = 1$, $x_{41} = 1$) provides the auditor assignment plan that will minimize the total number of hours of staff time expended. This solution is shown in Table 5.16.

You will see in Chapter 6 that the problem we have just solved is a special linear program known as the assignment problem. In Chapter 6 you will also see a special solution procedure that has been developed for this class of problems.

For the audit staff assignment problem Summers[2] offers a more extensive linear programming formulation and analysis than we have presented in this section. Summers shows how additional constraints, such as

1.   maximum hours of auditor availability,
2.   maximum hours of auditor utilization,
3.   allowances for auditor vacation,
4.   assignments to professional development, and
5.   assignments to specific audit activities

can be included in a linear programming formulation of the audit staff assignment problem. In addition, he discusses other alternatives for the objective function, such as billable time and intangible benefits.

The Accounting Point of View

In attempting to classify linear programming applications for business and industry, we have found that in terms of problem content most applications are probably more readily identified as finance, marketing, or management oriented problems. However, if you consider the data requirements of these

---

[2]Summers, E. L., "The Audit Staff Assignment Problem: A Linear Programming Analysis," *Accounting Review*, July, 1972.

applications (costs, profit margins, and so on) you should begin to realize the importance of the accounting function in formulating linear programming models. Can you imagine trying to determine an optimal product mix without the accountant's analysis of material costs, labor costs, factory overhead, selling, and administrative expenses and the resulting product profitability?

Even if the applications of linear programming are not solely accounting problems, the accountant must still be aware of the business applications of the technique. Any time any department or division of a firm undertakes a cost control or a profit maximization project, the firm's accountants will become involved in the problem. The accountants must therefore be thoroughly familiar with the assumptions underlying linear programming approaches to these problems. With this background the accountant can provide valuable assistance in the formulation and evaluation of linear programming models. Thus we feel that numerous linear programming problems are accounting related applications. We mean this in the sense that much of the data necessary for linear programming applications are provided by the accountant. Since the success of the application is critically dependent on the reliability of the data used, the accountant's role in linear programming applications can be quite significant.

5.5   Ingredient Mix Applications

The Blending Problem

Blending problems arise whenever a manager must decide how to blend two or more resources in order to produce one or more products. In these situations the resources contain one or more essential ingredients that must be blended in such a manner that the final products will contain specific percentages of the essential ingredients. In most of these applications, then, management must decide how much of each resource to purchase in order to satisfy product specifications and product demands at minimum cost.

These types of problems occur frequently in the petroleum industry (such as blending crude oil to produce different-octane gasolines), chemical industry (such as blending chemicals to produce fertilizers, weed killers, and so on), and food industry (such as blending input ingredients to produce soft drinks, soups, and so on). Because of their widespread application, our objective in this section is to illustrate how linear programming can be applied to solve these types of problems.

Consider the case of Beauty Suds, Inc., manufacturer of Wonderful Hair Shampoo. Beauty Suds is considering the production of a new product, Wonderful Plus Hair Shampoo. The new product is a blend of the company's standard shampoo base product, a new dandruff preventive, a perfume, and deionized water. The company has specified the following final product characteristics per gallon manufactured:

	Minimum	Maximum
Suds-forming ingredient, grams	100	150
Dandruff ingredient, grams	50	50
Perfume ingredient, grams	20	30
Shampoo viscosity, centipoise	400	600

The cost and general characteristics of the four raw materials are as follows:

	Shampoo Base	Dandruff Preventive	Perfume	Deionized Water
Suds ingredient, g/gal	150	0	0	0
Dandruff ingredient, g/gal	10	500	0	0
Perfume ingredient, g/gal	15	0	200	0
Viscosity, centipoise	700	600	400	5
Cost per gallon	$3.00	$15.00	$60.00	$0.25

Assuming that all quantities of ingredients blend linearly by volume, the management of Beauty Suds would like to know how much of each raw material should be in each gallon of the new shampoo product in order to meet product requirements at minimum cost.

In order to formulate a linear programming model for the Beauty Suds blending problem, we begin by defining appropriate decision variables. Let

x_1 = gallons of standard shampoo base per gallon of shampoo,

x_2 = gallons of dandruff preventive per gallon of shampoo,

x_3 = gallons of perfume per gallon of shampoo,

x_4 = gallons of deionized water per gallon of shampoo.

The objective function for our problem can then be written as follows:

$$\min 3x_1 + 15x_2 + 60x_3 + 0.25x_4$$

To meet the requirements for the minimum and maximum amounts of suds-forming ingredient, dandruff ingredient, perfume ingredient, and shampoo viscosity, we formulate the following set of constraints:

$$
\begin{aligned}
150x_1 & & \leq 150 & \quad \Big\} \text{ suds} \\
150x_1 & & \geq 100 & \\
10x_1 & + 500x_2 & = 50 & \quad \text{dandruff} \\
15x_1 & + 200x_3 & \leq 30 & \quad \Big\} \text{ perfume} \\
15x_1 & + 200x_3 & \geq 20 &
\end{aligned}
$$

$$700x_1 + 600x_2 + 400x_3 + 5x_4 \geq 400$$
$$700x_1 + 600x_2 + 400x_3 + 5x_4 \leq 600$$

viscosity

In addition, to guarantee that the amount of raw material blended will produce exactly one gallon of Wonderful Plus Hair Shampoo, we require that

$$x_1 + x_2 + x_3 + x_4 = 1.$$

At the optimal solution, then, if management requires 1000 gallons of the new product, they need only multiply the values of the decision variables by 1000. (Equivalently, we could have replaced the right-hand side of this constraint by 1000 and realized exactly the same solution.)

After adding the usual nonnegativity requirements, the complete linear programming model was solved using the Simplex method. The optimal solution is shown in Table 5.17.

We see that the optimal solution to the problem not only tells management how to blend the available resources to meet product specifications, but also provides the cost of doing so. This additional information is often the most critical piece of information from management's point of view. For example, suppose a priori that management felt that it could not market the product unless the cost of raw materials for the new product was less than $7 per gallon. Given this a priori assessment, should management produce the new product? Clearly the answer is yes, since the linear programming solution to the problem shows management that the raw materials cost to produce the new product is $6.16 per gallon.

In the Beauty Suds blending problem that we formulated as a linear programming model, we saw a problem situation wherein four different resources were blended to produce one product. In many blending problems, however, a number of different products must be produced. A descriptive approach to defining appropriate decision variables for these more general blending problems is to use double subscripted decision variables. The first subscript can be used to denote the resource and the second subscript to

TABLE 5.17   Optimal Solution for the
             Beauty Suds, Inc. Blending
             Problem

Material	Quantity (gallons)
Shampoo base	0.759
Dandruff preventive	0.085
Perfume	0.043
Water	0.113
Cost per gallon = $6.16	

denote the product. Thus we let x_{ij} be the amount (such as gallons) of resource i used to produce product j. Problem 15 at the end of this chapter describes a gasoline blending situation where decision variables of the above type can be applied.

The Diet Problem

The diet problem is presented in this chapter in order to introduce the reader to this well-known application of linear programming. Typically the diet problem, or in agricultural applications the feed mix problem, involves specifying a food or feed ingredient combination that will satisfy some minimal nutritional requirements at a minimum total cost. As a result, some authors view the diet problem as a special case of the general blending problem.

Let us consider the feed mix form of the diet problem encountered by Bluegrass Farms, Inc. in Lexington, Kentucky. This company is experimenting with a special diet for its race horses. The feed components available for the diet are a standard horse feed product, a vitamin enriched oat product, and a new vitamin and mineral feed additive. Table 5.18 shows the nutritional values and costs for the three components.

Suppose that the horse trainer sets the minimum daily diet requirement at 3 units of ingredient A, 6 units of ingredient B, and 4 units of ingredient C. Also suppose that for weight control the trainer does not want the total daily feed to exceed 6 pounds. What is the optimal daily mix of the three components?

A linear programming model of this diet problem can be formulated as follows: Let

$$x_1 = \text{pounds of the standard feed,}$$
$$x_2 = \text{pounds of the enriched oats,}$$
$$x_3 = \text{pounds of the additive.}$$

With the overall goal of minimizing cost, the objective function becomes

$$\min 0.25x_1 + 0.50x_2 + 3.00x_3.$$

TABLE 5.18   Units of Feed Ingredient per Pound of Feed Component

Diet Requirement	Standard	Feed Component Enriched Oats	Additive
Ingredient A	0.8	0.2	0
Ingredient B	1.0	1.5	3.0
Ingredient C	0.1	0.6	2.0
Cost per pound	$0.25	$0.50	$3.00

Using the information provided, the constraints for our problem are easily formulated as follows:

$$0.8x_1 + 0.2x_2 \qquad\qquad \geq 3 \qquad \text{ingredient A}$$
$$1.0x_1 + 1.5x_2 + 3.0x_3 \geq 6 \qquad \text{ingredient B}$$
$$0.1x_1 + 0.6x_2 + 2.0x_3 \geq 4 \qquad \text{ingredient C}$$
$$x_1 + \quad x_2 + \quad x_3 \leq 6 \qquad \text{total weight}$$
$$x_1, x_2, x_3 \geq 0.$$

The minimum-cost feed mix solution for the above linear programming model is given in Table 5.19.

As we saw in the blending problem, the optimal solution for the Bluegrass Farms linear programming model tells management not only how to mix the three components to produce the desired product but also the cost of doing so. This latter piece of information is often the first thing management wants to know. For example, if Bluegrass Farms is presently purchasing a feed mix with similar characteristics for a daily cost of less than $5.97, it is doubtful whether they would consider producing this new special diet except on an experimental basis.

5.6 Goal Programming Applications

Linear programming problems are limited to a single objective, such as the maximization of profit or the minimization of cost. However, on occasion, managers or decision makers face problem situations in which more than one objective exists. Goal programming has been developed as a procedure for handling multiple-objective situations within the general framework of linear programming. Each objective is viewed as a "goal." Then, given the usual resouce limitations or constraints, the manager attempts to develop decisions that provide the "best" solution in terms of coming *as close as possible* to reaching all goals. Although the goal programming philosophy for dealing with multiple objectives has been extended to nonlinear as well as linear programming models, we will limit our discussion in this text to linear goal programming problems.

To better understand the goal programming approach, let us consider a problem faced by McKenna Office Supplies, Inc. McKenna's management establishes monthly performance goals for its sales force. While each individual on the sales force has a volume quota for the month, McKenna

TABLE 5.19 Minimum-Cost Diet for Bluegrass Farms, Inc.

Standard feed, pounds	3.51
Enriched oats, pounds	0.95
Vitamin additive, pounds	1.54
Total, pounds	6.00
Daily cost = $5.97	

also specifies goals or quotas for the types of customers contacted. For example, McKenna's customer contact strategy for next month calls for the sales force to make 200 contacts with customers who have previously purchased supplies from the firm. In addition, the strategy calls for 120 contacts of new customers. The purpose of this latter quota or goal is to ensure that the sales force is continuing to investigate new sources of sales.

Making allowances for travel and waiting time, as well as for demonstration and direct sales time, McKenna has allocated two hours of sales force effort to each contact of a previous customer. New customer contacts tend to take longer and have an allocation rate of three hours per contact. For the upcoming month, McKenna projects a maximum of 640 hours of sales force time available for both previous and new customer contacts.

Although you might first think of the 200 previous customer contacts and the 120 new customer contacts as constraints, we will view them as objectives, or goals, for the next month. The question is, Does McKenna have sufficient sales force resources to realize both of these customer contact goals? The goals of 200 previous customer and 120 new customer contacts require a total of $2(200) + 3(120) = 760$ hours, but only 640 hours of sales force time is available. Thus, we see McKenna cannot satisfy both goals simultaneously. This is the type of situation for which the goal programming approach was developed; the goals are in conflict and cannot be achieved simultaneously. An allocation of sales force effort in the direction of reaching the new customer contact goal will reduce the time available and hence contacts possible for previous customers. The opposite effect occurs if the firm allocates sales force effort in the direction of reaching the contact goal for previous customers.

Let us proceed with a goal programming formulation of McKenna's problem. An important first step in goal programming is to explicitly state the goals. For the McKenna Office Supplies problem the goals can be stated as follows:

Goal 1:   Reach 200 previous customers,
Goal 2:   Reach 120 new customers.

Note that each goal has a stated target value: 200 and 120 in our example. This is a property of all goal programming models. That is, rather than stating objectives in terms of maximizing or minimizing some quantity or group of quantities, the objectives or goals are expressed in terms of reaching a desired quantity or level for each goal.

Once we have listed the goals with appropriate target values, we can proceed with the goal programming model. The next step is the key to a goal programming problem formulation: *each goal or objective is written in the form of a constraint.* Considering the first goal of reaching 200 previous customers and letting

x_1 = number of previous customers contacted,

we could write the constraint as

$$1x_1 = 200.$$

However, the above constraint form would require meeting the previous customer goal exactly, which we have seen may not be possible. Thus we add *deviation variables* which reflect the amount the final solution deviates from the stated goals. For example, for the previous customer contact goal, we would add the following deviation variables.

d_1^+ = number of previous customer contacts over the desired 200,

d_1^- = number of previous customer contacts under the desired 200.

Note that this notation associates the letter d with the deviation from the goal. A superscript of plus or minus is used to indicate whether the solution exceeds or falls below the stated goal. Including the deviation variables, we could write the constraint as

$$1x_1 = 200 + 1d_1^+ - 1d_1^-$$

Thus these deviation variables allow us to miss the goal and still obtain a feasible solution. For example, if $x_1 = 220$ in the final solution, d_1^+ would be 20 to reflect the overachievement of the goal by 20 contacts; d_1^- in this case would be zero. If $x_1 = 175$, then $d_1^- = 25$ and $d_1^+ = 0$ in order to reflect the 25 contacts short of the 200 goal.[3] Rewriting this constraint with all the variables on the left-hand side, the model constraint for the 200 previous customer contact goal would be written

$$1x_1 - 1d_1^+ + 1d_1^- = 200.$$

The next step is to develop a similar constraint in order to reflect the second goal of reaching 120 new customers, Letting

x_2 = number of new customers contacted,

d_2^+ = number of new customer contacts over the desired 120,

d_2^- = number of new customer contacts under the desired 120,

the constraint for the new customer goal would be written as follows:

$$1x_2 - 1d_2^+ + 1d_2^- = 120.$$

The sales force availability constraint can be handled just as in previous linear programming models. It would be written as

$$2x_1 + 3x_2 \leq 640.$$

We now have three constraints and six decision variables which combine to reflect the two goals and the one resource constraint. If we can now develop an objective function, we will have a linear goal programming model with six variables and three constraints. What is the appropriate objective function?

Recall that in the original discussion of the problem we identified two objectives or goals. Note that in terms of our deviation variables d_1^+, d_1^-, d_2^+,

---

[3]In using the Simplex method to solve this type of problem we will never have both d_1^+ and d_1^- positive. Such a solution would not make sense anyway, since we could not simultaneously over- and underachieve a goal.

and d_2^-, if we can make all of these variables zero, we have in fact reached the goals exactly with $x_1 = 200$ and $x_2 = 120$. However, even if the deviation variables cannot be reduced to zero, we can at least work to reduce them to their minimum possible values. Small values for the deviation variables are attractive because they imply small deviations from the goals. This is why the objective function in goal programming calls for minimizing the weighted sum of the deviation variables. The deviation variables portion of the objective function for McKenna's problem can be written as follows:

$$\text{min} \quad 0d_1^+ + 1d_1^- + 0d_2^+ + 1d_2^-.$$

Note that d_1^+ and d_2^+, which correspond to an overachievement of goals, have been given zero weights or coefficients. The reason for this is that there is no penalty for overachieving the two goals. On the other hand, the d_1^- and d_2^- variables have both been given weights of 1, indicating that management attaches equal importance to deviations from the two goals. Since the firm's overall objective is to minimize the combined underachievement of the two goals, the complete goal programming model can be written as follows:

$$\text{min} \quad 0x_1 + 0x_2 + 0d_1^+ + 1d_1^- + 0d_2^+ + 1d_2^-$$
$$\text{s.t.}$$
$$1x_1 \quad\quad - 1d_1^+ + 1d_1^- \quad\quad\quad\quad = 200$$
$$1x_2 \quad\quad\quad\quad - 1d_2^+ + 1d_2^- = 120$$
$$2x_1 + 3x_2 \quad\quad\quad\quad\quad\quad \leq 640$$
$$x_1, x_2, d_1^+, d_1^-, d_2^+, d_2^- \geq 0.$$

Since the above is a linear programming model, we can use the Simplex method to solve the problem. The optimal solution is as follows:

$$x_1 = 200$$
$$x_2 = 80$$
$$d_1^+ = 0$$
$$d_1^- = 0$$
$$d_2^+ = 0$$
$$d_2^- = 40$$

We see the previous customer contact goal is reached while the new customer contact goal is underachieved by $d_2^- = 40$.

With the goal programming approach to the McKenna problem in mind, let us summarize the characteristics common to all linear goal programming models:

1. Each goal appears in a separate constraint with the right-hand-side value indicating the target value for the goal.
2. Deviation variables d_i^+ and d_i^- are included for each goal in order to reflect the possible overachievement or underachievement of the goal.

3. Other constraints, reflecting resource capacities or other restrictions, are included just as they would be in any linear programming model.
4. The objective function requires minimizing the weighted sum of the deviation variables. Coefficients (weights) for the deviation variables in the objective function reflect the relative "cost" or "penalty" for each unit deviation from the corresponding goal's target value. Zero coefficients mean that the corresponding deviations from the target values carry no penalty.

In order to appreciate some of the flexibility offered by the goal programming approach, note that in the linear goal programming model of the McKenna problem we assigned a weight (coefficient) of 1 to a one-unit underachievement of each goal (d_1^- and d_2^-). This implied that a one-unit underachievement of one goal was just as undesirable as a one-unit under-achievement of the other goal. However, suppose McKenna's management was very much concerned about contacting new customers in order to provide growth in future sales. In fact, suppose that on a per-unit basis management felt the new customer contacts were twice as important as the previous customer contacts. The changed relative importance of the two goals can be reflected by altering the weights or coefficients for the deviation variables in the objective function. This reevaluation of the importance of new customer contacts could be expressed with the following objective function:

$$\text{min} \quad 0x_1 + 0x_2 + 0d_1^+ + 1d_1^- + 0d_2^+ + 2d_2^-.$$

Using the same three constraints and the revised objective function, the following goal programming solution is obtained:

$$x_1 = 140$$
$$x_2 = 120$$
$$d_1^+ = 0$$
$$d_1^- = 60$$
$$d_2^+ = 0$$
$$d_2^- = 0$$

The increased importance of goal 2 now leads to reaching the new customer goal while underachieving the previous customer goal by $d_1^- = 60$.

A further extension of goal programming provides the capability of specifying different priority levels for each of the goals or objectives. This extension is valuable in situations where one goal is so much more important than the others that the decision maker is unwilling to "trade off" satisfaction of the one goal for any amount of deviation reduction in another goal. In the McKenna problem, while we might select different objective function coefficients, or weights, to reflect the relative importance of the goals, the problem contained only one priority level, since the objective function and constraints permitted "trading off" the satisfaction of one goal for the satisfaction of the other.

In goal programming problems with priority levels the first priority (P_1) goals are treated in an objective function much like the one used in the McKenna problem. Second priority (P_2) goals are considered only after the optimal solution has been found using the P_1 goals. After the solution with P_1 goals is found, an objective function containing P_2 goals is then used. The solution is revised under the P_2 goal objective function as long as it does not cause a reduction in achievement of the P_1 goals. In this extension of goal programming, P_1 goals are considered first, then P_2 goals, then P_3 goals, etc. At each stage a solution revision can be made as long as it causes no reduction in achievement of the higher priority goals.

Solution procedures for goal programming problems with varying priority levels require some modification of the Simplex method. While we will not attempt to discuss the details of the modification in this text, realize that the goal programming problem presented in this section illustrates how multiple objectives may be important to the decision maker and how the goal programming approach extends the applications of linear programming to multiple objective problems.

5.7   Environmental Protection Application

While linear programming has been applied primarily in business and industrial settings, the technique is, of course, not limited to these fields. Applications of linear programming to health care, environmental protection, and a variety of other problems society is currently faced with have been made. In this section we describe a problem that, although similar to some of the industrial problems we have studied in earlier sections, incorporates environmental considerations. Specifically, the linear programming model we present will assist a firm in making policy decisions of an antipollution nature.

We consider the problem faced by Skillings Industrial Chemicals, Inc., a refinery located in southwestern Ohio near the Ohio River. The company's major product is manufactured from a chemical process that requires two raw materials, A and B. The production of 1 pound of product requires 1 pound of material A and 2 pounds of material B. The output of this process also yields 1 pound of liquid waste materials and a solid waste byproduct. The solid waste byproduct is given to a local fertilizer plant as payment for picking up the byproduct. Since the liquid waste material has virtually no market value, and since it is in liquid form, the refinery has been dumping it directly into the Ohio River. Skillings's manufacturing process is shown schematically in Figure 5.2.

Recent governmental pollution guidelines established by the Environmental Protection Agency will not permit this liquid waste disposal process to continue. Hence the refinery's research group has developed the following set of alternative uses for the waste material:

1. Produce a secondary product (K) by adding 1 pound of raw material A to every pound of liquid waste.

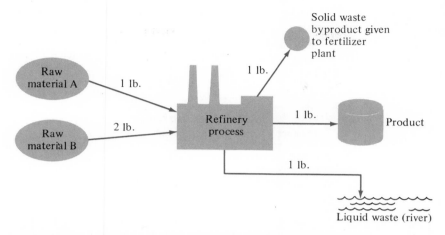

FIGURE 5.2 **Manufacturing Process at Skillings Industrial Chemicals, Inc.**

2. Produce another secondary product (M) by adding 1 pound of raw material B to every pound of liquid waste.
3. Specially treat the liquid waste so that it meets pollution standards before dumping it directly into the river.

These three alternatives are depicted in Figure 5.3.

The company's management knows that the secondary products will be low in quality and will probably not be very profitable. Management is also aware of the fact that the special treatment alternative will be a relatively expensive operation. The company's problem is to determine how to satisfy the pollution regulations and still maintain the highest possible profit. How should the waste material be handled? Should Skillings produce product K, product M, use the special treatment, or employ some combination of the three alternatives?

Since the waste disposal process will affect the production of the firm's primary product, the complete system—manufacturing process and waste disposal process—will have to be considered together in the analysis.

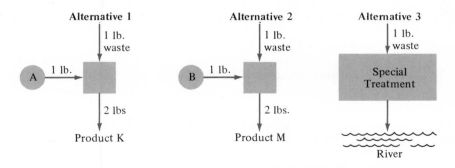

FIGURE 5.3 **Alternatives for Handling the Refinery Liquid Waste Material**

Skillings wants to be able to satisfy the antipollution requirements and still make a satisfactory profit.

Considering the selling price, material costs, and labor costs, the accounting department has prepared the following information with respect to product profit contribution:

Product	Profit Contribution per Pound
Primary	$2.10
Product K	−0.10
Product M	0.15

As you can see, the primary product is very profitable, while the secondary products are marginal. In fact, product K can be produced only at a loss. However, since product K provides a means for disposing of the waste material, it must still be considered as an alternative. Furthermore, suppose that the special treatment disposal cost is $0.25 per pound.

The ingredients required to make 1 pound of each product are summarized in Table 5.20.

Additional restrictions on our problem result from the fact that during any planning period the company will have limited amounts of raw materials available. During the production period of interest in our current problem, these maxima are 5000 pounds of material A and 7000 pounds of material B.

Let us see how we can formulate a linear programming model that will help management solve this problem. We let

x_1 = pounds of primary product,

x_2 = pounds of secondary product K,

x_3 = pounds of secondary product M,

x_4 = pounds of liquid waste material processed by the special treatment.

Assuming that the liquid waste material is a zero-cost, zero-profit by-product of the primary process, it will incur additional cost only if it has to be specially treated. Thus the objective function can be written as

$$\max \quad 2.10x_1 - 0.10x_2 + 0.15x_3 - 0.25x_4.$$

Table 5.20.　Pounds of Ingredient Required per Pound of Product

Ingredients	Primary Product	Product K	Product M
Raw material A	1	0.5	0.0
Raw material B	2	0.0	0.5
Waste	0	0.5	0.5

The raw material constraints are

$$1x_1 + 0.5x_2 \qquad \le 5000$$
$$2x_1 \qquad + 0.5x_3 \le 7000.$$

We note that the production of both product K (x_2) and product M (x_3) depends upon the amount of liquid waste material available. Hence we must include a constraint on the amount of products x_2, x_3, and x_4 that can be produced. Since all the liquid waste material must be disposed of, we must require that

$$0.5x_2 + 0.5x_3 + 1x_4 = \text{total liquid waste material available.}$$

Since the amount of total liquid waste material generated is equal to the amount of primary product produced (see Figure 5.2), we can write the above requirements as

$$0.5x_2 + 0.5x_3 + 1x_4 = 1x_1$$

or

$$- 1x_1 + 0.5x_2 + 0.5x_3 + 1x_4 = 0.$$

The solution to this four-variable, three-constraint linear programming model provides the most profitable production and pollution control plan. The complete solution is shown in Table 5.21.

We see that the optimal solution to our linear programming model involves the production of product K and specially treated waste, both of which result in losses for the company. Does this seem reasonable in view of the fact that product M will enable Skillings to dispose of waste and still realize some contribution to profit? Let us see if we can answer this question by analyzing the optimal solution a bit more carefully.

In our model the primary product was so profitable when compared to the alternatives that we produced as much primary product as possible. Since B was the limiting raw material resource, all of B was used up in the production of the primary product. Thus, since product M required raw

Table 5.21.   Optimal Production and Waste Management Plan for Skillings, Inc.

	Production (pounds)	Profit
Primary product	3500	$7350
Waste disposal		
Product K	3000	−$300
Specially treated waste	2000	−$500
	Total	$6550

material B, it was impossible to produce any amount of product M. Hence the waste material generated had to be disposed of using product K and the specially treated waste process.

Summary

In this chapter we have presented a broad range of situations which are illustrative of how linear programming can be a useful decision-making aid. Using a variety of application situations, we have formulated and solved problems from the areas of finance, marketing, management, and accounting. In addition, we have shown how linear programming can be applied to blending and diet problems. Goal programming was introduced to show how multiple objectives or goals could be handled with a linear programming solution technique. An application involving environmental protection showed the flexibility of linear programming in solving social problems.

All the illustrations presented in this chapter have been simplified versions of actual situations in which linear programming has been applied. In real-world applications the reader will find that the problem is not as concisely stated, that the data are not as readily available, and that the problem has a larger number of variables and constraints. However, a thorough study of the applications in this chapter is a good place for the reader who eventually hopes to apply linear programming to real-world problems to begin.

For the reader interested in learning about additional applications of linear programming, we suggest a text by Gass.[4] In this text the author presents a bibliography of over one hundred business and industrial applications of the linear programming technique.

Problems

1. *Product Mix.* A small job shop has purchased a new drill press which can be operated 40 hours per week. Two products are to be manufactured with this equipment. Product 1, which has a profit of 30 cents per unit, requires 1.2 minutes per unit, and product 2, which has a profit of 50 cents per unit, requires 1.5 minutes per unit. Based on current orders, 1000 units of product 1 and 500 units of product 2 must be manufactured each week.
   a. If the firm can sell all the units it produces, how many units of each product should be manufactured each week?
   b. What is the profit contribution of an overtime hour for the drill press? Is there an upper limit on the amount of overtime you would want? Explain.
2. *Media Selection.* The Westchester Chamber of Commerce periodically sponsors public service seminars and programs which are open to the public. Currently, promotional plans are under way for this year's program. Advertising alternatives include television, radio, and newspaper. Audience estimates, costs, and maximum

[4]Gass, S. J., *An Illustrated Guide to Linear Programming,* New York, McGraw-Hill, 1970.

media usage limitations are shown below:

	Television	Media Radio	Newspaper
Audience per advertisement	100,000	18,000	40,000
Cost per advertisement	$1,000	$150	$300
Maximum media usage limitation	10	20	10

If the promotional budget is limited to $10,000, how many commercial messages should be run on each medium in order to maximize total audience contact? What is the allocation of the $10,000 budget among the three media, and what is the total audience reached?

3. *Overtime Planning.* In Chapter 2 we presented a problem faced by Par, Inc. which involved production quantity decisions for standard (x_1) and deluxe (x_2) golf bags. The linear programming model for this problem is restated below:

$$\max \quad 10x_1 + 9x_2$$
$$\text{s.t.}$$
$$\tfrac{7}{10}x_1 + 1x_2 \le 630 \quad \text{cutting and dyeing}$$
$$\tfrac{1}{2}x_1 + \tfrac{5}{6}x_2 \le 600 \quad \text{sewing}$$
$$1x_1 + \tfrac{2}{3}x_2 \le 708 \quad \text{finishing}$$
$$\tfrac{1}{10}x_1 + \tfrac{1}{4}x_2 \le 135 \quad \text{inspection and packaging}$$
$$x_1, x_2 \ge 0$$

The optimal solution called for 540 standard bags and 252 deluxe bags, with an associated profit of $7668. The cutting and dyeing and the finishing departments were "bottleneck" departments in that all available production time in these departments was used.

Management now believes an additional 80 hours of finishing time can be obtained by having finishing department employees work overtime. However, because of differing wage rates between regular and overtime labor, standard bags produced with finishing department overtime will have a $3 added cost per bag, while deluxe bags produced with finishing department overtime will have a $2 added cost per bag. Let

x_1 = number of standard bags, regular time,

x_2 = number of deluxe bags, regular time,

x_3 = number of standard bags using finishing department overtime,

x_4 = number of deluxe bags using finishing department overtime.

Formulate a linear programming model that can be used to determine optimal production quantities in the finishing department if overtime is made available. What are the recommended production quantities, and what is the revised profit? What is the increase in profit if the overtime is used?

4. *Marketing Strategy.* In the marketing strategy problem encountered by Electronic Communications, Inc. (see Section 5.2) we found the advertising budget and sales

force availability were the limiting constraints. Assume an additional $2000 is available for advertising and an additional 300 hours is available in sales force effort. How does the optimal solution change?

5. *Investment and Loan Planning.* The employee credit union at State University is planning the usage of funds for the coming year. The credit union makes four types of loans to its members. In addition, it invests in "risk-free" securities in order to stabilize income. The various revenue producing investments together with annual rates of return are as follows:

Type of Loan/Investment	Annual Rate of Return (%)
Secured loans	
Automobile	8
Furniture	10
Other secured loans	11
Signature loans	12
"Risk-free" securities	9

State laws and credit union policies impose the following restrictions on the composition of the credit union's loans and investments:

1. "Risk-free" securities may not exceed 30% of the total funds.
2. Signature loans may not exceed 10% of total loans.
3. Furniture loans plus "other secured loans" may not exceed 50% of the total of the three types of secured loans.
4. Signature loans plus "other secured loans" may not exceed the amount invested in "risk-free" securities.

If the firm projects $2 million available for loans and investments during the coming year, how should the funds be allocated to each of the loan investment alternatives in order to maximize total annual return? What is the projected annual dollar return?

6. *Market Research Survey.* Market Surveys, Inc. specializes in evaluating consumer reaction to new products, services, and/or advertising campaigns. A client has just asked Market Survey to provide information on consumer reaction to a recently marketed new product. The client's contract calls for a door-to-door, personal interview survey with the following stipulations:

1. Survey at least 400 households with children.
2. Survey at least 200 households with no children.
3. The total number of households contacted during the evening should be at least as great as the number contacted during the day.
4. The total sample must be at least 1000 households.

Based upon previous interviews, management has developed the following interview costs:

Household	Interview Cost	
	Day	Evening
Children	$10	$12
No children	$ 8	$10

What household time-of-day survey plan should the company use in order to minimize interview costs while satisfying the contract requirements?

7. *Blending Problem.* Ajax Fuels, Inc. is developing a new additive for airplane fuels. The additive is a mixture of three liquid ingredients: A, B, and C. For proper performance, the total amount of additive (amount of A + amount of B + amount of C) must be at least 10 ounces per gallon of fuel. However, because of safety reasons, the amount of additive must not exceed 15 ounces per gallon of fuel. The mix or blend of the three ingredients is critical. At least 1 ounce of ingredient A must be used for every ounce of ingredient B. The amount of ingredient C must be greater than $\frac{1}{2}$ the amount of ingredient A. If the cost per ounce for ingredients A, B, and C is $0.10, $0.03, and $0.09, respectively, find the minimum cost mixture of A, B, and C for each gallon of airplane fuel.

8. *Labor Planning.* G Kunz and Sons, Inc. manufactures two products used in the heavy equipment industry. Both products require manufacturing operations in two departments. Production time in hours and profit figures for the two products are as follows:

	Product 1	Product 2
Profit/unit	$25	$20
Dept. A hours	6	8
Dept. B hours	12	10

For the coming production period, Kunz has a total of 900 hours of labor available which can be allocated to either of the two departments. Let b_1 be the hours assigned to department A and b_2 be the hours assigned to department B. Find the production plan and labor allocation (hours assigned in each department) that will maximize profits.

9. *Portfolio Selection.* National Insurance Associates carries an investment portfolio on a variety of stocks, bonds, and other investment alternatives. Currently $200,000 of funds has become available and must be considered for new investment opportunities. The four stock options National is considering and the relevant financial data are as follows:

	Investment Alternative			
	A	B	C	D
Price per share	$100	$50	$80	$40
Annual rate of return	0.12	0.08	0.06	0.10
Risk measure per dollar invested (higher values indicate greater risk)	0.10	0.07	0.05	0.08

The risk measure indicates the relative uncertainty associated with the stock in terms of its realizing the projected annual return. The risk measures are provided by the firm's top financial advisor.

National's top management has stipulated the following investment guidelines:

1. Annual rate of return for the portfolio must be at least 9%.

2. No one stock can account for more than 50% of the total dollar investment.

a. Use linear programming to develop an investment portfolio that minimizes risk.

b. If the firm ignores risk and uses a maximum return on investment strategy, what is the investment portfolio?

c. What is the dollar difference between the portfolio recommended in parts a and b? Why might the company prefer the model development in part a?

10. *Production Routing.* Lurix Electronics manufactures two products which can be produced on two different production lines. Both products have their lowest production costs when produced on the more modern of the two production lines. However, the modern production line does not have the capacity to handle the total production. As a result, some production will have to be routed to an older production line facility. Shown below are the data for total production requirements, production line capacities, and production costs.

	Production Cost/Unit		Minimum Production
	Modern Line	Old Line	Requirements
Product 1	$3.00	$5.00	500 units
Product 2	$2.50	$4.00	700 units
Production line capacities	800	600	

Formulate the linear programming model that can be used to make the production routing decision. What is the recommended decision and the total cost? (Use notation of the form x_{11} = units of product 1 produced on line 1.)

11. *Purchasing.* Edwards Manufacturing Company purchases two component parts from three different suppliers. The suppliers have limited capacity, and no one supplier can meet all of Edwards' needs. In addition, the suppliers differ in the prices charged for the components. Component price data are as follows:

	Supplier		
	1	2	3
Price/unit— component 1	$12	$13	$14
Price/unit— component 2	$10	$11	$10

Each supplier has a limited capacity in terms of the total number of components it can supply. However, as long as Edwards provides sufficient advance orders, each supplier can devote its capacity to component 1, component 2, or any mix or combination of two components as long as the total number of units ordered is within its capacity. Supplier capacities are as follows:

	Total Components Capacity
Supplier 1	600
Supplier 2	1000
Supplier 3	800

If the Edwards production plan for the next production period includes 1000 units of component 1 and 800 units of component 2, what purchases do you recommend? That is, how many units of each component should be ordered from each supplier? What is the total purchase cost for the components? (For practice in using double subscripted decision variables, use notation of the form x_{ij} = number of units of component i purchased from supplier j.)

12. *Sales Territory Assignments.* Wilson Distributors, Inc. is opening two new sales territories in the Western states. Three individuals currently selling in Midwest and Eastern states are being considered for promotion to regional sales manager positions in the two new sales territories. Management has estimated total annual sales (in thousands of dollars) for the assignment of each individual to each sales territory. The management sale projections are as follows:

Regional Managers	Sales Region	
	Northwest	Southwest
Bostock	$100	$95
McMahon	$85	$80
Miller	$90	$75

Which sales manager–sales territory assignments will maximize total sales? Formulate and solve a linear programming model for this problem. (Hint: This problem is similar to the auditor assignment problem of Section 5.4.)

13. *Investment Planning.* The management of the Bordon Investment Company has three investment opportunities to consider over the next eighteen months. The investments differ in terms of availability date, duration, rate of return, and maximum dollar amount. The data as summarized by one of the firm's financial analysts are as follows:

Investment	Available	Duration	Projected Annual Rate of Return	Maximum Amount
Mutual fund A	Now	No limit	0.09	No limit
Bond B	Now	12 months	0.12	$50,000
Stock C	6 months	No limit	0.14	$25,000

While the firm can purchase the mutual fund anytime and the stock anytime after the first six months, the bond investment is available only at the start of the eighteen-month period. If the bond investment is made, the investment plus interest will not be available for reinvesting until after twelve months.

a. If the firm has $60,000 to invest over the next eighteen months, develop the investment plan for each six-month period that will maximize the return. Note that since investment decisions are made every six months, the rate of return over each six-month period will be one-half the annual rate. Assume that the total funds available to the firm at the start of period 2 are the original $60,000 plus any six-month interest from the mutual fund and that the total funds available at the start of period 3 are the $60,000 plus interest from all previous investments. Show your investment recommendations in the following format, with the amounts invested appearing where the dashes are now:

Investment	Investment Plan		
	Period 1	Period 2	Period 3
Mutual fund A	—	—	—
Bond B	—	Same as period 1	Not available
Stock C	Not available	—	—

b. If the company changed the upper limit on the stock to a maximum of $50,000, what would happen? Use the shadow price to help you answer this before you resolve the problem.

14. *Make or Buy*. The Carson Stapler Manufacturing Company forecasts a 5000-unit demand for its Sure-Hold model during the next quarter. This stapler is assembled from three major components: base, staple cartridge, and handle. Until now Carson has manufactured all three components. However, the 5000 forecasted units is a new high in sales volume, and it is doubtful that the firm will have production capacity to make all the components. The company is considering contracting a local firm to produce at least some of the components.

The production time requirements per unit are as follows:

Departments	Base (hours)	Cartridge (hours)	Handle (hours)	Total Department Time Available (hours)
A	0.03	0.02	0.05	400
B	0.04	0.02	0.04	400
C	0.02	0.03	0.01	400

After considering the firm's overhead, material, and labor costs, the accounting department has determined the unit manufacturing cost for each component. These data, along with the purchase price quotations by the contracting firm, are as follows:

Component	Manufacturing Cost	Purchase Cost
Base	$0.75	$0.95
Cartridge	$0.40	$0.55
Handle	$1.10	$1.40

a. Determine the make-or-buy decision for Carson that will meet the 5000-unit demand at a minimum total cost. How many units of each component should be made and how many purchased?

b. Which departments are limiting the manufacturing volume? If overtime could be considered at the additional cost of $3 per hour, which department(s) should be allocated the overtime? Explain.

c. Suppose that up to 80 hours of overtime can be scheduled in department A. What do you recommend?

15. *Blending Problem.* Seastrand Oil Company produces two grades of gasoline: regular and high octane. Both types of gasoline are produced by blending two types of crude oil. Although both types of crude oil contain the two important ingredients required to produce both gasolines, the percentage of important ingredients in each type of crude oil differs, as well as the cost per gallon. The percentage of ingredients A and B in each type of crude oil, and the cost per gallon, are shown below.

Type of Crude Oil	Cost	Ingredient A	Ingredient B	
1	$0.10	20%	60%	Crude 1 is 60%
2	$0.15	50%	30%	ingredient B.

Each gallon of regular must contain at least 40% of A, whereas each gallon of high octane can contain at most 50% of B. Daily demand for regular octane gasoline is 800,000 gallons, and daily demand for high octane is 500,000 gallons. How many gallons of each type of crude oil should be used in regular and in high octane gasoline in order to satisfy daily demand at a minimum cost? Define the four decision variables as follows:

x_{11} = gallons of crude 1 used in regular gasoline,

x_{12} = gallons of crude 1 used in high octane gasoline,

x_{21} = gallons of crude 2 used in regular gasoline,

x_{22} = gallons of crude 2 used in high octane gasoline.

16. *Paper Trim Problem.* The Ferguson Paper Company produces rolls of paper for use in adding machines, desk calculators, and cash registers. The rolls, which are 200 feet long, are produced in widths of $1\frac{1}{2}$, $2\frac{1}{2}$, and $3\frac{1}{2}$ inches. The production process provides 200-foot rolls in 10-inch widths only. The firm must therefore cut the rolls to the desired final product sizes. The seven cutting alternatives and the amount of waste generated by each are as follows:

Cutting Alternative	Number of Rolls			Waste (inches)
	$1\frac{1}{2}$ in	$2\frac{1}{2}$ in	$3\frac{1}{2}$ in	
1	6	0	0	1
2	0	4	0	0
3	2	0	2	0
4	0	1	2	$\frac{1}{2}$
5	1	3	0	1
6	1	2	1	0
7	4	0	1	$\frac{1}{2}$

The minimum production requirements for the three products are as follows:

Roll Width (inches)	Units
1½	1000
2½	2000
3½	4000

a. If the company wants to minimize the number of units of the 10-inch rolls that must be manufactured, how many 10-inch rolls will be processed on each cutting alternative? How many rolls are required, and what is the total waste (inches)?

b. If the company wants to minimize the waste generated, how many 10-inch units will be processed on each cutting alternative? How many rolls are required, and what is the total waste (inches)?

c. What are the differences in approaches a and b to this trim problem? In this case, which objective do you prefer? Explain. What are the types of situations that would make the other objective the more desirable?

17. *Inspection.* The Get-Well Pill Company inspects capsule medicine products by passing the capsules over a special lighting table where inspectors visually check for cracked or partially filled capsules. Currently any of three inspectors can be assigned to the visual inspection task. The inspectors, however, differ in accuracy and speed abilities and are paid at slightly different wage rates. The differences are as follows:

Inspector	Speed (units per hour)	Accuracy (percent)	Hourly Wage
Davis	300	98	$5.90
Wilson	200	99	$5.20
Lawson	350	96	$5.50

Operating on a full eight-hour shift, the company needs at least 2000 capsules inspected with no more than 2% of these capsules having inspection errors. In addition, because of the fatigue factor of this inspection process, no one inspector can be assigned this task for more than four hours per day. How many hours should each inspector be assigned to the capsule inspection process during an eight-hour day if it is desired to minimize the cost of inspection? What volume will be inspected per day, and what is the daily capsule inspection cost?

18. *Equipment Acquisition.* The Two-Rivers Oil Company near Pittsburgh transports gasoline to its distributors by trucks. The company has recently received a contract to begin supplying gasoline distributors in southern Ohio and has $300,000 available to spend on the necessary expansion of its fleet of gasoline tank trucks. Three models of gasoline tank truck are available:

Truck Model	Capacity (gallons)	Purchase Cost	Monthly Operating Costs, Including Depreciation
Super Tanker	5000	$37,000	$550
Regular Line	2500	$25,000	$425
Econo-Tanker	1000	$16,000	$350

The company estimates that the monthly demand for the region will be a total of 550,000 gallons of gasoline. Due to the size and speed differences of the trucks, the different truck models will vary in terms of the number of deliveries or round trips possible per month. Trip capacities are estimated at 15 per month for the Super Tanker, 20 per month for the Regular Line, and 25 per month for the Econo-Tanker. Based on maintenance and driver availability, the firm does not want to add more than 15 new vehicles to its fleet. In addition, the company would like to make sure it purchases at least three of the new Econo-Tankers to use on the short-run low-demand routes. As a final constraint, the company does not want more than half of the new models to be Super Tankers.

a.   If the company wishes to satisfy the gasoline demand with a minimum monthly operating expense, how many models of each truck should be purchased?

b.   If the company did not require at least three Econo-Tankers and allowed as many Super Tankers as needed, what would the company strategy be?

19. *Production Scheduling.* The Silver Star Bicycle Company will be manufacturing both men's and women's models for their Easy-Pedal 10-speed bicycles during the next two months, and the company would like a production schedule indicating how many bicycles of each model should be produced in each month. Current demand forecasts call for 150 men's and 125 women's models to be shipped during the first month and 200 men's and 150 women's models to be shipped during the second month. Additional data are shown below:

Model	Production Costs	Labor Required for Manufacturing (hours)	Labor Required for Assembly (hours)	Current Inventory
Men's	$40	10	3	20
Women's	$30	8	2	30

Last month the company used a total of 4000 hours of labor. The company's labor relations policy will not allow the combined total hours of labor (manufacturing plus assembly) to increase or decrease by more than 500 hours from month to month. In addition, the company charges monthly inventory at the rate of 2% of the production cost based on the inventory levels at the end of the month. The company would like to have at least 25 units of each model in inventory at the end of the two months.

a.   Establish a production schedule that minimizes production and inventory costs and satisfies the labor smoothing, demand, and inventory requirements. What inventories will be maintained, and what are the monthly labor requirements?

b. If the company changed the constraints so that monthly labor increases and decreases could not exceed 250 hours, what would happen to the production schedule? How much will the cost increase? What would you recommend?

20. *Labor Balancing.* The Patriotic Doll Company manufactures two kinds of dolls: the Betsy Ross and the George Washington. The assembly process for each of these dolls requires two people. The assembly times are as follows:

	Assembler 1	Assembler 2
Betsy Ross doll	6 min	2 min
George Washington doll	3 min	4 min
Maximum hours available per day	8	8

The company policy is to balance workloads on all assembly jobs. In fact, management wants to schedule work so that no assembler will have more than thirty minutes more work per day than other assemblers. This means that in a regular eight-hour shift, all assemblers will be assigned at least $7\frac{1}{2}$ hours of work. If the firm makes a $2 profit for each George Washington doll and a $1 profit for each Betsy Ross doll, how many units of each doll should be produced per day? How much time will each assembler be assigned per day?

21. *Capital Budgeting.* The Ice-Cold Refrigerator Company can invest capital funds in a variety of company projects which have different capital requirements over the next four years. Faced with limited capital resources, the company must select the most profitable projects and budget for the necessary capital expenditures. The estimated project values, the capital requirements, and the available capital projections are as follows:

Project	Estimated Present Value	Capital Requirements			
		Year 1	Year 2	Year 3	Year 4
Plant expansion	$90,000	$15,000	$20,000	$20,000	$15,000
Warehouse expansion	$40,000	$10,000	$15,000	$20,000	$5,000
New machinery	$10,000	$10,000	0	0	$4,000
New product research	$37,000	$15,000	$10,000	$10,000	$10,000
Available capital funds		$30,000	$40,000	$30,000	$25,000

a. Which projects should the company select in order to maximize the present value of the invested funds? Show the capital budget for each year.

Hint: The decision must be made to accept or reject each project. This is similar to the auditor assignment problem (see Section 5.4), where we let $x = 1$ if the assignment was to be made and $x = 0$ if it was not to be made. Adopting a similar approach, we can let $x = 1$ if the project is accepted and $x = 0$ if it is rejected. Thus all variables must be constrained with $x \leq 1$. For this linear programming formulation of the capital budgeting problem the variables will be 0 (rejected), 1 (accepted), or a fraction between 0 and 1. Fractional values should be interpreted as insufficient funds for the complete project; therefore reject the project outright or proceed with the project in smaller increments, if possible. Actually, the method of integer programming (Chapter 8) could be used to require only 0 and 1 valued variables; however, a linear programming solution to the capital budgeting problem can still provide valuable information.

b. If the company could obtain an additional $10,000 in each of the four years, what would you recommend? What is the new solution?

22. *Goal Programming—Machine Location.* Morley Company is attempting to determine the best location for a new machine in an existing layout of three machines. The existing machines are located at the following x_1, x_2 coordinates on the shop floor:

$$\text{Machine 1:} \quad x_1 = 1, x_2 = 7$$
$$\text{Machine 2:} \quad x_1 = 5, x_2 = 9$$
$$\text{Machine 3:} \quad x_1 = 6, x_2 = 2$$

Let (x_1, x_2) represent the coordinates of the new machine.

a. Develop a goal programming model that can be solved to minimize the total distance of the new machine from the three existing machines. The distance is to be measured rectangularly. For example (see below), if the location of the new machine is $(x_1 = 3, x_2 = 5)$, it is considered to be a distance of four units from machine 1.

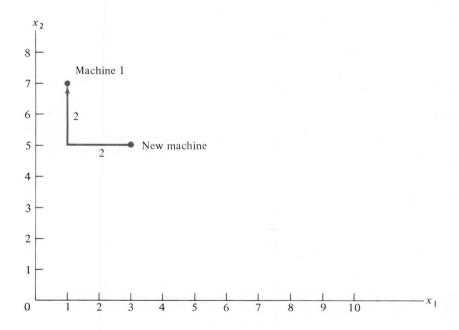

b. What is the optimal location for the new machine?

23. *Goal Programming—Store Location.* A fast-food chain is attempting to determine the best location for a new outlet. Management would like to determine the best location for drawing customers from three population centers. Letting (x_1, x_2)

represent the map coordinates of the three population centers, we can show their locations as follows:

$$\text{Population center 1:} \quad x_1 = 2, x_2 = 8$$
$$\text{Population center 2:} \quad x_1 = 6, x_2 = 6$$
$$\text{Population center 3:} \quad x_1 = 1, x_2 = 1$$

If the new outlet is located at coordinates $(x_1 = 3, x_2 = 2)$, then it is a distance of $(3 - 1) + (2 - 1) = 3$ miles from population center 3 (distance is measured as the sum of the east-west and north-south differences in coordinates).

a. Formulate and solve a goal programming model to determine what location for the new outlet will minimize the total distance from the three population centers. (Hint: Let x_1, x_2 represent the coordinates of the new location.)

b. Population center 1 is four times as large as center 3, and center 2 is twice as large as center 3. The firm feels that the importance of locating near a population center is proportional to its population. Develop and solve a new goal programming model where the weights on the deviations reflect this importance.

24. *Goal Programming—Work Force Smoothing.* The L. Young & Sons Manufacturing Company produces two products which have the following profit and resource requirement characteristics:

	Product 1	**Product 2**
Profit/unit	$4	$2
Dept. A hours/unit	1	1
Dept. B hours/unit	2	5

Last month's production schedule used 350 hours of labor in department A and 1000 hours of labor in department B.

Young's management has been experiencing work force morale and labor union problems during the past six months because of monthly departmental workload fluctuations. New hirings, layoffs, and interdepartmental transfers have been common because the firm has not attempted to stabilize departmental workload requirements.

Management would like to develop a production schedule for the coming month which will minimize deviations from the goals of maintaining department A workload at 350 hours and department B workload at 1000 hours.

a. Management has specified that a minimum of $1300 profit must be earned. Formulate and solve a goal programming model that will lead to minimum work force fluctuations subject to satisfying the profit requirement.

b. Suppose the firm ignores the workload fluctuations and considers the 350 hours in department A and the 1000 hours in department B as the maximum available. Formulate and solve a linear programming problem to maximize profit subject to these constraints.

c. Compare the approaches taken in parts a and b. Discuss which approach you favor and tell why.

Application

*Marathon Oil Company**
Findlay, Ohio

Marathon Oil Company was founded in 1887 when 14 oilmen pooled their properties to organize an oil-producing company in the Trenton Rock oil fields of Ohio. In 1924 Marathon entered the refining and marketing phase of the petroleum industry. Today, Marathon is a fully integrated oil company with significant international operations. It employs over 15,000 people, and company activities extend to six continents. In the United States the company markets petroleum products in 21 states, primarily in the Midwest and Southeast. Marathon had 1980 revenues of $8.8 billion. At year's end, assets totaled $5 billion.

Operations Research at Marathon Oil Company

Much of the computerized quantitative analysis work performed at Marathon is done by the Operations Research Department. This department was formed in 1963 to aid in solving problems for all components of the company. Approximately 50% of the problems solved involve linear programming. Typical applications are refinery models, distribution models, gasoline and fuel oil blending, and crude oil evaluation. Another 30% of the problems involve complex chemical engineering simulations of process operations. The remainder of the quantitative problems faced by the Operations Research Department involve solution techniques using nonlinear programming, network flow algorithms, and statistical techniques such as regression analysis and Box-Jenkins procedures.

A Marketing Planning Model

Marathon Oil Company has four refineries within the United States, operates 48 light products terminals, and has product demand at over 100 locations. The Marketing Operations Division is faced with the problem of determining which refinery should supply which terminal and at the same time determining which products should be transported via which pipeline, barge, or tanker in

*The authors are indebted to Jerry T. Ranney and Keith R. Weiss of Marathon Oil Company, Findlay, Ohio, for providing this application.

order to achieve a minimum cost. Product demand must be satisfied, and the supply capability of each refinery must not be exceeded. To help solve this difficult problem, Marathon's Operations Research Department developed a marketing planning model for the Marketing Operation Division.

The marketing planning model is a large-scale linear programming model that takes into account sales not only at Marathon product terminals but also at all exchange locations. An exchange contract is an agreement with other oil product marketers that involves exchanging or trading Marathon's products for theirs at different locations. Thus some geographical imbalance between supply and demand can be reduced. Both sides of the exchanges are represented, since this not only affects the net requirements at a demand location but in addition has important financial implications. All pipelines, barges, and tankers within Marathon's marketing area are also represented in the linear programming model.

The optimization of gasoline blending for each refinery, based on blendstock availabilities and the gasoline demand structure, is accomplished in the model by the inclusion of gasoline blending submodels. Thus the linear programming model is a combination of a blending model and a transportation model.

The objective of the linear programming model is to minimize the cost of meeting a given demand structure, taking into account sales price, pipeline tariffs, exchange contract costs, product demand, terminal operating costs, refining costs, and product purchases. The current linear programming matrix size is approximately 1800 rows by 6000 columns. The IBM MPSX/370 system solves the problem in less than three minutes using an IBM 370/168 computer system.

The marketing planning model is used to solve a wide variety of planning problems. These vary from evaluating gasoline blending economics to analyzing the economics of a new terminal or pipeline. Although the types of problems that can be solved are almost unlimited, the model is most effective in handling the following types of problems:

1. Evaluation of additional product demand locations, pipelines, refinery units, and exchange contracts.
2. Profitability of shifting sales from one product demand location to another.
3. Effects on refinery gasoline blending when octane requirements are increased, blendstock availabilities are decreased, or there is a major shift in the demand pattern.
4. The effects on supply and distribution when a pipeline increases its tariff.
5. Optimize production of the three grades of gasoline at the four refineries.

The linear programming model not only solves these problems, but gives the financial impact of each solution.

Benefits

With daily sales of about 15 million gallons of refined light product, a saving of even one-thousandth of a cent per gallon can result in significant long-term savings. At the same time, what may appear to be a savings in one area, such as refining or transportation, may actually add to overall costs when the effects are fully realized throughout the system. The marketing planning model allows a simultaneous examination of this total effect.

Chapter 6

The Assignment And Traveling Salesman Problems

In this chapter we introduce two special problems, referred to as the assignment and the traveling salesman problems. These two problems are important because they represent recurring situations that may exist in a variety of firms or organizations. After describing each of the two problems, we will develop the computational procedure or algorithm that may be used to establish the optimal solution or optimal decision for each problem. In solving the traveling salesman problem, we introduce the general branch-and-bound approach for problem solving. While in this chapter branch and bound will be applied specifically to the traveling salesman problem, it is a general solution procedure that may be used to solve other types of management science problems. In Chapter 8 it will be used to solve integer linear programming problems.

6.1 The Assignment Problem

The assignment problem arises in a variety of decision-making situations. For example, typical assignment problems involve assigning jobs to machines, assigning workers to tasks or projects, assigning sales personnel to sales territories, assigning contracts to bidders, and so on. A distinguishing feature of the assignment problem is that *one* job, worker, etc. is assigned to *one and only one* machine, project, etc. Specifically, we look for the assignment decisions that will optimize a stated objective such as minimize costs, minimize time, or maximize profits.

As an illustration of the assignment problem, let us consider the case of Fowle Marketing Research, Inc., which has just received requests for market research studies from three new clients. The company is faced with the task of assigning project leaders to each of these three new research studies. Currently, three individuals are relatively free from other major commitments and are available for the project leader assignments. Fowle's management realizes, however, that the time required to complete each study will depend upon the experience and ability of the project leader assigned to the study. Since the three projects have been judged to have approximately the same priority, the company would like to assign project leaders such that the total number of days required to complete all three projects is minimized. If one project leader is to be assigned to one and only one client, what assignments should be made?

In order to answer this assignment question, Fowle's management must first consider all possible project leader-client assignments and then estimate the corresponding project completion times. Fowle's assignment alternatives and estimated project completion times in days are summarized in Table 6.1. For example, it is estimated that Terry would require ten days to complete client A's project, while Carle would require approximately nine days for the same project.

Since there are only three clients and three project leaders, we can enumerate all possible assignment alternatives and then pick the one yielding the minimum total completion time. First we could consider assigning Terry to client A, B, or C, then assigning Carle to one of the remaining two clients,

TABLE 6.1   Estimated Project Completion Times (days) for the Fowle, Inc. Assignment Problem

	Client		
Project Leader	A	B	C
Terry	10	15	9
Carle	9	18	5
McClymonds	6	14	3

and finally assigning McClymonds to the remaining client. Thus in this case there are only a total of $3 \times 2 \times 1 = 6$ possible assignment solutions. Table 6.2 shows all assignment solutions and their associated total days of work.

The optimal solution is number 5, with Terry assigned to client B, Carle assigned to client C, and McClymonds assigned to client A. The total for all three projects is 26 days.

The above enumeration approach, which worked quite well for solving this small problem, is a very inefficient way to solve larger assignment problems. For example, a problem requiring the assignment of four leaders to four clients would require us to consider $4 \times 3 \times 2 \times 1 = 24$ alternative assignment solutions. In general there are $n! = n \times (n-1) \times (n-2) \times \cdots \times 3 \times 2 \times 1$ possible solutions to an assignment problem which require assigning n persons or objects to n tasks. For a relatively small problem with eight persons and eight tasks, there are $8! = 40,320$ possible solutions. Clearly it would be impractical to attempt to enumerate all possible solutions to such a problem by hand. Even for a large computer the enumeration approach is impractical, except for relatively small ($n \leq 15$) assignment problems.

TABLE 6.2   All Possible Assignment Solutions for the Fowle, Inc. Assignment Problem

	Assignment Solutions					
Project Leader	1	2	3	4	5	6
Terry	A(10)	B(15)	C(9)	A(10)	B(15)	C(9)
Carle	B(18)	A(9)	A(9)	C(5)	C(5)	B(18)
McClymonds	C(3)	C(3)	B(14)	B(14)	A(6)	A(6)
Total days for all projects	31	27	32	29	26	33

Minimum-time solution

6.2   An Assignment Problem Solution Algorithm

The *Hungarian method* is an efficient solution procedure for assignment problems. We will develop this specialized algorithm by showing how it may be used to solve the Fowle, Inc. problem. For convenience, we repeat below the estimated project completion times for the Fowle, Inc. assignment problem:

		COLUMNS		
		A	B	C
	Terry	10	15	9
ROWS	Carle	9	18	5
	McClymonds	6	14	3

A table or matrix such as this will be associated with every assignment problem. In a general framework, the rows will consist of the objects we want to assign, and the columns will denote the tasks or items we want to assign the objects to. The entries inside our table or matrix will be the values associated with making a particular assignment. We saw that in the Fowle, Inc. problem these values represented estimated project completion times. In other situations the values may represent costs, profits, parts produced, and so on.

The solution procedure involves what is called *matrix reduction*. By subtracting and adding appropriate numbers in the matrix, the algorithm determines an optimal solution to the general assignment problem. Basically there are three major steps associated with the procedure. Let us consider step 1, which shows the initial matrix reduction calculation.

Step 1:   Reduce the matrix by subtracting the smallest element in each row from every element in that row and then subtracting the smallest element in each column from every element in that column.

Thus we first reduce the numbers in the matrix by subtracting the minimum value in each row from each element in the row. With the minimum values of 9 for row 1, 5 for row 2, and 3 for row 3, our reduced matrix becomes

	A	B	C
Terry	1	6	0
Carle	4	13	0
McClymonds	3	11	0

The assignment problem represented by this reduced matrix is equivalent to our original assignment problem in the sense that the same solution will be optimal. The row 1 minimum element, 9, has been subtracted from every element in the first row. Since Terry must still be assigned to one of the clients, the only change is that in this revised problem the time for any assignment will be nine days less. Similarly Carle and McClymonds are shown with completion times requiring five and three less days, respectively.

Continuing Step 1 in the matrix reduction process, we subtract the minimum element in each column from every element in the column. This also leads to an equivalent assignment problem; that is, the same solution will still be optimal. With the minimum values of 1 for column 1, 6 for column 2, and 0 for column 3, the reduced matrix becomes

	A	B	C
Terry	0	0	0
Carle	3	7	0
McClymonds	2	5	0

In Table 6.3 we show all six assignment solutions for this reduced asignment problem. Our goal now is to continue reducing the matrix until the value of one of the solutions is zero. Then, as long as there are no negative elements in the matrix, the zero-valued solution will be optimal. The way in which we perform this further reduction and recognize when we have reached an optimal solution is described in the following two steps.

Step 2:   Find the *minimum* number of row and column straight lines necessary to cover all the zeros in the matrix. If the minimum number is the same as the number of rows (or equivalently,

TABLE 6.3   All Possible Assignment Solutions for the Reduced Fowle, Inc. Assignment Problem

	Assignment Solutions					
Project Leader	1	2	3	4	5	6
Terry	A(0)	B(0)	C(0)	A(0)	B(0)	C(0)
Carle	B(7)	A(3)	A(3)	C(0)	C(0)	B(7)
McClymonds	C(0)	C(0)	B(5)	B(5)	A(2)	A(2)
Total days for all projects in reduced matrix	7	3	8	5	2	9

Minimum-time solution

columns) in the matrix, an optimal assignment with value zero can be made. If the number of lines is *less* than the number of rows, go to step 3.

Applying step 2 we see, as shown below, that the minimum number of lines necessary to cover all the zeros is two. Thus we must continue to step 3:

	A	B	C
Terry	0	0	0
Carle	3	7	0
McClymonds	②	5	0

Two lines can be drawn to cover all zeros (step 2)

Step 3:   Subtract the value of the smallest *unlined* element from every *unlined* element and add this value to every element at the *intersection* of two lines. All other elements remain unchanged. Return to step 2 and continue until the minimum number of lines necessary to cover all the zeros in the matrix is equal to the number of rows.

The minimum unlined element is 2. Note that in our previous matrix we circled this element for convenience in carrying out the computations of step 3. Subtracting 2 from all unlined elements and adding 2 to the intersection element for Terry and client C produces the new matrix shown below:

	A	B	C
Terry	0	0	2
Carle	1	5	0
McClymonds	0	3	0

Returning to step 2, we find that the minimum number of straight lines necessary to cover all the zeros is 3. The following matrix illustrates the step 2 calculations:

	A	B	C
Terry	0	0	2
Carle	1	5	0
McClymonds	0	3	0

Three lines must be drawn to cover all zeros; therefore the optimal solution has been reached

According to step 2, then, it must be possible to find an assignment with a value of zero. Such an assignment can be found by first locating any row or column which contains only one zero. We draw a square around the zero, indicating an assignment, and eliminate that row or column from further consideration. Since row 2 has only one zero in the Fowle, Inc. problem, we assign Carle to C and eliminate row 2 and column 3 from further consideration. This leaves row 3 with only one zero; thus McClymonds is assigned to A, and row 3 and column 1 are removed from further consideration. Terry must then be assigned to B. The solution to the Fowle, Inc. problem is shown below:

	A	B	C
Terry	0	⊡0	2
Carle	1	5	⊡0
McClymonds	⊡0	3	0

If you make the mistake of drawing too many lines to cover the zeros in the reduced matrix and thus conclude an optimal solution has been reached when it has not, you will find you cannot identify a zero-value assignment. Thus if you think you have reached the optimal solution, but the zero-value assignments cannot be found, go back to the previous step and check to see if you have actually determined the *minimum* number of lines necessary to cover the zero elements.

Following steps 2 and 3 always leads to an assignment problem that is equivalent to the original assignment problem. That is, the optimal assignment solutions are the same for the original and all reduced assignment problems considered. The matrix reduction method enables us to consider successively reduced problems until the minimum zero-value assignment is observed. Table 6.4 lists all alternative assignment solutions for the final reduced Fowle, Inc. assignment problem.

The value of the optimal assignment can be found by referring to the original assignment problem and summing the solution times associated with the

TABLE 6.4   All Possible Assignment Solutions for the Completely Reduced Fowle, Inc. Assignment Problem

	Assignment Solutions					
Project Leader	1	2	3	4	5	6
Terry	A(0)	B(0)	C(2)	A(0)	B(0)	C(2)
Carle	B(5)	A(1)	A(1)	C(0)	C(0)	B(5)
McClymonds	C(0)	C(0)	B(3)	B(3)	A(0)	A(0)
Total days for all projects in reduced matrix	5	1	6	3	0	7

Minimum-time solution

optimal assignment; in this case Terry to B, Carle to C, and McClymonds to A. Thus we obtain the solution time of $15 + 5 + 6 = 26$ days.

We have seen how this assignment problem solution algorithm can be applied to the Fowle Marketing Research assignment problem in order to find an optimal assignment solution. The solution procedure we have outlined involves finding minimization assignments when we have the same number of leaders as clients. However, through some simple modifications we will show how to solve assignment problems when the number of people or objects (leaders) is not the same as the number of tasks (clients), and when the problem has a maximization objective.

Dummy Rows and Dummy Columns

The assignment solution algorithm we have just discussed requires an identical number of rows (people, objects, and so on) and columns (tasks, clients, and so on). Suppose that in the Fowle, Inc. example four project leaders had been available for assignment to the three new clients. Fowle still faces the same basic problem—namely, which project leaders should be assigned to which clients in order to minimize the total days required. The project completion time estimates with the new project leader alternative are shown in Table 6.5.

We have seen how to apply the assignment solution algorithm when the number of rows and columns are equal. Therefore we can apply the same procedure if we can add a new client, which would result in a 4×4 assignment problem. Since we do not have another client, we simply add a *dummy column* or a dummy client. Since this dummy client is nonexistent, the project leader assigned to the dummy client in the optimal assignment solution will in effect be the unassigned project leader.

What project completion time estimates should we show in this new dummy column? Actually any arbitrary value is acceptable as long as all project leaders are given the same completion time. However, since the dummy client assignment will not take place, a zero project completion time for all project leaders seems logical. The 4×4 Fowle, Inc. assignment problem is shown in Table 6.6.

Table 6.5   Estimated Project Completion Time (days) for the Fowle, Inc. Assignment Problem with Four Project Leaders

Project Leader	Client		
	A	B	C
Terry	10	15	9
Carle	9	18	5
McClymonds	6	14	3
Higley	8	16	6

Table 6.6   Estimated Project Completion Time (days) for the Fowle, Inc. Assignment Problem

Project Leader	Client			
	A	B	C	D ← ——Dummy client
Terry	10	15	9	0
Carle	9	18	5	0
McClymonds	6	14	3	0
Higley	8	16	6	0

Problem 3 at the end of the chapter asks you to use the Hungarian method to determine the optimal assignment solution to this problem.

Note that if we had considered the case of four new clients and only three project leaders, we would have had to add a *dummy row* or dummy project leader in order to apply the solution algorithm. The client receiving the dummy row assignment would not be assigned an immediate project leader and would have to wait until a new leader becomes available. Also note that in order to obtain an assignment problem form compatible with the solution algorithm, it may be necessary to add several dummy rows or dummy columns, but never both.

A Maximization Assignment Problem

Suppose that Salsbury Discounts, Inc. has just leased a new shopping center store and is attempting to determine where various departments should be located within the store. The store manager has four locations that have not yet been assigned a department and is considering five departments that might occupy the four locations. The departments under consideration are a shoe, a toy, an auto parts, a housewares, and a record department. The store manager would like to determine the optimal assignment of departments to locations in order to maximize profits. After a careful study of the layout of the remainder of the store, and based on his experience with similar stores, the store manager has made estimates of the expected annual profit for each department in each location. These are presented in Table 6.7.

We now have an assignment problem which requires a maximization objective. However, we have a problem involving more rows than columns. Thus we must first add a dummy column, corresponding to a dummy or fictitious location, in order to apply the Hungarian method solution procedure. We follow the procedure discussed for adding dummy rows and dummy columns. The 5×5 Salsbury Discount, Inc. assignment problem is shown in Table 6.8.

We can obtain an equivalent minimization assignment problem by converting all the elements in the matrix to *opportunity losses*. This conversion is accomplished by subtracting every element in each column from the largest element in the column.

Table 6.7   Estimated Annual Profit (thousands of dollars) for Each Department-Location Combination

Department	Location			
	1	2	3	4
Shoe	10	6	12	8
Toy	15	18	5	11
Auto parts	17	10	13	16
Housewares	14	12	13	10
Record	14	16	6	12

It turns out that finding the assignment that minimizes opportunity loss leads to the same solution that maximizes the value of the assignment in our original problem. Thus any maximization assignment problem can be converted to a minimization problem by converting the assignment matrix to one in which the elements represent opportunity losses. Hence we begin our solution to this maximization assignment problem by developing an assignment matrix where each element represents the opportunity loss from not making the "best" assignment. This matrix is presented in Table 6.9.

The opportunity loss from putting the shoe department in location 1 is $7000. That is, if we put the shoe department, instead of the best department (auto parts), in that location, we forego the opportunity to make an additional $7000 in profit. The opportunity loss associated with putting the toy department in location 2 is zero, since it yields the highest profit in that location. What about the opportunity losses associated with the dummy column? Well, the assignment of a department to this "dummy" location means that the department will not be assigned a store location in the optimal solution. Since all departments earn the

Table 6.8   Estimated Annual Profit (thousands of dollars) for Each Department-Location Combination, Including a Dummy Location

Department	Location					Dummy location
	1	2	3	4	5	
Shoe	10	6	12	8	0	
Toy	15	18	5	11	0	
Auto parts	17	10	13	16	0	
Housewares	14	12	13	10	0	
Record	14	16	6	12	0	

Table 6.9   Opportunity Loss (thousands of dollars) for Each
            Department-Location Combination

Department	Location					
	1	2	3	4	5	←Dummy location
Shoe	7	12	1	8	0	
Toy	2	0	8	5	0	
Auto parts	0	8	0	0	0	
Housewares	3	6	0	6	0	
Record	3	2	7	4	0	

same amount from this dummy location, zero, the opportunity cost for each department is zero.

Following steps 1, 2, and 3 of our assignment algorithm, we can proceed to determine the optimal maximum profit assignment solution. Since each row minimum and column minimum is already zero, the application of step 1 does not change our matrix. Continuing to step 2, we see that the minimum number of lines required to cover all the zeros is 4. Thus we cannot find a solution with a value of zero. The current matrix illustrating the results of step 2 is shown below (note that the minimum unlined element is 1):

Department	Location				
	1	2	3	4	5
Shoe	7	12	①	8	0
Toy	2	0	8	5	0
Auto parts	0	8	0	0	0
Housewares	3	6	0	6	0
Record	3	2	7	4	0

Performing step 3 leads to the following reduced assignment matrix:

Department	Location				
	1	2	3	4	5
Shoe	6	11	0	7	0
Toy	2	0	8	5	1
Auto parts	0	8	0	0	1
Housewares	3	6	0	6	1
Record	2	①	6	3	0

The minimum number of lines required to cover all the zeros is still 4. Repeating step 3 with the minimum unlined element of 1 yields a new matrix:

Department	Location				
	1	2	3	4	5
Shoe	5	10	0	6	0
Toy	2	0	9	5	2
Auto parts	0	8	1	0	2
Housewares	2	5	0	5	1
Record	1	0	6	2	0

The minimum number of lines required to cover all the zeros is still 4. We again repeat step 3 with 1 as the minimum element:

Department	Location				
	1	2	3	4	5
Shoe	4	10	0	5	0
Toy	1	0	9	4	2
Auto parts	0	9	2	0	3
Housewares	1	5	0	4	1
Record	0	0	6	1	0

The minimum number of lines needed is now five. Thus we can make an assignment with zero value. Hence we have found the optimal solution. The optimal solution, together with its resultant total profit, is presented in Table 6.10.

We note that since the optimal solution had the shoe department assigned to the dummy location, this department will not be included in the store layout.

Table 6.10   Maximum Profit Assignment for the Salsbury Discount Store

Department	Assigned Location	Estimated Profit
Toy	2	18
Auto parts	4	16
Housewares	3	13
Record	1	14
	Total	61

Unassigned: shoe department

Handling Unacceptable Assignments

Suppose that in the Salsbury Discounts, Inc. assignment problem the store manager believed that the toy department should not be considered for location 2 and the auto parts department should not be considered for location 4. Essentially, the store manager is saying that based on other considerations, such as size of area, adjacent departments, and so on, the two assignments are unacceptable alternatives.

You may recall that in the discussion of artificial variables for linear programming (see Chapter 3) we attempted to guarantee that variables would not appear in the optimal solution by assigning them extremely high costs in a minimization problem and extremely low profits in a maximization problem. Using this same approach for the assignment problem, we define a value of $+M$ for unacceptable minimization assignments and a value of $-M$ for unacceptable maximization assignments, where M is an arbitrarily large value. In fact, M is assumed so large that M minus any value is still extremely large. Thus an M-valued cell in an assignment matrix maintains its M value throughout the matrix reduction calculations. Since an M-valued cell can never be zero, it can never be an assignment in the final solution.

The Salsbury Discount Store assignment problem with the two unacceptable assignments is shown in Table 6.11.

When this assignment matrix is converted to the opportunity loss matrix, the $-M$ profit value will be changed to M. Problem 4 at the end of this chapter asks you to solve this assignment problem.

Summary of the Assignment Problem Solution Algorithm

We will now restate and summarize the complete step-by-step solution algorithm for the assignment problem. For convenience in describing the calculations, we will restate the procedure in terms of two stages, (1) preparing the problem for solution by the Hungarian method, and (2) using the Hungarian method to solve the problem.

Table 6.11   Estimated Profit for the Department-Location
Combinations

Department	Location				
	1	2	3	4	5
Shoe	10	6	12	8	0
Toy	15	$-M$	5	11	0
Auto parts	17	10	13	$-M$	0
Housewares	14	12	13	10	0
Record	14	16	6	12	0

Preparing the problem for solution

Step 1: Set up a matrix with the *m* objects (rows) to be assigned to *n* tasks (columns).

Step 2: Enter the cost, profit, or other measure of performance in the matrix cell corresponding to each object-task combination. Use a $-M$ profit or a $+M$ cost if the specific object-task combination is unacceptable.

Step 3: If the number of rows is not equal to the number of columns, add dummy rows or dummy columns until the number of rows and number of columns are equal. Use 0 values for the new elements in the assignment matrix.

Step 4: If the problem involves maximization, convert the matrix to an opportunity loss matrix by subtracting each column entry from the maximum value in the column.

The Hungarian solution procedure

Step 1: Subtract the smallest element in each row from every element in that row, and then subtract the smallest element in each column from every element in that column.

Step 2: Find the minimum number of row and column straight lines necessary to cover all the zeros in the matrix. If the minimum number is the same as the number of rows, the optimal solution can be found by using the zero-value assignments. Otherwise go to step 3.

Step 3: Locate the smallest unlined element. Subtract it from all unlined elements and add it to every element at the intersection of two lines. Repeat steps 2 and 3 until the optimal solution is found.

6.3 A Linear Programming Formulation of the Assignment Problem

In Section 5.4 we discussed how an audit staff assignment problem could be formulated and solved as a linear program. It was pointed out that the linear programming formulation of the problem, which involved decision variables that could take on only the values of 0 and 1, was really a zero–one integer programming problem (Chapter 8). However, it was also mentioned that the values of all the basic variables will be equal to 0 or 1 at the extreme points of the feasible region for such problems. Therefore, since the optimal solution to a linear program lies at an extreme point, the optimal solution to a linear programming formulation of the assignment problem will have the basic variables all equal to 0 or 1. Thus solving the linear programming formulation provides the optimal solution to the assignment problem.

   To expand on the linear programming approach in solving assignment problems, let us reconsider the Fowle Marketing Research problem with the four project leaders as shown in Table 6.5. Let us begin by defining the following decision variables:

$$x_{ij} = \begin{cases} 1 & \text{if project leader } i \text{ is assigned to client } j; \\ & i = 1, 2, 3, 4; j = 1, 2, 3 \\ 0 & \text{otherwise.} \end{cases}$$

Using the above decision variables, the objective function calling for the minimization of total days of labor can be written as

$$\begin{aligned} \min \quad & 10x_{11} + 15x_{12} + 9x_{13} \\ & + \ 9x_{21} + 18x_{22} + 5x_{23} \\ & + \ 6x_{31} + 14x_{32} + 3x_{33} \\ & + \ 8x_{41} + 16x_{42} + 6x_{43}. \end{aligned}$$

The constraints affecting this problem are that all clients must receive exactly one project leader and that the project leaders cannot be assigned to more than one client. The first condition is satisfied by the following linear constraints:

$$\begin{aligned} x_{11} + x_{21} + x_{31} + x_{41} &= 1 \qquad \text{client A,} \\ x_{12} + x_{22} + x_{32} + x_{42} &= 1 \qquad \text{client B,} \\ x_{13} + x_{23} + x_{33} + x_{43} &= 1 \qquad \text{client C.} \end{aligned}$$

The second condition is reflected in the following constraints:

$$\begin{aligned} x_{11} + x_{12} + x_{13} &\leq 1 \qquad \text{Terry,} \\ x_{21} + x_{22} + x_{23} &\leq 1 \qquad \text{Carle,} \\ x_{31} + x_{32} + x_{33} &\leq 1 \qquad \text{McClymonds,} \\ x_{41} + x_{42} + x_{43} &\leq 1 \qquad \text{Higley.} \end{aligned}$$

In addition, the nonnegativity constraints for the variables are included as usual.

The solution to this twelve-variable, seven-constraint linear programming model provides a project leader assignment plan that will allow Fowle to complete the three projects with a minimum total days of labor expended. Using the linear programming approach, we would obtain the same solution as obtained using the Hungarian method.

The general assignment problem is one that involves m objects and n tasks. If we let $x_{ij} = 1$ or 0 according to whether object i is assigned to task j or not, and if c_{ij} denotes the cost of assigning object i to task j, then we can write the general assignment model as follows:

$$\min \quad \sum_{i=1}^{m} \sum_{j=1}^{n} c_{ij} x_{ij}$$

s.t.

$$\sum_{j=1}^{n} x_{ij} \leq 1 \qquad i = 1, 2, \ldots, m$$

$$\sum_{i=1}^{m} x_{ij} = 1 \qquad j = 1, 2, \ldots, n$$

$$x_{ij} \geq 0 \qquad \text{for all } i \text{ and } j.$$

The above general model will not have a feasible solution if n exceeds m—that is, if the number of tasks exceeds the number of objects available for assignment. For example, if Fowle had five clients and only three project leaders available (that is, $n = 5$ and $m = 3$), our above model would not have a feasible solution. The equality constraints specify that each client must be assigned a project leader, and it is impossible to assign three project leaders to five clients unless we allow project leaders to be assigned to more than one client. Since our inequality constraints prohibit such assignments, we must conclude that we cannot obtain a feasible solution.

To get around this problem, we need only add two dummy project leaders to obtain a feasible linear programming solution. In the problem formulation, the cost for assigning the dummy leaders would be zero (that is, $c_{ij} = 0$ for all dummy project leaders). If this approach were employed, projects receiving a dummy project leader could not be started until a project leader became available sometime in the future.

We can handle the situation where some assignments are unacceptable by omitting the corresponding x_{ij} variables from the objective function and all the constraints. Thus these assignments will not be in the linear programming solution.

6.4   The Traveling Salesman Problem

Consider the problem of routing a salesman through a sequence of cities such that the total distance traveled is a minimum. If we define a *tour* as a sequence of cities which begins and ends with the same city and which also includes visits to all other cities once and only once, then the traveling salesman problem can be stated as follows: *find the minimum length tour for a given set of* n *cities.*

As an illustration of the traveling salesman problem, consider the following situation. Suppose Don Ryan, a traveling salesman, has his home office in city 1

Table 6.12   Intercity Distances (miles) for Ryan's Traveling Salesman Problem

(City 1 is the home office)

		To City					
		1	2	3	4	5	6
	1	0	22	34	42	30	60
	2	22	0	16	32	18	48
From City	3	29	16	0	28	22	55
	4	42	32	28	0	15	30
	5	30	18	25	15	0	42
	6	50	48	57	30	44	0

and desires to develop a tour through each of five other cities and back home in such a fashion that the total distance traveled is minimized. Table 6.12 shows the intercity distances for the cities in which Don must call on customer accounts.

Note that the intercity distances are not all symmetrical. For example, the distance from 1 to 6 is not equal to the distance from 6 to 1. Such situations may arise due to construction detours that increase the travel distance in one direction but not the other. A diagram showing the cities that Don must visit is presented in Figure 6.1.

In solving the traveling salesman problem we would like to determine the sequence in which the cities should be visited in order to minimize the total distance traveled. While several solution procedures are available for solving this problem, we will take this opportunity to introduce you to the important solution procedure referred to as branch and bound.

6.5   A Branch-and-Bound Solution Procedure

Branch and bound does not refer to a specific solution procedure for a specific problem. Rather it is an approach that has been applied successfully to a number of different types of problems, but it is not always applied in the same way. The branch-and-bound approach has been most widely used for what are termed combinatorial problems. These are problems were a finite number of solution possibilities exist. Thus while total enumeration is an alternative, it may be computationally infeasible, and a branch-and-bound approach may be quite helpful.

The branch-and-bound approach is based upon partitioning the set of all feasible solutions to a problem into smaller, mutually exclusive subsets. Then various rules are used to (1) identify the subsets which are most likely to contain the optimal solution and (2) identify the subsets that need not be explored because they could not possibly contain the optimal solution. We show how this is done by applying a branch-and-bound procedure to the traveling salesman problem.

Let us return to the Don Ryan traveling salesman problem and consider one possible solution, which is to visit each of the cities in numerical order; that is, the tour could be cities 1–2–3–4–5–6–1. This tour is depicted graphically in Figure 6.2.

By adding the distances between the pairs of cities visited, we find that Ryan would travel a total distance of 173 miles on this tour. Since we now know that 173 miles is the value of a feasible solution, the optimal solution to our traveling salesman problem cannot require Ryan to travel any farther than 173 miles; that is, the optimal solution must have a value of 173 miles or less. Thus this tour has established an *upper bound* on the value of the optimal solution to our problem. Of course we are now interested in determining if there are any better solutions.

First let us see how a *lower bound* on the value of the optimal solution can be established. Suppose that for the moment we think of our problem as one of assigning each city to some other city in such a fashion that the cost of assigning

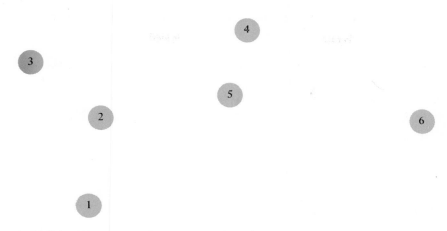

FIGURE 6.1   Diagram of Cities for Ryan's Traveling Salesman Problem

any city to some other city is given by the distance between the two cities. The assignment algorithm of Section 6.2 can be used to minimize the total intercity distances in such an assignment. In order to prohibit the assignment of any city to itself we can use the procedure discussed in Section 6.2 for handling unacceptable minimization assignments. That is, using the symbol M to denote an arbitrarily large value, we merely assign a distance of M to each of the diagonal elements in our matrix. The solution to such an assignment model would certainly be a lower bound on the optimal solution to our traveling salesman problem; if it consisted of a tour, it would be the optimal solution. However, since the optimal solution to the assignment problem might not require that all cities be visited before returning home, the optimal assignment might not provide a tour for the traveling salesman problem. Let us set up and solve an assignment model for Ryan's

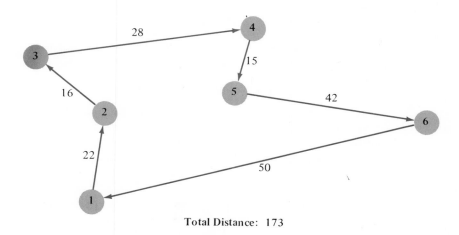

Total Distance: 173

FIGURE 6.2   Tour Resulting from Visiting Cities in Numerical Order

traveling salesman problem. The initial assignment matrix is presented below:

		To City					
		1	2	3	4	5	6
From City	1	M	22	34	42	30	60
	2	22	M	16	32	18	48
	3	29	16	M	28	22	55
	4	42	32	28	M	15	30
	5	30	18	25	15	M	42
	6	50	48	57	30	44	M

By applying the assignment algorithm of Section 6.2 we can obtain the optimal city-to-city assignment. The matrix reduction calculations are shown below:

Matrix 1   Row reductions:

	1	2	3	4	5	6	Row reductions
1	M	0	12	20	8	38	22
2	6	M	0	16	2	32	16
3	13	0	M	12	6	39	16
4	27	17	13	M	0	15	15
5	15	3	10	0	M	27	15
6	20	18	27	0	14	M	30

Matrix 2   Column reductions—identify minimum unlined element:

		1	2	3	4	5	6
	1	M	0	12	20	8	23
	2	0	M	0	16	2	17
Minimum unlined element	3	7	0	M	12	6	24
	4	21	17	13	M	0	0
	5	9	3	10	0	M	12
	6	14	18	27	0	14	M
Column reductions		6	0	0	0	0	15

Matrix 3   Unlined element reduction—identify minimum element:

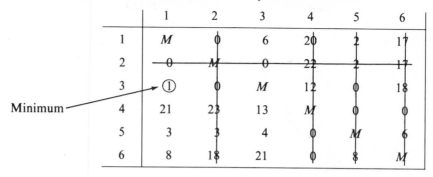

	1	2	3	4	5	6
1	M	0	6	20	2	17
2	0	M	0	22	2	17
3	①	0	M	12	0	18
4	21	23	13	M	0	0
5	3	3	4	0	M	6
6	8	18	21	0	8	M

Minimum → (points to the ① in row 3, column 1)

Matrix 4   Unlined element reduction—identify minimum element:

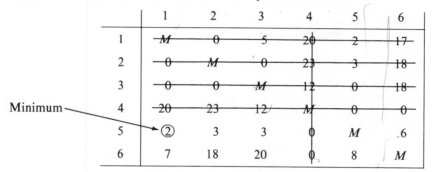

	1	2	3	4	5	6
1	M	0	5	20	2	17
2	0	M	0	23	3	18
3	0	0	M	12	0	18
4	20	23	12	M	0	0
5	②	3	3	0	M	6
6	7	18	20	0	8	M

Minimum → (points to the ② in row 5, column 1)

Matrix 5   Optimal solution:

	1	2	3	4	5	6
1	M	[0]	5	22	2	17
2	0	M	[0]	25	3	18
3	0	0	M	14	[0]	18
4	20	23	12	M	0	[0]
5	[0]	1	1	0	M	4
6	5	16	18	[0]	6	M

We see that the optimal solution assigns city 1 to city 2, city 2 to city 3, city 3 to city 5, city 4 to city 6, city 5 to city 1, and city 6 to city 4. Referring back to the original assignment matrix we see that if Ryan visits the cities in this order, 150 miles will be traveled. Unfortunately, this is *not* a tour, since he would not visit all the cities before returning home. Figure 6.3 provides a graphical representation of this solution.

The optimal solution to the assignment model includes two *subtours* and

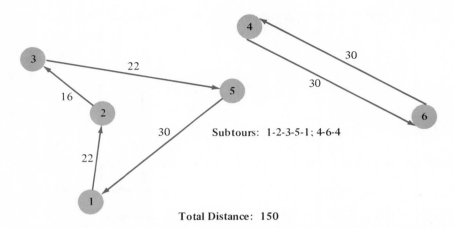

Subtours: 1-2-3-5-1; 4-6-4

Total Distance: 150

FIGURE 6.3   Optimal Solution to the Assignment Model Associated with Ryan's Traveling Salesman Problem

hence is not a feasible solution to the traveling salesman problem. But since every city must be assigned to some other city in any solution to the traveling salesman problem, this optimal solution provides a lower bound on the value of the optimal solution to the traveling salesman problem. Since our upper bound is 173, we now know that the most we can hope to improve over that solution is the difference between the upper bound and the lower bound, or 173 − 150 = 23. We can now show how the branch-and-bound approach can be used together with the assignment model to find the optimal solution.

The essential idea behind the branch-and-bound approach to the traveling salesman problem is that a sequence of assignment problems is formulated and solved in order to both increase the value of the lower bound and decrease the value of the upper bound. Since the upper bound always corresponds to a feasible solution (a tour), when we reach a point where the upper bound *equals* the lower bound, we are finished. In such a case the solution corresponding to the upper bound is optimal. The way in which we select the assignment problems to solve is the branching part of the branch-and-bound procedure.

The idea is to branch in such a way that the subtours are broken up and combined into a tour. We do this by breaking up the *smallest* subtour in the solution to the assignment model. In our problem this is the subtour 4–6–4. In Figure 6.4 we present the beginning of a *branch-and-bound tree* for Ryan's problem.

Note that the value of the solution to the assignment model is written inside the *circle* or *node* at the top of the tree. Below the node we have noted the subtours making up the optimal solution to the assignment model at this node. The two branches of the tree break up the shortest subtour. The left-hand branch corresponds to making the 4–6 route unacceptable, and the right-hand branch corresponds to making the 6-4 route unacceptable. Following the same approach we used to rule out the routes involving an assignment of a city to itself, we can move down the right-hand branch by creating a new assignment matrix which is

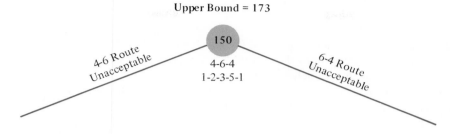

FIGURE 6.4   Initial Branch-and-Bound Tree for Ryan's Traveling Salesman Problem

the same as the initial matrix except for an M in the 6th row and the 4th column. However, since the M entries do not change in solving an assignment problem, all the work previously done in solving the assignment problem need not be repeated. That is, the solution to the new assignment model with an M in the 6th row and the 4th column can be obtained by starting with the previous *optimal* assignment matrix and placing an M in row 6, column 4. Doing so leads to the following matrix:

	1	2	3	4	5	6
1	M	0	5	22	2	17
2	0	M	0	25	3	18
3	0	0	M	14	0	18
4	20	23	12	M	0	0
5	0	1	1	0	M	4
6	5	16	18	M	6	M

An unacceptable
assignment

The matrix reduction calculations required to reach the optimal solution are shown below. Only a row reduction of 5 in row 6 was necessary.

Matrix 1   Row reduction (row 6 only)—optimal solution:

	1	2	3	4	5	6
1	M	[0]	5	22	2	17
2	0	M	[0]	25	3	18
3	0	0	M	14	[0]	18
4	20	23	12	M	0	[0]
5	0	1	1	[0]	M	4
6	[0]	11	13	M	1	M

The best solution ruling out the 6–4 route as unacceptable leads to a total distance of 155 and is a tour: 1–2–3–5–4–6–1. We can now add a node to the branch-and-bound tree. Note that since this solution provides a tour and has a value less than our previous upper bound of 173, we can reduce our upper bound to 155. In Figure 6.5 we show the current branch-and-bound tree.

We note that this branching process is actually partitioning the solutions to our assignment model. The top node corresponds to the optimal solution with all assignments, except a city to itself, acceptable. The left-hand branch corresponds to the partition where the 4–6 route is unacceptable, and the right-hand branch corresponds to the partition where the 6–4 route is unacceptable. Although we were able to decrease our upper bound, we cannot yet raise our lower bound, since there may be solutions on the left-hand branch which give a total distance of less than 155.

In order to solve the assignment problem corresponding to the left-hand branch, we can again return to the final assignment matrix corresponding to the top node and place an M in row 4, column 6. Doing so, we get the following initial matrix (only a column reduction of 4 in column 6 is necessary to find the optimal solution):

	1	2	3	4	5	6
1	M	0	5	22	2	17
2	0	M	0	25	3	18
3	0	0	M	14	0	18
4	20	23	12	M	0	M
5	0	1	1	0	M	4
6	5	16	18	0	6	M

An unacceptable assignment

Matrix 2   Column 6 reduction—optimal solution:

	1	2	3	4	5	6
1	M	[0]	5	22	2	13
2	0	M	[0]	25	3	14
3	[0]	0	M	14	0	14
4	20	23	12	M	[0]	M
5	0	1	1	0	M	[0]
6	5	16	18	[0]	6	M

The best solution ruling out the 4–6 route as unacceptable corresponds to a total distance of 154 and consists of two subtours: 1–2–3–1– and 4–5–6–4. We can now add another node to our branch-and-bound tree, as shown in Figure 6.6.

From the results of the assignment models for the two branches, we know that there can be no tours with total distance traveled less than 154. Thus we can

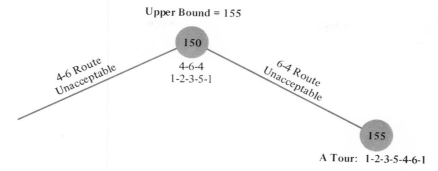

FIGURE 6.5   Modified Branch-and-Bound Tree after Making Route 6–4 Unacceptable

increase the lower bound to 154. However, we do not know if a tour exists with a value of 154. Hence we must continue branching from the node with value of 154 to investigate the possibility of a better solution.

Since this node contains two subtours of the same length, we arbitrarily select the subtour 1–2–3–1 to continue branching. To investigate other branches, we create three new subproblems, starting in each case with the optimal solution matrix obtained by *making the 4–6 route unacceptable:* (1) We make the 1–2 route unacceptable (thus both routes 4–6 and 1–2 are unacceptable) and obtain a new optimal solution. (2) Similarly, we make the 2–3 route unacceptable and resolve. (3) Finally, we make the 3–1 route unacceptable and obtain another optimal solution. In each case, carrying out these steps results in an optimal solution value of 159; in addition, each optimal solution contains two subtours: 1–3–2–1 and 4–5–6–4. We can now add three new nodes to our branch-and-bound tree to reflect the solution to the above three subproblems. Figure 6.7 illustrates the branch-and-bound tree.

We now see that there can be no tours with total distance traveled less than 155 miles. Thus we can increase the lower bound from 154 to 155. Since the upper and lower bounds are now equal, we have reached the optimal solution. The

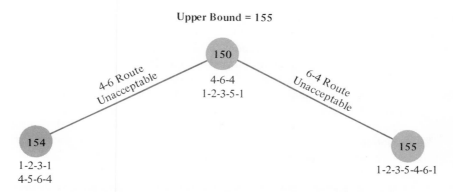

FIGURE 6.6   Modified Branch-and-Bound Tree after Making Route 4–6 Unacceptable

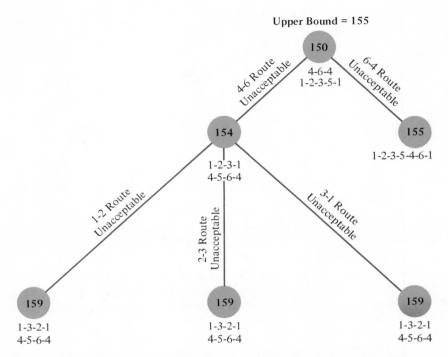

FIGURE 6.7   Final Branch-and-Bound Tree for Ryan's Traveling Salesman Problem

tour 1–2–3–5–4–6–1 corresponding to the upper bound is optimal. This optimal solution is depicted graphically in Figure 6.8.

The branch-and-bound procedure we have presented for solving the traveling salesman problem is known as the Eastman-Shapiro algorithm.[1] There are a number of other branch-and-bound schemes for the traveling salesman problem that differ in the way branches are created and/or upper and lower bounds are established. We now state in a step-by-step fashion the branch-and-bound algorithm we have presented for the traveling salesman problem:

Step 1:   Pick the value of the tour obtained by visiting each of the cities in numerical order as an initial upper bound.

Step 2:   Formulate an assignment model for assigning each city to some other city. Make the assignment of any city to itself unacceptable by placing an *M* in all the diagonal positions of the assignment matrix.

Step 3:   Solve the assignment model and write the value of the solution in the node. This value is a lower bound on the value of any solution that can be obtained by branching from that node. A lower bound for the entire problem is given by the node with the smallest value of all those from which we have not completed branching.

[1]For a discussion of this algorithm and other approaches to the traveling salesman problem, see Bellmore, M., and G. L. Nemhauser, "The Traveling Salesman Problem: A Survey," *Operations Research,* vol. 16, pp. 538–558, 1968.

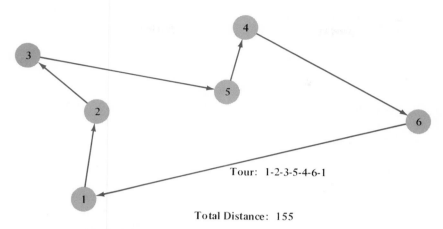

Tour: 1-2-3-5-4-6-1

Total Distance: 155

FIGURE 6.8   Optimal Solution to Ryan's Traveling Salesman Problem

Step 4:   If the solution to the assignment problem solved in step 3 is a tour and if the value of the solution is less than the current upper bound, set the new upper bound equal to the value of the solution corresponding to this new tour.

Step 5:   If the lower bound for the entire problem is equal to the upper bound, stop; the solution corresponding to the upper bound is optimal. If not, go on to step 6.

Step 6:   Branch from the node with the lowest value by breaking up the smallest subtour at that node. There will be one branch for each city-to-city trip in this subtour. Each branch will correspond to formulating a new assignment problem with one of the trips unacceptable. Return to step 3.

We close this section with a brief discussion of how the traveling salesman model can be applied to sequencing jobs on machines. The job-sequencing problem involves sequencing a fixed number of jobs, say n, on a machine in such a fashion that the total setup time is minimized. This is an important consideration when the setup times between jobs depend critically on the order in which the jobs are processed. To formulate this as a traveling salesman problem, we let the setup time between job i and job j correspond to the notion of the distance between city i and city j. We think of the machine the same way as we do of the salesman and try to find the best way to route the machine through the n jobs in order to minimize total setup time. Again, a branch-and-bound approach can be used to solve this problem.

Summary

In this chapter we have introduced you to two important problems, the assignment problem and the traveling salesman problem. Solution procedures were presented and demonstrated for each problem, with the general branch-and-bound solution procedure being applied to the traveling salesman problem.

Glossary

1. *Hungarian method*—An algorithm used to solve assignment problems.
2. *Matrix reduction*—The approach used by the Hungarian method which reduces the values of the assignments until a zero-valued assignment can be made.
3. *Dummy row(s)*—Extra row(s) added to an assignment problem to provide the equal number of rows and columns required by the solution procedure.
4. *Dummy column(s)*—Extra column(s) added to an assignment problem to provide the equal number of rows and columns required by the solution procedure.
5. *Opportunity loss*—The difference between the "best" assignment in the column and another assignment in the column. The measure is used to solve maximization assignment problems.
6. *Tour*—In a traveling salesman problem, a sequence of cities or locations starting and ending with the same city and including all other cities one and only one time.
7. *Subtour*—In a traveling salesman problem, a sequence of cities that does not include all cities (that is, the sequence is not a tour).
8. *Branch and bound*—A solution procedure usually applied to combinatorial problems which allows the analyst to partition possible solutions into subsets until the optimal solution is reached.
9. *Upper bound*—The value of the best *feasible* solution obtained thus far in a branch-and-bound procedure.

Problems

1. Scott and Associates, Inc. is an accounting firm which has three new clients. Three project leaders will be assigned to the three clients. Based on the different backgrounds and experiences of the leaders, the various leader-client assignments differ in terms of projected completion times. The possible assignments and the estimated completion time in days are shown below:

Project Leader	Client		
	A	B	C
Jackson	10	16	32
Ellis	14	22	40
Smith	22	24	34

a. Find the minimum time assignment by enumerating all possible assignment solutions.
b. Use the Hungarian method to obtain the optimal solution to this problem.

2. In Problem 1 assume that an additional employee is available for possible assignment. The following table shows the assignment alternatives and the estimated completion times:

Project Leader	Client A	B	C
Jackson	10	16	32
Ellis	14	22	40
Smith	22	24	34
Burton	14	18	36

a. What is the optimal assignment?

b. How did the assignment change compared to the best assignment possible in Problem 1? Was there any savings associated with considering Burton as one of the possible project leaders?

c. Which project leader remains unassigned?

3. Solve the Fowle Marketing Research, Inc. assignment problem when four project leaders are available for assignment to the three clients. The estimated project completion times in days are as follows:

Project Leader	Client A	B	C
Terry	10	15	9
Carle	9	18	5
McClymonds	6	14	3
Higley	8	16	6

4. Solve the Salsbury Discount, Inc. department-location assignment problem for the estimated annual profit data provided in Table 6.11.

5. In a job shop operation, four jobs may be performed on any of four machines. The number of hours required for each job on each machine are summarized below. What is the minimum total time job-machine assignment?

Job	Machine A	B	C	D
1	32	18	32	26
2	22	24	12	16
3	24	30	26	24
4	26	30	28	20

6. Mayfax Distributors, Inc. have four sales territories each of which must be assigned a sales representative. From past experience the firm's sales manager has estimated the sales volume for each sales representative in each sales territory. Find the sales representative-territory assignments that will maximize sales (data given in thousands).

Sales Representative	Sales Territory			
	A	B	C	D
Washington	44	80	52	60
Benson	60	56	40	72
Fredricks	36	60	48	48
Hodson	52	76	36	40

7. Each Monday the drivers of the Metor Bus System indicate their preferences for the various bus routes open during the coming week. With 1 indicating a first choice and 5 indicating a last choice, what is the driver-route assignment that minimizes the sum of the choice values?

Driver	Route				
	A	B	C	D	E
1	3	4	2	1	5
2	3	5	2	1	4
3	5	3	2	1	4
4	4	3	2	1	5
5	5	4	1	2	3

8. Four secretaries are available to type any of three company reports. Given the typing times in hours, what is the minimum total time secretary-report assignment?

Secretary	Report		
	A	B	C
Phyllis	24	12	10
Linda	19	11	11
Dave	25	16	16
Marlene	25	14	13

9. Four trucks must be dispatched to each of four customer locations. The assignments and the distances traveled by each truck in making the trips are shown below. What truck-customer assignments minimize the total distance traveled by the four trucks? Note that two unacceptable assignments are indicated because the specific truck involved is not equipped to carry the type of shipment involved. The unacceptable assignments show *M* as the distance traveled.

Truck	Customer			
	A	B	C	D
1	130	125	120	135
2	120	110	100	120
3	125	120	*M*	140
4	150	150	140	*M*

10. Manager Sparky Gibson of the Hamilton White Sox baseball team is trying to establish his starting pitchers for the crucial three-game series with the Mt. Washington Tigers. Sparky has the following five pitchers available:

    Minta—the ace of the staff, who just pitched last night's extra-inning game against the Northtown Giants.
    O'Donnel—the aging veteran, who has three wins and six losses this season.
    Banks—the relief ace, who has started only one game this season.
    Hudlow—the rookie, who just arrived from the Delphi farm team.
    Nash—a 10-win, 4-loss righthander who has been having arm problems.

    Sparky knows that the Tigers are saving their ace pitcher for the third game of the series. After considering the Tigers' probable lineup and pitchers, Sparky has estimated the probability of winning each of the three games with each of the five starting pitcher alternatives, as follows:

Starting Pitcher	Game 1	Game 2	Game 3
Minta	0.60	0.75	0.65
O'Donnel	0.40	0.45	0.45
Banks	0.50	0.45	0.35
Hudlow	0.30	0.50	0.20
Nash	0.40	0.45	0.30

    a. Assuming that each pitcher could only start one game in the series, what is the pitching rotation that will provide the highest winning probability for the Sox?
    b. If Nash reports that his arm is fine prior to the start of the first game and his probabilities of winning are revised to 0.60, 0.70, and 0.50 for the three games, how should Sparky alter the pitching rotation?

11. In Section 6.3 we stated that assignment problems can be formulated and solved by linear programming. In the linear programming formulation we let $x = 1$ if an assignment is made and $x = 0$ otherwise. Remember now that linear programming does not necessarily provide integer values for the variables. However, we will now illustrate that all the extreme points of the assignment formulation happen to be integer 0 or 1 solutions. Thus standard linear programming formulations of assignment problems will provide the necessary 0 or 1 solution values for the variables.

    Consider the simple assignment problem, given the following cost data:

Person	Job 1	Job 2
A	10	12
B	8	9

    a. Formulate the problem as a linear program.
    b. List all the basic feasible solutions for this problem.

12. The Lester City Steel Company has customers in Charlestown, Rossville, and Madison,

Pennsylvania. The distances in miles between the cities are summarized below:

From	To			
	Lester	Charlestown	Rossville	Madison
Lester	—	150	160	90
Charlestown	150	—	80	55
Rossville	160	80	—	120
Madison	90	55	120	—

The regional sales manager for Lester would like to visit all three customers and return to the Lester office in such a way that the total distance traveled will be minimized. What route should the sales manager select? Use the assignment algorithm and the branch-and-bound procedure to solve this traveling salesman problem.

13. Sue's School Bus Service provides students with rides to and from school each day. Sue leaves the school (the bus garage is located on the school grounds), picks up or drops off children at four bus stop locations, and returns to the school twice each day. With the following distances between bus stop locations, what is the route the bus should follow in order to minimize the total daily travel distance?

Bus Stop Locations	Distance in Miles				
	School	Maple	Terrace	Center	Applegate
School	—	2	1	6	5
Maple	2	—	2	5	4
Terrace	1	2	—	7	5
Center	6	5	7	—	2
Applegate	5	4	5	2	—

14. Four jobs must be processed on the same machine. The changeover or setup times between jobs are dependent upon the sequence in which the jobs are assigned to the machine. For example, the changeover time from job 1 to job 2 is 8 hours; however, if job 4 precedes job 2 on the machine, the changeover time is only 6 hours.

   Assume that the job you start with will be set up again after the other three jobs are processed. Thus the complete sequence of jobs can be viewed as a "tour." Given the changeover times in hours as shown below, use the traveling salesman solution procedure to find the sequence of jobs that will minimize the total changeover time:

From	To			
	1	2	3	4
1	—	8	6	4
2	1	—	5	5
3	1	7	—	4
4	1	6	3	—

Application

American Baseball League*
New York, New York

The American Baseball League consists of fourteen professional baseball teams organized into two divisions: the Western Division, with Seattle, Oakland, California, Texas, Kansas City, Minnesota, and Chicago, and the Eastern Division, with Milwaukee, Detroit, Cleveland, Toronto, Baltimore, New York, and Boston.

Management Science Applications in Professional Baseball

A variety of interesting scheduling problems occur in the operation of a professional baseball league. How can a schedule be developed that guarantees each team playing every other team in its division the same number of games with exactly half of the games being at home and half away? How can a schedule be developed that provides reasonable travel times and distances on road trips? How can each team have a balance of home stands and road trips throughout the season? How can the schedule of the American and National leagues be coordinated so that teams located in the same city (e.g., Chicago Cubs and Chicago White Sox) are not scheduled to play at home on the same date?

Solutions to the above rather complicated scheduling problems are often identified through the use of quantitative methods. In addition to its own staff, the American Baseball League uses management science consultants to assist with the scheduling decisions.

The Umpire Crew Assignment Problem

In addition to the schedules for each team, the American League must determine the best way to assign the umpire crews to the various games played throughout the league. Umpire crews are assigned to specific home-team cities for the two-, three-, or four-game series in that city but are not assigned on an individual-game basis. Since there are fourteen American League teams, there can be as many as seven "games" (doubleheaders count as one "game" in assigning crews); hence seven umpire crews must be assigned.

*The authors are indebted to James R. Evans, management science consultant to the American League, New York, N.Y., for providing this application.

Date	SEA	OAK	CAL	TEX	KC	MIN	CHI	MKE	DET	CLE	TOR	BAL	NY	BOS
Mon. April 27		CAL*		BOS*		SEA		TOR*	NY*	KC*		CHI*		
Tues. 28		CAL*		BOS*		SEA		TOR*	NY*	KC*		CHI*		
Wed. 29		CAL		BOS*		SEA		TOR*	NY			CHI*		
Thurs. 30	DET*		MKE*	KC*						CHI*		TOR*		MIN*
Fri. May 1	DET*	NY*	MKE*	KC*						CHI*		TOR*		MIN*
Sat. 2	DET*	NY	MKE*	KC*						CHI		TOR*		MIN
Sun. 3	DET	NY(2)	MKE	KC*						CHI		TOR		MIN
Mon. 4	MKE*	DET*	NY*		BOS*							MIN*		
Tues. 5	MKE*	DET*	NY*	CHI*	BOS*						CLE*	MIN*		
Wed. 6	MKE*	DET	NY*	CHI*	BOS*						CLE*	MIN*		
Thurs. 7	MKE*	DET	NY*	CHI*							CLE*			
Fri. 8	NY*	MKE*	DET*	BAL*		CLE*	KC*				BOS*			
Sat. 9	NY*	MKE	DET*	BAL*		CLE*	KC*				BOS			
Sun. 10	NY*	MKE	DET	BAL*		CLE	KC				BOS			
Mon. 11					TEX*		CLE*				BOS*			
Tues. 12					TEX*	BOS*	CLE*	CAL*	SEA*		BAL*		OAK*	
Wed. 13					TEX*	BOS*	CLE*	CAL*	SEA*		BAL*		OAK*	
Thurs. 14					TEX*	BOS	CLE	CAL	SEA*		BAL*		OAK*	

*Denotes night game or early-evening start
(2) Denotes doubleheader (two games in one day)

Figure 1   A Segment of the 1981 Schedule

Series	SEA	OAK	CAL	TEX	KC	MIN	CHI	MKE	DET	CLE	TOR	BAL	NY	BOS
6		CAL^5		BOS^3						KC^6		CHI^2		
7	DET^3	NY^2	MKE^7	KC^5		SEA^7		TOR^4	NY^1	CHI^6		TOR^4		MIN^1
8	MKE^2	DET^7	NY^3	CHI^6	BOS^5						CLE^1	MIN^4		
9	NY^7	MKE^3	DET^2	BAL^6		CLE^5	KC^4				BOS^1			
10					TEX	BOS	CLE	CAL	SEA		BAL		OAK	

Figure 2   Crew Assignments for Series 6–9

Several considerations are important in making the umpire crew assign-ments. Because of the amount of travel required, airline costs can be substantial. Thus from a cost point of view umpire crew assignments with minimum travel distances are desired. However, a second consideration in the assignment of the umpire crews is that there should be a balance such that each crew works approximately the same number of games with each team and in each city. The considerations of minimizing travel distances and at the same time balancing the crew assignments among the teams and cities are in conflict.

In addition to the above considerations, a number of constraints must also be satisfied. The most important of these constraints are as follows:

1. A crew cannot travel from city A to city B if the last game in city A is a night game and the first game in city B is an afternoon game on the next day.
2. A crew cannot travel from a West Coast location (Seattle, Oakland, or California) to Chicago or any Eastern Division city without a day off.
3. A crew traveling into or out of Toronto must have a day off unless they are coming from or going to New York, Boston, Detroit, or Cleveland. This constraint occurs because of flight scheduling problems.
4. Any crew traveling from a night game in Seattle, Oakland, or California cannot be assigned to Kansas City or Texas for a game on the next day.
5. No crew should be assigned to the same team for more than two series in a row.

Summarizing, the umpire assignment problem is to assign crews to series such that the above constraints are satisfied and the two considerations stated earlier (minimum distance traveled and balanced assignments) are achieved as closely as possible.

To better illustrate the nature of the umpire assignment problem, consider the assignment for one series. Suppose that the crews have already been scheduled for the first nine series of the 1981 schedule. Figure 1 shows a segment of the 1981 schedule, and Figure 2 shows the crew assignments for the sixth to ninth series and the pairings for the tenth series. The number next to each team identification in Figure 2 indicates the umpire crew assigned for that pairing. For example, for the ninth series crew 1 is assigned to the Boston-

Crew From	KC	MIN	CHI	To MKE	DET	TOR	NY
SEA (7)	M	1399	M	1694	1939	2124	2421
OAK (3)	1498	1589	M	1845	2079	2286	2586
CAL (2)	1363	1536	M	1756	1979	2175	2475
TEX (6)	M	853	798	843	982	1186	1383
MIN (5)	394	0	334	297	528	780	1028
CHI (4)	403	334	0	74	235	430	740
TOR (1)	M	M	M	M	206	M	366

Figure 3   A Cost Matrix for Crew Assignments for Series 10

Toronto games, crew 2 is assigned to the Detroit-California games, and so. How should we assign the crews to the games in series 10?

Enumeration of all possibilities would require evaluating 7! = 5040 assignments. Clearly it would be better to use an assignment model. Since mileage is one of the prime considerations, it is used as the "cost" of making the assignment. In choosing cost coefficients, an assignment violating any of the travel restrictions is handled as an unacceptable assignment by using M, an arbitrarily large number, as the intercity mileage. The cost matrix that results is shown in Figure 3. The unacceptable assignments stem from the following constraints:

> SEA to KC (restriction 4)
> SEA, OAK, CAL to CHI (restriction 2)
> TEX to KC (restriction 5)
> TOR to KC, CHI (series overlap)
> TOR to MIN, MKE (restriction 3)
> TOR to TOR (restriction 5)

What about the other principal objective of balance among teams? This objective may be incorporated into the assignment model by modifying the cost matrix to reflect imbalances. For instance, through May 10 crew 4 has already umpired three series with Kansas City and Milwaukee but only 0, 1, or 2 with the other teams. We may choose to designate the assignments from Chicago to Kansas City and Milwaukee as unacceptable. On the other hand, crew 5 has not been assigned any games with New York, Toronto, or Detroit. To guarantee that one of these series is assigned next, we would let all other costs in row 5 be M except for assignments to these teams. It is left as an exercise to the reader to find the minimum mileage assignment for this example.

The assignment problem described could be solved repeatedly, one series to the next, to generate a complete schedule. Solving the problem in this fashion, however, does not consider the schedule as a whole and could lead to some rather poor results. Nonetheless, the "one series at a time" approach does have some important advantages. First, it is easy to solve a sequence of assignment problems. Second, sensitivity analysis can easily be performed by manipulating the unacceptable assignments that are used to achieve balance. Finally, the minimum mileage obtained can be compared qualitatively with the resulting balance figures to help the scheduler trade off between the two conflicting objectives.

Chapter 7

The Transportation Problem

The problems and solution procedures we present in this chapter are concerned with the transportation or physical distribution of goods and services from several supply locations to several customer locations. Usually we have a fixed capacity or limited quantity of goods available at each supply location (*origin*) and a specified order quantity or demand at each customer location (*destination*). With a variety of transportation or shipping routes and a variety of costs for these routes, we would like to determine how many units should be shipped from each origin to each destination so that all destination demands are satisfied and the total transportation costs are minimized.

While the model and solution procedures presented in this chapter have been used to solve problems having nothing to do with the transportation of goods or services, the majority of problems or applications, as the name implies, have been used in transportation decision situations. Thus let us begin by considering a problem involving the distribution or transportation of a product from three plants to four distribution centers.

7.1   The Foster Generators, Inc. Transportation Problem

Foster Generators, Inc. is a firm that has production operations in Cleveland, Ohio; Bedford, Indiana; and York, Pennsylvania. Production capacities for these plants over the next three-month planning period for one particular type of generator are as follows:

Plant	Three-Month Production Capacity (units)
Cleveland	5000
Bedford	6000
York	2500
Total	13,500

Suppose that the firm distributes its generators through four regional distribution centers located in Boston, Chicago, St. Louis, and Lexington (Kentucky) and that the three-month forecasted demands for the distribution centers are as shown at the top of page 276.

Management would like to determine how much of its production should be shipped from each plant to each distribution center. Figure 7.1 shows graphically the distribution routes Foster can use.

With identical production costs at the three plants, the only variable costs involved are transportation costs. Thus the problem becomes one of determining the distribution routes to be used and the quantity to be shipped

Distribution Center	Forecasted Three-Month Demand (units)
Boston	6000
Chicago	4000
St. Louis	2000
Lexington	1500
Total	13,500

via each route so that all distribution center demands can be met with a minimum total transportation cost. The cost for each unit shipped on each route is given in Table 7.1.

We now discuss a solution procedure or algorithm that can be used to solve the Foster Generators transportation problem.

7.2   Transportation Problem Solution Algorithms

The solution algorithms for the transportation problem involve first finding an initial feasible solution and then proceeding iteratively to make improvements in the solution until an optimal solution is reached. In order to summarize the data conveniently and to keep track of the algorithm calculations, a *transportation tableau* is usually employed. The transportation tableau for the Foster Generators problem is presented in Table 7.2.

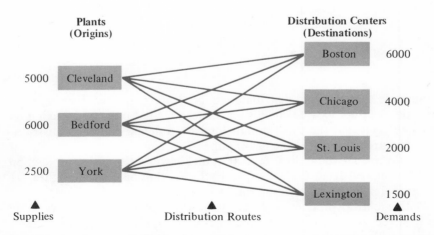

FIGURE 7.1   Possible Distribution Routes for the Foster Generators Transportation Problem

TABLE 7.1 Transportation Cost Per Unit for the Foster Generators Transportation Problem

From Origin	To Destination			
	Boston	Chicago	St. Louis	Lexington
Cleveland	3	2	7	6
Bedford	7	5	2	3
York	2	5	4	5

Note that the twelve *cells* in the tableau correspond to the twelve shipping routes shown in Figure 7.1; that is, each cell corresponds to the route from one plant to one distribution center. The entries at the right-hand border of the tableau represent the supply available at each plant, and the entries at the bottom border represent the demand at each distribution center. The entries in the upper right-hand corner of each cell represent the per unit cost of shipping over that specific route.

Once the transportation tableau is complete, we can proceed with the

TABLE 7.2 Transportation Tableau for the Foster Generators Transportation Problem

		To Destination				Origin Supply
		Boston	Chicago	St. Louis	Lexington	
From Origin	Cleveland	3	2	7	6	5000
	Bedford	7	5	2	3	6000
	York	2	5	4	5	2500
	Destination Demand	6000	4000	2000	1500	13,500

Cell corresponding to shipments from Bedford to Boston

Total supply and total demand

calculations necessary to determine the minimum-cost decision. As stated, the first phase of the solution procedure involves finding an initial feasible solution. This can be accomplished by either using the northwest corner rule or Vogel's approximation method.

The Northwest Corner Rule

The *northwest corner rule* for identifying an initial feasible solution requires that we begin in the upper left-hand corner or cell of the tableau (the *northwest corner* on a map) and allocate units to routes in a "move-to-the-right-and-down" fashion. For example, in the Foster Generators problem we begin by allocating as many units as possible to the northwest corner, that is, the Cleveland–Boston route. In this case we can ship only 5000 units over this cell or route, since the supply at Cleveland is only 5000. To indicate a shipment of 5000 units over the route, we write 5000 in the Cleveland–Boston cell of our transportation tableau. Since this reduces our supply at Cleveland from 5000 to 0, we cross out the 5000 supply value for Cleveland in the tableau and replace it with the new revised value of 0. In addition, since 5000 units shipped along this route still leaves a demand of 1000 unsatisfied at Boston, we cross out the 6000 Boston demand value and replace it with 1000. Our transportation tableau now appears as shown below:

	Boston	Chicago	St. Louis	Lexington	Supply
Cleveland	3 5000	2	7	6	0 ~~5000~~
Bedford	7	5	2	3	6000
York	2	5	4	5	2500
Demand	~~6000~~ 1000	4000	2000	1500	

We continue the procedure by "moving down" the Boston column and shipping as many units as possible over the cell in row 2 and column 1: the Bedford–Boston route. Since the remaining Boston demand is only 1000 units, we ship 1000 over the Bedford–Boston route and "move to the right" in the Bedford row, shipping as many as possible, 4000, over the Bedford–

Chicago cell or route. The resulting tableau appears below:

	Boston	Chicago	St. Louis	Lexington	Supply
Cleveland	3 5000	2	7	6	0 ~~5000~~
Bedford	7 1000	5 4000	2	3	1000 ~~5000~~ ~~6000~~
York	2	5	4	5	2500
Demand	~~6000~~ ~~1000~~ 0	~~4000~~ 0	2000	1500	

Continuing in this "right-and-down" fashion, we obtain the following initial feasible transportation solution using the northwest corner rule:

	Boston	Chicago	St. Louis	Lexington	Supply
Cleveland	3 5000	2	7	6	0 ~~5000~~
Bedford	7 1000	5 4000	2 1000	3	0 ~~1000~~ ~~5000~~ ~~6000~~
York	2	5	4 1000	5 1500	0 ~~1500~~ ~~2500~~
Demand	~~6000~~ ~~1000~~ 0	~~4000~~ 0	~~2000~~ ~~1000~~ 0	~~1500~~ 0	

This solution is feasible, since all the demand is satisfied and all the supply is used. However, we would be very fortunate indeed if this turned out to be the optimal solution. The total transportation cost that would result from this solution is calculated in Table 7.3 on page 282.

The major advantage of using the northwest corner rule to find an initial feasible solution is that it is quick and easy to use. However, you might suspect that the initial feasible solution obtained using this procedure will not be very good, since the costs of shipping over each of the routes were totally ignored. This is the major shortcoming of the northwest corner rule. Vogel's approximation method overcomes this shortcoming by taking costs into account in the development of an initial feasible solution.

Vogel's Approximation Method

Vogel's approximation method (VAM) attempts to find a low-cost initial transportation solution by considering the costs associated with the transportation route alternatives. In order to apply VAM we first calculate for each row and column the penalty that will be incurred if, instead of shipping over the *best* route, we are forced to ship over the *second-best* route. Let us apply VAM to develop an initial feasible solution for the Foster Generators problem. An initial set of row and column penalties for this problem have been calculated in the tableau below:

	Boston	Chicago	St. Louis	Lexington	Supply	Row Penalties
Cleveland	3	2	7	6	5000	1
Bedford	7	5	2	3	6000	1
York	2	5	4	5	2500	2
Demand	6000	4000	2000	1500		
Column Penalties	1	3	2	2		

For row 1 we see that the best or lowest-cost route is the Cleveland–Chicago route, at a cost of $2 per unit. If we are not allowed to ship any of the Cleveland production over this route and must ship over the second-best route instead (the Cleveland–Boston route, at $3 per unit), the penalty we pay is $1 per unit. Similarly, Bedford–St. Louis is the best route in row 2. If we are not allowed to ship over this best route, we will have to pay a penalty of at least $1 per unit; that is, the incremental cost is $1 per unit for shipping over the second-best route, Bedford–Lexington.

The penalties for each column are calculated similarly. For example, in column 3 the cheapest way to satisfy the St. Louis demand is to ship from Bedford. If we do not ship over this route, we must pay a penalty of at least $2 per unit, corresponding to the incremental cost of shipping over the second best route, York–St. Louis. Thus the column penalty is 2.

Once *all* the row and column penalties have been calculated, we make an allocation to the cell for which the penalty would be greatest if we did not select this cell or route. That is, we locate the row or column with the largest penalty and then allocate the maximum number of units possible to the best cell in that row or column. In our problem, column 2 has the largest penalty, 3, and the Cleveland–Chicago route is the best in that column. Thus we allocate the maximum number of units possible, 4000, to this cell. Hence in our transportation tableau we write 4000 in the Cleveland–Chicago cell.

The allocation of 4000 units to the Cleveland–Chicago route satisfies all the Chicago demand, and hence we can line out column 2 and ignore it in the remainder of the calculations. In addition, we reduce the supply available at Cleveland by the amount shipped. The revised supply at Cleveland is now 5000 − 4000 = 1000 units. The resulting transportation tableau is shown below:

	Boston	Chicago	St. Louis	Lexington	Supply	Row Penalties
Cleveland	3	2 — 4000	7	6	1000 ~~5000~~	X̶ 3
Bedford	7	5	2	3	6000	X̶ 1
York	2	5	4	5	2500	2̶ 2
Demand	6000	~~4000~~ 0	2000	1500		
Column Penalties	1	3	2	2		

Once column 2 has been lined out and the Cleveland supply and Chicago demand have been revised, we must recalculate the penalties in

TABLE 7.3. Total Cost of Initial Feasible Solution Obtained Using the Northwest Corner Rule

Route		Units	Per Unit	Total
From	To	Shipped	Cost	Cost
Cleveland	Boston	5000	$3	$15,000
Bedford	Boston	1000	$7	7000
Bedford	Chicago	4000	$5	20,000
Bedford	St. Louis	1000	$2	2000
York	St. Louis	1000	$4	4000
York	Lexington	1500	$5	7500
			Total	$55,500

order to determine the next allocation. The recalculated row penalties are shown in the above tableau. Note that the *column* penalties remain unchanged, since a *column* was lined out in the previous step.

Row 1 now has the largest penalty, and thus we select the Cleveland–Boston route as the best cell or route. The maximum amount we can ship over this route is the remaining supply of 1000 units at Cleveland. Thus 1000 units are allocated to the cell in row 1 and column 1. Since all the Cleveland production has been shipped, we line out the Cleveland row and ignore it in the remainder of the calculations. The Boston demand can now be revised to 6000 − 1000 = 5000 units. Our resulting transportation tableau is shown below:

	Boston	Chicago	St. Louis	Lexington	Supply	Row Penalties
~~Cleveland~~	3 1000	2 4000	7	6	0 ~~1000~~ ~~5000~~	~~1~~ 3
Bedford	7	5	2	3	6000	~~1~~ 1
York	2	5	4	5	2500	~~2~~ 2
Demand	6000 5000	~~4000~~ 0	2000	1500		
Column Penalties	1	3	2	2		

Once row 1 has been lined out and the Cleveland supply and the Boston demand have been revised, we must calculate new column penalties in order to determine the next allocation. A new tableau with the recalculated column penalties is presented below. Note that since column 1 turns out to have the maximum penalty, we have selected the York–Boston route as the best cell, and hence have allocated 2500 units over this route. Since this exhausts our supply at York, we have lined out the York row in this revised tableau:

	Boston	Chicago	St. Louis	Lexington	Supply	Row Penalties
~~Cleveland~~	3 1000	2 4000	7	6	0 ~~1000~~ ~~5000~~	~~1~~ 3
Bedford	7	5	2	3	6000	~~1~~ 1
~~York~~	2 2500	5	4	5	0 ~~2500~~	~~2~~ 2
Demand	~~6000~~ ~~5000~~ 2500	~~4000~~ 0	2000	1500		
Column Penalties	~~1~~ 5	3	~~2~~ 2	~~2~~ 2		

TABLE 7.4 Total Cost of Initial Feasible Solution Obtained Using Vogel's Approximation Method

Route		Units	Per Unit	Total
From	To	Shipped	Cost	Cost
Cleveland	Boston	1000	$3	$ 3000
Cleveland	Chicago	4000	$2	8000
Bedford	Boston	2500	$7	17,500
Bedford	St. Louis	2000	$2	4000
Bedford	Lexington	1500	$3	4500
York	Boston	2500	$2	5000
			Total	$42,000

Since we have only one row left, it is not necessary to recalculate row or column penalties. All that we have to do to obtain an initial feasible solution is to allocate the 6000 units of supply at Bedford to the Boston, St. Louis, and Lexington destinations. Carrying out these remaining allocations results in the following transportation tableau.

	Boston	Chicago	St. Louis	Lexington	Supply	Row Penalties
~~Cleveland~~	3 ~~1000~~	2 ~~4000~~	7	6	0 ~~1000~~ ~~5000~~	~~1~~ 3
Bedford	7 2500	5	2 2000	3 1500	~~6000~~	~~1~~ 1
~~York~~	2 ~~2500~~	5	4	5	0 ~~2500~~	~~2~~ 2
Demand	~~6000~~ ~~5000~~ ~~2500~~	~~4000~~ 0	~~2000~~	~~1500~~		
Column Penalties	~~1~~ 5	3	~~2~~ 2	~~2~~ 2		

This solution is feasible, since all the demand is satisfied and all the supply is used. The total transportation cost resulting from this solution is calculated in Table 7.4.

Comparing Tables 7.3 and 7.4, we see that the initial feasible solution obtained using Vogel's approximation method results in a cost savings of $13,500. Considering only these cost savings, one is tempted to conclude that VAM is obviously the best way to find an initial feasible solution. However, neither method guarantees us the optimal solution. Thus further calculations will be necessary regardless of whether the northwest corner rule or VAM is used to find an initial feasible solution.

In most, but not all, cases VAM will give a better initial feasible solution and also will tend to minimize the calculations necessary to reach the optimal solution. The major drawback of Vogel's approximation method is that it takes many more calculations to find an initial feasible solution than does the northwest corner rule. There are some studies that seem to indicate that the extra work necessary in using VAM to find an initial feasible solution is more than compensated for by the reduction in work necessary in the second phase of the solution procedure, where we must iterate from the initial feasible solution to the optimal solution.

Summary of Initial Feasible Solution Procedures

Before moving on to the second phase of the solution procedure and attempting to improve the initial feasible solution, let us restate the steps of the northwest corner rule and Vogel's approximation method for obtaining an initial transportation solution.

Northwest corner rule

Step 1: Starting with the upper left-hand cell (northwest corner) of the transportation tableau, assign as many units to this cell as possible. The amount assigned is the smaller of the row supply available or the column demand requirement.

Step 2: Reduce the row supply and the column demand by the amount assigned to the cell.

Step 3: If the row supply is now zero, move down the column to the next cell; if the column demand is now zero, move to the right on the row to the next cell; if both the row supply and the column demand are zero, move down one cell and to the right one cell, to the next cell.

Step 4: For the next cell, as identified by step 3, assign as many units as possible and return to step 2 until an initial feasible solution is obtained.

Vogel's approximation method

Step 1: For each row and column of the transportation tableau, compute a penalty cost, which is the difference between the unit cost on the *second-best* route in the row or column and the *best* route in the row or column.

Step 2: Identify the row or column with the highest penalty cost and assign as many units as possible to the *best* cell or route in the identified row or column.

Step 3: Reduce the row supply and the column demand by the amount assigned to the cell.

Step 4: If the row supply is now zero, eliminate the row; if the column demand is now zero, eliminate the column; if both the row supply and the column demand are zero, eliminate both the row and the column.

Step 5: Compute the new row and column penalty costs for the transportation tableau after the step 4 reduction and return to step 2 until an initial feasible solution is obtained.

The Stepping-Stone Method

The *stepping-stone method* provides an iterative method for moving from the northwest corner or VAM initial feasible solution to an optimal solution. As we will discuss in detail later, this method can be implemented only if the initial feasible solution of an m-origin, n-destination transportation problem uses $m + n - 1$ transportation routes. This condition requires the Foster Generators transportation problem to have $3 + 4 - 1 = 6$ transportation routes in the initial solution. For the Foster problem both the northwest corner rule solution (Table 7.3) and the VAM solution (Table 7.4) satisfy this condition; thus we may proceed with the stepping-stone method. Later we will show what to do if the initial solution does not consist of $m + n - 1$ transportation routes.

We will use the stepping-stone method to evaluate the economics of shipping via transportation routes that are not currently part of the transportation solution. If we can find cost-reducing routes, the current solution is revised by making shipments via these new routes. By continuing to evaluate the costs associated with routes that are not in the current solution, we will know that we have reached the optimal solution when all routes not in the current solution would increase costs if they were brought into the solution.

To see how the stepping-stone method works, let us return to the VAM initial solution for the Foster Generators problem as presented below:

	Boston	Chicago	St. Louis	Lexington	Supply
Cleveland	3 1000	2 4000	7	6	5000
Bedford	7 2500	5	2 2000	3 1500	6000
York	2 2500	5	4	5	2500
Demand	6000	4000	2000	1500	

Suppose we were to allocate 1 unit to the route or cell in row 2 and column 2; that is, ship one unit on the currently unused route from Bedford to Chicago. In order to satisfy the Chicago demand exactly, we would have to reduce the number of units in the Cleveland–Chicago cell to 3999. But then we would have to increase the amount in the Cleveland–Boston cell to 1001 so that the total Cleveland supply of 5000 units could be shipped.

Finally, we would reduce the Bedford–Boston cell by 1 in order to exactly satisfy the Boston demand. The tableau below summarizes the series of adjustments just described:

	Boston	Chicago	St. Louis	Lexington	Supply
Cleveland	1001 ~~1000~~ [3]	3999 ~~4000~~ [2]	[7]	[6]	5000
Bedford	2499 ~~2500~~ [7]	[5]	2000 [2]	1500 [3]	6000
York	2500 [2]	[5]	[4]	[5]	2500
Demand	6000	4000	2000	1500	

What is the added or reduced cost that will result from using the Bedford–Chicago route? Let us calculate the cost per unit change resulting from the one unit addition to the Bedford–Chicago route. The cost adjustments are as follows:

	Changes	Effect on Cost
Add 1 unit	Bedford–Chicago	+5
Reduce 1 unit	Cleveland–Chicago	−2
Add 1 unit	Cleveland–Boston	+3
Reduce 1 unit	Bedford–Boston	−7
	Net effect	−1

Thus this analysis tells us that the transportation costs can be reduced by $1 for every unit shipped over the Bedford–Chicago route if corresponding changes are made in other routes as shown.

Before making additions to this new route, let us consider the general procedure for evaluating the costs associated with a new cell or route and then check all currently unused routes to find the best route to add to our current transportation solution.

The method we have just demonstrated for evaluating the Bedford–Chicago route is known as the stepping-stone method. Note that in considering the addition of this new route, we evaluated its effect on other routes *currently in the transportation solution,* referred to as *occupied* cells. In total we considered changes in four cells, the new cell and three *current solution* or *occupied* cells. In effect, we can view these four cells as forming a path or *stepping-stone path* in the tableau, where the corners of the path are current solution cells. The idea is to view the tableau as a pond with the current solution cells as stones sticking up in the pond. To identify the stepping-stone path for a new cell, we move in horizontal and vertical directions using current solution cells as the stones at the corners of the path by which we can step from stone to stone and return to the new cell we initially started with. The dotted line in the following tableau represents the stepping-stone path for the Cleveland–St. Louis route or cell. In terms of a transportation tableau, the stepping-stone path represents the sequence of adjustments that are necessary to maintain a feasible solution, given that one unit is to be shipped through a new or currently unoccupied cell.

	Boston	Chicago	St. Louis	Lexington	Supply
Cleveland	3 1000	2 4000	7	6	5000
Bedford	7 2500	5	2 2000	3 1500	6000
York	2 2500	5	4	5	2500
Demand	6000	4000	2000	1500	

By using the stepping-stone path for a new cell, we can evaluate the costs associated with a one-unit addition to the new cell. For example, the Cleveland–St. Louis cell would result in the following changes:

	Changes	Effect on Cost
Add 1 unit	Cleveland–St. Louis	+7
Reduce 1 unit	Bedford–St. Louis	−2
Add 1 unit	Bedford–Boston	+7
Reduce 1 unit	Cleveland–Boston	−3
	Net effect	+9

Thus we see that the Cleveland–St. Louis route is unattractive, in that use of this route will result in a $9 per unit increase in the transportation cost.

Finding the stepping-stone path for each possible new cell enables us to identify the cost effect for each new cell or route. Evaluating this cost effect for all possible new cells leads to the following transportation tableau. The per unit cost effect for each possible new cell is circled in the cell.

	Boston	Chicago	St. Louis	Lexington	Supply
Cleveland	3 1000	2 4000	7 (+9)	6 (+7)	5000
Bedford	7 2500	5 (−1)	2 2000	3 1500	6000
York	2 2500	5 (+4)	4 (+7)	5 (+7)	2500
Demand	6000	4000	2000	1500	

On the basis of the calculated per unit changes, we see that the best cell in terms of cost reduction is the Bedford–Chicago cell, with a $1 decrease in cost for every unit shipped on this route. The question now is, How much should we ship over this new route? Since the total cost decreases by $1 per unit shipped, we would like to ship the maximum possible number of units. We know from our previous stepping-stone calculation that each unit shipped over the Bedford–Chicago route results in an increase of one unit shipped from Cleveland to Boston and a decrease of one unit in both the amount shipped from Bedford to Boston (currently 2500) and the amount shipped from Cleveland to Chicago (currently 4000). Because of this, the

TABLE 7.5 Optimal Solution to the Foster Generators Transportation Problem

Route		Units	Per Unit	Total
From	To	Shipped	Cost	Cost
Cleveland	Boston	3500	$3	$10,500
Cleveland	Chicago	1500	$2	3000
Bedford	Chicago	2500	$5	12,500
Bedford	St. Louis	2000	$2	4000
Bedford	Lexington	1500	$3	4500
York	Boston	2500	$2	5000
				$39,500

maximum we can ship over the Bedford–Chicago route is 2500, which results in no units being shipped from Bedford to Boston. The tableau corresponding to this new solution is presented below:

	Boston	Chicago	St. Louis	Lexington	Supply
Cleveland	3 3500	2 1500	7	6	5000
Bedford	7	5 2500	2 2000	3 1500	6000
York	2 2500	5	4	5	2500
Demand	6000	4000	2000	1500	

Note that the only changes from the previous tableau are located on the stepping-stone path originating in the Bedford–Chicago cell. We can now use the stepping-stone method to recalculate the per unit changes resulting from attempting to add new cells or routes to this new solution. Doing so we get the tableau below. Note that the stepping-stone path used to evaluate the York–St. Louis cell is indicated by the dashed line in the tableau.

	Boston	Chicago	St. Louis	Lexington	Supply
Cleveland	3 3500	2 1500	7 (8)	6 (6)	5000
Bedford	7 (1)	5 2500	2 2000	3 1500	6000
York	2 2500	5 (4)	4 (6)	5 (6)	2500
Demand	6000	4000	2000	1500	

The per unit change for every possible new cell is now greater than or equal to zero. Thus since there is no new route which will decrease the total cost, we have reached the optimal solution. The optimal solution together with its total cost is summarized in Table 7.5 on page 289.

The most difficult part of the solution procedure we have outlined is the identification of every stepping-stone path so that we can calculate the cost per unit change in each new cell. There is an easier way to make these cost per unit calculations; it is called the modified distribution (MODI) method. While we will not derive the method, we will demonstrate how it can be used to calculate the per unit changes for the new or unoccupied cells.

Modified Distribution (MODI) Method

The MODI method requires that we define an index u_i for each row of the tableau and an index v_j for each column of the tableau. The values of these indices are found by requiring that the cost coefficient for each current solution (or occupied) cell equal $u_i + v_j$. If we define c_{ij} to be the per unit cost of shipping from plant i to distribution center j, then we require that $u_i + v_j = c_{ij}$ for each occupied cell in order to calculate the per unit changes in the final tableau of the Foster Generators problem.

Requiring that $u_i + v_j = c_{ij}$ for all the occupied cells in the final tableau of the Foster Generators problem leads to a system of six equations and seven variables:

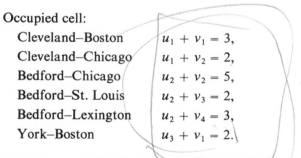

Occupied cell:

    Cleveland–Boston $u_1 + v_1 = 3,$
    Cleveland–Chicago $u_1 + v_2 = 2,$
    Bedford–Chicago $u_2 + v_2 = 5,$
    Bedford–St. Louis $u_2 + v_3 = 2,$
    Bedford–Lexington $u_2 + v_4 = 3,$
    York–Boston $u_3 + v_1 = 2.$

Since there is one more variable than equation in the above system, we can freely pick a value for one of the variables and then solve for the others. Thus we shall always choose $u_1 = 0$ and then solve for the values of the other variables. Setting $u_1 = 0$, we get the following system of equations:

$$0 + v_1 = 3,$$
$$0 + v_2 = 2,$$
$$u_2 + v_2 = 5,$$
$$u_2 + v_3 = 2,$$
$$u_2 + v_4 = 3,$$
$$u_3 + v_1 = 2.$$

Solving these equations leads to the following values for $u_1, u_2, u_3, v_1, v_2,$

v_3, and v_4:

$$u_1 = 0, \qquad v_1 = 3,$$
$$u_2 = 3, \qquad v_2 = 2,$$
$$u_3 = -1, \qquad v_3 = -1,$$
$$v_4 = 0.$$

Now let us define $e_{ij} = c_{ij} - u_i - v_j$, where the value of e_{ij} represents the per-unit change in total cost resulting from allocating one unit to the unoccupied cell in row i and column j. Rewriting the final tableau for the Foster Generators problem and replacing the previous marginal information with the values of u_i and v_j we obtain

u_i \ v_j	3	2	−1	0
0	3 ⟶ 3500	2 ⟶ 1500	7 ⟶ ⑧	6 ⟶ ⑥
3	7 ⟶ ①	5 ⟶ 2500	2 ⟶ 2000	3 ⟶ 1500
−1	2 ⟶ 2500	5 ⟶ ④	4 ⟶ ⑥	5 ⟶ ⑥

Once again the per-unit cost effect for each new cell (e_{ij}) has been circled.

Note how much easier it is to compute the net changes using the MODI method. For example, $e_{13} = c_{13} - u_1 - v_3 = 7 - 0 - (-1) = 8$ represents the net change in the total cost that would result from allocating one unit to cell 1,3. We also observe that these e_{ij} calculated by the MODI method are exactly the same as the net changes calculated by the stepping-stone method. It is still necessary to search for a stepping-stone path to determine which route to close once the best route to open has been identified. However, it is not necessary to generate a stepping-stone path for any of the other unoccupied cells. Thus a considerable savings in the work required at each iteration can be obtained by employing the MODI method in the calculation of the e_{ij} for each unoccupied cell.

Summary of the Stepping-Stone and MODI Algorithms

The stepping-stone and modified distribution methods were presented as procedures for improving an initial feasible transportation solution until an optimal solution is reached. Below we restate the detailed steps of these algorithms.

Stepping-Stone Method   Given the transportation tableau with an initial solution and $m + n - 1$ occupied cells, the stepping-stone method is as follows:

Step 1:   For each unoccupied cell, identify its stepping-stone path through the transportation tableau.

Step 2:   Compute the per unit change (e_{ij}) from adding one unit to each unoccupied cell as follows:

    a.   Label the starting or unoccupied cell under consideration as cell 1 and number sequentially 2, 3, 4, . . . the occupied cells on the corners of its stepping-stone path.

    b.   The per unit change from adding one unit to the unoccupied cell is found by adding the unit shipping costs of all *odd* numbered cells on the path and subtracting the unit shipping costs of all *even* numbered cells on the path.

Step 3:   In a minimization problem, if the per unit changes for all unoccupied cells are nonnegative, the solution is optimal. However, if negative per unit changes exist, identify the best cell (most negative per unit change) and continue.

Step 4:   For the best cell, identify the sequentially numbered occupied cells on the corners of its stepping-stone path as under step 2. Determine the even-numbered stepping-stone cell over which the smallest quantity is being shipped. Add this quantity to the new cell and all odd numbered cells. Subtract this quantity from all even numbered cells. Return to step 1.

Modified Distribution (MODI) Method   Given the transportation tableau with an initial solution and $m + n - 1$ occupied cells, the MODI method is as follows:

Step 1:   Letting $u_1 = 0$, use the occupied cells of the transportation tableau to compute row indices $u_2, u_3, \ldots$ and column indices $v_1, v_2, v_3, \ldots$ such that

$$u_i + v_j = c_{ij}$$

for all occupied cells.

Step 2:   Compute the cost e_{ij} of adding one unit to each unoccupied cell by

$$e_{ij} = c_{ij} - u_i - v_j.$$

Step 3:   Follow step 3 of the stepping-stone method.

Step 4:   Follow step 4 of the stepping-stone method.

7.3   Handling Special Situations

We will now discuss how to handle the following special transportation problem situations:

1.   Total supply not equal to total demand;
2.   Maximization objective;
3.   Unacceptable transportation routes;
4.   Transportation tableaus with less than $m + n - 1$ occupied cells.

One situation that often occurs is the case where the total supply is not equal to the total demand. This situation can be handled easily by our solution procedure if we first introduce a dummy plant or dummy distribution center. If total supply is greater than total demand, we introduce a *dummy destination* (distribution center) with demand exactly equal to the excess of supply over demand. Similarly, if total demand is greater than total supply, we introduce a *dummy origin* (plant) with supply exactly equal to the excess of demand over supply. In either the excess demand or excess supply case, we assign cost coefficients of zero to every route into a dummy distribution center and every route out of a dummy plant. This is because no shipments will actually be made from a dummy plant or to a dummy distribution center when the solution is implemented.

The transportation model can also be used to solve problems involving maximization of an objective. The only modification in our solution procedure necessary for problems of this type is in the selection of an unoccupied cell to allocate units to. Instead of picking the cell with the most negative e_{ij} value, we pick that cell for which e_{ij} is largest. That is, we pick the cell which will cause the largest per unit increase in the objective function.

In the assignment problem, we saw that unacceptable assignments carry an extremely large cost of M in order to keep them out of solution. Thus if we have a transportation route from an origin to a destination that for some reason cannot be used, we simply assign this route a value of M, and thus this route will not enter the solution. Unacceptable routes would be assigned a value of $-M$ in a maximization problem.

A final difficulty that can occur when applying our solution procedure is referred to as *degeneracy*. This happens when there are less than $m + n - 1$ occupied cells in an m-origin, n-destination transportation tableau and causes problems in that there are not enough cells to identify all stepping-stone paths or all u_i and v_j in the MODI method. To handle this situation, we artificially create an occupied cell; that is, we place a 0, representing nothing being shipped, in one of the unoccupied cells and then treat it as if it were occupied. Note, however, that we must choose the unoccupied cell in which to place the 0 so that once it is placed, all stepping-stone paths and all the u_i and v_j can be determined.

Let us now illustrate with another example how the above difficulties can be resolved. Suppose we have three plants (origins) with production capacities as follows:

Plants	Production Capacity
P_1	50
P_2	40
P_3	30
Total	120

We also have demand for our product at three retail outlets. The demand forecasts for the current planning period are presented below:

Retail Outlets	Forecasted Demand
R_1	45
R_2	15
R_3	30
Total	90

The production cost at each plant is different, and the sales prices at the retail outlets vary. Taking prices, production costs, and shipping costs into consideration, the profits for producing one unit at plant i, shipping it to retail outlet j, and selling it at retail outlet j are presented in Table 7.6.

We note first that the total production capacity exceeds the total demand at the retail outlets. Thus we must introduce a dummy retail outlet with demand exactly equal to the excess of production capacity. We therefore add retail outlet R_4 with a demand of 30 units. The per unit profit for shipping from each plant to retail outlet R_4 is set to zero, since these units will not actually be shipped. An initial feasible solution for this problem obtained by the northwest corner rule is presented below:

	R_1		R_2		R_3		R_4		Supply
		2		8		10		0	
P_1	45		5						50
		6		11		6		0	
P_2			10		30				40
		12		7		9		0	
P_3							30		30
Demand	45		15		30		30		

Table 7.6 Profit Per Unit for Producing at Plant *i* and Selling at Retail Outlet *j*

	Retail Outlets		
	R$_1$	R$_2$	R$_3$
P$_1$	2	8	10
P$_2$	6	11	6
P$_3$	12	7	9

With this solution as a starting point we can attempt to use the MODI method to calculate the row and column indices u_i and v_j. Unfortunately, whenever the number of occupied cells is less than the number of rows plus the number of columns minus 1, it will not be possible to calculate all the u_i and v_j; that is, degeneracy occurs. In this case, since the number of rows is 3 and the number of columns is 4, anytime the number of occupied cells is less than 6 we will have a degenerate solution. From the tableau below we see that it is not possible to calculate u_3 or v_4 using the initial feasible solution:

u_i \ v_j	2	8	3		Supply
0	2 45	8 5	10	0	50
3	6	11 10	6 30	0	40
	12	7	9	0 30	30
Demand	45	15	30	30	

We must artificially create a sixth occupied cell by placing a 0 in any cell that will allow us to complete the calculation of the u_i and v_j. Thus we place a 0 in row 3 and column 3 and treat the corresponding cell as if it were occupied. Then we can complete our calculations of the u_i and v_j. The result of this calculation, together with the e_{ij} for each unoccupied cell, is presented on page 297.

Since this is a maximization problem, we pick the cell with the largest e_{ij} to make an allocation; that is, the route from P$_1$ to R$_3$ with $e_{13} = 7$ should be selected. Applying the stepping-stone procedure, we see that the maxi-

First tableau:

u_i \\ v_j	2	8	3	−6	Supply
0	2 · 45	8 · 5	10 · ⑦	0 · ⑥	50
3	6 · ①	11 · 10	6 · 30	0 · ③	40
6	12 · ④	7 · (−7)	9 · 0	0 · 30	30
Demand	45	15	30	30	

mum amount we can ship over this route before the cell in row 1 and column 2 becomes occupied is 5. Making the appropriate adjustments and recalculating the e_{ij}, we obtain a new tableau

Second tableau:

u_i \\ v_j	2	15	10	1	Supply
0	2 · 45	8 · (−7)	10 · 5	0 · (−1)	50
−4	6 · ⑧	11 · 15	6 · 25	0 · ③	40
−1	12 · ⑪	7 · (−7)	9 · 0	0 · 30	30
Demand	45	15	30	30	

The route from P_3 to R_1 with $e_{31} = 11$ now results in the largest increase. Our stepping-stone path (dashed line) indicates that 0 units is the maximum that can be shipped over this route if we are to maintain a feasible solution in our tableau; that is, if we attempted to ship any positive amount we would end up with the amount shipped from P_3 to R_3 being negative.

Making the appropriate adjustments for 0 units being shipped, and recalculating the e_{ij}, we obtain a new tableau. Note that we no longer have an entry in the P_3-R_3 cell, since the 0 units previously there have been moved to the P_3-R_1 cell.

In iterating to this tableau we see that there is really no change in the shipping pattern. However, the maximum net change is now $e_{24} = 14$. Thus we make an allocation to the route P_2-R_4. Note from the stepping-stone path that we will ship 25 units. Also since cell P_3-R_1 is on the stepping-stone path, we will increase the number of units shipped from P_3 to R_1 from 0 to 25. Our new tableau is given below:

We next allocate to the P_1-R_4 route, since e_{14} is the largest e_{ij}. The maximum that can be shipped over this route is 5. The next tableau is shown below:

u_i \ v_j	2	11	10	0	Supply
0	2 / 15	8 / ⊝-3	10 / 30	0 / 5	50
0	6 / ④	11 / 15	6 / ⊝-4	0 / 25	40
10	12 / 30	7 / ⊝-14	9 / ⊝-11	0 / ⊝-10	30
Demand	45	15	30	30	

We now ship 15 units over the route P_2-R_1. The result of this iteration is the following tableau:

u_i \ v_j	6	11	10	0
0	2 / ⊝-4	8 / ⊝-3	10 / 30	0 / 20
0	6 / 15	11 / 15	6 / ⊝-4	0 / 10
6	12 / 30	7 / ⊝-10	9 / ⊝-7	0 / ⊝-6

Since all the e_{ij} are now less than or equal to zero, we have reached the optimal solution to this maximization transportation problem.

When you apply the above procedures to solve a transportation problem it may happen that there are alternate optimal solutions to the problem. We will discover this condition whenever the e_{ij} for an unoccupied cell is equal to zero in the final transportation tableau. This condition implies that we could allocate units to the unoccupied cell with a zero e_{ij} without causing a change in the value of the solution. Hence another optimal solution could be found by allocating units to that route.

Summary of Solution Procedure for Transportation Problems

Let us now summarize in a step-by-step fashion the solution procedure that we have developed for transportation problems.

Step 1:   Find an initial feasible solution using either the northwest corner rule or Vogel's approximation method.

Step 2:   Use the MODI method to determine the per unit change in the value of the current solution that would result from making an allocation to any unoccupied cell. If degeneracy occurs, it will be necessary to artificially create an occupied cell by shipping 0 units over a route in order to calculate all the u_i and v_j.

Step 3:   Determine if making an allocation to any of the unoccupied cells will cause an improvement in the value of the current solution. If not, the optimum has been reached.

Step 4:   Allocate as many units as possible to that unoccupied cell that will cause the greatest per unit improvement in the value of the solution. Use the stepping-stone method to determine which currently occupied cell becomes unoccupied. Return to step 2.

7.4   A Linear Programming Formulation of the Transportation Problem

Like the assignment problem, the transportation problem can be formulated and solved using linear programming. In order to show the linear programming formulation of the transportation problem, we must introduce some additional notation. Let

i = index for origins, $i = 1, 2, \ldots, m$,

j = index for destinations, $j = 1, 2, \ldots, n$,

x_{ij} = number of units shipped from origin i to destination j,

c_{ij} = cost per unit of shipping from origin i to destination j,

s_i = supply or capacity in units at origin i,

d_j = demand in units at destination j.

The general linear programming formulation of the m-origin, n-destination transportation problem is

$$\min \quad \sum_{i=1}^{m} \sum_{j=1}^{n} c_{ij} x_{ij}$$

s.t.

$$\sum_{j=1}^{n} x_{ij} \leq s_i \qquad i = 1, 2, \ldots, m \quad \text{(supply)},$$

$$\sum_{i=1}^{m} x_{ij} = d_j \qquad j = 1, 2, \ldots, n \quad \text{(demand)},$$

$$x_{ij} \geq 0 \qquad \text{for all } i \text{ and } j.$$

You might note that the supply constraints are inequalities in this formulation. As long as total supply is at least as great as total demand, a feasible solution will result, and all demands will be met. It is not necessary to introduce a dummy origin in the case where total supply is greater than total demand. If we encounter a transportation problem where total supply ($\sum_{i=1}^{m} s_i$) is less than total demand ($\sum_{j=1}^{n} d_j$), there will be no feasible solution to the problem. That is, we know in advance that demands cannot be satisfied unless

$$\sum_{i=1}^{m} s_i \geq \sum_{j=1}^{n} d_j.$$

We can still generate a minimum transportation-cost solution for the available supply and at the same time identify the destinations that will not receive the requested demand by creating a dummy origin or source with a supply exactly equal to the difference between the total demand and the total supply. If we let s_{m+1} indicate the fictitious supply, then

$$s_{m+1} = \sum_{j=1}^{n} d_j - \sum_{i=1}^{m} s_i.$$

Essentially, we create a dummy origin with a capacity of s_{m+1}.

The result of introducing this dummy origin is to make total supply equal to total demand. Thus the modified linear programming model will have a feasible solution. Since no shipments will actually be made from the dummy origin, all objective function cost coefficients for this source can be set equal to zero. Thus

$$c_{m+1,1} = c_{m+1,2} = \cdots c_{m+1,n} = 0.$$

In the linear programming formulation of the transportation problem, the case of unacceptable routes is easy to handle. We simply remove the x_{ij} corresponding to an unacceptable route from the problem formulation. Then it will not be possible for the optimal solution to include units shipped over the unacceptable route.

In the case where some routes have a limited shipping capacity, additional constraints can be added to the linear programming model. For example, suppose that the route from origin 2 to destination 3 had a maximum shipping capacity of 50 units. The following constraint can be added to guarantee that the route capacity will be met:

$$x_{23} \le 50.$$

In general, if L_{ij} represents the route capacity from origin i to destination j, additional constraints of the form

$$x_{ij} \le L_{ij}$$

will be needed.

Summary

In this chapter we have introduced the transportation problem and have presented a number of approaches to solving decision-making problems that can be formulated in the framework of a general transportation situation. It should be apparent that the assignment problem discussed in Chapter 6 is really a special case of the transportation problem; that is, an assignment problem can be viewed as a transportation problem where each origin has exactly one unit to ship and each destination has a demand for exactly one unit. Hence the solution methods developed for the transportation problem could also be used to solve the assignment problem. The chapter concluded with a discussion of how a transportation problem could be formulated as a linear program and hence solved using the Simplex method described in Chapter 3.

Glossary

1. *Origin*—A source or supply location in a transportation problem.
2. *Destination*—A customer or demand location in a transportation problem.
3. *Transportation tableau*—A table showing origins, destinations, routes, costs, supplies, and demands in a transportation problem. The tableau is used to facilitate the solution algorithm calculations.
4. *Cell*—A section of a transportation tableau corresponding to a route between a specific origin and a specific destination.
5. *Occupied cell*—A cell indicating that some quantity is assigned to its corresponding route.
6. *Northwest corner rule*—An algorithm used to find an initial feasible solution to a transportation problem.
7. *Vogel's approximation method*—An algorithm used to find an initial feasible solution to a transportation problem.

8. *Stepping-stone method*—An algorithm used to find the optimal solution to a transportation problem.
9. *Stepping-stone path*—A path in a transportation tableau beginning and ending with the same unoccupied cell and having occupied cells on the corners of the path.
10. *Modified distribution method (MODI)*—An algorithm used to find the optimal solution to a transportation problem.
11. *Degeneracy*—A situation that occurs when there are less than $m + n - 1$ occupied cells in a transportation tableau.
12. *Dummy origin*—An origin added to make total supply equal to total demand in a transportation problem. The supply at the dummy origin is equal to the excess of demand over the current supply.
13. *Dummy destination*—A destination added to make total supply equal total demand in a transportation problem. The demand at the dummy destination is equal to the excess of supply over the demand.

Problems

1. Consider the following initial transportation tableau:

Origins		Destinations			Supply
		Fairport	Mendon	Penfield	
	Corning	16	10	14	600
	Geneva	12	12	20	200
	Demand	3000	200	300	

   a. Use the northwest corner rule to find an initial solution.
   b. Use the stepping-stone method to find an optimal solution.
2. a. For Problem 1 use Vogel's approximation method to find an initial solution.
   b. Use the MODI method to evaluate all unassigned routes.
3. Vogel's approximation method takes cost into account in developing an initial feasible solution. Thus it usually leads to a better initial feasible solution than the northwest corner rule. However, this problem shows that it is sometimes possible to get a better initial feasible solution using the northwest corner rule.

   For the minimum-cost transportation problem represented by the tableau below find an initial feasible solution using both the northwest corner rule and Vogel's approximation method. Compare the values of the initial solutions found and comment on your results.

	Warehouses (Destinations)			Origin supply
	W_1	W_2	W_3	
P_1	20	16	24	300
P_2	10	10	8	500
P_3	12	18	10	100
Destination demand	200	400	300	900

Plants (Origins)

4. Consider the following transportation problem:

		Destinations			Supply
		Boston	Atlanta	Houston	
	Detroit	5	2	3	100
Origins	St. Louis	8	4	3	300
	Denver	9	7	5	300
	Demand	300	200	200	

   a. Use the northwest corner rule to find an initial solution.
   b. Use the stepping-stone method to find an optimal solution.
   c. How would the optimal solution change if we want to ship 100 units on the Detroit–Atlanta route?

5. a. Use Vogel's approximation method to find an initial solution to Problem 4.
   b. Use the MODI method to find an optimal solution.
   c. Compare the northwest corner rule and Vogel's approximation method in terms of their relative advantages.

6. Suppose that in Problem 4 a labor dispute temporarily eliminates the Denver–Boston and the St. Louis–Atlanta routes. How should the firm revise its shipping schedules in order to maintain a minimum total transportation cost solution? The transportation tableau with an M unit cost assigned to the unacceptable routes is as follows:

		Destinations			
		Boston	Atlanta	Houston	Supply
	Detroit	5	2	3	100
Origins	St. Louis	8	M	3	300
	Denver	M	7	5	300
	Demand	300	200	200	

What effect did the elimination of these two routes have on the firm's total transportation costs?

7. Consider the following transportation problem:

		Destinations			
		Los Angeles	San Francisco	San Diego	Supply
	San Jose	4	10	6	100
Origins	Las Vegas	8	16	6	300
	Tucson	14	18	10	300
	Demand	200	300	200	700

a. Use the northwest corner rule to find an initial solution.
b. Use the stepping-stone method to find an optimal solution.
c. How would the optimal solution change if we want to ship 100 units on the San Jose–Los Angeles route?

8. Consider the transportation tableau with the feasible solution shown below:

	D_1	D_2	D_3	
O_1	6 150	8 100	8	250
O_2	18	12 100	14 50	150
O_3	8	12	10 100	100
	150	200	150	

a. Use the MODI method and the initial feasible solution given above to find the minimum cost solution to this problem.
b. Using your solution to part a, identify an alternate optimal solution.

9. Solve the following minimum cost transportation problem:

		Destinations			
		D_1	D_2	D_3	Supply
	O_1	1	3	4	200
Origins	O_2	2	6	8	500
	O_3	2	5	7	300
	Demand	200	100	400	

a. Identify any degenerate solutions that occur in your search for an optimal solution.

b. Since total supply (1000 units) exceeds total demand (700 units), which origins may consider alternate uses for their excess supply and still maintain a minimum total transportation cost solution?

10. Klein Chemicals, Inc. produces a special oil-base material that is currently in short supply. Four of Klein's customers have already placed orders which in total exceed the combined capacity of Klein's two plants. Klein's management faces the problem of deciding how many units it should supply to each customer. Since the four customers are in different industries, the pricing structure enables different prices to be charged to different customers. However, slightly different production costs at the two plants and varying transportation costs between the plants and customers make a "sell to the highest bidder" strategy unacceptable. After considering price, production costs, and transportation costs, Klein has established the following profit per unit for each plant-customer alternative.

		Customers			
		D_1	D_2	D_3	D_4
Plant	Clifton Springs	$32	$34	$32	$40
	Danville	$34	$30	$28	$38

The plant capacities and customer orders are as follows:

Plant Capacity	Orders	
Clifton Springs: 5000 units	D_1	2000 units
Danville: 3000 units	D_2	5000 units
	D_3	3000 units
	D_4	2000 units

How many units should each plant produce for each customer in order to *maximize* profits? Which customer demands will not be met?

11. Sound Electronics, Inc. produces a battery-operated tape recorder at plants located in Martinsville, North Carolina; Plymouth, New York; and Franklin, Missouri. The unit transportation cost for shipments from the three plants to distribution centers in Chicago, Dallas, and New York are as follows:

		To	
From	Chicago	Dallas	New York
Martinsville	1.45	1.60	1.40
Plymouth	1.10	2.25	0.60
Franklin	1.20	1.20	1.80

After considering transportation costs, management has decided that under no circumstances will it use the Plymouth–Dallas route. The plant capacities and distributor orders for the next month are as follows:

Plant	Capacity (units)	Distributor	Orders (units)
Martinsville	400	Chicago	400
Plymouth	600	Dallas	400
Franklin	300	New York	400

Because of different wage scales at the three plants, the unit production cost varies from plant to plant. If the costs are \$29.50/unit at Martinsville, \$31.20/unit at Plymouth, and \$30.35/unit at Franklin, find the production and distribution plan that minimizes production and transportation costs.

12. The Ace Manufacturing Company has orders for three similar products:

Product	Orders (units)
A	2000
B	500
C	1200

Three machines are available for the manufacturing operations. All three machines can produce all the products at the same production rate. However, due to varying defect percentages of each product on each machine, the unit costs of the products vary depending upon the machine used. Machine capacities for the next week, and the unit costs, are as follows:

Machine	Capacity (units)
I	1500
II	1500
III	1000

		Products		
		A	B	C
	I	1.00	1.20	0.90
Machine	II	1.30	1.40	1.20
	III	1.10	1.00	1.20

a. Use the transportation model to develop the minimum-cost production schedule for the products and machines.

b. Do alternate optimal production schedules exist? If the production manager would like the minimum-cost schedule to have the smallest possible number of changeovers of products on machines, which solution would you recommend?

13. Consider the following transportation problem:

		Destinations			
		A	B	C	Supply
Origins	1	10	15	9	1
	2	9	18	5	1
	3	6	14	3	1
	Demand	1	1	1	

a. Use the northwest corner rule to find an initial solution.
b. Use the MODI method to find an optimal solution. Note that the initial solution is degenerate. Two cells must be artificially occupied with zeros in order to calculate the u_i and v_j's.
c. Could this problem have been solved using the assignment algorithm of Chapter 6?

14. Forbelt Corporation has a 1-year contract to supply motors for all refrigerators produced by the Ice Age Corporation. Ice Age manufactures the refrigerators at four locations around the country: Boston, Dallas, Los Angeles, and St. Paul. Plans call for the following number (in thousands) of refrigerators to be produced at each location:

Boston	50
Dallas	70
Los Angeles	60
St. Paul	80

Forbelt has three plants that are capable of producing the motors. The plants and production capacities (in thousands) are as follows:

Denver	100
Atlanta	100
Chicago	150

Because of varying production and transportation costs, the profit Forbelt earns on each lot of 1000 units depends on which plant it was produced at and which destination it was shipped to. The following table gives the accounting department estimates of the profit per unit (shipments will be made in lots of 1000 units):

	Shipped To			
Produced At	Boston	Dallas	Los Angeles	St. Paul
Denver	7	11	8	13
Atlanta	20	17	12	10
Chicago	8	18	13	16

Given profit maximization as a criterion, Forbelt would like to determine how many motors should be produced at each plant and how many motors should be shipped from each plant to each destination.

a. Develop an initial transportation tableau for this problem.
b. Find an initial feasible solution using Vogel's approximation method. Use the MODI method to determine if this solution is optimal.
c. Find an initial feasible solution using the northwest corner rule and then use the MODI method to find the optimal solution. Do you prefer Vogel's method for finding an initial feasible solution to this problem?
d. Develop a linear programming model of this problem.

Chapter 8

Integer
Linear
Programming

In this chapter we turn our attention to a class of problems that could be modeled as linear programs except for the requirement that some or all of the variables must take on integer values. Such problems are called *integer* linear programming problems. For many years management scientists have known that there are a large number of practical applications for which mathematical models involving integer variables could be developed. However, in spite of the large number of applications, it has only been in recent years that practitioners have begun to use integer linear programming models extensively. The reason for this implementation lag is that efficient computerized solution procedures have only recently become widely available. Now many problems with up to several hundred integer variables can be solved with available commercial computer codes such as IBM's MPSX/370–MIP/370.

The plan of this chapter is to provide an applications-oriented introduction to integer linear programming. After a short section describing the different types of integer linear programming (ILP) models, we show how a graphical procedure can be used to solve problems involving two-decision variables. We then discuss, in some detail, two common ILP applications: capital budgeting and distribution system design. Finally, we have included a section detailing the branch-and-bound solution procedure for ILPs with more than two variables. This is the solution procedure employed by almost all commercial ILP computer codes available today and is regarded as the most efficient general purpose solution procedure.

8.1 Types of Integer Programming Models

The only difference between the problems studied in this chapter and the ones studied in the earlier chapters on linear programming is that some of the variables are required to assume integer values. If all of the variables are required to be integer, we say we have an *all-integer linear program*. Stated below is a two-variable, all-integer linear programming model:

$$
\begin{aligned}
\max \quad & 2x_1 + 3x_2 \\
\text{s.t.} \quad & \\
& 3x_1 + 3x_2 \le 12 \\
& \tfrac{2}{3}x_1 + 1x_2 \le 4 \\
& 1x_1 + 2x_2 \le 6 \\
& x_1, x_2 \ge 0 \text{ and integer.}
\end{aligned}
$$

You will note that if the statement "and integer" is dropped from the above model, we are left with the familiar two-variable linear program. The linear program which results from dropping the integer requirements for the variables is referred to as the *LP Relaxation* of the ILP.

If some, but not all, of the variables in a problem are required to be integer, we say we have a *mixed integer linear program* (MILP). Stated on p. 313 is a two-variable MILP:

$$\text{max} \quad 3x_1 + 4x_2$$
$$\text{s.t.}$$
$$-1x_1 + 2x_2 \le 8$$
$$1x_1 + 2x_2 \le 12$$
$$2x_1 + 1x_2 \le 16$$
$$x_1, x_2 \ge 0 \text{ and } x_2 \text{ integer.}$$

The LP Relaxation of the above MILP is given by dropping the requirement that x_2 take on integer values.

In many applications, the integer variables are only permitted to assume the values zero or one. In such cases we say we have a *binary* or a *0-1 integer linear program*. Zero-one ILPs may be either of the all-integer or MILP type. Both the capital budgeting and distribution system design problems discussed in a later section of this chapter make use of 0-1 variables.

8.2 Graphical Solution of Integer Linear Programs

Security Realty Investors currently has $910,000 which is available for new rental property investments. After an initial screening, Security has reduced the investment alternatives to a series of townhouses and a group of apartment buildings in a large apartment complex. The townhouses can be purchased in blocks of three for the price of $130,000 per block, but there are only four blocks of townhouses available for purchase at this time. Each building in the apartment complex contains 12 dwelling units and sells for $182,000. The individual apartment buildings can be purchased separately, and the complex developer has agreed to build as many 12-unit buildings as Security would like to purchase.

Security's property manager is free to devote 140 hours per month to these investments. Each block of townhouses will require 4 hours of the property manager's time each month, while each apartment building will require 40 hours per month. The yearly cash flow (after deducting mortgage payments and operating expenses) is estimated at $2000 per block of townhouses and $3000 per apartment building. Security would like to allocate its investment funds to apartment buildings and townhouses in order to maximize the yearly cash flow.

In order to develop an appropriate mathematical model for this problem, let us introduce the following definitions for the decision variables:

x_1 = number of blocks of townhouses purchased,

x_2 = number of apartment buildings purchased.

The objective function, measuring cash flow in thousands of dollars, can be written as

$$\text{max} \quad 2x_1 + 3x_2.$$

There are three constraints that must be satisfied:

$$130x_1 + 182x_2 \leq 910 \quad \text{(funds available in thousands of dollars)},$$
$$4x_1 + 40x_2 \leq 140 \quad \text{(manager's time in hours)},$$
$$x_1 \quad\quad \leq 4 \quad \text{(townhouse availability in blocks)}.$$

In addition, the variables must be restricted to nonnegative values. Also, since fractional values for the blocks of townhouses and/or number of apartment buildings are unacceptable, the decision variables x_1 and x_2 must be integer. Thus we see that the proper model for the Security Realty problem is the following all-integer linear program:

$$
\begin{aligned}
\max \quad & 2x_1 + 3x_2 \\
\text{s.t.} \quad & \\
& 130x_1 + 182x_2 \leq 910 \\
& 4x_1 + 40x_2 \leq 140 \\
& x_1 \leq 4 \\
& x_1, x_2 \geq 0 \text{ and integer.}
\end{aligned}
$$

A first approach to solving such a problem might be to drop the integer requirements and solve the resulting LP Relaxation. You might then round off the decision variables in an attempt to find the optimal solution to the ILP. However, as we shall see, such an approach may not yield the optimal solution. In fact, rounding off values of the decision variables could actually result in an infeasible solution.

The linear program resulting from dropping the integer requirements for the decision variables (the LP Relaxation) is written as follows:

$$
\begin{aligned}
\max \quad & 2x_1 + 3x_2 \\
\text{s.t.} \quad & \\
& 130x_1 + 182x_2 \leq 910 \\
& 4x_1 + 40x_2 \leq 140 \\
& x_1 \leq 4 \\
& x_1, x_2 \geq 0.
\end{aligned}
$$

The optimal solution to the LP Relaxation (see Figure 8.1) is given by $x_1 = 2.44$ and $x_2 = 3.26$. The objective function value of this solution is 14.66, corresponding to a cash flow of \$14,660. However, this solution is not feasible for our ILP problem, since the decision variables assume fractional values.

Rounding the decision variables to the nearest integer value yields a solution of $x_1 = 2$ and $x_2 = 3$, for an objective function value of 13, or a \$13,000 annual cash flow.

In Figure 8.2 we show the feasible solution points that provide integer values for x_1 and x_2. Is the rounded solution of $x_1 = 2$ and $x_2 = 3$ the optimal integer solution? The answer is no! As can be seen in Figure 8.2, the optimal integer solution is $x_1 = 4$ and $x_2 = 2$, with an objective function value of

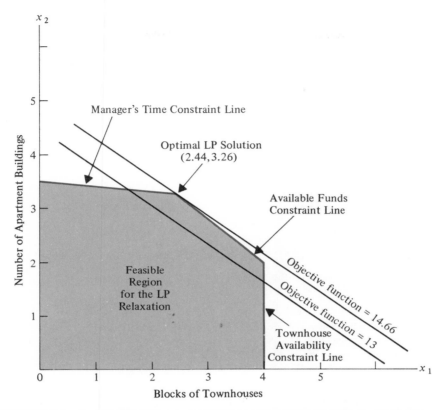

FIGURE 8.1   **Graphical Solution to the LP Relaxation of the Security Realty Problem**

14:00, or a $14,000 annual cash flow. For Security Realty, the approach of rounding the linear programming solution to the nearest integer solution was not a good strategy. The rounded solution of $x_1 = 2$ and $x_2 = 3$ would have cost Security Realtors $1000 a year in cash flow.

As can be seen from the Security Realty problem, the graphical procedure for solving two-variable ILPs is quite similar to the graphical procedure for linear programs. First a graph of the feasible region for the LP Relaxation is constructed. Then the feasible integer points are denoted by heavy dots. The integer solution point on the best objective function line can then be located; this point is the optimal solution to the ILP problem.

Also from our analysis of the Security Realty Investment problem, an important observation can be made about the relationship between the value of the optimal integer solution and the value of the optimal LP Relaxation solution. This observation is stated for *maximization problems*[1] as property 1.

---

[1] For minimization problems, property 1 would be stated with greater than or equal to substituted for less than or equal to.

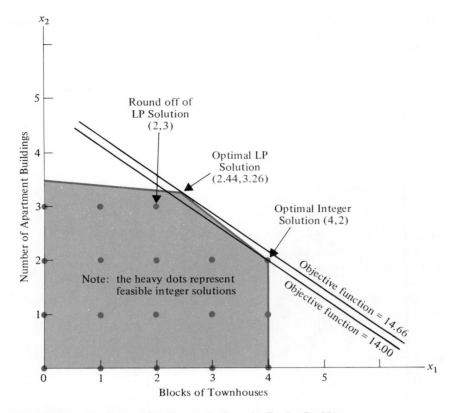

FIGURE 8.2   The Integer Solution to the Security Realty Problem

Property 1. The value of the optimal solution to any integer or mixed integer linear program yields a value *less than or equal to* the value of the optimal solution to its LP Relaxation.

The above property means that an *upper bound* on the value of any maximization integer or mixed integer linear program can be found by solving its associated LP Relaxation. This property can be seen in Figure 8.2. The optimal LP solution is on the highest objective function line and has a value of $14.66. The optimal integer solution is on a lower objective function line and has a smaller value, $14.00. As we shall see, property 1 is used in the branch-and-bound solution procedure for solving ILPs.

We note in closing this section that mixed integer linear programs with two-decision variables can be solved by a simple modification of the graphical procedure outlined above. Problem 5 at the end of the chapter requires the graphical solution of an MILP.

8.3   Applications of Integer Linear Programming

In the previous section we saw an illustration of an all-integer linear program: the Security Realty Investors problem. In this section we discuss

TABLE 8.1   Project Present Values, Capital Requirements, and Available Capital Projections for the Ice-Cold Refrigerator Company

Project	Estimated Present Value ($)	Capital Requirements ($)			
		Year 1	Year 2	Year 3	Year 4
Plant expansion	90,000	15,000	20,000	20,000	15,000
Warehouse expansion	40,000	10,000	15,000	20,000	5,000
New machinery	10,000	10,000	0	0	4,000
New product research	37,000	15,000	10,000	10,000	10,000
Available capital funds		40,000	50,000	40,000	35,000

two applications involving 0-1 or binary integer variables: the capital budgeting and distribution system design problems. We have chosen these applications because they represent two areas in which ILP has been used widely in practice. Through these applications you should begin to develop an appreciation of the flexibility in model development provided by 0-1 variables.

Capital Budgeting

Capital budgeting is an area where the management science approach has often led to considerable savings and/or increased profits. In Chapter 5, Problem 21, a linear programming formulation of the capital budgeting problem was presented. To get an idea of what is involved in capital budgeting, let us recall this capital budgeting problem and review its linear programming formulation.

The Ice-Cold Refrigerator Company can invest capital funds in a variety of company projects which have varying capital requirements over the next four years. Faced with limited capital resources, the company must select the most profitable projects and budgets for the capital expenditures. The estimated present values of the projects, the capital requirements, and the available capital projections[2] are shown in Table 8.1.

The following definitions are chosen for the decision variables:

x_1 = 1 if the plant expansion project is accepted; 0 if rejected.

x_2 = 1 if the warehouse expansion project is accepted; 0 if rejected.

x_3 = 1 if the new machinery project is accepted; 0 if rejected.

x_4 = 1 if the new product research project is accepted; 0 if rejected.

The linear programming formulation of this capital budgeting problem has a separate constraint for each year's available funds and a separate constraint

---

[2]The estimated present value is the net return for the project discounted back to the beginning of year 1.

requiring each variable to be less than or equal to 1. The LP formulation is given below (monetary units are expressed in thousands of dollars).

$$\max \quad 90x_1 + 40x_2 + 10x_3 + 37x_4$$
$$\text{s.t.}$$
$$15x_1 + 10x_2 + 10x_3 + 15x_4 \leq 40$$
$$20x_1 + 15x_2 + 10x_4 \leq 50$$
$$20x_1 + 20x_2 + 10x_4 \leq 40$$
$$15x_1 + 5x_2 + 4x_3 + 10x_4 \leq 35$$
$$x_1 \leq 1$$
$$x_2 \leq 1$$
$$x_3 \leq 1$$
$$x_4 \leq 1$$
$$x_1, x_2, x_3, x_4 \geq 0.$$

The optimal solution to this linear programming problem is given by $x_1 = 1$, $x_2 = 0.5$, $x_3 = 0.5$, and $x_4 = 1$, with a total present value of $152,000. The difficulty with a linear programming approach to the capital budgeting problem is now readily apparent. Unless it is possible to implement the warehouse expansion and new machinery projects in 50% increments, the current solution is not feasible. Thus some adjustment in the LP solution, such as rounding off (possibly leading to a nonoptimal solution), must be made prior to implementation.

A more preferable approach is to reformulate the Ice-Cold Refrigerator Company problem as a 0-1 integer linear program. The 0-1 ILP formulation is shown below:

$$\max \quad 90x_1 + 40x_2 + 10x_3 + 37x_4$$
$$\text{s.t.}$$
$$15x_1 + 10x_2 + 10x_3 + 15x_4 \leq 40$$
$$20x_1 + 15x_2 + 10x_4 \leq 50$$
$$20x_1 + 20x_2 + 10x_4 \leq 40$$
$$15x_1 + 5x_2 + 4x_3 + 10x_4 \leq 35$$
$$x_1, x_2, x_3, x_4 = 0,1.$$

The optimal integer solution[3] is given by $x_1 = 1$, $x_2 = 1$, $x_3 = 1$, and $x_4 = 0$ with a total present value of $140,000. We note that this optimal solution could not have been discovered by simply rounding off the linear programming solution. In fact, the best feasible solution that can be found by considering all possible roundings of the fractional variables in the linear programming solution is $x_1 = 1$, $x_2 = 0$, $x_3 = 0$, $x_4 = 1$, with a total present value of $127,000. This is substantially less than the value of the optimal integer solution to the capital budgeting problem.

---

[3]This solution was found using the branch-and-bound solution procedure presented in Section 8.4. Problem 8 asks you to develop the branch-and-bound solution of this problem.

The ability to avoid fractional values is one of two main reasons that an integer programming formulation is usually preferred for capital budgeting problems. The second reason most management scientists prefer a 0-1 integer programming model for the capital budgeting problem is the flexibility provided in developing certain nonbudgetary constraints. These constraints are often important in capital budgeting problems and can be formulated only through the use of 0-1—sometimes called logical—variables.

Multiple choice constraints   Suppose that instead of one warehouse expansion project, the Ice-Cold Refrigerator Company actually has three warehouse expansion projects under consideration. One of the warehouses must be expanded because of increasing product demand, but there is not sufficient new demand to make expansion of more than one warehouse profitable. The following variable definitions and multiple choice constraint could be incorporated into our previous 0-1 ILP model to reflect this situation. Let

$x_2 = 1$ if warehouse 1 is expanded; 0 if not.

$x_5 = 1$ if warehouse 2 is expanded; 0 if not.

$x_6 = 1$ if warehouse 3 is expanded; 0 if not.

The multiple choice constraint reflecting the requirement that one and only one of these projects must be selected is written as follows:

$$x_2 + x_5 + x_6 = 1.$$

It is easy to see why this is called a multiple choice constraint. Since x_2, x_5, and x_6 are allowed to assume only the values 0 or 1, one and only one of these projects must be selected from among the three choices. Note that if fractional values (as in linear programming) were allowed for the decision variables, we could not enforce the requirement of selecting one and only one project (e.g., $x_2 = 1/3$, $x_5 = 1/3$, $x_6 = 1/3$ would satisfy the constraint).

If it had not been required that one warehouse be expanded, then our multiple choice constraint could be modified as follows:

$$x_2 + x_5 + x_6 \leq 1.$$

This modification allows for the case of no warehouse expansion ($x_2 = x_5 = x_6 = 0$), but does not permit more than one warehouse to be expanded. This type of constraint is often called a *mutually exclusive constraint*.

k *out of* **n** *alternatives constraint*   A slight extension of the notion of a multiple choice constraint can be used to model situations in which k out of a set of n projects must be selected. Suppose x_2, x_5, x_6, x_7, and x_8 represent five potential warehouse expansion projects and it is considered necessary to accept two of the five projects. The following constraint ensures satisfaction of this new requirement:

$$x_2 + x_5 + x_6 + x_7 + x_8 = 2.$$

If it is required that no more than two of the projects be selected, we would use the following less-than-or-equal-to constraint

$$x_2 + x_5 + x_6 + x_7 + x_8 \leq 2.$$

Once again, each of the above variables must be restricted to 0-1 values.

Conditional constraints   Sometimes the acceptance of one project is conditional upon the acceptance of another. For example, suppose for the Ice-Cold Refrigerator Company that the warehouse expansion project was conditional on the plant expansion project. That is, the company will not consider expanding the warehouse unless the plant is expanded. With x_1 representing plant expansion and x_2 representing warehouse expansion, the following conditional constraint could be introduced to enforce this requirement:

$$x_2 \leq x_1$$

or

$$x_2 - x_1 \leq 0.$$

Since both x_1 and x_2 are required to be 0 or 1, we see that whenever x_1 is 0, x_2 will be forced to 0. When x_1 is 1, x_2 is also allowed to be 1; thus, both the plant and the warehouse can be expanded. However, we note that the above constraint does not force the warehouse expansion project (x_2) to be accepted if the plant expansion project (x_1) is.

If it were required that the warehouse expansion project be accepted whenever the plant expansion project was, and vice versa, then we would say that x_1 and x_2 represented *corequisite* projects. To model such a situation we simply write the above constraint as an equality

$$x_2 = x_1$$

or

$$x_2 - x_1 = 0.$$

This constraint forces x_1 and x_2 to take on the same value.

Cautionary note on sensitivity analysis   Sensitivity analysis is often more critical for ILP problems than for linear programming problems. A very small change in one of the coefficients in the constraints can cause a relatively large change in the value of the optimal solution. To see why this is so, consider the following integer programming model of a simple capital budgeting problem involving four projects and a budgetary constraint for a single time period:

$$\max \quad 40x_1 + 60x_2 + 70x_3 + 160x_4$$
$$\text{s.t.}$$
$$16x_1 + 35x_2 + 45x_3 + 85x_4 \leq 100$$
$$x_1, x_2, x_3, x_4 = 0,1.$$

The optimal solution to this problem can be quickly found by enumerating the alternatives. It is $x_1 = 1$, $x_2 = 1$, $x_3 = 1$, and $x_4 = 0$, with an objective function value of $170. However, note that if the budget available is increased by $1.00 (from 100 to 101), the optimal solution changes to $x_1 = 1$, $x_2 = 0$, $x_3 = 0$, and $x_4 = 1$, with an objective function value of $200. That is, one additional dollar in the budget would lead to a $30 increase in the return. Surely management, when faced with such a situation, would increase the budget by $1.00. Because of the extreme sensitivity of the value of the optimal solution to the constraint coefficients, practitioners usually recommend resolving the ILP problem several times with slight variations in the coefficients before attempting to choose an optimal solution for implementation.

Distribution System Design

In Chapter 7 the following linear programming formulation for the transportation problem was developed:

$$\min \quad \sum_{i=1}^{m} \sum_{j=1}^{n} c_{ij} x_{ij}$$

s.t.

$$\sum_{j=1}^{n} x_{ij} \leq s_i \qquad i = 1, 2, \ldots, m \quad \text{(supply)},$$

$$\sum_{i=1}^{m} x_{ij} = d_j \qquad j = 1, 2, \ldots, n \quad \text{(demand)},$$

$$x_{ij} \geq 0 \qquad \text{for all } i \text{ and } j,$$

where

$i = $ index for origins, $i = 1, 2, \ldots, m$,

$j = $ index for destinations, $j = 1, 2, \ldots, n$,

$x_{ij} = $ number of units shipped from origin i to destination j,

$c_{ij} = $ cost per unit of shipping from origin i to destination j,

$s_i = $ supply or capacity in units at origin i,

$d_j = $ demand in units at destination j.

In the transportation problem it is assumed that the origins and destinations are fixed. Consequently the problem is to determine how much of the product to ship from each origin to each destination in order to minimize the total transportation cost. However, in more general distribution system design problems, it is necessary to select the best locations for the origins as well as the amounts to ship from each origin to each destination.

Suppose the origins represent m potential locations for plants with capacities s_i and the destinations represent n retail outlets with demand d_j. A more complex distribution system design problem must now be solved. If site

i is selected for a plant location, there will be a fixed cost associated with plant construction and then a variable cost associated with the number of units shipped from plant i to the various retail outlets. On the other hand, if site i is not selected, then there is no fixed cost and no units can be shipped from site i. The introduction of one integer 0-1 variable for each potential plant location allows us to develop an MILP model for this distribution system design problem. Let

$y_i = 1$ if a plant is constructed at site i, 0 otherwise.

f_i = fixed cost of constructing a plant at site i with capacity s_i.

To represent the constraint that nothing can be shipped from site i if a plant is not constructed, the supply constraints in the transportation model are modified as follows:

$$\sum_{j-1}^{n} x_{ij} \leq s_i y_i \qquad i = 1, 2, \ldots, m,$$

or

$$\sum_{j-1}^{n} x_{ij} - s_i y_i \leq 0 \qquad i = 1, 2, \ldots, m.$$

Also, another term must be added to the objective function to represent the fixed cost of plant construction at each site selected:

$$\text{fixed cost of plant construction} = \sum_{i-1}^{m} f_i y_i.$$

The complete model for our distribution system design problem can now be written:

$$\min \quad \sum_{i-1}^{m} \sum_{j-1}^{n} c_{ij} x_{ij} + \sum_{i-1}^{m} f_i y_i$$

s.t.

$$\sum_{j-1}^{n} x_{ij} - s_i y_i \leq 0 \qquad i = 1, 2, \ldots, m \quad \text{(plant capacities)}$$

$$\sum_{i-1}^{m} x_{ij} = d_j \qquad j = 1, 2, \ldots, n \quad \text{(demand at retail outlets)}$$

$$x_{ij} \geq 0 \text{ for all } i \text{ and } j$$

$$y_i = 0, 1, \quad i = 1, 2, \ldots, m.$$

This basic model can be expanded to accommodate distribution systems involving shipments from plants to warehouses to retail outlets, and multiple products.[4] Using the special properties of 0-1 variables, it can also be expanded to accommodate a variety of configuration constraints on the plant locations. For example, suppose site 1 was in Dallas and site 2 was

---

[4]A model of this type was used by a large food chain and resulted in substantial savings in distribution system costs. See Geoffrion and Graves, "Distribution System Design by Benders Decomposition," *Management Science*, Jan. 1974.

in Ft. Worth. A company might not want to locate plants in both Dallas and Ft. Worth because the cities are so close together. To prevent this, the following constraint can be added to the model:

$$y_1 + y_2 \leq 1.$$

This constraint was called a *mutually exclusive* constraint in the previous subsection. It allows either y_1 or y_2 to equal 1 but not both. If we had written the constraint as an equality, it would be the same as the multiple choice constraint we encountered in the capital budgeting problem. Other constraints such as the conditional or corequisite constraint can be introduced to satisfy managerially specified requirements on the configuration of plant locations.

8.4   Branch-and-Bound Solution of Integer Linear Programs

As with linear programs, integer linear programs involving three variables are awkward to solve graphically. Moreover, since larger problems are impossible to solve using a graphical approach, other solution procedures must be employed. Branch and bound is currently the most efficient general purpose solution procedure for ILPs and MILPs. Almost all commercially available integer programming computer codes employ the branch-and-bound approach.

The branch-and-bound solution procedure was first introduced in Chapter 6, where we used a branch-and-bound approach to solve the traveling salesman problem. As was pointed out in that section, branch and bound does not refer to a specific solution procedure for a specific problem. Rather it is an approach to problem solving that is based on the notion of partitioning the set of all feasible solutions to a problem into smaller, mutually exclusive subsets of solutions. Upper and lower bounds on the value of the best solution in each subset are then determined, and the branch-and-bound procedure is used to systematically eliminate subsets from consideration.

In this section we show how the branch-and-bound approach can be used to solve integer programming problems by applying it to the all-integer Security Realty Investment problem. We then comment on how it can be extended to MILPs and present a flowchart summarizing the steps in the procedure.

The branch-and-bound procedure begins by solving the LP Relaxation of the ILP. The LP Relaxation of the Security Realty Investors problem is restated below:

$$\begin{aligned}
\max \quad & 2x_1 + 3x_2 \\
\text{s.t.} \quad & \\
& 130x_1 + 182x_2 \leq 910 \\
& 4x_1 + 40x_2 \leq 140 \\
& x_1 \qquad\quad \leq 4 \\
& x_1, x_2 \geq 0.
\end{aligned}$$

The solution is $x_1 = 2.44$ and $x_2 = 3.26$, with an objective function value equal to 14.66. Had the optimal solution to the LP Relaxation satisfied the integer requirements, we would have had the optimal solution to the ILP. But this did not occur, and we will continue with the branch-and-bound procedure. As a first step, note that property 1 in Section 8.2 indicates that solving the LP Relaxation of an ILP provides an upper bound on the value of the solution to the ILP problem. Thus we know that the value of the integer optimal solution to the Security Realty problem cannot exceed 14.66.

Since the coefficients of all the variables in the constraints are nonnegative and since the constraints are all of the ≤ type, a feasible integer solution can be found by rounding down for each decision variable; that is, rounding down can only reduce the left-hand side of the inequality and hence must always provide a feasible solution. The feasible solution found by rounding down is $x_1 = 2$ and $x_2 = 3$, with an objective function value of 13. The value of this feasible solution provides a lower bound on the value of the optimal ILP solution, since we know that the value of the optimal solution must yield a value greater than or equal to the value of any feasible solution. Thus a lower bound of 13 can be established. The first node of our branch-and-bound solution tree appears as shown below, where UB refers to upper bound and LB to lower bound.

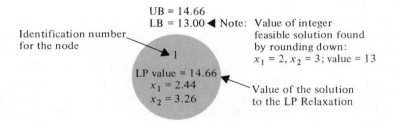

We now know that the value of the optimal solution must be between the upper bound of 14.66 and the lower bound of 13.00. Although we have already found a feasible solution with a value of 13, we must continue to see if a better solution can be found. This is where the branching part of the branch-and-bound solution procedure comes into play.

The set of feasible solutions to the LP Relaxation is partitioned into two subsets. These subsets are created by choosing the decision variable that is furthest from being integral to branch on; hence x_1 with a value of 2.44 is selected. In the optimal integer solution x_1 must be integer, so we see that either x_1 will be less than or equal to 2 or x_1 will be greater than or equal to 3. Thus two branches and two *descendant nodes* are created for our branch-and-bound solution tree. One descendant node corresponds to that subset of solutions with $x_1 \leq 2$; the other corresponds to the subset of solutions with $x_1 \geq 3$. Since x_1 must be integral, the optimal solution must be contained in one of these two subsets.

The first branch is created by adding the constraint $x_1 \le 2$ to the Security Realty problem. We will refer to the node created as node 2. Thus at node 2 the LP Relaxation of this problem is solved.

LP at node 2:

$$
\begin{aligned}
\max \quad & 2x_1 + 3x_2 \\
\text{s.t.} \quad & \\
& 130x_1 + 182x_2 \le 910 \\
& 4x_1 + 40x_2 \le 140 \\
& x_1 \qquad\quad \le 4 \\
& x_1 \qquad\quad \le 2 \\
& x_1, x_2 \ge 0.
\end{aligned}
$$

We note that the added constraint $(x_1 \le 2)$ makes the constraint $x_1 \le 4$ redundant. This is just a coincidence and does not always happen. The solution to this linear program yields $x_1 = 2$ and $x_2 = 3.30$, with value equal to 13.90.

The second branch from node 1 is created by adding the constraint $x_1 \ge 3$ to the Security Realty problem. Thus at node 3 the following LP Relaxation of this problem is solved.

LP at node 3:

$$
\begin{aligned}
\max \quad & 2x_1 + 3x_2 \\
\text{s.t.} \quad & \\
& 130x_1 + 182x_2 \le 910 \\
& 4x_1 + 40x_2 \le 140 \\
& x_1 \qquad\quad \le 4 \\
& x_1 \qquad\quad \ge 3 \\
& x_1, x_2 \ge 0.
\end{aligned}
$$

The solution to this linear program yields $x_1 = 3$ and $x_2 = 2.86$, with value equal to 14.58.

From Property 1 we know that the LP value at node 2 is an upper bound on all solutions with $x_1 \le 2$, and the LP value at node 3 is an upper bound on all solutions with $x_1 \ge 3$. Since these two subsets include all solutions to the problem, we can compute a new upper bound. It is the maximum of the LP value for node 2 (LP value = 13.90) and the LP value for node 3 (LP value = 14.58). Hence our new upper bound on the value of the ILP solution to the Security Realty problem is 14.58. In general, we will recompute the upper bound each time all the branches from a node have been completed.

At this time the lower bound is also recomputed. The new value for the lower bound is the maximum value of all feasible integer solutions found so far. Since the LP solutions at nodes 2 and 3 did not yield a feasible integer solution, the lower bound of 13 established at node 1 is not revised. At this point of the branch-and-bound solution procedure we have UB = 14.58 and LB = 13.00. The current partial branch-and-bound solution tree is shown in Figure 8.3.

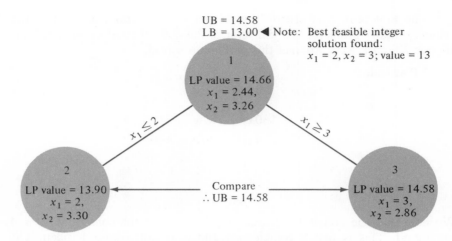

UB = 14.58
LB = 13.00 ◀ Note: Best feasible integer
solution found:
$x_1 = 2, x_2 = 3$; value = 13

1
LP value = 14.66
$x_1 = 2.44$,
$x_2 = 3.26$

$x_1 \leq 2$

$x_1 \geq 3$

2
LP value = 13.90
$x_1 = 2$,
$x_2 = 3.30$

Compare
∴ UB = 14.58

3
LP value = 14.58
$x_1 = 3$,
$x_2 = 2.86$

FIGURE 8.3   Partial Branch-and-Bound Solution Tree for Security Realty Problem

We have established (at node 2) that 13.90 is an upper bound on all solutions with $x_1 \leq 2$ and (at node 3) that 14.58 is an upper bound on all
solutions with $x \geq 3$. Property 2 below shows how these results can be used in
continuing with the branch-and-bound solution procedure.

Property 2. The LP value at each node is an upper bound on the LP
value at any descendant node.

Using this property, we see that if we were to branch from node 2 we
could not find any solution with a value greater than 13.90. If we were to
branch from node 3 no solution with a value greater than 14.58 could be
found. Since node 3 could potentially lead to a better solution we choose to
select it (rather than node 2) to branch from. In general we will always select
the node with the largest LP value to continue branching.

Since x_2 is the only variable with a fractional value at node 3 we choose
to branch on it. Thus two branches are created from node 3: one with $x_2 \leq 2$
and another with $x_2 \geq 3$. Two descendant nodes are then created by solving
the following linear programs at nodes 4 and 5.

LP at node 4:

$$
\begin{aligned}
\max \quad & 2x_1 + 3x_2 \\
\text{s.t.} \quad & \\
& 130x_1 + 182x_2 \leq 910 \\
& 4x_1 + 40x_2 \leq 140 \\
& x_1 \leq 4 \\
& x_1 \geq 3 \\
& x_2 \leq 2 \\
& x_1, x_2 \geq 0.
\end{aligned}
$$

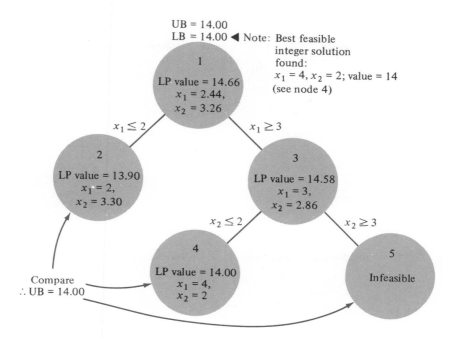

FIGURE 8.4 **Complete Branch-and-Bound Solution Tree for Security Realty Problem**

LP at node 5:

$$\begin{array}{ll} \max & 2x_1 + 3x_2 \\ \text{s.t.} \\ & 130x_1 + 182x_2 \le 910 \\ & 4x_1 + 40x_2 \le 140 \\ & x_1 \le 4 \\ & x_1 \ge 3 \\ & x_2 \ge 3 \\ & x_1, x_2 \ge 0. \end{array}$$

After solving these linear programming problems we can construct the branch-and-bound solution tree shown in Figure 8.4.

At this point we have found a feasible solution ($x_1 = 4$, $x_2 = 2$) with a value of 14.00 (see node 4). From UB = 14.00 we know that the optimal solution cannot yield a value greater than 14.00. Therefore the solution $x_1 = 4$, $x_2 = 2$ with value 14.00 has been found to be optimal for the Security Realty problem. We can now state the stopping rule for the branch-and-bound solution procedure.

Stopping Rule. When UB = LB the optimal solution has been found. It is the feasible solution with value equal to LB.

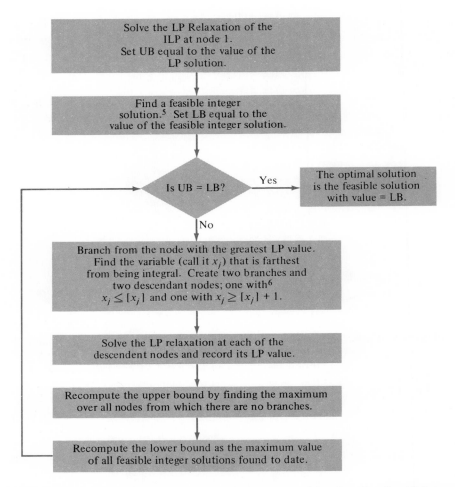

FIGURE 8.5   Flowchart of Branch-and-Bound Solution Procedure for the All-Integer Linear Program

We have seen how the branch-and-bound solution procedure is applied to solve the all-integer Security Realty Investors problem. A summary of the general procedure for the all-integer linear program is presented in flowchart form in Figure 8.5.

Extension to Mixed Integer Linear Programs

A big advantage of the branch-and-bound solution procedure for integer programming is that it is applicable to both the all-integer and the mixed

---

[5]In case the constraints are all of the $\leq$ type with nonnegative coefficients, the solution found by rounding down will be feasible. Otherwise some knowledge of the particular application may provide a feasible integer solution.

[6]The notation $[x_j]$ means the greatest integer less than or equal to x_j; for example, $[2.86] = 2$.

integer linear program. To see how the branch-and-bound approach can be applied to an MILP, let us return to the Security Realty problem and suppose that x_2 was not required to be integer. This would be the case if fractional shares could be purchased in the apartment buildings. In this situation the LP Relaxation solved at node 1 would be exactly the same, yielding a value of 14.66 as an upper bound. But the lower bound would be found by rounding down on x_1 only. Thus the value of the lower bound at node 1 would be 13.78, given by the feasible mixed integer solution $x_1 = 2$, $x_2 = 3.26$. This is shown below:

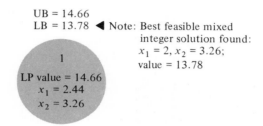

In order to branch we now restrict consideration to only those variables that are required to be integer. Selecting the integer variable with the largest fractional part leads us to again branch on x_1; we require $x_1 \le 2$ on one branch and $x_1 \ge 3$ on the other. Thus the LP Relaxations solved at nodes 2 and 3 would be the same as before (see Figure 8.6). However, we now have a feasible mixed integer solution whenever the LP solution at a node yields x_1 integer. Thus the solutions at both nodes 2 and 3 are feasible for the MILP. A new lower bound of LB = 14.58 can be established by comparing the values of all the feasible mixed integer solutions found. A new upper bound of UB = 14.58 can be established by comparing the LP values at nodes 2 and

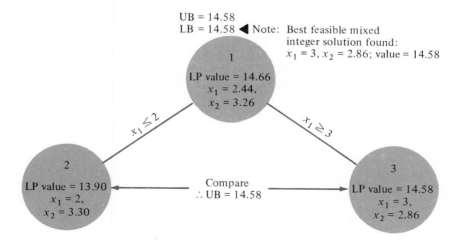

FIGURE 8.6   **Branch-and-Bound Tree for Security Realty Mixed Integer Linear Program (x_1 Integer, x_2 Not Integer)**

3. Since the upper and lower bounds are equal the optimal solution to the Security Realty problem with only x_1 required to be integer has been found. It is given by $x_1 = 3$, $x_2 = 2.86$, with an objective function value of 14.58. The branch-and-bound tree for this MILP is shown in Figure 8.6.

Summary

We have introduced an important extension of the linear programming model, the integer linear program. The only difference between the integer linear programming problem and the linear programming problem studied in previous chapters is the added restriction on some of the variables. If all of the variables are required to be integer we have an all-integer ILP; if some but not all of the variables are required to be integer we have a mixed integer linear program (MILP). Finally, in case the integer variables are only permitted to assume the values 0 or 1, we have a 0-1 (binary) ILP. Binary ILPs may be either all integer or mixed integer.

Two primary reasons for studying ILPs were presented. First, in many applications fractional values of the decision variables are not permitted. Since we have seen that rounding off the LP solution can provide poor results, methods for finding the optimal integer solution are needed. For any two-variable problem it was shown how a simple extension of the graphical procedure for linear programs could be used to find solutions. The branch-and-bound solution procedure was presented for solving larger ILPs. A major advantage of the branch-and-bound solution procedure is its flexibility; it can be used for both the all-integer and the mixed integer linear programs. Almost all existing commercial ILP computer codes employ the branch-and-bound approach.

A second reason mentioned for studying ILP was that it provides increased modeling flexibility through the use of 0-1 variables. In our discussion of the capital budgeting and distribution system design problems, we saw how a number of important managerial considerations could be incorporated through the use of multiple choice constraints, conditional constraints, and so on.

In recent years, with the availability of commercial ILP computer codes, we have seen a rapid growth in the use of ILP. As researchers develop solution procedures capable of solving ILPs with larger numbers of variables we can expect to see a continuation of this rapid growth and the development of many new applications.

Glossary

1. *All-integer linear program*—An ILP in which all the decision variables are required to assume integer values.

2. *LP Relaxation*—The linear program that results from dropping the integer requirements on the variables. For each binary variable x_j the requirement $x_j \leq 1$ must be added. For a maximization problem, the value of

the optimal solution to the LP Relaxation is an upper bound on the value of the optimal integer solution.

3. *Mixed integer linear program (MILP)*—An ILP in which some, but not all, of the variables are required to be integer.

4. *0-1 Integer linear program*—An all-integer or mixed integer linear program in which the integer variables are only permitted to assume the values 0 or 1.

5. *Upper bound*—A value that is known to be greater than or equal to the value of any feasible solution. The solution to the LP Relaxation of an ILP provides an upper bound for a maximization problem.

6. *Multiple choice constraint*—A constraint requiring that the sum of two or more 0-1 variables equal 1. Thus any feasible solution makes a choice of one of these variables to set equal to 1.

7. *Mutually exclusive constraint*—A constraint requiring that the sum of two or more 0-1 variables be less than or equal to 1. Thus if one of the variables equals 1 the others must equal 0. However, all variables could equal 0.

8. k *out of* n *alternatives constraint*—An extension of the multiple choice constraint. This constraint requires that the sum of n 0-1 variables equal k.

9. *Conditional constraints*—Constraints involving 0-1 variables which do not allow certain variables to equal 1 unless certain other variables are equal to 1.

10. *Corequisite constraint*—A constraint requiring that two 0-1 variables be equal. Thus they are both in or out of solution together.

11. *Branch and bound*—A solution procedure for ILPs which sequentially partitions the set of feasible solutions into smaller and smaller subsets until the optimal solution is found.

12. *Lower bound*—A value that is less than or equal to the value of the optimal solution. For a maximization problem, the value of any feasible integer solution to an ILP is a lower bound. The largest of these is a greatest lower bound.

13. *Descendant node*—A node created in a branch-and-bound solution tree by branching from another node by adding a constraint to the LP Relaxaton solved at the previous node.

Problems

1. Indicate which of the following are all-integer linear programs, which are mixed integer linear programs, and which are ordinary linear programs. For each of the all-integer and mixed integer linear programs write the LP Relaxation. (Do not attempt to solve.)

    a.   max $30x_1 + 25x_2$
         s.t.

$$3x_1 + 1.5x_2 \leq 400$$
$$1.5x_1 + 2x_2 \leq 250$$
$$1x_1 + 1x_2 \leq 150$$
$$x_1, x_2 \geq 0 \text{ and } x_2 \text{ integer.}$$

b. min $3x_1 + 4x_2$
   s.t.
   $$2x_1 + 4x_2 \geq 8$$
   $$2x_1 + 6x_2 \geq 12$$
   $$x_1, x_2 \geq 0 \text{ and integer.}$$

c. min $30x_1 + 4x_2$
   s.t.
   $$3x_1 + 2x_2 \geq 50$$
   $$0.1x_1 + 0.2x_2 \geq 2$$
   $$x_1, x_2 \geq 0 \text{ and } x_1 \text{ integer.}$$

d. max $3x_1 + 4x_2$
   s.t.
   $$-1x_1 + 2x_2 \leq 8$$
   $$1x_1 + 2x_2 \leq 12$$
   $$2x_1 + 1x_2 \leq 16$$
   $$x_1, x_2 \geq 0 \text{ and integer.}$$

e. max $20x_1 + 5x_2$
   s.t.
   $$5x_1 + 1x_2 \leq 15$$
   $$6x_1 + 4x_2 \leq 24$$
   $$1x_1 + 1x_2 \leq 5$$
   $$x_1, x_2 \geq 0.$$

2. Consider the all-integer linear program given below:

$$\text{max} \quad 5x_1 + 8x_2$$
$$\text{s.t.}$$
$$6x_1 + 5x_2 \leq 30$$
$$9x_1 + 4x_2 \leq 36$$
$$1x_1 + 2x_2 \leq 10$$
$$x_1, x_2 \geq 0 \text{ and integer.}$$

a. Graph the constraints for this problem. Indicate with heavy dots all the feasible integer solutions.
b. Find the optimal solution to the LP Relaxation. Round down to find a feasible integer solution.
c. Find the optimal integer solution. Is it the same as the solution found in part b above by rounding down?

3. Consider the all-integer linear program given below:

$$\text{max} \quad 1x_1 + 1x_2$$
$$\text{s.t.}$$
$$4x_1 + 6x_2 \leq 22$$
$$1x_1 + 5x_2 \leq 15$$
$$2x_1 + 1x_2 \leq 9$$
$$x_1, x_2 \geq 0 \text{ and integer.}$$

a. Graph the constraints for this problem. Indicate with heavy dots all the feasible integer solutions.
b. Solve the LP Relaxation of this problem.
c. Find the optimal integer solution.

4. Consider the ILP given below:

$$\begin{array}{ll} \max & 10x_1 + 3x_2 \\ \text{s.t.} & \\ & 6x_1 + 7x_2 \leq 40 \\ & 3x_1 + 1x_2 \leq 11 \\ & x_1, x_2 \geq 0 \text{ and integer.} \end{array}$$

a. Formulate and solve the LP Relaxation of the problem. Solve it graphically. Round down to find a feasible solution. State upper and lower bounds on the value of the optimal solution.

b. Solve the ILP graphically. Compare the value of this solution with the solution found in part a.

c. Suppose the objective function changes to max $3x_1 + 6x_2$. Repeat parts a and b above.

5. Consider the MILP given below:

$$\begin{array}{ll} \max & 2x_1 + 3x_2 \\ \text{s.t.} & \\ & 4x_1 + 9x_2 \leq 36 \\ & 7x_1 + 5x_2 \leq 35 \\ & x_1, x_2 \geq 0 \text{ and } x_1 \text{ integer.} \end{array}$$

a. Graph the constraints for this problem. Indicate on your graph all feasible mixed integer solutions.

b. Find the optimal solution to the LP Relaxation. Round the value of x_1 down to find a feasible mixed integer solution. Is this solution optimal? Why or why not?

c. Find the optimal solution for the MILP.

6. Consider the MILP given below.

$$\begin{array}{ll} \max & 1x_1 + 1x_2 \\ \text{s.t.} & \\ & 7x_1 + 9x_2 \leq 63 \\ & 9x_1 + 5x_2 \leq 45 \\ & 3x_1 + 1x_2 \leq 12 \\ & x_1, x_2 \geq 0 \text{ and } x_2 \text{ integer.} \end{array}$$

a. Graph the constraints for this problem. Indicate on your graph all feasible mixed integer solutions.

b. Find the optimal solution to the LP Relaxation. Round the value of x_2 down to find a feasible mixed integer solution. Specify upper and lower bounds on the value of the optimal solution to the MILP.

c. Find the optimal solution to the MILP.

7. Consider again the all-integer linear program in Problem 4. It is restated below:

$$\begin{array}{ll} \max & 10x_1 + 3x_2 \\ \text{s.t.} & \\ & 6x_1 + 7x_2 \leq 40 \\ & 3x_1 + 1x_2 \leq 11 \\ & x_1, x_2 \geq 0 \text{ and integer.} \end{array}$$

Solve this problem using the branch-and-bound procedure.

8. The integer programming formulation of the Ice-Cold Refrigerator Company capital budgeting problem is presented below:

$$\max \quad 90x_1 + 40x_2 + 10x_3 + 37x_4$$

s.t.

$$15x_1 + 10x_2 + 10x_3 + 15x_4 \leq 40$$
$$20x_1 + 15x_2 \qquad\quad + 10x_4 \leq 50$$
$$20x_1 + 20x_2 \qquad\quad + 10x_4 \leq 40$$
$$15x_1 + 5x_2 + 4x_3 + 10x_4 \leq 35$$
$$x_1, x_2, x_3, x_4 = 0,1.$$

Solve this problem using the branch-and-bound procedure. Note that in the case of variables restricted to 0 or 1 each branch corresponds to setting one of the variables equal to 0 or 1. Thus the branching variable is treated as a constant in the linear programming problem solved at the descendant node.

9. Consider the MILP given below:

$$\max \quad 1x_1 + 2x_2 + 1x_3$$

s.t.

$$7x_1 + 4x_2 + 3x_3 \leq 28$$
$$4x_1 + 7x_2 + 2x_3 \leq 28$$
$$x_1, x_2, x_3 \geq 0 \text{ and } x_1, x_2 \text{ integer.}$$

Solve this problem using the branch-and-bound procedure.

10. The Martin-Beck Company is in the process of planning for new production facilities and developing a more efficient distribution system design. At present they have one plant at St. Louis with a capacity of 30,000 units. But because of increased demand, management is considering four potential new plant sites: Detroit, Denver, Toledo, and Kansas City. The transportation tableau below summarizes the projected plant capacities, the cost per unit of shipping from each plant to each destination, and the demand forecasts over a one-year planning horizon.

	Boston	Atlanta	Houston	Capacities
Detroit	5	2	3	10,000
Toledo	4	3	4	20,000
Denver	9	7	5	30,000
Kansas City	10	4	2	40,000
St. Louis	8	4	3	30,000
Demand	30,000	20,000	20,000	

Suppose that the fixed costs of constructing the new plants are

Detroit	$175,000,
Toledo	$300,000,
Denver	$375,000,
Kansas City	$500,000.

The Martin-Beck Company would like to minimize the total cost of plant construction and distribution of goods.

a. Develop a 0-1 mixed integer linear programming model of this problem. (Do not attempt to solve.)

b. Modify your formulation in part a to account for the policy restriction that one plant but not both must be located in Detroit or in Toledo. (Do not attempt to solve.)

c. Modify your formulation in part a to account for the policy restriction that at most two plants can be located in Denver, Kansas City, and St. Louis. (Do not attempt to solve.)

d. Suppose that there are two possible sizes for the Denver plant, the one mentioned earlier with a capacity of 30,000 and a cost of 375,000, and another with a capacity of 60,000 and a cost of 550,000. Modify your formulation in part a to account for this consideration. (Do not attempt to solve.)

11. Spencer Enterprises is attempting to choose among a series of new investment alternatives. The potential investment alternatives, the net present value of the future stream of returns, the capital requirements, and the available capital funds over the next three years are summarized below:

Alternative	Net Present Value ($)	Capital Requirements ($)		
		Year 1	Year 2	Year 3
Limited warehouse expansion	4,000	3,000	1,000	4,000
Extensive warehouse expansion	6,000	2,500	3,500	3,500
Test market new product	10,500	6,000	4,000	5,000
Advertising campaign	4,000	2,000	1,500	1,800
Basic research	8,000	5,000	1,000	4,000
Purchase new equipment	3,000	1,000	500	900
Capital funds available		10,500	7,000	8,750

a. Develop an integer programming model for maximizing the net present value. (Do not solve.)

b. Assume that only one of the warehouse expansion projects can be implemented. Modify your model of part a.

c. Suppose that if the test marketing of the new product is carried out, then the advertising campaign must also be conducted. Modify your formulation of part b to reflect this new situation.

12. The following questions refer to a capital budgeting problem with six projects represented by 0-1 variables $x_1, x_2, x_3, x_4, x_5, x_6$.

a. Write constraints modeling a situation where project 4 cannot be undertaken unless projects 1 and 3 are also.

b. Revise the requirement in part a to accommodate the case in which, when projects 1 and 3 are undertaken, project 4 must also be undertaken.

c. Write a constraint modeling a situation in which two of the projects 1, 3, 5, and 6 must be undertaken.

d. Write a constraint modeling a situation in which projects 3 and 5 must be undertaken simultaneously.

e. Write a constraint modeling a situation in which project 1 or 4 must be undertaken but not both.

Application

Ketron[*]
Arlington, Virginia

Ketron, Inc. is an operations research consulting firm with several branch offices located throughout the United States. An important part of Ketron's business is involved with national defense and other government operations research applications.

The Management Science Systems division of Ketron is responsible for the maintenance, development, enhancement, and marketing of MPSIII, a proprietary mathematical programming system for use on IBM computers. Members of the Management Science Systems division consult with users of MPSIII and assist them in developing and implementing solutions to their problems. One such mixed integer programming (MIP) application developed for a major sporting equipment company is outlined below.

A Customer Order Allocation Model

A major sporting equipment company satisfies demand for its products by making shipments from its factories and other locations around the country where inventories are maintained. The company markets approximately 300 products and has about 30 sources of supply (factory and warehouse locations). The problem of interest is to determine how to best allocate customer orders to the various sources of supply such that the total manufacturing cost is minimized. Although transportation cost is not directly considered, it can be accounted for indirectly by not including variables corresponding to shipments from distant locations. Figure 1 provides a graphical representation of this problem. Note in the figure that each customer can receive shipments only from a few of the various sources of supply. For example, we see that customer 1 may be supplied by sources A or B, customer 2 may be supplied only by source A, and so on.

The customer order allocation problem is solved periodically. In a typical period, there are between 30 and 40 customers to be supplied. Since most customers require several products, there are usually between 600 and 800 orders that must be assigned to the sources of supply.

The sporting equipment company classifies each customer order as either a "guaranteed" or a "secondary" order. Guaranteed orders are single-source orders in that they must be filled by a single supplier to ensure the complete order will be delivered to the customer at one time. It is this "single source" requirement that necessitates the use of integer variables in

*The authors are indebted to J. A. Tomlin, Ketron, Inc., San Bruno, California, for providing this application.

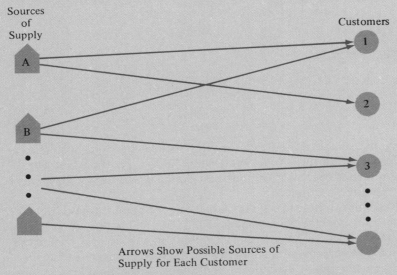

Sources of Supply

Customers

Arrows Show Possible Sources of Supply for Each Customer

FIGURE 1   Graphical Representation of the Customer Order Allocation Problem

the model. Approximately 80% of the company's orders are guaranteed orders.

Secondary orders can be split between the various sources of supply. These orders are made by customers restocking inventory, and there is no problem in receiving partial shipments from different sources at different times. The total of all secondary orders for a given product is treated as a goal or target in the model formulation. Deviations below the goal are permitted, but a penalty cost is associated with these deviations in the objective function. When deviations occur in the optimal solution, the secondary orders will not be completely satisfied; the "shortfall" is spread among customers in specified proportions.

Manufacturing considerations are such that raw material availability and the type of process used constrain the amount of production. In addition, groups of items which are similar may belong to a "model group" which must be jointly constrained at some factories. There are also several restrictions on international shipping. For various policy reasons, shipments between sources and customers in certain countries may not be made. This reduces the number of variables in the model but necessitates extensive data checking to ensure that all "guaranteed" orders have a permissible source. If they do not, some means must be found to make the problem feasible before even beginning to solve the mixed integer programming model.

The primary objective of the model is to minimize the total manufacturing costs, subject to the requirement that the guaranteed orders be met. As indicated previously, the deviations below the secondary demand goals are dealt with by defining "shortfall" variables with an associated cost. This cost represents a penalty for not having the item in inventory when it is required.

A description of the constraints and the objective function for the model is presented below.

Constraints

Guaranteed orders: Each customer's order for each product is assigned to a single supplier. (This is a multiple choice constraint.)

Secondary orders: For each product the total amount of secondary demand assigned plus the shortfall must equal the total demand goal (target).

Raw material capacities: The amount of each type of raw material used at a supply source cannot exceed the amount available.

Manufacturing capacities: At each supply source the capacity for each type of production process cannot be exceeded.

Individual product capacities: The amount of product produced at a site cannot exceed that site's capacity for the product.

Group capacities: The total production for a group of similar products at a site cannot exceed that site's capacity for the group of products.

Objective Function

The objective is to minimize the sum of (1) the manufacturing cost for guaranteed orders, (2) the manufacturing cost for secondary orders, and (3) the penalty cost for unsatisfied secondary demand.

Model Solution

It is unreasonable to expect to obtain an optimal solution for a problem of this complexity. Furthermore, the goal programming methodology for handling the secondary demand means that an "optimum" is of questionable interpretation. What is needed is a "good" feasible mixed integer solution. This is one of the advantages of the branch-and-bound approach. If an integer solution is found whose value is within a few percent of the value of the linear programming relaxation, the room for improvement is obviously small.

The solution procedure used is to make a sequence of runs, each beginning where the previous one terminated. Each run allows at most 40 linear programming evaluations (boundings), though many more variables will usually be set to some integer value (branched on). In almost every case the first such run, which includes finding the linear programming relaxation solution, produces a solution satisfactory to the user.

A fairly typical problem has about 800 constraints, 2000 0–1 assignment variables for the guaranteed orders, and 500 continuous variables associated with the secondary orders. This model is solved using the BLOODHOUND branch-and-bound mixed integer programming module of Ketron's MPSIII system. The computer time consumed in producing a solution is approximately 6 minutes on an IBM 3033. Almost half of this time, however, is used to generate the model, optimize the linear programming relaxation, and produce extensive solution reports.

Implementation Notes

In large-scale applications such as this, considerable systems work is involved in generating the data for the model and the managerial reports. Special data processing languages are often available to ease the programming burden of these phases. The DATAFORM language facility of MPSIII is used to generate the data for this model and to prepare the reports.

In this application it is necessary to make a competely separate preprocessing run to check for internal consistency and errors in the data. Only when the data appear logically error-free is the model generated and solved. Although tedious, this kind of preprocessing effort is critical for mixed integer models, since the cost of solving the wrong model can be significant. Furthermore, in some cases the data preprocessing step permits the size of the model to be reduced. Such a reduction is possible in this application when a demand for a product has only one legitimate source. The computational benefits of such reductions can be substantial.

Chapter 9

Network Models I: PERT/CPM

Many managerial problems in the areas of project scheduling and control, transportation systems design, and communication systems design have been successfully solved with the aid of network models and network analysis techniques. As you will see, a *network* is basically a graphical representation or description of a problem situation. By employing special network analysis algorithms, solutions can be obtained for the particular problems.

PERT (Program Evaluation and Review Technique) and CPM (Critical Path Method) are two well-known network analysis techniques used to assist managers in planning, scheduling, and controlling large-scale construction projects, research and development projects, and so on. Other network models have been applied to problems dealing with finding the shortest route from one point to another (for example, finding the shortest route in miles from New York to San Francisco), finding the maximal amount of flow over some system (for example, the maximum number of vehicles that can travel over a particular highway system), and finding the best configuration for newly designed communication systems.

In this chapter we begin our discussion of network models by investigating how PERT and CPM can be used to assist managers in project planning, scheduling, and control. The application of the other types of network models referred to above will be discussed in Chapter 10.

9.1   Project Management with PERT/CPM

In many situations managers assume the responsibility for planning, scheduling, and controlling projects that consist of numerous separate jobs or tasks performed by a variety of departments, individuals, etc. Often these projects are so large and/or complex that the manager cannot possibly keep all the information pertaining to the plan, schedule, and progress of the project in his or her head. In these situations the techniques of PERT and CPM have proved to be extremely valuable in assisting managers in carrying out their project management responsibilities.

PERT and CPM have been used to plan, schedule, and control a wide variety of projects, such as

1. Research and development of new products and processes;
2. Construction of plants, buildings, highways, etc.;
3. Maintenance of large and complex equipment;
4. Design and installation of new systems such as manufacturing, computers, accounting, etc.

In projects such as these, project managers must schedule and coordinate the various jobs or activities so that the entire project is completed on time. A complicating factor in carrying out this task is the interdependence of the activities; for example, some activities depend upon the completion of other activities before they can be started. When we realize that projects can have as many as several thousand specific activities, we see why project managers look for procedures that will help them answer questions such as the following:

1. What is the expected project completion date?
2. What is the scheduled start and completion date for each specific activity?
3. Which activities are "critical" and must be completed *exactly* as scheduled in order to keep the project on schedule?
4. How long can "noncritical" activities be delayed before they cause a delay in the total project?

As you will see, PERT and CPM can be used to help answer the above questions.

While PERT and CPM have the same general purpose and utilize much of the same terminology, the techniques were actually developed independently. PERT was introduced in the late 1950s specifically for planning, scheduling, and controlling the Polaris missile project. Since many jobs or activities associated with the Polaris missile project had never been attempted previously, it was difficult to predict the time to complete the various jobs or activities. Consequently, PERT was developed with an objective of being able to handle uncertainties in activity completion times.

On the other hand, CPM was developed primarily for scheduling and controlling industrial projects where job or activity times were considered known. CPM offered the option of reducing activity times by adding more workers and/or resources, usually at an increased cost. Thus a distinguishing feature of CPM was that it enabled time and cost trade-offs for the various activities in the project.

In today's usage the distinction between PERT and CPM as two separate techniques has largely disappeared. Computerized versions of the PERT/CPM approach often contain options for considering uncertainty in activity times as well as activity time-cost trade-offs. In this regard, modern project planning, scheduling, and controlling procedures have essentially combined the features of PERT and CPM such that a distinction between the two techniques is no longer necessary.

9.2 PERT/CPM Networks

The first step in the PERT/CPM project scheduling process is to determine all specific jobs or activities that make up the project. As a simple illustration involving the process of buying a small business, consider the list of four activities shown in Table 9.1. The development of an accurate list of activities such as this is a key step in any project. Since we will be planning the entire project and estimating the project completion date based on our list of activities, poor planning and omission of activities will be disastrous and lead to completely inaccurate schedules. We will assume that careful planning has been completed for our example problem and that Table 9.1 lists all activities for the small business project.

TABLE 9.1   Activity List for the Sample Project of Buying a Small Business

Activity	Description	Immediate Predecessors
A	Develop a list of sources for financing	—
B	Analyze the financial records of the business	—
C	Develop a business plan (e.g., sales projections, cash flow, etc.)	B
D	Submit a proposal to a lending institution	A, C

Note that Table 9.1 contains additional information in the column labeled immediate predecessors. The *immediate predecessors* for a particular activity are the activities that must be completed immediately prior to the start of the given activity. For example, the information in Table 9.1 tells us we can start work on activities A and B anytime, since neither of these activities depend upon the completion of prior activities. However, activity C cannot be started until activity B has been completed, and activity D cannot be started until both activities A and C have been completed. As you will see, immediate predecessor information must be known for each activity in order to describe the interdependencies among the activities in the project.

In Figure 9.1 we have drawn a picture that not only depicts the activities listed in Table 9.1 but also portrays the predecessor relationships among the activities. We refer to this graphical representation as the *network* for the project. As you can see, the network consists of numbered circles which are interconnected by several arrows. In general network terminology, the circles are called *nodes* and the arrows connecting the nodes are called *branches* or *arcs*. In a PERT/CPM network the arrows correspond to the activities in the project and the completion of several activities which lead into a node is referred to as an *event*. For example, node 2 refers to the event that activity B has been completed, and node 3 refers to the event that both activities A and C have been completed.

While the case did not arise in the network of our example project, we may encounter other PERT/CPM networks where two activities appear to

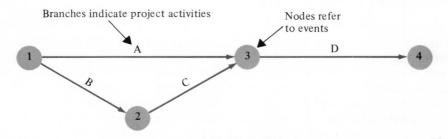

FIGURE 9.1   PERT/CPM Network for the Example Project of Buying a Small Business

have the same starting and ending nodes. For example, consider the following portion of a project activity table:

Activity	Immediate Predecessors
A	—
B	—
C	A
D	A, B

Note that for this project, activities C and D both have activity A as a common predecessor. A network corresponding to this situation might appear as follows:

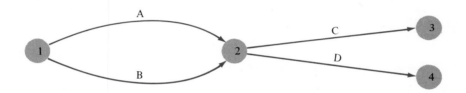

This network causes no particular problem for activity D, since it shows activities A and B as the correct immediate predecessors. However, the network incorrectly shows both activities A and B as immediate predecessors for activity C. Note from the activity list that this is incorrect since activity A should be the only predecessor for activity C.

We can avoid the above type of problem by never allowing two activities to have the same starting and ending nodes. This is accomplished by inserting *dummy activities,* which, as the name implies, are not actual activities but rather are fictitious activities used to ensure that the proper activity relationships are depicted in the network. For example, in the above illustration a dummy activity can be inserted in the network so that activities A and B no longer have the same starting and ending nodes. The resulting network is as follows:

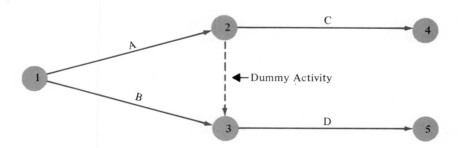

The dummy activity, represented by the dashed arrow, enables the network to show the correct activity relationships. That is, activity C can begin as soon as activity A is completed, whereas activity D can begin only after both activities A and B are completed. Although dummy activities may not be required for all PERT/CPM networks, larger and/or more complex projects may require several dummy activities in order to depict the proper activity relationships.

9.3   Project Scheduling with Uncertain Activity Times—PERT

In this section we will consider the details of project scheduling for a problem involving the research and development of a new product. Because many of the activities in this project have never been previously attempted, the project manager wants to identify and account for the uncertainties in the activity times. Since handling uncertainties in activity times was developed as part of the PERT technique, we will refer to the analysis in this section as the PERT approach to project scheduling.

An Example—The Daugherty Porta-Vac Project

The H. S. Daugherty Company has manufactured industrial vacuum cleaning systems for a number of years. Recently a member of the company's new-product research team submitted a report suggesting the company consider manufacturing a cordless vacuum cleaner that could be powered by a rechargeable battery. The vacuum cleaner, referred to as a Porta-Vac, could be used for light industrial cleaning and could contribute to Daugherty's expansion into the household market. Management hoped that the new product could be manufactured at a reasonable cost and that its portability and no-cord convenience would make it extremely attractive.

Daugherty's top management would like to initiate a project to study the feasibility of proceeding with the Porta-Vac idea. The end result of the feasibility project will be a report recommending the action to be taken for the new product. In order to complete this project, we will need information from the firm's research and development (R&D), product testing, manufacturing, cost estimating, and market research groups. How long do you think this feasibility study project will take? When should we tell the product testing group to schedule their work? Obviously, we do not have enough information to answer these questions at this time. In the following discussion we will learn how PERT can be used to answer these questions and provide the complete schedule and control information for the project.

The first step in the project scheduling process is to determine all the activities that make up the project as well as the immediate predecessors for each activity. For the Porta-Vac project, these data are shown in Table 9.2.

The network for the Porta-Vac project is shown in Figure 9.2. Check for yourself to see that the network does in fact maintain the immediate predecessor relationships shown in Table 9.2.

TABLE 9.2   Activity List for the Daugherty Porta-Vac Project

Activity	Description	Immediate Predecessors
A	R&D product design	—
B	Plan market research	—
C	Routing (manufacturing engineering)	A
D	Build prototype model	A
E	Prepare marketing brochure	A
F	Cost estimates (industrial engineering)	C
G	Preliminary product testing	D
H	Market survey	B, E
I	Pricing and forecast report	H
J	Final report	F, G, I

Activity Times

Once we have established a network for our project, we will need information on the time required to complete each activity. This information will be used in the calculation of the duration of the entire project and the scheduling of the specific activities. Accurate activity time estimates are essential for successful project management. Errors in activity time estimates will cause errors in scheduling and project completion date projections.

For repeat projects, such as construction and/or maintenance projects, managers may have the experience and historical data necessary to provide accurate activity time estimates. However, for new or unique projects, activity time estimation may be significantly more difficult. In fact, in many cases activity times are uncertain and are perhaps best described by a range of possible values rather than one specific activity time estimate. In these

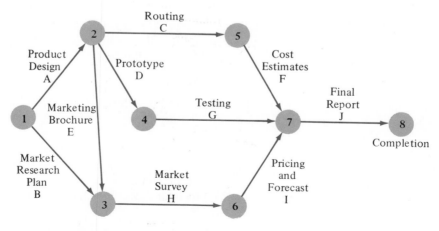

FIGURE 9.2   Network for the Porta-Vac Project

TABLE 9.3   Optimistic, Most Probable, and Pessimistic Activity Time Estimates (in Weeks) for the Porta-Vac Project

Activity	Optimistic (*a*)	Most Probable (*m*)	Pessimistic (*b*)
A	4	5	12
B	1	1.5	5
C	2	3	4
D	3	4	11
E	2	3	4
F	1.5	2	2.5
G	1.5	3	4.5
H	2.5	3.5	7.5
I	1.5	2	2.5
J	1	2	3

instances the uncertain activity times are treated as random variables with associated probability distributions, and the PERT procedure is used to provide probability statements about the project meeting specific completion dates.

In order to incorporate uncertain activity times into the PERT network model, we will need to obtain three time estimates for each activity. The three estimates are

Optimistic time (*a*)—the activity time if everything progresses in an *ideal* manner;

Most probable time (*m*)—the most likely activity time under normal conditions;

Pessimistic time (*b*)—the activity time if we encounter significant breakdowns and/or delays.

The three estimates enable the manager to develop a best guess of the most likely activity time and then express his or her uncertainty by providing estimates ranging from the best (optimistic) possible time to the worst (pessimistic) possible time.

As an illustration of the PERT procedure with uncertain activity times, let us consider the optimistic, most probable, and pessimistic time estimates for the Porta-Vac activities as presented in Table 9.3.

Using the product design activity A as an example, we see that management estimates that this activity will require from 4 weeks (optimistic) to 12 weeks (pessimistic), with the most likely time 5 weeks. If the activity could be repeated a large number of times, what would be the average time for the activity? The PERT procedure estimates this average or *expected time* (*t*) from the following formula:

$$t = \frac{a + 4m + b}{6}.$$

(9.1)

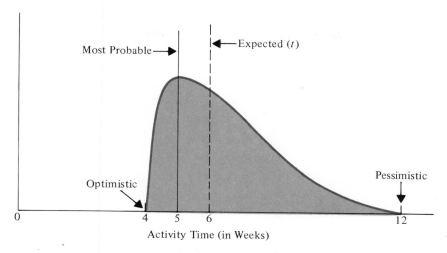

FIGURE 9.3   **Activity Time Distribution for Product Design Activity A of the Porta-Vac Project**

For activity A we have an estimated average or expected completion time of

$$t = \frac{4 + 4(5) + 12}{6} = \frac{36}{6} = 6 \text{ weeks.}$$

Equation (9.1) is based on the PERT assumption that the uncertain activity times are best described by a *beta probability distribution;* that is, equation (9.1) provides the average time for the special case of a beta probability distribution as the best description of the variability in activity times. This distribution assumption, which was judged to be reasonable by the developers of PERT, provides the time distribution for activity A as shown in Figure 9.3.

For uncertain activity times we can use the common statistical measure of the *variance* to describe the dispersion or variation in the activity time values. In PERT we compute the variance of the activity times from the following formula[1]:

$$\text{Variance of activity time} = \left(\frac{b - a}{6}\right)^2. \tag{9.2}$$

As you can see, the difference between the pessimistic (*b*) and optimistic (*a*) time estimates greatly affects the value of the variance. With large differences in these two values, management has a high degree of uncertainty in the activity time. Accordingly, the variance given by equation (9.2) will be large.

---

[1]The variance equation is based on the notion that a standard deviation is approximately ⅙ of the difference between the extreme values of the distribution: $(b - a)/6$. The variance is simply the square of the standard deviation.

TABLE 9.4 Expected Times and Variances for the Porta-Vac Activities

Activity	Expected Time (t) (in weeks)	Variance (V)
A	6	1.78
B	2	0.44
C	3	0.11
D	5	1.78
E	3	0.11
F	2	0.03
G	3	0.25
H	4	0.69
I	2	0.03
J	2	0.11
Total	32	

Referring to activity A we see that the measure of uncertainty—that is, the variance—of this activity, denoted σ_A^2, is

$$\sigma_A^2 = \left(\frac{12 - 4}{6}\right)^2 = \left(\frac{8}{6}\right)^2 = 1.78.$$

The expected times and variances for the Porta-Vac activities as computed using the data in Table 9.3 and equations (9.1) and (9.2) are given in Table 9.4.

A network depicting the Porta-Vac project and expected activity times is shown in Figure 9.4. Note that above each arrow or arc we write the letter of the corresponding activity, and directly under the arc and the letter we write the expected time of the activity.

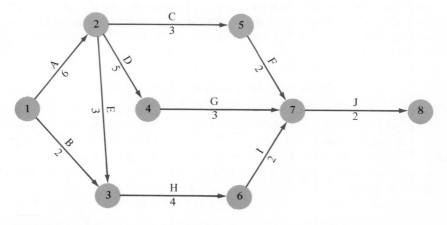

FIGURE 9.4 Porta-Vac Project Network with Expected Activity Times

The Critical Path Calculation

Once we have the network and the expected activity times, we are ready to proceed with the calculations necessary to determine the expected project completion date and a detailed activity schedule. In our initial calculations we will treat the expected activity time (Table 9.4) as the *fixed length* or *known duration* of each activity. Later we will analyze the effect of activity time variability.

While Table 9.4 indicates that the total expected time to complete all the work for the Porta-Vac project is 32 weeks, we can see from the network (Figure 9.4) that several of the activities can be conducted simultaneously (A and B, for example). Being able to work on two or more activities simultaneously will have the effect of making the total project completion time shorter than 32 weeks. However, the desired project completion time information is not directly available from the data in Table 9.4.

In order to arrive at a project duration estimate we will have to analyze the network and determine what is called its critical path. A *path* is a sequence of connected activities that lead from the starting node (1) to the completion node (8). The connected activities defined by nodes 1–2–5–7–8 form a path consisting of activities A, C, F, and J. Nodes 1–2–4–7–8 define the path associated with activities A, D, G, and J. Since *all* paths must be traversed in order to complete the project, we need to analyze the amount of time the various paths require. In particular, we will be interested in the longest path through the network. Since all other paths are shorter in duration, the longest path determines the expected total time or expected duration of the project. If activities on the longest path are delayed, the entire project will be delayed. Thus the longest path activities are the *critical activities* of the project and the longest path is called the *critical path* of the network. If managers wish to reduce the total project time, they will have to reduce the length of the critical path by shortening the duration of the critical activities. The following discussion presents a step-by-step procedure or algorithm for finding the critical path of a project network.

Starting at the network's origin (node 1) and using a starting time of 0, compute an *earliest start* and *earliest finish* time for each activity in the network. Let

$$ES = \text{earliest start time for a particular activity,}$$
$$EF = \text{earliest finish time for a particular activity,}$$
$$t = \text{expected activity time for the activity.}$$

The following expression can be used to find the earliest finish time for a given activity:

$$EF = ES + t. \tag{9.3}$$

For example, for activity A, $ES = 0$ and $t = 6$; thus the earliest finish time for activity A is $EF = 0 + 6 = 6$.

We will write the earliest start and earliest finish times directly on the network in brackets next to the letter of the activity. Using activity A as an example, we have

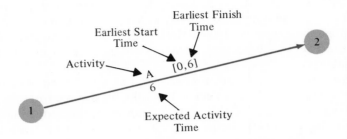

Since activities leaving a node cannot be started until *all* immediately preceding activities have been completed, the following rule can be used to determine the earliest start times for activities:

Earliest Start Time Rule: The earliest start time for an activity leaving a particular node is equal to the *largest* value of the earliest finish times for all activities entering the node.

Applying this rule to the portion of the network involving nodes 1, 2, 3, and 6, we obtain the following:

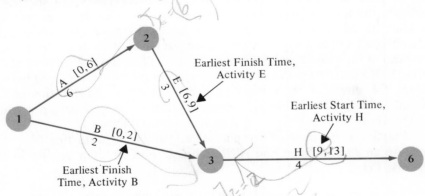

Note that applying the earliest start time rule at node 3 shows that the earliest start time for activity H is equal to the largest value of the earliest finish times for the two entering activities, B and E.

Proceeding in a *forward pass* through the network, we can establish first an earliest start and then an earliest finish time for each activity. The Porta-Vac network with ES and EF values is shown in Figure 9.5. Note that the earliest finish time for activity J, the last activity, is 17 weeks. Thus the earliest completion time for the entire project is 17 weeks.

We now continue the algorithm for finding the critical path by making a *backward pass* calculation. Starting at the completion point (node 8) and

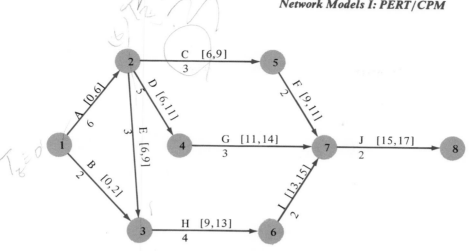

FIGURE 9.5   Porta-Vac Network with Earliest Start and Earliest Finish Times Shown Above Activities

using a latest finish time of 17 for activity J, we trace back through the network computing a latest start and latest finish time for each activity. Let

LS = latest starting time for a particular activity,

LF = latest finishing time for a particular activity.

The following expression can be used to find the latest start time for a given activity:

$$LS = LF - t. \tag{9.4}$$

Given LF = 17 and $t = 2$ for activity J, the latest start time for this activity can be computed as LS = 17 − 2 = 15.

The following rule is necessary in order to determine the latest finish time for any activity in the network:

Latest Finish Time Rule: The latest finish time for an activity entering a particular node is equal to the *smallest* value of the latest starting times for all activities leaving the node.

Logically the above rule states that the latest time an activity can be finished is equal to the earliest (smallest) value for the latest start time of following activities. The complete network with the LS and LF backward pass calculations is shown in Figure 9.6. The latest start and latest finish times for the activities are written in brackets directly under the earliest start and earliest finish times.

Note the application of the latest finish time rule at node 2. The latest finish time for activity A (LF = 6) is the smallest value of the latest start times for the activities that leave node 2; that is, the smallest LS value for activities C (LS = 10), D (LS = 7), and E (LS = 6) is 6.

After obtaining the start and finish activity times as summarized in Figure 9.6, we can find the amount of slack or free time associated with each

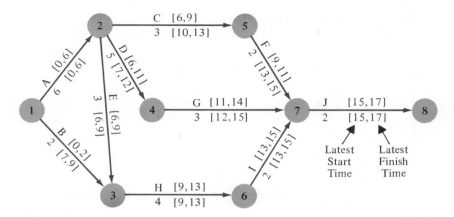

FIGURE 9.6   Porta-Vac Network with Latest Start and Latest Finish Times Shown Below Activities

of the activities. *Slack* is defined as the length of time an activity can be delayed without affecting the completion date for the project. The amount of slack for each activity is computed as follows:

$$\text{Slack} = \text{LS} - \text{ES} = \text{LF} - \text{EF}. \tag{9.5}$$

For example, we see that the slack associated with activity C is LS − ES = 10 − 6 = 4 weeks. This means that activity C, the routing activity, can be delayed up to 4 weeks (start anywhere between weeks 6 and 10) and the entire project can still be completed in 17 weeks. This activity is not a critical activity and is not part of the critical path. Using equation (9.5), we see that the slack associated with activity E is LS − ES = 6 − 6 = 0. Thus activity E, the marketing brochure activity, has no slack time and must be held to the 6-week start time schedule. Since this activity cannot be delayed without affecting the entire project, it is a critical activity and is on the critical path. In general, the critical path activities are the activities with zero slack.

The start and finish times shown on the network in Figure 9.6 provide a detailed schedule for all activities. That is, from Figure 9.6, we know the earliest and latest starting and finishing times for the activities. Putting this information in tabular form provides the activity schedule shown in Table 9.5. Note that by computing the slack associated with each activity, we see that activities A, E, H, I, and J each have zero slack; hence these activities form the critical path in the Porta-Vac network. Note that Table 9.5 also shows the slack or delay that can be tolerated for the noncritical activities before these activities will cause a project delay.

Variability in the Project Completion Date

While during the critical path calculations we treated the activity times as fixed at their expected values, we are now ready to consider the uncertainty

TABLE 9.5 Activity Schedule (in Weeks) for the Porta-Vac Project

Activity	Earliest Start	Latest Start	Earliest Finish	Latest Finish	Slack (LS − ES)	Critical Path?
A	0	0	6	6	0	Yes
B	0	7	2	9	7	
C	6	10	9	13	4	
D	6	7	11	12	1	
E	6	6	9	9	0	Yes
F	9	13	11	15	4	
G	11	12	14	15	1	
H	9	9	13	13	0	Yes
I	13	13	15	15	0	Yes
J	15	15	17	17	0	Yes

in the activity times and determine the effect this uncertainty or variability has on the project completion date. Recall that the critical path determines the duration of the entire project. For the Porta-Vac project the critical path of A–E–H–I–J resulted in an expected project completion time of 17 weeks.

Just as the critical path activities govern the expected project completion date, variation in critical path activities can cause variation in the project completion date. Variation in noncritical path activities will ordinarily have no effect on the project completion date because of the slack time associated with these activities. However, if a noncritical activity were delayed long enough to expend all of its slack time, then that activity would become part of a new critical path, and further delays would extend the project completion date. Variability leading to a longer than expected total time for the critical path activities will always extend the project completion date. On the other hand, variability in critical path activities resulting in a shorter critical path will enable an earlier than expected completion date, unless the activity times on the other paths become critical. The PERT procedure uses the variance in the critical path activities to determine the variance in the project completion date.

If we let T denote the project duration, then T, which is determined by the critical activities A–E–H–I–J in the Porta-Vac problem, has the expected value of

$$T = t_A + t_E + t_H + t_I + t_J$$
$$= 6 + 3 + 4 + 2 + 2 = 17 \text{ weeks.}$$

Similarly the variance in the project duration is given by the sum of the variance of the critical path activities. Thus the variance (σ^2) for the Porta-Vac project completion time is given by

$$\sigma^2 = \sigma_A^2 + \sigma_E^2 + \sigma_H^2 + \sigma_I^2 + \sigma_J^2$$
$$= 1.78 + 0.11 + 0.69 + 0.03 + 0.11 = 2.72.$$

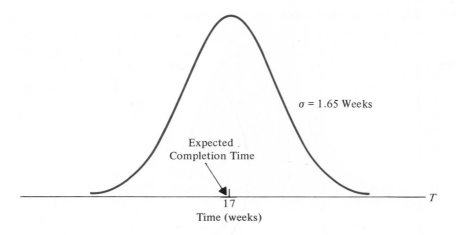

FIGURE 9.7   PERT Normal Distribution of the Project Completion Time Variation for the Porta-Vac Project

This formula is based on the assumption that all the activity times are independent. If two or more activities are dependent, the formula only provides an approximation to the variance of the project completion time. The closer the activities are to being independent, the better the approximation.

Since we know that the standard deviation is the square root of the variance, we can compute the standard deviation (σ) for the Porta-Vac project completion time as follows:

$$\sigma = \sqrt{\sigma^2} = \sqrt{2.72} = 1.65.$$

A final assumption of PERT, that the distribution of the project completion time T follows a normal or bell-shaped distribution,[2] allows us to draw the distribution shown in Figure 9.7. With this distribution we can compute the probability of meeting a specified project completion date. For example, suppose that management has allotted 20 weeks for the Porta-Vac project. While we expect completion in 17 weeks, what is the probability that we will meet the 20-week deadline? Using the normal distribution from Figure 9.7, we are asking for the probability that $T \leq 20$. This is shown graphically as the shaded area in Figure 9.8. The z value for the normal distribution at $T = 20$ is given by

$$z = \frac{20 - 17}{1.65} = 1.82.$$

Using $z = 1.82$ and the tables for the normal distribution (see Appendix A), we see that the probability of the project meeting the 20-week deadline is

---

[2]The use of the normal distribution as an approximation is based on the central limit theorem, which indicates that the sum of independent activity times follows a normal distribution as the number of activities becomes large.

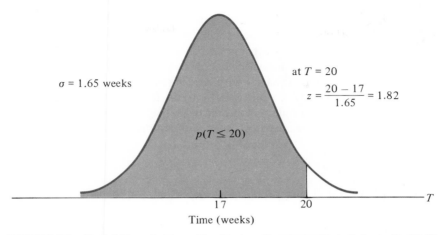

FIGURE 9.8   Probability of a Porta-Vac Project Completion Date Prior to the 20-Week Deadline

$0.4656 + 0.5000 = 0.9656$. Thus while activity time variability may cause the project to exceed the 17-week expected duration, there is an excellent chance that the project will be completed before the 20-week deadline. Similar probability calculations can be made for other project deadline alternatives.

Summary of PERT Procedure

Before discussing the contributions of PERT, let us briefly review the process of analyzing a project using the PERT procedure. In analyzing *any* project using PERT, we perform the following steps:

Step 1:   Develop a list of activities that make up the project, including immediate predecessors.

Step 2:   Draw a network corresponding to the activity list developed in Step 1.

Step 3:   Estimate the expected activity time and the variance for each activity.[3]

Step 4:   Using the expected activity time estimates, determine the earliest start time and the earliest finish time for each activity. The earliest finish time for the complete project corresponds to the earliest finish time for the last activity. This is the expected project completion time.

---

[3]While we have illustrated PERT with variability in activity times, the manager may choose to provide the expected time estimates directly. In this case, the variance calculations cannot be made, and Step 7 of the PERT procedure would be ignored. The critical path can be computed, but completion time probabilities cannot.

Step 5:   Using the project completion time as the latest finishing time for the last activity, work backward through the network to compute the latest start and latest finish time for each activity.

Step 6:   Compute the slack associated with each activity. The critical path activities are the activities with zero slack.

Step 7:   Use the variability in the activity times to estimate the variability of the project completion date; then, using this estimate, compute the probability of meeting a specified completion date.

Contributions of PERT

In Section 9.1 we stated that project managers look for procedures that will help them answer many important questions regarding the planning, scheduling, and controlling of projects. Let us reconsider these questions in light of the information our PERT analysis has provided about the Porta-Vac project:

1.   What is the expected project completion date?

  Answer: PERT has shown management that the expected project duration is 17 weeks.

2.   What is the scheduled start and completion date for each specific activity?

  Answer: PERT has provided management with a detailed activity schedule that shows the earliest start, latest start, earliest finish, and latest finish times for each activity (Table 9.5).

3.   Which activities are "critical" and must be completed *exactly* as scheduled in order to keep the project on schedule?

  Answer: PERT has provided management with the critical activities A–E–H–I–J.

4.   How long can "noncritical" activities be delayed before they cause a delay in the total project?

  Answer: The detailed activity schedule (Table 9.5) shows management the slack time available for each activity.

In addition to the above information, management has also been provided with information about the probability of meeting the 20-week deadline. The probability is 0.9656.

In the management of any project, the above information is important and valuable. While larger projects may substantially increase the time required to draw the PERT network and to make the necessary calculations, the PERT procedure and contributions in the larger projects are identical to those observed in the Porta-Vac project. Furthermore, computer packages currently exist that carry out the steps of the PERT procedure, thus relieving the applications analyst from having to carry out the details of the technique using hand calculation procedures.

TABLE 9.6   **Activity List for a Two-Machine Maintenance Project**

Activity		Immediate Predecessor	Expected Time (in days)
A	Overhaul machine I	—	7
B	Adjust machine I	A	3
C	Overhaul machine II	—	6
D	Adjust machine II	C	3
E	Test system	B, D	2

9.4   Considering Time–Cost Trade-Offs

As we mentioned earlier, the CPM approach to project scheduling provides the project manager with the capabilities of adding resources to selected activities in an attempt to reduce activity, and thus project, completion times. Since added resources such as more workers, overtime, and so on generally increase project costs, the decision to reduce activity times must take into consideration the additional cost involved. In effect, the project manager has to make a decision that involves trading off decreased activity time against increased project cost.

In the Porta-Vac project, the 17-week scheduled completion time could be reduced if management were willing to add resources to shorten any of the critical path activities: A, E, H, I, and J. Since the Porta-Vac project has a high probability of meeting the 20-week project deadline, it is doubtful that management would be willing to add costs to reduce activity times for this particular project. Thus let us consider another project where time–cost trade-offs would most likely need to be considered.

Table 9.6 defines a two-machine maintenance project consisting of five activities. Since management has had substantial experience with similar projects, the maintenance activities times are considered known; hence only a single time estimate is provided for each activity. The network for this project is shown in Figure 9.9.

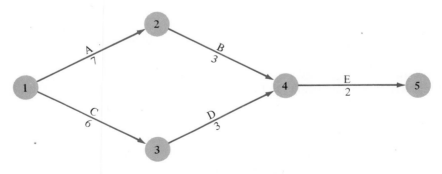

FIGURE 9.9   **Network of a Two-Machine Maintenance Project**

TABLE 9.7   Activity Schedule for the Maintenance Project

Activity	Earliest Start	Latest Start	Earliest Finish	Latest Finish	Slack (LS − ES)	Critical Path?
A	0	0	7	7	0	Yes
B	7	7	10	10	0	Yes
C	0	1	6	7	1	
D	6	7	9	10	1	
E	10	10	12	12	0	Yes

Critical path calculations for the maintenance project network are computed following the procedure we used to find the critical path in the Porta-Vac network. Making the forward pass and backward pass calculations, we can obtain the activity schedule shown in Table 9.7. As you can see, the zero slack times, and thus the critical path, are associated with activities A–B–E or nodes 1–2–4–5. The length of the critical path, and thus the project, is 12 days.

Crashing Activity Times

Now suppose that the current production levels make it imperative for the maintenance project to be completed within 2 weeks, or 10 working days. By looking at the length of the critical path of the network (12 days), we realize that it is impossible to meet the project completion date unless we can shorten selected activity times. This shortening of activity times, which usually can be achieved by adding resources such as manpower or overtime, is referred to as *crashing* the activity times. However, since the added resources associated with crashing activity times usually result in added project costs, we will want to identify the activities that cost least to crash and then crash only the amount necessary to meet the desired project completion date.

In order to determine just where and how much to crash activity times, we will need information on how much each activity can be crashed and how much the crashing process costs. Possibly the best way to accomplish this is to ask management for the following information on each activity:

1. Estimated activity cost under the normal or expected activity time;
2. Activity completion time under maximum crashing (that is, shortest possible activity time);
3. Estimated activity cost under maximum crashing.

Let

$$\tau = \text{normal activity time,}$$
$$\tau' = \text{crashed activity time (at maximum crashing),}$$
$$C_n = \text{normal activity cost,}$$
$$C_c = \text{crashed activity cost (at maximum crashing).}$$

We can compute the *maximum* possible activity time reduction M due to crashing as follows:

$$M = \tau - \tau'. \tag{9.6}$$

On a per-unit-time basis (for example, per day), the crashing cost K for each activity is given by

$$K = \frac{C_c - C_n}{M}. \tag{9.7}$$

For example, if activity A has a normal activity time of 7 days at a cost of $500 and a maximum crash activity time of 4 days at a cost of $800, we have $\tau = 7$, $\tau' = 4$, $C_n = 500$, and $C_c = 800$. Thus, using equations (9.6) and (9.7) we see that activity A can be crashed a maximum of

$$M_A = 7 - 4 = 3 \text{ days}$$

at a crashing cost of

$$K_A = \frac{800 - 500}{3} = \frac{300}{3} = \$100 \text{ per day.}$$

We will make the assumption that any portion or fraction of the activity crash time can be achieved for a corresponding portion of the activity crashing cost. For example, if we decided to crash activity A by only 1½ days, we would assume that this could be accomplished with an added cost of 1½($100) = $150, which results in a total activity cost of $500 + $150 = $650. Figure 9.10 shows the graph of the time–cost relationship for activity A.

The complete normal and crash activity data for our example project are given in Table 9.8.

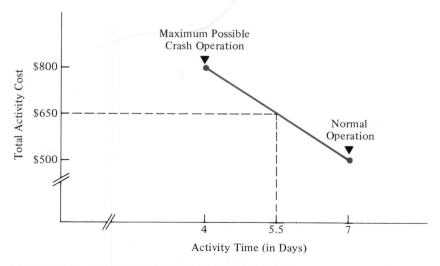

FIGURE 9.10   Time–Cost Relationship for Activity A

TABLE 9.8   Normal and Crash Activity Data for the Maintenance Project

Activity	Normal Time, τ	Crash Time, τ'	Total Normal Cost, C_n	Total Crash Cost, C_c	Maximum Crash Days $M = \tau - \tau'$	Crash Cost per Day, $K = \dfrac{C_c - C_n}{M}$
A	7	4	$500	$800	3	$100
B	3	2	$200	$350	1	$150
C	6	4	$500	$900	2	$200
D	3	1	$200	$500	2	$150
E	2	1	$300	$550	1	$250
			$1700	$3100		

Now the question is, which activities would you crash, and how much should these activities be crashed in order to meet the 10-day project completion deadline at minimum cost? Your first reaction to this question is possibly to consider crashing the critical path activities A, B, or E. Since activity A has the lowest crashing costs of the three, crashing this activity by 2 days will reduce the A–B–E path to the desired 10 days. While this is correct, be careful: as you crash the current critical path activities, other paths may become critical. Thus you will need to check the critical path in the revised network and perhaps either identify additional activities to crash or modify your initial crashing decision. While in a small network you may be able to use this trial-and-error approach to making crashing decisions, in larger networks you will need a mathematical procedure in order to arrive at the optimal decision. The following discussion shows how linear programming can be used to solve the network crashing problem.

A Linear Programming Model for Crashing Decisions

While several solution procedures and variations exist for the crashing procedure, the following linear programming model is one approach used to help make crashing decisions. First we define the decision variables. Let

x_i = time of occurrence of event i, $i = 1,2,3,4,5$,

y_j = amount of crash time used for activity j, $j =$ A,B,C,D,E.

Since the total normal time project cost is fixed at $1700 (see Table 9.8), we can minimize the total project cost (normal cost plus crash cost) simply by minimizing the crashing costs. Thus our linear programming objective function becomes

$$\min \sum_j K_j y_j \tag{9.8}$$

or

$$\min 100 y_A + 150 y_B + 200 y_C + 150 y_D + 250 y_E, \tag{9.9}$$

where K_j is the crash cost for activity j, j = A,B,C,D,E, on a per-unit-time basis.[4]

The constraints on the model involve describing the network, limiting the activity crash times, and meeting the project completion date. Of these, the constraints used to describe the network are perhaps the most difficult. These constraints are based on the following conditions:

1. The time of occurrence of event i (x_i) must be greater than or equal to the activity completion time for all activities leading into the node or event.
2. An activity start time is equal to the occurrence time of its preceding node or event.
3. An activity time is equal to its normal time less the length of time it is crashed.

Using an event occurrence time of zero at node 1 ($x_1 = 0$), we can create the following set of network description constraints:

Event 2:

$$x_2 \geq \underbrace{\tau_A - y_A}_{} + 0$$

Occurrence time for event 2 — Actual time for activity A — Start time for activity A ($x_1 = 0$)

$$x_2 \geq 7 - y_A$$

or

$$x_2 + y_A \geq 7. \tag{9.10}$$

Event 3:

$$x_3 \geq \tau_C - y_C + 0$$

$$x_3 + y_C \geq 6. \tag{9.11}$$

Since two activities enter event or node 4, we have the following two constraints:

Event 4:

$$x_4 \geq \tau_B - y_B + x_2$$

$$x_4 \geq \tau_D - y_D + x_3 \tag{9.12}$$

or

$$-x_2 + x_4 + y_B \geq 3$$

$$-x_3 + x_4 + y_D \geq 3. \tag{9.13}$$

Event 5:

$$x_5 \geq \tau_E - y_E + x_4$$

or

$$-x_4 + x_5 + y_E \geq 2. \tag{9.14}$$

---

[4]Note that the x_i variables indicating event occurrences do not result in costs; thus they have zero coefficients in the objective function.

The five constraints (9.10)–(9.14) are necessary to describe our CPM network.

The maximum allowable crash time constraints are

$$y_A \leq 3 \tag{9.15}$$

$$y_B \leq 1 \tag{9.16}$$

$$y_C \leq 2 \tag{9.17}$$

$$y_D \leq 2 \tag{9.18}$$

$$y_E \leq 1 \tag{9.19}$$

and the project completion date provides another constraint:

$$x_5 \leq 10. \tag{9.20}$$

Adding the nonnegativity restrictions and solving the above 9-variable, 11-constraint (9.10)–(9.20) linear programming model provides the following solution:

$$
\begin{array}{ll}
x_2 = 5 & y_A = 2 \\
x_3 = 6 & y_B = 0 \\
x_4 = 8 & y_C = 0 \\
x_5 = 10 & y_D = 1 \\
& y_E = 0
\end{array}
$$

Objective function = \$350.

The solution values of $y_A = 2$ and $y_D = 1$ tell us activity A must be crashed 2 days (\$200) and activity D must be crashed 1 day (\$150) in order to meet the 10-day project completion deadline. Because of this crashing, the time for activity A will be reduced to $7 - 2 = 5$ days, while the time for activity D will be reduced to $3 - 1 = 2$ days. The total project cost (normal cost plus crashing cost) will be \$1700 + \$200 + \$150 = \$2050. To generate the new activity schedule under crashing, we use the crashed activity times and repeat the critical path calculations for the network. Doing this provides the activity schedule shown in Table 9.9. Note that in our final solution all

TABLE 9.9 New Activity Schedule for the Maintenance Project after Crashing Activities A and D

Activity	Time After Crashing	ES	LS	EF	LF	Slack
A	5	0	0	5	5	0
B	3	5	5	8	8	0
C	6	0	0	6	6	0
D	2	6	6	8	8	0
E	2	8	8	10	10	0

activities are critical. Resolving the linear programming model with alternate project completion dates [constraint (9.20)] will show the project manager the costs associated with crashing the project to meet alternate deadlines.

Due to the substantial formulation and computational effort associated with activity crashing, most applications of this technique use specialized computer programs developed to handle crashing and the related network analyses.

9.5 PERT/Cost

As you have seen, PERT and CPM concentrate on the *time* aspect of a project and provide information which can be used to schedule and control individual activities so that the entire project is completed on time. While project time and the meeting of a scheduled completion date are primary considerations for almost every project, there are many situations in which the *cost* associated with the project is just as important as time. In this section, we show how the technique referred to as PERT/Cost can be used to help plan, schedule, and control project costs. The ultimate objective of a PERT/Cost system is to provide information which can be used to maintain project costs within a specified budget.

Planning and Scheduling Project Costs

The budgeting process for a project usually involves identifying all costs associated with the project and then developing a schedule or forecast of when the costs are expected to occur. Then at various stages of project completion, the actual project costs incurred can be compared to the scheduled or budget costs. If actual costs are exceeding budgeted costs, corrective action may be taken to keep costs within the budget.

The first step in a PERT/Cost control system is to break the entire project into components that are convenient in terms of measuring and controlling costs. While a PERT/CPM network may already show detailed activities for the project, we may find that these activities are too detailed for conveniently controlling project costs. In such cases related activities which are under the control of one department, subcontractor, etc., are often grouped together to form what are referred to as *work packages*. By identifying costs of each work package, a project manager can use a PERT/Cost system to help plan, schedule, and control project costs.

Since the projects we discuss in this chapter have a relatively small number of activities, we will find it convenient to define work packages as having only one activity. Thus in our discussion of the PERT/Cost technique we will be treating each activity as a separate work package. Realize, however, that in large and complex projects we would almost always group related activities so that a cost control system could be developed for a more reasonable number of work packages.

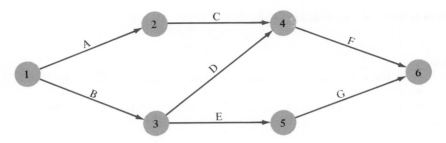

FIGURE 9.11   A Project Network

In order to illustrate the PERT/Cost technique, let us consider the research and development project network shown in Figure 9.11. We are assuming that each activity is an acceptable work package and that a detailed cost analysis has been made on an activity basis. The activity cost estimates, along with the expected activity times, are shown in Table 9.10. In using the PERT/Cost technique we will be assuming that activities (work packages) are defined such that costs occur at a constant rate over the duration of the activity. For example, activity B, which shows an estimated cost of $30,000 and an expected 3-month duration, is assumed to have a cost rate of $30,000/3 = $10,000 per month. The cost rates for all activities are provided in Table 9.10. Note that the total estimated or budgeted cost for the project is $87,000.

Using the expected activity times, we can compute the critical path for the project. A summary of the critical path calculations and the resulting activity schedule is shown in Table 9.11. Activities B, D, and F determine the critical path and provide an expected project duration of 8 months.

We are now ready to develop a budget for the project which will show when costs should occur during the 8-month project duration. First let us assume that all activities begin at their earliest possible starting date. Using the monthly activity cost rates shown in Table 9.10 and the earliest start times, we can prepare the month-by-month cost forecast as shown in Table 9.12. For example, using the earliest start date for activity A as 0, we expect

TABLE 9.10   Activity Time and Cost Estimates

Activity	Expected Time (Months)	Budgeted or Estimated Cost	Budgeted Cost per Month
A	2	$10,000	$ 5,000
B	3	30,000	10,000
C	1	3,000	3,000
D	3	6,000	2,000
E	2	20,000	10,000
F	2	10,000	5,000
G	1	8,000	8,000
	Total Project Budget =	$87,000	

TABLE 9.11   Activity Schedule

Activity	Earliest Start	Latest Start	Earliest Finish	Latest Finish	Slack	Critical Path?
A	0	3	2	5	3	
B	0	0	3	3	0	Yes
C	2	5	3	6	3	
D	3	3	6	6	0	Yes
E	3	5	5	7	2	
F	6	6	8	8	0	Yes
G	5	7	6	8	2	

activity A, which has a 2-month duration, to show a cost of $5000 in each of the first 2 months of the project. By similarly using the earliest starting date and monthly cost rate for each activity, we are able to complete Table 9.12 as shown. Note that by summing the costs in each column we obtain the total cost anticipated for each month of the project. Finally, by accumulating the monthly costs, we can show the budgeted total cost schedule, provided all activities are started at the *earliest* starting times. Table 9.13 shows the budgeted total cost schedule when all activities are started at the *latest* starting times.

Provided the project progresses on its PERT or CPM time schedule, each activity will be started somewhere between its earliest and latest starting times. This implies that the total project costs should occur at levels between the earliest start and latest start costs schedules. For example, using the data in Tables 9.12 and 9.13, we see that by month 3, total project costs should be between $30,000 (latest starting date schedule) and $43,000 (earliest starting date schedule). Thus at month 3 a total project cost between $30,000 and $43,000 would be expected.

In Figure 9.12 we show the forecasted total project costs for both the

TABLE 9.12   Budgeted Costs for an Earliest Starting Date Schedule ($ $\times$ 10³)

Activity	Month 1	2	3	4	5	6	7	8
A	5	5						
B	10	10	10					
C			3					
D				2	2	2		
E				10	10			
F							5	5
G						8		
Monthly Cost	15	15	13	12	12	10	5	5
Total Project Cost	15	30	43	55	67	77	82	87

TABLE 9.13   Budgeted Costs for a Latest Starting Date Schedule ($ × 10³)

Activity	1	2	3	4	5	6	7	8
A				5	5			
B	10	10	10					
C						3		
D				2	2	2		
E						10	10	
F							5	5
G								8
Monthly Cost	10	10	10	7	7	15	15	13
Total Project Cost	10	20	30	37	44	59	74	87

earliest and latest starting time schedules. The shaded region between the two cost curves shows the possible budgets for the project. If the project manager is willing to commit activities to specific starting times, a specific project cost forecast or budget can be prepared. However, based on the above analysis we know that such a budget will have to be in the feasible region shown in Figure 9.12.

Controlling Project Costs

The information that we have developed thus far is helpful in terms of planning and scheduling total project costs. However, if we are going to have

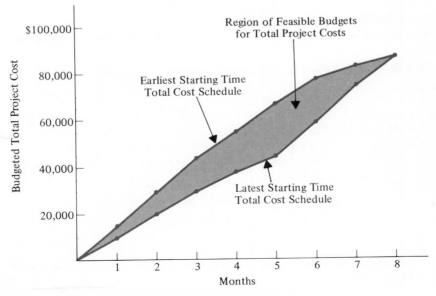

FIGURE 9.12   **Feasible Budgets for Total Project Costs**

TABLE 9.14 Activity Cost Estimates

Activity	Budgeted Cost	Activity	Budgeted Cost
A	$10,000	E	$20,000
B	30,000	F	10,000
C	3000	G	8000
D	6000		

an effective cost control system, we will need to identify costs on a much more detailed basis. For example, information that the project's actual total cost is exceeding the budgeted total cost will be of little value unless we can identify the activity or group of activities that are causing the cost overruns.

The PERT/Cost system provides the desired cost control by budgeting and then recording actual costs on an activity (i.e., work package) basis. Periodically throughout the project's duration, actual costs for all completed and in-process activities are compared to the appropriate budgeted costs. The project manager is then provided with up-to-date information on the cost status of each activity. If at any point in time actual costs exceed budgeted costs, a cost overrun has occurred. On the other hand, if actual costs are less than the budgeted costs, we have a condition referred to as a cost underrun. By identifying the sources of cost overruns and cost underruns, the manager can take corrective action where necessary. Note that the budgeted or estimated activity costs for the R&D project network of Figure 9.11 are shown in Table 9.14.

Now at any point during the project's duration the manager can use a PERT/Cost procedure to obtain an activity cost status report by collecting the following information for *each activity:*

1. Actual cost to date;
2. Percent completion to date.

A PERT/Cost system will require periodic—perhaps biweekly or monthly—collection of the above information. Let us suppose we are at the end of the fourth month of the project and have the actual cost and percent completion data for each activity, as shown in Table 9.15. This current status information shows that activities A and B have been completed, activities C, D, and E are in process, and activities F and G have not yet been started.

In order to prepare a cost status report we will need to compute the value for all work completed to date. Let

V_i = value of work completed for activity i,

p_i = percent completion for activity i,

B_i = budget for activity i.

The following relationship is used to find the value of work completed for each activity:

$$V_i = p_i(100)B_i. \tag{9.21}$$

TABLE 9.15   Activity Cost and Percent Completion
Data at the End of Month 4

Activity	Actual Cost	Percent Completion
A	$12,000	100
B	30,000	100
C	1000	50
D	2000	33
E	10,000	25
F	0	0
G	0	0
Total Actual Cost = $55,000		

For example, the values of work completed for activities A and C are as follows[5]:

$$V_A = (^{100}/_{100})(\$10,000) = \$10,000,$$
$$V_C = (^{50}/_{100})(\$3000) = \$1500.$$

Cost overruns and cost underruns can now be found by comparing the actual cost of each activity with its appropriate budget value. Let

AC_i = actual cost to date for activity i,

D_i = difference in actual and budget value for activity i.

We have

$$D_i = AC_i - V_i. \tag{9.22}$$

A positive D_i indicates the activity has a cost *overrun*, while a negative D_i indicates a cost *underrun*. $D_i = 0$ indicates that actual costs are in agreement with the budgeted costs.

For example,

$$D_A = AC_A - V_A = \$12,000 - \$10,000 = \$2000$$

shows activity A, which has already been completed, has a $2000 cost overrun. However, activity C, with $D_C = \$1000 - \$1500 = -\$500$, is currently showing a cost underrun, or savings, of $500. A complete cost status report such as the one shown in Table 9.16 can now be prepared for the project manager.

This cost report shows the project manager that the costs to date are $6500 over the estimated or budgeted costs. On a percentage basis, we would say the project is experiencing a ($6500/$48,500) × 100 = 13.4% cost overrun, which for most projects is a serious situation. By checking each

---

[5]Equation (9.21) and the succeeding calculations are based on the PERT/Cost assumption that activity costs occur at a constant rate over the duration of the activity. For details regarding this assumption see Wiest, J. D. and F. K. Levy, *A Management Guide to PERT/CPM*, Englewood Cliffs, N.J., Prentice-Hall, 2nd ed., 1977.

TABLE 9.16   Project Cost Status Report at Month 4

Activity	Actual Cost (AC)	Budgeted Value $[V = (p/100)B]$	Differences (D)
A	$12,000	$10,000	$2,000
B	30,000	30,000	0
C	1,000	1,500	−500
D	2,000	2,000	0
E	10,000	5,000	5,000
F	0	0	0
G	0	0	0
Totals	$55,000	$48,500	$6,500

Total Project Cost
Overrun to Date

activity, we see that activities A and E are causing the cost overrun. Since activity A has been completed, its cost overrun cannot be corrected; however, activity E is in process and is only 25% complete. Thus activity E should be reviewed immediately. Corrective action for activity E can help to bring actual costs closer to the budgeted costs. The manager may also want to consider cost reduction possibilities for activities C, D, F, and G in order to keep the total project cost within the budget.

While the PERT/Cost procedure described above can be an effective cost control system, it is not without possible drawbacks and implementation problems. First, the activity-by-activity cost recording system can require significant clerical effort, especially for firms with large and/or numerous projects. Thus the personnel and other costs associated with maintaining a PERT/Cost system may offset some of the advantages. Second, questions can arise as to how costs should be allocated to activities or work packages. Overhead, indirect, and even material costs can cause cost allocations and measurement problems. Third, and perhaps most critical, is the fact that PERT/Cost requires a system of cost recording and control that is significantly different from most cost accounting systems. Firms using departments or other organizational units as cost centers will need a substantially revised accounting system to handle the PERT/Cost activity-oriented system. Problems of modifying accounting procedures and/or carrying dual accounting systems are not trivial matters.

Summary

In this chapter we have introduced PERT, CPM, and PERT/Cost as network based procedures designed to assist in the project planning, scheduling, and control process. PERT, which includes capabilities for handling variable or uncertain activity times, was developed primarily for new and/or unique projects such as those encountered in research and development. CPM, which provided the capability of reducing project completion times by crashing selected activities under increased but known costs, used a single activity time estimate and was developed for industrial-type projects where experience with activity times and resource requirements was readily available. However, in today's usage, the distinction between PERT and CPM as being two separate techniques has all but disappeared. In the final section of this chapter we described how the PERT/Cost technique can be used to help plan, schedule, and control project costs. Because of the numerous computations associated with planning, updating, and revising PERT/CPM and/or PERT/Cost networks, computer programs are frequently used to implement these project management techniques.

Glossary

1. *Network*—A graphical description of a problem or situation consisting of numbered circles (nodes) interconnected by a series of lines (branches or arcs).

2. *Nodes*—The intersection or junction points of a network.

3. *Program evaluation and review technique (PERT)*—A network based project management procedure.

4. *Activities*—Specific jobs or tasks that are components of a project. These are represented by arcs in a PERT network.

5. *Immediate predecessors*—The activities that must immediately precede another given activity.

6. *Branches*—The lines connecting the nodes which in general carry the flow through the network.

7. *Arcs*—Same as branches.

8. *Event*—An event occurs when *all* the activities leading into a node have been completed.

9. *Dummy activity*—A fictitious activity with zero activity time used to create a PERT-type network.

10. *Optimistic time*—A PERT activity time estimate based on the assumption that the activity will progress in an ideal manner.

11. *Most probable time*—A PERT activity time estimate for the most likely activity time.

12. *Pessimistic time*—A PERT activity time estimate based on the assumption that the most unfavorable conditions occur.

13. *Expected activity time*—The average activity time.

14. *Beta distribution*—A probability distribution used to describe PERT activity times.

15. *Path*—A sequence of branches (activities) connecting the origin and destination of a network.

16. *Critical path*—The longest sequence of activities or path in a project management (PERT/CPM) network. The time it takes to traverse this path is the estimated project duration.

17. *Critical activities*—The activities on the critical path.

18. *Earliest start time*—The earliest time at which an activity may begin.

19. *Earliest finish time*—The earliest time at which an activity may be completed.

20. *Latest start time*—The latest time at which an activity may begin without holding up the complete project.

21. *Latest finish time*—The latest time at which an activity may be completed without holding up the complete project.

22. *Forward pass*—A calculation procedure moving forward through the network which determines the early start and early finish times for each activity.

23. *Backward pass*—A calculation procedure moving backwards through the network which determines the latest start and latest finish times for each activity.

24. *Slack*—The length of time an activity can be delayed without affecting the project completion date.

25. *Critical path method (CPM)*—A network-based project management procedure which includes the capability of crashing a network.

26. *Crashing*—The process of reducing an activity time by adding resources and hence usually cost.

27. *PERT/Cost*—A technique designed to assist in the planning, scheduling, and controlling of project costs.

28. *Work package*—A natural grouping of interrelated project activities for purposes of cost control. A work package is a unit of cost control in a PERT/Cost system.

Problems

1. The Mohawk Discount Store chain is designing a management training program for individuals at its corporate headquarters. The company would like to design the program so that the trainees can complete it as quickly as possible. There are important precedence relationships that must be maintained between assignments or activities in the program. For example, a trainee cannot serve as an assistant to the store manager until after obtaining experience in the credit department and at least one sales department. The activities shown below are the assignments that must be completed by each trainee in the program:

Activity	Immediate Predecessor
A	—
B	—
C	A
D	A, B
E	A, B
F	C
G	D, F
H	E, G

Construct a PERT/CPM network for this problem. Do not attempt to perform any further analysis.

2. Construct a PERT/CPM network for a project having the following activities:

Activity	Immediate Predecessor
A	—
B	—
C	A
D	A
E	C, B
F	C, B
G	D, E

The project is completed when both activities F and G are complete.

3. Assume that the project in Problem 2 has the following activity times:

Activity	Time (months)
A	4
B	6
C	2
D	6
E	3
F	3
G	5

a. Find the critical path for the project network.
b. The project must be completed in 1½ years; do you anticipate difficulty in meeting the deadline? Explain.

4. Management Decision Systems (MDS) is a consulting company specializing in the development of decision support systems. MDS has just obtained the contract to develop a computer system to assist the management of a large company in formulating its capital-expenditure plan. The project leader has developed the following list of activities and immediate predecessors:

Activity	Immediate Predecessor
A	—
B	—
C	—
D	B
E	A
F	B
G	C, D
H	B, E
I	F, G
J	H

Construct a PERT/CPM network for this problem.

5. Consider the following project network (the times shown are in weeks):

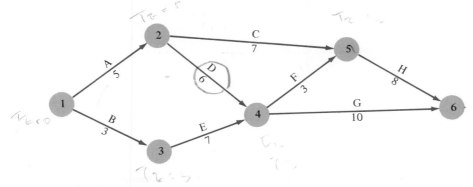

a. Identify the critical path.
b. How long will it take to complete this project?
c. Can activity D be delayed without delaying the entire project? If so, how many days?
d. Can activity C be delayed without delaying the entire project? If so, how many days?
e. What is the schedule for activity E (that is, start and completion times)?

6. The following estimates of activity times (days) are available for a small project:

Activity	Optimistic	Most Probable	Pessimistic
A	4	5	6
B	8	9	10
C	7	7.5	11
D	7	9	10
E	6	7	9
F	5	6	7

a. Compute the expected activity completion times and the variance for each activity.
b. The management science staff has found that the critical path consists of activities B–D–F. Compute the expected project completion time and the variance.

7. Suppose that the following estimates of activity times (weeks) were provided for the network shown in Problem 5:

Activity	Optimistic	Most Probable	Pessimistic
A	4	5	6
B	2.5	3	3.5
C	6	7	8
D	5	5.5	9
E	5	7	9
F	2	3	4
G	8	10	12
H	6	7	14

What is the probability that the project will be completed within
a.   21 weeks?
b.   22 weeks?
c.   25 weeks?

8.   Consider the project network given below:

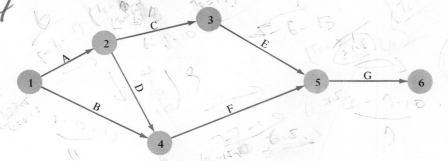

The appropriate managers have made estimates of the optimistic, most probable, and pessimistic times (in days) for completion of the activities. These times are as follows:

Activity	Optimistic	Most Probable	Pessimistic
A	5	6	7
B	5	12	13
C	6	8	10
D	4	10	10
E	5	6	13
F	7	7	10
G	4	7	10

a.   Find the critical path.
b.   How much slack time, if any, is there in activity C?
c.   Determine the expected project completion time and the variance.
d.   Find the probability that the project will be completed in 30 days or less.

9.   Refer to the Porta-Vac project network shown in Figure 9.2. Suppose Daugherty's management revises the activity time estimates as follows:

Activity	Optimistic	Most Probable	Pessimistic
A	3	7	11
B	2	2.5	6
C	2	3	4
D	6	7	14
E	2	3	4
F	2.5	3	3.5
G	2.5	4	5.5
H	4.5	5.5	9.5
I	1	2	3
J	1	2	3

a. What are the expected times and variances for each activity?

b. What are the critical path activities?

c. What is the expected project completion date?

d. What is the new probability that the project will be completed before the 20-week deadline?

e. Show the new detailed activity schedule (see Table 9.5).

10. Doug Casey is in charge of planning and coordinating next spring's sales management training program for his company. Doug has listed the following activity information for this project:

| | | | Times (weeks) | | |
| | | Immediate | | Most | |
Activity	Description	Predecessors	Optimistic	Likely	Pessimistic
A	Plan topic	—	1.5	2	2.5
B	Obtain speakers	A	2	2.5	6
C	List meeting locations	—	1	2	3
D	Select location	C	1.5	2	2.5
E	Speaker travel plans	B, D	0.5	1	1.5
F	Final check with speakers	E	1	2	3
G	Prepare and mail brochure	B, D	3	3.5	7
H	Take reservations	G	3	4	5
I	Last-minute details	F, H	1.5	2	2.5

a. Show the PERT/CPM network for this project.

b. What are the critical path activities and the expected project completion time?

c. Prepare the activity schedule for this project.

d. If Doug wants a 0.99 probability of completing the project on time, how far ahead of the scheduled meeting date should he begin working on the project?

11. Hamilton County Parks is planning to develop a new park and recreational area on a recently purchased 100-acre tract. Activities making up the park development project include clearing playground and picnic areas, road construction, shelter house construction, picnic equipment purchases, and so on. The PERT/CPM network shown below is being used to assist in the planning, scheduling, and controlling of this project:

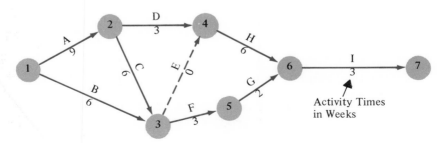

a. What is the critical path for this network?
b. Show the activity schedule and slack for each activity.
c. The park commissioner would like to open the park to the public within six months from the time the work on the project is started. Does this opening date appear feasible? Explain.

12. The product development group at Landon Corporation has been working on a new computer software product that has the potential to capture a large market share. Through outside sources, Landon's management has learned that a competitor is working to bring a similar product to the market. As a result, Landon's top management has increased its pressure on the product development group. The group's leader has turned to PERT/CPM as an aid to the scheduling of the activities remaining before the new product can be brought to the market. The PERT/CPM network developed is shown below:

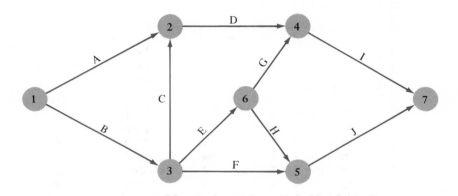

The activity time estimates in weeks are given below:

Activity	Optimistic	Most Probable	Pessimistic
A	3	4	5
B	3	3.5	7
C	4	5	6
D	2	3	4
E	6	10	14
F	7.5	8.5	12.5
G	4.5	6	7.5
H	5	6	13
I	2	2.5	6
J	4	5	6

a. Develop an activity schedule for this project and identify the critical path activities.
b. What is the probability that the project will be completed so that Landon Corporation may introduce the new product within 25 weeks? 30 weeks?

13. Consider the following network with activity times shown in days:

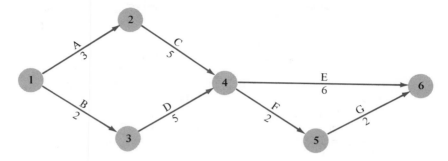

The crash data for this project are as follows:

Activity	Normal Time	Crash Time	Total Normal Cost, $	Total Crash Cost, $
A	3	2	800	1400
B	2	1	1200	1900
C	5	3	2000	2800
D	5	3	1500	2300
E	6	4	1800	2800
F	2	1	600	1000
G	2	1	500	1000

  a. Find the critical path and the expected project duration.
  b. What is the total project cost using the normal times?

14. Refer to Problem 13. Assume that management desires a 12-day project completion time. Formulate a linear programming model that can be used to assist with the crashing decisions.

15. Assume that the following crash data are available for the project described in Problem 3:

Activity	Normal Time	Crash Time	Total Normal Cost ($ \times 10^3$)	Total Crash Cost ($ \times 10^3$)
A	4	2	50	70
B	6	3	40	55
C	2	1	20	24
D	6	4	100	130
E	3	2	50	60
F	3	3	25	25
G	5	3	60	75

a. Show a linear programming model that could be used to make the crash decisions if the project has to be completed in T months.

b. If $T = 12$ months, what activities should be crashed, what is the crashing cost, and what are the critical activities?

16. For the Daugherty Porta-Vac project shown in Figure 9.2, suppose expected activity costs are as follows:

Activity	Expected Cost ($\$ \times 10^3$)
A	90
B	16
C	3
D	100
E	6
F	2
G	60
H	20
I	4
J	2

Develop a total cost budget based on both an earliest start and a latest start schedule. Show the graph of feasible budgets for the total project cost.

17. Using the Daugherty Porta-Vac project cost data given in Problem 16, prepare a PERT/Cost analysis for each of the following three points in time. For each case, show the percent overrun or underrun for the project to date and indicate any corrective action that should be undertaken. Note: If an activity is not listed below, assume that it has not been started.

a. At the end of the fifth week:

Activity	Actual Cost ($\$ \times 10^3$)	Percent Completion
A	62	80
B	6	50

b. At the end of the tenth week.

Activity	Actual Cost ($\$ \times 10^3$)	Percent Completion
A	85	100
B	16	100
C	1	33
D	100	80
E	4	100
H	10	25

c. At the end of the 15th week:

Activity	Actual Cost ($\times 10^3$)	Percent Completion
A	85	
B	16	
C	3	
D	105	
E	4	100
F	3	
G	55	
H	25	
I	4	

18. The two-machine maintenance project discussed in Section 9.4 is shown below:

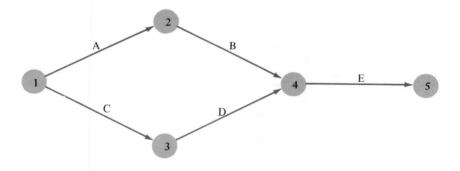

The recommended crashed schedule is shown in Table 9.9. Final times and costs for the project are as follows:

Activity	Expected Time (Days)	Cost ($)
A	5	700
B	3	200
C	6	500
D	2	350
E	2	300
	Total	2050

a. Show the graph of feasible budgets for the project's total cost. Does this represent a usual or an unusual feasible budget region? Explain.

b.   Suppose at the start of day 8 we find the following activity status report:

Activity	Actual Cost ($)	Percent Completion
A	800	100
B	100	67
C	450	100
D	250	50
E	0	0

In terms of both time and cost, is the project on schedule? What action is recommended?

19.   A firm is modifying its warehouse operation with the installation of an automated stock handling system. Specific activities include redesigning the warehouse layout, installing the new equipment, testing the new equipment, etc. The project management network is shown below:

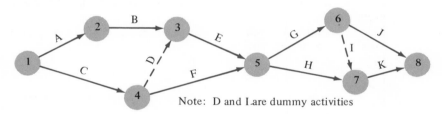

Note: D and I are dummy activities

Pertinent time and cost data are as follows:

Activity	Expected Time (Weeks)	Variance	Budgeted Cost ($)
A	3	0.3	6,000
B	2	0.5	4,000
C	8	2.0	16,000
D	0	0.0	0
E	6	1.0	18,000
F	4	0.2	20,000
G	5	0.4	15,000
H	1	0.1	2,000
I	0	0.0	0
J	5	1.0	5,000
K	6	0.6	12,000

a.   Develop an activity schedule for the project.
   (1)   What is the critical path?
   (2)   What is the expected completion date?
   (3)   What is the probability of meeting a desired 6-month (26-week) completion date?
b.   Develop a PERT/Cost budget for total project costs over the project's duration. What should the range be for expenditures after 12 weeks of the project?

20. Refer to the network in Problem 17. Suppose that after 12 weeks of operation the following data are available on all completed and in-process activities:

Activity	Actual Cost ($)	Percent Completion
A	5,000	100
B	4,000	100
C	18,000	100
E	9,000	50
F	18,000	75

Is the project in control based on both time and cost considerations? What corrective action, if any, is desirable?

21. Because Landon Corporation (see Problem 12) is being pressured to complete the product development project at the earliest possible date, the project leader has requested an evaluation of the possibility of crashing the project.

a. Develop a linear programming model that could be used to help in making the crash decisions.

b. What information would have to be provided before the linear programming model could be implemented?

Application

Seasongood
&
Mayer
Cincinnati, Ohio

Seasongood & Mayer, established in 1887, is an investment securities firm that engages in the following areas of municipal finance:

1. Underwriting new issues of municipal bonds;
2. Trading—for example, acting as a market maker for the buying and selling of previously issued bonds;
3. Investment banking—that is, the process of obtaining money from the capital markets at the lowest possible cost.

The major applications of quantitative analysis at Seasongood & Mayer are in the investment banking area. One particular application involves the use of PERT/CPM in the introduction of a 31 million dollar hospital revenue bond issue.

Scheduling the Introduction of a Bond Issue

In any major building project there are certain common steps:

1. Defining the project;
2. Determining the cost of the project; and
3. Financing the project.

The role of the investment banker in building projects is to develop a method of financing that will result in the owner receiving the necessary funds in a timely manner. In a hospital building project, such as the one we will be discussing, the typical method of financing is tax-free hospital revenue bonds.

The construction cost for the building project is an important factor in determining the best approach to financing. Normally, the construction cost is based on a bid submitted by a contractor or a construction manager. However, this cost is usually guaranteed only for a specified period of time, such as 60–90 days. The major function of the hospital's investment banker is to arrange the timing of the financing in such a way that the proceeds of the bond issue can be made available within the time limit of the guaranteed-

TABLE 1 Activities for the Providence Hospital Project

Activity	Time (Weeks)	Description of Activity	Immediate Predecessor(s)
A	4	Drafting and distribution of legal documents	—
B	3	Preparation and distribution of unaudited financial statements of hospital	—
C	2	Draft and distribution of hospital history, description of services, and existing facilities for Preliminary Official Statement (POS)	—
D	8	Draft and distribution of demand portion of feasibility study	—
E	4	Review (additions/deletions) and approval as to form of legal documents	A
F	1	Review (additions/deletions) and approval of hospital history, etc. for POS	C
G	4	Review (additions/deletions) and approval of demand portion of feasibility study	D
H	2	Draft and distribution of financial portion (as to form) of feasibility study	E, G
I	2	Drafting and distribution of plan of financing and all pertinent facts relevant to the bond transaction for POS	E
J	0.5	Review and approval of unaudited financial statements	B
K	20	Firm price received for cost of project	—
L	1	Review (additions/deletions), approval and completion of financial portion of feasibility study	H, K
M	1	Draft of POS completed	F, I, J, L
N	0.14	All material sent to bond rating services	M
O	0.28	POS printed and distributed to all interested parties	M
P	1	Presentation to bond rating services (Standard & Poor, Moody's)	N
Q	1	Bond rating received	P
R	2	Marketing of bonds	O, Q
S	0*	Purchase Contract executed	R
T	0.14	Final Official Statement authorized and completed, legal documents completed	S

TABLE 1   (continued)

Activity	Time (Weeks)	Description of Activity	Immediate Predecessor(s)
U	3	Fulfillment of all terms and conditions of Purchase Contract	S
V	0*	Bond proceeds available to hospital	T, U
W	0*	Hospital's ability to sign construction contract	T, U

*Occurs instantaneously.

price construction bid. Since most hospitals must have the proceeds of their permanent long-term financing in hand prior to committing to major construction contracts, the investment banker plays a very significant role.

To arrange for the financing, the investment banker must coordinate the activities of hospital attorneys, the bond counsel, and so on. The cooperation of all parties and the coordination of project activities is best achieved if everyone recognizes the interdependency of the activities and the necessity of completing individual tasks in a timely manner. Seasongood & Mayer has found the critical path method (CPM) to be useful in scheduling and coordinating such a project.

As managing underwriter for a $31,050,000 issue of Hospital Facilities Revenue Bonds for Providence Hospital in Hamilton County, Ohio (December, 1980), Seasongood & Mayer utilized a critical path analysis to coordinate and schedule the project financing activities. Descriptions of the activities, times required, and immediate predecessors are given in Table 1. The complete CPM network is shown in Figure 1. The critical path activities

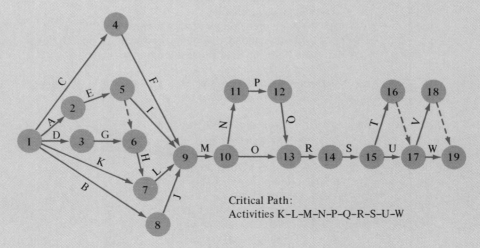

Critical Path:
Activities K–L–M–N–P–Q–R–S–U–W

FIGURE 1   Seasongood & Mayer CPM Network for Providence Hospital Project

K-L-M-N-P-Q-R-S-U-W resulted in a scheduled project completion time of 29.14 weeks; thus, the funds for the project are received approximately 64 days after the receipt of a firm construction price. Specific schedules showing start and finish times for all activities were used to keep the entire project on schedule. The use of CPM was instrumental in helping Seasongood & Mayer obtain financing for this project within the time specified in the construction bid.

Chapter 10

Network Models II: Other Topics

This chapter continues the previous chapter's discussion of the application of network models. Three new problems are introduced: the shortest route problem, the maximal flow problem, and the minimal spanning tree problem. We show how network models of each of these problems can be developed and illustrate the application of each to a practical problem.

10.1 The Shortest Route Problem

PERT/CPM network analysis procedures concentrated on the critical or longest path of the network. In other network applications, such as in the design of transportation systems, the *shortest path* or *shortest route* through the network is of primary interest.

Let us consider a problem faced by the Gorman Construction Company. Gorman operates several construction projects located throughout a three-county area. Construction sites are sometimes located as far as 50 miles from Gorman's main office. With multiple daily trips carrying personnel, equipment, and supplies to and from the construction locations, the costs associated with the transportation activity have been significant. For any given construction site, the travel alternatives between the site and the office can be described by a network of roads, streets, and highways. Suppose that the network shown in Figure 10.1 describes the travel alternatives to and from six of Gorman's newest construction sites. The roads, streets, and highways appear as arcs in the network while the length or distance for each is shown above the corresponding arc. Note that the lengths of the arcs are not necessarily drawn proportional to the travel distances. If Gorman wishes to minimize the total travel distance from the office to each site, what are the shortest routes for the given transportation network?

A Shortest Route Algorithm

In order to solve Gorman's problem, we will need to determine the shortest route from Gorman's office, node 1, to each of the other nodes in the network. The algorithm we present uses a labeling procedure to find the shortest distance from node 1 to each of the other nodes. As we perform the steps of the labeling procedure, we will identify a *label* for each node consisting of two numbers enclosed in brackets. The first number in the label for a particular node indicates the distance from node 1 to that node, while the second number indicates the preceding node on the route from node 1 to that node. We will show the label for each node directly above or below the node in the network. For example, a label for a particular node might appear as shown in Figure 10.2.

Whenever the algorithm has determined the shortest distance from node 1 to a particular node, the node is said to have a *permanent* label. If, however, the shortest distance from node 1 to a particular node has not yet been determined, the node is said to have a *tentative* label. Now that we have

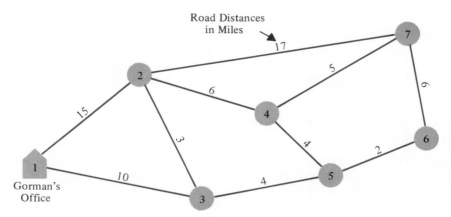

Note: The length of each arc is not necessarily drawn
proportional to the distance associated with the arc

FIGURE 10.1   Road Network for the Gorman Company Shortest Route Problem

an idea of what a label is, let us see how labels are computed and how the labeling process can be used to determine the shortest route from node 1 to each of the other nodes in the network.

We begin the labeling process by associating with node 1 the permanent label $[0, S]$. The S simply indicates that node 1 is the starting node and the 0 reflects the distance from node 1 to itself is zero. All other nodes in the network are initially assigned the tentative label $[M, —]$. The M is an arbitrarily large value, indicating that at the start of our solution procedure we do not know the distance from node 1 to the node in question. The "—" in the label indicates that we have not as yet identified a route from node 1 to the node. To distinguish between tentatively and permanently labeled nodes, we follow the practice of shading all permanently labeled nodes in the network. In addition, an arrow will be used to point to the permanently labeled node being investigated at each step of the labeling algorithm. The initial identification of Gorman's network is shown in Figure 10.3.

To perform the first step or iteration of the labeling procedure, we must consider every node that can be reached directly from node 1; hence we look at nodes 2 and 3. Consider for the moment node 2. Currently, the distance portion of the label at node 2 shows M, an arbitrarily large number, as the

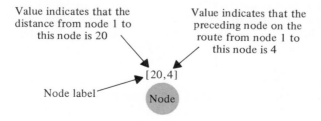

FIGURE 10.2   An Example of a Node Label

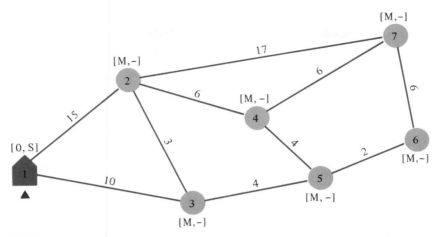

FIGURE 10.3   Initial Network Identification for Gorman's Shortest Route Problem

distance from node 1 to node 2. However, we now see that we can go directly from node 1 to node 2 with a distance of 15 miles. Thus we can revise the tentative label at node 2 to [15,1]. Note that the second number in the label indicates that the preceding node on the route to node 2 is node 1. Next, considering node 3, we find that we can go directly from node 1 to node 3 in 10 miles. Thus we revise the tentative label at node 3 to [10,1]. Figure 10.4 shows the results of these label changes.

Refer to Figure 10.4. We now consider all tentatively labeled nodes and identify the node with the smallest distance value in its label; this is node 3. The tentative label associated with node 3 indicates that we can reach node 3 from node 1 by traveling a distance of 10 miles. Could we get to node 3 following a shorter route? Since any other route to node 3 would require

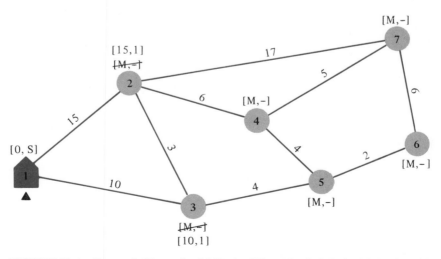

FIGURE 10.4   Gorman's Network with Revised Tentative Labels for Nodes 2 and 3

passing through other nodes, and since the distance from node 1 to all other nodes is greater than or equal to 10, there could be no shorter route to node 3 found by first going to some other node. Thus we have identified the best, or shortest, route to node 3, and accordingly node 3 is permanently labeled with a distance of 10 miles. Shading node 3 to indicate it is a permanently labeled node, and adding an arrow to indicate that node 3 will be used to start the next step of the labeling process, provides the network as shown in Figure 10.5.

We proceed by considering all tentatively labeled nodes that can be reached directly from node 3. Thus we consider nodes 2 and 5. Note that 3 miles is the direct distance from node 3 to node 2 and 4 miles is the direct distance from node 3 to node 5. Since the permanent label for node 3 indicates that the shortest distance to node 3 is 10, we see that we can reach node 2 in 10 + 3 = 13 miles and node 5 in 10 + 4 = 14 miles. Thus the label at node 2 is revised to [13,3] to indicate that we have now found a route from node 1 to node 2 with a distance of 13 miles and that the preceding node on the route is node 3. Similarly, the new tentative label for node 5 is [14,3]. Figure 10.6 shows the network computations up to this point.

We next consider all tentatively labeled nodes in order to identify the node having the smallest distance value. From Figure 10.6, we see this is node 2 with a distance value of 13 miles. Node 2 is now declared permanently labeled because we can guarantee that node 2 can be reached from node 1 in the shortest possible distance of 13 miles by going through node 3.

The next step or iteration begins at node 2, the most recently permanently labeled node. As before, we consider every tentatively labeled node that can be reached directly from node 2; that is, nodes 4 and 7. Starting with the distance value of 13 in the permanent label at node 2, and adding

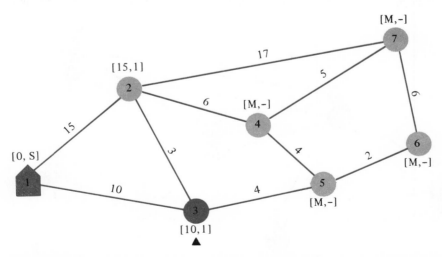

FIGURE 10.5   Gorman's Network with Node 3 Identified as a Permanently Labeled Node

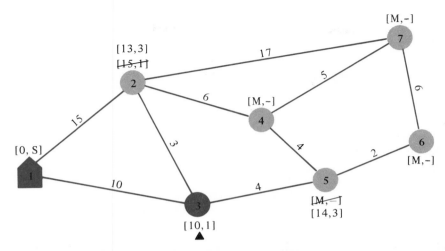

FIGURE 10.6 Gorman's Network with New Tentative Labels for Nodes 2 and 5

the direct distance from node 2 to each of nodes 4 and 7, shows us node 4 can be reached in $13 + 6 = 19$ miles, while node 7 can be reached in $13 + 17 = 30$ miles. Thus the tentative labels at nodes 4 and 7 are revised as shown in Figure 10.7.

From among the remaining tentatively labeled nodes (nodes 4, 5, 6, and 7), we select the node with the smallest distance value and declare that node permanently labeled. Thus node 5 becomes the new permanently labeled node. From node 5, then, we recompute labels for all tentatively labeled nodes that can be reached directly from node 5. Figure 10.8 depicts these calculations.

Identifying the smallest distance for the remaining tentatively labeled

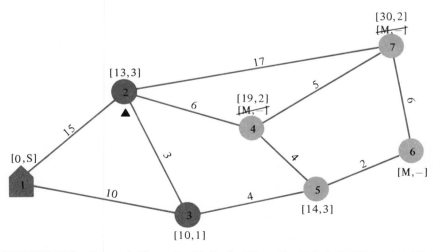

FIGURE 10.7 Gorman's Network with Revised Tentative Labels for Nodes 4 and 7

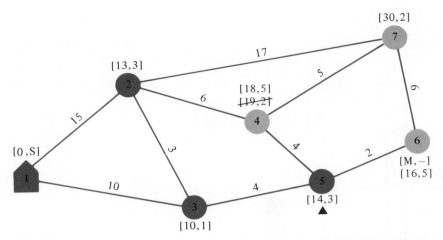

FIGURE 10.8   Gorman's Network with Revised Tentative Labels for Nodes 4 and 6 Identified from Node 5

nodes results in node 6 being permanently labeled. From node 6 we can determine a new tentative label for node 7. After this step, the network appears as shown in Figure 10.9.

We now have only two remaining nodes with tentative labels. Since the distance portion of the label at node 4 is smaller than the corresponding value at node 7, node 4 becomes the new permanently labeled node. Moreover, since node 7 is the only remaining tentatively labeled node that can be reached directly from node 4, we compare the current labeled distance of 22 for node 7 with the sum of the distance in the label on node 4, and the direct distance from node 4 to node 7. Note in this case the [22,6] tentative label already existing at node 7 has the smaller distance value; thus

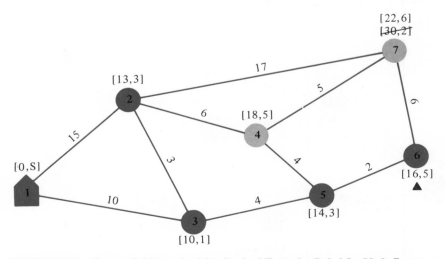

FIGURE 10.9   Gorman's Network with a Revised Tentative Label for Node 7

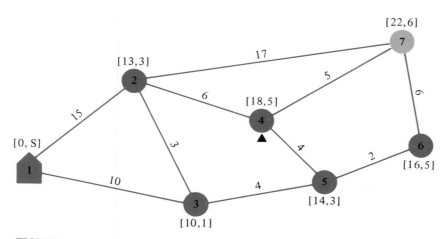

FIGURE 10.10 Gorman's Network with Tentative Labels Identified from Node 4

the tentative label at node 7 remains unchanged. Figure 10.10 shows the network at this point in time.

Since node 7 is the only remaining node with a tentative label, it is now permanently labeled. Whenever all nodes have been permanently labeled, we have found the shortest route from node 1 to every node in the network. Figure 10.11 shows the final network with all nodes being permanently labeled.

We can now use the information in the permanent labels to find the shortest route from node 1 to each of the nodes in the network. For example, the permanent label at node 7 tells us the shortest distance from node 1 to node 7 is 22 miles. To find the particular route that enables us to reach node 7 in 22 miles, we start at node 7 and note that the label tells us we reach node 7 by coming from node 6. Moving back through the network to node 6, we

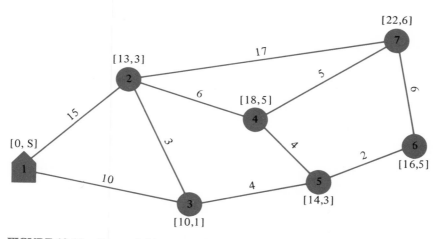

FIGURE 10.11 Gorman's Network with All Nodes Permanently Labeled

see from its permanent label that we reach node 6 by coming from node 5. Continuing this process, we note that we reach node 5 from node 3 and finally that we reach node 3 from node 1. Therefore the shortest route from node 1 to node 7 is 1–3–5–6–7. Using this approach, the following shortest routes are identified for the Gorman transportation network:

Node	Shortest Route from Node 1	Distance in Miles
2	1–3–2	13
3	1–3	10
4	1–3–5–4	18
5	1–3–5	14
6	1–3–5–6	16
7	1–3–5–6–7	22

Perhaps for a problem as small as the Gorman problem you could have found the shortest routes just as fast, if not faster, by inspection. The reason is that with only seven nodes there are few alternate routes. However, when we begin to investigate problems with 15 to 20 or more nodes, it becomes very time consuming to attempt to find the shortest routes by inspection. In fact, because of the increased number of alternate routes in a larger network, it is very easy to miss one or more routes and come up with the wrong answer. Thus for larger problems a systematic procedure such as the labeling procedure described above is required. Even with the labeling procedure, we find that as the networks grow in size it becomes necessary to implement the algorithm on a computer.

In summarizing our shortest route labeling procedure in general terms, let us think of a network consisting of N nodes. The following procedure can be used to find the shortest route from node 1 to each of the other nodes in the network.

Step 1: Assign node 1 the permanent label $[0, S]$ and tentatively label all other nodes $[M, —]$.

Step 2: For nodes that can be reached directly from node 1, compare the distance portion of their tentative labels with the sum of the distance portion of the node 1 label (that is, 0) and the direct distance from node 1 to the node in question. The smaller of the two numbers is the new distance portion of the tentative label for the node in question.

Step 3: If the distance portion of a tentative label is changed, identify the preceding node that resulted in the change by writing its number in the label.

Step 4: Determine the tentatively labeled node with the smallest distance value and declare that node permanently labeled. If all nodes are permanently labeled, go to step 6.

Step 5:   Identify all tentatively labeled nodes that can be directly reached from the new permanently labeled node identified in step 4. Compare the distance portion of the current tentative label with the sum of the distance value at the new permanently labeled node and the direct distance from the new permanently labeled node to each node in question; the smaller of the two numbers is the new tentative label distance. Go to step 3.

Step 6:   The permanent labels identify the shortest distance to each node and the preceding node for each node in the network. The shortest route to a given node can be found by starting at the given node and moving to its preceding node. Continuing this backward movement through the network will provide the shortest route from node 1 to the node in question.

The above steps will determine the shortest distance from node 1 to each of the other nodes in the network. Note that $N-1$ iterations of the algorithm are required to find the shortest distance to all other nodes. If the shortest distance is not needed to every node, the algorithm can be stopped when those nodes of interest have been permanently labeled. The algorithm can also be easily modified to find the shortest distance from any node, say node k, to all other nodes in the network. To make such a change, we would merely begin by labeling node k with the permanent label $[0, S]$ and tentatively labeling all other nodes $[M, —]$. Then by applying the steps of the algorithm, we can find the shortest route from node k to each of the other nodes in the network.

One final comment is in order before we close this section. In the Gorman problem we used distance as the measure of primary interest. The same algorithm can be used for other criteria such as travel time, travel cost, and so on. In these situations the labeling algorithm would generate minimum travel time routes, minimum cost routes, and so on. Sometimes, in these cases, the quantitative analyst will encounter networks in which some of the arcs have negative values. This could happen in a cost minimization problem where a negative arc value would indicate a profit for traveling over the associated arc. The labeling algorithm we have presented works only for arc values that are nonnegative. Algorithms have been developed to solve problems with negative arc values, but a discussion of these is beyond the scope of this text.

10.2   The Maximal Flow Problem

Consider a network with one input or *source* node and one output or *sink* node. The maximal flow problem asks, What is the maximum amount of flow (that is, vehicles, messages, fluid, and so on) that can enter and exit from the network system in a given period of time? In this problem we attempt to transmit flow through all branches of the network as efficiently as possible. The amount of flow is limited due to capacity restrictions on the various branches of the network. For example, highway types limit vehicle flow in a transportation system, while pipe sizes limit oil flow in an oil distribution system. The maximum or upper limit on the flow in a branch is referred to as the *flow capacity* of the branch. While we do not specify capacities for the nodes, we do assume that the flow out of a node is equal to the flow into the node.

As an example of the maximal flow problem, consider the north-south interstate-highway system passing through Cincinnati, Ohio. The north-south vehicle flow reaches a level of 15,000 vehicles per hour at peak times. Due to a planned summer highway-maintenance program calling for the temporary closing of lanes and lower speed limits, a network of alternate routes through Cincinnati has been proposed by a transportation planning committee. The alternate routes include other highways as well as city streets. Because of differences in speed limits and traffic patterns, flow capacities vary depending upon the particular streets or roads used. The proposed network with branch flow capacities is shown in Figure 10.12.

The flow capacities are based on the direction of the flow. For example, highway section or branch 1–2 shows a capacity of 5000 vehicles per hour in the 1–2 direction; however, a 0 capacity exists in the 2–1 direction. This means that the highway network planners do not want vehicles flowing from node 2 into node 1. Logically speaking, since node 1 is the input, or source, and a potential traffic jam location, it would be undesirable to permit traffic flow into the node 1 intersection from node 2. The directional capacities on branch 1–2 can also be interpreted as indicating a one-way street leading from the node 1 intersection. In any case, this example shows that the flow capacities of branches can be dependent upon the direction of the flow. Do you believe the highway system network shown in Figure 10.12 can accom-

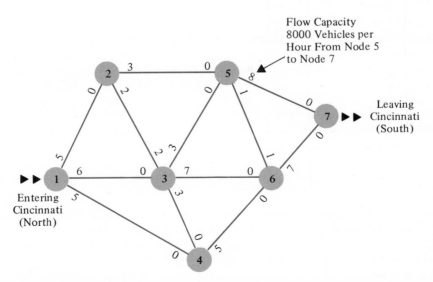

FIGURE 10.12   Network of Highway System and Flow Capacities (in 1000s/Hour) for Cincinnati

modate the north-south maximum flow of 15,000 vehicles per hour? What is the maximal flow in vehicles per hour for the network? How much flow should go over each branch?

A Maximal Flow Algorithm

As we shall see, the maximal flow algorithm presented in this section uses the following common sense type solution approach:

1. Find any path from the input (source) node to the output (sink) node which has flow capacities in the direction of the flow greater than zero for all branches on the path.
2. Increase the flow along the path by as much as possible.
3. Continue looking for source-to-sink paths that still have remaining flow capacities in the direction of the flow greater than zero for all branches and increase the flow along these paths as much as possible.
4. Stop when it is no longer possible to find a source-to-sink path with flow capacities in the direction of the flow greater than zero for all branches on the path.

Before presenting the details of the maximal flow algorithm, let us briefly discuss a procedure that will ensure that the above intuitive steps result in a optimal solution to the problem of finding the maximal flow from the source to the sink node.

The procedure permits previously assigned flow to take an alternate route by permitting fictional flows in the reverse direction. For example, consider the 3–6 branch:

Here we see that the initial flow capacity in the 3–6 direction is 7000 vehicles per hour, while no flow is permitted in the 6–3 direction.

If we choose to let 6000 vehicles per hour flow in the 3–6 direction, we will revise the flow capacities as follows:

Note that we have decreased the flow capacity in the 3–6 direction by 6000 vehicles per hour and simultaneously increased the flow capacity in the 6–3 direction by the same amount. The revised flow capacity of 1000 vehicles per hour in the 3–6 direction is readily interpreted as the remaining flow capacity in the branch. However, note that the 6–3 direction which had an initial flow capacity of 0 now shows a revised flow capacity of 6000 vehicles per hour. This revised capacity in the 6–3 direction is actually indicating that a fictitious flow of up to 6000 vehicles per hour is permitted in this direction.

Fictitious flow would not send vehicles in the 6–3 direction, but rather simply decrease the amount of flow originally committed to the 3–6 branch direction. In effect, fictitious flow in the 6–3 direction would result in flow which was originally committed to the 3–6 direction being diverted to other branches in the network.

The above process of tracking flow capacities is an important part of the maximal flow algorithm. For example, in an earlier step of the algorithm we might commit flow along a certain branch. Later, due to flows identified in other branches it may be desirable to decrease the flow along the original branch. The procedure we have described above will identify the extent to which our original decision to commit some flow needs to be revised in order to increase the total flow through the network.

Let us look now at the steps of the maximal flow algorithm.

Step 1:   Find any path from the source node to the sink node that has flow capacities in the direction of the flow greater than zero for all branches on the path. If no path is available, the optimal solution has been reached.

Step 2:   Find the smallest branch capacity, P_f, on the path selected in step 1. Increase the flow through the network by sending an amount P_f over the path selected in step 1.

Step 3:   For the path selected in step 1, reduce all branch flow capacities in the direction of flow by P_f and increase all branch flow capacities in the reverse direction by P_f. Go to step 1.

While the procedure will vary depending upon the analyst's choice of paths in step 1, the algorithm will eventually provide the maximal flow solution. Our calculations for the highway flow network are as follows:

Iteration 1:   The path selected is 1–3–6–7; P_f, determined by branch 1–3, is 6. The revised network is as follows:

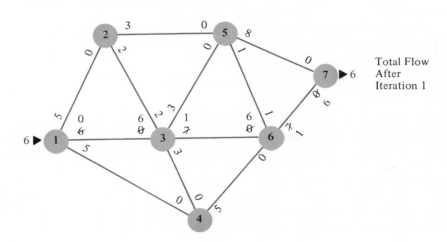

Total Flow
After
Iteration 1

Iteration 2: The path selected is 1–2–5–7; P_f, determined by branch 2–5, is 3. The revised network is as follows:

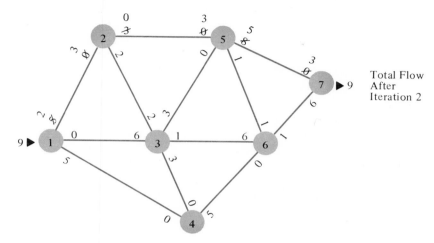

Total Flow After Iteration 2

Note that the total flow through the network can be found by summing the P_f values from each iteration.

While we will not show our revised network after each iteration, you should attempt to update the network flow capacities as you follow the discussion. For example, what will this network look like after the following three iterations?

Iteration 3: The path selected is 1–2–3–5–7; P_f, determined by branch 1–2 (or 2–3), is 2.

Iteration 4: The path selected is 1–4–6–7; P_f, determined by branch 6–7, is 1.

Iteration 5: The path selected is 1–4–6–5–7; P_f, determined by branch 6–5, is 1.

At this point we have a total flow of 13,000 vehicles per hour, and the revised network capacities are as follows:

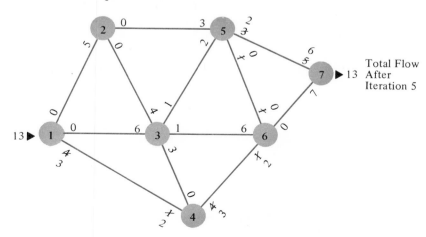

Total Flow After Iteration 5

Are there any other paths from node 1 to node 7 that have flow capacities in the direction of the flow greater than 0? Try 1–4–6–3–5–7 with a flow of $P_f = 1$ determined by branch 3–5. This increases the flow to 14,000 vehicles per hour. However, as you can see from the following revised network, there are no more paths from node 1 to node 7 that have flow capacities greater than 0 on all branches of the path; thus 14,000 vehicles per hour is the maximal flow for this network.

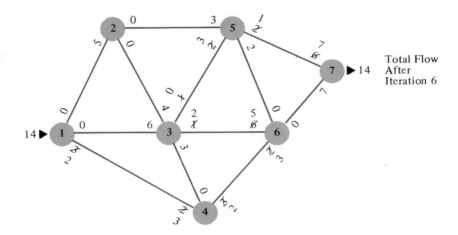

Total Flow
After
Iteration 6

Note that in iteration 6 a flow of 1000 vehicles per hour was permitted in the 6–3 direction. From our initial network, however, we know that the flow capacity in the 6–3 direction is 0; thus the 1000 units of flow in the 6–3 direction represents a fictitious flow. The real effect of this flow is to divert 1000 units of flow originally commmitted to the 3–6 branch in iteration 1 along the 3–5 branch in order to enable us to get 1000 units more of flow through the network. Let us now determine the amount and direction of flow in each branch so that the total flow of 14,000 vehicles per hour can be attained.

Branch flows for the maximal flow solution can be found by comparing the final branch flow capacities with the initial branch flow capacities. If the final flow capacity is *less* than the initial flow capacity, flow is occurring in the branch with an amount equal to the difference between the initial and final flow capacities. For example, consider the 3–6 branch with initial flow and final flow capacities shown below:

Initial capacities:

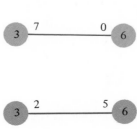

Since the final flow capacity in the 3–6 direction is less than the initial flow capacity, the branch has a flow of $7 - 2 = 5$ in the 3–6 direction. This branch flow is summarized as follows:

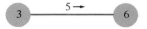

Comparing final and initial branch flow capacities for all branches in the network enables us to determine the final flow pattern as shown in Figure 10.13.

The results of the maximal flow analysis indicate that the planned highway network system will not handle the peak flow of 15,000 vehicles per hour. The transportation planners will have to expand the highway network, increase current branch flow capacities, or be prepared for serious traffic jam problems. If the network is extended or modified, another maximal flow analysis will determine the extent of any improved flow.

10.3   The Minimal Spanning Tree Problem

In network terminology, the minimal spanning tree problem involves using the branches of the network to reach *all* nodes of the network in such a fashion that the total length of all branches used to reach the nodes is minimal. To better understand this problem, let us consider the communications system design problem encountered by a regional computer center.

The Southwestern Regional Computer Center must have special computer communications lines installed in order to connect five satellite users with a new central computer. The telephone company will install the new communications network. However, the installation is an expensive operation. In order to reduce costs, the center's management group wants the total length of the new communications lines to be as small as possible.

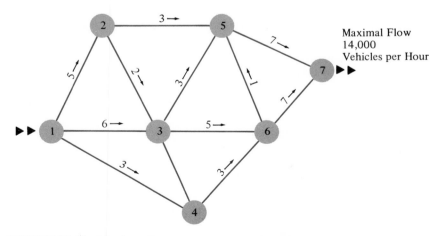

FIGURE 10.13   Maximal Flow Pattern for the Highway System Network

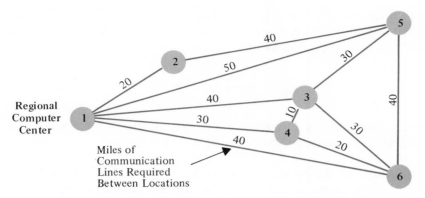

FIGURE 10.14   Communications Network for the Regional Computer System

While the central computer could be connected directly to each user, it appears to be more economical to install a direct line to some users and let other users tap into the system by linking with the users that are already connected to the system.

The determination of this minimal length communications system design is an example of the *minimal spanning tree* problem. The network for this problem with possible connection alternatives and distances is shown in Figure 10.14. A direct distance table corresponding to this network is shown in Table 10.1. As in the shortest route algorithm, if no arc directly connects two nodes, the direct distance is entered as a very large number, M.

A Minimal Spanning Tree Algorithm

This network algorithm is relatively easy in that it simply adds the closest unconnected node to those that are already connected. The steps of the algorithm are as follows:

Step 1:   Prepare a table of direct distances. Add a column to the left-hand side of the table and label this column with the word "connected."

Step 2:   Select any arbitrary node and consider it connected. Place a ✓ in the left-hand column beside the node number and cross out the column corresponding to this connected node.

Step 3:   For all rows corresponding to the connected nodes (that is, the ✓ rows), find the smallest value in the columns not crossed out and circle it. The column containing the circled element is the new connected node.

Step 4:   Place a ✓ in the left-hand column beside the new connected node number and cross out the column corresponding to this connected node. Return to Step 3 until all nodes are connected.

Step 5:   The minimal spanning tree solution is given by the connections identified by the circled elements; the total length of the connection is given by the sum of the circled elements.

TABLE 10.1. Direct Distance Table for the Regional Computer System

		To Node					
		1	2	3	4	5	6
	1	0	20	40	30	50	40
	2	20	0	M	M	40	M
From	3	40	M	0	10	30	30
Node	4	30	M	10	0	M	20
	5	50	40	30	M	0	40
	6	40	M	30	20	40	0

The following calculations were made for the Regional Computer Center's minimal spanning tree problem:

Step 1: We prepared a table of direct distances (Table 10.1).
Step 2: We started the algorithm with node 1, although any starting node is acceptable. Thus node 1 was considered connected and column 1 was crossed out.
Step 3: For row 1 the minimum value was 20, corresponding to node 2.
Step 4: Node 2 was considered connected and column 2 was crossed out.

At this point the revised distance table was as follows:

	Connected		To Node					
			1	2	3	4	5	6
	✓	1	0	(20)	40	30	50	40
	✓	2	20	0	M	M	40	M
From		3	40	M	0	10	30	30
Node		4	30	M	10	0	M	20
		5	50	40	30	M	0	40
		6	40	M	30	20	40	0

The algorithm continues from this point with a return to Step 3.

Step 3: For connected rows 1 and 2, the minimum value in the columns not crossed out is 30, corresponding to node 4.
Step 4: Node 4 is considered connected and column 4 is crossed out.

Repeating Steps 3 and 4 results in the following final table.

	Connected		To Node					
			1	2	3	4	5	6
From Node	✓	1	0	㉑	40	㉚	50	40
	✓	2	20	0	M	M	40	M
	✓	3	40	M	0	10	㉚	30
	✓	4	30	M	⑩	0	M	⑳
	✓	5	50	40	30	M	0	40
	✓	6	40	M	30	20	40	0

Referring to Step 5, we see that the circled elements provide the optimal solution. In our case node 1 connects with nodes 2 and 4, node 4 connects with nodes 3 and 6, and, finally, node 3 makes a connection with node 5. The minimal length of the spanning tree is given by the sum of the circled elements, which is 110 miles for our example problem.

The minimal spanning tree design for the Regional Computer Center's communications network is shown in Figure 10.15.

Summary

In this chapter we have extended the discussion, begun in Chapter 9, of the use of network models in managerial decision making. We introduced the shortest route, maximal flow, and minimal spanning tree problems and presented a specialized solution procedure for each of these problems. We

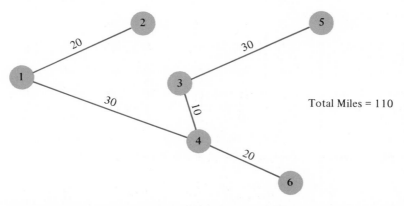

FIGURE 10.15   Minimal Spanning Tree Communications Network for the Regional Computer Center

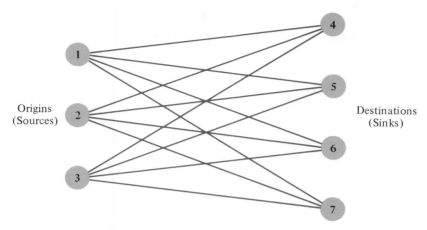

FIGURE 10.16 **Network Representation of a Transportation Problem**

mention here that linear programming models of these problems can also be developed. One of the advantages of the specialized algorithms presented here is that no background in linear programming, or any other technique, is necessary to understand and apply them.

The key to success in network approaches to problem solving is in realizing how the problem can be represented in a network format. While some network applications are obvious, other problems may require substantial ingenuity to develop the appropriate network representation. In any case, once the network representation has been developed, special solution algorithms are readily available to arrive at a network solution to the problem.

As a final note, it is well to realize that other typical management science problems can be approached as network problems. For example, a network model of a transportation problem with three origins (sources) and four destinations (sinks) is shown in Figure 10.16. The assignment and traveling salesman problems can also be solved using network models; however, as you saw in Chapters 6 and 7, these problems also have specialized solution algorithms.

Glossary

1. *Shortest route*—Shortest path between two nodes in a network.
2. *Maximal flow*—The maximum amount of flow that can enter into or exit from a network system during a given period of time.
3. *Arc capacity*—The maximum flow for an arc of the network. The arc capacity in one direction may not equal that in the reverse direction.
4. *Source*—An origin node (that is, no prior nodes exist).
5. *Sink*—A destination node (that is, no following nodes exist).
6. *Spanning tree*—A set of branches that connect every node in the network with all other nodes.
7. *Minimal spanning tree*—The spanning tree with the minimum length.

Problems

1. Find the shortest route from node 1 to each of the other nodes in the transportation network shown below.

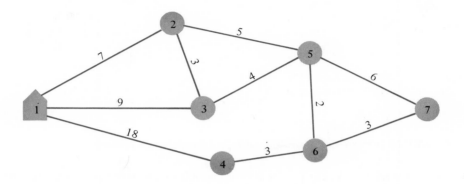

2. For the Gorman Construction Company problem (see Figure 10.1), assume node 7 is the Company's warehouse and supply center. Often several daily trips are made from node 7 to the other nodes or construction sites. Using node 7 as the starting node, find the shortest route from this node to each of the other nodes in the network.

3. In the original Gorman Construction Company problem, we found the shortest distance from the office (node 1) to each of the other nodes or construction sites. Because some of the roads are highways and others are city streets, the shortest distance routes between the office and the construction sites may not necessarily provide the quickest or shortest time routes. Shown below is the Gorman road network with travel time values rather than distance values. Find the shortest route from Gorman's office to each of the construction sites if the objective is to minimize travel time rather than distance.

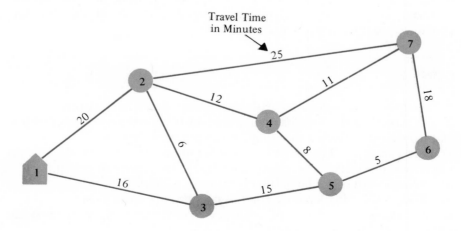

4. Find the shortest route between nodes 1 and 8 in the following network:

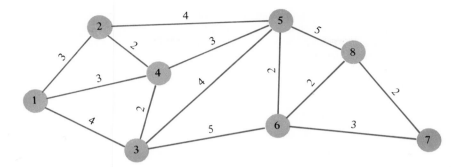

5. Find the shortest route between nodes 1 and 10 in the following network:

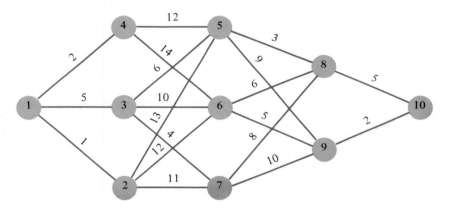

6. Morgan Trucking Company operates a special fast-service pickup and delivery truck service between Chicago and any of 10 other cities located in a four-state area. When Morgan receives a request for service, it dispatches a truck from Chicago to the city requesting service as soon as possible. Since both fast service and minimum travel costs are objectives for Morgan, it is important that the dispatched truck take the shortest route from Chicago to the specified city. Assume that the following network (not drawn to scale) with distances given in miles represents the highway network for this problem:

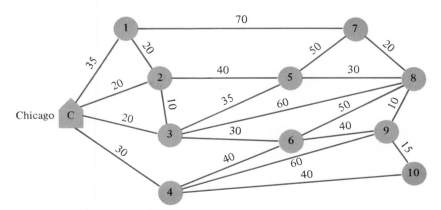

    a.   Find the shortest route distances from Chicago to all 10 cities.

    b.   What is the shortest route to city 7? city 9?

7.   The north-south highway system passing through Albany, New York, can accommodate the capacities shown in the figure below.

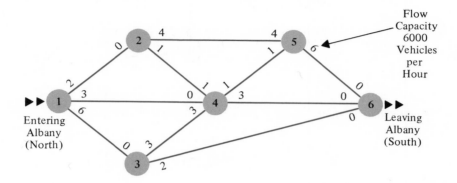

Do you believe the highway system network can accommodate a north-south flow of 10,000 vehicles per hour?

8.   If the Albany highway network system problem has flow capacities revised as shown in the following network, what is the maximal flow in vehicles per hour through the system?

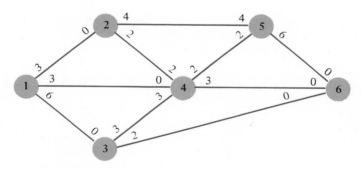

How many vehicles per hour must travel over each road (branch) in order to obtain this maximal flow?

9.   The High-Price Oil Company owns a pipeline network which is used to transmit oil from its source to several storage locations. A portion of the network is as follows:

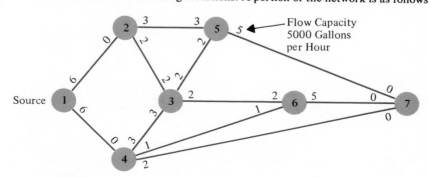

Due to the varying pipe sizes the flow capacities also vary. By selectively opening and closing sections of the pipeline network, the firm can supply any of the storage locations.

a. If the firm wants to supply storage location 7 and fully utilizes the network system capacity, how long will it take to satisfy a location 7 demand of 100,000 gallons? What is the maximal flow for this pipeline system?

b. If a break occurs on line 2–3 and it is closed down, what is the maximal flow for the system? How long will it take to transmit 100,000 gallons to location 7?

10. For the highway network system shown below determine its maximal flow in vehicles per hour.

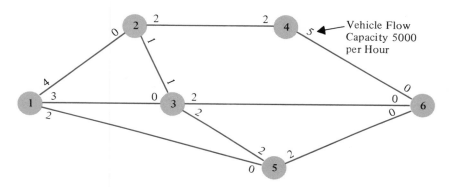

The highway commission is considering expanding highway section 3–4 to permit a flow of 2000 vehicles per hour or, at an additional cost, a flow of 3000 vehicles per hour. What is your recommendation for the 3–4 branch of the network?

11. The State of Ohio has recently purchased land for a new state park. Planners of the park have identified the ideal locations for the lodge, cabins, picnic groves, boat dock, and scenic points of interest. These locations are represented by the nodes of the network below. The branches of the network represent possible road alternatives in the park. If the state park designers want to minimize the total road miles that must be constructed in the park and still permit access to all facilities (nodes), which road alternatives should be constructed? (That is, find the minimal spanning tree for this network.)

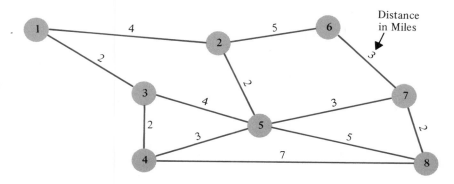

12. In a large soap products plant, quality control inspectors sample various products from the different production areas and then return the samples to the lab for analysis. The inspection process is slow, and the inspectors spend substantial time

transporting samples from the production areas to the labs. The company is considering installing a pneumatic tube conveyor system that could be used to transport the samples between the production areas and the lab. The network below shows the locations of the lab and the production areas (nodes) where the samples must be collected. The branches are the alternatives being considered for the conveyor system. What is the minimum total length and layout of the conveyor system that would enable all production areas to send samples to the lab?

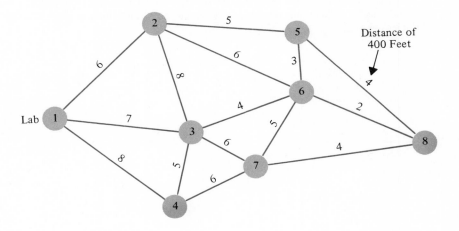

Chapter 11

Decision Theory

Decision theory or decision analysis can be used to determine optimal strategies when a decision maker is faced with several decision alternatives and an uncertain or risk-filled pattern of future events. For example, a manufacturer of a new style or line of seasonal clothing would like to manufacture large quantities of the product if consumer acceptance and consequently demand for the product are going to be high. However, the manufacturer would like to produce much smaller quantities if consumer acceptance and demand for the product are going to be low. Unfortunately, the seasonal clothing items require the manufacturer to make a production quantity decision before the demand is actually known. The actual consumer acceptance of the new product will not be determined until the items have been placed in the stores and the buyers have had the opportunity to purchase them. The selection of the best production volume decision from among several production volume alternatives when the decision maker is faced with the uncertainty of future demand is a problem suited for a decision theory analysis. In this chapter we will introduce the concepts and procedures associated with the decision theory approach to problem solving.

We begin our study of decision theory by considering problem situations in which there are reasonably few decision alternatives and possible future events. The concept of a payoff table is introduced to provide a structure for this type of decision situation and to illustrate the fundamentals involved in the decision theory approach to any situation. This analysis is then extended to show how additional information obtained through experimentation can be combined with the decision maker's preliminary information in order to develop an optimal decision strategy.

11.1 Structuring the Decision Situation: Payoff Tables

In order to illustrate the decision theory approach, let us consider the case of Political Systems, Inc. (PSI), a newly formed computer service firm specializing in information services such as surveys, data analysis, and so on for individuals running for political office. PSI is in the final stages of selecting a computer system for its midwest branch located in Chicago. While the firm has decided on a computer manufacturer, it is currently attempting to determine the size of the computer system that would be the most economical to lease. We will use decision theory to help PSI make its computer leasing decision.

The first step in the decision theory approach for a given problem situation is to identify the alternatives that may be considered by the decision maker. For PSI, the final decision will be to lease one of three computer systems which differ in size and capacity. The three decision alternatives, denoted d_1, d_2, and d_3, are as follows:

d_1 = lease the large computer system,

d_2 = lease the medium-sized computer system,

d_3 = lease the small computer system.

Obviously, the determination of the best decision will depend upon what PSI management foresees as the possible market acceptance of their service and consequently the possible demand or load on the PSI computer system. Often the future events associated with a problem situation are uncertain. That is, while a decision maker may have an idea of the variety of possible future events, the decision maker will often be unsure as to which particular event will occur. Thus the second step in a decision theory approach is to identify the future events that might occur. These future events, which are not under the control of the decision maker, are referred to as the *states of nature* for the problem. It is assumed that the list of possible states of nature includes everything that can happen and that the individual states of nature do not overlap; that is, the states of nature are defined so that one and only one of the listed states of nature will occur.

When asked about the states of nature for the PSI decision problem, management viewed the possible acceptance of their service as an either-or situation. That is, PSI management believed that the firm's overall level of acceptance in the market place would be one of two possibilities: high acceptance or low acceptance. Thus the PSI states of nature, denoted s_1 and s_2, are as follows:

$$s_1 = \text{high customer acceptance of PSI services,}$$
$$s_2 = \text{low customer acceptance of PSI services.}$$

Given the three decision alternatives and the two states of nature, which computer system should PSI lease? In order to answer this question, we will need information on the profit associated with each combination of a decision alternative and a state of nature. For example, what profit would PSI experience if the firm decided to lease the large computer system d_1 and market acceptance was high s_1? What profit would PSI experience if the firm decided to lease the large computer system d_1 and market acceptance was low s_2? And so on.

In decision theory terminology, we refer to the outcome resulting from making a certain decision and the occurrence of a particular state of nature as the *payoff*. Using the best information available, management of PSI has estimated the payoffs or profits for the PSI computer leasing problem. These estimates are presented in Table 11.1. A table of this form is referred to as a *payoff table*. In general, entries in a payoff table can be stated in terms of profits, costs, or any other measure of output that may be appropriate for the particular situation being analyzed. The notation we will use for the entries in the payoff table is $V(d_i, s_j)$, which denotes the payoff associated with decision alternative d_i and state of nature s_j. Using this notation we see that $V(d_3, s_1) = \$100,000$.

The identification of the decision alternatives, the states of nature, and the determination of the payoff associated with each decision alternative and state of nature combination are the first three steps in the decision theory approach. The question we now turn to is the following: How can the decision maker best utilize the information presented in the payoff table to

Table 11.1 Payoff Table for the PSI Computer Leasing Problem

| | | States of Nature | |
| | | High Acceptance (s_1) | Low Acceptance (s_2) |
Decision Alternatives			
Lease a large system	d_1	$200,000	$-20,000
Lease a medium-sized system	d_2	$150,000	$ 20,000
Lease a small system	d_3	$100,000	$ 60,000

Profit or payoff

arrive at a decision? As we shall see, there are several criteria that may be used.

11.2 Types of Decision-Making Situations

Before discussing specific decision-making criteria, let us consider the types of decision-making situations that we may encounter. The classification scheme for decision-making situations is based upon the knowledge the decision maker has about the states of nature. In this regard, there are two types of decision-making situations:

1. Decision making under certainty—The process of choosing a decision alternative when the state of nature is known;
2. Decision making under uncertainty—The process of choosing a decision alternative when the state of nature is not known.

In the case of decision making under certainty there will only be one column in the payoff table, and the optimal decision is the one corresponding to the best payoff in the column. For example, if PSI knew for certain that market acceptance of its service was going to be high, column s_2 could be removed from the payoff table and the optimal solution would be the large system d_1, since d_1 provides the largest profit ($200,000) in the s_1 column.

Most situations in which the decision theory approach is applied involve decision making under uncertainty. In these cases the selection of the best alternative is more difficult. First the decision maker must select a criterion. Then he or she must determine which decision alternative is best under the chosen criterion.

11.3 Criteria for Decision Making Under Uncertainty Without Using Probabilities

In some situations of decision making under uncertainty the decision maker may have very little confidence in her or his ability to assess the probabilities of the various states of nature. In such cases, the decision maker might prefer to choose a decision criterion that does not require any knowledge of the probabilities of the states of nature. Three of the most popular criteria available for these cases are maximin (or minimax), maximax (or minimin), and minimax regret.

Because different criteria will sometimes lead to different decision recommendations, it is important for the decision maker to know the criteria available and then select the specific criterion which, according to his or her judgment, is the most appropriate. We now discuss the above three criteria for decision making under uncertainty by showing how each could be used to solve the PSI computer leasing problem.

Maximin

The *maximin* decision criterion is a pessimistic or conservative approach to arriving at a decision. In this approach the decision maker attempts to *maxi*mize the *mini*mum possible profits; hence the term maximin. Using the information contained in the payoff table, the decision maker would first list the minimum payoff that is possible for each decision alternative. The decision maker would then select the decision from the new list that results in maximum payoff. Table 11.2 illustrates this process for the PSI problem.

Since $60,000, corresponding to the decision to lease a small system, yields the maximum of the minimum payoffs, the decision to lease a small system is recommended as the maximin decision. This decision criterion is considered conservative because it concentrates on the worst possible payoffs and then recommends the decision alternative that avoids the possibility of extremely "bad" payoffs. In using the maximin criterion PSI is guaranteed a profit of at least $60,000. While PSI may still make more, it *cannot* make less than the maximin criterion value of $60,000.

For problems in which costs are to be minimized, the conservative maximin approach is reversed in that the decision maker first lists the maximum cost for each decision alternative. The recommended decision then corresponds to the *mini*mum of the *maxi*mum costs. Thus this criterion used for minimization problems is referred to as *minimax*.

Maximax

While maximin offers a pessimistic decision criterion, maximax provides an optimistic criterion. Using this criterion for maximization problems, the

Table 11.2   PSI Minimum Payoff for Each Decision Alternative

Decision Alternatives		Minimum Payoff	
Large system	d_1	$ -20,000	Maximum of the
Medium system	d_2	$ 20,000	minimum payoff
Small system	d_3	$ 60,000	values

Table 11.3   PSI Maximum Payoff for Each Decision Alternative

Decision Alternatives		Maximum Payoff	
Large system	d_1	$200,000 ←	Maximum of the
Medium system	d_2	$150,000	maximum payoff
Small system	d_3	$100,000	values

decision maker selects the decision that *maxi*mizes the *max*imum payoff; hence the name *maximax*. In applying this criterion, the decision maker first determines the maximum payoff possible for each decision alternative. The decision maker then identifies the decision that provides the overall maximum payoff. Table 11.3 shows the result of applying this criterion for the PSI problem.

Since $200,000, corresponding to the decision to lease a large system, yields the maximum of the maximum payoffs, the decision to lease a large system is the recommended maximax decision. This decision criterion reflects an optimistic point of view because it simply recommends the decision alternative that provides the possibility of obtaining the best of all payoffs, $200,000. While the use of this criteron provides the opportunity for a large payoff, it also exposes the company to the possibility of a $20,000 loss. Hence we would definitely not recommend using this criterion if information was available indicating that state of nature s_2 was highly likely.

For minimization problems, the maximax criterion reverses to the *mini*mum of the *mini*mum cost values, or the *minimin* criterion.

Minimax Regret

Suppose we make the decision to lease the small system d_3 and afterwards learn that market acceptance of the PSI service is high, s_1. Table 11.1 shows the resulting profit to be $100,000. However, now that we know state of

Table 11.4   Regret or Opportunity Loss for the PSI Problem

Decision Alternatives		States of Nature	
		High Acceptance (s_1)	Low Acceptance (s_2)
Large system	d_1	0	$80,000
Medium system	d_2	$50,000	$40,000
Small system	d_3	$100,000	0

Table 11.5 PSI Maximum Regret or Opportunity Loss for Each Decision Alternative

Decision Alternatives		Maximum Regret or Opportunity Loss	
Large system	d_1	$ 80,000	
Medium system	d_2	$ 50,000 ←	Minimum of the maximum regret
Small system	d_3	$100,000	

nature s_1 has occurred, we see that the large system decision d_1 yielding a profit of $200,000 would have been the optimal decision. This difference between the optimal payoff ($200,000) and the payoff experienced ($100,000) is referred to as the *opportunity loss* or *regret* associated with our d_3 decision when state s_1 occurs ($200,000 − $100,000 = $100,000). If we had made decision d_2 and state of nature s_1 had occurred, the opportunity loss or regret for this decision and state of nature would have been $200,000 − $150,000 = $50,000.

The general expression for opportunity loss or regret is given by

$$R(d_i, s_j) = V^*(s_j) - V(d_i, s_j) \tag{11.1}$$

where

$R(d_i, s_j)$ = regret associated with decision alternative d_i and state of nature s_j,

$V^*(s_j)$ = best payoff value under state of nature s_j.[1]

For our d_3 decision and state of nature s_1, $V^*(s_1) = \$200,000$ and $V(d_3, s_1) = \$100,000$. Thus

$$R(d_3, s_1) = \$200,000 - \$100,000 = \$100,000.$$

Using equation (11.1) we can compute the regret associated with all combinations of decision alternatives d_i and states of nature s_j. We simply replace each entry in the payoff table with the value found by subtracting the entry from the largest entry in its column. Table 11.4 shows the regret, or opportunity loss, table for the PSI problem.

The next step in applying the minimax regret criterion requires the decision analyst to identify the maximum regret for each decision alternative. These data are shown in Table 11.5. The final decision is made by selecting the alternative corresponding to the *mini*mum of the *maxi*mum *regret* values; hence the name *minimax regret*. For the PSI problem, the decision to lease a medium-sized computer system, with a corresponding regret of $50,000, is the recommended minimax regret decision.

Note that the three decision criteria discussed in this section have each

---

[1]In cost minimization problems $V^*(s_j)$ will be the smallest entry in column j. Thus for minimization problems, formula (11.1) must be changed to $R(d_i, s_j) = V(d_i, s_j) - V^*(s_j)$.

led to different recommendations. This is not in itself bad. It simply reflects the difference in decision-making philosophies that underlie the various criteria. Ultimately, the decision maker will have to choose the most appropriate criterion and then make the final decision accordingly. The major criticism of the criteria discussed in this section is they do not consider any information about the probabilities of the various states of nature. In the next section we discuss criteria that utilize probability information in selecting a decision alternative.

11.4   Criteria for Decision Making Under Uncertainty Using Probabilities

In many situations good probability estimates can be developed for the states of nature. Two decision criteria which make use of these probability estimates in the selection of a decision alternative are expected monetary value and expected opportunity loss. Let us now see how these criteria can be applied when making decisions under uncertainty.

Expected Monetary Value

The *expected monetary value* criterion requires the analyst to compute the expected value for each decision alternative and then select the alternative yielding the best expected value. Let

$$P(s_j) = \text{probability of occurrence for state of nature } s_j,$$
$$N = \text{number of possible states of nature.}$$

Since one and only one of the N states of nature can occur, the associated probabilities must satisfy the following two conditions:

$$P(s_j) \geq 0 \qquad \text{for all states of nature } j \tag{11.2}$$

$$\sum_{j=1}^{N} P(s_j) = P(s_1) + P(s_2) + \cdots + P(s_N) = 1. \tag{11.3}$$

The expected monetary value (EMV) of a decision alternative d_i is given by

$$\text{EMV}(d_i) = \sum_{j=1}^{N} P(s_j) V(d_i, s_j). \tag{11.4}$$

In words, the expected monetary value of a decision alternative is the sum of weighted payoffs for the alternative. The weight for a payoff is the probability of the associated state of nature and therefore the probability that the payoff occurs. Let us now return to the PSI problem to see how the expected monetary value criterion can be applied.

Suppose that PSI management believes that the high acceptance state of nature, while very desirable, has only a 0.3 probability of occurrence, while the low acceptance state of nature has a 0.7 probability. Thus $P(s_1) = 0.3$ and $P(s_2) = 0.7$. Using the payoff values $V(d_i, s_j)$ shown in Table 11.1

and equation (11.4), expected monetary values for the three decision alternatives can be calculated:

$$\text{EMV}(d_1) = 0.3(200,000) + 0.7(-20,000) = \$46,000,$$
$$\text{EMV}(d_2) = 0.3(150,000) + 0.7(20,000) = \$59,000,$$
$$\text{EMV}(d_3) = 0.3(100,000) + 0.7(60,000) = \$72,000.$$

Thus according to the expected monetary value criterion the small system decision d_3 with an expected monetary value of \$72,000 is the recommended decision.

Note, however, that if the probabilities of the states of nature change, a different decision alternative might be selected. For example, if $P(s_1) = 0.6$ and $P(s_2) = 0.4$, we find the following expected monetary values:

$$\text{EMV}(d_1) = 0.6(200,000) + 0.4(-20,000) = \$112,000,$$
$$\text{EMV}(d_2) = 0.6(150,000) + 0.4(20,000) = \$98,000,$$
$$\text{EMV}(d_3) = 0.6(100,000) + 0.4(60,000) = \$84,000.$$

We now see that decision alternative d_1 with an expected monetary value of \$112,000 is the recommended decision with these probabilities.

Expected Opportunity Loss

In Section 11.3 we defined the concept of an opportunity loss or regret associated with each decision alternative and state of nature combination. For PSI we developed the opportunity loss table shown in Table 11.4. The *expected opportunity loss* criterion uses the probabilities of the states of nature as weights for the opportunity loss values and computes the expected value of the opportunity loss (EOL) as follows:

$$\text{EOL}(d_i) = \sum_{j=1}^{N} P(s_j)R(d_i, s_j) \qquad (11.5)$$

where $R(d_i, s_j)$ denotes the regret or opportunity loss for decision alternative d_i and state of nature s_j [see equation (11.1)].

Again using $P(s_1) = 0.3$ and $P(s_2) = 0.7$ for PSI and the opportunity loss data of Table 11.4, the expected opportunity losses for the three decision alternatives become

$$\text{EOL}(d_1) = 0.3(0) + 0.7(80,000) = \$56,000,$$
$$\text{EOL}(d_2) = 0.3(50,000) + 0.7(40,000) = \$43,000,$$
$$\text{EOL}(d_3) = 0.3(100,000) + 0.7(0) = \$30,000.$$

Since we would want to minimize the expected opportunity loss, the small system decision d_3, with the smallest loss of \$30,000, is recommended.

While expected opportunity loss offers an alternate criterion and approach to decision making under uncertainty, the optimal decision using the expected opportunity loss criterion will *always* be the same as the optimal decision using the expected monetary value criterion. Since the recommended decisions are identical, only one criterion need be applied in a given decision-making situation. In practice the expected monetary value has been the most widely used and accepted criterion for decision making under uncertainty. However, the expected opportunity loss provides the same result, and as we will see in Section 11.6, the EOL associated with the best decision provides an indication of the value of collecting additional information about the probabilities for the states of nature.

11.5   Decision Trees

While decision problems involving a modest number of decision alternatives and a modest number of states of nature can be analyzed by using payoff tables, they can also be analyzed by using a graphical representation of the decision-making process called a *decision tree*.

Figure 11.1 shows a decision tree for the PSI computer leasing problem. Note that the tree shows the natural or logical progression that will occur in the decision-making process. First the firm must make its decision (d_1, d_2, or d_3); then, once the decision is implemented, the state of nature (s_1 or s_2) will occur. The number at each end point of the tree represents the payoff associated with a particular chain of events. For example, the topmost payoff of 200,000 arises whenever management makes the decision to purchase a large system (d_1) and market acceptance turns out to be high (s_1). The next lower terminal point of $-20,000$ is reached when management has made the decision to lease the large system (d_1) and the true state of nature turns out to be a low degree of market acceptance (s_2). Thus we see that each possible sequence of events for the PSI problem is represented in the decision tree.

Using the general terminology associated with decision trees, we will refer to the intersection or junction points of the tree as *nodes* and the arcs or connectors between the nodes as *branches*. Figure 11.2 shows the PSI decision tree with the nodes numbered 1 to 4 and the branches labeled as decision or state-of-nature branches. When the branches *leaving* a given

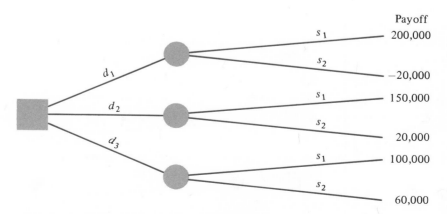

Figure 11.1   Decision Tree for the PSI Problem

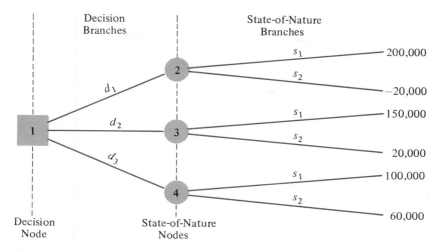

Figure 11.2   PSI Decision Tree with Node and Branch Labels

node are decision branches, we refer to the node as a decision node. Decision nodes are denoted by squares. Similarly, when the branches leaving a given node are state-of-nature branches, we refer to the node as a *state-of-nature node*. State-of-nature nodes are denoted by circles. Using this node-labeling procedure, node 1 is a decision node, whereas nodes 2, 3, and 4 are state-of-nature nodes.

At decision nodes the decision maker selects the particular decision branch (d_1, d_2, or d_3) that will be taken. Selecting the best branch is equivalent to making the best decision. However the state-of-nature branches are not controlled by the decision maker; thus the specific branch followed from a state-of-nature node depends upon the probabilities associated with the branches. Using $P(s_1) = 0.3$ and $P(s_2) = 0.7$ we show the PSI decision tree with state-of-nature branch probabilities in Figure 11.3.

We will now use the branch probabilities and the expected monetary value criterion to arrive at the optimal decision for PSI. Working *backward*

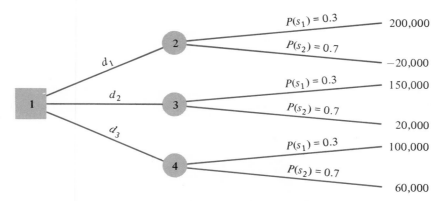

Figure 11.3   PSI Decision Tree with State-of-Nature Branch Probabilities

through the decision tree, we first compute the expected monetary value at each state-of-nature node. That is, at each state-of-nature node we weigh the possible payoffs by their chance of occurrence. The expected monetary values for nodes 2, 3, and 4 are computed as follows:

$$EMV(\text{node } 2) = 0.3(200,000) + 0.7(-20,000) = 46,000,$$
$$EMV(\text{node } 3) = 0.3(150,000) + 0.7(\ 20,000) = 59,000,$$
$$EMV(\text{node } 4) = 0.3(100,000) + 0.7(\ 60,000) = 72,000.$$

We now continue backward through the tree to the decision node. Since the expected monetary values for nodes 2, 3, and 4 are known, the decision maker can view decision node 1 as follows:

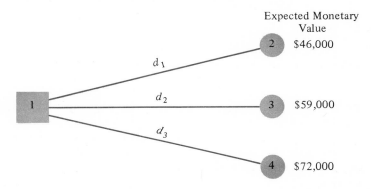

Since the decision maker controls the branch leaving a decision node and since we are trying to maximize expected profits, the best decision branch at node 1 is d_3. Thus the decision tree analysis leads us to recommend d_3 with an expected monetary value of $72,000. Note that this is the same recommendation that was obtained using the expected monetary value criterion in conjunction with the payoff table.

We have seen how decision trees can be used to analyze a decision under uncertainty. While other decision problems may be substantially more complex than the PSI problem, if there are a reasonable number of decision alternatives and states of nature, the decision tree approach outlined in this section can be used. First, the analyst must draw a decision tree consisting of decision and state-of-nature nodes and branches that describe the sequential nature of the problem. Assuming the expected monetary value criterion is to be used, the next step is to determine the probabilities for each of the state-of-nature branches and compute the expected monetary value at each state-of-nature node. The decision branch leading to the state-of-nature node with the best expected monetary value is then selected. The decision alternative associated with this branch is the best decision using the expected monetary value criterion.

11.6   Expected Value of Perfect Information

At the end of Section 11.4 we mentioned that the expected opportunity loss criterion was useful in determining the value of collecting additional information about the probabilities of the states of nature. Suppose now that PSI had the opportunity to conduct a market research study to thoroughly evaluate consumer needs for its service. Such a study could help by improving the current probability assessments for the states of nature. On the other hand, if the cost of obtaining such information exceeded its value, PSI should not seek it.

To help determine the maximum possible value of additional information for PSI we have reproduced PSI's opportunity loss table as Table 11.6. Recall that the optimal decision using either the expected monetary value or expected opportunity loss criterion was to lease the small system, d_3, when $P(s_1) = 0.3$ and $P(s_2) = 0.7$. Let us now concentrate on the losses associated with this decision.

We see that if state of nature s_1 occurs, d_3 will not have been the best decision and PSI will have an opportunity loss of $100,000 due to the fact that d_1 was not selected. That is, given perfect information that s_1 was going to occur, PSI could increase its profit $100,000 by selecting d_1 instead of d_3. On the other hand, if state of nature s_2 occurs, d_3 will have been the best decision and the opportunity loss will be $0. Thus perfect information that s_2 was going to occur would be of no value to the company since PSI would have made the optimal decision without it.

What is the expected value of this perfect information? Using $P(s_1) = 0.3$ and $P(s_2) = 0.7$ and the opportunity loss values, we see that 30% of the time PSI could save $100,000 while 70% of the time the savings would be $0. Thus, the *expected value of perfect information* (EVPI) for PSI's problem is given by

$$\text{EVPI} = (0.3)(\$100,000) + (0.7)(\$0) = \$30,000.$$

In the table below we summarize what is involved in computing the expected value of perfect information:

Possible Information	Action and Payoff if Decision is Made Before Information is Available	Action and Payoff if Decision is Made After Information is Available	Value of Perfect Information (Opportunity Loss of d_3)	Probability of Information
High Acceptance	Lease small system $100,000	Lease large system $200,000	$100,000	0.3
Low Acceptance	Lease small system $60,000	Lease small system $60,000	$0	0.7

$$\text{EVPI} = 0.3(100,000) + 0.7(0) = \$30,000$$

Note that EVPI is the same as the *expected opportunity loss of the optimal decision* (i.e., d_3; see Section 11.4). Thus if we had used expected opportu-

TABLE 11.6   Opportunity Loss Table for the PSI Problem

| | | States of Nature | |
		High Acceptance (s_1)	Low Acceptance (s_2)
Decision Alternatives			
Large system	d_1	0	$80,000
Medium system	d_2	$ 50,000	$40,000
Small system	d_3	$100,000	0

nity loss as a decision criterion, or if in our analysis we had computed the expected opportunity loss of the optimal decision, we would have already computed the expected value of perfect information.

Generally speaking, we would not expect a market research study to provide "perfect" information, but the information provided might be worth a good portion of the $30,000. In any case, PSI's management knows it should never pay more than $30,000 for any information, no matter how good. Provided the market survey cost is reasonably small—say $5000 to $10,000—it appears economically desirable for PSI to consider the market research study.

Before leaving this section we note the general expression for computing the expected value of perfect information (EVPI) from a payoff table. Let

d^* = optimal decision for the problem prior to obtaining information,

$P(s_j)$ = probability of state of nature j,

N = number of states of nature, and

$R(d^*, s_j)$ = opportunity loss or regret value for decision d^* and state of nature s_j.

Then we have the following expression for EVPI:

$$\text{EVPI} = \sum_{j=1}^{N} P(s_j)R(d^*, s_j). \tag{11.6}$$

11.7   Decision Theory With Experiments

In decision theory situations involving decision making under uncertainty, we have seen how probability information about the states of nature affects the expected value calculations and thus possibly the decision recommendation. Frequently decision makers have preliminary or prior probability estimates for the states of nature which are initially the best probability values available. However, in order to make the best possible decision, the decision maker may want to seek additional information about the states of nature. This new information can be used to revise or update the prior probabilities so that the final decision is based upon more accurate probability estimates for the states of nature.

The seeking of additional information is most often accomplished through experiments designed to provide the most current data available about the states of nature. Raw material sampling, product testing, and test market research are examples of experiments that may enable a revision or updating of the state-of-nature probabilities. In the remaining sections of this chapter we will reconsider the PSI computer leasing problem and show how new information can be used to revise the state-of-nature probabilities. We will then show how these revised probabilities can be used to develop an optimal decision strategy for PSI.

Recall that management had assigned a probability of 0.3 to the state of nature s_1 and a probability of 0.7 to the state of nature s_2. At this point, we will refer to these initial probability estimates, $P(s_1)$ and $P(s_2)$, as the *prior* probabilities for the states of nature. Using these prior probabilities we found that the decision to lease the small system d_3 was optimal, yielding an expected monetary value of \$72,000. Applying the criterion of minimizing expected opportunity loss, we obtained the same decision recommendation and also learned that the expected opportunity loss (EOL) of the optimal decision d_3 was \$30,000. In addition, we showed that since the expected value of perfect information was equal to the EOL of the optimal decision, the expected value of new information about the states of nature could potentially be worth as much as \$30,000.

Suppose that PSI decides to consider hiring a market research firm to study the potential acceptance of the PSI service. The market research study will provide new information which can be combined with the prior probabilities through a Bayesian procedure to obtain updated or revised probability estimates for the states of nature. These revised probabilities are called *posterior* probabilities. The complete process of revising probabilities is depicted in Figure 11.4.

We usually refer to the new information obtained through research or experimentation as an *indicator*. Since in many cases the experiment conducted to obtain the additional information will consist of taking a statistical sample, the new information is also often referred to as *sample information*.

Using the indicator terminology, we can denote the outcomes of the PSI marketing research study as follows:

I_1 = favorable market research report; i.e., in the market research study the individuals contacted generally express considerable interest in PSI's services.

I_2 = unfavorable market research report; i.e., in the market research study the individuals contacted generally express little interest in PSI's services.

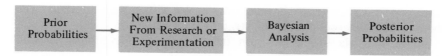

Figure 11.4   Probability Revision Based on New Information

Given one of these possible indicators, our objective is to provide improved estimates of the probabilities of the various states of nature based upon the findings of the market research study. The end result of the Bayesian revision process depicted in Figure 11.4 is a set of posterior probabilities of the form $P(s_j | I_k)$, where $P(s_j | I_k)$ represents the conditional probability that state of nature s_j will occur given that the outcome of the market research study was indicator I_k.

To make effective use of this indicator information we must know something about the probability relationships between the indicators and the states of nature. For example, in the PSI problem, given that the state of nature ultimately turns out to be high customer acceptance, what is the probability that the market research study will result in a favorable report? In this case we are asking about the conditional probability of indicator I_1 given state of nature s_1, written $P(I_1 | s_1)$. In order to carry out the analysis, we will need conditional probability relationships for all indicators given all states of nature, i.e., $P(I_1 | s_1)$, $P(I_1 | s_2)$, $P(I_2 | s_1)$, and $P(I_2 | s_2)$. Historical relative frequency data and/or subjective probability estimates are usually the primary source for these conditional probability values.

In the PSI case the past record of the marketing research company on similar studies has led to the following estimates of the relevant conditional probabilities:

| | Market Research Report | |
States of Nature	Favorable (I_1)	Unfavorable (I_2)
High acceptance s_1	$P(I_1 | s_1) = 0.8$	$P(I_2 | s_1) = 0.2$
Low acceptance s_2	$P(I_1 | s_2) = 0.1$	$P(I_2 | s_2) = 0.9$

Note that these probability estimates indicate that a great degree of confidence can be placed in the market research report. When the true state of nature is s_1, the market research report will be favorable 80% of the time and unfavorable only 20%. When the true state is s_2, the report will make the correct indication 90% of the time. Now let us see how this additional information can be incorporated into the decision-making process.

11.8 Developing a Decision Strategy

A decision strategy is simply a policy or decision rule that is to be followed by the decision maker. In the PSI case a decision strategy would consist of a rule to follow based on the outcome of the market research study. The rule would recommend a particular decision based upon whether the market research report was favorable or unfavorable. We will employ a decision tree analysis to find the optimal decision strategy for PSI.

Figure 11.5 shows the decision tree for the PSI computer leasing problem provided a market research study is conducted. Note that as you move from left to right the tree shows the natural or logical order that will

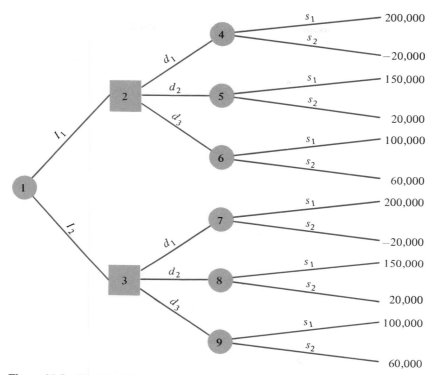

Figure 11.5   Decision Tree for the PSI Problem

occur in the decision-making process. First, the firm will obtain the market research report indicator (I_1 or I_2); then a decision (d_1, d_2, or d_3) will be made; finally, the state of nature (s_1 or s_2) will occur. The decision and the state of nature combine to provide the final profit or payoff.

Using decision tree terminology, we have now introduced an *indicator node*, node 1, and *indicator branches, I_1 and I_2.* Since the branches emanating from indicator nodes are not under the control of the decision maker but are determined by chance, these nodes are depicted by a circle just like the state-of-nature nodes. We see that nodes 2 and 3 are decision nodes, while nodes 4, 5, 6, 7, 8, and 9 are state-of-nature nodes. For decision nodes the decision maker must select the specific branch d_1, d_2, or d_3 that will be taken. Selecting the best decision branch is equivalent to making the best decision. However, since the indicator and state-of-nature branches are not controlled by the decision maker, the specific branch leaving an indicator or a state-of-nature node will depend upon the probability associated with the branch. Thus before we can carry out an analysis of the decision tree and develop a decision strategy, we must compute the probability of each indicator branch $P(I_k)$ and the probability of each state-of-nature branch. Note from the decision tree that the state-of-nature branches occur *after* the indicator branches. Thus when we attempt to compute state-of-nature branch probabilities, we will need to consider which indicator was previously observed. That is, we will express state-of-nature probabilities in terms of the probability of state of nature s_j given indicator I_k was observed. Thus all state-of-nature probabilities will be expressed in a $P(s_j | I_k)$ form.

Computing Branch Probabilities: The Decision Tree Approach

The prior probabilities for the states of nature in the PSI problem were given as $P(s_1) = 0.3$ and $P(s_2) = 0.7$. In Section 11.7 we identified the relationship between the market research indicator and states of nature with the probabilities

$$P(I_1 | s_1) = 0.8, \qquad P(I_2 | s_1) = 0.2,$$
$$P(I_1 | s_2) = 0.1, \qquad P(I_2 | s_2) = 0.9.$$

However, in order to develop the decision tree in Figure 11.5, we need indicator branch probabilities $P(I_k)$ and state-of-nature branch probabilities $P(s_j | I_k)$. The problem now facing us is how to use the given prior probability estimates $P(s_j)$ and the given conditional probability estimates $P(I_k | s_j)$ to calculate the branch probabilities $P(I_k)$ and $P(s_j | I_k)$.

Let us concentrate on computing the state-of-nature branch probabilities $P(s_j | I_k)$. In the process, we will also compute the indicator branch probabilities $P(I_k)$. We will illustrate the procedure by calculating $P(s_1 | I_1)$, the probability that market acceptance is high (s_1) given the market research report is favorable (I_1). Shown in equation (11.7) is the basic expression for conditional probability. You may recall the use of this expression in previous courses dealing with probability and statistics. Using conditional probability, we can write

$$P(s_1 | I_1) = \frac{P(I_1 \cap s_1)}{P(I_1)}, \tag{11.7}$$

where $P(I_1 \cap s_1)$ is referred to as the joint probability. The value of $P(I_1 \cap s_1)$ gives the probability I_1, favorable market research report, and s_1, high consumer acceptance, both occur.

Unfortunately, we cannot use equation (11.7) directly to compute $P(s_1 | I_1)$, since both $P(I_1 \cap s_1)$ and $P(I_1)$ are unknown. However, reversing I_1 and s_1 in equation (11.7) provides the following conditional probability expression:

$$P(I_1 | s_1) = \frac{P(I_1 \cap s_1)}{P(s_1)}. \tag{11.8}$$

Using equation (11.8) and solving for $P(I_1 \cap s_1)$, we have

$$P(I_1 \cap s_1) = P(I_1 | s_1) P(s_1). \tag{11.9}$$

By substituting equation (11.9) for $P(I_1 \cap s_1)$ in equation (11.7), we have

$$P(s_1|I_1) = \frac{P(I_1|s_1)P(s_1)}{P(I_1)}.$$ (11.10)

We are now a step closer to finding $P(s_1|I_1)$ since we have been given values of $P(I_1|s_1) = 0.8$ and $P(s_1) = 0.3$. However, we still need a value for the indicator branch probability $P(I_1)$.

In order to see how we find $P(I_1)$, first recognize that there are only two outcomes that correspond to I_1, namely

1. The market research report is favorable (I_1) and the state of nature turns out to be high acceptance (s_1), written ($I_1 \cap s_1$);
2. The market research report is favorable (I_1) and the state of nature turns out to be low acceptance (s_2), written ($I_1 \cap s_2$).

The probabilities of these two outcomes are written $P(I_1 \cap s_1)$ and $P(I_1 \cap s_2)$, respectively.

Since the ($I_1 \cap s_1$) and ($I_1 \cap s_2$) results are mutually exclusive (if one occurs, the other cannot), the probability the market research report is favorable is given by

$$P(I_1) = P(I_1 \cap s_1) + P(I_1 \cap s_2).$$ (11.11)

Recall that in equation (11.9) we showed that

$$P(I_1 \cap s_1) = P(I_1|s_1)P(s_1).$$

Using this expression form with s_2 instead of s_1, we have

$$P(I_1 \cap s_2) = P(I_1|s_2)P(s_2).$$

Thus equation (11.11) can now be revised as follows:

$$P(I_1) = P(I_1|s_1)P(s_1) + P(I_1|s_2)P(s_2).$$ (11.12)

Since $P(I_1|s_1)$, $P(I_1|s_2)$, $P(s_1)$, and $P(s_2)$ are known, equation (11.12) can be used to calculate $P(I_1)$. Then equation (11.10) can be used to calculate $P(s_1|I_1)$.

Before making these calculations let us examine the general form of equations (11.12) and (11.10). Specifically, we want to be able to calculate any indicator branch probability $P(I_k)$ and any state-of-nature branch probability $P(s_j|I_k)$. Assuming we have N states of nature, $s_1, s_2, \ldots, s_N$, equation (11.11) generalizes to

$$P(I_k) = P(I_k \cap s_1) + P(I_k \cap s_2) + \ldots + P(I_k \cap s_N).$$ (11.13)

Using the relationship established by equation (11.9) we can write

$$P(I_k) = P(I_k|s_1)P(s_1) + P(I_k|s_2)P(s_2) + \ldots + P(I_k|s_N)P(s_N)$$ (11.14)

or

$$P(I_k) = \sum_{j=1}^{N} P(I_k|s_j)P(s_j).$$ (11.15)

Thus equation (11.10) generalizes to

$$P(s_j | I_k) = \frac{P(I_k | s_j)P(s_j)}{P(I_k)}, \tag{11.16}$$

where $P(I_k)$ is computed from either equation (11.14) or (11.15). Equation (11.16) is known as Bayes's rule or Bayes's theorem and provides a general expression for computing the conditional probability of state of nature s_j given indicator I_k has occurred. Thus given prior probabilities $P(s_j)$ and conditional probabilities of the form $P(I_k | s_j)$, the Bayesian procedures defined in equations (11.15) and (11.16) can be used to compute indicator probabilities $P(I_k)$ and revised or posterior state-of-nature probabilities $P(s_j | I_k)$.

Let us return to the PSI decision where we have been given the prior probabilities $P(s_1) = 0.3$ and $P(s_2) = 0.7$ and the conditional probabilities $P(I_1 | s_1) = 0.8$, $P(I_2 | s_1) = 0.2$, $P(I_1 | s_2) = 0.1$, and $P(I_2 | s_2) = 0.9$. Moving from left to right through the decision tree (Figure 11.5), we can use equation (11.15) to first find the probabilities of the indicator branches:

$$P(I_1) = P(I_1 | s_1)P(s_1) + P(I_1 | s_2)P(s_2)$$
$$= (0.8)(0.3) + (0.1)(0.7) = 0.31$$

and

$$P(I_2) = P(I_2 | s_1)P(s_1) + P(I_2 | s_2)P(s_2)$$
$$= (0.2)(0.3) + (0.9)(0.7) = 0.69.$$

Note that after we obtained $P(I_1)$, we could have found $P(I_2)$ by using the fact that there are only two indicators, I_1 and I_2. Thus $P(I_1) + P(I_2) = 1$, and hence $P(I_2) = 1 - P(I_1) = 1 - 0.31 = 0.69$.

The above calculations tell us that based upon the given prior probabilities for the states of nature, $P(s_j)$, and the conditional probabilities, $P(I_k | s_j)$, the probability of a favorable market research report I_1 is 0.31 and the probability of an unfavorable report is 0.69.

Now we can use equation (11.16) to compute the revised or posterior probabilities for the state-of-nature branches, given an indicator of I_1 or I_2 from the market research study. For example, if indicator I_1 occurs, we have

$$P(s_1 | I_1) = \frac{P(I_1 | s_1)P(s_1)}{P(I_1)} = \frac{(0.8)(0.3)}{(0.31)} = 0.7742$$

and

$$P(s_2 | I_1) = \frac{P(I_1 | s_2)P(s_2)}{P(I_1)} = \frac{(0.1)(0.7)}{(0.31)} = 0.2258.$$

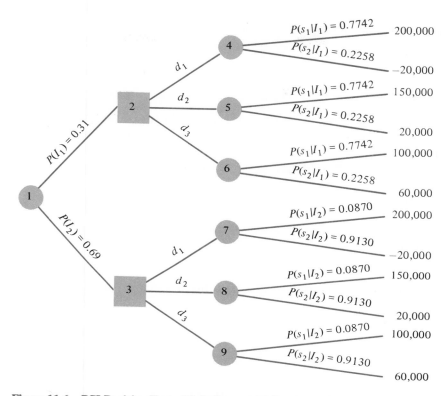

Figure 11.6   PSI Decision Tree with Indicator and State-of-Nature Branch Probabilities

Similar calculations for the indicator I_2 will show $P(s_1 \mid I_2)$ = 0.0870 and $P(s_2 \mid I_2)$ = 0.9130.

These revised probabilities provide the probability estimates of the state-of-nature branches after the market study is complete. For example, if the report is favorable, $P(s_1 \mid I_1)$ = 0.7742 indicates that there is a 0.7742 probability that the market acceptance will be high (s_1). However, we realize that the final market acceptance of the PSI service may be low, even though the market research report is favorable. This probability is given by $P(s_2 \mid I_1)$ = 0.2258. Note, however, that the state-of-nature probabilities given I_1 have been substantially revised from the prior values of $P(s_1)$ = 0.3 and $P(s_2)$ = 0.7. Similar interpretations can be made for the case when the market research report is unfavorable (I_2). Figure 11.6 shows the PSI decision tree after all indicator and state-of-nature branch probabilities have been computed.

Although the above procedure can be used to compute branch probabilities for decision theory problems when the decision tree approach is employed, the calculations can become quite cumbersome as the problem size grows larger. Thus in order to assist in applying Bayes' rule to compute branch probabilities, we present a tabular procedure that will make it easier to carry out the computations, especially for large decision theory problems.

A Tabular Procedure for Computing Branch Probabilities

The procedure used for computing the probabilities of the indicator and state-of-nature branches can be carried out by utilizing the following tabular approach. First, for each indicator I_k we form a table consisting of the following five column headings:

> *Column 1:* States of nature s_j;
> *Column 2:* Prior probabilities $P(s_j)$;
> *Column 3:* Conditional probabilities $P(I_k | s_j)$;
> *Column 4:* Joint probabilities $P(I_k \cap s_j)$;
> *Column 5:* Posterior probabilities $P(s_j | I_k)$.

Then, the following procedure can be utilized to calculate $P(I_k)$ and the $P(s_j | I_k)$ values.

Step 1. In column 1 list the states of nature appropriate to the problem being analyzed.
Step 2. In column 2 enter the probability corresponding to each state of nature listed in column 1.
Step 3. In column 3 write the appropriate value of $P(I_k | s_j)$ for each state of nature specified in column 1.
Step 4. To compute each entry in column 4, multiply each entry in column 2 by the corresponding entry in column 3.
Step 5. Add the entries in column 4. The sum is the value of $P(I_k)$. For convenience, write the sum under the last column entry.
Step 6. To compute each entry in column 5 divide the corresponding entry in column 4 by $P(I_k)$.

We will now illustrate the above procedure to compute $P(I_1)$ and the revised probabilities corresponding to I_1 for the PSI, Inc. problem.

Steps 1, 2, and 3:

s_j	$P(s_j)$	$P(I_1 \| s_j)$	$P(I_1 \cap s_j)$	$P(s_j \| I_1)$
s_1	0.3	0.8		
s_2	0.7	0.1		

Steps 4 and 5:

s_j	$P(s_j)$	$P(I_1 \| s_j)$	$P(I_1 \cap s_j)$	$P(s_j \| I_1)$
s_1	0.3	0.8	0.24	
s_2	0.7	0.1	0.07	
			$P(I_1) = 0.31$	

Step 6:

s_j	$P(s_j)$	$P(I_1 \| s_j)$	$P(I_1 \cap s_j)$	$P(s_j \| I_1)$
s_1	0.3	0.8	0.24	$= {}^{0.24}\!/_{0.31}$
				$= 0.7742$
s_2	0.7	0.1	0.07	$= {}^{0.07}\!/_{0.31}$
				$= 0.2258$
			$\overline{P(I_1) = 0.31}$	

Note that $P(I_1)$, $P(s_1 \| I_1)$, and $P(s_2 \| I_1)$ are exactly the same as we calculated by applying equations (11.15) and (11.16) directly.

An Optimal Decision Strategy

Regardless of the approach used to compute the branch probabilities, we can now use the branch probabilities and the expected monetary value criterion to arrive at the optimal decision for PSI. Working *backward* through the decision tree, we first compute the expected monetary value at each state-of-nature node. That is, at each state-of-nature node the possible payoffs are weighted by their chance of occurrence. Thus the expected monetary values for nodes 4 through 9 are computed as follows:

EMV(node 4) $= (0.7742)(200,000) + (0.2258)(-20,000) = 150,324,$
EMV(node 5) $= (0.7742)(150,000) + (0.2258)(20,000) = 120,646,$
EMV(node 6) $= (0.7742)(100,000) + (0.2258)(60,000) = 90,968,$
EMV(node 7) $= (0.0870)(200,000) + (0.9130)(-20,000) = -860,$
EMV(node 8) $= (0.0870)(150,000) + (0.9130)(20,000) = 31,310,$
EMV(node 9) $= (0.0870)(100,000) + (0.9130)(60,000) = 63,480.$

We now continue backward through the decision tree to the decision nodes. Because the expected values for nodes 4, 5, and 6 are known, the decision maker can view decision node 2 as follows:

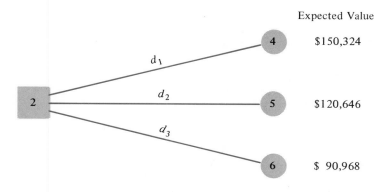

Since the decision maker controls the branch leaving a decision node, and since we are trying to maximize expected profits, the optimal decision at node 2 is d_1. Thus since d_1 leads to an expected value of $150,324, we say EMV(node 2) = $150,324 if the optimal decision of d_1 is made.

A similar analysis of decision node 3 shows that the optimal decision branch at this node is d_3. Thus EMV(node 3) becomes $63,480 provided the optimal decision of d_3 is made.

As a final step, we can continue working backward to the indicator node and establish its expected value. The branches at node 1 are as follows:

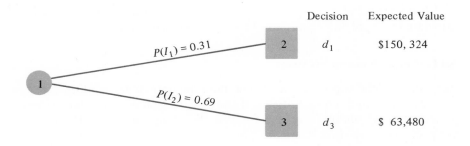

	Decision	Expected Value
2	d_1	$150, 324
3	d_3	$ 63,480

Since node 1 has probability branches, we cannot select the best branch. Rather, we must compute the expected value over all possible branches. Thus we have

$$\text{EMV(node 1)} = (0.31)(\$150,324) + (0.69)(\$63,480) = \$90,402.$$

The value of $90,402 is viewed as the expected value of the optimal decision strategy when the market research study is used or the expected monetary value using sample information (i.e., that provided by the market research report).

Note that the final decision has not yet been determined. We will need to know the results of the market research study before deciding to lease a large system (d_1) or a small system (d_3). The results of the decision theory analysis at this point, however, have provided us with the following optimal *decision strategy* if the market research study is conducted.

Decision Strategy	
If	Then
Report favorable (I_1)	Lease large system (d_1)
Report unfavorable (I_2)	Lease small system (d_3)

Thus we have seen how the decision tree approach can be used to develop optimal decision strategies for decisions under uncertainty when experiments are used to provide additional information. While other decision strategy problems may not be as simple as the PSI problem, the approach we have outlined is still applicable. First, draw a decision tree consisting of indicator, decision, and state-of-nature nodes and branches such that the tree describes the specific decision-making process. Posterior probability calculations must be made in order to establish indicator and state-of-nature branch probabilities. Then by working backward through the tree, computing expected values at state-of-nature and indicator nodes, and selecting the best decision branch at decision nodes, the analyst can determine an optimal decision strategy and the associated expected value for the problem.

11.9   Expected Value of Sample Information

In the PSI problem, management now has a decision strategy of leasing the large computer system if the market research report is favorable and leasing the small computer system if the market research report is unfavorable. Since the additional information provided by the market research firm will result in an added cost for PSI in terms of the fee paid to the research firm, PSI management may question the value of this market research information.

The value of information is often measured by calculating what is referred to as the *expected value of sample information* (EVSI). For maximization problems[2]

$$\text{EVSI} = \begin{bmatrix} \text{expected value of the} \\ \text{optimal decision } with \\ \text{sample information} \end{bmatrix} - \begin{bmatrix} \text{expected value of the} \\ \text{optimal decision } without \\ \text{sample information} \end{bmatrix} \quad (11.17)$$

For PSI the market research information is considered the "sample" information. The decision tree calculations indicated that the expected value of the optimal decision with the market research information was $90,402, while the expected value of the optimal decision without the market research information was $72,000. Using equation (11.17), the expected value of the market research report is

$$\text{EVSI} = \$90,402 - \$72,000 = \$18,402.$$

Thus PSI should be willing to pay up to $18,402 for the market research information.

Efficiency of Sample Information

In Section 11.6 we saw that the expected value of perfect information (EVPI) for the PSI problem was $30,000. While we never expected the market research report to obtain perfect information, we can use an *efficiency* measure to express the value of the report. With perfect information having an efficiency rating of 100%, the efficiency rating (E) for sample

---

[2]In minimization problems the expected value with sample information will be less than or equal to the expected value without sample information. Thus in minimization problems

$$\text{EVSI} = \begin{bmatrix} \text{expected value of the} \\ \text{optimal decision } without \\ \text{sample information} \end{bmatrix} - \begin{bmatrix} \text{expected value of the} \\ \text{optimal decision } with \\ \text{sample information} \end{bmatrix}$$

information is computed as follows:

$$E = \frac{\text{EVSI}}{\text{EVPI}} \times 100.$$

For our PSI example,

$$E = \frac{18,402}{30,000} \times 100 = 61\%.$$

In other words, the information from the market research firm is 61% as "efficient" as perfect information.

Low efficiency ratings for information might lead the decision maker to look for other types of information. On the other hand, high efficiency ratings indicate that the information is almost as good as perfect information, and additional sources of information are probably not worth searching for.

11.10   Other Topics in Decision Theory

In our discussion of decision theory models, we have only considered decision situations where the states of nature are finite and can be listed. The next step would be to consider situations where the states of nature were so numerous that it would be impractical, if not impossible, to treat the states of nature as a discrete random variable consisting of a finite number of values. For example, let us suppose that we were attempting to price a new product and were concerned with the potential sales volume we might experience at different prices. We might think of the states of nature as being all possible sales volumes from 0 to 200,000 units. Although there are a finite number of states of nature, no units sold, one unit sold, and so on, we recognize that attempting to deal with this large number of possible states of nature is extremely impractical. The solution procedure that is used in such circumstances is to treat the state of nature as a continuous random variable. For example, perhaps a reasonable approximation of the state of nature (that is, sales volume) is that sales are normally distributed with a mean of 100,000 units and a standard deviation of 25,000 units. Although decision theory techniques have been developed to handle such situations, we shall not attempt to present these procedures in this chapter.

Another area of decision theory is concerned with alternative measures of the payoffs in a decision theory situation. In our PSI example we used profit in dollars as the measure of the payoff. Then the criterion of best expected *monetary* value was used to select the best decision. While decision theory applications are often based on expected monetary value, perhaps there are other measures of payoff that should be used.

For example, let us consider a situation in which we have two alternative investments. Investment A yields a fixed profit of $50,000; investment B yields a 50% chance of making $100,002, but also a 50% chance of making nothing. Thus the expected value for B is

$$E(B) = 0.5(100,002) + 0.5(0)$$
$$= \$50,001.$$

Using the expected monetary value criterion as the measure of the payoff, we would select decision alternative B. However, many decision makers, if not most, would select alternative A; that is, some decision makers prefer the no-risk $50,000 profit over the 50–50 chance of a $100,002 profit. In decision theory terminology, if alternative A is preferred, we say that alternative A has a higher *utility,* where utility is a measure of the decision maker's preference considering monetary value as well as the risk involved. Ideally we would like to measure payoffs in terms of the decision maker's utility and select optimal decision strategies based on expected utility rather than expected monetary value. However, attempting to assess realistic utility functions for the decision maker can be very difficult, and we shall not attempt to present utility theory in this text.

Summary

In this chapter we have introduced the decision theory or decision analysis approach to decision making. We have discussed in detail the decision theory procedures designed to solve problems with a limited number of decision alternatives and a finite list of possible states of nature. The goal of the decision theory approach was to identify the best decision alternative given an uncertain or risk-filled pattern of future events (that is, states of nature).

After defining decision making under certainty and uncertainty, we discussed the decision criteria of maximin, maximax, and minimax regret for solving problems of decision making under uncertainty without using probabilities. We then discussed the use of expected value and expected opportunity loss as criteria for solving problems of decision making under uncertainty using probabilities. We also showed how additional information about the states of nature can be used to revise or update the probability estimates and develop an optimal decision strategy for the problem. The notions of expected value of sample information, expected value of perfect information, and efficiency were used to evaluate the contribution of the additional information.

Glossary

1. *States of nature*—The uncontrollable future events that can affect the outcome of a decision.

2. *Payoff*—The outcome measure such as profit, cost, etc. Each combination of a decision alternative and a state of nature has a specific payoff.

3. *Payoff table*—A tabular representation of the payoffs for a decision problem.

4.   *Decision making under certainty*—The process of choosing a decision alternative when the state of nature is known.

5.   *Decision making under uncertainty*—The process of choosing a decision alternative when the state of nature is not known.

6.   *Maximin*—A maximization decision criterion for decisions under uncertainty that seeks to maximize the minimum payoff.

7.   *Minimax*—A minimization decision criterion for decisions under uncertainty that seeks to minimize the maximum payoff.

8.   *Maximax*—A maximization decision criterion for decisions under uncertainty that seeks to maximize the maximum payoff.

9.   *Minimin*—A minimization decision criterion for decisions under uncertainty that seeks to minimize the minimum payoff.

10.   *Opportunity loss or regret*—The amount of loss (lower profit or higher cost) due to not making the best decision for each state of nature.

11.   *Minimax regret*—A maximization or minimization decision criterion for decisions under uncertainty that seeks to minimize the maximum regret.

12.   *Expected monetary value*—A decision criterion for decisions under uncertainty. The expected monetary value weights the payoff for each decision by its probability of occurrence.

13.   *Expected opportunity loss*—The expected value criterion applied to opportunity loss or regret values. Also a decision criterion for decisions under uncertainty. It yields the same optimal decision as the expected monetary value criterion.

14.   *Decision tree*—A graphical representation of the decision-making situation from decision to state-of-nature to payoff.

15.   *Nodes*—The intersection or junction points of the decision tree.

16.   *Branches*—Lines or arcs connecting nodes of the decision tree.

17.   *Expected value of perfect information (EVPI)*—The expected value of information that would tell the decision maker exactly which state of nature was going to occur (that is, perfect information). EVPI is equal to the expected opportunity loss of the best decision alternative when no additional information is available.

18.   *Indicators*—Information about the states of nature obtained by experimentation. An indicator may be the result of a sample.

19.   *Prior probabilities*—The probabilities of the states of nature prior to obtaining experimental information.

20.   *Posterior (revised) probabilites*—The probabilities of the states of nature after using Bayes theorem to adjust the prior probabilities based upon given indicator information.

21.   *Bayesian revision*—The process of adjusting prior probabilities to create the posterior probabilities based upon information obtained by experimentation.

22.   *Expected value of sample information (EVSI)*—The difference between the expected value of an optimal strategy based on new information and the "best" expected value without any new information. It is a measure of the economic value of new information.

23.   *Efficiency*—The ratio of EVSI to EVPI; perfect information is 100% efficient.

Problems

1. Suppose that a decision maker faced with four decision alternatives and four states of nature develops the following profit payoff table:

		States of Nature			
		s_1	s_2	s_3	s_4
	d_1	14	9	10	5
	d_2	11	10	8	7
Decisions	d_3	9	10	10	11
	d_4	8	10	11	13

   If the decision maker knows nothing about the chances or probability of occurrence of the four states of nature, what is the recommended decision under each of the following criteria?
   a. Maximin.
   b. Maximax.
   c. Minimax regret.
   Which decision criterion do you prefer? Explain. Is it important for the decision maker to establish the most appropriate decision criterion before analyzing the problem? Explain.

2. Assume the payoff table in Problem 1 provides *cost* rather than profit payoffs. What is the recommended decision under each of the following criteria?
   a. Minimax.
   b. Minimin.
   c. Minimax regret.

3. Suppose that the decision maker in Problem 1 obtains some information that enables the following probability estimates to be made: $P(s_1) = 0.5$, $P(s_2) = 0.2$, $P(s_3) = 0.2$, $P(s_4) = 0.1$.
   a. Use the expected monetary value criterion to determine the optimal decision.
   b. Now assume the entries in the payoff table are costs and use the expected monetary value criterion to determine the minimum cost solution.
   c. Show that the expected opportunity loss criterion leads to the same decisions recommended by the expected monetary value criterion in parts a and b.

4. Hale's TV Productions is considering producing a pilot for a comedy series for a major TV network. While the network may reject the pilot and the series, it may also purchase the program for one or two years. Hale may decide to produce the pilot or transfer the rights for the series to a competitor for $100,000. Hale's profits are summarized in the following payoff table:

		States of Nature			
		Reject	1 Year	2 Years	
Produce pilot	d_1	−100	50	150	Profit in
Sell to competitor	d_2	100	100	100	$ × 10³

   If the probability estimates for the states of nature are $P(\text{reject}) = 0.2$, $P(1 \text{ year}) = 0.3$, $P(2 \text{ year}) = 0.5$, what should the company do? What is the maximum Hale should be willing to pay for inside information on what the network will do?

5. McHuffter Condominiums, Inc., of Pensacola, Florida, has recently purchased land near the Gulf of Mexico and is attempting to determine the size of the condominium development it should build. Three sizes of developments are being considered: small (d_1), medium (d_2), and large (d_3). At the same time an uncertain economy makes it difficult to ascertain the demand for the new condominiums. McHuffter's management realizes that a large development followed by a low demand could be very costly to the company. However, if McHuffter makes a conservative small development decision and then finds a high demand, the firm's profits will be lower than they might have been. With the three levels of demand—low, medium, and high—McHuffter's management has prepared the following payoff table:

		Demand		
		Low	Medium	High
	Small	400	400	400
Decision	Medium	100	600	600
	Large	−300	300	900

Profit in $ × 10^3

   a. If nothing is known about the demand probabilities, show the decision recommendations under the maximin, maximax, and minimax regret criteria.
   b. If $P(\text{low}) = 0.20$, $P(\text{medium}) = 0.35$, and $P(\text{high}) = 0.45$, what is the decision recommended under the expected monetary value criterion?
   c. What is the expected value of perfect information?

6. Construct a decision tree for the McHuffter Condominiums problem (Problem 5). What is the expected value at each state-of-nature node? What is the optimal decision?

7. Martin's Service Station is considering investing in a heavy-duty snowplow this fall. Martin has analyzed the situation carefully and feels this would be a very profitable investment if the snowfall is heavy. A small profit could still be made if the snowfall is moderate, but Martin would lose money if snowfall is light. Specifically, Martin forecasts a profit of $7000 if snowfall is heavy and $2000 if it is moderate, and a $9000 loss if it is light. Based on the weather bureau's long-range forecast Martin estimates $P(\text{heavy snowfall}) = 0.4$, $P(\text{moderate snowfall}) = 0.3$, and $P(\text{light snowfall}) = 0.3$.
   a. Prepare a decision tree for Martin's problem.
   b. Using the expected monetary value criterion, would you recommend that Martin invest in the snowplow?

8. Refer again to the investment problem faced by Martin's Service Station (Problem 7). Martin can purchase a blade to attach to his service truck that can also be used to plow driveways and parking lots. Since this truck must also be available to start cars, etc., Martin will not be able to generate as much revenue plowing snow if he elects this alternative. But he will keep his loss smaller if there is light snowfall. Under this alternative Martin forecasts a profit of $3500 if snowfall is heavy and $1000 if it is moderate, and a $1500 loss if snowfall is light.
   a. Prepare a new decision tree showing all three alternatives.
   b. Using the expected monetary value criterion, what is the optimal decision?
   c. Develop a table showing the opportunity loss for each decision-state of nature combination. Which decision minimizes expected opportunity loss?
   d. What is the expected value of perfect information?

9. The Gorman Manufacturing Company must decide whether it should purchase a component part from a supplier or manufacture the component at its Milan, Michigan, plant. If demand is high, it would be to Gorman's advantage to manufacture the component. However, if demand is low, Gorman's unit manufacturing cost will be high due to under-utilization of equipment. The projected profit in thousands of dollars for Gorman's make or buy decision is shown below:

	Demand		
	Low	Medium	High
Manufacture component	−20	40	100
Purchase component	10	45	70

The states of nature have the following probabilities: $P(\text{low demand}) = 0.35$, $P(\text{medium demand}) = 0.35$, and $P(\text{high demand}) = 0.30$.

a. Use a decision tree to recommend a decision.

b. Use EVPI to determine whether Gorman should attempt to obtain a better estimate of demand.

10. In order to save on gasoline expenses, Rona and Jerry agreed to form a car pool for traveling to and from work. After limiting the travel routes to two alternatives, Rona and Jerry could not agree on the best way to travel to work. Jerry preferred the expressway, since it was usually the fastest; however, Rona pointed out that traffic jams on the expressway sometimes led to long delays. Rona preferred the somewhat longer, but more consistent, Queen City Avenue. While Jerry still preferred the expressway, he agreed with Rona that they should take Queen City Avenue if the expressway had a traffic jam. Unfortunately, they did not know the state of the expressway ahead of time. The following payoff table provides the one-way time estimates for traveling to or from work:

		States of Nature	
		Expressway Open s_1	Expressway Jammed s_2
Expressway	d_1	25	45
Queen City Avenue	d_2	30	30

(Travel time in minutes

After driving to work on the expressway for 1 month (20 days), they found the expressway jammed three times. Assuming that these days are representative of future days, should they continue to use the expressway for traveling to work? Explain. Would it make sense not to adopt the expected value criterion for this particular problem? Explain.

11. In Problem 10, suppose that Rona and Jerry wished to determine the best way to return home in the evenings. In 20 days of traveling home on the expressway they found the expressway jammed six times. Using the travel time table shown in Problem 10, what route would you recommend they take on their way home in the evening? If they had perfect information about the traffic condition of the expressway, what would be their savings in terms of expected travel time?

12. A firm produces a perishable food product at a cost of $10 per case. The product sells for $15 per case. For planning purposes the company is considering possible demands of 100, 200, or 300 cases. If the demand is less than production, the excess production is lost. If demand is more than production, the firm, in an attempt to maintain a good service image, will satisfy the excess demand with a special production run at a cost of $18 per case. The product, however, always sells at $15 per case.

   a. Set up the payoff table for this problem.

   b. If $P(100) = 0.2$, $P(200) = 0.2$, and $P(300) = 0.6$, use the expected opportunity loss criterion to determine the solution.

   c. What is the EVPI?

13. The Kremer Chemical Company has a contract with one of its customers to supply a unique liquid chemical product that will be used by the customer in the manufacturing of a lubricant for airplane engines. Because of the chemical process used by the Kremer Company, batch sizes for the liquid chemical product must be 1000 pounds. The customer has agreed to adjust manufacturing to the full batch quantities and will order either 1, 2, or 3 batches every six months. Since an aging process of two months exists for the product, Kremer will have to make its production (how much to make) decision before its customer places an order. Thus Kremer can list the product demand alternatives of 1000, 2000, or 3000 pounds, but the exact demand is unknown.

   Kremer's manufacturing costs are $15 per pound, and the product sells at the fixed contract price of $20 per pound. If the customer orders more than Kremer has produced, Kremer has agreed to absorb the added cost of filling the order by purchasing a higher quality substitute product from another chemical firm. The substitute product, including transportation expenses, will cost Kremer $24 per pound. Since the product cannot be stored more than four months without spoilage, Kremer cannot inventory excess production until the customer's next six-month order. Therefore if the customer's current order is less than Kremer has produced, the excess production will be reprocessed and is valued at $5 per pound.

   The inventory decision in this problem is how much should Kremer produce given the above costs and the possible demands of 1000, 2000, or 3000 pounds? Based on historical data and an analysis of the customer's future demands Kremer has assessed the following probability distribution for demand.

Demand	Probability
1000	0.3
2000	0.5
3000	0.2
Total	1.0

   a. Develop a payoff table for the Kremer problem.

   b. How many batches should Kremer produce every six months?

   c. How much of a discount should Kremer be willing to allow the customer for specifying in advance exactly how many batches will be purchased?

14. A quality control procedure involves 100% inspection of parts received from a supplier. Historical records show the following defective rates have been observed.

Defective	Probability
0	0.15
1	0.25
2	0.40
3	0.20

The cost for the quality control 100% inspection is $250 for each shipment of 500 parts. If the shipment is not 100% inspected, defective parts will cause rework problems later in the production process. The rework cost is $25 for each defective part.

a. Complete the following payoff table, where the entries represent the total cost of inspection and reworking:

	Defective			
	0%	1%	2%	3%
100% Inspection	$250	$250	$250	$250
No Inspection				

b. The plant manager is considering eliminating the inspection process in order to save the $250 inspection cost per shipment. Do you support this action? Use EMV to justify your answer.

c. Show the decision tree for this problem.

15. Milford Trucking, located in Chicago, has requests to haul two shipments, one to St. Louis and one to Detroit. Because of a scheduling problem, Milford will only be able to select one of these assignments. The St. Louis customer has guaranteed a return shipment, but the Detroit customer has not. Thus if Milford accepts the Detroit shipment and cannot find a Detroit-to-Chicago return shipment, the truck will return to Chicago empty. The payoff table showing profit is as follows:

		Return Shipment From Detroit s_1	No Return Shipment From Detroit s_2
St. Louis	d_1	2000	2000
Detroit	d_2	2500	1000

a. If the probability of a Detroit return shipment is 0.4, what should Milford do?

b. What is the expected value of information that would tell Milford whether or not Detroit had a return shipment?

16. Suppose you are given a decision situation with three possible states of nature: s_1, s_2, and s_3. The prior probabilities are $P(s_1) = 0.2$, $P(s_2) = 0.5$, and $P(s_3) = 0.3$. Indicator information I is obtained and it is known that $P(I|s_1) = 0.1$, $P(I|s_2) = 0.05$, and $P(I|s_3) = 0.2$. Compute the revised or posterior probabilities: $P(s_1|I)$, $P(s_2|I)$, and $P(s_3|I)$.

17. The payoff table for a decision problem with two states of nature and three decision alternatives is presented below:

	s_1	s_2
d_1	15	10
d_2	10	12
d_3	8	20

The prior probabilities for s_1 and s_2 are $P(s_1) = 0.8$ and $P(s_2) = 0.2$.
a. Using only the prior probabilities and the expected monetary value criterion, find the optimal decision.
b. Find the EVPI.
c. Suppose some indicator information I is obtained with $P(I|s_1) = 0.2$ and $P(I|s_2) = 0.75$. Find the posterior probabilities $P(s_1|I)$ and $P(s_2|I)$. Recommend a decision alternative based on these probabilities.

18. Consider the following decision tree representation of a decision theory problem with two indicators, two decision alternatives, and two states of nature:

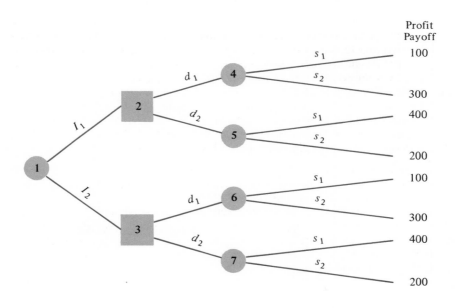

Assume the following probability information is given:

$$P(s_1) = 0.4, \qquad P(I_1|s_1) = 0.8, \qquad P(I_2|s_1) = 0.2,$$
$$P(s_2) = 0.6, \qquad P(I_1|s_2) = 0.4, \qquad P(I_2|s_2) = 0.6.$$

a. What are the values for $P(I_1)$ and $P(I_2)$?
b. What are the values of $P(s_1|I_1)$, $P(s_2|I_1)$, $P(s_1|I_2)$, and $P(s_2|I_2)$?
c. Use the decision tree approach and determine the optimal decision strategy. What is the expected value of your solution?

19. The payoff table for Problem 18 is as follows:

	s_1	s_2
d_1	100	300
d_2	400	200

   a. What is your decision without the indicator information?
   b. What is the expected value of the indicator or sample information EVSI?
   c. What is the expected value of perfect information EVPI?
   d. What is the efficiency of the indicator information?

20. The payoff table for Hale's TV Productions (Problem 4) is as follows:

		States of Nature		
		s_1	s_2	s_3
Produce pilot	d_1	-100	50	150
Sell to competitor	d_2	100	100	100
Probability of states of nature		0.2	0.3	0.5

For a consulting fee of $2500 an agency will review the plans for the comedy series and indicate the overall chances of a favorable network reaction to the series. If the special agency review results in a favorable (I_1) or an unfavorable (I_2) evaluation, what should Hale's decision stategy be? Assume Hale believes the following conditional probabilities are realistic appraisals of the agency's evaluation accuracy:

$$P(I_1|s_1) = 0.3, \qquad P(I_2|s_1) = 0.7,$$
$$P(I_1|s_2) = 0.6, \qquad P(I_2|s_2) = 0.4,$$
$$P(I_1|s_3) = 0.9, \qquad P(I_2|s_3) = 0.1.$$

   a. Show the decision tree for this problem.
   b. What is the recommended decision strategy and the expected value, assuming the agency information is obtained?
   c. What is the EVSI? Is the $2500 consulting fee worth the information? What is the maximum Hale should be willing to pay for the consulting information?

21. McHuffter Condominiums (Problem 5) is conducting a survey which will help evaluate the demand for the new condominium development. McHuffter's payoff table (profit) is as follows:

			States of Nature		
			Low	Medium	High
			s_1	s_2	s_3
	Small	d_1	400	400	400
Decision	Medium	d_2	100	600	600
	Large	d_3	-300	300	900
Probability of states of nature			0.20	0.35	0.45

The survey will result in three indicators of demand [weak (I_1), average (I_2), or strong (I_3)], where the conditional probabilities are as follows:

	$P(I_k\|s_k)$		
	I_1	I_2	I_3
s_1	0.6	0.3	0.1
s_2	0.4	0.4	0.2
s_3	0.1	0.4	0.5

a. What is McHuffter's optimal strategy?
b. What is the value of the survey information?
c. What are the EVPI and the efficiency of the survey information?

22. The payoff table for Martin's Service Station (Problems 7 and 8) is as follows:

		Snowfall		
		Heavy	Moderate	Light
		s_1	s_2	s_3
Purchase snowplow	d_1	7000	2000	−9000
Do not invest	d_2	0	0	0
Purchase snowplow with blade	d_3	3500	1000	−1500
Probabilities of states of nature		0.4	0.3	0.3

Suppose Martin decides to wait to check the September temperature pattern before making a final decision. Estimates of the probabilities associated with an unseasonably cold September (I) are as follows: $P(I\,|\,s_1) = 0.30$; $P(I\,|\,s_2) = 0.20$; $P(I\,|\,s_3) = 0.05$. If Martin observes an unseasonably cold September, what is the recommended decision? If Martin does not observe an unseasonably cold September, what is the recommended decision?

23. A food processor considers daily production runs of 100, 200, or 300 units. Possible demands for the product are 100, 200, or 300 cases. The payoff table is as follows:

			Demand (cases)		
			100	200	300
			s_1	s_2	s_3
	d_1	100	500	200	−100
Production	d_2	200	−400	800	700
	d_3	300	−1000	−200	1600

a. If $P(s_1) = 0.20$, $P(s_2) = 0.20$, and $P(s_3) = 0.60$, what is your recommended production quantity?
b. On some days the firm receives phone calls for advance orders and on some days it does not. Let I_1 = advance orders are received and I_2 = no advance

orders are received. If $P(I_2|s_1) = 0.80$, $P(I_2|s_2) = 0.40$, and $P(I_2|s_3) = 0.10$, what is your recommended production quantity for days the company does not receive any advance orders?

24. The Gorman Manufacturing Company (Problem 9) has the following payoff table for a make-or-buy decision:

		Demand		
		Low	Medium	High
		s_1	s_2	s_3
Manufacture component	d_1	-20	40	100
Purchase component	d_2	10	45	70
Probabilities		0.35	0.35	0.30

A test market study of the potential demand for the product is expected to report either a favorable (I_1) or unfavorable (I_2) condition. The relevant conditional probabilities are as follows:

$$P(I_1|s_1) = 0.10 \quad P(I_2|s_1) = 0.90,$$
$$P(I_1|s_2) = 0.40 \quad P(I_2|s_2) = 0.60,$$
$$P(I_1|s_3) = 0.60 \quad P(I_2|s_3) = 0.40.$$

a. What is the probability the market research report will be favorable?
b. What is Gorman's optimal decision strategy?
c. What is the expected value of the market research information?
d. What is the efficiency of the information?

25. The traveling time to work for Rona and Jerry has the following time payoff table (Problem 10):

		States of Nature for Expressway	
		Open	Jammed
		s_1	s_2
Expressway	d_1	25	45
Queen City Avenue	d_2	30	30
Probability of states of nature		0.85	0.15

After a period of time Rona and Jerry noted that the weather seemed to affect the traffic conditions on the expressway. They identified three weather conditions (indicators) with the following conditional probabilities:

I_1 = clear,
I_2 = overcast,
I_3 = rain,
$P(I_1|s_1) = 0.8$, $\quad P(I_2|s_1) = 0.2$, $\quad P(I_3|s_1) = 0$,
$P(I_1|s_2) = 0.1$, $\quad P(I_2|s_2) = 0.3$, $\quad P(I_3|s_2) = 0.6$.

a. Show the decision tree for the problem of traveling to work.
b. What is the optimal decision strategy and the expected travel time?
c. What is the efficiency of the weather information?

26. The research and development manager for Beck Company is trying to decide whether or not to fund a project to develop a new lubricant. It is assumed the project will be a major technical success, a minor technical success, or a failure. The company has estimated that the value of a major technical success is $150,000, since the lubricant can be used in a number of products the company is making. If the project is a minor technical success, its value is $10,000, since Beck feels the knowledge gained will benefit some other ongoing projects. If the project is a failure, it will cost the company $100,000.

Based on the opinion of the scientists involved and the manager's own subjective assessment, the assigned prior probabilities are as follows:

$$P(\text{major success}) = 0.15,$$
$$P(\text{minor success}) = 0.45,$$
$$P(\text{failure}) \qquad\ = 0.40.$$

a. Using the expected monetary value criterion, should the project be funded?
b. Suppose that a group of expert scientists from a research institute could be hired as consultants to study the project and make a recommendation. If this study will cost $30,000, should the Beck Company consider hiring the consultants?

27. Consider again the problem faced by the R&D manager of Beck Company (Problem 26). Suppose an experiment can be conducted to shed some light on the technical feasibility of the project. There are three possible outcomes for the experiment:

I_1 = prototype lubricant works well at all temperatures,

I_2 = prototype lubricant works well only at temperatures above 10°F,

I_3 = prototype lubricant does not work well at any temperature.

Suppose that we can determine the following conditional probabilities:

$$P(I_1 | \text{major success}) = 0.70,$$
$$P(I_1 | \text{minor success}) = 0.10,$$
$$P(I_1 | \text{failure}) \qquad\ = 0.10,$$

$$P(I_2 | \text{major success}) = 0.25,$$
$$P(I_2 | \text{minor success}) = 0.70,$$
$$P(I_2 | \text{failure}) \qquad\ = 0.30,$$

$$P(I_3 | \text{major success}) = 0.05,$$
$$P(I_3 | \text{minor success}) = 0.20,$$
$$P(I_3 | \text{failure}) \qquad\ = 0.60.$$

a. Assuming the experiment is conducted and the prototype lubricant works well at all temperatures, should the project be funded?
b. Assuming the experiment is conducted and the prototype lubricant works well only at temperatures above 10°F, should the project be funded?
c. Develop a decision strategy that Beck's R&D manager can use to recommend a funding decision based on the outcome of the experiment.
d. Find the EVSI for the experiment. How efficient is the information in the experiment?

28. The payoff table for the Kremer Chemical Company (Problem 13) is as follows:

		Demand		
Production		1,000	2,000	3,000
Quantity		s_1	s_2	s_3
1000	d_1	5,000	1,000	$-3,000$
2000	d_2	$-5,000$	10,000	6,000
3000	d_3	$-15,000$	0	15,000
Probabilities		0.30	0.50	0.20

Kremer has identified a pattern in the demand for the product based on the customer's previous order quantity. Let

I_1 = customer's last order was 1000 pounds,

I_2 = customer's last order was 2000 pounds,

I_3 = customer's last order was 3000 pounds.

The conditional probabilities are as follows:

$P(I_1|s_1) = 0.10,$ $P(I_2|s_1) = 0.30,$ $P(I_3|s_1) = 0.60,$

$P(I_1|s_2) = 0.30,$ $P(I_2|s_2) = 0.30,$ $P(I_3|s_2) = 0.40,$

$P(I_1|s_3) = 0.80,$ $P(I_2|s_3) = 0.20,$ $P(I_3|s_3) = 0.00.$

a. Develop an optimal decision strategy for Kremer.
b. What is the EVSI?
c. What is the efficiency of the information for the most recent order?

29. Milford Trucking Co. (Problem 15) has the following payoff table:

		Return Shipment from Detroit	No Return Shipment from Detroit
		s_1	s_2
St. Louis	d_1	2000	2000
Detroit	d_2	2500	1000
Probabilities		0.40	0.60

a. Milford can phone a Detroit truck dispatch center and determine if the general Detroit shipping activity is busy (I_1) or slow (I_2). If the report is busy, the chances of obtaining a return shipment will increase. Suppose the following conditional probabilities are given:

$P(I_1|s_1) = 0.6,$ $P(I_2|s_1) = 0.4,$

$P(I_1|s_2) = 0.3,$ $P(I_2|s_2) = 0.7.$

What should Milford do?
b. If the Detroit report is busy (I_1), what is the probability that Milford obtains a return shipment if it makes the trip to Detroit?
c. What is the efficiency of the phone information?

30. The quality control inspection process (Problem 14) has the following payoff table:

		Percent Defective			
		0%	1%	2%	3%
		s_1	s_2	s_3	s_4
100% Inspection	d_1	250	250	250	250
No inspection	d_2	0	125	250	375
Probabilities		0.15	0.25	0.40	0.20

Suppose a sample of five parts is selected from the shipment and one defect is found.

a. Let I = one defect in a sample of 5. Use the binomial probability distribution to compute $P(I|s_1)$, $P(I|s_2)$, $P(I|s_3)$, and $P(I|s_4)$, where the state-of-nature identifies the value for p.

b. If I occurs, what are the revised probabilities for the states of nature?

c. Should the entire shipment be 100% inspected whenever one defect is found in a sample of size 5?

d. What is the cost savings associated with the sample information?

Chapter 12

Inventory Models With Deterministic Demand

Expenses associated with financing and maintaining inventories are a substantial part of the cost of doing business for most companies. In large companies, especially those with many or expensive products, the costs associated with raw material, in-process, and finished goods inventories can run into the millions of dollars. To gain an appreciation of how these costs arise and what managers can do to control them, let us consider the situation faced by the R & B Beverage Company. R & B Beverage is a distributor of beer, wine, and soft-drink products in central Ohio. From a main warehouse located in Columbus, R & B supplies nearly 1000 retail stores with beverage products.

R & B's beer inventory, which constitutes about 40% of the company's total inventory, currently consists of approximately 50,000 cases. Since the average cost per case is roughly $5.00, R & B estimates the value of its beer inventory to be $250,000.

There are a number of costs associated with maintaining or carrying a given level of inventory. Taken together, these costs are usually referred to as the *inventory holding costs*. First, there is the cost of financing. If money is borrowed to maintain the inventory investments, an interest charge is incurred. If the firm's own money is used, there is an opportunity cost associated with not being able to use the money for other investments. In either case, a financing charge exists in the form of an interest cost for the capital tied up in inventory. The *cost of capital* is usually expressed as a percentage of the amount invested. Since R & B estimates its cost of capital at an annual rate of 18%, this portion of the inventory cost is $0.18 ($250,000) = $45,000 per year.

There are a number of other costs such as insurance, taxes, breakage, pilferage, and warehouse overhead which also depend for the most part on the value of the inventory. R & B estimates these other costs at an annual rate of approximately 7% of the value of its inventory. Thus total inventory holding cost for the R & B beer inventory is 25% of its value, or 0.25 ($250,000) = $62,500 per year. When we consider that the beer constitutes only about 40% of R & B's total inventory, we can begin to see that inventory holding cost is a major expense for the R & B Beverage Company.

Inventory holding cost is a concern to every manager who finds some form of inventory under his or her control. Certainly, all managers are aware that inventories, which can be defined as any idle goods or materials that are waiting to be used, are necessary and important for the efficiency of business operations. Thus managers are faced with the dual problems of maintaining sufficient inventories to meet demand for goods and at the same time incurring the lowest possible inventory cost. Basically, managers attempt to solve these problems by making the best possible decisions with respect to the following:

1. How much should be ordered when the inventory for a given item is replenished?
2. When should the inventory for a given item be replenished?

The purpose of this chapter is to introduce you to how quantitative models can assist in making the above decisions. While there are many basic similarities in all inventory systems, each system also has unique operating characteristics that prevent us from applying one or two general inventory decision models to all situations. In this chapter you will be introduced to the fundamental inventory decision models and some of the more common and most useful variations.

12.1   Economic Order Quantity (EOQ) Model

Undoubtedly the best known and most fundamental inventory decision model is the *economic order quantity (EOQ) model*. This model is potentially applicable when the entire quantity ordered arrives in the inventory at one point in time and when the demand for the item has a constant, or nearly constant, rate. The *constant demand rate* condition simply means that the same number of units are taken from inventory each period of time, such as 5 units every day, 25 units every week, 100 units every four-week period, and so on.

Let us see how the EOQ model can be applied by the R & B Beverage Company. R & B's warehouse manager has conducted a preliminary analysis of overall inventory costs and has decided to do a detailed study of one product for the purpose of establishing the *how-much*-to-order and *when*-to-order decision rules that will result in the lowest possible inventory cost for the product. The manager has selected R & B's number one selling beer, Bub, for this study.

In a meeting with the R & B purchaser in charge of Bub the manager found that since Bub was the company's number one selling beer, the purchaser tended to order large quantities ahead of time and always maintain a sizable inventory so that the company would never experience a shortage. Actually no attention was being given to the costs associated with placing purchase orders or holding the inventory. Records showed that over the past year the purchaser had placed 13 orders of 8000 cases each (ordering about every four weeks) with a purchase price of $5.00 per case.

The historical demand data for Bub during the past 10 weeks are as follows:

Week	Demand (cases)
1	2000
2	2025
3	1950
4	2000
5	2100
6	2050
7	2000
8	1975
9	1900
10	2000
Total cases	20,000
Average cases per week	2000

Strictly speaking, the above weekly demand figures do not show a constant demand rate. However, given the relatively low variability exhibited by the weekly demands, inventory planning with a constant demand rate of 2000 cases per week appears acceptable.

In practice you will find that the real inventory situation seldom, if ever, satisfies the assumptions of the model exactly. Thus in any particular application it is the job of the manager and the management scientist to determine whether the model assumptions are close enough to reality for the model to be useful. In this situation, since demand varies from a low of 1900 cases to a high of 2100 cases, it appears that the assumption of constant demand of 2000 cases per week is a reasonable approximation.

The how-much-to-order decision involves selecting an order quantity that draws a compromise between (1) keeping small inventories and ordering frequently and (2) keeping large inventories and ordering infrequently. The first alternative would probably result in undesirably high ordering costs, while the second alternative would probably result in undesirably high inventory holding costs. In order to find an optimal compromise between these conflicting alternatives, let us develop a mathematical model that will show the total cost[1] as the sum of the inventory holding cost and the ordering cost.

Inventory holding or *inventory carrying costs* are costs that are dependent upon the size of the inventory; that is, larger inventories require larger inventory holding costs. Since R & B estimated its annual inventory holding costs to be 25% of the value of its inventory and since the cost of one case of Bub beer is $5.00, 0.25 ($5.00) = $1.25 is the cost of holding or carrying one case of Bub beer in inventory for one year. Note that defining the inventory holding cost as a percentage of value of the product is convenient because it is easily transferable to other products. For example, a case of Carle's Red Ribbon Beer ($4.20/case) would have an annual inventory holding cost of 0.25 ($4.20) = $1.05 per case.

The next step in our inventory analysis is to determine the cost of placing an order. For R & B the largest portion of this cost involves the salaries of the purchasers. An analysis of the purchasing process showed that a purchaser spends approximately 45 minutes preparing and processing an order for Bub beer. This amount of time is required regardless of the number of cases ordered. With a wage rate and fringe benefit cost for purchasers of $16.00 per hour, the labor portion of the ordering cost is $12.00. Making allowances for paper, postage, telephone, and transportation costs at $8.00 per order, the manager estimated the cost of ordering to be $20.00 per order. That is, R & B is paying $20.00 per order regardless of the quantity requested in the order.

The inventory holding costs, the order costs, and the demand information are the three data items that must be prepared prior to the use of any

---

[1]While management scientists typically refer to "total cost" models for inventory systems, often these models describe only the total *variable* or total *relevant* costs for the decision being considered. Costs which are not affected by the how-much-to-order decision are considered fixed or constant and are not included in the model.

EOQ model. Since these data have now been developed for our R & B example, let us see how they are used to develop a total cost model. We shall begin by defining the symbol Q to be the size of the order quantity. Thus the *how-much*-to-order decision involves trying to find that value of Q which will minimize the sum of inventory holding and ordering costs.

The inventory level for Bub will have a maximum value of Q units when the order of size Q is received from the manufacturer. R & B will then supply its customers from inventory until the inventory is depleted, at which time another shipment of Q units will be received. With the assumption of a constant demand rate of 2000 units per week or, assuming R & B is open five days each week, 400 units per day, the sketch of the inventory level for Bub beer is shown in Figure 12.1.

Note that the sketch indicates that the average inventory level for the period in question is $\frac{1}{2} Q$. This should appear reasonable to you since the maximum inventory level is Q, the minimum is 0, and the inventory level declines at a constant rate over the period.

Figure 12.1 shows the inventory pattern during one order cycle period of length T. As time goes on, this pattern will repeat. The complete inventory pattern is shown in Figure 12.2. If the average inventory during each cycle is $\frac{1}{2} Q$, the average inventory level over any number of cycles is also $\frac{1}{2} Q$. Thus, as long as the time period involved contains an integral number of order cycles, the average inventory for the period will be $\frac{1}{2} Q$.

The inventory holding cost can be calculated using the average inventory level. That is, we can calculate the inventory holding cost by multiplying the average inventory by the cost of carrying one unit in inventory for the stated period. The period of time selected for the model is up to you; it could be one week, one month, one year, or more. However, since the inventory carrying costs for many industries and businesses are often expressed as an

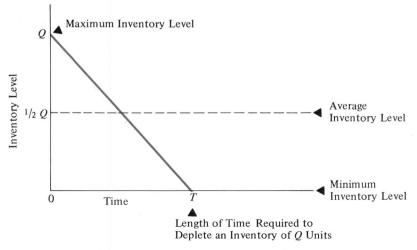

FIGURE 12.1   Sketch of the Inventory Level for Bub Beer

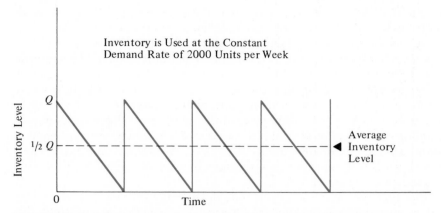

FIGURE 12.2   Inventory Pattern for the EOQ Inventory Decision Model

annual percentage or rate, you will probably find most inventory models developed on an *annual cost* basis.

Let

I = annual inventory carrying charge (25% for R & B),

C = unit cost of the inventory item ($5.00 for Bub beer).

The cost of storing or holding one unit in inventory for the year, denoted by C_h, is given by $C_h = IC$, which for Bub is 0.25($5.00) = $1.25. Thus the general equation for annual inventory holding cost is as follows:

$$\begin{pmatrix} \text{Annual inventory} \\ \text{holding cost} \end{pmatrix} = \begin{pmatrix} \text{average} \\ \text{inventory} \end{pmatrix} \begin{pmatrix} \text{annual holding} \\ \text{cost} \\ \text{per unit} \end{pmatrix}$$

$$= \tfrac{1}{2}\, QC_h. \tag{12.1}$$

To complete our total cost model, we must now include the ordering cost. Our goal is to express this cost in terms of the order quantity Q. Since the inventory holding cost was expressed as an annual cost, we need to express ordering costs on an annual basis. The first question is, how many orders will be placed during the year? Let D denote the annual demand for the product [for R & B, D = (52 weeks)(2000 per week) = 104,000]. We know that by ordering Q units each time we order, we will have to place D/Q orders. For example, if Q = 52,000, we would need to order only twice a year to satisfy demand for Bub beer. If C_0 is the cost of placing one order ($20.00 for R & B), the general equation for the annual ordering cost is as follows:

$$\begin{pmatrix} \text{Annual ordering} \\ \text{cost} \end{pmatrix} = \begin{pmatrix} \text{Number of} \\ \text{orders} \\ \text{per year} \end{pmatrix} \begin{pmatrix} \text{cost} \\ \text{per} \\ \text{order} \end{pmatrix}$$

$$= \left(\frac{D}{Q}\right) C_0. \tag{12.2}$$

Thus the total annual cost—inventory holding cost plus ordering cost—can be expressed as follows:

$$TC = \tfrac{1}{2}\, QC_h + \frac{D}{Q}\, C_0. \qquad (12.3)$$

Using the Bub data, the total cost model becomes

$$TC = \tfrac{1}{2}\, Q(\$1.25) + \frac{104{,}000}{Q}(\$20) = 0.625\, Q + \frac{2{,}080{,}000}{Q}. \qquad (12.4)$$

The development of the above total cost model has gone a long way toward helping solve the inventory problem. We now are able to express the total annual cost as a function of one of the decisions, *how much* should be ordered. The development of a realistic total cost model is perhaps the most important part of applying quantitative techniques to inventory decision making. Equation (12.3) is the general total cost equation for inventory situations in which the assumptions of the economic order quantity model are valid.

The How-Much-to-Order Decision

The next step is to find the order quantity Q that does in fact minimize the total cost as stated in equation (12.4). Using a trial-and-error approach we can compute the total cost for several possible order quantities. As a starting point, let us use the current purchase policy for Bub which is $Q = 8000$. The total annual cost is

$$TC = 0.625\,(8000) + \frac{2{,}080{,}000}{8000} = \$5{,}260.$$

A trial with an order quantity of 5000 gives

$$TC = 0.625\,(5000) + \frac{2{,}080{,}000}{5000} = \$3{,}541.$$

The results of several other trial order quantities are shown in Table 12.1. As

Table 12.1 Inventory Holding and Ordering Costs for Various Order Quantities of Bub Beer

Order Quantity	Annual Inventory Holding Cost	Annual Ordering Cost	Annual Total Cost
5000	$3125	$ 416	$3541
4000	2500	520	3020
3000	1875	693	2568
2000	1250	1040	2290
1000	625	2080	2705

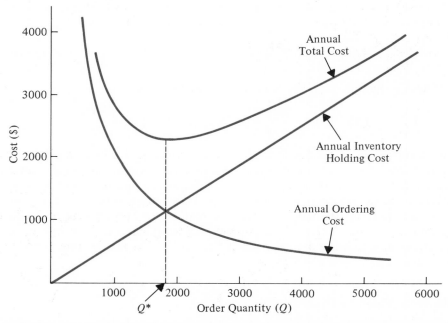

FIGURE 12.3 **Graph of Annual Inventory Holding, Ordering, and Total Cost for Bub Beer**

can be seen, the lowest cost solution is around 2000 units. Graphs of the inventory holding, ordering, and total costs are shown in Figure 12.3.

The advantage of the trial-and-error approach is that it is rather easy to do and provides the total cost for a number of possible order quantity decisions. Also, we can see that approximately 2000 units appears to be the minimum cost order quantity. The disadvantage of this approach, however, is that it does not provide the exact minimum cost order quantity.

Refer to Figure 12.3. You can see that the minimum total cost order quantity is an order size of Q^*. By using differential calculus it can be shown (see Appendix 12.1) that the value of Q^* which minimizes the total cost is given by the formula

$$Q^* = \sqrt{\frac{2DC_0}{C_h}}. \tag{12.5}$$

This formula is well known by management scientists and is referred to as the economic order quantity (EOQ) formula.

For Bub beer the minimum total cost order quantity is

$$Q^* = \sqrt{\frac{2(104,000)20}{1.25}} = \sqrt{3,328,000} \approx 1824.$$

Use of an order quantity of 1824 in equation (12.4) shows that the minimum cost inventory policy for Bub beer results in a total cost of $2280. Note that this inventory decision—that is, $Q^* = 1824$—results in a $5260 - $2280 = $2980, or 56.7% cost reduction from the current purchase policy of $Q = 8000$. Also, you might note that this value of Q^* has balanced the inventory holding and ordering costs. Check for yourself to see that these costs are equal.[2] Problem 2 at the end of the chapter will ask you to show that this is a general property of the EOQ model.

The When-to-Buy Decision

Now that we know how much to order, we want to answer the second question of *when* to order. The when-to-order decision is most often expressed in terms of a *reorder point*—the inventory level at which a new order should be placed.

The manufacturer of Bub beer guarantees a two-day delivery on any order placed by R & B. Hence, assuming a constant demand rate of 2000 cases per week or 400 cases per day, we expect (2 days) (400 cases/day) = 800 cases of Bub to be sold during the two days it takes a new order of Bub to reach the R & B warehouse. In inventory terminology, the two-day delivery period is referred to as the *lead time* for a new order, and 800 cases of demand anticipated during this period is referred to as the *lead time demand*. Thus R & B should order a new shipment of Bub beer from the manufacturer when the inventory on hand reaches a level of 800 cases. For inventory systems using the constant demand rate assumption and a fixed lead time, the reorder point is the same as the lead time demand. The general expression for the reorder point is given as follows:

$$r = dm, \qquad (12.6)$$

where

r = reorder point,

d = demand per day,

m = lead time for a new order in days.

The question of how frequently the order will be placed can now be answered. This period between orders is referred to as the *cycle time*. Previously [see equation (12.2)] we defined D/Q as the number of orders that will be placed in a year. Thus $D/Q^* = 104,000/1824 = 57$ is the number of orders R & B will place for Bub each year. If we place 57 orders over 365 days, we will order approximately every $365/57 = 6.4$ days. Thus the cycle time is computed to be 6.4 days. The general expression[3] for a cycle

---

[2]Actually, Q^* from equation (12.5) is 1824.28, but since we cannot order fractional cases of beer, a Q^* of 1824 is shown. This value of Q^* may cause a few cents deviation between the two costs. If Q^* is used at its exact value, the inventory holding and ordering costs will be exactly the same.

[3]This general expression for cycle time is based upon 365 days per year. If the firm operated 250 days per year and wanted to express cycle time in terms of working days, the cycle time would be given by $T = 250Q^*/D$.

time of T days is given by

$$T = \frac{365}{D/Q^*} = \frac{365Q^*}{D}. \qquad (12.7)$$

Sensitivity Analysis in the EOQ Model

Even though substantial time has been spent in arriving at the cost per order ($20.00) and inventory holding cost (25%) figures, we should realize that these figures are at best good estimates. Thus we may want to consider how much the order size recommendation would change if the estimated ordering and holding costs had been different. To determine this, we can calculate the recommended order quantity under several different cost conditions. These calculations are shown in Table 12.2. As you can see from the table, the value of Q^* appears relatively stable, even with some variations in the cost estimates. Based on these results it appears that the best order quantity for Bub is somewhere around 1700 to 2000 units and definitely not near the current order quantity of 8000 units. If operated properly, the total cost for the Bub inventory system should be close to $2280 per year. We also note that there is very little risk associated with implementing the calculated order quantity of $Q = 1824$. In the worst case (when the true optimal order quantity $Q^* = 1908$), there is only a $3 increase in the total annual cost; that is, $2292 − $2289 = $3.

From the above analysis we would say that this EOQ model is insensitive to small variation or errors in the cost estimates. This is property of EOQ models in general, which indicates that if we have at least reasonable estimates of ordering and inventory holding costs, we should obtain a good approximation of the true minimum cost order quantity.

The Manager's Use of the EOQ Model

The inventory model and analysis has led to a recommended order quantity of 1824 units. Is this the final decision, or should the manager's judgment enter into the establishment of the final inventory policy decisions? Although

Table 12.2   Economic Order Quantities for Several Cost Possibilities

Possible Inventory Holding Cost (Percent)	Possible Cost per Order	Optimal Order Quantity (Q^*)	Projected Total Cost	
			Using Q^*	Using $Q = 1824$
24	$19	1815	$2178	$2178
24	$21	1908	$2289	$2292
26	$19	1744	$2267	$2269
26	$21	1833	$2383	$2383

the model has provided us with a good order quantity recommendation, it may not have taken into account all aspects of the inventory situation. As a result, the decision maker should feel free to modify the final order quantity recommendation to meet the unique circumstances of his inventory situation. In this case the warehouse manager felt that it would be desirable to increase the order quantity from 1824 units to 2000 units in order to have an order quantity equal to five days' demand. By doing so, R & B can maintain a 7-day, or weekly order cycle.

The warehouse manager also realized that the EOQ model was based on the constant demand rate assumption of 2000 units per week. While this was close to the actual case, sometimes the demand might exceed this amount. If a reorder point of 800 units is used, we would be expecting an 800-unit demand during the lead time and the new order to arrive exactly when the inventory level reached zero. Such close timing would leave little room for error, and the scheduling of arrivals would be very critical if stockouts are to be avoided. To protect against shortages due to higher than expected demands or slightly delayed incoming orders, the warehouse manager recommended a 1200-unit reorder point. Thus under normal conditions R & B will order 2000 cases of Bub whenever the current inventory reaches 1200 units. During the expected two-day lead time 800 units should be demanded, and thus 400 units should be in inventory when an order arrives. The extra 400 units serves as a safety precaution against a higher than expected demand or a delayed incoming order. In general the amount by which the reorder point exceeds the expected lead time demand is referred to as *safety stock*.

The decision to adjust the order quantity and reorder point were purely management judgment decisions and were not necessarily made with a minimum cost objective in mind. However, they are examples of how judgment might interface with the inventory decision model to arrive at a sound inventory policy. The final decision of $Q = 2000$ with a 400-unit safety stock resulted in a total cost of $2790.[4] This was still a $5260 - $2790 = $2470, or 47%, savings over the current inventory policy with $Q = 8000$.

How Has the EOQ Decision Model Helped?

The EOQ model has objectively included inventory holding and ordering costs and, with the aid of some management judgment, has led to a cost-saving inventory decision. In addition, the general optimal order quantity model, equation (12.5), is potentially applicable to other R & B products. For example, Red Ribbon beer ($4.20/case), which has an ordering cost of $20.00, a constant demand rate of 1200 cases per week (62,400 cases/year), and a two-day lead time period, has a recommended

---

[4]A Q of 2000 units resulted in a total cost of $2290 (see Table 12.1). The additional safety stock inventory of 400 units increases the average inventory by 400 units, since it is on hand all year long. Thus the inventory carrying charge is increased by 1.25(400) = $500, and the total cost of the revised policy is $2290 + $500 = $2790.

order quantity of

$$Q^* = \sqrt{\frac{2(62,400)(20.00)}{(0.25)(4.20)}} = 1542 \text{ cases,}$$

a cycle time of $T = (1542/62,400)\ 365 = 9$ days, and a reorder point of $r = (240)\ (2) = 480$ cases.

We will now investigate additional inventory decision models that are designed to make *how-much-* and *when-*to-order decisions for other types of inventory systems.

12.2 Economic Production Lot Size Model

The following inventory decision model is similar to the first model in that we are attempting to determine *how much* we should order or produce and *when* the order should be placed. Again we will make the assumption of a constant demand rate. However, instead of the goods arriving at the warehouse in a shipment of size Q^* as assumed in the EOQ model, we will assume that units are supplied to inventory at a constant rate over several days or several weeks. The *constant supply rate* assumption implies that the same number of units is supplied to inventory each period of time (for example, 10 units every day, 50 units every week, and so on). This model is designed for production situations in which once an order is placed, production begins and a constant number of units is added to inventory each day until the production run has been completed.

If we have a production system that produces 50 units per day and we decide to schedule 10 days of production each time we want additional units, we have a $50(10) = 500$-unit production run size. Alternative terminology may refer to the 500 units as the *production lot size* or *lot quantity*.

If, in general we let Q indicate the production lot quantity, our approach to the inventory decisions will be similar to the EOQ model; that is, we will attempt to build an inventory holding and ordering cost model that expresses the total annual cost as a function of the production quantity. Then we will attempt to find the quantity that minimizes the total cost.

One other condition that should be mentioned at this time is that the model will only apply to production situations in which the production rate is greater than the demand rate. Stated more simply, the production system must be able to satisfy the demand. For example, if our constant demand rate is 2000 units per week, the production rate has to be at least 2000 units per week if we are going to satisfy our demand.

Since we have assumed that the production rate will exceed the demand rate, each day during a production run we will be manufacturing more units than we ship. Thus we will put the excess production in inventory, resulting in a gradual inventory buildup during the production period. When the production run is completed, the inventory will show a gradual decline until a new production run is started. The inventory pattern for this system is shown in Figure 12.4.

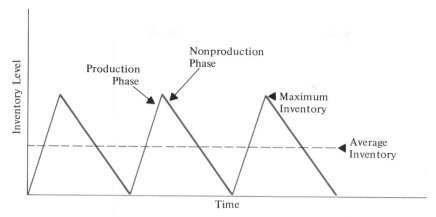

FIGURE 12.4   Inventory Pattern for the Production Lot Size Inventory Model

As in the EOQ model, we are now dealing with two costs, the inventory holding cost and the ordering cost. While the inventory holding cost is identical to our definition in the EOQ model, the interpretation of the ordering cost is slightly different. In fact, in a production situation the ordering cost may be more correctly referred to as production setup cost. This cost, which includes hours of labor, material, and lost production costs incurred while preparing the production system for operation, is a fixed cost which occurs for every production run, regardless of the production quantity.

Building the Total Cost Model

Let us begin building our model by attempting to write the inventory holding cost in terms of our production quantity Q. Again, our approach will be to develop an expression for average inventory, and then establish the holding costs associated with the average inventory level. We will use a one-year time period and an annual cost for our model.

We saw in the EOQ model that the average inventory was simply one-half the maximum inventory or $\frac{1}{2} Q$. Since Figure 12.4 shows a constant inventory buildup rate during the production run and a constant inventory depletion rate during the nonproduction period, the average inventory for the production lot size model will also be one-half of the maximum inventory level. However, in this inventory system the production quantity Q does not go into inventory at one point in time, and thus the inventory level never reaches a level of Q units.

Let us see if we can compute the maximum inventory level. First we define the following symbols:

d = daily demand rate for the product,

p = daily production rate for the product,

t = number of days for a production run.

Since we are assuming p will be larger than d, the excess production each day is $p - d$, which is the daily rate of inventory buildup. If we run production for t days and place $p - d$ units in inventory each day, the inventory level at the end of the production run will be $(p - d)t$. From Figure 12.4 we can see that the inventory level at the end of the production run is also the maximum inventory level. Thus we can write

$$\text{Maximum inventory} = (p - d)t. \tag{12.8}$$

If we know we are producing a production quantity of Q units at a daily production rate of p units, then $Q = pt$, and we can compute the length of the production run t to be

$$t = Q/p \text{ days.} \tag{12.9}$$

Thus

$$\begin{aligned}\text{Maximum inventory} &= (p - d)t = (p - d)(Q/p) \\ &= (1 - d/p)Q. \end{aligned} \tag{12.10}$$

The average inventory, which is one half of the maximum inventory, is given by

$$\text{Average inventory} = \tfrac{1}{2}(1 - d/p)Q. \tag{12.11}$$

With an annual inventory holding cost of $C_h = IC$ per unit, the general equation for annual inventory holding cost is as follows:

$$\begin{gathered} \begin{array}{c}\text{Annual inventory} \\ \text{holding cost}\end{array} = \left(\begin{array}{c}\text{average} \\ \text{inventory}\end{array} \right)\left(\begin{array}{c}\text{annual holding} \\ \text{cost} \\ \text{per unit}\end{array} \right) \\ = \tfrac{1}{2}(1 - d/p)QC_h. \end{gathered} \tag{12.12}$$

If D is the annual demand for the product and C_0 is the setup cost for a production run, then the total annual setup cost, which takes the place of the total annual ordering costs of the EOQ model, is as follows:

$$\begin{gathered}\text{Annual setup cost} = \left(\begin{array}{c}\text{number of production} \\ \text{runs per year}\end{array} \right)\left(\begin{array}{c}\text{setup cost} \\ \text{per run}\end{array} \right) \\ = \left(\frac{D}{Q} \right) C_0. \end{gathered} \tag{12.13}$$

Thus the total annual cost (TC) model is

$$\text{TC} = \tfrac{1}{2}\left(1 - \frac{d}{p} \right)QC_h + \frac{D}{Q} C_0. \tag{12.14}$$

Suppose that a plant operates 250 days per year; 115 days are idle due to weekends and holidays. Then we could write daily demand d in terms of annual demand D as follows:

$$d = D/250.$$

If we let P denote the annual production for the product if it were produced every day, then

$$P = 250p \quad \text{or} \quad p = P/250.$$

Thus[5]

$$\frac{d}{p} = \frac{D/250}{P/250} = \frac{D}{P}.$$

Therefore we could write the total annual cost as follows:

$$TC = \frac{1}{2}\left(1 - \frac{D}{P}\right)QC_h + \frac{D}{Q}C_0. \tag{12.15}$$

Equations (12.14) and (12.15) are equivalent. However, equation (12.15) may be used more frequently since an *annual* cost model tends to make the analyst think in terms of collecting *annual* demand (D) and *annual* production (P) data rather than daily rate data.

Finding the Economic Production Lot Size

Given the estimates of the inventory holding cost C_h, setup cost C_0, annual demand rate D, and annual production rate P, we can use a trial-and-error approach to compute the total annual cost for various lot sizes Q. However, we may also use the minimum cost formula for Q^* which has been developed using differential calculus (see Appendix 12.2). The equation is as follows:

$$Q^* = \sqrt{\frac{2DC_0}{(1 - D/P)C_h}}. \tag{12.16}$$

An Example Beauty Bar Soap is produced on a production line that has an annual capacity of 60,000 cases. The annual demand is estimated at 26,000 cases, with the demand rate essentially constant throughout the year. The cleaning, preparation, and setup of the production line costs approximately \$135.00. The manufacturing cost per case is \$4.50, and an annual inventory holding cost is figured at a 24% rate. Thus $C_h = IC = 0.24$ (\$4.50) = \$1.08. What is your recommended production lot size?

Using equation (12.15) we have

$$Q^* = \sqrt{\frac{2(26,000)(135)}{\left(1 - \frac{26,000}{60,000}\right)(1.08)}} = \sqrt{\frac{7,020,000}{0.612}} = 3387$$

The total annual cost using equation (12.15) and $Q^* = 3387$ is estimated to be \$2073.

---

[5]The ratio $d/p = D/P$ regardless of the number of days of operation; 250 days was used here merely as an illustration.

Other relevant data include a one-week lead time to schedule and set up a production run. Thus a one-week demand of $26,000/52 = 500$ cases is the reorder point. The cycle time between production runs, using equation (12.7), is estimated to be $T = [(365)(3387)]/26,000$, or about 47 days. Thus we should plan a production run of 3300 to 3400 units about every 47 days.

Certainly the manager will want to review the model recommendations. Adjusting the recommended $Q* = 3387$ to a slightly more practical figure and/or adding safety stock may be desirable.

12.3   An Inventory Model with Planned Shortages

In many inventory situations a shortage or stockout—a demand that cannot be supplied from inventory or production—is undesirable and should be avoided if at all possible. However, there are other cases in which it may be desirable—from an economic point of view—to plan for and allow shortages. In practice these types of situations are most commonly found where the value per unit of the inventory is very high and hence the inventory holding cost is high. An example of this type of situation is a new car dealer's inventory. It is not uncommon for a dealer not to have the specific car you want in stock. However, if you are willing to wait a few weeks, the dealer will generally order a car for you.

The specific model developed in this section allows the type of shortage known as a *backorder*. In a backorder situation an assumption is made that when a customer places an order and discovers that the supplier is out of stock, the customer does not withdraw the order. Rather, the customer waits until the next shipment arrives, and then the order is filled. Frequently the waiting period in backordering situations will be relatively short and, by promising the customer top priority and immediate delivery when the goods become available, companies can convince customers to wait for the order. In these cases the backorder assumption is valid. If for a particular product a firm finds that a shortage causes the customer to withdraw the order and a lost sale results, the backorder model would not be the appropriate inventory decision model.

Using the backorder assumption for shortages, we will now develop an extension to the EOQ model presented in Section 12.1. The EOQ model assumptions of the goods arriving in inventory all at one time and a constant demand rate for the product will be used. If we let S indicate the amount of the shortage or the number of backorders that have accumulated when a new shipment of size Q is received, then the inventory system for the backorder case has the following characteristics:

1. With S backorders existing when a new shipment of size Q arrives, the S backorders will be shipped to the appropriate customers immediately and the remaining $Q - S$ units will be placed in inventory.
2. $Q - S$ will be the maximum inventory level.

3. The inventory cycle of T days will be divided into two distinct phases; t_1 days when inventory is on hand and orders are filled as they occur and t_2 days when there is a stockout and all orders are placed on backorder.

The inventory pattern for this model, where negative inventory represents the number of backorders, is shown in Figure 12.5.

With the inventory pattern now defined, we should be able to proceed with the basic step of all inventory models; namely, the development of a total cost expression. For the inventory model with backorders we will encounter the usual inventory holding costs and ordering costs. In addition, we will incur a backordering cost in terms of labor and special delivery costs directly associated with the handling of the backorders. Another portion of the backorder cost can be expressed as a loss of goodwill with customers due to the fact that customers will have to wait for their orders. Since the *goodwill cost* depends upon how long the customer has to wait, it is customary to adopt the convention of expressing all backorder costs in terms of how much it costs to have a unit on backorder for a stated period of time. This method of costing backorders on a time basis is similar to the method we have used to compute the inventory holding cost.

Using this method for approaching backorder costs, we can compute a total annual cost of backorders once the average backorder level and the backorder cost per unit per unit time are known. As you will recall, this is the same type of information that is needed to calculate inventory holding costs.

Admittedly, the backorder cost rate (especially the goodwill cost) is difficult to determine in practice. However, noting that EOQ models are rather insensitive to the cost estimates (see Table 12.2) we should feel confident that reasonable estimates of the backorder cost will lead to a good approximation of the overall minimum cost inventory decision.

Let us begin the development of our total cost model by showing how to calculate the inventory holding costs. First we use a small hypothetical example to suggest a procedure for computing the average inventory level. If

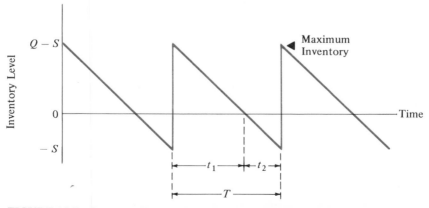

FIGURE 12.5   Inventory Pattern for an Inventory Model with Backorders

we have an average inventory of 2 units for three days and no inventory on the fourth day, what is our average inventory level over the four-day period? You should say

$$\frac{2 \text{ units} (3 \text{ days}) + 0 \text{ units} (1 \text{ day})}{4 \text{ days}} = \frac{6}{4} = 1.5 \text{ units.}$$

Refer to Figure 12.5. You can see that this is exactly what happens in the backorder model. With a maximum inventory of $Q - S$ units during the t_1 days we have inventory, an average inventory of $(Q - S)/2$ is on hand for the t_1 days. No inventory is carried for the t_2 days in which we experience backorders. Thus over the total cycle time of $T = t_1 + t_2$ days, we can compute the average inventory level as follows:

$$\frac{\text{Average inventory}}{\text{level}} = \frac{\frac{1}{2}(Q - S) t_1 + 0 t_2}{T} = \frac{\frac{1}{2}(Q - S) t_1}{T}. \quad (12.17)$$

Can we find other ways of expressing t_1 and T? Since we know that the maximum inventory is $Q - S$ and that d represents the constant daily demand, we have

$$t_1 = \frac{Q - S}{d} \text{ days.} \quad (12.18)$$

That is, the maximum inventory level of $Q - S$ units will be used up in $(Q - S)/d$ days. Since Q units are ordered and shipped each cycle, we know the length of a cycle must be

$$T = Q/d \text{ days.} \quad (12.19)$$

Using equations (12.18) and (12.19) with equation (12.17), we can write the following:

$$\frac{\text{Average}}{\text{inventory}} = \frac{\frac{1}{2}(Q - S)[(Q - S]/d]}{Q/d} = \frac{(Q - S)^2}{2Q}. \quad (12.20)$$
$$\text{level}$$

Thus the average inventory level is expressed in terms of two inventory decisions, how much we order (Q) and the maximum number of backorders we will allow (S).

The formula for the annual number of orders placed under this model is identical to that for the EOQ model. With D representing the annual demand we have

$$\text{Annual number of orders} = D/Q. \quad (12.21)$$

The next step is to develop an expression for the average backorder level. Since there is a maximum of S backorders, we can use the same logic that we used to establish average inventory to find the average number of backorders. We have an average number of backorders during the period t_2 of $\frac{1}{2}$ the maximum number of backorders or $\frac{1}{2} S$. Since we do not have any backorders during the t_1 days we have inventory, we can calculate the average backorder level in a manner similar to equation (12.17). Using this approach we have

$$\text{Average backorder level} = \frac{0t_1 + (S/2)t_2}{T} = \frac{(S/2)t_2}{T}. \quad (12.22)$$

Since we let the maximum number of backorders reach an amount S at a daily rate of d, the length of the backorder portion of the inventory cycle is

$$t_2 = S/d. \quad (12.23)$$

Using equations (12.23) and (12.19) in equation (12.22), we have

$$\text{Average backorder level} = \frac{(S/2)(S/d)}{Q/d} = \frac{S^2}{2Q}. \quad (12.24)$$

Let

$$C_b = \text{cost to maintain one unit on backorder for one year.}$$

Our total annual cost expression (TC) for the inventory model with backorders becomes

$$\text{TC} = \frac{(Q-S)^2}{2Q}C_h + \frac{D}{Q}C_0 + \frac{S^2}{2Q}C_b. \quad (12.25)$$

Given the cost estimates C_h, C_0, and C_b and the annual demand D, we can begin to determine the minimum cost values for our inventory decisions, Q and S. With two decision components a trial-and-error approach, while valid, becomes cumbersome. Using calculus, management scientists have established the following minimum cost formulas for the order quantity Q^* and the planned backorders S^*:

$$Q^* = \sqrt{\frac{2DC_0}{C_h}\left(\frac{C_h + C_b}{C_b}\right)} \quad (12.26)$$

and

$$S^* = Q^*\left(\frac{C_h}{C_h + C_b}\right). \quad (12.27)$$

An Example   Suppose the Higley Radio Components Company has a product for which the assumptions of the inventory model with backorders are valid. Information obtained by the company is as follows:

$$D = 2000 \text{ units per year,}$$
$$I = 20\% \text{ per year,}$$
$$C = \$50 \text{ per unit,}$$
$$C_h = \text{IC} = \$10 \text{ per unit per year,}$$
$$C_0 = \$25 \text{ per order.}$$

The company is considering the possibility of allowing some backorders to occur for the product. A manager, using a one-week backorder cost estimate of roughly \$0.50 to \$0.60 per unit, estimates the annual unit backorder cost at \$30 per unit per year. Using equations (12.26) and (12.27) we have

$$Q^* = \sqrt{\frac{2(2000)(25)}{10}\left(\frac{10 + 30}{30}\right)} = \sqrt{10,000\left(\frac{40}{30}\right)} = 115$$

and

$$S^* = 115\,\frac{10}{10 + 30} = 115\,\frac{10}{40} = 29.$$

If this solution is implemented, the system will operate with the following properties:

$$\text{Maximum inventory} = Q - S = 115 - 29 = 86,$$

$$\text{Cycle time} = T = (Q/D)(365) = 21 \text{ days.}$$

The total annual cost is

$$\text{Inventory holding cost} = \frac{(86)^2}{2(115)}(10) = \$322$$

$$\text{Ordering cost} \quad = \frac{2000}{115}(25) \quad = \$435$$

$$\text{Backorder cost} \quad = \frac{(29)^2}{2(115)}(30) = \underline{\$110}$$

$$\text{Total cost} \quad\quad\quad = \$867$$

If the company had chosen to prohibit backorders and had adopted the regular EOQ model, the recommended inventory decision would have been

$$Q^* = \sqrt{\frac{2DC_0}{C_h}} = \sqrt{10,000} = 100.$$

This order quantity would have resulted in an inventory holding cost and ordering cost of \$500 each or a total annual cost of \$1000. Thus in this example, allowing backorders is projecting a \$1000 − \$867 = \$133 or 13.3% savings in cost from the no-stockout EOQ model. The above comparison and conclusion is based on the assumption that the backorder model (no lost sales) with an annual cost per backordered unit of \$30 is a valid model for the actual inventory situation. If the company has strong fears that stockouts might lead to lost sales, then the above savings might not be enough to warrant switching to an inventory policy that allowed for planned shortages.

Note that as the backordering cost C_b becomes large relative to the inventory holding cost C_h, the quantity $C_h/(C_h + C_b)$ in equation (12.27) will be relatively small, and thus S^* will also be small. In this case the backorder model and the regular EOQ model provide very similar results. Also note that as the holding costs ($C_h = IC$) become large, the number of backorders S becomes larger. This explains why many items which have a very high per unit cost C are handled on a backorder basis.

12.4   Quantity Discounts for the EOQ Model

Quantity discounts occur in numerous businesses and industries where suppliers provide an incentive for large purchase quantities by offering lower unit costs when items are purchasesd in larger lots or quantities. In this section we show how the basic EOQ model can be used when quantity discounts are offered.

Assume that we have a product where the basic EOQ model is applicable, but instead of a fixed unit cost, our supplier quotes the following discount schedule.

Discount Category	Order Size	Discount	Unit Cost
1	0 to 999	0	$5.00
2	1000 to 2499	3%	$4.85
3	2500 and over	5%	$4.75

The 5% discount for the 2500-unit minimum order quantity looks tempting; however, realizing that higher order quantities give us higher inventory carrying costs, we should prepare a thorough cost analysis before making a final ordering and inventory policy recommendation.

Suppose our data and cost analysis show an inventory holding cost rate of 20% per year, ordering costs of $49 per order, and an annual demand of 5000 units; what order quantity should we select? The following three-step procedure shows the calculations necessary to make this decision. In our preliminary calculations we will use Q_1 to indicate the order quantity for discount category 1, Q_2 for discount category 2, and Q_3 for discount category 3.

Step 1.   Compute a Q^* using the EOQ formula for the unit cost associated with each discount category.

Recall the EOQ model $Q^* = \sqrt{2DC_0/C_h}$. In this case,

$$Q_1^* = \sqrt{\frac{2(5000)49}{(0.20)(5.00)}} = 700$$

$$Q_2^* = \sqrt{\frac{2(5000)49}{(0.20)(4.85)}} = 711$$

$$Q_3^* = \sqrt{\frac{2(5000)49}{(0.20)(4.75)}} = 718.$$

Since the only differences in the models are slight differences in the inventory holding costs, the economic order quantities resulting from this step will be approximately the same. However, the calculated order quantities will usually not all be of the size necessary to qualify for the discount price assumed. In the above case, both Q_2^* and Q_3^* are insufficient order quantities to obtain their assumed unit costs of \$4.85 and \$4.75, respectively. For those order quantities for which the assumed price is incorrect, the following procedure must then be used.

Step 2.   For those Q^*'s which are too small to qualify for the assumed discount price, adjust the order quantity upward to the nearest order quantity which will allow the product to be purchased at the assumed price.

In our example this causes us to set

$$Q_2^* = 1000$$

and

$$Q_3^* = 2500.$$

If a calculated Q^* for a given price is larger than the *highest* order quantity providing the particular discount price, this discount price need not be considered any further, since it cannot lead to an optimal solution. While this may not be obvious, it does turn out to be a property of the EOQ quantity discount model. Problem 19 at the end of the chapter will ask you to show that this property is true.

In our previous inventory models we have ignored the annual purchase cost of the item because it was constant and never affected by the inventory-order policy decision. However, in the quantity-discount model total annual purchase cost will vary with the order quantity decision and the associated unit cost. Thus annual purchase cost (annual demand $D \times$ unit cost C) is included in the total cost model as shown below:

$$\text{TC} = \frac{Q}{2} C_h + \frac{D}{Q} C_0 + DC. \qquad (12.28)$$

Using this total cost formula we can determine the optimal order quantity for the EOQ discount model in Step 3 below.

Step 3.   For each of the order quantities resulting from Step 1 and Step 2, compute the total annual cost using the unit price from the appropriate discount category and equation (12.28). The order quantity yielding the minimum total annual cost is the optimal order quantity.

The Step 3 calculations for our example problem are summarized in Table 12.3. As you can see, a decision to order 1000 units at the 3% discount rate yields the minimum cost solution. While the 2500-unit order quantity

TABLE 12.3   Total Annual Cost Calculations for the EOQ Quantity Discount Model

Category	Unit Cost	Order Quantity	Annual Inventory Cost	Annual Ordering Cost	Annual Purchase Cost	Total Annual Cost
1	$5.00	700	$ 350	$350	$25,000	$25,700
2	$4.85	1000	$ 485	$245	$24,250	$24,980
3	$4.75	2500	$1188	$ 98	$23,750	$25,036

would result in a 5% discount, its excessive inventory holding cost makes it the second best solution.

12.5   Material Requirements Planning

Each of the approaches to inventory management discussed in Sections 12.1–12.4 use what is generally referred to as the *order point* approach to inventory planning and control. That is, whenever the inventory level for a given product reaches its order point, an order of fixed size is placed. In practice, order point techniques have been found to be useful and most appropriate for controlling inventories of finished goods. However, in manufacturing environments, where the objective is to control the production and the inventories of the components that make up the finished product, the order point approaches have not been found to be effective inventory planning and control aids. Consequently, new methods have been developed to handle the unique aspects of manufacturing inventories. One of the most important of the new techniques is the *material requirements planning* method, abbreviated as MRP. To see why approaches like MRP are needed, let us consider some of the unique aspects of manufacturing environments.

The purpose of a manufacturing inventory system differs substantially from that of a marketing or finished goods inventory system where the purpose is to maintain inventory to meet customer demand. The major function of a manufacturing inventory system is to translate the demand for finished goods into detailed inventory requirements for the components that make up the finished goods. In manufacturing, the statement of how many finished items are to be produced and when they are to be produced is referred to as the *master production schedule*. Once the master production schedule is determined, the production requirements for the components that make up the finished product can be scheduled and controlled by the firm. Consequently, this schedule is a key element in the development of an MRP system.

Another important input to an MRP system is the bill of materials. Basically, a *bill of materials* is a structured parts list; however, it differs from an ordinary parts list in that it shows the manner in which the finished product is actually put together. To develop a better understanding of the role the master production schedule and the bill of materials play in the

MRP approach to inventory control, let us consider the production and inventory situation for the Spiecker Manufacturing Company.

An Example of the MRP Approach

Spiecker Manufacturing Company is a major producer of snowblowers. In Figure 12.6 we have shown a graphic representation for a portion of the bill of materials for model 140, a 14″ snowblower. Note that the bill of materials depicts how the product is exploded into the parts necessary for its assembly and the hierarchy of steps required. For example, we see that in order to produce the air cleaner subassembly, the filter housing must be complete; in order to produce the engine assembly, the air cleaner assembly must be complete; and so on.

Let us assume that the master production schedule calls for the final assembly of 5000 units of model 140 during week 21 of the current production period; hence, to meet this schedule, the four main assemblies depicted in Figure 12.6 must be completed no later than the end of week 20. We will now examine in detail the production and inventory control aspects for the engine assembly, concentrating on how the MRP approach can be applied. Relevant data regarding the number of units in inventory and lead time are given in Table 12.4.

An important aspect of the current example involves how the components relate to one another. Ultimately, these relationships will help us determine appropriate inventory levels for each of the components. For example, the order point approach to inventory control assumes that each item in inventory is independent of all other items. However, this is not the situation in our example. In fact, the Spiecker snowblower problem is an illustration of demand for one component being dependent upon the demand

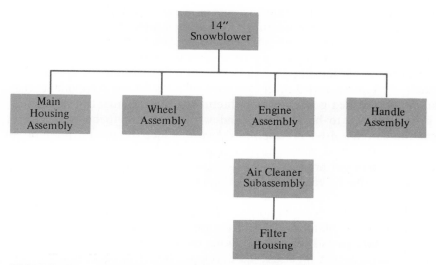

FIGURE 12.6   A Portion of the Bill of Materials for the 14″ Snowblower

TABLE 12.4   Inventory on Hand and Lead Time for the Spiecker Manufacturing Example

Component	Units in Inventory	Lead Time (weeks)
Engine assembly	1800	8
Air cleaner subassembly	1000	2
Filter housing	2000	4

of other components, all of which are ultimately dependent upon the demand for the finished good.

Before the advent of the MRP approach to inventory management, the net requirement for each component was often found using the formula

$$
\begin{array}{l}
\text{Net component} \\
\text{requirement}
\end{array} =
\left(
\begin{array}{c}
\text{number of components} \\
\text{required to meet} \\
\text{demand for} \\
\text{finished good}
\end{array}
\right)
-
\left(
\begin{array}{c}
\text{number of} \\
\text{components} \\
\text{in inventory}
\end{array}
\right)
$$

Thus the net requirements based on 5000 snowblowers would be calculated as follows:

Components	$\left(\begin{array}{c}\text{Number of components} \\ \text{required to meet} \\ \text{demand of} \\ \text{5000 snowblowers}\end{array}\right)$	−	$\left(\begin{array}{c}\text{Number in} \\ \text{inventory}\end{array}\right)$	=	Net requirement
Engines	5000	−	1800	=	3200
Air cleaners	5000	−	1000	=	4000
Filter housings	5000	−	2000	=	3000

However, note that this approach does not recognize the nature of dependent demand—e.g., the fact that the number of filter housings required is dependent upon the number of air cleaners produced, etc.

The approach to determining net requirements whenever a dependent demand situation exists is shown below:

$$
\begin{array}{l}
\text{Net component} \\
\text{requirement}^{6}
\end{array} =
\left(
\begin{array}{c}
\text{gross component} \\
\text{requirement}
\end{array}
\right)
-
\left(
\begin{array}{c}
\text{number of components} \\
\text{in inventory}
\end{array}
\right)
$$

[6]The net component requirement is usually written as

$$
\begin{array}{l}
\text{Net component} \\
\text{requirement}
\end{array} =
\left(
\begin{array}{c}
\text{gross component} \\
\text{requirement}
\end{array}
\right)
-
\left(
\begin{array}{c}
\text{scheduled} \\
\text{receipts}
\end{array}
\right)
-
\left(
\begin{array}{c}
\text{number of} \\
\text{components} \\
\text{in inventory}
\end{array}
\right)
$$

For simplicity, we have ignored discussing the effect of scheduled receipts or inventory previously ordered.

where the gross component requirement is the quantity of the component needed to support production at the next higher level of assembly. For example, the gross component requirement for the filter housing is the number of filter housings required to meet the net requirement for the air cleaner subassembly; the gross component requirement for the air cleaner sub-assembly is the number of air cleaners needed to meet the net requirement for the engine assembly; and so on. Let us see how these requirements can be computed for the Spiecker Company:

Quantity of snowblowers to be produced:	5000	
Gross requirements, engines:	5000	
Less engines in inventory:	1800	
Net requirements, engines:	3200	← Engines
Gross requirements, air cleaners:	3200	
Less air cleaners in inventory:	1000	
Net requirements, air cleaners:	2200	← Air cleaners
Gross requirements, filter housings:	2200	
Less filter housings in inventory:	2000	
Net requirements, filter housings:	200	← Filter housings

While the net requirements for engines under the MRP approach is still 3200 units, note how MRP has used the dependent demand information to show that fewer air cleaners and filter housings will be needed. In addition to considering dependent demand in the determination of net requirements for components, an MRP system also determines when the net requirements are needed. MRP handles this aspect of production and inventory control using a procedure referred to as *time phasing*.

Time phasing is an approach the enables an organization to determine the specific point in time at which an order must be placed for a component. By starting with the time that the finished product must be completed, we can work backward in order to determine when an order for each component must be placed. For example, the time-phasing calculations for the Spiecker snowblower problem might appear as shown at the top of page 479.

Until the development of large-scale computers, the sheer volume of calculations prohibited the implementation of an MRP system. For example, even in our small illustration, you can begin to appreciate the complexity involved in keeping track of the production and inventory status for every component in the Spiecker Company. Fortunately, because of modern computer technology, we find that what was an unmanageable problem for earlier manual approaches is now routinely handled by an MRP system.

In practice, the time-phasing calculations are somewhat more complex than our example implies, since the individual components may be used in

	Week	
Complete order for engines:	20	
Minus lead time for engines:	8	
Place an order for engines:	12	← Order engines

Complete order for air cleaners:	12	
Minus lead time of air cleaners:	2	
Place an order for air cleaners:	10	← Order air cleaners

Complete order for filter housings:	10	
Minus lead time for filter housings:	4	
Place an order for filter housings:	6	← Order filter housings

more than one final product. However, a complete discussion of the details regarding time phasing is beyond the scope of the text. The interested reader is referred to *Material Requirements Planning* by Joseph Orlicky (McGraw-Hill Book Company, 1975).

To appreciate another important aspect of using an MRP system, assume that during the manufacture of the filter housing component, a machine breakdown occurs that will delay production of the housings for one week. Perhaps the only alternative management has for maintaining the current schedule is to hire an outside contractor to produce the remaining number of required filter housings; however, the increased costs associated with using an outside contractor are significant. What should management do?

Before reaching a decision regarding the use of an outside contractor, management should analyze the effects a one-week delay in the production of the filter housings would bring about. Because an MRP system maintains information on all items in inventory, this data can now be made available to management. For example, the MRP system would examine the bill of materials in order to determine the impact a one-week delay in the filter housing would have in terms of the production schedule for all other components. In addition, if management elects to delay production by one week, all components affected by the change would then be updated by the MRP system to reflect new production schedules.

In essence, then, an MRP system is implemented as a computerized data processing and information system whose function is to monitor the status of production and inventory. By recognizing the dependent nature of demand inherent in most manufacturing environments and the subsequent importance of timing, MRP offers a better alternative to production and inventory control than do traditional types of EOQ models.

Currently, there are many computer manufacturers that offer computer programs that will carry out the calculations required to implement the MRP approach. Although the use of any of these software packages can greatly simplify the development and implementation of an MRP type of system, the development of an MRP system can be an expensive and time-consuming project. Properly implemented, however, the MRP approach can provide significant inventory planning and control advantages for the firm.

Summary

In this chapter you have seen some of the approaches operations researchers take in attempting to develop inventory decision models that will assist managers in establishing low-cost operating policies for inventory systems. We first studied cases where the demand for the product occurs at a rather stable or constant known rate. In analyzing these inventory systems, operations researchers attempt to develop total cost models which include ordering cost, inventory holding cost, and, in some cases, backordering cost, and then use differential calculus to develop minimum cost formulas for the order quantity Q. A reorder point r can be established by considering the lead time demand for the item.

We pointed out that the order point type of approaches referred to above are most applicable for controlling finished goods inventory. For manufacturing inventories, where dependent demand exists, methods such as MRP offer significant advantages.

In closing this chapter we reemphasize that inventory and inventory systems can be an extremely expensive phase of a firm's operation. It is of utmost economic importance for managers to be aware of the cost of inventory systems and to make the best possible operating policy decisions for the inventory system. Quantitative inventory decision models, as presented in this chapter, can help managers to develop good inventory policies.

Glossary

1. *Inventory holding or inventory carrying cost*—All costs associated with maintaining an inventory investment: cost of the capital investment in the inventory, insurance, taxes, warehouse overhead, and so on. This cost may be stated as a percentage of the inventory investment or a cost per unit.

2. *Cost of capital*—The cost a firm incurs, usually interest payments on borrowed funds or dividend payments on stocks, in order to obtain capital for investment. The cost of capital, which may be stated as an annual percentage rate, is part of the holding cost associated with maintaining inventory levels.

3. *Economic order quantity (EOQ)*—The order quantity which minimizes the total inventory costs in the most fundamental inventory decision model.

4. *Constant demand rate*—An assumption of many inventory decision models which states that the same number of units are taken from inventory in each period of time.

5. *Ordering cost*—The fixed cost (salaries, paper, transportation, and so on) associated with placing an order for an item.

6. *Reorder point*—The inventory level at which a new order should be placed.

7. *Lead time*—The time between the placing of an order and its receipt in the inventory system.

8. *Lead time demand*—The number of units demanded during the lead time period.

9. *Cycle time*—The length of time between the placing of two consecutive orders.

10. *Safety stock*—Inventory maintained in order to reduce the number of stockouts resulting from higher than expected demand during leadtime.

11. *Constant supply rate*—The situation in which the inventory is built up at a constant rate over a period of time. This assumption applies to the production lot size model of this chapter.

12. *Backorder*—The receipt of an order for a product when there are no units on hand in inventory. These backorders become shortages which are eventually satisfied when a new supply of the product becomes available.

13. *Quantity discounts*—Discounts or lower unit costs offered by the manufacturer when a customer purchases larger quantities of the product.

14. *Goodwill cost*—A cost associated with a backorder, a lost sale, or any form of stockout or unsatisfied demand. This cost may be used to reflect the loss of future profits due to the fact a customer experienced an unsatisfied demand.

15. *Material requirements planning (MRP)*—A computerized data processing system whose function is to schedule production and control the level of inventory for components with dependent demand.

16. *Master production schedule*—A statement of how many finished items are to be produced and when.

17. *Bill of materials*—A structured parts list that shows the manner in which the product is actually put together.

18. *Dependent demand*—The demand for one component depends upon the demand for another component.

19. *Time phasing*—Adding the dimension of time to inventory status data in an MRP environment.

Problems

1. Suppose R & B Beverage Company has a soft-drink product that has a constant annual demand rate of 3600 cases. A case of the soft drink costs R & B $3.00. If ordering costs are $20.00 and inventory holding costs are charged at 25%, what is the economic order quantity and cycle time in days for this product?

2. A general property of the EOQ inventory model is that total inventory holding and total ordering costs are equal or balanced at the optimal solution. Use the data in Problem 1 to show that this result is observed for this problem. Use equations (12.1), (12.2), and (12.5) to show in general that total inventory holding costs and total ordering costs are equal whenever Q^* is used.

3. The XYZ Company purchases a component used in the manufacturing of automobile generators directly from the supplier. XYZ's generator production operation, which is operated at a constant rate, will require 1000 components per month throughout the year (12,000 units annually). If ordering costs are $25.00 per order, unit cost is $2.50 per component, and annual inventory holding costs are charged at 20%, answer the following inventory policy questions for XYZ:
   a. What is the EOQ for this component?
   b. What is the length of cycle time in months?
   c. What are the total annual inventory holding and ordering costs associated with your recommended EOQ?

4. Assuming 250 days of operation per year and a lead time of 5 days, what is the reorder point for the XYZ Company in Problem 3?

5. Suppose that XYZ's management in Problem 3 likes the operational efficiency of ordering in quantities of 1000 units and ordering once each month. How much more expensive would this policy be than your EOQ recommendation? Would you recommend in favor of the 1000-unit order quantity? Explain. What would the reorder point be if the 1000-unit quantity were acceptable?

6. Tele-Reco is a new specialty store which sells television sets, videotape recorders, video games, and other television related products. A new Japanese manufactured videotape recorder costs Tele-Reco $600 per unit. Tele-Reco's inventory carrying cost is figured at an annual rate of 22%. Ordering costs are estimated to be $70 per order.
   a. If demand for the new videotape recorder is expected to be constant with a rate of 20 units per month, what is the recommended order quantity for the tape recorder?
   b. What is the estimated annual cost for inventory and ordering costs associated with this product?
   c. How many times will orders be placed per year, and what is the cycle time for this product?

7. A large distributor of oil-well drilling equipment has operated over the past two years with EOQ policies based on an annual inventory carrying charge of 22%. Under the EOQ policy, a particular product has been ordered with a $Q^* = 80$. A recent evaluation of carrying costs shows that because of an increase in the interest rate associated with bank loans, the inventory carry charge should be 27%.
   a. What should be the new Q^* for the above product?
   b. Develop a general expression showing how the economic order quantity changes when the inventory carrying cost is changed from I to I'.

8. Nation-Wide Bus Lines is proud of its six-week bus driver training program that it conducts for all new Nation-Wide drivers. A six-week training program costs Nation-Wide $22,000 for instructors, equipment, and so on and is independent of the number of new drivers in the class as long as the class size remains less than or equal to 35. The Nation-Wide training program must provide the company with approximately five new fully trained drivers per month. After completing the training program, new drivers are paid $1600 per month but do not work until a full-time driver position is open. Nation-Wide views the $1600 per month paid to each idle new driver as a holding cost necessary to maintain a supply of newly

trained drivers available for immediate service. Viewing new drivers as inventory-type units, how large should the training classes be in order to minimize Nation-Wide's total annual training and new driver idle-time costs? How many training classes should the company hold each year? What is the total annual cost of your recommendation?

9. All-Star Bat Manufacturing, Inc. supplies baseball bats to major and minor league baseball teams. After an initial order in January, demand over the eight-month baseball season is approximately constant at 1000 bats per month. Assuming that the bat production process can handle up to 4000 bats per month, the bat production setup costs are $150 per setup, the production cost is $10 per bat, and assuming that All-Star uses a 24% annual or 2% monthly inventory holding cost, what production lot size would you recommend to meet the demand during the baseball season? How often will the production process operate, and what.is the length of a production run?

10. Assume a production line operates such that the production lot size model of Section 12.2 is applicable. Given $D = 6400$ units per year, $C_0 = \$100$, and $C_h = \$2.00$ per unit per year, compute the minimum cost production lot size for each of the following production rates:

    a.   8000 units per year.
    b.   10,000 units per year.
    c.   32,000 units per year.
    d.   100,000 units per year.

Compute the EOQ recommended lot size using equation (12.5). What two observations can you make about the relationship between the EOQ model and the production lot size model?

11. Assume you are reviewing the production lot size decision associated with a production operation where $P = 8000$ units per year, $D = 2000$ units per year, $C_0 = \$300$, and $C_h = \$1.60$ per unit per year. Also assume current practice calls for production runs of 500 units every three months. Would you recommend changing the current production lot size? Why or why not? How much could be saved by converting to your production lot size recommendation?

12. A well-known manufacturer of several brands of toothpaste uses the production lot size model to determine production quantities for its various products. The product known as Extra White is currently being run in production lot sizes of 5000 units. The length of the production run for this quantity is 10 days. Because of a recent shortage of a particular raw material, the supplier of the material has announced a cost increase that will be passed along to the manufacturer of Extra White. Current estimates are that the new raw material cost will increase the manufacturing cost of the toothpaste products by 23% per unit. What will be the effect of this price increase on the production lot sizes for Extra White? What is the new length of the production run?

13. Suppose the XYZ Company of Problem 3, with $D = 12,000$ units per year, $C_h = (2.50)(0.20) = \$0.50$, and $C_0 = \$25.00$, decided to operate with a backorder inventory policy. Backorder costs are estimated to be $5 per unit per year. Identify the following:

    a.   Minimum cost order quantity.
    b.   Maximum number of backorders.
    c.   Maximum inventory level.
    d.   Cycle time.
    e.   Total annual cost.

14. Assuming 250 days of operation per year and a lead time of 5 days, what is the reorder point for the XYZ Company in Problem 13? Show the general formula for the reorder point for the EOQ model with backorders. In general, is the reorder point when back orders are allowed greater than or less than the reorder point when backorders are not allowed? Explain.

15. A manager of an inventory system believes inventory models are important decision-making aids. While he frequently uses the EOQ policy, he has never considered a backorder model because he has always felt backorders were "bad" and should be avoided. However, with upper management's continued pressure for cost reduction, he has asked you to analyze the economics of a backordering policy for some products that he believes can possibly be backordered. For a specific product with $D = 800$ units per year, $C_0 = \$150$, $C_h = \$3.00$, and $C_b = \$20$, what is the economic difference in the EOQ and the planned backorder model? If the manager puts constraints that no more than 25% of the units can be backordered and that no customer will have to wait more than 3 weeks (21 days) for an order, should the backorder inventory policy be adopted?

16. If the lead time for new orders is one month for the inventory system discussed in Problem 15, find the reorder point for both the EOQ and the planned backorder models.

17. Assume that the following quantity discount schedule is appropriate:

Order Size	Discount	Unit Cost
0 to 49	0	$30.00
50 to 99	5%	$28.50
over 99	10%	$27.00

If annual demand is 120 units, ordering cost is $20 per order, and annual inventory carrying cost is 25%, what order quantity would you recommend?

18. Apply the EOQ model to the following quantity discount situation:

Category	Order Size	Discount	Unit Cost
1	0 to 99	0	$10.00
2	over 99	3%	9.70

$D = 500$ units per year, $C_0 = \$40$, and an annual inventory holding cost of 20% are given. What order quantity do you recommend?

19. In the EOQ model with quantity discounts we stated that if the Q^* for a price category is larger than necessary to qualify for the category price, the category cannot be optimal. Use the two discount categories in Problem 18 to show that this is true. That is, plot the total cost curves for the two categories and show that if the category 2 minimum cost Q is an acceptable solution, we do not have to consider category 1.

20. Consider the Spiecker Manufacturing example of Section 12.5. Determine the net requirements for the engine assembly, the air cleaner subassembly, and the filter housing if the number of units in inventory were 2000, 1500, and 1000, respectively. Assume that 5000 units of model 140 are still required in week 21.

21. For the Spiecker Manufacturing example of Section 12.5, determine the effect on time phasing if lead times were 10 for the engine assembly, 3 for the air cleaner subassembly, and 5 for the filter housing.

22. C & D Lawn Products manufactures a rotary spreader for applying fertilizer. A portion of the bill of materials is shown below:

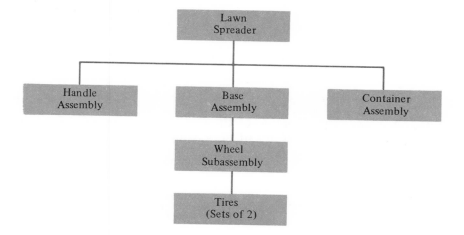

If 3000 lawn spreaders are needed to satisfy a customer's order, determine the net requirements for the base assembly, wheel subassembly, and tires (sets of 2). Assume that 1000 base assemblies, 1500 wheel subassemblies, and 800 tires (sets of 2) are currently in inventory.

23. In Problem 22, assume that the lead time for the base assembly, wheel subassembly, and tires are 2 weeks, 4 weeks, and 5 weeks, respectively. If all components must be completed no later than week 15 of the current production period, determine when orders must be placed to meet the production schedule.

Appendix 12.1   Development of the Optimal Order Quantity (Q^*) Formula for the EOQ Model

Given equation (12.3) as the general total annual cost formula for the EOQ model,

$$TC = \frac{1}{2} QC_h + \frac{D}{Q} C_0,$$ (12.3)

we can find the order quantity Q that minimizes the total cost by setting the derivative $d\text{TC}/dQ$ equal to zero and solving for Q^*.

$$\frac{d\text{TC}}{dQ} = \frac{1}{2} C_h - \frac{D}{Q^2} C_0 = 0$$

$$\frac{1}{2} C_h = \frac{D}{Q^2} C_0$$

$$C_h Q^2 = 2DC_0$$

$$Q^2 = \frac{2DC_0}{C_h}$$

Hence

$$Q^* = \sqrt{\frac{2DC_0}{C_h}} \,. \tag{12.5}$$

The second derivative is

$$\frac{d^2\text{TC}}{dQ^2} = \frac{2D}{Q^3}\, C_0.$$

Since the value of the second derivative is greater than zero for D, C_0, and Q greater than zero, Q^* from equation (12.5) is in fact the minimum cost solution.

Appendix 12.2 Development of the Optimal Lot Size Q^* for the Production Lot Size Model

Given equation (12.15) as the total annual cost formula for the production lot size model,

$$\text{TC} = \frac{1}{2}\left(1 - \frac{D}{P}\right)QC_h + \frac{D}{Q}\, C_0 \tag{12.15}$$

we can find the order quantity Q that minimizes the total cost by setting the derivative $d\text{TC}/dQ$ equal to zero and solving for Q^*.

$$\frac{d\text{TC}}{dQ} = \frac{1}{2}\left(1 - \frac{D}{P}\right)C_h - \frac{D}{Q^2}\, C_0 = 0.$$

Solving for Q^* we have

$$\frac{1}{2}\left(1 - \frac{D}{P}\right)C_h = \frac{D}{Q^2}\, C_0$$

$$\left(1 - \frac{D}{P}\right)C_h Q^2 = 2DC_0$$

$$Q^2 = \frac{2DC_0}{(1 - D/P)C_h} \,.$$

Hence

$$Q^* = \sqrt{\frac{2DC_0}{(1 - D/P)C_h}} \,. \tag{12.16}$$

The second derivative is

$$\frac{d^2\text{TC}}{dQ^2} = \frac{2DC_0}{Q^3} \,.$$

Since the value of the second derivative is greater than zero for D, C_0, and Q greater than zero, Q^* from equation (12.16) is a minimum cost solution.

Appendix 12.3 Development of the Optimal Order Quantity ($Q*$) and Optimal Backorders ($S*$) Formulas for the Planned Shortage Model

Given equation (12.25) as the total annual cost model for the planned shortage case,

$$TC = \frac{(Q - S)^2}{2Q} C_h + \frac{D}{Q} C_0 + \frac{S^2}{2Q} C_b \tag{12.25}$$

we have two inventory decision variables Q and S. To find the Q and S values that minimize equation (12.25) we must set the two partial derivatives $\partial TC/\partial Q$ and $\partial TC/\partial S$ equal to zero.

First, let us rewrite equation (12.25) as follows:

$$TC = \left(\frac{Q^2 - 2QS + S^2}{2Q}\right) C_h + \frac{D}{Q} C_0 + \frac{S^2}{2Q} C_b$$

$$= \frac{Q}{2} C_h - SC_h + \frac{C_h}{2Q} S^2 + \frac{DC_0}{Q} + \frac{C_b}{2Q} S^2$$

$$= \left(\frac{C_h + C_b}{2Q}\right) S^2 - SC_h + \frac{QC_h}{2} + \frac{DC_0}{Q}.$$

Then, setting $\partial TC/\partial S = 0$, we get

$$\frac{\partial TC}{\partial S} = \left(\frac{C_h + C_b}{Q}\right) S - C_h = 0.$$

Solving for $S*$, we have

$$\left(\frac{C_h + C_b}{Q}\right) S = C_h.$$

Thus

$$S* = Q\left(\frac{C_h}{C_h + C_b}\right). \tag{12.27}$$

Setting $\partial TC/\partial Q = 0$, we get

$$\frac{\partial TC}{\partial Q} = \frac{-(C_h + C_b) S^2}{2Q^2} + \frac{C_h}{2} - \frac{DC_0}{Q^2} = 0.$$

Substituting $S*$ of equation (12.27), we have

$$\frac{\partial TC}{\partial Q} = \frac{-(C_h + C_b)Q^2(C_h)^2/(C_h + C_b)^2}{2Q^2} + \frac{C_h}{2} - \frac{DC_0}{Q^2} = 0.$$

Solve for $Q*$ as follows:

$$\frac{-(C_h)^2}{2(C_h + C_b)} + \frac{C_h}{2} = \frac{DC_0}{Q^2}$$

$$\frac{-(C_h)^2 + C_h(C_h + C_b)}{2(C_h + C_b)} = \frac{DC_0}{Q^2}$$

$$Q^2 = \frac{2(C_h + C_b)DC_0}{C_h C_b}$$

$$= \frac{2C_h DC_0}{C_h C_b} + \frac{2C_b DC_0}{C_h C_b}$$

$$= \frac{2DC_0}{C_h}\left(\frac{C_h}{C_b} + \frac{C_b}{C_b}\right).$$

Hence

$$Q^* = \sqrt{\frac{2DC_0}{C_h}\left(\frac{C_h + C_b}{C_b}\right)}. \qquad (12.26)$$

The second-order conditions will show equations (12.26) and (12.27) to be the minimum cost solutions.

Chapter 13

Inventory Models With Probabilistic Demand

In this chapter we will consider inventory decision models in which the exact demand for the item is not known in advance and therefore can only be described in probabilistic terms. The decision models used to analyze these inventory systems are referred to as *probabilistic demand* models. However, even when probabilistic demands exist, the inventory manager will be attempting to make the how-much-to-order and/or when-to-order decisions that will enable an efficient operation of the inventory system. Under a minimum cost objective, the relevant cost components, just as with the EOQ model, are ordering and inventory holding costs.

13.1 Order Quantity–Reorder Point Models

Since the level of mathematical sophistication required for an exact formulation of order quantity–reorder point inventory models with probabilistic demand is beyond the scope of this text, we will restrict our discussion of these inventory decision problems to a heuristic procedure that should enable you to obtain good, workable solutions without relying upon more advanced mathematical techniques. While this solution procedure can only be expected to provide approximations to the optimal inventory decisions, it has been found to yield very good decisions in many practical situations.

Let us consider the case of Dabco Industrial Lighting Distributors. Suppose Dabco purchases a special high-intensity light bulb for industrial lighting systems from a well-known light bulb manufacturer. Dabco would like a recommendation on how much it should order and when it should place an order so that a low-cost inventory operation can be realized. Pertinent facts are that ordering costs are $12.00 per order, one bulb costs $6.00, and Dabco uses a 20% annual holding cost rate for its inventory ($C_h = 0.20 \times 6.00 = \$1.20$). Dabco, which has over 1000 different customers, experiences a probabilistic demand in that the number of orders will vary considerably from day to day and week to week. While demand is not specifically known, historical sales data indicate that an annual demand of 8000 bulbs, while not exact, can be used as a good estimate of the anticipated annual volume.

The How-Much-to-Order Decision

Although we are in a probabilistic demand situation, we have a good estimate of the expected annual volume of 8000 units. As an approximation of the best order quantity we can apply the EOQ model with the expected annual volume substituted for the annual demand D. In Dabco's case,

$$Q^* = \sqrt{\frac{2DC_0}{C_h}} = \sqrt{\frac{2(8000)(12)}{(0.20)(6.00)}} = 400 \text{ units.}$$

When we studied the sensitivity of the EOQ models, we learned that the total cost of operating an inventory system was relatively insensitive to order quantities that were in the neighborhood of Q^*. Using this knowledge, we expect 400 units per order to be a good approximation of the optimal order quantity. Even if annual demand were as low as 7000 units or as high as 9000 units, an order quantity of 400 units should be a relatively good low-cost order size. Thus, given our best estimate of annual demand at 8000 units, we will use $Q^* = 400$.

We have established the 400-unit order quantity by ignoring the fact that demand is probabilistic. Using $Q^* = 400$, Dabco can anticipate placing approximately $D/Q^* = 8000/400 = 20$ orders per year with an average of approximately $365/20 = 18$ days between orders.

The When-to-Order Decision

We now want to establish a when-to-order decision rule or reorder point that will trigger the ordering process. Further pertinent data indicate that it usually takes one week for Dabco to receive a new supply of light bulbs from the manufacturer. With an average weekly demand of 8000/52 weeks = 154 units, you might first suggest a 154-unit reorder point. However, it now becomes extremely important to consider the probabilities of the various demands. If 154 is the average weekly demand, and if the demands are symmetrically distributed about 154, then weekly demand will be more than 154 units roughly 50% of the time.

When the demand during the one-week lead time exceeds 154 units, Dabco will experience a shortage or stockout. Thus with a reorder point of 154 units approximately 50% of the time (10 of the 20 orders a year) Dabco will be short of bulbs before the new supply arrives. This shortage rate would most likely be viewed as unacceptable. In order to determine a reorder point with a reasonably low likelihood or probability of a stockout it is necessary to establish a probability distribution for the lead time demand and analyze stockout probabilities.

Using historical data and some judgment, the *lead time demand distribution* for Dabco's light bulbs is assumed to be a normal distribution with a mean of 154 units and a standard deviation of 25 units. This is shown in Figure 13.1.

While the normal distribution of lead time demand is used in the Dabco problem, any demand probability distribution is acceptable. By collecting historical data on actual demands during the lead time period, an analyst should be able to determine if the normal distribution or some other probability distribution is the most realistic picture of the lead time demand distribution.

Given the lead time demand probability distribution, we can now determine how the reorder point r affects the probability of stocking out of the item. Since stockouts occur whenever the demand during the lead time exceeds the reorder point, we can find the probability of a stockout by using the lead time demand distribution to compute the probability of demand exceeding r.

We could now approach the when-to-order problem by defining a cost per stockout and then attempting to include this cost in a total-cost equation.

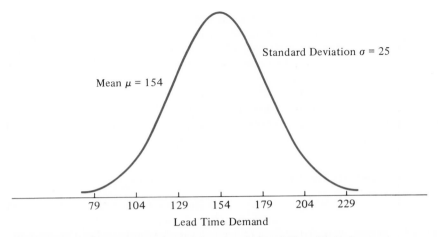

Figure 13.1   Distribution of Demand During the Lead Time for Dabco

Possibly a more practical approach is to ask management to define an acceptable *service level,* where the service level refers to the average number of stockouts we are willing to allow per year. If demand for a product is probabilistic, a manager who says he will never tolerate a stockout is being somewhat unrealistic because attempting to avoid stockouts completely will require high reorder points, high inventory levels, and an associated high inventory holding cost.

Suppose in this case that Dabco management is willing to tolerate an average of one stockout per year. This service level can be maintained if 1 out of the 20 planned orders, 5% of the orders, result in a stockout. This implies that for any one order there can be a 5% chance of a stockout. Thus the reorder point r can be found by using the lead time demand distribution to find the value of r for which there is only a 5% chance of having a lead time demand exceeding it. This situation is shown graphically in Figure 13.2.

From the normal distribution tables in Appendix A, we see that an r value that is 1.645 standard deviations above the mean will allow stockouts 5% of the time. Therefore, for the assumed normal distribution for lead time demand with $\mu = 154$ and $\sigma = 25$, the reorder point r is determined by

$$r = 154 + 1.645(25) = 195.$$

If a normal distribution is used for lead time demand, the general equation for r is

$$r = \mu + z\sigma \qquad (13.1)$$

where z is the number of standard deviations necessary to achieve the acceptable stockout probability.

Thus the recommended inventory decision is to order 400 units whenever the inventory level reaches the reorder point of 195. Since the

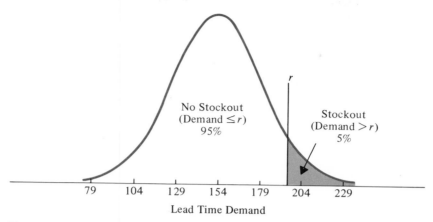

Figure 13.2   Reorder Point *r* that Allows a 5% Chance of Stockout for Dabco Light Bulbs

mean or expected demand during the lead time is 154 units, the $195 - 154 = 41$ units serve as a safety stock which absorbs higher than usual demand during the lead time. Roughly 95% of the time the 195 units will be able to satisfy demand during the lead time. The anticipated annual cost for this system is as follows:

Ordering cost	$(D/Q)C_0 = (8000/400)12$	$= \$240.00$
Holding cost—normal inventory	$(Q/2)C_h = (400/2)(1.20)$	$= \$240.00$
Holding cost—safety stock	$(41)C_h = 41(1.20)$	$= \underline{\$\ 49.20}$
		$\$529.20$

If Dabco could have assumed that a known, constant demand rate of 8000 units per year existed for the light bulbs, a $Q^* = 400$, $r = 154$, and total annual cost of $\$240 + \$240 = \$480$ would have been expected. When demand is uncertain and can only be expressed in probabilistic terms, a larger total cost can be expected. The larger cost occurs in the form of larger inventory holding costs due to the fact that more inventory must be maintained in order to prevent frequent stockouts. For Dabco this additional inventory or safety stock was 41 units with an additional annual inventory holding cost of $49.20.

13.2   Single-Period Inventory Models

In our previous treatment of inventory problems we have assumed that the inventory system operates continuously and that we will have many repeating cycles or periods. Furthermore, we have assumed the inventory may be carried for one or more repeat periods and that we will be placing repeat orders for the product in the future. The *single-period* inventory model refers to inventory situations in which *one* order is placed for the product; and at the end of the period the product has either sold out or there is a surplus of unsold items which will be sold for a salvage value. The single-period models occur in situations involving seasonal or perishable items that cannot be carried in inventory and sold in future periods. Seasonal clothing (such as bathing suits, winter coats, and so on) are typically handled in a single-period manner. In these situations a buyer places one preseason order for each item and then experiences a stockout or holds a clearance sale on the surplus stock at the end of the season. No items are carried in inventory and sold the following year. Newspapers are another example of a product that is ordered one time and is either sold or not sold during the single period. While newspapers are ordered daily, they cannot be carried in inventory and sold in later periods. Thus newspaper orders may be treated as a sequence of single-period models; that is, each day or period is separate, and a single-period inventory decision must be made each period (day). Since we only order once for the period, the only inventory decision we must make is *how much* of the product to order at the start of the period.

Obviously, if the demand were known for our single-period inventory situation, the solution would be easy: we would simply order the amount we knew we were going to sell. However, in most single-period models, the exact demand will not be known. In fact, forecasts may show that demand can have a wide variety of values. If we are going to analyze this type of inventory decision problem in a quantitative manner, we will need information about the probabilities associated with the various demand possibilities. Thus the single-period model is another type of probabilistic demand model.

The solution procedures for the single-period probabilistic demand model are based on either a payoff table analysis or the more general method of incremental analysis. We show how to use both of these solution procedures in the following two single-period examples.

Payoff Table Analysis

The payoff table analysis of single-period inventory models can be used when there are a finite number of possible demand values; that is, the probability distribution for demand is discrete. Hence each possible demand value and its associated probability can be tabulated.

For example, the Kremer Chemical Company has a contract with one of its customers to supply a unique liquid chemical product that will be used by the customer in the manufacturing of a lubricant for airplane engines. Because of the chemical process used by the Kremer Company, batch sizes for the liquid chemical product must be 1000 pounds. The customer has agreed to adjust manufacturing to the full batch quantities and will order either 1, 2, or 3 batches every six months. Since an aging process of two months exists for the product, Kremer will have to make its production (how much-to-order) decision before its customer places an order. Thus Kremer can list the product demand alternatives of 1000, 2000, or 3000 pounds, but the exact demand is unknown.

Kremer's manufacturing costs are $15 per pound, and the product sells at the fixed contract price of $20 per pound. If the customer orders more than Kremer has produced, Kremer has agreed to absorb the added cost of filling the order by purchasing a higher quality substitute product from another chemical firm. The substitute product, including transportation expenses, will cost Kremer $24 per pound. Since the product cannot be stored more than four months without spoilage, Kremer cannot inventory excess production until the customer's next six-month order. Therefore if the customer's current order is less than Kremer has produced, the excess production will be reprocessed and will be valued at $5 per pound.

The inventory decision in this problem is, how much should Kremer produce or order given the above costs and the possible demands of 1000, 2000, or 3000 pounds? While Kremer will be making similar ordering decisions every six months, the fact that the product cannot be carried in inventory between ordering decisions means that each order must be treated as a single-period model.

Our philosophy for finding the best order size now changes over the previous inventory models we have studied. Since no matter how much we order or produce we will order only once, ordering costs are fixed and can be ignored. The inventory holding cost during the two-month aging period can be allocated on a per unit basis and included as part of the cost per unit. Thus since we are dealing with uncertain demand and uncertain sales, the objective for the single-period inventory problems is often stated in terms of maximizing profits rather than attempting to identify and minimize ordering and inventory holding costs. As a result, we need to compute the profit that will be realized under any given order quantity. The optimal order quantity will be the one providing the highest profit.

Since we know that the demand alternatives or states of nature are 1000, 2000, or 3000 pounds, what order quantities should we consider? Actually, for the Kremer Company case the batch size restrictions of 1000 pounds makes 1000, 2000, or 3000 pounds the only alternatives.

Let us now see what profit or payoff Kremer may realize under each different order size and demand possibility. Let

p = selling price per pound,

c = cost per pound (includes an inventory holding cost),

c' = cost per pound if outside supplier used,

s = salvage value per pound,

Q = Kremer's production quantity,

D = customer's demand.

The profit or payoff (P) equations are as follows:
If $Q = D$,

$$P = \text{(sales)} - \text{(production cost)}$$
$$= pD - cQ = 20D - 15Q.$$

If $Q < D$,

P = (sales) − (production cost) − (purchase cost for shortage)

$= pD - cQ - c'(D - Q)$

$= 20D - 15Q - 24(D - Q) = -4D + 9Q.$

If $Q > D$,

P = (sales) − (production cost) + (salvage value of surplus)

$= pD - cQ + s(Q - D)$

$= 20D - 15Q + 5(Q - D) = 15D - 10Q.$

The above profit equations are used to compute Kremer's profit under all combinations of order quantity Q and demand D. The profit calculations are summarized in Table 13.1. The final column is the computed profit for each combination of order quantity and demand. Since the profit is conditional on the specific order size-demand outcome, the profit values are referred to as the *conditional profit* or *payoff*. A complete payoff table for our problem is shown in Table 13.2.

In order to make the final decision on the order quantity we need to know the probabilities of the various demand alternatives. As in all probabilistic demand models, we must define the probability distribution for the demand. Suppose Kremer has historical data on the customer's demand pattern. With a managerial assessment of the customer's future demands,

TABLE 13.1   **Profit Calculations in Thousands of Dollars for Trial Order Quantities for the Kremer Company**

Trial Order Quantity Q	Possible Demand D	$20D$ Sales ($\times 1000$)	$15Q$ Production Cost ($\times 1000$)	If $Q < D$ 24 $(D - Q)$ Shortage Cost ($\times 1000$)	If $Q > D$ 5 $(Q - D)$ Salvage Value ($\times 1000$)	Total Profit P ($\times 1000$)
1000	1000	20	15	0	0	5
1000	2000	40	15	24	0	1
1000	3000	60	15	48	0	−3
2000	1000	20	30	0	5	−5
2000	2000	40	30	0	0	10
2000	3000	60	30	24	0	6
3000	1000	20	45	0	10	−15
3000	2000	40	45	0	5	0
3000	3000	60	45	0	0	15

TABLE 13.2   Payoff Table of Conditional Profits for the Kremer Chemical Company

		Demand D		
		1000	2000	3000
	1000	5000	1000	−3000
Trial Order Quantities (Q)	2000	−5000	10,000	6000
	3000	−15,000	0	15,000

Kremer defines the probability distribution for demand as follows:

D	Probability
1000	0.3
2000	0.5
3000	0.2

We can now compute the expected profit for each order quantity by weighting the conditional profits by their probabilities. The expected profits are as follows:

Expected profit $(Q = 1000) = 0.3(5000) + 0.5(1000) + 0.2(-3000) = \$1400$,

Expected profit $(Q = 2000) = 0.3(-5000) + 0.5(10{,}000) + 0.2(6000) = \$4700$,

Expected profit $(Q = 3000) = 0.3(-15{,}000) + 0.5(0) + 0.2(15{,}000) = -\$1500$.

Thus for the Kremer Chemical Company a $Q = 2000$ pounds is the recommended single-period order quantity in that it shows the highest expected profit.

The above payoff table approach to the single-period inventory decision model was applicable because the demand alternatives of 1000, 2000, and 3000 could be listed and the demand probability distribution defined. The optimal order quantity will always be one of the demand alternatives; that is, order quantities between demand alternatives can never be optimal. Therefore using trial order quantities equal to the demand alternative will provide the optimal solution without having to consider other order quantities.

Incremental Analysis

In the payoff table analysis of the single-period inventory model we stressed that we must be able to list the alternative demand levels for the item in order to use this approach. Each demand level corresponded to a column in our payoff table. Thus the payoff table approach is applicable only in situations in which the probability distribution of demand is discrete. In many other inventory situations the number of values demand can take on is so large that it is best to approximate the demand with a continuous probability distribution. Since a continuous demand distribution would mean we would need an infinite number of columns in a payoff table to represent all possible demand levels, the payoff table approach is not feasible. *Incremental* or *marginal* analysis offers an efficient way of developing formulas for making the how-much-to-order decision in these cases. We show how this approach can be applied by developing and using it to solve the ordering problem faced by the Johnson Shoe Company.

Suppose that the Johnson Shoe Company is considering ordering a new white fashion shoe for men that has just been shown at a buyers' meeting in New York City. The shoe will be part of the company's spring–summer promotion and will be sold through nine retail stores in the Chicago area. The shoes will cost $20 per pair and retail for $30 per pair. If all the shoes are not sold by July 15, the company will have a July–August clearance sale and will be able to sell all surplus shoes at $15 per pair. How many shoes would you order for this single-period inventory problem?

The obvious question at this time is, what are the possible levels of demand that we might experience for this shoe and what are the probabilities associated with these levels? We will certainly need this demand information before we can intelligently attempt to answer the question of how much to order. The first question, then, is, how do we obtain the demand probability distribution data?

Based on previous experience with other fashion shoes and a general management anticipation of the possible acceptance of this particular shoe, assume we can establish a minimum and maximum sales volume for any particular size of shoe. For example, suppose that for shoe size 10D the estimated range for the demand is 700 to 1300 pairs of shoes. Thus we can establish limits on our demand. However, we still have not established the complete probability distribution on specific shoe demands. Since it would be impractical and virtually impossible for anyone to estimate the probability of exactly 700 units, 701 units, 702 units . . ., our next step is to break the range of sales into several intervals and attempt to use managerial judgment to provide probability estimates for each of the intervals. For example, suppose we divide our demand for the size 10D shoe into the following intervals:

at least 700 but less than 900

at least 900 but less than 1100

at least 1100 but no more than 1300

Since the amount of subjective information required is reduced by breaking the range of sales into intervals, it should be easier to obtain management probability estimates for demands in these intervals. Thus suppose the following estimated probability data were obtained:

Interval	Estimated Probability
At least 700 but less than 900	0.25
At least 900 but less than 1100	0.50
At least 1100 but no more than 1300	0.25

The graph of this probability distribution is shown in Figure 13.3. While we have limited our demand intervals in this example to three, it is often desirable to use a finer breakdown. However, more than six to eight intervals will make it increasingly difficult for managers to provide probability estimates for the intervals.

Incremental analysis attacks the how-much-to-order problem by determining the cost or loss associated with stocking and not stocking *one additional unit.* Suppose we decide to order the average or expected number of shoes demanded. Figure 13.3 shows that this expected demand would be 1000 pairs of size 10D white shoes. Next, suppose a manager asks us to consider incrementing the order size by 1 to an order quantity of 1001 pairs of shoes. Is it economically desirable to make this one-unit increment in the order size? We can make this decision by analyzing the incremental effect of the one additional unit in terms of the cost or loss that might result. Suppose we decide to stock the one additional unit and then find it is not needed. What is our loss? Your answer should be $5, the $20 cost per unit minus $15 salvage value per unit. The $5 cost is the loss associated with stocking an extra unit when it is not needed. Now suppose we decide not to stock the one

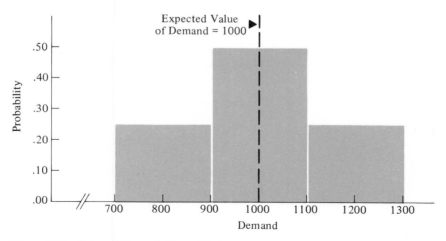

Figure 13.3   Interval Demand Probabilities for Johnson Shoe Company Size 10D White Shoes

additional unit. A loss associated with this decision will occur if we find later that the unit could have been sold. In this case we have lost the opportunity to make a sale and its associated profit. Losses of this type are referred to as opportunity losses. Therefore if we do not stock a unit that could have been sold, we have at least lost the profit of $10 we could have made on the sale of this unit. An unsatisfied demand could also result in a loss of goodwill which could be reflected as an increase in the opportunity loss.

The general expressions for the two types of losses are as follows:

$$L_S = c - s, \tag{13.2}$$

$$L_{NS} = (p - c) + g. \tag{13.3}$$

where

L_S = loss of *stocking* one unit and finding it *could not* be sold,
L_{NS} = loss of *not stocking* one unit and finding it *could have been* sold,
p = selling price per unit,
s = salvage value per unit,
c = cost per unit,
g = goodwill or other added cost per unit due to shortage.

Assume that the Johnson Shoe Company did not specify a goodwill cost; thus the opportunity loss of not stocking an additional unit when it is needed is $10.

When working with uncertain demands, we know we have to consider the probability of obtaining specific demands and thus the probability of obtaining the losses associated with these demands. For example, when considering order sizes of 1000 or 1001 units, the loss of $5 associated with stocking the extra unit can occur only when the demand is less than or equal to 1000 and the extra unit is not sold. Similarly, the $10 loss associated with not stocking the extra unit can occur only when the demand exceeds 1000 and the unstocked unit could have been sold. These conditions are summarized below:

Order Quantity	Possible Loss	Probability Loss Occurs
Incremental unit stocked ($Q = 1001$)	$L_S = \$5$	$P(\text{demand} \leq 1000)$
Incremental unit not stocked ($Q = 1000$)	$L_{NS} = \$10$	$P(\text{demand} > 1000)$

By looking at the demand probability distribution in Figure 13.3, we see that $P(\text{demand} \leq 1000) = 0.50$ and therefore $P(\text{demand} > 1000) = 1 - P(\text{demand} \leq 1000) = 0.50$. By multiplying the possible losses by the probability of obtaining the loss, we have the expected value of the loss or what we call the *expected loss* (EL). Thus

$$\text{EL}(Q = 1001) = L_\text{S}P(\text{demand} \leq 1000) = \$5(0.5) = \$2.50,$$
$$\text{EL}(Q = 1000) = L_\text{NS}P(\text{demand} > 1000) = \$10(0.5) = \$5.00.$$

Now what is our decision: do we order $Q = 1001$ or $Q = 1000$? Since the expected loss is greater for $Q = 1000$, we want to avoid this loss, and thus we should stock the additional unit, making $Q = 1001$. The manager might ask us to again consider incrementing our order by one additional unit to $Q = 1002$.

While we could follow the process of a unit-by-unit analysis, it would be very time consuming and cumbersome. We would have to evaluate $Q = 1001$ versus $Q = 1002$, $Q = 1002$ versus $Q = 1003$, and so on, until we found the expected loss of an incremental unit equal to the expected loss without the incremental unit; that is, the optimal order quantity Q^* occurs when the incremental analysis shows

$$\text{EL}(Q^* + 1) = EL(Q^*) \tag{13.4}$$

and there is no economic advantage to increasing the order quantity by the incremental unit.

Using D to indicate demand, the general expression for equation (13.4) is

$$L_\text{S}P(D \leq Q^*) = L_\text{NS}P(D > Q^*).$$

Since we know

$$P(D > Q^*) = 1 - P(D \leq Q^*),$$

we have

$$L_\text{S}P(D \leq Q^*) = L_\text{NS}[1 - P(D \leq Q^*)].$$

Solving for $P(D \leq Q^*)$, we have

$$P(D \leq Q^*) = \frac{L_\text{NS}}{L_\text{S} + L_\text{NS}} \tag{13.5}$$

Since we have already calculated the losses to be

$$L_\text{NS} = \$10 \quad \text{and} \quad L_\text{S} = \$5,$$

equation (13.5) becomes

$$P(D \leq Q^*) = \frac{10}{5 + 10} = 2/3.$$

Thus we can find the optimal order quantity Q^* by returning to the assumed probability distribution shown in Figure 13.3 and finding a Q^* that will provide $P(D \leq Q^*) = 2/3$. In order to do this, we recall the simplifying assumption for the demand intervals: the probability of any specific demand within an interval is assumed to be *equal* for all values in the interval. For example, this assumption states that the interval 900 but less than 1100 has a 0.5 probability as shown and that all demands in the interval 900, 901, ... , 1000, 1001, ... have the same probability.

Where should Q^* be in order to have $P(D \le Q^*)$ = ⅔ or 0.67? The following tabular format should help us answer that question:

Q	P(D < Q) Lower Limit	P(D < Q) Upper Limit	
700–900	0	0.25	
900–1100	0.25	0.75 ←	Q^* is in
1100–1300	0.75	1.00	this interval

You can see that Q^* must be in the interval from 900 to 1100 units in order for $P(D \le Q^*)$ = 0.67. Since each value of demand in the interval is equally likely, Q^* is given by

$$Q^* = \left(\frac{0.67 - 0.25}{0.50}\right) 200 + 900 = 1068.$$

The general expression for Q^* using incremental analysis and interval demand probabilities is

$$Q^* = LL + \left(\frac{P(D \le Q^*) - LL_p}{I_p}\right) I, \qquad (13.6)$$

where after finding the interval containing Q^*, we define

LL = lower limit of the interval (LL = 900 in the Johnson Shoe problem)

LL_p = probability of $D \le Q$ when Q is the lower limit (LL_p = 0.25 in the Johnson Shoe problem)

I = interval size ($1100 - 900 = 200$ in the Johnson Shoe problem)

I_p = probability that D is in the interval (I_p = 0.50 in the Johnson Shoe problem).

In summary, the key equation in incremental analysis is equation (13.5) where Q^* is found to be at that point where $P(D \le Q^*) = L_{NS}/(L_S + L_{NS})$, or the $L_{NS}/(L_S + L_{NS})$ fractile of the probability distribution of demand. In applying the incremental approach, we would first determine L_{NS} and L_S and then compute $P(D \le Q^*)$. Given this critical probability value, we would refer to the assumed probability distribution in order to find Q^*. The critical probability value $P(D \le Q^*)$ is independent of the probability distribution assumed; that is, if Johnson Shoe Company had assumed a different demand probability distribution we would still want the Q^* where $P(D \le Q^*)$ = 0.67.

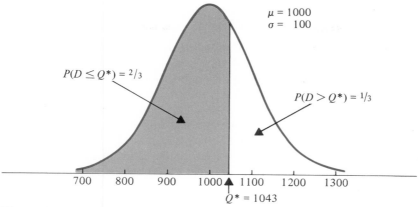

$\mu = 1000$
$\sigma = 100$

$P(D \leq Q^*) = {}^2/_3$

$P(D > Q^*) = {}^1/_3$

700   800   900   1000   1100   1200   1300

$Q^* = 1043$

Figure 13.4 **Normal Distribution of Demand for Johnson Shoe Company Size 10D White Shoes**

For example, suppose that for the same Johnson Shoe Company problem management had decided that a normal distribution with mean $\mu = 1000$ and standard deviation $\sigma = 100$ was a good approximation to the probability distribution of demand for the size 10D shoes (see Figure 13.4).

From Appendix A we see that $2/3$ of the area under the curve for a normal distribution lies below $Z = 0.43$ standard deviations above the mean. Since the average demand is given by $\mu = 1000$ and the standard deviation is $\sigma = 100$,

$$Q^* = \mu + Z\sigma$$
$$= 1000 + 0.43(100) = 1043.$$

Thus with this assumed normal probability distribution of demand the Johnson Shoe Company should order 1043 pairs of the 10D white shoes.

In solving the Johnson Shoe Company problem, we have used two types of continuous demand probability distributions: the interval demand probabilities and the normal probability distribution. The first case gave $Q^* = 1068$ units while the second approach gave $Q^* = 1043$ units. While we have been working on the same basic problem, you may want to ask why we obtained different recommended order quantities. If you look closely at our quantitative procedure you will note that the incremental analysis gave $P(D \leq Q^*) = 2/3$ for both; however, the two approaches assumed different probability distributions for demand. Thus in probabilistic inventory decision models the assumptions about the demand probability distributions are critical and can affect the recommended inventory decision. For the Johnson Shoe Company example, which is the best solution? Actually it depends upon which demand distribution assumption is closest to reality. Thus in applying quantitative approaches to inventory problems with probabilistic demands we must exercise care in selecting the probability distribution that is the best approximation to reality.

Summary

In this chapter you have seen inventory decision models where a known demand could not be assumed, and thus it was expressed by a probability distribution. The critical facet of the probabilistic demand model is obtaining the probability distribution that most realistically approximates the actual demand distribution. We saw that interval demand distributions as well as other specific probability distributions could be used in these models. Solution procedures were presented for approximating the order quantity and reorder point decisions under probabilistic demand. In addition, solution procedures were presented for the single-period probabilistic demand model.

Given a specific inventory problem, our first approach would be to consider the constant demand rate inventory models of Chapter 12. If the assumptions of these models were close approximations to the realities of the inventory problem, we would apply the most representative constant demand rate decision model. If the constant demand rate assumption were not met, we would proceed to *carefully* establish a probability distribution for the demand and then apply the appropriate probabilistic inventory decision model.

If you attempt to apply a constant demand rate inventory model when demand only approximately meets this condition, a manager may become uncomfortable with your demand assumptions and ask you to view the problem in a manner that does not make the known demand assumptions. You would then be correct to point out to him that probabilistic demand models exist that do not require the known demand assumption. On the surface, the manager may view the probabilistic demand model as "closer to reality" and therefore a better approach to the inventory decision problem. However, here is the catch: the probabilistic demand models *require* specification of the probabilities associated with various demand alternatives. When you work with a manager in order to establish the probabilities of selling 100 units, 150 units, and so on, you will encounter assumptions or estimates about the demand probabilities and ultimately find that probabilistic demand models are not necessarily better approximations of the real inventory situation. The trick, of course, is to learn to exercise good judgment in selecting the best inventory decision model for the specific inventory problem.

Glossary

1. *Probabilistic demand*—Situations in which demand for the inventory item is not known exactly and probabilities must be used to describe the demand alternatives for the product.
2. *Lead time demand distribution*—In probabilistic inventory models, this is the distribution of demand that occurs during the lead time period.

3. *Service level*—The average number of stockouts we are willing to allow per year.

4. *Single-period inventory models*—Inventory models in which it is assumed that only one order is placed for the product, and at the end of the period the item has either sold out or there is a surplus of unsold items which will be sold for a salvage value.

5. *Incremental or marginal analysis*—The solution technique whereby the analyst considers the marginal profit or costs associated with incrementing the order quantity by 1 unit.

Problems

1. Floyd Distributors, Inc. provides a variety of auto parts to small local garages. Floyd purchases from the manufacturers according to the EOQ model and then ships from a regional warehouse direct to its customers. For a particular type of muffler, Floyd's EOQ analysis recommends orders with $Q* = 25$ to satisfy an annual demand of 200 mufflers (average demand is approximately 4 units per week). Floyd has a three-week lead time on all orders placed with the muffler supplier.

   a. What is the reorder point if Floyd assumes a constant demand of 4 units per week?

   b. Suppose Floyd's muffler demand shows some variability such that the lead time demand follows a normal distribution with $\mu = 12$ and $\sigma = 2.5$. If Floyd's management can tolerate one stockout per year, what is the revised reorder point?

   c. What is the safety stock for part b? If $C_h = \$5/\text{unit}/\text{year}$, what is the extra cost due to the uncertainty of demand?

2. For Floyd Distributors in Problem 1, we were given $Q* = 25$, $D = 200$, $C_h = \$5$, and a normal lead time demand distribution with $\mu = 12$ and $\sigma = 2.5$.

   a. What is Floyd's reorder point if the firm is willing to tolerate two stockouts during the year?

   b. What is Floyd's reorder point if the firm wants to restrict the probability of a stockout on any one cycle to 1%?

   c. What are the safety stock levels and the annual safety stock costs for the reorder points found in parts a and b?

3. A firm with an annual demand of approximately 1000 units has $C_0 = \$25.50$ and $C_h = 8$. The demand exhibits some variability such that the lead time demand follows a normal distribution with $\mu = 25$ and $\sigma = 5$.

   a. What is the recommended order quantity?

   b. What is the reorder point and safety stock if the firm desires a 2% probability of stockout on any given order cycle?

   c. If a manager sets the reorder point at 30, what is the probability of a stockout on any given order cycle? How many times would you expect to stockout during the year if this reorder point were used?

4. The B&S Novelty and Craft Shop in Bennington, Vermont, sells a variety of quality handmade items to tourists. B&S will sell approximately 300 hand-carved minia-ture replicas of a colonial soldier each year, but the demand pattern during the year is uncertain. The replicas sell for $20 each, and B&S uses a 15% annual inventory holding cost rate. Ordering costs are $5 per order, and demand during the lead time

follows a uniform distribution with the demand alternatives from 6 to 25 each having approximately the same probability of occurrence.

a.   What is the recommended order quantity?

b.   If B&S is willing to have a stockout roughly twice a year, what reorder point would you recommend? What is the probability B&S will have a stockout on any one order cycle?

c.   What are the safety stock and annual safety stock costs for this product?

5.   Suppose the following payoff table represents the profits associated with various production order quantity decisions in a single-period inventory problem:

		Demand D			
		100	200	300	400
	100	150	100	50	0
Order	200	0	300	250	200
Quantities Q	300	−300	0	450	400
	400	−600	−300	0	600

The probability of demand is given by $P(100) = 0.2$, $P(200) = 0.4$, $P(300) = 0.1$, and $P(400) = 0.3$. Use the expected value criterion to arrive at the recommended order quantity.

6.   Refer to the Kremer Chemical Company in Section 13.2. Suppose the following revised cost-profit information has been made available:

Manufacturing cost $25 per pound
Sales price $30 per pound
Purchase of substitute product $40 per pound
Value of excess production $10 per pound.

If possible demands are still 1000, 2000, or 3000 with $P(1000) = 0.4$, $P(2000) = 0.3$, and $P(3000) = 0.3$, what is the new recommended decision and the revised expected profit? Should Kremer reconsider its policy of guaranteeing orders in excess of its production? What would your recommendation be if Kremer supplied only from its production?

7.   The J&B Card Shop sells calendars with different colonial pictures shown for each month. The once-a-year order for each year's calendar is placed in September. From past experience the demand for the calendars can be approximated by a normal distribution with $\mu = 500$ and $\sigma = 120$. The calendars cost $1.50 each, and J&B sells them for $3.00 each.

a.   If J&B throws out all unsold calendars at the end of the year (that is, salvage value is zero), how many calendars should be ordered?

b.   If J&B reduces the calendar price to $1.00 in July of each year and can sell all surplus calendars at this price, how many calendars should be ordered?

8.   The Gilbert Air-Conditioning Company is considering the purchase of a special shipment of portable air conditioners manufactured in Japan. Each unit will cost Gilbert $80 and it will be sold for $125. Gilbert does not want to carry surplus air conditioners over until the following year. Thus all supplies will be sold to a wholesaler who has agreed to take all surplus units for $50 per unit. The probability

distribution for air conditioner demand is as follows:

Interval	Estimated Probability
0 but less than 10	0.30
10 but less than 20	0.35
20 but less than 30	0.20
30 but less than 40	0.10
40 to 50	0.05

Use incremental analysis to find the recommended order quantity for Gilbert.

9. Refer to Problem 8. Suppose the air conditioner demand had been approximated by a normal distribution with $\mu = 20$ and $\sigma = 8$.
   a. What is the recommended order quantity under this assumed demand distribution?
   b. What is the probability Gilbert will sell all units it orders?

10. A popular newsstand in a large metropolitan area is attempting to determine how many copies of the Sunday paper it should purchase each week. Demand for the newspaper on Sundays can be approximated by a normal distribution with $\mu = 450$ and $\sigma = 100$. The newspaper costs the newsstand 35¢ a copy and sells for 50¢ a copy. The newsstand does not receive any value from suplus papers and thus absorbs a 100% loss on all unsold papers.
   a. How many copies of the Sunday paper should be purchased each week?
   b. What is the probability that the newsstand has a stockout?
   c. The manager of the newsstand is concerned about the newsstand's image if the probability of stockout is high. The customers often purchase other items after coming to the newsstand for the Sunday paper. Frequent stockouts would cause customers to go to another newsstand. The manager agrees that a $0.50 loss of goodwill cost should be assigned to any stockout. What is the new recommended order quantity and the new probability of a stockout?

11. A perishable dairy product is ordered daily at a particular supermarket. The product, which costs $1.19 per unit, sells for $1.65 per unit. If units are unsold at the end of the day, the supplier takes them back at a rebate of $1 per unit. Assume that daily demand is approximately normally distributed with $\mu = 150$ and $\sigma = 30$.
   a. What is your recommended daily order quantity for the supermarket?
   b. What is the probability that the supermarket sells all the units it orders?
   c. In problems such as these, why would the supplier offer a rebate as high as $1? For example, why not offer a nominal rebate of, say, 25 cents per unit? What happens to the supermarket order quantity as the rebate is reduced?

12. A retail outlet sells a seasonal product for $10 per unit. The cost of the product is $8 per unit. All units not sold during the regular season are sold for half the retail price in an end-of-season clearance sale. Assume that demand for the product is normal with $\mu = 500$ and $\sigma = 100$.
   a. What is the recommended order quantity?
   b. What is the probability that at least some customers will ask to purchase the product after the outlet is sold out? That is, what is the probability of a stockout using your order quantity in part a?

c. Suppose the owner's policy is that in order to keep customers happy and returning to the store later, stockouts should be avoided if at all possible. What is your recommended order quantity if you get the owner to agree to a 0.15 probability of stockout?

d. Using your answer to part c, what is the goodwill cost you are assigning to a stockout? That is, how many dollars per unit is the owner implying he would pay to avoid a stockout?

13. The McCormick Hardware Store places one order for riding lawn mowers each February. The lawn mowers being purchased this year cost $300 and sell for $425. In the past, McCormick has always been able to sell all surplus lawn mowers during the September "end-of-summer" sale. The clearance sale price for these lawn mowers will be $250. If the following probability distribution for demand is assumed, how many lawn mowers should McCormick order?

Demand	Probability
0	0.10
1	0.15
2	0.30
3	0.20
4	0.15
5	0.10

Application

Informatics Inc.*
Woodland Hills, California

Informatics Inc. was formed in 1962 as a computer software company. Today it has offices located throughout the United States and in several foreign countries. In 1980, the company's revenues were over $125 million.

Informatics has concentrated its business activities in three areas:

1. Software products—selling computer software packages;
2. Information processing—selling computer timesharing services and turnkey systems;
3. Professional services—providing consultants, computer programmers, and other trained personnel.

The application that follows describes the use of an Informatics system known as DISTRIBUTION IV. This computerized system has been used for effective inventory management and merchandise distribution in several of Informatics' client companies.

An Inventory Management Application

Medi-$ave Pharmacies, part of National Medical Enterprises, distributes prescription and over-the-counter merchandise to drugstores across the United States. The company was experiencing profitability problems stemming from a very rapid growth rate. The total number of distribution outlets had climbed to 86, and the company was handling more than 7000 items in its inventory.

To improve bottom-line profits, Medi-$ave attacked the problem of poorly controlled expansion by working toward resource concentration. The company moved away from small chain store distribution and began to develop a business base with leased pharmacy departments in major discount stores.

One of the key factors in making the resource concentration strategy successful was to meticulously control the flow of goods from inventory to drug outlet. To achieve tight inventory control, Medi-$ave installed the merchandise management reporting system called DISTRIBUTION IV. DISTRIBUTION IV is a computerized information system developed for the wholesale and retail distribution industry by Informatics Inc. With the DISTRIBUTION IV system, Medi-$ave generates as many as 500 different reports

*The authors are indebted to Carol Hays of Informatics Inc., for providing this application.

which provide all types of inventory status information. Many of these reports not only provide raw information, but also analyze it. For instance, DISTRIBU-TION IV generates "picking" reports that give instructions to warehouse workers as each merchandise order is received. The picking report tells the worker exactly where to find the merchandise by aisle and bin location. "Screened" picking reports instruct the worker on how many items to draw from that location. For example, a report might list an order for five bottles of aspirin, show that only three bottles are in inventory, and then instruct the worker to pick all three bottles.

Medi-$ave also uses a billing system report that issues billings at the retail rate for each store. These billings come from store-by-store state-ments that show the number of items ordered and the number shipped, and they include a supply of retail price stickers.

An inventory management system issues reports on low stock, dead items, and items with excessive demand. These are examples of raw information reports which are analyzed by an inventory manager. The reports can be issued in any number of variations—by department, by age of inventory, by dollar amount in inventory—and the variation is selectable at any time.

Medi-$ave also analyzes its stock by velocity code. Velocity codes define the typical demand and movement of certain types of stock. For instance, an item coded "A" is ordered regularly and usually in large amounts, "B" coded items have less movement than "A" items, and "C" items less movement than "B" items. Velocity code reports provide informa-tion on the amount of time each coded item remains in stock, helping to determine reorder rates.

The scientific buying module of DISTRIBUTION IV is an example of analytical reporting. Records on the history of activity levels for each item in inventory are analyzed and recommendations on purchases are made based on past demand. An objective of this scientific buying module is to make the inventory replenishment decisions in such a fashion that the contribution margin on inventory investment is maximized. What has evolved is a system known as "cycle time max." Under this system, 80%–85% of the inventory replenishment orders are placed at a specified point in time. With such an ordering policy, larger orders are placed, resulting in quantity discounts and other concessions from suppliers.

The 15%–20% of the inventory items that are not under the "cycle time max" system are handled by the scientific buying module on an exception basis. These items are generally the high volume items which require standard order quantity and reorder level rules based on inventory carrying and ordering costs.

All of the reports provided by the DISTRIBUTION IV system have helped Medi-$ave to achieve tight controls on methods of inventory. Prescription merchandise is now shipped from the Medi-$ave warehouse in Baton Rouge, Louisiana, to all stores five days a week. Over-the-counter merchandise is shipped once every two weeks. Stores place their orders at prearranged times each day through direct order entry devices. At the same time, management information on store sales, number of prescriptions, purchases for the day, and bank deposits are also transmitted to the Medi-$ave headquarters.

With the new reporting system, Medi-$ave has been able to track the gross margin return on investment for every inventoried item and every vendor. Consequently, Medi-$ave has decided to concentrate on leased pharmacy departments of discount stores, minimizing activity with freestanding drugstores. In addition, the discount stores themselves stock health and beauty aids, allowing Medi-$ave to eliminate these items from its own inventory.

As a result of Medi-$ave's strategy, the total number of outlets was cut from 86 to 64. Inventory was reduced from 7000 items to 4500. These efforts have had positive effects on profit figures for Medi-$ave. Over the five years the company has conducted the program, profits have increased by 35.3%, and return on investment for the most recent year was up by 16.1%.

Sales per square foot are $286, as compared to the National Association of Chain Drug Stores (NACDS) reported national median of $158, and Medi-$ave now has a net pretax profit-to-sales ratio of 3.6% (versus the NACDS median of 2.3%).

The DISTRIBUTION IV merchandise management system was first introduced by Informatics in 1971. Today it is being used for the inventory control and management of over one million items.

Chapter 14

Computer Simulation

The management science techniques presented in the other chapters of this text emphasize the formulation and solution of a mathematical model of the system under study. Frequently, the "solution" process employs an analytical procedure which identifies an optimal solution for the model. Although this process of formulating and solving a mathematical model has been successfully applied in many practical situations, there are other systems that are so complex they cannot be modeled and solved in this manner. Computer simulation has proven to be a valuable management science tool in these instances.

As with all models, the purpose of a computer simulation model is to provide a representation of a real system. Great care is usually taken to ensure that the simulation model is descriptive of the real system. Then, through a series of computer runs, or experiments, we study the behavior of the simulation model. The operating characteristics of the simulation model are then used to make inferences about the operating characteristics of the real system. The more representative the simulation model is of the real system, the better the inferences will be.

The surveys of current uses of management science techniques referred to in Chapter 1 indicate that computer simulation is one of the most popular and frequently used problem-solving tools. Some of the reasons why computer simulation is so widely used are as follows:

1. Computer simulation can be used to obtain good solutions to problems that are too complex to be solved with procedures such as linear programming, inventory models, etc.
2. The simulation approach is relatively easy to explain and understand. As a result management confidence is increased, and consequently acceptance of the technique is more easily obtained.
3. Computer manufacturers have developed extensive software packages which consist of specialized simulation programming languages, thus facilitating use by analysts.
4. Simulation is a very flexible technique which can be applied to a wide variety of situations. For example, the technique has been used to describe the behavior of production systems, financial systems, inventory systems, waiting-line systems, and so on.

In this chapter we will introduce the concepts and procedures of computer simulation by studying how the approach can be applied to a waiting-line system and an inventory system. Analytic techniques for these problems are presented in Chapters 12, 13, and 15. The analytic techniques should be used when the mathematical model is not too complex and its underlying assumptions are satisfied. In other cases the simulation approach, as described in this chapter, is a viable alternative.

14.1   County Beverage Drive-Thru

County Beverage Drive-Thru, Inc. is a company that is building a chain of beverage supply stores throughout an area in northern Illinois. The stores are

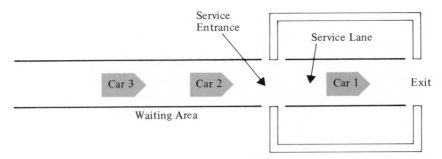

FIGURE 14.1   Layout of County Beverage Drive-Thru

designed to enable customers to pick up beverages, snacks, and party supplies without getting out of their cars. A typical store design is shown in Figure 14.1. A service lane runs through the middle of the store, and soft drinks, beer, and other supplies are stored at various locations along both sides of the service lane. When a customer drives into the store, the store clerk takes the order, fills the order, and collects the money. The customer remains in the car while receiving service. When additional customers arrive at the store, they wait in a line outside the store until the preceding customer's order is complete. Then the next customer in line drives into the store for service.

The County Beverage Drive-Thru operation is an example of a *waiting-line* or *queueing system*. This particular waiting-line configuration has one service lane and is therefore referred to as a *single-channel waiting line*. If we are willing to assume that the number of cars arriving at the store has a Poisson probability distribution and that the length of time that the customer is actually in the store (service time) has an exponential probability distribution, the mathematical models presented in the next chapter can be used to study this waiting-line system. However, for the County Beverage Drive-Thru we are not willing to make these assumptions; thus we will be using computer simulation to study the operation of the store.

The specific situation we will simulate is a new store that will be located near a major shopping center. Construction of the store will not begin for approximately three months. County Beverage's president has requested planning information on the projected operation of the store, including estimates of the number of customers served, profitability of the store, and the number of lost sales due to long waiting lines.

In modeling the system we will study the store's operation in terms of what happens during time periods of three minutes each. That is, we will count the number of customer arrivals, count the number of customers lost, and determine whether or not a customer is being serviced during each three-minute interval. A simulation model which increments time in fixed intervals is referred to as a *fixed-time simulation model.*[1]

Based on a study of traffic flow, the company has estimated the

---

[1] Simulation models which increment time based on the occurrence of the next event (time of next arrival, time of next service, and so on) are referred to as *next-event simulation models.* Next-event simulation models will not be discussed in detail in this text.

TABLE 14.1   Probability Distribution for the Number of Customers Arriving at the County Beverage Drive-Thru During a Three-Minute Period

Number of Customers Arriving	Probability
0	0.19
1	0.39
2	0.19
3	0.15
4	0.08
	1.00

probability distribution of customer arrivals to be as shown in Table 14.1. This probability distribution is believed to be representative of the number of arrivals during the peak business period occurring in the late afternoon and early evening. As the data show, there is a 0.19 probability of no customers arriving during a given three-minute period, a 0.39 probability of one customer arriving during the same three-minute period, and so on.

Sales records from the company's other stores show that customers vary in terms of the size of the order placed. For three classes of order size (small, medium, and large), the probabilities for the various order sizes, the average times to fill the orders, and the average profit per order are shown in Table 14.2.

As an additional operating condition, experience with other company stores indicates that customers will wait for service only if there are less than four cars in the waiting line. If a customer arrives and there are already four cars in the waiting area, the customer will drive off. This failure to enter the waiting line is referred to as *balking* and results in a lost customer and a lost profit.

Simulation of Customer Arrivals

Before developing the complete simulation model, let us concentrate on simulating the number of customers that arrive at the store during any

TABLE 14.2   Order Size Data for the County Beverage Drive-Thru

Order Size	Probability	Time to Fill Order	Average Profit
Small	0.39	3 minutes	$0.75
Medium	0.50	6 minutes	$1.50
Large	0.11	9 minutes	$3.00
	1.00		

three-minute period. In simulating the customer arrival process for County Beverage we will also be demonstrating how the probabilistic component of a real-world process or system is modeled.

The technique used to simulate customer arrivals is based on the use of random numbers. Almost everyone who has been exposed to simple random sampling and basic statistics is familiar with tables of random digits or random numbers.[2] We have included a table of random numbers in Appendix B. Twenty random numbers from the first line of this table are as follows:

$$63271 \quad 59986 \quad 71744 \quad 51102.$$

The specific digit appearing in a given position is a random selection of the digits 0, 1, 2, . . . , 9, with each digit having an equal chance of selection. The grouping of the numbers in sets of five is simply for the convenience of making the table easier to read.

Suppose we select random numbers from our table in sets of two digits. There are 100 two-digit random numbers from 00 to 99, with each two-digit random number having a $1/100 = 0.01$ chance of occurring. While we could select two-digit random numbers from any part of the random number table, suppose we start by using the first row of random numbers from Appendix B. The first ten of the two-digit random numbers would be

$$63, \quad 27, \quad 15, \quad 99, \quad 86, \quad 71, \quad 74, \quad 45, \quad 11, \quad 02.$$

Now let us see how we can simulate the number of customers arriving in a three-minute period by associating a given number of arrivals with each of these two-digit random numbers. For example, let us consider the possibility of no customers arriving during a three-minute interval. The probability distribution in Table 14.1 shows this event to have a 0.19 probability. Since each of the two-digit random numbers has a 0.01 probability of occurrence, we can let 19 of the 100 possible two-digit random numbers correspond to no customers arriving. Any 19 numbers from 00 to 99 will do, but for convenience we associate the arrival of 0 customers with the first 19 two-digit numbers: 00, 01, 02, 03, . . . , 18. Thus any time one of these two-digit numbers is observed in a random selection, we will say that no customers arrived during that period. Since the numbers 00 to 18 include 19% of the possible two-digit random numbers, we expect the arrival of no customers for any given three-minute interval to have a probability of 0.19.

Now consider the possibility of one customer arriving during a three-minute period, an event which has a 0.39 probability of occurring (See Table 14.1). Letting 39 of the 100 two-digit numbers (such as 19, 20, 21, 22, . . . , 57) correspond to a simulated arrival of one customer will provide a 0.39 probability for one customer arrival. Continuing to assign the number of customers arriving to sets of two-digit numbers according to the probability

---

[2]See, for example, *A Million Random Digits with 100,000 Normal Deviates,* Rand Corporation, 1955.

TABLE 14.3   Random Number Assignments for the Number of Customers Arriving at the County Beverage Drive-Thru During a Three-Minute Time Period

Interval	Simulated Arrivals	Probability
00–18	0	0.19
19–57	1	0.39
58–76	2	0.19
77–91	3	0.15
92–99	4	0.08
		1.00

distribution shown in Table 14.1 results in the number and customer arrival assignments shown in Table 14.3.

Using Table 14.3 and the two-digit random numbers in the first row of Appendix B (63, 27, 15, 99, 86, . . .), we can simulate the number of customers arriving during the three-minute periods. The results for 10 such three-minute periods, or ½ hour of store operation, are shown in Table 14.4. The first two-digit random number, 63, is in the interval 58–76; thus according to Table 14.3 this corresponds to two customers arriving during the first three-minute period. The second random number, 27, is in the interval 19–57; thus the number of simulated customer arrivals during the second period is one, and so on.

By selecting a two-digit random number for each three-minute period, we can simulate the number of customer arrivals during that period. In doing so, the simulated probability distribution for the number of customer arrivals

TABLE 14.4   Simulated Customer Arrivals for 10 Three-Minute Periods at the County Beverage Drive-Thru

Period	Random Number	Simulated Customer Arrivals
1	63	2
2	27	1
3	15	0
4	99	4
5	86	3
6	71	2
7	74	2
8	45	1
9	11	0
10	02	0
	Total arrivals (30 minutes)	15

is the same as the given probability distribution shown in Table 14.1. In this manner, the simulation of customer arrivals has the same characteristics as the specified distribution of customer arrivals. Simulations that use a random-number procedure to generate probabilistic inputs such as the number of customer arrivals are referred to as *Monte Carlo simulations*.

For any simulation model it is relatively easy to apply the above random-number procedure to simulate values of a random variable. First develop a table similar to Table 14.3 by associating an interval of random numbers with each possible value of the random variable. In doing so, be sure that the probability of selecting a random number from each interval is the same as the actual probability associated with the value of the random variable. Then each time a value of the random variable is needed, we simply select a new random number and use the corresponding interval of random numbers to find the value of the random variable.

Using a similar procedure, we see that the random-number intervals given in Table 14.5 can be used to simulate order sizes for customers stopping at the County Beverage Drive-Thru.

A Simulation Model for County Beverage Drive-Thru

Now that we know how to simulate the number of customers arriving and the customer order size, let us proceed with the development of the logic for the County Beverage simulation model. We will develop the model in a step-by-step manner. In doing so, we will carry out the necessary calculations to demonstrate how the simulation process is working.

Whenever we need to generate a value for the number of customers arriving and/or the order size, we will use the random numbers from row 10 of Appendix B. Tables 14.3 and 14.5 will be used to determine the corresponding number of customer arrivals and the order sizes. For convenience, the first five two-digit random numbers from row 10 are reproduced here:

81,   62,   83,   61,   00.

In developing the logic and mathematical relationships for the simulation model, we follow the logic and relationships of the actual operation as closely as possible. To demonstrate the simulation process, we begin with an

TABLE 14.5   Random-Number Assignments for the Order Size of Customers of County Beverage Drive-Thru

Interval	Simulated Order Size	Probability
00–38	Small	0.39
39–88	Medium	0.50
89–99	Large	0.11
		1.00

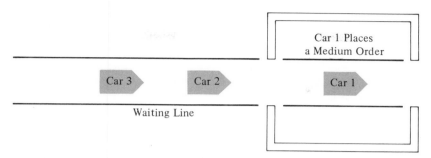

FIGURE 14.2 **Status of the Operation for the First Three-Minute Simulation Period**

idle or empty store and simulate what happens for each of the first three periods. Try to follow the logic of the model and see if you agree with the statements under the column labeled "Things that Happen."

Period 1 (see Figure 14.2).

Random Number	Things that Happen
81	Three cars arrive for service; thus the first car, identified as car 1, gets immediate service.
62	Car 1 places a medium order and hence will not finish service until the end of period 2 (6 minutes).
	Cars 2 and 3 still want service and consequently are in the waiting line.

Period 2 (see Figure 14.3).

Random Number	Things that Happen
83	Three more cars, identified as cars 4, 5, and 6, arrive for service.
	The Drive-Thru is still busy serving the customer from period 1; thus a total of five cars (two waiting plus three new customers) are wanting service this period.

FIGURE 14.3 **Status of the Operation for the Second Three-Minute Simulation Period**

Too many cars are attempting to get service; hence one customer (car 6) will be lost and four cars will remain in the waiting line.

Car 1 completes service at the end of this period; a profit of $1.50 is recorded.

Period 3 (see Figure 14.4).

Random Number	Things that Happen
61	Two more cars, identified as cars 7 and 8, arrive for service.
	The service area is free at the beginning of the period, since the customer from period 1 (car 1) has completed service and left the Drive-Thru.
	One car from the waiting line (car 2) begins service, leaving five cars still wanting service; hence, one customer (car 8) will be lost and four cars will remain in the waiting line.
00	The customer in car 2 places a small order; thus car 2 will finish service at the end of this period. Total profit as of the end of this period will be $1.50 (car 1) + $0.75 (car 2) = $2.25.

The flowchart of the simulation model we have been using is shown in Figure 14.5. Continue to use the random numbers from row 10 of Appendix B and see if you can conduct the simulation calculations for the first ten periods of operation. Your simulation results should agree with those shown in Table 14.6.

At this point we have succeeded in simulating ten periods, or a total of 30 minutes of operation. Although the results in Table 14.6 show evidence of long waiting lines and high lost customer rates (eight in the first half-hour), a 30-minute simulation period is too short a time frame to draw general conclusions about the operation of the store. In order to take full advantage of the simulation procedure we must continue to simulate the store's operation for many more time periods. But even for this relatively small simulation problem continuing the hand simulation computations as we have

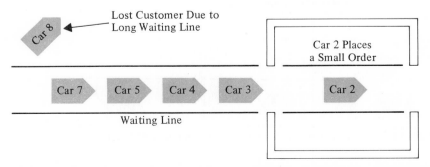

FIGURE 14.4   Status of the Operation for the Third Three-Minute Simulation Period

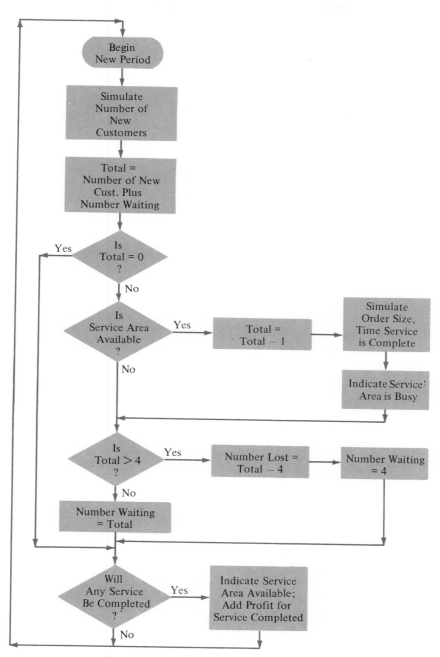

FIGURE 14.5   Flowchart of the County Beverage Simulation Model

TABLE 14.6 Simulation Results from Ten Three-Minute Periods of Operation for the County Beverage Drive-Thru

Period	Random Number	Number of New Customers	Is Service Area Available?	Random Number	Order Size	Service Periods	Number of Lost Customers	Number Waiting	Was Service Completed This Period?	Profit
1	81	3	Yes	62	Medium	2	0	2	No	—
2	83	3	No	—	—	—	1	4	Yes	$1.50
3	61	2	Yes	00	Small	1	1	4	Yes	0.75
4	39	1	Yes	25	Small	1	0	4	Yes	0.75
5	45	1	Yes	68	Medium	2	0	4	No	—
6	35	1	No	—	—	—	1	4	Yes	1.50
7	37	1	Yes	63	Medium	2	0	4	No	—
8	60	2	No	—	—	—	2	4	Yes	1.50
9	24	1	Yes	21	Small	1	0	4	Yes	0.75
10	98	4	Yes	06	Small	1	3	4	Yes	0.75

Total customers served   7

Total profit $7.50

Total lost customers   8

been doing is unrealistic, if not practically impossible. Thus we will look to the computer to provide the computational assistance necessary to conduct the simulation process.

Computer Simulation—Generating Pseudorandom Numbers

If a computer procedure is going to be used to perform the simulation calculations, we will need a way for the computer to generate random numbers and values for the probabilistic components of the model. While the computer could be programmed to store random-number tables and then follow the procedure outlined previously, the computer storage space required would result in an inefficient use of computer resources. For this reason, computer simulations make use of mathematical formulas that generate numbers which, for all practical purposes, have the same properties as the numbers selected from random-number tables. These numbers are called *pseudorandom numbers*. In computer simulations pseudorandom numbers are used in exactly the same way as we used the random numbers selected from random-number tables in our hand simulation.

Most mathematical formulas designed to generate pseudorandom numbers produce numbers from 0 up to but not including 1. Thus we must consider a somewhat different approach in order to simulate the number of customer arrivals and the order size. We must now associate an interval of pseudorandom numbers with each number of arrivals so that the probability of generating a pseudorandom number in the interval will be equal to the probability of the corresponding number of arrivals. Table 14.7 shows how this would be done for the number of cars arriving at the County Beverage Drive-Thru. Note that Table 14.7 shows a pseudorandom number less than 0.19 corresponds to no arrivals, a pseudorandom number greater than or equal to 0.19 but less than 0.58 corresponds to one arrival, and so on. Table 14.8 provides the pseudorandom number intervals that can be used to simulate the order sizes for County Beverage customers.

TABLE 14.7   Pseudorandom Number Intervals and the Associated Number of Customers Arriving at the County Beverage Drive-Thru

Interval of Pseudorandom Numbers	Simulated Customer Arrivals	Probability
0.00 but less than 0.19	0	0.19
0.19 but less than 0.58	1	0.39
0.58 but less than 0.77	2	0.19
0.77 but less than 0.92	3	0.15
0.92 but less than 1.00	4	0.08
		1.00

```
C
C     THIS PROGRAM SIMULATES
C     THE OPERATION OF THE COUNTY BEVERAGE DRIVE-THRU

      HOUR=-1
      WORK=0
      WAIT=0
      FINISH=0
   1  TSERVD=0
      TPROF=0
      TLOST=0
   2  TIME=0
      IF(FINISH.GE.20) FINISH=FINISH-20
C
C     SIMULATE THE NUMBER OF CARS ARRIVING IN A TIME PERIOD
C
   5  TIME=TIME+1
      RN=RAND(1.)
      IF(RN.LT..19) CAR=0
      IF(RN.GE..19.AND.RN.LT..58) CAR=1
      IF(RN.GE..58.AND.RN.LT..77) CAR=2
      IF(RN.GE..77.AND.RN.LT..92) CAR=3
      IF(RN.GE..92) CAR=4
      TOTAL=WAIT+CAR
      IF(TOTAL.EQ.0) GO TO 10
      IF(WORK.EQ.1) GO TO 20
      TOTAL=TOTAL-1
C
C     SIMULATE THE ORDER SIZE OF THE NEXT CAR TO BE SERVICED
C
      RN=RAND(1.)
      IF(RN.LT..39) LENGTH=1
      IF(RN.GE..39.AND.RN.LT..89) LENGTH=2
      IF(RN.GE..89) LENGTH=3
      FINISH=TIME+LENGTH-1
      WORK=1
C
C     CALCULATE THE NUMBER OF LOST CUSTOMERS AND NUMBER WAITING
C
  20  IF(TOTAL.GT.4) GO TO 30
      WAIT=TOTAL
      GO TO 10
  30  LOST=TOTAL-4
      WAIT=4
      TLOST=TLOST+LOST
C
C     RELEASE A CAR COMPLETING SERVICE AND RECORD THE PROFIT
C
  10  IF(FINISH.NE.TIME) GO TO 5
```

Figure 14.6   See legend facing page.

TABLE 14.8   Pseudorandom Number Intervals and the Associated
Order Sizes for County Beverage Customers

Interval of Pseudorandom Numbers	Simulated Order Size	Probability
0.00 but less than 0.39	Small	0.39
0.39 but less than 0.89	Medium	0.50
0.89 but less than 1.00	Large	0.11
		1.00

Computer Simulation—Computer Program and Results

A computer *simulator* is a computer program written to conduct simulation
computations. For the County Beverage simulation we need a computer
program with the logic as shown in Figure 14.5. Such a program would
perform the calculations and keep track of the simulation results in a form
similar to that shown in Table 14.6. Figure 14.6 shows a computer program

```
      IF(LENGTH.EQ.1) PROFIT=.75
      IF(LENGTH.EQ.2) PROFIT=1.5
      IF(LENGTH.EQ.3) PROFIT=3
      TPROF=TPROF+PROFIT
      TSERVD=TSERVD+1
      WORK=0
C
C     SIMULATION RUN OF 20 TIME PERIODS PER HOUR
C
      IF(TIME.LT.20) GO TO 5
      HOUR=HOUR+1
      IF(HOUR.EQ.0) GO TO 1
C
C     WRITE SUMMARY RESULTS OF SIMULATION RUN
C
      IF(HOUR.LT.30) GO TO 2
      ASERVD=TSERVD/30
      PSERVD=TSERVD/(TSERVD+TLOST)*100
      ALOST=TLOST/30
      PLOST=100-PSERVD
      APROF=TPROF/30
      WRITE(6, 35)
   35 FORMAT('1',////////,10X,'ITEM OF INTEREST',5X,'TOTAL',5X,'PERCENT'
     ,5X,'HOURLY AVERAGE',///)
      WRITE(6,40) TSERVD,PSERVD,ASERVD
   40 FORMAT(14X,'SERVED',F16.0,F11.1,F15.1,/)
      WRITE(6,45) TLOST,PLOST,ALOST
   45 FORMAT(14X,'LOST',F18.0,F11.1,F15.1,/)
      WRITE(6,50) TPROF,APROF
   50 FORMAT(14X,'PROFIT',F18.2,9X,F16.2)
      STOP
      END
```

FIGURE 14.6   FORTRAN Program for Simulation of the County Beverage Drive-Thru

TABLE 14.9   Computer Simulation Results for 30 Hours of Operation

Item of Interest	Total	Percent	Hourly Average
Number served	365	38.8	12.17
Number lost	575	61.2	19.17
Profit	$488.25	—	$16.28

written in the FORTRAN language which will simulate the County Beverage operation.

Results from the computer simulation are shown in Table 14.9. The store's operation was simulated for a total of 30 hours (600 three-minute time periods). Based on the simulation results, we are able to make the following observations about the behavior of the system:

1. 365 customers were serviced during the 30 hours of simulated operation. However, 575 cars (61.2%) were lost because of long waiting lines.

2. The average profit was $16.28 per hour or $1.34 per car serviced ($488.25/365 = $1.34).

3. The biggest problem with the store's operation appears to be the number of lost customers (an average of 19.17 per hour). An estimate of the average dollar loss per hour due to lost customers is 19.17 ($1.34 per car) = $25.69.

Recall for a moment that a primary objective of simulation is to describe the behavior of a real system. In the County Beverage Drive-Thru simulation this is exactly what we have done. We have not determined an optimal solution or decision for the store; we have simply simulated what could happen in 30 hours of actual operation of the Drive-Thru. If the actual operation behaves as the simulation model indicates, County Beverage will have a significant waiting-line problem with a sizable lost profit.

14.2   Some Practical Considerations

Before proceeding with any further discussion and analysis of the County Beverage simulation model, let us describe some other aspects of simulation that are encountered in almost every simulation study.

Selecting a Simulation Language

In developing the computer program or simulator, a decision must be made as to the computer language that will be used. General purpose programming languages such as FORTRAN and PL/1 can be used to develop the computer programs. However, as the growth of simulation applications and interest has increased, users as well as computer manufacturers have recognized that most computer simulations have many common features: values of random variables must be generated from probability distributions; tables are needed to keep track of simulation results; and so on. Thus special programming languages have been developed to enable analysts and programmers to more easily describe simulation models in computer form.

Some of the more common simulation languages in use today are GPSS, SIMSCRIPT, DYNAMO, and GASP. These special simulation languages frequently have automatic or built-in time indicators, simplified procedures for generating probabilistic components, and automatic collection and printout of statistical results. One programming statement of a simulation language often performs the computation and record keeping that would require several FORTRAN or PL/1 statements to duplicate. There are complete textbooks devoted to a discussion of the use of computer languages in simulation, and the interested reader can refer to one of the references listed at the end of this text.

Validation

An important step in any simulation study is the validation of the simulation model. Validation involves verifying that the simulation model accurately represents the real-world system it is designed to simulate. Models that do not adequately reflect the behavior of the real system cannot be expected to provide worthwhile information. Thus before implementing any simulation results the analyst must be sure that a thorough job of model validation has been done.

If the simulation model applies to a system currently in operation, the simulation results can be compared with the current and the past behavior of the system in order to determine the validity of the model. The procedure usually followed is to run the simulation model using an actual set of past observations. In this way the output of the simulation model can be directly compared to the behavior of the actual system. Any major difference in the results is indicative of problems in the model.

Another approach to model validation is to have the overall model reviewed by people who are most familiar with the operation of the real system. This review is subjective in nature, with the appropriate individuals evaluating the reasonableness of the simulation model and the simulation results.

In addition, careful attention should also be paid to the programming of the simulation model. Even if the model is formulated correctly, improper programming of the model can lead to inaccurate results. Standard quality control steps and good programming practice can be the best safeguards against this type of error.

A further check in the validation procedure is to compare the simulated distributions for the probabilistic components with the corresponding distributions in the real system. For example, in the County Beverage study, the

TABLE 14.10 Model-Validation Step Showing a Comparison of the Simulated Relative Frequencies and the Actual Probability Distribution for the Number of Customer Arrivals at the County Beverage Drive-Thru

Number of Customer Arrivals	Number of Simulated Periods Having This Number of Arrivals	Simulated Relative Frequencies	Actual Probabilities (See Table 14.1)
0	124	0.207	0.19
1	229	0.382	0.39
2	104	0.173	0.19
3	86	0.143	0.15
4	57	0.095	0.08
Simulated periods	600	1.000	1.00

probability distribution for the number of cars arriving in a three-minute period was considered known and an important input for the simulation model. Recall that the simulation results shown in Table 14.9 were based on 30 hours of simulated operation. Since each hour has 20 three-minute periods, the total simulation contained 30(20) = 600 three-minute periods. Thus if the simulation model is correctly simulating the number of customers arriving at the store, the relative frequencies of the number of cars arriving should approximate the probability distribution for the real system as shown in Table 14.1.

Table 14.10 shows the relative frequencies for the number of customers that arrived during the 600 three-minute periods in the simulation run. A comparison of the simulated distribution and the actual probability distribution from Table 14.1 shows no major differences. Thus we conclude that the number of customer arrivals is being simulated correctly.[3] A similar comparison of the actual and simulated distributions for the size of the customer orders resulted in the conclusion that the model was valid in terms of its simulation of this probabilistic component.

Start-Up Problems

Most simulation studies are concerned with the operation of a system during its normal, or *steady-state,* condition. In the County Beverage example, the firm is interested in what happens during a "normal" hour of operation. Recall, however, that when we started the hand simulation calculations we assumed that no cars were waiting and that no cars were being served. Therefore data collected during the first part of the simulation can be expected to differ from the data collected during time intervals later in the

---

[3]Standard statistical procedures, such as the chi-square goodness-of-fit test, can be performed to test whether the results observed are expected. The use of such tests is described in most standard statistics texts. For example, see Anderson, D.R., Sweeney, D.J., and Williams, T.A., *Introduction to Statistics: An Applications Approach,* St. Paul, Minn., West Publishing Company, 1981.

simulation. The usual way to avoid start-up difficulties is to run the simulation model for a specified time period without collecting any data. The length of this start-up period must be sufficient for the system to have stabilized. Data are then collected on the system after it has reached a stable, or steady-state, condition. For the County Beverage simulation, the first hour of operation was considered a start-up period. The data for the 30 hours of simulation reported in Table 14.9 are the simulation results for hours 2 through 31.

Statistical Considerations

The results of any simulation run actually represent a sample. For example, the simulation results in Table 14.9 can be viewed as a sample of 30 hours of operation. Thus $16.28 is an estimate of the mean hourly profit for the County Beverage operation. The important thing to keep in mind is that different values for average hourly profit would be observed if the simulation was run again using a different sequence of random numbers. Nonetheless, by running the simulation for long periods, large sample sizes are obtained, and most analysts are willing to use the values obtained from the simulation run to estimate the true mean value of interest.

Determining the best statistical approach to estimating the value of some quantity (such as hourly profit) is not a simple problem. A complete study of this issue would require a background in the area of statistics referred to as experimental design. Consequently, the interested reader is referred to one of the more advanced texts on simulation listed at the end of this book.

14.3 County Beverage Drive-Thru—Additional Simulation Results

The primary conclusion from the simulation results presented in Section 14.1 for the County Beverage operation is that the store cannot handle the amount of business that is anticipated. Undoubtedly, County Beverage management would like to explore alternative operating policies that might improve service and hence company profits. Certainly, the addition of a second store clerk should help the performance of the system. In addition, since construction of the building has not begun, management could consider a possible redesign of the store. Thus the following two operating policies and store layouts are being considered.

System A (see Figure 14.7)   Two clerks will operate the store during the peak business period. Two cars will be permitted into the store area for servicing at the same time. Bottlenecks may still occur because both cars must use the same lane. If the second car completes service before the first car, it will have to wait for the first car to complete service before it can leave the store. Also, if the first car finishes service first, it can leave the store, but

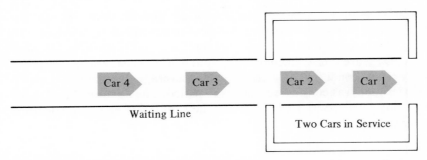

FIGURE 14.7   Proposed Design, System A, for the County Beverage Drive-Thru

a new customer cannot enter the store until the car in the second position has its order filled.

System B (see Figure 14.8)   Two clerks will operate the store during the peak period. The service lane of the store will be widened to permit two cars to be serviced simultaneously, with each car being permitted to leave the store as soon as it is finished. Waiting cars move into the store as soon as either lane opens up.

In order to help the company determine which system should be adopted, simulation models were developed for both systems. Tables 14.11 and 14.12 show the results of 30 hours of simulation for each system. These simulation results provide critical information to the individual responsible for the final design decision.

System A shows an average profit of $27.88 per hour, an increase of $11.60 per hour over the original one-lane, one-server system. However, 302 customers (32.8%) were lost because of long waiting lines. Although system B shows a higher average profit ($34.48) and a lower lost customer rate (15.9%), the advantage of system B may be offset by the added construction cost required to widen the service lane. The final decision may still take more study, but the simulation results provide important information for the decision maker. Perhaps a creative person could come up with an idea for

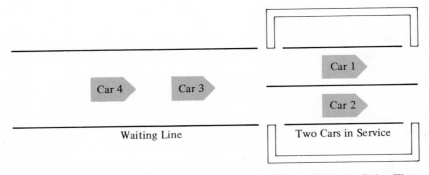

FIGURE 14.8   Proposed Design, System B, for the County Beverage Drive-Thru

Table 14.11 Computer Simulation Results for 30 Hours of Operation at the County Beverage Drive-Thru Under System A

Item of Interest	Total	Percent	Hourly Average
Number served	618	67.2	20.60
Number lost	302	32.8	10.07
Profit	$836.25	—	$27.88

modifying the single service lane operation to increase the number of cars served and still avoid the costly two-lane construction. If such an idea occurs, a simulation model could be developed to evaluate its effectiveness.

14.4   An Inventory Simulation Model

In this section we present a simulation model of an inventory system being operated by an auto supply company. While we are interested in understanding how the inventory system operates, we are also interested in making decisions concerning the reorder point and order quantity for a particular inventory item. By designing a set of experiments, we will simulate the operation of the inventory system for a variety of reorder point and order quantity alternatives. Upon completion of the experiments with the simulation model we should be able to select a good reorder point and order quantity for the item.

Art's Auto Supplies, Inc. is a specialty auto supplies store that carries over 1000 items in inventory. While the store's manager has used inventory models to determine how-much-to-order and when-to-order decisions for most of the products, the manager has become especially concerned about the inventory problem for a deluxe tool cabinet. Demand for the cabinets has been relatively low but subject to some variability. While on approximately one-half of the days the store is open for business no one orders a cabinet, about one day per month three or four orders occur. If variable demand were the only source of uncertainty, the store manager believes the order quantity

Table 14.12 Computer Simulation Results for 30 Hours of Operation at the County Beverage Drive-Thru Under System B

Item of Interest	Total	Percent	Hourly Average
Number served	785	84.1	26.17
Number lost	148	15.9	4.93
Profit	$1034.25	—	$34.48

and reorder point decisions could be based on an inventory model, perhaps similar to the inventory model discussed in Section 13.1. However, the tool cabinet inventory problem is further complicated by the fact that the lead time—the time between order placement and order arrival—also varies. Historically the length of the lead time has been anywhere between one and five days. These lead times have caused the store to run out of inventory on several occasions. Orders received during the out-of-stock period have caused lost sales. Thus given this situation, the store manager would like to establish order quantity and reorder point decisions that minimize total relevant inventory cost—that is, ordering, holding, and stockout or shortage costs.

After an analysis of delivery charges and other costs associated with each order, the store manager was able to estimate an order cost at $20 per order. An analysis of interest, insurance, and other inventory carrying costs led to an estimate for the holding cost of $0.10 per unit per day. Finally, the shortage cost was estimated to be $50 per unit. The total cost of the system is given by the sum of the ordering cost, the holding cost, and the shortage cost. The objective is to find the order quantity and reorder point combination that will result in the lowest possible total cost.

A first step in the simulation approach to this problem is to develop a model that can be used to simulate the total costs corresponding to a specific order size and reorder point. Then, using this model, the two decision variables can be varied systematically in order to determine what appears to be the lowest cost combination. Let us see what is involved in developing such a model to carry out a one-day simulation of the inventory process.

Assume that a specific reorder point and order quantity have already been selected. We must begin each day of the simulation by checking whether any inventory that had been ordered has just arrived. If so, the current inventory on hand must be increased by the quantity of goods received. Note that this assumes that orders are received and inventory on hand is updated at the start of each day. If this assumption is not appropriate, a different model, perhaps calling for goods to be received at the end of the day, would have to be developed.

Next our simulator must generate a value for the daily demand from the appropriate probability distribution. If there is sufficient inventory on hand to meet the daily demand, the inventory on hand will be decreased by the amount of the daily demand. If, however, inventory on hand is not sufficient to satisfy all the demand, we will satisfy as much of the demand as possible. The inventory will then be zero, and a shortage cost will be computed for all unsatisfied demand. In using this procedure we are assuming that if a customer orders more cabinets than the store has in inventory, the customer will take what is available and shop elsewhere for the remainder of the order. With another auto supply store only two blocks away, the store manager is sure unsatisfied demand will result in lost sales, and a $50 goodwill cost for each shortage is believed to be appropriate.

After the daily order has been processed, the next step is to determine if the ending inventory has reached the reorder point and a new order should be placed. However, prior to placing a new order, we must check to see if the

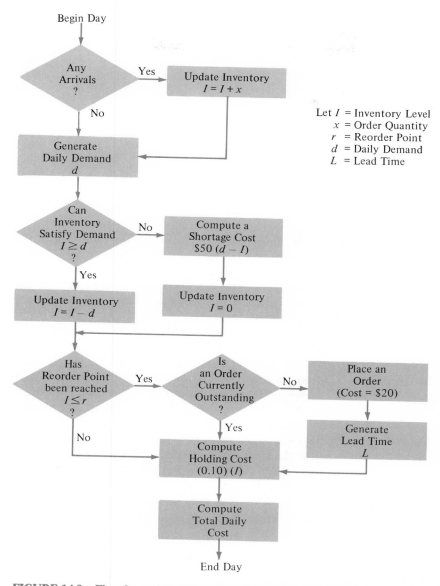

Begin Day

Any Arrivals ? — Yes → Update Inventory $I = I + x$

No

Generate Daily Demand d

Let I = Inventory Level
x = Order Quantity
r = Reorder Point
d = Daily Demand
L = Lead Time

Can Inventory Satisfy Demand $I \geq d$? — No → Compute a Shortage Cost $\$50 \, (d - I)$

Yes

Update Inventory $I = I - d$ Update Inventory $I = 0$

Has Reorder Point been reached $I \leq r$? — Yes → Is an Order Currently Outstanding ? — No → Place an Order (Cost = \$20)

No   Yes   Generate Lead Time L

Compute Holding Cost $(0.10) \, (I)$

Compute Total Daily Cost

End Day

FIGURE 14.9 **Flowchart of the Simulation of One Day of Operation for the Art's Auto Supplies Inventory System**

most recent order is outstanding and should be arriving shortly. If so, we do not place an order.[4] Otherwise, an order is placed and the company incurs an ordering cost. If a new order is placed, a lead time must be randomly generated to reflect the time between the placement and the receipt of the goods.

[4]We are assuming that it will never be necessary to have two orders outstanding simultaneously. However, in other simulation models, having several orders outstanding may be an entirely appropriate assumption.

Table 14.13   Frequency and Relative Frequency Distributions for Demand in Art's Auto Supplies Problem

Demand (units)	Frequency (days)	Relative Frequency
0	150	0.50
1	75	0.25
2	45	0.15
3	15	0.05
4	15	0.05
	300	1.00

Finally, an inventory holding cost, which is $0.10 for each unit in the daily ending inventory, is computed. The sum of the shortage costs, ordering costs, and inventory holding costs becomes the total daily cost for the simulation. Performing the above sequence of operations would complete one day of simulation. Figure 14.9 depicts this daily simulation process for the deluxe tool cabinet inventory operation.

The daily simulation process should be repeated for as many days as are necessary to obtain meaningful results. The output from the simulation will show the total cost involved in using one particular order quantity and reorder point combination. By simulating the inventory operation with different order quantity–reorder point combinations, we can compare total operating costs and select the apparent "best" order quantity and reorder point decisions for the deluxe tool cabinets.

Suppose the store has a complete set of records showing the demand for the deluxe tool cabinets for the past year (300 days). Furthermore, suppose the records also show the number of days between placement and receipt of each order over the same period. Table 14.13 shows the frequency and relative frequency distributions for demand, and Table 14.14 shows the frequency and relative frequency distributions for lead time.

Table 14.14   Frequency and Relative Frequency Distributions for Lead Time in Art's Auto Supplies Problem

Lead Time (days)	Frequency (days)	Relative Frequency
1	6	0.20
2	3	0.10
3	12	0.40
4	6	0.20
5	3	0.10
	30	1.00

TABLE 14.15 Pseudorandom Numbers and Associated Daily Demands for Art's Auto Supplies Problem

Daily Demand	Relative Frequency	Interval of Pseudorandom Numbers	Probability of Selecting a Psuedorandom Number in Interval
0	0.50	0.00 but less than 0.50	0.50
1	0.25	0.50 but less than 0.75	0.25
2	0.15	0.75 but less than 0.90	0.15
3	0.05	0.90 but less than 0.95	0.05
4	0.05	0.95 but less than 1.00	0.05
	1.00		1.00

In order to carry out the simulation steps depicted in Figure 14.9, we must develop the procedure for generating values from the demand and lead time distributions. As before, we shall associate with each value of the random variable an interval of pseudorandom numbers such that the probability of generating a pseudorandom number in that interval is the same as the relative frequency of the associated demand and lead time. The intervals of pseudorandom numbers are shown in Tables 14.15 and 14.16.

To appreciate how the simulation method works for this problem, we will follow a ten-day simulation of the process. Let us assume that the store manager wants to determine the effect of using an order quantity of five units with a reorder point of three units. For purposes of starting the simulation, let us assume that we have a beginning inventory of 5 units at the start of day 1 of our ten-day simulation.

Refer to the flowchart in Figure 14.9. The first step is to check to see if any shipments have arrived. Since this is the first day of the simulation, we

TABLE 14.16 Pseudorandom Number Intervals and Associated Lead Times for Art's Auto Supplies Problem

Lead Time (days)	Relative Frequency	Interval of Pseudorandom Numbers	Probability of Selecting a Pseudorandom Number in Interval
1	0.20	0.00 but less than 0.20	0.20
2	0.10	0.20 but less than 0.30	0.10
3	0.40	0.30 but less than 0.70	0.40
4	0.20	0.70 but less than 0.90	0.20
5	0.10	0.90 but less than 1.00	0.10
	1.00		1.00

assume no arrivals, and generate the daily demand for day 1. Let us assume we use a computer to generate pseudorandom numbers between 0 and 0.999 · · · and that the first number generated is 0.093. From Table 14.15 we see that this pseudorandom number corresponds to a demand of 0 units. Note that we have no shortage costs to compute since the inventory on hand (5 units) is greater than the reorder point (3 units); thus we do not place an order. The holding costs for day 1 are computed to be ($0.10) 5, or $0.50. With no shortages and no ordering, the total cost for day 1 is just the holding cost of $0.50. Continuing our simulation in this manner, we obtained the computer generated results shown in Table 14.17.

At the start of day 4 the beginning inventory was 4 units. The random number selected to generate daily demand was 0.528; thus a daily demand of 1 unit was generated. As a result, the ending inventory dropped to 3 units and an order for 5 units was placed. Generating another random number, in this case 0.620, indicates (see Table 14.16) a lead time of 3 days, which means that the new order will be available on day 7. The day 4 costs are ($0.10) 3 = $0.30 for the inventory holding cost and $20.00 for the ordering cost. Since there was not shortage cost, the total cost for the day was $20.30. The figures at the bottom of Table 14.17 provide the average holding cost, average order cost, average shortage cost, and average total cost for the ten-day simulation. Prior to drawing any firm conclusions based on these limited simulation results, we should run the simulation for many more days. Also we will want to test many other order quantity–reorder point combinations.

A computer programmer could develop a computer simulation program or simulator that would enable the store to explore a variety of order quantities and reorder points for a large number of simulated days. In Table 14.18 we present output from a simulator that was developed to solve inventory problems such as the auto supplies problem. In this simulator the

TABLE 14.17   Computer Simulation Results for Ten Days of Operation of Art's Auto Supplies with an Order Quantity of 5 and Reorder Point of 3

Day	Beg Inv	Units Rcvd	Rndm Numb	Units Demd	End Inv	Rndm Numb	Lead Time	Holding Cost	Order Cost	Short Cost	Total Cost
1	5	0	0.093	0	5			0.50	0.00	0.00	0.50
2	5	0	0.681	1	4			0.40	0.00	0.00	0.40
3	4	0	0.292	0	4			0.40	0.00	0.00	0.40
4	4	0	0.528	1	3	0.620	3	0.30	20.00	0.00	20.30
5	3	0	0.866	2	1			0.10	0.00	0.00	0.10
6	1	0	0.975	4	0			0.00	0.00	150.00	150.00
7	0	5	0.622	1	4			0.40	0.00	0.00	0.40
8	4	0	0.819	2	2	0.939	5	0.20	20.00	0.00	20.20
9	2	0	0.373	0	2			0.20	0.00	0.00	0.20
10	2	0	0.353	0	2			0.20	0.00	0.00	0.20
			Average cost for 10 simulated days					0.27	4.00	15.00	19.27

TABLE 14.18 Simulated Average Daily Cost for 1000 Days of Art's Auto Supplies Inventory Problem

Reorder Level	Order Quantity									
	5	10	15	20	25	30	35	40	45	50
1	14.35	8.30	6.58	5.20	5.35	4.16	3.30	4.42	3.98	5.22
2	11.51	5.93	5.46	3.92	3.91	3.44	2.96	3.69	3.62	3.71
3	9.34	5.64	3.37	3.01	3.03	2.84	3.96	3.29	2.90	3.07
4	6.90	4.12	3.47	2.78	3.14	2.79	3.29	3.25	3.37	3.42
5	5.41	3.31	2.85	2.42	2.61	3.24	3.25	2.93	3.18	3.22
6	4.72	2.75	2.69	2.60	(2.39)	2.74	2.93	3.06	3.13	3.34
7	4.72	2.85	2.52	2.60	2.76	2.71	3.06	2.99	3.02	3.28
8	5.50	2.89	2.66	2.50	2.62	2.75	2.99	3.05	3.33	3.56
9	4.36	3.11	2.62	2.62	2.66	2.77	3.05	3.18	3.34	3.49
10	4.68	3.05	2.75	2.72	2.80	2.85	3.18	3.28	3.31	3.72

decision maker has the option of selecting a variety of order quantities and reorder points. For purposes of illustration, the computer simulation output is shown for simulations with order quantities of from 5 units to 50 units in increments of 5 and for reorder points of from 1 to 10 in increments of 1. A total of 1000 days is represented in the simulation of each order quantity–reorder point combination.

We see that the results of this computer simulation indicate that the lowest cost solution occurs at an order quantity of 25 units and a reorder point of 6 units; in this case the resulting average total cost is $2.39 per day. After studying these results, the store manager might wish to explore other order quantities near the apparent "best" order quantity of 25. In Table 14.19 the results of varying the order quantity from 21 to 30 in increments of 1 and reorder points from 4 to 8 are shown. The smallest simulated average total cost of $2.33 now occurs when the order quantity is 22 units and the reorder point is 6 units. Note, however, that in this second set of simulation experiments the previously best order quantity of 25 units and reorder point of 6 units has a total cost of $2.75 per day. Since different random numbers

TABLE 14.19 Simulated Average Daily Cost for 1000 Days of Art's Auto Supplies Inventory Problem

Reorder Level	Order Quantity									
	21	22	23	24	25	26	27	28	29	30
4	2.94	3.02	3.13	2.74	2.89	2.56	2.74	3.07	2.67	3.24
5	2.59	2.58	2.84	2.70	2.66	2.59	2.88	2.57	2.48	2.75
6	2.55	(2.33)	2.87	2.35	2.75	2.45	2.81	2.79	2.61	2.60
7	2.52	2.45	2.47	2.51	2.57	2.62	2.61	2.63	2.62	2.67
8	2.50	2.69	2.48	2.49	2.63	2.57	2.63	2.69	2.69	2.71

were used in the two simulations, different total costs are to be expected. The selection of the "best" order quantity and reorder point is now up to the analyst. What decisions would you make? While you might want to run more or longer simulations, the simulation data of Tables 14.18 and 14.19 indicate that good solutions apparently exist with order quantities around 20 to 25 units and reorder points around 6 or 7 units. Thus while simulation has not guaranteed an optimal solution, it has enabled us to identify apparent low-cost or "near-optimal" decisions for the inventory problem. The final decision for an order quantity and reorder point will be based on the store manager's preference from among the good or "near-optimal" solutions.

14.5   Advantages and Disadvantages of Computer Simulation

A primary advantage of computer simulation is that it is applicable in complex cases where analytical procedures cannot be employed. For example, the County Beverage waiting-line system and the Art's Auto Supply inventory system were sufficiently complex that the analytical approaches discussed in other chapters of this text did not apply. That is, the forms of the probability distributions involved do not satisfy the assumptions of the analytical models. In general, as the number of probabilistic components in the system becomes larger, the more likely it is that simulation will be the best approach.

Another advantage of the simulation approach is that the simulation model and simulator provide a convenient experimental laboratory. Once the computer program has been developed, it is usually relatively easy to experiment with the model. For example, if we wanted to know the effect of an increase in shortage cost on the recommended solution to our inventory problem, we could have simply changed the shortage cost input value and rerun the simulation. The effect of experimental changes in other inputs, such as the probability distributions of customer arrivals, lead time, and so on, could also be investigated.

Simulation is not without its disadvantages. One obvious disadvantage is that someone must develop the computer program. For large simulation projects this is usually a substantial undertaking. Hence one should certainly not attempt to develop a simulation model unless the potential gains promise to outweigh the costs of model development. This disadvantage has been reduced in recent years with the development of computer simulation languages such as GPSS and SIMSCRIPT. The use of these languages often leads to considerable savings in time and money as the computer program or simulator is developed.

Another disadvantage of simulation is that it does not guarantee an optimal solution to a problem. One usually selects those values of the decision variables to test in the model that have a good chance of being near the optimal solution. However, since it is usually too costly to try all values of the decision variables, and since different simulations may provide different results, there is no guarantee that the best simulation solution found is the overall optimal solution. Nonetheless, the danger of obtaining bad solutions is slight if good judgment is exercised in developing and running the simulation model. The decision maker usually has a good idea of reasonable values to try for the decision variables, and it is usually possible to run the simulation long enough to identify the apparent best decisions.

Summary

In this chapter we have seen how two different problems could be analyzed and solved using the computer simulation technique. Based on these two simulation models, we can make the following general observations about the simulation approach to decision making:

1. Simulation is most appropriate when the problem is too complex or difficult to solve using another quantitative technique.
2. A model must be developed to represent the various relationships existing in the problem situation.
3. A process such as a random-number procedure must be employed to generate values for the probabilistic components in the model.
4. A bookkeeping procedure must be developed to keep track of what is happening in the simulation process (see Table 14.6).
5. Because of the numerous calculations required in most simulations, a computer program or simulator is required.
6. The simulation process must be conducted for many days or periods in order to establish the long-run averages for the decision alternatives or other changes in the system.

Simulation should not necessarily be thought of as another technique for finding optimal solutions to problems. However, once a simulation model has been developed, a quantitative analyst may vary certain key design parameters and observe the effect on the output of the computer runs. Through a series of experiments with the simulation model good values may be selected for the key design parameters of the system. In the County Beverage problem, simulation experiments helped to identify the two-lane design as the one yielding the highest average hourly profit. In the simulation of Art's Auto Supply, the simulation experiments helped identify an order quantity of 22 and a reorder level of 6 as a good low cost inventory policy. Thus through these two examples we have shown how simulation experiments can be used to provide information on how to improve the performance of a system.

In both problems studied in this chapter, the probabilistic components resulted from discrete probability distributions; that is, the random variables involved could take on only a finite number of values. In many computer simulation experiments probabilistic components are encountered that follow continuous distributions such as the normal or exponential probability distributions. The basic simulation approach we have developed in this chapter is still appropriate for these situations. The only difference concerns the method of generating random values from the appropriate continuous probability distributions.

Glossary

1. *Simulation*—A technique used to describe the behavior of a real-world system over time. Most often this technique employs a computer program to perform the simulation computations.
2. *Monte Carlo simulation*—Simulations that use a random number procedure to create values for the probabilistic components.
3. *Pseudorandom numbers*—Computer-generated numbers developed from mathematical expressions which have the properties of random numbers.
4. *Simulator*—The computer program written to perform the simulation calculations.
5. *GPSS, SIMSCRIPT, DYNAMO, GASP*—Specially designed computer programming languages used for simulation studies.

Problems

Most of the problems in this section are designed to enable you to perform simulations with hand calculations. To keep the calculations reasonable, we will ask you to consider only a few decision alternatives and relatively short periods of simulation. While this should give you a good understanding of the simulation process, the simulation results will not be sufficient for you to make final conclusions or decisions about the problem situation. If you have access to a computer, we suggest that you develop a computer simulation model for some of the problems. Then, by using the model to test several decision alternatives over a much longer simulated period of time, you will be able to obtain the desired decision-making information.

1. A retail store has experienced the following historical daily demand for a particular product:

Sales (Units)	Frequency (Days)
0	4
1	6
2	14
3	12
4	7
5	5
6	2
Total	50

a. Develop a relative frequency distribution for the above data.
b. Use the random numbers from row 4 of Appendix B to simulate daily sales for a 10-day period.

2. A study was conducted in order to investigate the number of cars arriving at the drive-in window of Community Savings Bank. The following data were collected for 100 randomly selected five-minute intervals.

Number of Arrivals	Number of Occurrences
0	12
1	24
2	37
3	19
4	8
Total	100

a. Develop a relative frequency distribution for the above data.
b. Use random numbers to simulate the number of customers that arrive between 9:00 A.M. and 9:15 A.M. on a given day.

3. Decca Industries has experienced the following weekly absenteeism frequency over the past 20 weeks:

Number of Employees Absent	Frequency
1	2
2	4
3	7
4	3
5	2
6	2
Total	20 weeks

a. Develop a relative frequency distribution for the above data.
b. Use random numbers to simulate weekly absenteeism for a 15-week period.

4. Given below are 50 weeks of historical sales data for cars sold by Domoy Motors, Inc., a new car dealer in Newton, Ohio.

Number of Sales	Number of Weeks
0	2
1	5
2	8
3	22
4	10
5	3
Total	50

a. Develop the relative frequency distribution for these data.
b. Use a random-number procedure to simulate weekly automobile sales for a 12-week period.

5. Charlestown Electric Company is building a new generator for its Mt. Washington plant. Even with good maintenance procedures, the generator will have periodic failures or breakdowns. Historical figures for similar generators indicate that the relative frequency of failures during a year is as follows:

Number of Failures	Relative Frequency
0	0.80
1	0.15
2	0.04
3	0.01

Assume that the useful lifetime of the generator is 25 years. Use simulation to estimate the number of breakdowns that will occur in the 25 years of operation. Is it common to have 5 or more consecutive years of operation without a failure?

6. Use row 15 of Appendix B to simulate 15 minutes of operation for the County Beverage Drive-Thru application presented in Section 14.1. Show your simulation results in the format of Table 14.6.

7. A service technician for a major photocopier company is trained to service two models of copier: the X100 and the Y200. Approximately 60% of the technician's service calls are for the X100, and 40% are for the Y200. The service time distributions for the two models are as follows:

X100		Y200	
Time (Minutes)	Relative Frequency	Time (Minutes)	Relative Frequency
25	0.50	20	0.40
30	0.25	25	0.40
35	0.15	30	0.10
40	0.10	35	0.10

a. Show the random-number intervals that can be used to simulate the type of machine to be serviced and the length of the service time.

b. Simulate 20 service calls. What is the total service time the technician spends on the 20 calls?

8. Bushnell's Sand and Gravel (BSG) is a small firm that supplies sand, gravel, and topsoil to contractors and landscape firms. BSG maintains an inventory of high quality screened topsoil which is used to supply the weekly orders for two companies: Bath Landscaping Service and Pittsford Lawn Care, Inc. The problem BSG has is to determine how many cubic yards of screened topsoil to have in inventory at the beginning of each week in order to satisfy the needs of both of its customers. BSG would like to select the lowest possible inventory level that would have a 0.95 probability of satisfying the combined weekly orders from both customers. The demand distributions for the two customers are as follows:

	Weekly Demand	Relative Frequency
Bath Landscaping	10	0.20
	15	0.35
	20	0.30
	25	0.10
	30	0.05
Pittsford Lawn Care	30	0.20
	40	0.40
	50	0.30
	60	0.10

Simulate 20 weeks of operation for beginning inventories of 70 and of 80 cubic yards. Based upon your limited simulation results, how many cubic yards should BSG maintain in inventory? Discuss what you would want to do in a full-scale simulation of this problem.

9. Paula Williams is currently completing the design for a drive-in movie theater to be located in Big Flats, New York. Paula has purchased the land and is now in the planning stages of determining the number of automobiles to accommodate. Each automobile location requires installing a speaker system at a total cost of $250 per location. Based upon her experience with the five other drive-ins she has been operating for the past eight years, Paula estimates that the nightly attendance will range from 100 to 500 automobiles with the relative frequencies shown below:

Approximate Number of Automobiles	Relative Frequency
100	0.10
200	0.25
300	0.40
400	0.15
500	0.10

a. Simulate 20 days of attendance for capacities of 300, 400, and 500.
b. In the 20 days of simulated operation, how many daily demands of 300 would you have expected? Did you observe this many in your simulation? Should you have? Explain.
c. After considering personnel and other operating costs, the average profit is $1 per car. Using your 20 days of simulated data, what is the average nightly profit for the capacities of 300, 400, and 500? How many days of operation will it take Paula to recover the speaker installation cost if all profits are allocated to this cost?

10. A door-to-door magazine salesperson has the following historical sales record. If the salesperson talks to the woman of the house, there is a 15% chance of making a sale. Furthermore, if the salesperson convinces the woman of the house to purchase some

magazines, the relative frequency distribution for the number of subscriptions ordered is as follows:

Number of Subscriptions	Relative Frequency
1	0.60
2	0.30
3	0.10

On the other hand, if the man of the house answers the door, the salesperson's chances of making a sale are 25%. In addition, the relative frequency distribution for the number of subscriptions ordered is as follows:

Number of Subscriptions	Relative Frequency
1	0.10
2	0.40
3	0.30
4	0.20

The salesperson has found that no one answers the door at about 30% of the houses contacted. However, of the people who do answer the door, 80% are women and 20% are men. The salesperson's profit is $2.00 for each subscription sold.

a. Prepare a simulation model flowchart (see Figure 14.5) for this problem. The output of the model should be the total profit the salesperson makes from calling upon N houses.

b. Simulate this problem and show the house-by-house results for 25 calls. What is the total profit projected for the 25 calls?

c. Based upon your results from part b, how many subscriptions should the salesperson expect to sell by calling on 100 houses per day? What is the salesperson's expected daily profit?

11. For the Art's Auto Supplies problem in Section 14.4, develop a ten-day simulation when the following demand distribution is assumed:

Demand	Relative Frequency
0	0.25
1	0.50
2	0.15
3	0.05
4	0.05

Using an order quantity of 5 and a reorder point of 3, show your results in the format of Table 14.17.

12. Bristol Bikes, Inc. would like to develop an order quantity and reorder point policy that would minimize the total costs associated with the company's inventory of exercise bikes. The relative frequency distribution for retail demand on a weekly basis is shown below:

Demand	Probability
0	0.20
1	0.50
2	0.10
3	0.10
4	0.05
5	0.05

The relative frequency distribution for lead time is as follows:

Lead Time (weeks)	Relative Frequency
1	0.10
2	0.25
3	0.60
4	0.05

The inventory holding costs are $1 per unit per week, the ordering cost is $20 per order, the shortage cost is $25 per unit, and the beginning inventory is 7 units. Using an order quantity of 12 and a reorder point of 5, simulate 10 weeks of operation of this inventory system.

13. Stollar's Bakery Shop would like to determine how many 10-inch white cakes should be produced each day in order to maximize profits. The production costs are $2.50 per cake, and the selling price is $4.50. Any cakes that are not sold at the end of the day are sold for $1.50 to a local store that specializes in day-old goods. Assume that the bakery has available the following data showing the daily demand during the past month (20 days of operation):

Daily Demand	Frequency (number of days observed)
0	1
1	2
2	1
3	2
4	3
5	6
6	3
7	1
8	1
	$\overline{20}$ days

Develop a ten-day simulation for production sizes ranging from 1 to 8 cakes per day. Use the following random numbers to generate daily demand:

48, 12, 77, 24, 32, 43, 96, 03, 62, 77.

What appears to be the best production size?

14. Domoy Motors, Inc. purchases a certain model automobile for $5778. In order to finance the purchase of cars of this model, Domoy must pay an 18% annual interest rate on borrowed capital. This interest rate amounts to approximately $20 per car per week. Orders for additional cars can be placed each week, but a minimum order size of five cars is required on any given order. It currently takes three weeks to receive a new shipment of cars after the order is placed. The cost of placing an order is $50. If Domoy runs out of cars in inventory, a shortage cost of $300 per car is incurred. Currently Domoy has 20 cars of this model in inventory. Historical data showing the weekly demand were given in Problem 4.

   a. Assuming an order quantity of 15 cars and a reorder point of 10 cars, perform a 12-week simulation of Domoy's operation. Use the first 12 two-digit random numbers from row 2 of Appendix B. Show your simulation results in the format of Table 14.17.

   b. Write a computer program to simulate weekly sales at Domoy Motors. Use the program to determine the order policy that appears to minimize Domoy's overall costs.

15. Mt. Washington Garage sells regular and unleaded gasoline. Pump number one, a self-service facility, is used by customers who want to pump their own gas. Pump number two, a full-service facility, is used by customers who are willing to pay a higher cost per gallon in order to have an attendent pump the gas, check the oil, and so on. Both pumps can service one car at a time. Based upon past data, the owner of the garage estimates that 70% of the customers select the self-service pump and 30% want full service. The arrival rate of cars for each minute of operation is given by the following probability distribution:

Number of Arrivals in One Minute of Operation	Probability
0	0.10
1	0.20
2	0.35
3	0.30
4	0.05
	1.00

The time to service a car, which depends upon whether the self-service or full-service facility is used, is given by the following probability distribution:

Self-Service Pump Service Time (minutes)	Probability	Full-Service Pump Service Time (minutes)	Probability
2	0.10	3	0.20
3	0.20	4	0.30
4	0.60	5	0.35
5	0.10	6	0.10
	1.00	7	0.05
			1.00

Study the operation of the system for 10 minutes using simulation. As part of your analysis consider the following types of questions. What is the average number of cars waiting for service per minute at both facilities? What is the average amount of time a car must wait for service? Prepare a brief report for Mt. Washington Garage that describes your analysis and any conclusions.

16. A medical consulting firm has been asked to determine the facilities required in the x-ray laboratory of a new hospital. In particular, the firm should provide recommendations on the number of x-ray units for the laboratory. How could computer simulation assist in reaching a good decision? What factors would you consider in a simulation model of this problem?

17. Consider a medium-sized community that currently has only one fire station. You have been hired by the city manager to assist in the determination of the best location for a second fire station. What would be your objective for this problem? Explain how computer simulation might be used to evaluate alternative locations and help identify the best location.

18. A bus company is considering adding a new ten-stop route to its operation. The bus will be scheduled to complete the route once each hour. If the company has determined the approximate demand distribution for each location, discuss how simulation might be used to project the hourly profit associated with the new route. If the company can assign a regular bus or a more economical minibus to this route, discuss how simulation might help make this decision. Note that with the minibus the company's management is concerned about being unable to pick up customers if the bus is already carrying its maximum number of riders.

Application

*Champion International Corporation**
New York, New York

Champion International Corporation is one of the largest forest products companies in the world, employing over 41,000 people in the United States, Canada, and Brazil. Champion manages over three million acres of timberlands in the United States. Its objective is to maximize the return of this timber base by converting trees into three basic product groups: (1) building materials, such as lumber and plywood; (2) white paper products, including printing and writing grades of white paper; (3) brown paper products, such as linerboard and corrugated containers. Given the highly competitive markets within the forest products industry, survival dictates that Champion must maintain its position as a low-cost producer of quality products. This requires an ambitious capital program to improve the timber base and to build additional modern, cost-effective timber conversion facilities.

Management Science Function

The Management Science function at Champion International Corporation is organizationally structured within the Corporate Planning Department and operates as an internal consulting service within the company. Approximately 40% of the project activity is involved with facility and production planning, 30% with physical distribution, 20% with process improvement, and 10% with capital budgeting. The primary techniques used are mathematical programming (e.g., linear programming), simulation, and statistical analyses.

A Simulation Application

An integrated pulp and paper mill is a facility in which wood chips and chemicals are processed in order to produce paper products or dried pulp. To begin with, wood chips are cooked and bleached in the pulp mill; the resulting pulp is piped directly into storage tanks, as shown in Figure 1. From the storage tanks the pulp is sent to either the paper mill or a dryer. In the

*The authors are indebted to Bill Griggs and Walter Foody of Champion International for providing this application.

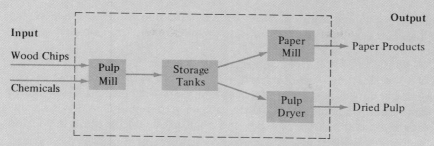

FIGURE 1 The Champion Integrated Pulp and Paper Mill Facility

paper mill the pulp is routed to one or more paper machines which produce the finished paper products. Alternatively, the pulp is sent to a dryer, and the dried pulp is then sold to other paper mills which do not have the capability of producing their own pulp. The total system, referred to as an integrated pulp and paper mill, is a large facility costing several hundreds of million dollars.

One of Champion's major pulp and paper facilities is presently comprised of a pulp mill, three paper machines, and a dryer. As the facility developed, it was found that the pulp mill could produce more pulp than the combination of paper machines and the dryer could use. A study was undertaken to determine whether it would be worthwhile to invest in improvements which would increase the capacity of the dryer. One of the first questions to be answered in the study was, How much additional pulp could be produced and dried, given each possible capacity increase on the dryer?

A simple approach to this question is to look at average flows. For example, the pulp mill has a capacity of 940 tons[1] per day (TPD), the three paper machines together average 650 TPD of pulp use, and the dryer can handle 200 TPD. Based on average flows for each ton of increased dryer capacity, we can produce one more ton of pulp in the pulp mill. Note, however, that this is only true until the capacity of the dryer reaches 290 TPD, after which further improvements to the dryer will have no benefit.

The above analysis is inadequate because it ignores the day-to-day deviations from the average. That is, all of the equipment in the mill is subject to downtime and to variations in efficiency. For example, suppose that on one day the pulp mill is inoperable for more than the average length of time and on the same day the paper machines are experiencing less than the usual downtime. In this case there will be very little pulp available for the dryer, regardless of its capacity. This lack of pulp will not "average out" on days when the opposite conditions occur, since there will be far more pulp available than the pulp dryer can handle. Consequently, the pulp storage tanks will become full, and the pulp mill will have to shut down.

Based upon the above analysis, we can conclude that in order not to reduce the production on the paper machines the ratio of additional pulp production to the increase in dryer capacity will be less than 1. Since the benefits of any investment in the dryer are directly proportional to this ratio, a

[1]All numerical values have been modified to protect proprietary information.

simulation was undertaken in order to estimate this ratio as precisely as possible. The simulation model that was developed had the following components:

Pulp Mill   The pulp mill was assumed to have an average production rate of 1044 TPD when it is operating, with an average of 10% downtime. The actual downtime used in the model in each time period simulated was drawn randomly from a sample of actual downtimes experienced by the pulp mill over several months. Thus one day the pulp mill might be down 2% of the time, the next day 20%, etc.

Paper Machine   The rate of pulp flow to the paper machines in a time period is a function of the particular type of paper being made and the amount of downtime on the paper machines. In the simulation, the rate of pulp flow was input to the model based on a typical schedule of types of paper to be made. The downtime for each machine was drawn from a sample of actual downtimes.

Pulp Dryer   In each run of the model, downtime on the dryer was drawn from a sample of actual downtimes. The capacity of the dryer was set at different levels in different runs.

Storage Tanks   The connecting link between the pulp mill, the paper machines, and the dryer is the pulp storage tanks. In the model all pulp produced by the pulp mill is added to the inventory in these tanks. All pulp drawn by the dryer and paper machines is subtracted from this inventory. If the storage tanks are empty, the model must shut down the paper machines. If the tanks are full, the pulp mill must be shut down. The actual rate at which the dryer is operated at any moment must be set by the model (as it is in reality) to try to keep the storage tanks from becoming "too empty or too full."

Results

A PL/1 computer program was developed to simulate the above process. The simulation program was run at various levels of dryer capacity. The simulation results showed that for every TPD of additional pulp capacity, approximately 0.8 TPD of additional pulp could actually be dried without reducing the production on the paper machines. This number was then used by management in comparing the costs and benefits of the capital investment necessary to increase the pulp dryer capacity. Note that if the "average basis" analysis had been used, the benefits of the project would have been overstated by 25%.

Chapter 15

Waiting Line Models

Everyone has experienced waiting line situations such as a line of customers at a supermarket checkout counter, a line of customers at a teller window of a bank, or a line of cars at a traffic light. In these and many other situations, *waiting* time is undesirable for all parties concerned. For example, the customer in the supermarket checkout line can become very annoyed with excessive waiting times. In addition, the excessive waiting times, while indicative of the presence of many customers, are equally undesirable for the manager of the supermarket. The manager realizes that long waiting lines mean that customers are not being promptly serviced. Eventually, these long waiting times may cause potential repeat customers to seek better service elsewhere, thus proving costly in terms of lost future sales.

If the manager in our supermarket example is concerned about the existence of long waiting lines, one obvious solution would be to add more checkout counters. The added service capability should provide better service and correspondingly shorter customer waiting lines. However, additional supermarket checkout counters will lead to greater costs in terms of additional personnel, equipment, and space requirements. Thus the supermarket waiting line problem will require the manager to balance the benefits of better service with the added costs involved.

Quantitative models have been developed to help managers understand and make better decisions concerning the operation of waiting lines. In operations research terminology, *queueing theory* involves the study of waiting lines, where the waiting line is referred to as the *queue*. Thus in our supermarket example, customers in the waiting line could have been referred to as the customers in the queue.

For a given waiting line problem, queueing models may be used to identify the system's *operating characteristics,* such as

1. The percentage of time or probability that the service facilities (checkout counters) are idle;
2. The probability of a specific number of units (customers) in the system[1];
3. The average number of units in the system;
4. The average time each unit spends in the system (waiting time plus service time);
5. The average number of units in the waiting line or queue;
6. The average time each unit spends in the waiting line;
7. The percentage of time or probability that an arriving unit will have to wait.

Given the above information together with service cost estimates, customer waiting line limitations, and customer waiting time costs, the manager will be better equipped to make decisions that balance desirable service levels with service costs.

In this chapter we will discuss how analytical and simulation models of

---

[1]The system includes the waiting line and the service facility.

waiting lines can assist in developing good decisions for waiting line problems. As an illustration of an application of a waiting line model, let us consider the problem Schips, Inc. is presently having with the truck dock at the company's Western Hills store.

15.1 The Schips, Inc. Truck Dock Problem

Schips, Inc., is a large department store chain which has six branch stores located throughout the city. The company's Western Hills store, which was built some years ago, has recently been experiencing some problems in its receiving and shipping department because of the substantial growth in the branch's sales volume. Unfortunately, the store's truck dock was designed to handle only one truck at a time, and the branch's increased business volume has led to a bottleneck in the truck dock area. At times the branch manager has observed as many as five Schips trucks waiting to be loaded or unloaded. As a result, the manager would like to consider various alternatives for improving the operation of the truck dock and reducing the truck waiting times.

One alternative the manager is considering is to speed up the loading/unloading operation by installing a conveyor system at the dock. As a second alternative, the manager is considering adding a second dock area and dock crew so that two trucks could be loaded and/or unloaded simultaneously.

What should the manager do in order to improve the operation of the truck dock? Obviously more information is needed before a course of action can be taken. While the alternatives being considered should reduce the truck waiting times, they will also increase the cost of operating the dock. Thus the manager will want to know how each alternative will affect the waiting times before making a final decision. Let us see how a waiting line model of the truck dock operation can assist the manager in making this decision.

15.2 The Single-Channel Waiting Line

Schip's current receiving and shipping operation is an example of a *single-channel* or *single-server* waiting line. By this we mean that each truck entering the system must pass through *one* server—the one loading dock—in order to complete the loading and/or unloading process. The trucks form a waiting line and wait for the loading dock to become available. A diagram of the Schips single-channel waiting line system is shown in Figure 15.1.

In order to develop a waiting line model for the truck dock operation, we will need to identify some important characteristics of the system: (1) the arrival distribution for the trucks; (2) the service time distribution for the truck loading and unloading operation; and (3) the waiting line or queue discipline for the trucks. This information will be necessary to determine which of many waiting line models is most representative of the Schips truck dock waiting line.

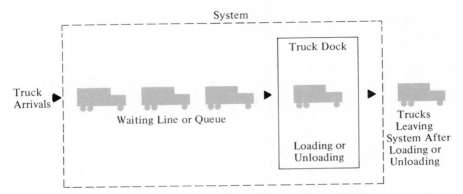

FIGURE 15.1.   Diagram of Schips Single-Channel Truck Dock Waiting Line

15.3   Arrival Distribution

Defining the arrival distribution for a waiting line involves determining how many units arrive for service in a given period of time. For example, in the Schips waiting line problem we will be interested in determining the number of trucks that arrive at the loading dock in a 1-hour period. Since the number of trucks arriving each hour is not necessarily constant, we will need to define a probability distribution that describes the hourly truck arrivals.

For many waiting lines, the arrivals occurring in a given period of time appear to have a *random pattern*—that is, while we may have a good estimate of the total number of arrivals expected, each arrival is independent of other arrivals and we cannot predict when the arrival will occur. In such cases, operations researchers have found that the *Poisson* probability distribution provides a good description of the arrival pattern.

The Poisson probability distribution is defined as follows:

$$P(x) = \frac{\lambda^x e^{-\lambda}}{x!} \qquad \text{for } x = 0, 1, 2, \ldots, \tag{15.1}$$

where, in waiting line applications,

x = number of arrivals in a specific period of time,

λ = average or expected number of arrivals for the specific period of time,

$e \cong 2.71828$.

In the Schips loading dock problem, busy periods would often have as many as seven or eight trucks arriving at the loading dock in a one-hour period. However, during slow times, it was common to have no arrivals during a one-hour period. Since truck arrivals were not scheduled and occurred in an unpredictable fashion, a random arrival pattern appeared to exist. Thus the Poisson distribution should provide a good description of the arrival pattern. Since arrivals occur at an average rate of 24 trucks per

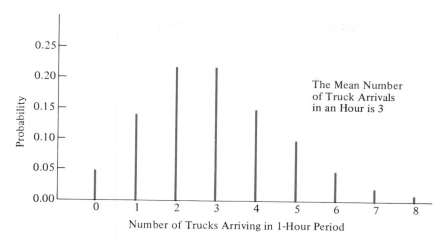

FIGURE 15.2.   **Poisson Distribution of Truck Arrivals for Schips**

8-hour day, or 3 trucks per hour ($\lambda = 3$), we can use the following Poisson distribution to compute the probability of x truck arrivals in an hour[2]:

$$P(x) = \frac{3^x e^{-3}}{x!}.$$

The probabilities for 0, 1, and 2 trucks arriving in an hour are as follows:

$$P(x = 0) = \frac{3^0 e^{-3}}{0!} = e^{-3} \approx 0.0498$$

$$P(x = 1) = \frac{3^1 e^{-3}}{1!} = 3e^{-3} \approx 0.1494$$

$$P(x = 2) = \frac{3^2 e^{-3}}{2!} = \frac{9e^{-3}}{2} \approx 0.2241$$

Using the Poisson probability distribution we would expect no arrivals in an hour 4.98% of the time, exactly one arrival in an hour 14.94% of the time, exactly two arrivals in an hour 22.41% of the time, and so on. Continuing these probability calculations will show that the probability of nine or more truck arrivals in one hour is only 0.0038. Figure 15.2 shows the arrival distribution for Schips trucks based on the Poisson distribution assumption.

In the analysis that follows, we will use the Poisson distribution to describe the truck arrivals for Schips. You will see that the assumption of a Poisson arrival distribution will help simplify our analysis of the waiting line problem. In practice you would want to record the actual number of arrivals per time period for several days or weeks and compare the frequency

[2]Values of $e^{-\lambda}$ are provided in Appendix C.

distribution of the observed number of arrivals to the Poisson distribution to see if the Poisson distribution is a good approximation of the arrival distribution for the waiting line.

15.4   Service Time Distribution

A service time probability distribution is needed to describe how long it takes to load or unload (that is, service) a truck once the dock crew begins the loading or unloading operation. Since the trucks carry different quantities of different items, the loading and unloading service times will vary. Operations researchers have found that the *exponential* probability distribution often provides a good description of the service time distribution. The exponential probability distribution is defined as follows:

$$f(x) = \mu e^{-\mu x} \qquad \text{for } x \geq 0. \tag{15.2}$$

In waiting line applications

x = service time,

μ = average or expected number of units that the service facility can handle in a specific period of time,

$e \simeq 2.71828$.

If we use an exponential service time distribution, *the probability of a service being completed within a specific period of time, t, is given by*

$$P(\text{service time} \leq t) = 1 - e^{-\mu t}. \tag{15.3}$$

Suppose that after collecting data on loading and unloading times for Schips trucks, we find that when working continuously the dock crew can service an average of four trucks per hour. Then using $\mu = 4$, the probability of a service being completed within time t [see equation (15.3)] is as follows:

$$P(\text{service time} \leq t) = 1 - e^{-4t}.$$

Using this equation we can compute the probability that a truck is loaded and/or unloaded (serviced) within any specified time t. For example,

$$P(\text{service time} \leq 0.1 \text{ hours}) = 1 - e^{-4(0.1)} = 1 - e^{-0.4} \simeq 0.3297$$

$$P(\text{service time} \leq 0.3 \text{ hours}) = 1 - e^{-4(0.3)} = 1 - e^{-1.2} \simeq 0.6988$$

$$P(\text{service time} \leq 0.5 \text{ hours}) = 1 - e^{-4(0.5)} = 1 - e^{-2} \simeq 0.8647.$$

Thus using the exponential distribution we would expect 32.97% of the trucks to be serviced in 6 minutes or less ($t = 0.1$), 69.88% in 18 minutes or less ($t = 0.3$), and 86.47% in 30 minutes or less ($t = 0.5$). Figure 15.3 shows graphically the probability that t hours or less will be required to service a Schips truck.

In the analysis of a specific waiting line the quantitative analyst will want to collect data on actual service times to see if the exponential

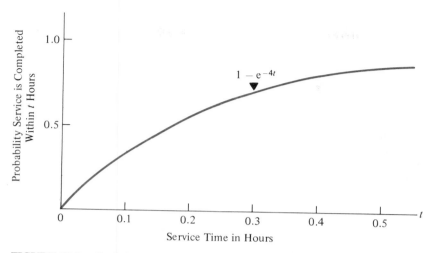

FIGURE 15.3. **Probability that a Schips Truck Will Be Serviced within *t* Hours**

distribution assumption is appropriate. If you find that other service time patterns (such as a normal service time distribution or a constant service time) exist, the exponential distribution should not be used. For the Schips problem we will assume that it has already been determined that the exponential distribution is the most appropriate representation of the service times.

15.5 Queue Discipline

In describing a waiting line, we must define the manner in which the waiting units are ordered for service. For the Schips, Inc. problem, and in general for most customer-oriented waiting lines, the waiting units are ordered on a first-come first-served basis, which is referred to as a first-in-first-out (FIFO) queue discipline. When people wait in line for an elevator, it is usually the last one in line that is the first one serviced (that is, first to leave the elevator). This is an example of a last-in-first-out (LIFO) queue discipline. Other types of queue disciplines assign priorities to the waiting units and service the unit with the highest priority first. We will restrict our attention to waiting lines with a FIFO queue discipline. In situations where the FIFO queue discipline is not appropriate, waiting line models other than those discussed in this chapter must be used.

15.6 The Single-Channel Waiting Line Model with Poisson Arrivals and Exponential Service Times

The waiting line model presented in this section can be applied to waiting lines where the following conditions exist:

1. Single-channel waiting line,
2. Poisson distribution of arrivals,

3. Exponential distribution of service times,
4. First-in-first-out (FIFO) queue discipline.

Since we assumed that the above conditions were applicable to the Schips problem, we will show how this waiting line model can be used to analyze the loading dock operation.

The quantitative methodology used in the development of most waiting line models is rather complex. However, our purpose in this chapter is not to provide the theoretical development of waiting line models, but rather to show how some of the expressions that have been developed and can be applied to waiting line problems such as the one encountered at Schips, Inc.

Let us begin by reviewing some of our notation:

λ = expected number of arrivals per time period
(mean arrival rate)

μ = expected number of services possible per time period
(mean service rate).

For the Schips problem we have already found $\lambda = 3$ and $\mu = 4$.

Using the assumptions of Poisson arrivals and exponential service times, operations researchers have developed the following expressions which define the operating characteristics of a single-channel waiting line[3]:

1. The probability that the service facility is idle (that is, the probability of 0 units in the system):

$$P_0 = \left(1 - \frac{\lambda}{\mu}\right).$$
(15.4)

2. The probability of n units in the system:

$$P_n = \left(\frac{\lambda}{\mu}\right)^n P_0 = \left(\frac{\lambda}{\mu}\right)^n \left(1 - \frac{\lambda}{\mu}\right).$$
(15.5)

3. The average number of units in the system:

$$L = \frac{\lambda}{\mu - \lambda}.$$
(15.6)

4. The average time a unit spends in the system (waiting time plus service time):

$$W = \frac{1}{\mu - \lambda} = \frac{L}{\lambda}.$$
(15.7)

5. The average number of units in the queue waiting for service:

$$L_q = \frac{\lambda^2}{\mu(\mu - \lambda)} = L - \frac{\lambda}{\mu}.$$
(15.8)

[3]These equations apply to the *steady-state* operation of a waiting line, which occurs after a start-up or transient period at the beginning of the waiting line operation.

6. The average time a unit spends in the queue waiting for service:

$$W_q = \frac{\lambda}{\mu(\mu - \lambda)} = \frac{L_q}{\lambda} = W - \frac{1}{\mu} \qquad (15.9)$$

7. The probability that an arriving unit has to wait for service:

$$P_w = \frac{\lambda}{\mu}. \qquad (15.10)$$

The values of the mean arrival rate λ and the mean service rate μ are clearly important components in the above formulas. From equation (15.10) we see that the ratio of these two values, λ/μ, is simply the probability that the server is busy. Thus λ/μ is often referred to as the *utilization factor* for the waiting line.

Since we know the probability that the server is busy, λ/μ, cannot be greater than 1, we see that we cannot consider a utilization factor of $\lambda/\mu > 1$ in equations (15.4)–(15.10). In addition, if we attempt to use $\lambda/\mu = 1$, or $\lambda = \mu$, we see from equations (15.6) and (15.7) that the number of units in the system L and the average time a unit spends in the system W both become infinitely large. This tells us that if we attempt to operate a single-channel waiting line system with Poisson arrivals and exponential service times at a utilization factor of $\lambda/\mu = 1$, both the waiting line and the waiting time will grow without limit.

Based on the above discussion it should be clear that the formulas for determining the operating characteristics of a single-channel waiting line presented in equations (15.4)–(15.10) are applicable only when $\lambda/\mu < 1$. This condition occurs when the mean service rate μ is greater than the mean arrival rate λ, and hence the service rate is sufficient to process or service all arrivals.

Returning to the Schips loading dock problem, we see that with $\lambda = 3$ trucks per hour, $\mu = 4$ trucks per hour, and $\lambda/\mu = \frac{3}{4}$, we can use equations (15.4)–(15.10) to determine the operating characteristics of the loading dock operation. This is done as follows:

$$\text{utilization factor} = \frac{\lambda}{\mu} = \frac{3}{4} = 0.75$$

$$P_0 = \left(1 - \frac{\lambda}{\mu}\right) = \left(1 - \frac{3}{4}\right) = 0.25$$

$$L = \frac{\lambda}{\mu - \lambda} = \frac{3}{4 - 3} = 3 \text{ trucks}$$

$$W = \frac{L}{\lambda} = \frac{3}{3} = 1 \text{ hour per truck}$$

$$L_q = L - \frac{\lambda}{\mu} = 3 - \frac{3}{4} = 2.25 \text{ trucks}$$

$$W_q = W - \frac{1}{\mu} = 1 - \frac{1}{4} = 0.75 \text{ hour per truck}$$

$$P_w = \frac{\lambda}{\mu} = \frac{3}{4} = 0.75.$$

By looking at the above data for the waiting line, we can learn several important things about the loading dock operation. In particular, the fact that trucks wait an average of 0.75 hour or 45 minutes before being loaded or unloaded appears excessive and undesirable. In addition, the facts that the average waiting line is 2.25 trucks and that 75% of the arriving trucks have to wait for service are indicators that something should be done to improve the efficiency of the loading dock operation.

In an effort to improve the operation of the loading dock the branch manager is considering the use of a conveyor system to speed up the loading/unloading process. Table 15.1 was prepared to help the manager better understand the potential benefits of this alternative. In particular, note that as the mean service rate increases (i.e., more trucks loaded/unloaded per hour), the average waiting time per truck, the average number of trucks waiting, and the probability of an arriving truck having to wait all improve. For example, if installing the conveyor system will increase the service rate to 6 trucks per hour, Table 15.1 shows that the average time a truck spends in the system can be reduced from 1 hour to 0.33 hour, or 20 minutes. In addition, we see that the percentage of trucks having to wait for service would be reduced from 75% to 50%.

In evaluating a specific proposal for a conveyor system, the manager can use the projected service rate (μ) and the information in Table 15.1 to determine what improvements can be anticipated in the truck dock operation. The added cost of the proposed changes can be compared with the corresponding benefits to help the manager determine whether or not the specific proposal is worthwhile.

What if the manager learns that the cost of the new conveyor system is too great for the performance benefits obtained? In this case the manager

TABLE 15.1   Waiting Line System Characteristics for the Schips Truck Dock Problem

Mean Service Rate μ, Trucks per Hour	4	6	8	10
Utilization factor	0.75	0.5	0.375	0.3
Probability that the crew is idle, P_0	0.25	0.5	0.625	0.7
Average number of trucks in system, L	3	1	0.6	0.429
Average time a truck spends in system, W, hours	1	0.33	0.2	0.143
Average number of trucks in queue, L_q	2.25	0.5	0.225	0.129
Average time a truck spends in queue, W_q, hours	0.75	0.167	0.075	0.043
Probability that an arriving unit has to wait for service, P_w	0.75	0.5	0.375	0.3

might want to consider the alternative of expanding the dock area to create a two-channel operation.

15.7   The Multiple-Channel Waiting Line Model with Poisson Arrivals and Exponential Service Times

A logical extension of the single-channel waiting line is the *multiple-channel waiting line*. By multiple-channel waiting lines we mean that two or more channels or service locations are present. Although items arriving for service wait in a single waiting line, they may move to the first available channel to be serviced. For the Schips loading dock problem, a multiple-channel waiting line model could be applied if the branch manager implemented an expansion of the dock area and dock crew such that two trucks could be loaded and/or unloaded simultaneously. The trucks arriving for service would form a waiting line and wait for either of the two loading areas to become available. A diagram of the Schips two-channel waiting line system is shown in Figure 15.4.

   If we make the assumptions that the multiple servers are identical in terms of providing exponential service times with the same mean service rate, that the arrival distribution can be described by the Poisson distribution, and that a first-in-first-out queue discipline is appropriate, we have the basic multiple-channel waiting line with Poisson arrivals and exponential service times. Operations researchers have developed the following formulas for determining the operating characteristics of this type of multiple-channel

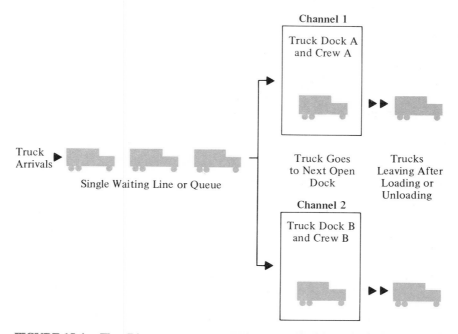

FIGURE 15.4.   Flow Diagram of Schips Two-Channel Waiting Line System

waiting line. Let

$$k = \text{number of channels,}$$
$$\lambda = \text{mean arrival rate for the system,}$$
$$\mu = \text{mean service rate for } each \text{ channel (service rates are assumed to be identical).}$$

Then we have the following expressions:

1. The probability that all k service channels are idle (that is, the probability of zero units in the system):

$$P_0 = \frac{1}{\left[\displaystyle\sum_{n=0}^{n=k-1} \frac{1}{n!}\left(\frac{\lambda}{\mu}\right)^n\right] + \frac{1}{k!}\left(\frac{\lambda}{\mu}\right)^k \frac{k\mu}{k\mu - \lambda}} \qquad \text{for } k\mu > \lambda \quad (15.11)$$

2. The probability of n units in the system:

$$P_n = \frac{1}{k!\,k^{n-k}}\left(\frac{\lambda}{\mu}\right)^n P_0 \qquad \text{for } n > k \qquad (15.12)$$

$$P_n = \frac{1}{n!}\left(\frac{\lambda}{\mu}\right)^n P_0 \qquad \text{for } n \le k. \qquad (15.13)$$

3. The average number of units in the system:

$$L = \frac{\lambda\mu(\lambda/\mu)^k}{(k-1)!(k\mu - \lambda)^2}\, P_0 + \frac{\lambda}{\mu} \qquad (15.14)$$

4. The average time a unit spends in the system (waiting time + service time):

$$W = \frac{\mu(\lambda/\mu)^k}{(k-1)!(k\mu - \lambda)^2}\, P_0 + \frac{1}{\mu} = \frac{L}{\lambda}. \qquad (15.15)$$

5. The average number of units in the queue waiting for service:

$$L_q = L - \frac{\lambda}{\mu}. \qquad (15.16)$$

6. The average time a unit spends in the queue waiting for service:

$$W_q = W - \frac{1}{\mu} = \frac{L_q}{\lambda} = W - \frac{1}{\mu}. \qquad (15.17)$$

7. The probability that an arriving unit has to wait for service:

$$P_w = \frac{1}{k!}\left(\frac{\lambda}{\mu}\right)^k \frac{k\mu}{k\mu - \lambda}\, P_0. \qquad (15.18)$$

While the equations describing the operating characteristics of a multiple-channel waiting line with Poisson arrivals and exponential service times are somewhat more complex than the single-channel equations, they provide the same information and are used exactly like we used the results from the single-channel model. In fact, the single-channel model is a special case of the general multiple-channel model where $k = 1$; that is, if we use $k = 1$ in equations (15.11)–(15.18), we will generate the corresponding single-channel results of equations (15.4)–(15.10).

For an application of the multiple-channel waiting line model we return to the Schips loading dock problem. Suppose the manager wishes to consider the desirability of expanding the loading dock area to provide space to load and/or unload two trucks simultaneously. If this were done, the manager would assign a crew to each of the two docks and operate with a two-channel waiting line. How does this alternative compare to the single-channel alternative presented in the previous section?

We can answer this question by applying equations (15.11)–(15.18) specifically for the two-channel ($k = 2$) waiting line. Using $\lambda = 3$ trucks per hour and $\mu = 4$ trucks per hour for each crew, we have the following operating conditions:

$$P_0 = \frac{1}{\left[\sum_{n=0}^{1} \frac{1}{n!}\left(\frac{3}{4}\right)^n\right] + \frac{1}{2!}\left(\frac{3}{4}\right)^2 \frac{2(4)}{2(4) - 3}}$$

$$= \frac{1}{1 + \frac{3}{4} + \frac{1}{2}\left(\frac{3}{4}\right)^2 \left(\frac{8}{8 - 3}\right)} = 0.4545$$

$$L = \frac{3(4)(3/4)^2}{(1)!(8 - 3)^2} (0.4545) + \frac{3}{4} = 0.873 \text{ trucks}$$

$$W = \frac{0.873}{3} = 0.291 \text{ hours}$$

$$L_q = 0.873 - \frac{3}{4} = 0.123 \text{ trucks}$$

$$W_q = 0.291 - \frac{1}{4} = 0.041 \text{ hours}$$

$$P_w = \frac{1}{2!}\left(\frac{3}{4}\right)^2 \frac{2(4)}{(2(4) - 3)} (0.4545) = 0.2045.$$

Shown below are some of the benefits of the two-channel loading dock operation as compared to the current single-channel system:

1. The average time a truck waits before being loaded or unloaded is reduced from 45 minutes to 0.041 hour, or 2.46 minutes.
2. The average length of the waiting line is reduced from 2.25 trucks to 0.123 truck.

3. The percentage of trucks having to wait for service is reduced from 75% to 20.45%.
4. The average time a truck is at the loading dock (waiting time plus loading/unloading time) is reduced from 1 hour to 0.291 hour, or 17.46 minutes).

The advantages are clear. The two-channel system will greatly improve the operating characteristics. However, before implementing the two-dock system, the manager will undoubtedly want to consider the economic aspects of such a change.

15.8   Economic Analysis of Waiting Lines

As we stated earlier in this chapter, the solution to a waiting line problem may require the manager to balance or trade off the cost reductions resulting from better service with the increased cost of achieving the better service. In defining the costs of the Schips loading dock problem, we will want to consider the waiting time cost for the trucks, both in the queue and while being serviced at the dock, and the costs for the loading dock operation. We can develop a mathematical model that will enable us to compare the costs of Schips single-channel and two-channel truck dock operations as follows: Let

c_1 = truck cost per hour,

L = average number of trucks in the system,

c_2 = crew cost per hour,

k = number of channels (also the number of dock crews).

Then

$$\text{Total hourly cost for trucks waiting and being loaded/unloaded} = c_1 L$$

$$\text{Total hourly cost for the dock crews} = c_2 k$$

$$\text{Total operating cost per hour} = c_1 L + c_2 k. \quad (15.19)$$

By evaluating the above total cost model for the one- and two-channel systems we will be able to obtain cost information helpful in making the decision regarding the truck dock operation. For example, suppose that the Schips trucks are operated at a cost of $25 per hour and that a dock crew is paid a total of $30 per hour. Table 15.2 summarizes the costs associated with the Schips loading dock alternatives. These cost projections tell us that the hourly costs will be reduced by $105.00 − 81.83 = $23.17 per hour in changing to the two-channel system. This is a 22% reduction in costs resulting from an improved loading dock operation. Assuming an annual operation of 40 hours per week for 52 weeks a year, this hourly saving results in a total savings of (40)(52)($23.17) = $48,193.60 per year. Although the manager must now consider the cost of expanding the operation to the two-channel system, the projected $48,193.60 makes the two-dock operation an attractive alternative.

TABLE 15.2 Total Hourly Cost Summary for the Schips Truck Dock Problem

System	Average Number of Trucks in System	Truck Cost/Hour	Number of Crews	Total Crew Cost/Hour	Total Cost/Hour
Single-channel	3.00	3.00 ($25) = $75	1	1($30) = $30	$105.00
Two-channel	0.873	0.873 ($25) = $21.83	2	2($30) = $60	81.83

15.9 Other Waiting Line Models

In this chapter you have been exposed to single-channel and multiple-channel waiting lines with Poisson arrivals and exponential service times. However, many variations of these specific systems exist in actual waiting line situations. Operations researchers have analyzed a wide variety of possible waiting lines and developed general expressions for average customer waiting time, average number of customers in the system, percent of the time servers are idle, and other operating characteristics of the system. Specifically, models are available covering some of the following types of waiting line situations:

1. Arrivals other than Poisson;
2. Service times other than exponential;
3. Arrivals in bulk quantities rather than one at a time;
4. Limited or finite waiting lines, called *truncated queues;*
5. Mean arrival and service rates that vary with the number of the units waiting for service;
6. Queue disciplines other than first-in-first-out;
7. Sequential waiting lines, where units pass through a fixed sequence or series of servers.

D. G. Kendall suggested a special notation for classifying waiting line models. In short, the Kendall system is a shorthand notation for identifying the waiting line model being considered. While the Kendall notation cannot completely describe all waiting line configurations, it has been adopted as a common method for classifying the arrival distribution, service distribution, and number of parallel servers in a waiting line system. The three symbol Kendall notation is as follows:

$$\underline{\hspace{3cm}} \; / \; \underline{\hspace{3cm}} \; / \; \underline{\hspace{2cm}}$$

| code indicating arrival distribution | code indicating service distribution | number of parallel servers |

With *M* being the code for both the Poisson arrival distribution and also the exponential service time distribution, the single-channel waiting line discussed in Section 15.6 is the $M/M/1$ waiting line model. The two-truck dock problem of Section 15.7 is an example of the $M/M/2$ model. Several other arrival and service time distributions are possible and are denoted by other code letters.

With many models of waiting lines available, a decision maker with a specific waiting line problem should attempt to identify a model that closely approximates the specific problem; that is, the decision maker should attempt to identify a model with an arrival distribution, service time distribution, number of servers, queue discipline, and so on that closely approximates the actual situation. Even with the numerous waiting line models in existence, many practical waiting line problems are so complex that management scientists have been unable to develop the analytical expressions necessary to determine the operating characteristics. If the decision maker is unable to find an analytical model applicable to the specific waiting line, a computer simulation model of the problem may be used to develop the necessary operating characteristics.

15.10   Simulation of Waiting Lines

Computer simulation models offer an attractive alternative to the use of mathematical models when studying the behavior and operating characteristics of waiting lines. In Chapter 14 we saw how a simulation model could be used to study the waiting line situation at the County Beverage Drive-Thru. The attractiveness of computer simulation models rests primarily with their versatility. Although we pointed out that mathematical models have been developed for waiting line situations that differ from the Poisson-exponential systems described in this chapter, the complexity and diversity of waiting lines often prohibits an analyst from finding an existing model that fits the specific situation being studied. Even when models that appear to be good approximations of the problem can be identified, the mathematics of the models are often so complex that many practitioners are unable to determine whether the models are applicable or not. Thus a computer simulation model of a waiting line problem offers another approach to studying waiting line situations.

Let us consider a deviation from the assumptions which enabled us to utilize existing mathematical models for the Schips truck dock waiting line. One key assumption was that the service times in the Schips problem were essentially random *and* independent of all other conditions. This enabled us to use the same exponential distribution and mean service rate for all trucks. Let us suppose that the Schips truck dock crew does not work independently of the number of trucks waiting to be serviced. That is, suppose that management has observed that as the length of the waiting line increases, the rate at which the dock crew loads and unloads also increases. Thus our previous assumption that service times are always exponentially distributed with a mean service rate of 4 trucks per hour would not reflect the actual situation. Hence while the decision maker might still elect to use the

Poisson-exponential model as a rough approximation, it may be desirable to develop a computer simulation model that attempts to account for the varying work rates of the crew.

Also recall that the waiting line models in this chapter employ a first-in-first-out queue discipline. Suppose the branch manager wanted to evaluate the policy of having the dock crews load customer delivery trucks before unloading incoming shipments from the central warehouse. How would the waiting times and operating costs be affected by this policy? We cannot answer this question with a waiting line model that assumes a first-in-first-out queue discipline. However, a computer simulation model could be used to test this new priority policy.

Finally, suppose that we collected actual arrival and service time data for the Schips trucks for a two-week period and found that arrivals did not follow a Poisson distribution and the service times did not follow an exponential distribution. We might try to identify the general distributions that these data follow and attempt to identify an existing waiting line model based on these distributions. However, if an existing model cannot be found or if the arrivals and/or service times do not follow any recognizable probability distribution, we could input the observed relative frequency data for the arrival and service times into a simulation model and use computer simulation to generate the operating characteristics of the loading dock.

Although we have mentioned only a few specific changes in the characteristics of the Schips waiting line problem, it should be apparent that many other possibilities could be considered. Again, this is where computer simulation starts to become especially attractive as a solution procedure. Instead of using an existing waiting line model that is perhaps a poor approximation of the waiting line being studied, we develop a computer simulation model that more closely reflects the true characteristics of the waiting line.

Summary

Waiting line problems occur in a variety of practical situations in which customers or other units may wait for a service. Queueing models have been developed which provide information regarding waiting times, idle time, number of people waiting, and other operating characteristics of a waiting line. This information, along with cost data, may be used to balance the benefits of improved service with the cost necessary to improve the service.

In this chapter we have presented models for single-channel and multiple-channel waiting lines with Poisson arrivals and exponential service times. In addition, we pointed out that models exist which are applicable in a variety of other waiting line situations. However, a computer simulation model of the waiting line is recommended if the assumptions of existing waiting line models do not closely approximate the specific problem under study.

Glossary

1. *Queueing theory*—The operations research term for the study of waiting lines.
2. *Queue*—A waiting line.
3. *Single-channel line*—A waiting line with only one server.
4. *Multiple-channel line*—A waiting line with two or more parallel identical servers.
5. *Mean arrival rate*—The expected number of customers or units arriving or entering the system in a given period of time.
6. *Poisson distribution*—A probability distribution used to describe the random arrival pattern for some waiting lines.
7. *Mean service rate*—The expected number of customers or units that can be serviced by one server in a given period of time.
8. *Exponential distribution*—A probability distribution used to describe the pattern or service times for some waiting lines.

Problems

The following waiting line problems are all based upon the assumptions of Poisson arrivals and exponential service times:

1. The demand for access to a time-sharing computer occurs at a mean rate of three requests for service per 5-minute period.
    a. What is the probability that no one will attempt to use the system in a given 5-minute period?
    b. What is the probability of exactly one request? Exactly two requests?
    c. What is the probability the computer facility will have three or more requests in a 5-minute period?
2. Computer programs require on the average of 10 minutes of computer time.
    a. What is the mean service rate in programs per hour?
    b. What percentage of the programs will be completed in 5 minutes or less ($t \leq 0.083$ hour)?
    c. What percentage in 10 minutes or less?
    d. What percentage of the computer programs will require *more than* 30 minutes to complete?
3. Phone calls come into the dispatcher's office at the Madeira Cab Company at the rate of five calls per 15-minute interval. Answer the following questions:
    a. What is the probability of three calls during a 15-minute interval?
    b. What is the probability of three calls during a 6-minute interval?
    c. What is the probability of five calls during a 3-minute interval?
4. The reference desk of a large library receives requests for assistance at a mean rate of 10 requests per hour. Assuming that the reference desk has a mean service rate of 12 requests per hour, consider the following questions:
    a. What is the utilization factor for the reference desk?
    b. What is the probability that the reference desk is idle?
    c. What is the average waiting time plus service time for a request for assistance?
    d. What is the average number of requests that will be waiting in the queue?

5. Trucks using a single-channel loading dock have a mean arrival rate of 12 per day. The loading/unloading rate is 18 per day.
   a. What is the proability the dock will be idle?
   b. What is the probability of one truck in the system?
   c. What is the probability that at least one truck will be waiting (that is, the probability of at least two trucks in the system)?
   d. What is the probability a new arrival will have to wait?

6. A mail-order nursery specializes in European beech trees. New orders, which are processed by a single shipping clerk, have a mean arrival rate of 30 per week and a mean service rate of 40 per week. Assume a week consists of 5 working days.
   a. What is the average time in days an order spends in the system?
   b. What is the average time in days an order spends in the queue waiting for the clerk to begin service?
   c. Verify that the answer to part a is equal to the answer to part b plus $1/\mu$. Does this make sense? Explain.

7. For the Schips single-channel waiting line, assume the mean arrival rate is four trucks per hour and the mean service rate for the crew is five trucks per hour.
   a. What is the probability the dock crew will be idle?
   b. What is the average number of trucks in the system?
   c. What is the average time a truck spends in the system?
   d. What is the average number of trucks in the queue?
   e. What is the average time a truck spends in the queue waiting for service?
   f. What is the probability an arriving truck will have to wait?
   g. What is the probability that at least one unit will be waiting?
   h. Does this waiting line provide more or less service than the original Schips crew operation (see Table 15.1)?

8. The City Beverage Drive-Thru is considering a two-channel system. Cars arrive at the beverage store at the mean rate of six per hour. The service rate for each channel or server is ten per hour.
   a. What is the probability of an empty system?
   b. What is the probability that an arriving car will have to wait?

9. Consider a two-channel waiting line with a mean arrival rate of 50 per hour and a mean service rate of 75 per hour for each channel.
   a. What is the probability of an empty system?
   b. What is the probability that an arrival will have to wait?
   c. Would the answers to parts a and b change if the mean arrival rate were 2 per hour and the mean service rate were 3 per hour? Why?

10. For a two-channel waiting line with a mean arrival rate of 15 per hour and a mean service rate of 10 per hour per channel, determine the probability that an arrival has to wait. What is the probability of waiting if the system is expanded to three channels?

11. Pete's market is a small local grocery store with only one checkout counter. Assume that shoppers arrive at the checkout lane at an average rate of 15 customers per hour and that the average order takes 3 minutes to ring up and bag. What information would you develop for Pete to aid him in analyzing his current operation? If Pete does not want the average waiting time in the queue to exceed 5 minutes, what would you tell Pete about his current system?

12. In Problem 11 we analyzed the checkout waiting line for Pete's market. After reviewing our analysis, Pete felt it would be desirable to hire a full-time person to assist in the checkout operation. Pete believed that if the new employee assisted the checkout cashier, service time could be reduced to 2 minutes. However, Pete was also considering installing a second checkout lane which could be operated by the

new person. This second alternative would provide a two-channel system with the average service time of 3 minutes for each server. Should Pete use the new employee to assist on the current checkout counter or operate a second counter? Justify your recommendation.

13. Keuka Park Savings and Loan currently has one drive-in teller window. The arrival of cars occurs at a mean rate of 10 cars per hour. The mean service rate is 12 cars per hour.
   a. What is the probability the service facility will be idle?
   b. If you were to drive up to the facility, what is the expected number of cars you would see waiting and being serviced?
   c. What is the probability that at least one car will be waiting to be serviced?
   d. What is the average time in the queue waiting for service?
   e. As a potential customer of the system, would you be satisfied with the above waiting line characteristics? How do you think management could go about assessing the feelings of its customers with respect to the operation of the current system?

14. In order to improve the service to the customer, Keuka Park Savings and Loan wants to investigate the effect of a second drive-in teller window. Assume a mean arrival rate of 10 cars per hour and a mean service rate of 12 cars per hour for each drive-in window. What effect would the addition of a new teller window have upon the system? Does this system appear acceptable?

15. Fore and Aft Marina is a newly planned marina that is to be located on the Ohio River near Madison, Indiana. Assume that Fore and Aft decides to build one docking facility and that a mean arrival rate of 5 boats per hour and a mean service rate of 10 boats per hour are expected. Consider the following questions:
   a. What is the probability that the boat dock will be idle?
   b. What is the average time a boat will spend waiting for service? What is the average time a boat will spend at the dock?
   c. What is the average number of boats that will be waiting in the queue for service?
   d. If you were the management of Fore and Aft Marina and believed that the above arrival and service rates were accurate, would you be satisfied with the service level your system would be providing?

16. Management of the Fore and Aft Marina project in Problem 15 wants to investigate the possibility of adding a second dock. Assume a mean arrival rate of 5 boats per hour and a mean service rate of 10 boats per hour for each channel.
   a. What is the probability that a boat that stops for fuel will have to wait?
   b. What is the average waiting time a boat will spend in the queue?
   c. What is the probability the system is idle?
   d. Would you consider this good service? Is it too good?

17. Big Al's Quickie Car Wash has two wash areas with a mean rate of 15 cars per hour. Cars arrive at a station at the rate of 10 cars per hour on the average, join the waiting line, and select the next open wash area when it becomes available.
   a. What is the probability a station will be empty?
   b. What is the probability that a customer who arrives at a station will have to wait?
   c. As a customer of Big Al's Quickie Car Wash, do you think the service of the system favors the customer? If you were Al, what would your attitude be relative to this service level?

18. In Section 15.7, we developed the operating characteristics for a two-channel model of the Schips loading dock operation. Use the results $P_0 = 0.4545$ and $P_W = 0.2045$ and compute the probability that one of the two dock crews is idle.

19. In Sections 15.7 and 15.8 we determined the operating characteristics and prepared an economic analysis of the Schips problem for the case of two loading docks. One of the assumptions that was implicit in our analysis was that the crews would not work together. Suppose, however, that when one of the dock crews was idle and the other was busy, the idle crew would help the busy crew with its loading and unloading. Thus none of the dock workers would be idle unless there were no trucks in the system.

   The formulas presented in Section 15.7 are not applicable to this new situation and hence should not be applied. This is a case in which a simulaton model would be useful.

   a. Discuss in a step-by-step fashion how you would develop a simulation model to determine the operating characteristics of this waiting line system.

   b. What type of output would you like to have as a result of the simulation?

*Goodyear Tire & Rubber Company**
Akron, Ohio

The Goodyear Tire & Rubber Company had its beginning in an old converted strawboard factory in 1898. Its first product was bicycle tires. Since 1926 it has been the world's largest rubber company and one of the nation's leading industrial corporations.

Although tires are Goodyear's biggest single product line, the company has become a highly diversified corporate enterprise. The company's product line has changed from the original bicycle tires, carriage tires, and horseshoe pads to tires of all types, chemicals, industrial rubber products, defense products, packaging films, foam cushioning, shoe soles and heels, flooring and counter tops, metal rims and wheels, aircraft brakes and wheels, aerospace products, and atomic energy.

Goodyear has more than 129 production facilities—about half in the United States, half overseas—and approximately 155,000 employees. Its sales and distribution operations cover virtually all areas of the free world. Corporate headquarters are in Akron, Ohio.

Familiar to millions of people are the company airships, named the *Enterprise, Columbia,* and *America,* which are stationed in the United States, and the *Europa,* which is stationed in Europe. These airships are made by Goodyear Aerospace Corporation, a subsidiary of The Goodyear Tire & Rubber Company.

Quantitative Analysis at Goodyear

Goodyear has many departments that perform quantitative analyses. Most analyses are performed by one of the computer programming departments under the guidance of a user (client) department. These computer programming departments are involved in a variety of applications from

---

*The authors are indebted to Dr. Walt Fenske of The Goodyear Tire & Rubber Company for providing this application.

routine data collection and systems maintenance to queueing analysis. For example, one department is responsible for maintaining a system that gathers records of orders and sales; another department is responsible for forecasting and assisting production schedulers; and a third department is responsible for quality control. The waiting line (queueing) application discussed in the remainder of this presentation was the responsibility of yet another department. Many of the applications performed by the departments are interrelated, and one department will often use data generated by another department.

A Waiting Line Application

The application discussed involves a system for dispatching maintenance personnel to fix machines. Under the then current manual system, whenever a machine needed repair a production supervisor used a phone intercom system to call an individual referred to as a dispatcher. The dispatcher recorded the information provided by the production supervisor on cards. Then, whenever maintenance personnel called the dispatcher to request a new assignment, the information on these cards was used by the dispatcher to tell the maintenance personnel which machine should be repaired.

Due primarily to a need to develop a computerized data base that could be analyzed to improve the maintenance function, Goodyear decided to replace the manual system with a computer controlled system. In the computer controlled system the dispatcher function is performed by a person called a coordinator. The function of the coordinator is to enter service information when received into the computer using a remote computer terminal. The need for more information to be entered causes the coordinator's task to be more time-consuming than the dispatcher's function in the old system. However, the computer controlled system offers many potential advantages in other areas because of the wide variety of information entered by the coordinator.

Quantitative analysis was used in designing the computer controlled system. The problem to be solved was to determine how many coordinators (and consequently, remote computer terminals) were needed. If there are not enough coordinators, production supervisors and maintenance personnel will have difficulty reaching a coordinator. If the computer system is to be a success, people trying to reach the coordinator should not have long waits. However, if there are too many coordinators, excessive coordinator and computer terminal expenses will be incurred. Some of the questions which had to be answered were the following:

1. What percentage of the time will the coordinator be busy?
2. What is the maximum number of people waiting to reach the coordinator?
3. What is the average time spent waiting to reach the coordinator?
4. How many calls does the coordinator receive?

5. How many callers have to wait longer than 4 minutes to reach the coordinator?
6. How many callers do not have to wait to reach the coordinator?

These questions suggest that the design of the new system may be aided by use of a waiting line model. In a waiting line model of this situation, the coordinators are the servers, and the people waiting to talk to the coordinators constitute the waiting line. Thus if one coordinator is used, the model is a single-channel waiting line model. Otherwise it is a multiple-channel waiting line model.

The complexity of the proposed computer system can best be understood by considering the four types of arrivals that must be handled. The first type of arrival is a call received from a production supervisor stating that a machine needs repair. At this time a *work order is initiated.* The second type of arrival is a call from a maintenance person stating that the repair work is being started; this is referred to as placing the *work order in process.* The third type of arrival, referred to as *completing a work order,* is a call from a maintenance person stating that the repair work has been completed. The fourth type of arrival is any other type of call. Note that each work order generates three calls to the coordinator.

For this problem the arrivals were known to differ from the Poisson distribution. In addition, there were a number of other complicating factors that precluded the use of the waiting line models introduced in this chapter. However, a simulation model of the system, built on many of the basic queueing principles in this chapter, was implemented. The General Purpose Simulation System (GPSS) was the programming language used for the simulation model.

Computer simulation runs were performed for a system with one coordinator and a system with two coordinators. In the one-coordinator system the simulation runs showed the coordinator would be busy about 69% of the time and that the average waiting time to reach the coordinator would be 4.9 minutes. The average waiting time for the one-coordinator system was considered to be much too high.

For the two-coordinator system the simulation results indicated that each coordinator would be busy approximately 35% of the time. However, the average waiting time to reach a coordinator dropped to 42 seconds. In fact, it was found that a call would get through immediately about 90% of the time. Since management believed that these times were reasonable, the system was designed to have two coordinators and two remote computer terminals.

Chapter 16

Dynamic Programming

Dynamic programming is an approach to problem solving that permits decomposing one large mathematical model which may be very difficult to solve into a number of smaller problems which are usually much easier to solve. Moreover, the dynamic programming approach allows us to break up a large problem in such a fashion that once all the smaller problems have been solved, we are left with an optimal solution to the large problem. We shall see that each of the smaller problems created is identified with a *stage* of the dynamic programming solution procedure. As a consequence, the technique has been applied to many decision problems that are multistage in nature. Often the multiple stages are created by the fact that a sequence of decisions must be made over time. For example, a problem óf determining an optimal decision over a one-year time horizon might be broken into 12 smaller stages, where each stage requires an optimal decision over a one-month time horizon. In most cases each of these smaller problems cannot be considered to be completely independent of the others, and this is where the dynamic programming approach is helpful. Let us begin by discovering how to solve a shortest route problem using a dynamic programming approach.

16.1 A Shortest Route Problem

In Chapter 10 we studied a labeling algorithm for solving the shortest route problem. Let us now illustrate the dynamic programming approach by using it to solve a shortest route problem. Consider the network presented in Figure 16.1. Assuming that the numbers above each arc denote the direct distance in miles between two nodes, find the shortest route from node 1 to node 10.

Before attempting to solve this problem, let us note an important characteristic of shortest route problems. This characteristic is actually a restatement of Richard Bellman's famous *principle of optimality* as it applies to the shortest route problem[1]:

> *The Principle of Optimality.* If a particular node is on the optimal route, then the shortest path from that node to the end is also on the optimal route.

The dynamic programming approach to this problem essentially involves treating each node as if it were on the optimal route and making calculations accordingly. In doing so we work backward; that is, we start at the terminal node, node 10, and work backward, calculating the shortest route from each node to node 10 until we reach the origin, node 1. Then we will have solved the original problem of finding the shortest route from node 1 to node 10.

As we stated in the introduction to this chapter, the dynamic programming approach decomposes the original problem into a number of smaller problems which are much easier to solve. In the shortest route problem for

[1]See Dreyfus, S., *Dynamic Programming and the Calculus of Variations*, New York, Academic Press, 1965.

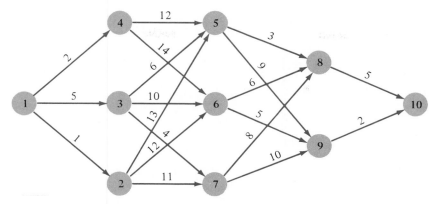

Figure 16.1   Network for the Shortest Route Problem

the network in Figure 16.1 the smaller problems that we will create define a four-stage dynamic programming problem. The first stage begins with nodes that are exactly one arc away from the destination and ends at the destination node. Note from Figure 16.1 that only nodes 8 and 9 are exactly one arc away from node 10. The second stage begins with all nodes that are exactly two arcs away from the destination and ends with all nodes that are exactly one arc away. Hence in dynamic programming terminology nodes 5, 6, and 7 would be considered the input nodes for stage 2 and nodes 8 and 9 would be considered output nodes for stage 2. The output nodes for stage 2 are the input nodes for stage 1. The input nodes for our third-stage problem are those that are exactly three arcs away from the destination, that is, nodes 2, 3, and 4. The output nodes, all of which are one arc closer to the destination, are nodes 5, 6, and 7. Finally, the input to stage 4 is node 1 and the output nodes are 2, 3, and 4. The decision problem we shall want to solve at each stage is to determine which arc it is best to travel over in moving from each particular input node to an output node. Let us consider the stage 1 problem.

We arbitrarily begin the stage 1 calculations with node 9. Since there is only one way to travel from node 9 to node 10, this is obviously the shortest route and requires us to travel a distance of 2 miles. Similarly there is only one path from node 8 to node 10. The shortest route from node 8 to the end is thus the length of that route, or 5 miles. The stage 1 decision problem is solved. For each input node we have identified an optimal decision, that is, the best arc to travel over to reach the output node. The stage 1 results are summarized below.

Stage 1

Input Nodes	Arc Decision	Shortest Distance to Node 10 (miles)
8	8–10	5
9	9–10	2

To begin the solution to the stage 2 problem, we move to node 7. (We could have selected nodes 5 or 6; the order of the nodes selected at any stage is arbitrary.) There are two arcs that leave node 7 and are connected to input nodes for stage 1. These are arc 7–8, which has a length of 8, and arc 7–9, which has a length of 10. If we select arc 7–8, we will have a distance from node 7 to node 10 which is 8 (that is, the length of arc 7–8) plus the shortest distance to node 10 from node 8. Thus the decision to select arc 7–8 has a total associated distance of 8 + 5 = 13. With a distance of 10 for arc 7–9 and stage 1 results showing a distance of 2 from node 9 to node 10, the decision to select arc 7–9 has an associated distance of 10 + 2 = 12. Thus given we are at node 7, we should select arc 7–9, since it is on the path that will reach node 10 in the shortest distance (12 miles). By performing similar calculations for nodes 5 and 6, we can generate the following stage 2 results:

Stage 2

Input Nodes	Arc Decision	Output Nodes	Shortest Distance to Node 10 (miles)
5	5–8	8	8
6	6–9	9	7
7	7–9	9	12

In Figure 16.2 the number in the square by each node considered so far indicates the length of the shortest route from that node to the end. We have completed the solution to our first two subproblems (stages 1 and 2). We now know the shortest route from nodes 5, 6, and 7 to node 10.

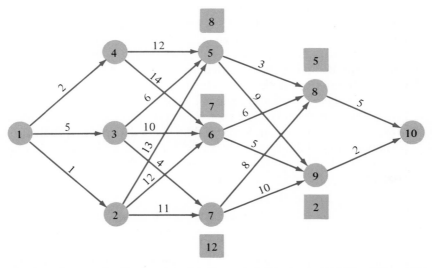

Figure 16.2   Intermediate Solution to the Shortest Route Problem Using Dynamic Programming

To begin our third stage, let us start with node 2. To find the shortest route from node 2 to node 10, we must make three calculations because we have three arcs that connect node 2 to stage 2 input nodes. If we select arc 2–7 and then follow the shortest route to the end we will travel $11 + 12 = 23$ miles. Similarly, selecting arc 2–6 requires $12 + 7 = 19$ miles, and selecting arc 2–5 requires $13 + 8 = 21$ miles. Thus the shortest route from node 2 to node 10 is 19 miles, which indicates that arc 2–6 is the best decision, given that we are at node 2. Similarly, we find that the shortest route from node 3 to node 10 is given by $\min\{4 + 12, 10 + 7, 6 + 8\} = 14$; the shortest route from node 4 to node 10 is given by $\min\{14 + 7, 12 + 8\} = 20$. This completes our stage 3 calculations. The results are summarized below:

Stage 3

Input Nodes	Arc Decision	Output Nodes	Shortest Distance to Node 10 (miles)
2	2–6	6	19
3	3–5	5	14
4	4–5	5	20

In solving the stage 4 subproblem we find that the shortest route from node 1 to node 10 is given by $\min\{1 + 19, 5 + 14, 2 + 20\} = 19$. Thus the optimal decision at stage 4 is to select arc 1–3. By moving through the network from stage 4 to stage 3 to stage 2 to stage 1, we can identify the best decision at each stage and therefore the shortest route from node 1 to node 10. This is as follows:

Stage	Arc Decision
4	1–3
3	3–5
2	5–8
1	8–10

Thus the shortest route is through nodes 1–3–5–8–10 with a distance of $5 + 6 + 3 + 5 = 19$ miles.

Note how the calculations at each successive stage made use of the calculations at prior stages. This characteristic is an important part of the dynamic programming procedure. Figure 16.3 illustrates the final network calculations. Note that we have now determined the shortest route from every node to node 10.

The dynamic programming approach, while enumerating or evaluating several paths at each stage, did not require us to enumerate all possible paths from node 1 to node 10. Returning to our stage 4 calculations, we considered

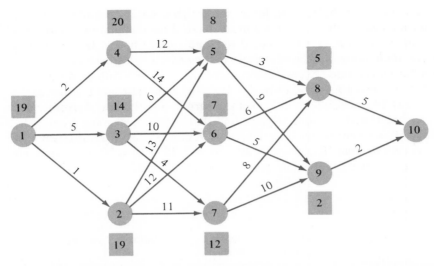

Figure 16.3   Final Solution to the Shortest Route Problem Using Dynamic Programming

three alternatives for leaving node 1. The complete route associated with each of these alternatives is presented below.

Arc Alternatives at Node 1	Complete Path to Node 10	Distance (miles)	
1–2	1–2–6–9–10	20	
1–3	1–3–5–8–10	19	←—— Selected as
1–4	1–4–5–8–10	22	best

However, when you realize that there are a total of 16 alternate routes from node 1 to node 10, you can see that dynamic programming has provided substantial computational savings over a total enumeration of all possible solutions.

The fact that we did not have to evaluate all the paths at each stage as we moved backward from node 10 to node 1 is illustrative of the power of dynamic programming. Using dynamic programming, we need only make a small fraction of the number of calculations that would be required using total enumeration. If our example network had been larger, the savings would have been even greater.

16.2   Dynamic Programming Notation

Perhaps one of the most difficult aspects of learning how to apply dynamic programming involves understanding the notation used to develop the approach. The notation we will use is the same as that used by Nemhauser[2] and is fairly standard.

[2]See Nemhauser, G. L., *Introduction to Dynamic Programming,* New York, Wiley, 1966.

The *stages* of a dynamic programming solution procedure are formed by decomposing the original problem of interest into a number of subproblems. Associated with each subproblem is a stage in the dynamic programming solution procedure. For example, the shortest route problem introduced in the preceding section was solved using a four-stage dynamic programming solution procedure. We had a four-stage procedure because we decomposed the original problem into the following four subproblems:

1. *Stage 1 Problem:* Where should we go from nodes 8 and 9 so that we will reach node 10 along the shortest route?

2. *Stage 2 Problem:* Using the results of stage 1, where should we go from nodes 5, 6, and 7 so that we will reach node 10 along the shortest route?

3. *Stage 3 Problem:* Using the results of stage 2, where should we go from nodes 2, 3, and 4 so that we will reach node 10 along the shortest route?

4. *Stage 4 Problem:* Using the results of stage 3, where should we go from node 1 so that we will reach node 10 along the shortest route?

Let us look closely at what occurs at the stage 2 problem. Consider the following representation of this stage.

Input	Decision Problem	Output
(a location in the network, node 5, 6, or 7)	For a given input, which arc should we select to reach stage 1? *Decision Criterion* Shortest distance to destination (arc value plus shortest distance from output node to destination)	(a location in the network, node 8 or 9)

Using dynamic programming notation, we define

x_2 = input to stage 2. x_2 represents our location in the network at the beginning of stage 2 (node 5, 6, or 7). Note that the input to stage 2 is the output of stage 3.

d_2 = decision variable at stage 2. This represents the arc selected to move to stage 1.

x_1 = output for stage 2. This will be the node we reach (node 8 or 9) after considering the input x_2 and the decision d_2. This will also be the input to stage 1.

Using this notation the stage 2 problem can be partially represented as follows:

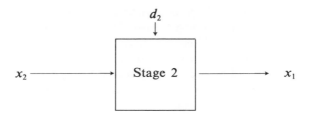

Recall that in the dynamic programming approach to the shortest route problem we worked backward through the stages, beginning at node 10. When we reached stage 2 we did not know x_2 because the stage 3 problem had not yet been solved. The approach used was to consider *all* alternatives for the input x_2. Then we determined the best decision d_2 for each of the inputs x_2. Later, when we moved forward through the system to recover the optimal sequence of decisions, we saw that the stage 3 decision provided a specific x_2, node 5, and from our previous analysis we knew the best decision (d_2) to make as we continued on to stage 1.

Let us consider a general dynamic programming problem with N stages and adopt the following general notation:

$$x_n = \text{input to stage } n \text{ (output from stage } n + 1\text{)},$$
$$d_n = \text{decision at stage } n.$$

The general N-stage problem is decomposed as follows:

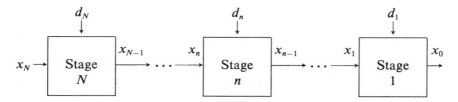

The four-stage shortest route problem can be represented as follows:

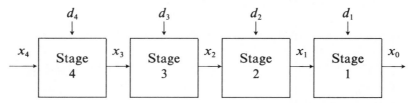

The values of the input and output variables x_4, x_3, x_2, x_1, and x_0 are important because they couple the four subproblems together. At any stage we will ultimately need to know the input x_n in order to make the best decision d_n. These x_n variables can be thought of as defining the *state* or condition of the system as we move from stage to stage. Accordingly, these variables are referred to as the *state variables* of the problem. In our shortest route problem, the state variables represented our location in the network at each stage (that is, a particular node).

TABLE 16.1 Table Showing Output Node Corresponding to Each Input Node and Decision, $x_1 = t_2(x_2, d_2)$

	x_1	Output State	
	x_2	8	9
	5	5–8	5–9
Input State	6	6–8	6–9
	7	7–8	7–9

d_2

At stage 2 of the shortest route problem we considered the input x_2 and made the decision d_2 that would provide the shortest distance to the destination. The output x_1 was based upon a combination of the input and the decision; that is, x_1 was a function of x_2 and d_2. In dynamic programming notation we could write

$$x_1 = t_2(x_2, d_2)$$

where $t_2(x_2, d_2)$ is the function at stage 2 that determines the stage 2 output.

Since $t_2(x_2, d_2)$ is the function that "transforms" the input to the stage into the output, this function is referred to as the *stage transformation function*. The general expression for this function is

$$x_{n-1} = t_n(x_n, d_n). \tag{16.1}$$

The mathematical form of the stage transformation function is dependent upon the particular dynamic programming problem. In our shortest route problem, the transformation function was based upon a tabular type of calculation. For example, Table 16.1 shows the stage transformation function $t_2(x_2, d_2)$ for stage 2.

Each stage also has a return associated with it. In our shortest route problem the return was the arc distance traveled in moving from an input node to an output node. For example, if node 7 were the input state for stage 2 and we selected arc 7–9 as d_2, the return for that stage would be the arc length, 10 miles. The return at a stage, which may be thought of as the payoff or value for a stage, is represented by the general notation $r_n(x_n, d_n)$.

Using the stage transformation function and the *return function*, our shortest route problem can be shown as follows.

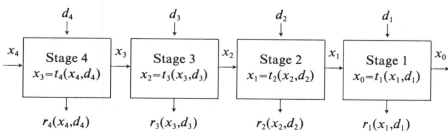

If we view a system or a process as consisting of N stages, we can represent a dynamic programming formulation schematically as follows:

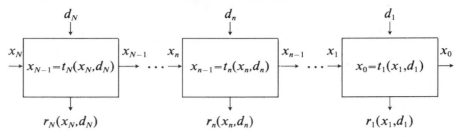

Each of the squares in the diagram represents a stage in the process. As indicated, there are two inputs to each stage: the state variable and the decision variable. There are also two outputs: a new value for the state variable and a return for the stage. The new value for the state variable is determined as a function of the inputs using $t_n(x_n, d_n)$. The value of the return for a stage is also determined as a function of the inputs using $r_n(x_n, d_n)$.

In addition we will use the notation $f_n(x_n)$ to represent the optimal total return from stage n and all remaining stages, given an input of x_n to stage n. For example, in our shortest route problem $f_2(x_2)$ represents the optimal total return (that is, the minimum distance) from stage 2 and all remaining stages, given an input of x_2 to stage 2. Thus we see from Figure 16.3 that $f_2(x_2 = \text{node } 5) = 8$, $f_2(x_2 = \text{node } 6) = 7$, and $f_2(x_2 = \text{node } 7) = 12$. These are just the values in the squares at nodes 5, 6, and 7. Let us now turn to a well-known dynamic programming problem and use the notation just developed.

16.3   The Knapsack Problem

The knapsack problem is often encountered in dynamic programming applications. The basic idea is that there are N different types of items that can be put into a knapsack. Each item has a certain weight associated with it as well as a value. The problem is to determine how many units of each item to place in the knapsack in order to maximize the total value. A constraint is placed on the maximum weight permissible.

Consider a manager of a manufacturing operation who must make a biweekly selection of jobs to process during the following two-week period. A list of the jobs waiting to be processed at the beginning of the current week is presented in Table 16.2. The estimated time required for completion and the value rating associated with each category of job are also shown in the table.

The value rating assigned to each job is a subjective score assigned by the supervisor. A scale from 1 to 20 is used to measure the value of each job, where 1 represents jobs of the least value, and 20 represents jobs of most value. The value of a job depends upon such things as expected profit, length of time the job has been waiting to be processed, priority, and so on. In this

Table 16.2   Job Data for the Manufacturing Operation

Job	Number of Jobs to Be Processed	Estimated Completion Time per Job (days)	Value Rating
Category 1	4	1	2
Category 2	3	3	8
Category 3	2	4	11
Category 4	2	7	20

situation we would like to make a selection of jobs to process during the next two weeks such that all the jobs selected can be processed within ten days and that the total value of the jobs selected is maximized. In knapsack problem terminology we are in essence selecting the best jobs for our two-week knapsack, where the knapsack has a capacity equal to the ten-day production capacity. Let us formulate and solve this problem using a dynamic programming solution procedure.

This problem can be formulated as a dynamic programming problem involving four stages. At stage 1 we must decide how many jobs from category 1 to process, at stage 2 we must decide how many jobs from category 2 to process, and so on. Thus we let d_n denote the number of jobs in category n selected (that is, the decision variable at stage n). The state variable x_n is defined as the number of days of processing time remaining when we reach stage n.

Thus with a two-week production period, $x_4 = 10$ represents the total number of days that are available for processing jobs. The stage transformation functions are then defined so that

$$Stage\ 4 \quad x_3 = t_4(x_4, d_4) = x_4 - 7d_4$$
$$Stage\ 3 \quad x_2 = t_3(x_3, d_3) = x_3 - 4d_3$$
$$Stage\ 2 \quad x_1 = t_2(x_2, d_2) = x_2 - 3d_2$$
$$Stage\ 1 \quad x_0 = t_1(x_1, d_1) = x_1 - 1d_1.$$

The return at each stage is based on the value rating of the jobs and the number of jobs selected at each stage. The return functions are as follows:

$$Stage\ 4 \quad r_4(x_4, d_4) = 20d_4$$
$$Stage\ 3 \quad r_3(x_3, d_3) = 11d_3$$
$$Stage\ 2 \quad r_2(x_2, d_2) = 8d_2$$
$$Stage\ 1 \quad r_1(x_1, d_1) = 2d_1.$$

Figure 16.4 shows a schematic representation of the problem.

As with the shortest route problem in Section 16.1, we will apply a backward solution procedure; that is, we will begin by considering the stage 1 decision. A restatement of the principle of optimality can be made in terms of this problem. That is, regardless of whatever decisions have been made at

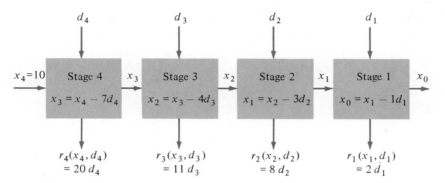

Figure 16.4   Schematic Presentation of the Dynamic Programming Formulation of the Manufacturing Problem

previous stages, if our decision at stage n is to be part of an optimal overall strategy, the decision made at stage n must necessarily be optimal for all remaining stages.

Let us set up a table which will help us calculate the optimal decisions for stage 1.

Stage 1   Note that the input to stage 1, x_1, which is the number of days of processing time available at stage 1, is unknown because we have not yet identified the decisions at the previous stages. Therefore in our analysis at stage 1 we will have to consider all possible values of x_1 and identify the best decision d_1 for each case; $f_1(x_1)$ will be the total return after decision d_1 is made. The possible values of x_1 and the associated d_1 and $f_1(x_1)$ values are as follows:

x_1	d_1^*	$f_1(x_1)$
0	0	0
1	1	2
2	2	4
3	3	6
4	4	8
5	4	8
6	4	8
7	4	8
8	4	8
9	4	8
10	4	8

The d_1^* column gives the optimal values of d_1 corresponding to a particular value of x_1, where x_1 can range from 0 to 10. The specific value of x_1 will depend upon how much processing time has been used by the jobs in the other categories selected in stages 2, 3, and 4. Since each stage 1 job requires one day of processing time and has a positive return of 2 per job, we always select as many jobs at this stage as possible. The number of jobs selected will depend upon the processing time available up to the maximum number of jobs of 4 for category 1.

Recall that $f_1(x_1)$ represents the value of the optimal total return from stage 1 and all remaining stages, given an input of x_1 to stage 1. Therefore $f_1(x_1) = 2x_1$ for all possible values of $x_1 \le 4$. Thus the optimization of stage 1 is accomplished. Let us now move on to stage 2 and carry out the optimization at that stage.

Stage 2   Again we will use a table to help identify the optimal decision. Since the input to stage 2, x_2, is unknown, we have to consider all possible values from 0 to 10. Also we have to consider all possible values of d_2 (that is, 0, 1, 2, or 3). The entries under the heading $r_2(x_2, d_2) + f_1(x_1)$ represent the total return that will be forthcoming from the final two stages, given the input of x_2 and the decision of d_2. For example, if stage 2 were entered with $x_2 = 7$ days of processing time remaining, and if a decision were made to select two jobs from category 2, that is, $d_2 = 2$, the total return for stages 1 and 2 would be 18.

x_2 \ d_2	$r_2(x_2,d_2) + f_1(x_1)$				d_2^*	$f_2(x_2)$	$x_1 = t_2(x_2,d_2^*)$ $= x_2 - 3d_2^*$
	0	1	2	3			
0	⓪	—	—	—	0	0	0
1	②	—	—	—	0	2	1
2	④	—	—	—	0	4	2
3	6	⑧	—	—	1	8	0
4	8	⑩	—	—	1	10	1
5	8	⑫	—	—	1	12	2
6	8	14	⑯	—	2	16	0
7	8	16	⑱	—	2	18	1
8	8	16	⑳	—	2	20	2
9	8	16	22	㉔	3	24	0
10	8	16	24	㉖	3	26	1

The return for stage 2 would be $r_2(x_2, d_2) = 8d_2 = 8(2) = 16$, and with $x_2 = 7$ and $d_2 = 2$, we would have $x_1 = x_2 - 3d_2 = 7 - 6 = 1$. From the previous table we see that the optimal return from stage 1 with $x_1 = 1$ is $f_1(1) = 2$. Thus the total return corresponding to $x_2 = 7$, $d_2 = 2$ is given by $r_2(7, 2) + f_1(1) = 16 + 2 = 18$. Similarly with $x_2 = 5$, and $d_2 = 1$, we get $r_2(5, 1) + f_1(2) = 8 + 4 = 12$. Note that some combinations of x_2 and d_2 are not feasible. For example, with $x_2 = 2$ days, $d_2 = 1$ is infeasible because category 2 jobs each require 3 days to process. The infeasible solutions are indicated by a dash.

After all the total returns in the rectangle have been calculated, we can determine an optimal decision at this stage for each possible value of the input or state variable x_2. For example, if $x_2 = 9$ there are four possible values we can select for d_2: 0, 1, 2, or 3. Clearly $d_3 = 3$ with a value of 24 yields the maximum total return for the last two stages. Therefore we record this value in the d_2^* column. For additional emphasis we circle the element inside the rectangle corresponding to the optimal return. The optimal total return, given that we are in state $x_2 = 9$ and must pass through two more stages, is thus 24, and we record this value in the $f_2(x_2)$ column. Given that we enter stage 2 with $x_2 = 9$ and make the optimal decision $d_2^* = 3$, we will enter stage 1 with $x_1 = t_2(9, 3) = x_2 - 3d_2 = 9 - 3(3) = 0$. This value is recorded in the last column in our table. We can now go on to stage 3.

Stage 3 The table we construct here is much the same as for stage 2. The entries under the heading $r_3(x_3, d_3) + f_2(x_2)$ represent the total return over stages 3, 2, and 1 for all possible inputs x_3 and all possible decisions d_3.

x_3 \ d_3	$r_3(x_3,d_3) + f_2(x_2)$			d_3^*	$f_3(x_3)$	$x_2 = t_3(x_3,d_3^*)$ $= x_3 - 4d_3^*$
	0	1	2			
0	⓪	—	—	0	0	0
1	②	—	—	0	2	1
2	④	—	—	0	4	2
3	⑧	—	—	0	8	3
4	10	⑪	—	1	11	0
5	12	⑬	—	1	13	1
6	⑯	15	—	0	16	6
7	18	⑲	—	1	19	3
8	20	21	㉒	2	22	0
9	㉔	23	㉔	0,2	24	9,1
10	26	㉗	26	1	27	6

There are some features of interest in this table which were not present at stage 2. We note that if the state variable $x_3 = 9$, then there are two decisions that will lead to an optimal total return from stages 1, 2, and 3; that is, we may elect to process no jobs from category 3, in which case we will obtain no return from stage 3 but will enter stage 2 with $x_2 = 9$. Since $f_2(9) = 24$, the selection of $d_3 = 0$ would result in a total return of 24.

However, a selection of $d_3 = 2$ also leads to a total return of 24. We obtain a return of $11(d_3) = 11(2) = 22$ for stage 3 and a return of 2 for the remaining two stages, since $x_2 = 1$. To show that there are alternate optimal solutions at this stage we have placed two entries in the d_3^* and $x_2 = t_3(x_3, d_3^*)$ columns. The other entries in this table are calculated in the same manner as at stage 2. Let us now move on to the last stage.

Stage 4   Since we know that there are 10 days available in the planning period, the input to stage 4 is $x_4 = 10$. Thus we have to consider only one row in the table, corresponding to stage 4.

d_4 x_4	$r_4(x_4,d_4) + f_3(x_3)$ 0	1	d_4^*	$f_4(x_4)$	$x_3 = t_4(x_4, d_4)$ $= 10 - 7d_4^*$
10	27	⑱	1	28	3

The optimal decision, given $x_4 = 10$, is $d_4^* = 1$.

We have completed our dynamic programming solution of this problem. In order to identify the overall optimal solution, we must now trace back through the tables beginning at stage 4. The optimal decision at stage 4 is $d_4^* = 1$. Thus $x_3 = 10 - 7d_4^* = 3$, and we enter stage 3 with 3 days available for processing. With $x_3 = 3$ we see that the best decision at stage 3 is $d_3^* = 0$. Thus we enter stage 2 with $x_2 = 3$. The optimal decision at stage 2 with $x_2 = 3$ is $d_2^* = 1$, resulting in $x_1 = 0$. Finally the decision at stage 1 must be $d_1^* = 0$. The optimal strategy for our manufacturing operation is then as follows:

Decision	Return
$d_1^* = 0$	0
$d_2^* = 1$	8
$d_3^* = 0$	0
$d_4^* = 1$	20
Total return	28

We should schedule one job from category 2 and one job from category 4 for processing over the next ten-day planning period.

Another advantage of the dynamic programming approach can now be illustrated. Suppose that we wanted to schedule the jobs to be processed over an eight-day period only. We can solve this new problem simply by making a recalculation at stage 4. The new stage 4 table would appear as follows:

d_4 x_4	0	1	d_4^*	$f_4(x_4)$	$x_3 = t_4(x_4,d_4^*)$ $= 8 - 7d_4^*$
8	㉒	㉒	0,1	22	8,1

Actually, we are testing the sensitivity of our optimal solution to a small change in the total number of days available for processing. We have here the case of alternate optimal solutions. One solution can be found by setting $d_4^* = 0$ and tracing through the tables. Doing so, we obtain the following:

Decision	Return
$d_1^* = 0$	0
$d_2^* = 0$	0
$d_3^* = 2$	2
$d_4^* = 0$	0
Total return	22

A second optimal solution can be found by setting $d_4^* = 1$ and tracing back through the tables. Doing so, we obtain another solution (which has exactly the same total return):

Decision	Return
$d_1^* = 1$	2
$d_2^* = 0$	0
$d_3^* = 0$	0
$d_4^* = 1$	20
Total return	22

From the shortest route and the knapsack examples you should start to become familiar with the basic stage-by-stage solution procedure of dynamic programming. In the next section we see how dynamic programming can be used to solve a production and inventory control problem.

16.4   A Production and Inventory Control Problem

In the chapter covering inventory decision models with deterministic demand, we commented on problems where the demand was considered known but fluctuated from period to period. The dynamic programming approach developed in this section makes solving this type of production and inventory control problem possible.

Suppose that we have developed forecasts of the demand for a particular product over a certain number of periods and that we would like to decide upon a production quantity for each of the periods so that demand can be satisfied at a minimum cost. There are two costs to be considered: production costs and inventory holding costs. We will assume that one production setup will be made each period, and thus setup costs will be constant. As a result, setup costs are not considered in the analysis.

We will allow the production and inventory holding costs to vary across periods. This makes our model more flexible since it also allows for the

Table 16.3   Data for the Production and Inventory Control Problem

Month	Demand	Production Capacity	Storage Capacity	Production Cost per Unit	Holding Cost per Unit
January	2	3	2	$175	$30
February	3	2	3	$150	$30
March	3	3	2	$200	$40

The beginning inventory for January is 1 unit.

possibility of using different facilities for production and storage in different periods. Production and storage capacity constraints, which may vary across periods, will be included in the model. Let us adopt the following notation:

N = number of periods (stages in our dynamic programming formulation),

D_n = demand during stage n; $n = 1, 2, \ldots, N$

x_n = a state variable representing the amount of inventory on hand at the beginning of stage n; $n = 1, 2, \ldots, N$

d_n = decision variable for stage n; the production quantity for the corresponding period; $n = 1, 2, \ldots, N$

P_n = production capacity in stage n; $n = 1, 2, \ldots, N$

W_n = storage capacity at the end of stage n; $n = 1, 2, \ldots, N$

C_n = production cost per unit in stage n; $n = 1, 2, \ldots, N$

H_n = holding cost per unit of ending inventory for stage n; $n = 1, 2, \ldots, N$

We will develop the dynamic programming solution for a problem covering three months of operation. The data for our problem are presented in Table 16.3.

We can think of each month in our problem as a stage in a dynamic programming formulation. Figure 16.5 shows a schematic representation of such a formulation. Note that the beginning inventory in January is 1 unit.

In Figure 16.5 we have numbered the periods backward; that is, stage 1

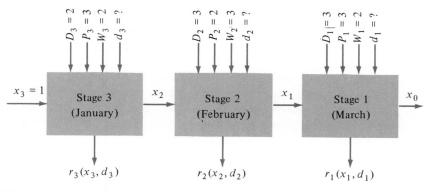

Figure 16.5   Schematic Representation of the Product and Inventory Control Problem as a Three-Stage Dynamic Programming Problem

corresponds to March, stage 2 corresponds to February, and stage 3 corresponds to January. The stage transformation functions take the form of ending inventory = beginning inventory + production − demand. Thus we have

$$x_3 = 1$$
$$x_2 = x_3 + d_3 - D_3 = x_3 + d_3 - 2$$
$$x_1 = x_2 + d_2 - D_2 = x_2 + d_2 - 3$$
$$x_0 = x_1 + d_1 - D_1 = x_1 + d_1 - 3.$$

The return functions for each stage represent the sum of production and inventory holding costs for the month. For example, in stage 1 (March) $r_1(x_1, d_1) = 200d_1 + 40(x_1 + d_1 - 3)$ represents the total production and holding costs for the period. The production costs are \$200 per unit and the holding costs are \$40 per unit of ending inventory. The other return functions are

$$r_2(x_2, d_2) = 150d_2 + 30(x_2 + d_2 - 3) \qquad \text{stage 2—February}$$
$$r_3(x_3, d_3) = 175d_3 + 30(x_3 + d_3 - 2) \qquad \text{stage 3—January.}$$

This problem is particularly interesting because there are three constraints that must be satisfied at each stage as we perform the optimization procedure. Two are fairly straightforward, while the third is a little tricky. The first constraint is that the ending inventory must be less than or equal to the warehouse capacity. Mathematically we have

$$x_n + d_n - D_n \le W_n$$

or

$$x_n + d_n \le W_n + D_n \tag{16.2}$$

The second constraint is that the production level in each period may not exceed the production capacity. Mathematically we have

$$d_n \le P_n \tag{16.3}$$

The most difficult constraint to handle is the requirement that beginning inventory plus production must exceed demand for each period. The difficulty with this constraint becomes clear if we study stage 2. The demand for this period is 3, but the production capacity is 2. Therefore we must require that the beginning inventory x_2 be greater than or equal to 1. In general, for each stage this means we must have a constraint that requires beginning inventory plus production to be greater than or equal to demand. Mathematically this constraint can be written as

$$x_n + d_n \ge D_n \tag{16.4}$$

Let us now begin the stagewise solution procedure. At each stage we want to minimize $r_n(x_n, d_n) + f_{n-1}(x_{n-1})$ subject to the constraints given by equations (16.2), (16.3), and (16.4).

Stage 1   The stage 1 problem is as follows:

$$\min \quad r_1(x_1, d_1) = 200d_1 + 40(x_1 + d_1 - 3)$$

s.t.

$$x_1 + d_1 \leq 5 \qquad \text{warehouse constraint}$$
$$d_1 \leq 3 \qquad \text{production constraint}$$
$$x_1 + d_1 \geq 3 \qquad \text{satisfy demand constraint.}$$

Combining terms in the objective function, we can rewrite the problem:

$$\min \quad r_1(x_1, d_1) = 240d_1 + 40x_1 - 120$$

s.t.

$$x_1 + d_1 \leq 5$$
$$d_1 \leq 3$$
$$x_1 + d_1 \geq 3.$$

Following the tabular approach we adopted in Section 16.3, we will consider all possible inputs to stage 1 (x_1) and make the corresponding minimum cost decision. Since we are attempting to minimize cost, we will want the decision variable d_1 to be as small as possible and still satisfy the demand constraint. Thus the table for stage 1 is as follows:

x_1	d_1^*		$f_1(x_1) = r_1(x_1, d_1^*)$ $240d_1 + 40x_1 - 120$
0	3		600
1	2	Production	400
2	1	capacity of 3	200
3	0	for stage 1	0

Warehouse
capacity of 3
from stage 2

Demand constraint: $x_1 + d_1 \geq 3$

Now let us proceed to stage 2.

Stage 2

$$\min \quad r_2(x_2, d_2) + f_1(x_1) = 150d_2 + 30(x_2 + d_2 - 3) + f_1(x_1)$$
$$= 180d_2 + 30x_2 - 90 + f_1(x_1)$$

s.t.

$$x_2 + d_2 \leq 6$$
$$d_2 \leq 2$$
$$x_2 + d_2 \geq 3.$$

The stage 2 calculations are summarized in the table below:

x_2 \ d_2	$r_2(x_2, d_2) + f_1(x_1)$ 0	1	2	d_2^*	$f_2(x_2)$	$x_1 = x_2 + d_2^* - 3$
0	—	—	—	—	M	—
1	—	—	⟨900⟩	2	900	0
2	—	750	⟨730⟩	2	730	1

Production capacity of 2 for stage 2

Warehouse capacity of 2 from stage 3

Check demand constraint $x_2 + d_2 \geq 3$ for each x_2, d_2 combination (—indicates an infeasible solution)

The detailed calculations for $r_2(x_2, d_2) + f_1(x_1)$ when $x_2 = 1$ and $d_2 = 2$ are as follows:

$$r_2(1, 2) + f_1(0) = 180(2) + 30(1) - 90 + 600 = 900.$$

For $r_2(x_2, d_2) + f_1(x_1)$ when $x_2 = 2$ and $d_2 = 1$, we have

$$r_2(2, 1) + f_1(0) = 180(1) + 30(2) - 90 + 600 = 750.$$

For $x_2 = 2$ and $d_2 = 2$, we have

$$r_2(2, 2) + f_1(1) = 180(2) + 30(2) - 90 + 400 = 730.$$

Note that an arbitrarily high cost M is assigned to the $f_2(x_2)$ column for $x_2 = 0$. Since an input of 0 to stage 2 does not provide a feasible solution, the M cost associated with the $x_2 = 0$ input will prevent $x_2 = 0$ from occurring in the optimal solution.

Stage 3

$$\min \quad r_3(x_3, d_3) + f_2(x_2) = 175d_3 + 30(x_3 + d_3 - 2) + f_2(x_2)$$
$$= 205d_3 + 30x_3 - 60 + f_2(x_2)$$

s.t.

$$x_3 + d_3 \leq 4$$
$$d_3 \leq 3$$
$$x_3 + d_3 \geq 2$$

Table 16.4   Optimal Production and Inventory Control Policy

Month	Beginning Inventory	Pro- duction	Pro- duction Cost	Ending Inven- tory	Holding Cost	Total Monthly Cost
January	1	2	$ 350	1	$30	$ 380
February	1	2	300	0	0	300
March	0	3	600	0	0	600
Totals			$1250		$30	$1280

With $x_3 = 1$ already defined by the beginning inventory level, the table for stage 3 becomes

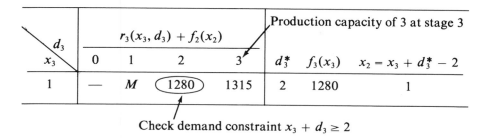

d_3 x_3	$r_3(x_3, d_3) + f_2(x_2)$					Production capacity of 3 at stage 3		
	0	1	2	3		d_3^*	$f_3(x_3)$	$x_2 = x_3 + d_3^* - 2$
1	—	M	1280	1315		2	1280	1

Check demand constraint $x_3 + d_3 \geq 2$

Thus we find that the total cost associated with the optimal production and inventory policy is \$1280. To find the optimal decisions and inventory levels for each period, we may trace back through each stage and identify x_n and d_n^* as we go. Table 16.4 summarizes the optimal production and inventory policy.

Summary

Dynamic programming is an attractive approach to problem solving when it is possible to break a large problem up into smaller multiple stages. The solution procedure then proceeds recursively, solving one of the smaller problems at each stage. Dynamic programming is not a specific algorithm, but rather an approach to problem solving. Thus the recursive optimization may be carried out differently for different problems. While we have used a tabular approach to determine optimal decisions at each stage, other dynamic programming problems might use linear programming, branch and bound, calculus, and other methods to solve the subproblems. In any case it is almost always easier to solve a series of smaller problems than one large one. This is how the dynamic programming approach obtains its power.

Glossary

1. *Dynamic programming*—An approach to problem solving that permits decomposing one large mathematical model which may be very difficult to solve into a number of smaller problems which are usually easier to solve.
2. *Principle of optimality*—Regardless of the decisions that have been made at the previous stages, if the decision made at stage *n* is to be part of an overall optimal solution, the decision made at stage *n* must be optimal for all remaining stages.
3. *Stages*—When a large problem is decomposed into a number of smaller problems, the dynamic programming solution approach creates a stage to correspond to each of the subproblems.

4. *State variables x_n and x_{n-1}*—An input state variable x_n and an output state variable x_{n-1} together define the condition of the process at the beginning and end of stage n.

5. *Decision variable d_n*—A variable representing the possible decisions that can be made at stage n.

6. *Stage transformation function $t_n(x_n, d_n)$*—The rule or equation that relates the output state variable x_{n-1} for stage n to the input state variable x_n and the decision variable d_n.

7. *Return function $r_n(x_n, d_n)$*—A value (such as profit or loss) associated with making decision d_n at stage n for a specific value of the input state variable x_n.

8. *Knapsack problem*—N items, each of which has a different weight and value, are to be placed into a knapsack with limited weight capacity so as to maximize the total value of the items placed in the knapsack.

Problems

1. In Section 16.1 we solved a shortest route problem using dynamic programming. Find the optimal solution to this problem by total enumeration; that is, list all possible routes from the origin, node 1, to the destination, node 10, and pick the one with the smallest value. Explain why the dynamic programming approach results in fewer computations for this problem.

2. Consider the following network. The numbers above each arc represent the distance between the connected nodes.

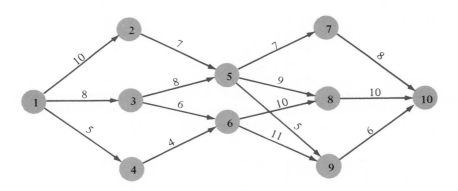

   a. Find the shortest route from node 1 to node 10 using dynamic programming.
   b. What is the shortest route from node 4 to node 10?
   c. Enumerate all possible routes from node 1 to node 10. Explain how dynamic programming has reduced the number of computations below that required by total enumeration.

3. A firm has just hired eight new employees and would like to determine how to allocate the new employees to four activities. The firm has prepared the table below, which gives the estimated profit for each activity as a function of the number of new employees allocated to it:

Activities	Number of New Employees								
	0	1	2	3	4	5	6	7	8
1	22	30	37	44	49	54	58	60	61
2	30	40	48	55	59	62	64	66	67
3	46	52	56	59	62	65	67	68	69
4	5	22	36	48	52	55	58	60	61

a. Use dynamic programming to determine the optimal allocation of new employees to the activities.

b. Suppose there were only six new employees hired. Which activities would you assign to these six employees?

4. A sawmill receives logs in 20-foot lengths, cuts them to smaller lengths, and then sells these smaller lengths to a number of manufacturing companies. The lengths which the company has orders for are

$$l_1 = 3 \text{ ft}$$

$$l_2 = 7 \text{ ft}$$

$$l_3 = 11 \text{ ft}$$

$$l_4 = 16 \text{ ft}$$

The sawmill currently has an inventory of 2000 logs in 20-foot lengths and would like to select a cutting pattern that will maximize the profit made on this inventory. Assuming the sawmill has sufficient orders available, its problem becomes one of determining the cutting pattern that will maximize profits. The per unit profit for each of the smaller lengths is as follows:

Length (feet)	Profit
3	$1
7	3
11	5
16	8

Any cutting pattern is permissible as long as

$$3d_1 + 7d_2 + 11d_3 + 16d_4 \le 20$$

where d_i is the number of pieces of length l_i cut, $i = 1, 2, 3, 4$.

a. Set up a dynamic programming model of this problem and solve it. What are your decision variables? What is your state variable?

b. Explain breifly how this model can be extended to find the best cutting pattern in cases where the overall length l can be cut into N lengths, $l_1, l_2, \ldots, l_N$.

5. A large manufacturing company has a very well developed management training program. Each trainee is expected to complete a four-phase program, but there are a number of different assignments each trainee can be given at each phase of the training program. The assignments available and the estimated completion times in months at each phase of the program are shown at the top of page 598.

Phase I	Phase II	Phase III	Phase IV
A–13	E–3	H–12	L–10
B–10	F–6	I–6	M–5
C–20	G–5	J–7	N–13
D–17		K–10	

Assignments made at subsequent phases depend upon the previous assignment. For example, a trainee who completes assignment A at phase I may only go on to assignments F or G at phase II. That is, there is a precedence relationship for each assignment as shown below:

Assignment	Feasible Succeeding Assignments
A	F, G
B	F
C	G
D	E, G
E	H, I, J, K
F	H, K
G	J, K
H	L, M
I	L, M
J	M, N
K	N
L	Finish
M	Finish
N	Finish

a. The company would like to determine the sequence of assignments that will minimize the time in the training program. Formulate and solve this as a dynamic programming problem. (Hint: Develop a network representation of the problem where each node represents completion of an activity.)

b. If a trainee has just completed assignment C and would like to complete the remainder of the training program in the shortest possible time, which assignment should be chosen next?

6. Crazy Robin, the owner of a small chain of Robin Hood Sporting Goods stores in Des Moines and Cedar Rapids, Iowa, has just purchased a new supply of top line golf balls. Because she was willing to purchase the entire amount of a production overrun, Robin was able to buy the golf balls at one-half the usual price.

    Three of Robin's stores do a good business in the sale of golf equipment and supplies and, as a result, Robin has decided to retail the balls at these three stores. Thus Robin is faced with the problem of determining how many dozen balls to allocate to each store. The following estimates show the expected profit from allocating 100, 200, 300, 400, or 500 dozen to each store:

	Number of Dozens of Golf Balls				
	100	200	300	400	500
Store 1	$600	$1100	$1550	$1700	$1800
Store 2	500	1200	1700	2000	2100
Store 3	550	1100	1500	1850	1950

Assuming the lots cannot be broken into any sizes smaller than 100 dozen each, how many dozen golf balls should Crazy Robin send to each store?

7. The Max X. Posure Advertising Agency is conducting a ten-day advertising campaign for a local department store. The agency has determined that the most effective campaign would possibly include placing ads in four media: daily newspaper, Sunday newspaper, radio, and television. $8000 has been made available for this campaign, and the agency would like to distribute this in $1000 increments across the media in such a fashion that an advertising exposure index is maximized. Research that has been conducted by the agency permits the following estimates to be made of the exposure per each $1000 expenditure in each of the media.

	Thousands of Dollars Spent							
Media	1	2	3	4	5	6	7	8
Daily newspaper	24	37	46	59	72	80	82	82
Sunday newspaper	15	55	70	75	90	95	95	95
Radio	20	30	45	55	60	62	63	63
Television	20	40	55	65	70	70	70	70

a. How much should the agency spend on each medium in order to maximize the department store's exposure?

b. How would your answer change if only $6000 were budgeted?

c. How would your answers in parts a and b change if television was not considered as one of the media?

8. Suppose that we have a three-stage process where the yield for each stage is a function of the decision made. In mathematical notation we may state our problem as follows:

$$\max \quad r_1(d_1) + r_2(d_2) + r_3(d_3)$$
$$\text{s.t.}$$
$$d_1 + d_2 + d_3 \le 1000.$$

The possible values the decision variables may take on at each stage and the corresponding returns are presented in tabular form below:

Stage 1		Stage 2		Stage 3	
d_1	$r_1(d_1)$	d_2	$r_2(d_2)$	d_3	$r_3(d_3)$
0	0	100	120	100	175
100	110	300	400	500	700
200	300	500	650		
300	400	600	700		
400	425	800	975		

a. Use total enumeration to list all feasible sequences of decisions for this problem. Which one is optimal [that is, maximizes $r_1(d_1) + r_2(d_2) + r_3(d_3)$]?
b. Use dynamic programming to solve this problem.

9. Recall the production and inventory control problem of Section 16.4. Mills Manufacturing Company has just such a production and inventory control problem for an armature the company manufactures as a component for a generator. The available data for the next three-month planning period are presented below:

Month	Demand	Production Capacity	Warehouse Capacity	Production Cost per Unit	Holding Cost per Unit
1	20	30	40	$2.00	$0.30
2	30	20	30	1.50	0.30
3	30	30	20	2.00	0.20

Using the dynamic programming approach outlined in Section 16.4 find the optimal production quantities and inventory levels in each period for the Mills Manufacturing Company. Assume there is a beginning inventory of 10 units on hand at the beginning of month 1 and that production runs are completed in multiples of 10 units (that is, 10, 20, or 30 units).

10. A chemical processing plant is considering introducing a new product on the market. However, before making a final decision, management has requested you to provide estimates of profits associated with different process designs. The general flow process is represented below.

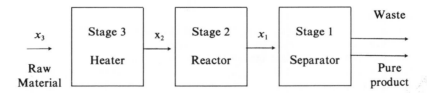

Raw material is fed into a heater at the rate of 4500 pounds per week. The heated material is then routed to a reactor where a portion of the raw material is converted to pure product. A separator then withdraws the finished product for sale. The unconverted material is discarded as waste.

Profit considerations are to be based on a two-year payback period on investments; that is, all capital expenditures must be recovered in 2 years (100 weeks). All calculations will be based on weekly operations. Raw material costs are expected to stay fixed at $1 per pound, and it has been forecast that the finished product will sell for $6 per pound.

It is your responsibility to determine the process design that will yield maximum profit per week. You and your coworkers have collected the following preliminary data.

At stage 3 one heater with an initial cost of $12,000 is being considered. Two temperatures, 700°F and 800°F, are feasible. The operating costs for the heater depend directly on the temperature to be attained. These costs are presented on page 601.

Operating Costs at Stage 3

| | | Decisions at Stage 3 | |
		700°F	800°F
Input x_3	4500 lb	$280/week	$380/week

The output from stage 3, x_2, which is also the input to stage 2, may be expressed as 4500 pounds of raw material heated to either 700°F or 800°F. One of the decisions you must make is to what temperature the raw material should be heated.

For stage 2 a reactor, which can operate with either of two catalysts, C1 or C2, is to be used. The initial cost of this reactor is $50,000. The operating costs of this reactor are independent of the input x_2 and depend only upon the catalyst selected. The costs of the catalysts are included in the operating costs. The output will be expressed in pounds of converted (or pure) material. The percent of material converted depends on the incoming temperature and the catalyst used. The tables below summarize the pertinent information. Thus a second decision you must make is to specify which catalyst should be used.

Percent Conversion

| | | Decisions at Stage 2 | |
		C1	C2
x_2	(4500 lb, 700°F)	20%	40%
	(4500 lb, 800°F)	40%	60%

Operating Costs

| Decision at Stage 2 | |
C1	C2
$450/week	$650/week

One of two separators, S1 or S2, will be purchased for stage 1. S1 has an initial cost of $20,000 and a weekly operating cost of $0.10 per pound of pure product to be separated. Comparatively, S2 has an initial cost of $5000 and a weekly operating cost of $0.20 per pound of pure product to be separated. Included in these operating costs is the expense of discarding the unconverted raw material as waste.

Develop a dynamic programming model for this problem. What is your recommendation for best temperature for the heater? best catalyst to use with the reactor? best separator to purchase? What is the maximum weekly profit?

Chapter 17

Markov Processes

Markov process models are useful in studying the evolution of certain systems over repeated trials. These repeated trials are often successive time periods where the state or outcome of the system in any particular time period cannot be determined with certainty. Rather, a set of transition probabilities is used to describe the manner in which the system makes transitions from one period to the next. Hence we talk about the probability of the system being in a particular state at a given time period.

Markov processes have been used to describe the probability that a machine which is functioning in one period will continue to function or will break down in the next period. They have also been used to describe the probability that a consumer purchasing brand A in one period will purchase brand B in the next period. In this chapter we will study a marketing application of Markov process models that involves an analysis of the store switching behavior of supermarket customers. As a second illustration of Markov process models, we will consider an accounting application that is concerned with the transitioning of accounts receivable dollars to different aging categories.

Since an in-depth treatment of Markov processes is beyond the scope of this text, our analysis in both illustrations will be restricted to Markov processes in which there are a finite number of states, the transition probabilities remain constant over time, and the probability of being in a particular state at any one time period depends only upon the state of the process in the immediately preceding period. Such Markov processes are often referred to as Markov chains with stationary transition probabilities.

17.1   Market Share Analysis

Suppose that we are interested in analyzing the market share and customer loyalty for Murphy's Foodliner and Ashley's Supermarket, the only two grocery stores in a small town. We focus our attention on the sequence of shopping trips of one customer. We assume that the customer makes one shopping trip each week and that the customer will select either Murphy's Foodliner or Ashley's Supermarket, but not both, on each weekly trip.

Using the terminology of Markov processes, we refer to the weekly time periods or shopping trips as the *trials of the process*. Thus at each trial the customer will shop at either Murphy's Foodliner or Ashley's Supermarket. The particular store selected in a given week is referred to as the *state of the system* in that time period. Since the customer has two shopping alternatives at each trial, we say the system has two possible states. Since the number of states is finite, we can list and identify each state in detail. The two possible states are

> State 1:   The customer shops at Murphy's Foodliner;
> State 2:   The customer shops at Ashley's Supermarket.

If we say the system is in state 1 at trial 3, we are simply saying that the customer shops at Murphy's during the third weekly shopping period.

As we continue the shopping trip process into the future, we cannot say for certain where the customer will shop during a given week or trial. In fact, we realize that during any given week, the customer may be either a Murphy's customer or an Ashley's customer. However, using a Markov process model we will be able to compute the probability that the customer shops at each store during any time period. For example, we may find there is a 0.6 probability that the customer will shop at Ashley's during a particular week and a 0.4 probability that the customer will shop at Murphy's.

In order to determine the probabilities of the various states occurring at successive trials of the Markov process, we need information on the probability that a customer remains with the same store or switches to the competing store as the process continues from trial to trial or week to week.

Suppose as part of a market research study we collect data from 100 shoppers over a 10-week period. Suppose further that these data show each customer's weekly shopping-trip pattern in terms of the sequence of visits to Murphy's and Ashley's. In order to develop a Markov process model for the sequence of weekly shopping trips, we need to express the probability of selecting each store (state) in a given time period solely in terms of the store (state) that was selected during the previous time period. In reviewing the data, suppose we find that out of all customers who shopped at Murphy's in a given week, 90 percent shopped at Murphy's the following week while 10 percent switched to Ashley's. Suppose that similar data for the customers who shopped at Ashley's in a given week show that 80 percent shopped at Ashley's the following week while 20 percent switched to Murphy's. Probabilities based on these data are shown in Table 17.1. Since these are the probabilities that a customer moves or makes a transition from a state in a given period to a state in the following period, these probabilities are given the special name of *transition probabilities*.

An important property of the table of transition probabilities is that the sum of the entries in each row is 1; this indicates that each row of the table provides a probability distribution. For example, a customer who shops at Murphy's one week must shop at either Murphy's or Ashley's the next week.

TABLE 17.1   Transition Probabilities for Murphy's and Ashley's Food Stores

		Next Weekly Shopping Period	
		Murphy's Foodliner	Ashley's Supermarket
Current Weekly Shopping Period	Murphy's Foodliner	0.9	0.1
	Ashley's Supermarket	0.2	0.8

The entries in row 1 give the probabilities associated with each of these events.

The 0.9 and 0.8 probabilities in Table 17.1 can be interpreted as measures of store loyalty in that they indicate the probability of a repeat visit to the same store. Similarly, the 0.1 and 0.2 probabilities are measures of the store switching characteristics of customers.

It is important to realize that in developing a Markov process model for our problem, we are assuming that the transition probabilities will be the same for any customer and that the transition probabilities will not change over time; that is, at any point in time, the transition probabilities can be used to assess the probability a customer will shop at Murphy's or Ashley's in the next period, given we know where the customer is shopping during the current time period.

Note that the table of transition probabilities, Table 17.1, has one row and one column for each state of the system. We will use the symbol p_{ij} to represent the individual transition probabilities and the symbol P to represent the matrix (table) of transition probabilities; that is,

p_{ij} = probability of making a transition from state i in a given time period to state j in the next time period.

For our supermarket problem we have

$$P = \begin{bmatrix} p_{11} & p_{12} \\ p_{21} & p_{22} \end{bmatrix} = \begin{bmatrix} 0.9 & 0.1 \\ 0.2 & 0.8 \end{bmatrix}.$$

Using the matrix of transition probabilities, we can now determine the probability that a customer will be a Murphy's or an Ashley's customer at some time period in the future. Let us begin by assuming that we have a customer whose last weekly shopping trip was to Murphy's. What is the probability that this customer will shop at Murphy's on the next weekly shopping trip, time period 1? In other words, what is the probability that the system will be in state 1 after the first transition? The matrix of transition probabilities indicates that this probability is $p_{11} = 0.9$.

Now let us consider the state of the system in period 2. A useful way of depicting what can happen on the second weekly shopping trip is to draw a tree diagram of the possible outcomes (see Figure 17.1). Using this tree diagram, we see that the probability that the customer shops at Murphy's during both the first and second weeks is $(0.9)(0.9) = 0.81$. Also, note that the probability of the customer switching to Ashley's on the first trip and then switching back to Murphy's on the second trip is $(0.1)(0.2) = 0.02$. Since these are the only two ways that the customer can be in state 1 (shopping at Murphy's) during the second period, the probability of the system being in state 1 during the second period is $0.81 + 0.02 = 0.83$. Similarly, the probability of the system being in state 2 during the second period of the process is $0.09 + 0.08 = 0.17$.

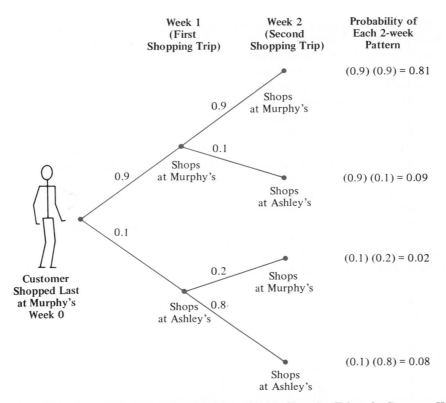

	Week 1 (First Shopping Trip)	Week 2 (Second Shopping Trip)	Probability of Each 2-week Pattern

FIGURE 17.1   Tree Diagram Depicting Two Weekly Shopping Trips of a Customer Who Shopped Last at Murphy's

As desirable as the tree diagram approach may be from an intuitive point of view, this approach becomes very cumbersome when we want to extend the analysis three, four, etc., periods into the future. Fortunately, there is an easier way to calculate the probabilities of the system being in state 1 or state 2 for any subsequent period. First, we introduce notation that will allow us to represent the probability of the system being in state 1 or state 2 for any given period of time. Let

$$\pi_i(n) = \text{probability that the system is in state } i \text{ at the } n\text{th period.}$$

index
denotes
the state
denotes the time
period or number of transitions

For example, $\pi_1(1)$ would represent the probability of the system being in state 1 in period 1 (that is, after 1 transition), while $\pi_2(1)$ denotes the probability of the system being in state 2 after one transition. Since $\pi_i(n)$ is the probability that the system is in state i at period n, this probability is referred to as a *state probability*.

$\pi_1(0)$ and $\pi_2(0)$ will denote the probability of the system being in state 1 or state 2 at some initial or starting time period. Period or week 0 represents the most recent time period, when we are beginning the analysis of a Markov process. If we set $\pi_1(0) = 1$ and $\pi_2(0) = 0$, we are saying that as an initial condition the customer shopped last week at Murphy's; whereas if we set $\pi_1(0) = 0$ and $\pi_2(0) = 1$, we would be starting the system with a customer who shopped last week at Ashley's. In our tree diagram of Figure 17.1 we considered the situation where the customer shopped last at Murphy's. Thus

$$[\pi_1(0) \quad \pi_2(0)] = [1 \quad 0]$$

is a vector that represents the initial state probabilities of our system. In general, we use the notation

$$\Pi(n) = [\pi_1(n) \quad \pi_2(n)]$$

to denote the vector of state probabilities for the system at period n. In our shopping example, $\Pi(1)$ is a vector representing the state probabilities for the first week, $\Pi(2)$ is a vector representing the state probabilities for the second week, and so on.

Using this notation, we can find the state probabilities for period $n + 1$ by simply multiplying the known state probabilities for period n by the transition probability matrix. Using the vector of state probabilities and the matrix of transition probabilities, this multiplication[1] can be expressed as follows:

$$\Pi(\text{next period}) = \Pi(\text{current period})P$$

or

$$\Pi(n + 1) = \Pi(n)P. \tag{17.1}$$

Beginning with the system in state 1 at period 0, we have $\Pi(0) = [1 \quad 0]$. We can compute the state probabilities for period 1 as follows:

$$\Pi(1) = \Pi(0)P$$

or

$$[\pi_1(1) \quad \pi_2(1)] = [\pi_1(0) \quad \pi_2(0)] \begin{bmatrix} p_{11} & p_{12} \\ p_{21} & p_{22} \end{bmatrix}$$

$$= [1 \quad 0] \begin{bmatrix} 0.9 & 0.1 \\ 0.2 & 0.8 \end{bmatrix}$$

$$= [0.9 \quad 0.1]$$

The state probabilities $\pi_1(1) = 0.9$ and $\pi_2(1) = 0.1$ are the probabilities that

---

[1]Appendix E provides the step-by-step procedure for vector and matrix multiplication.

a customer shops at Murphy's or Ashley's during week 1, given that he or she shopped at Murphy's during week 0.

Using equation (17.1), we can compute the state probabilities for the second week as follows:

$$\Pi(2) = \Pi(1)P$$

or

$$[\pi_1(2) \quad \pi_2(2)] = [\pi_1(1) \quad \pi_2(1)] \begin{bmatrix} p_{11} & p_{12} \\ p_{21} & p_{22} \end{bmatrix}$$

$$= [0.9 \quad 0.1] \begin{bmatrix} 0.9 & 0.1 \\ 0.2 & 0.8 \end{bmatrix}$$

$$= [0.83 \quad 0.17]$$

We see that the probability of shopping Murphy's during the second week is 0.83, while the probability of shopping Ashley's during this time period is 0.17. These same results were previously obtained using the tree diagram of Figure 17.1. By continuing to apply equation (17.1), we can easily compute the state probabilities for any future time period; that is,

$$\Pi(3) \quad = \Pi(2)P,$$

$$\Pi(4) \quad = \Pi(3)P,$$

$$\vdots \qquad \vdots$$

$$\Pi(n + 1) = \Pi(n)P.$$

Table 17.2 shows the result of carrying out these calculations for a number of periods in the future.

The vectors $\Pi(1)$, $\Pi(2)$, $\Pi(3)$, ... contain the probabilities that a customer who started out as a Murphy customer will be in state 1 or state 2 in the first period, the second period, the third period, and so on. In Table 17.2 we see that after a large number of periods these probabilities do not change much from one period to the next. In fact, the probability of the system being in state 1 or state 2 is approaching $\frac{2}{3}$ and $\frac{1}{3}$ after a large number of shopping periods.

If we had started with 1000 Murphy customers—that is, 1000 consumers who last shopped at Murphy's—our analysis indicates that during the fifth subsequent weekly shopping period 723 would be customers of Murphy's and 277 would be customers of Ashley's. Moreover, after a large number of shopping periods, approximately 667 would be customers of Murphy's and 333 customers of Ashley's.

Now let us repeat our analysis, but this time we will begin the process with a customer who shopped last at Ashley's. Thus

$$\Pi(0) = [\pi_1(0) \quad \pi_2(0)] = [0 \quad 1].$$

TABLE 17.2   Probabilities of States for Future Periods Beginning Initially with a Murphy's Customer, $\Pi(0) = [1 \quad 0]$

State Probability	0	1	2	3	4	5	Period (n) 6	7	8	9	10	Large n
$\pi_1(n)$	1	0.9	0.83	0.781	0.747	0.723	0.706	0.694	0.686	0.680	0.676	$\rightarrow \frac{2}{3}$
$\pi_2(n)$	0	0.1	0.17	0.219	0.253	0.277	0.294	0.306	0.314	0.320	0.324	$\rightarrow \frac{1}{3}$

TABLE 17.3   Probabilities of States for Future Periods Beginning Initially with an Ashley's Customer, $\Pi(0) = [0 \quad 1]$

State Probability	0	1	2	3	4	5	Period (n) 6	7	8	9	10	Large n
$\pi_1(n)$	0	0.2	0.34	0.438	0.507	0.555	0.589	0.612	0.628	0.640	0.648	$\rightarrow \frac{2}{3}$
$\pi_2(n)$	1	0.8	0.66	0.562	0.493	0.445	0.411	0.388	0.372	0.360	0.352	$\rightarrow \frac{1}{3}$

Using equation (17.1), the probability of the system being in state 1 or state 2 in period 1 is given by

$$\Pi(1) = \Pi(0)P$$

or

$$[\pi_1(1) \quad \pi_2(1)] = [\pi_1(0) \quad \pi_2(0)] \begin{bmatrix} p_{11} & p_{12} \\ p_{12} & p_{22} \end{bmatrix}$$

$$= [0 \quad 1] \begin{bmatrix} 0.9 & 0.1 \\ 0.2 & 0.8 \end{bmatrix}$$

$$= [0.2 \quad 0.8].$$

Proceeding as before we can calculate subsequent state probabilities. Doing so, we obtain the results shown in Table 17.3.

In the fifth shopping period the probability that the customer will be shopping at Murphy's is 0.555 and the probability that the customer will be shopping at Ashley's is 0.445. After a large number of shopping periods the probability of the system being in state 1 approaches $\frac{2}{3}$ and the probability of it being in state 2 approaches $\frac{1}{3}$. These are the same as the probabilities obtained after a large number of transitions when the system started in state 1. Thus we see that the probability of the system being in a particular state after a large number of periods is independent of beginning state of the system. The probabilities that we approach after a large number of transitions are referred to as *steady-state probabilities*. We shall denote the steady-state probability for state 1 with the symbol π_1 and the steady-state probability for state 2 with the symbol π_2. We simply omit the period designation from $\pi_i(n)$, since it is no longer necessary.

Thus if we have 1000 customers in the system, the Markov process model tells us that in the long run, with steady-state probabilities $\pi_1 = \frac{2}{3}$ and $\pi_2 = \frac{1}{3}$, approximately two-thirds, or 667 customers, would be Murphy's, while approximately one-third, or 333 customers, would be Ashley's. These steady-state probabilities can be interpreted as the market shares for the two stores.

The analysis of Tables 17.2 and 17.3 indicates that as n gets larger, the difference between the state probabilities for the nth shopping period and the $(n+1)$th period becomes increasingly smaller. This leads us to the conclusion that as n gets extremely large, the state probabilities at the $(n+1)$th period are equal to those at the nth period. This observation provides the basis for a simple method for computing the steady-state probabilities without having to actually carry out a large number of calculations.

In general we know from equation (17.1) that

$$[\pi_1(n+1) \quad \pi_2(n+1)] = [\pi_1(n) \quad \pi_2(n)] \begin{bmatrix} p_{11} & p_{12} \\ p_{21} & p_{22} \end{bmatrix}.$$

Since for sufficiently large n the difference between $\Pi(n+1)$ and $\Pi(n)$ is negligible, we see that in the steady state $\pi_1(n + 1) = \pi_1(n) = \pi_1$ and $\pi_2(n + 1) = \pi_2(n) = \pi_2$. Thus we have

$$[\pi_1 \quad \pi_2] = [\pi_1 \quad \pi_2] \begin{bmatrix} p_{11} & p_{12} \\ p_{21} & p_{22} \end{bmatrix}$$

$$= [\pi_1 \quad \pi_2] \begin{bmatrix} 0.9 & 0.1 \\ 0.2 & 0.8 \end{bmatrix}.$$

After carrying out the above multiplications we obtain

$$\pi_1 = 0.9\pi_1 + 0.2\pi_2 \qquad (17.2)$$

and

$$\pi_2 = 0.1\pi_1 + 0.8\pi_2. \qquad (17.3)$$

However, we also know that

$$\pi_1 + \pi_2 = 1, \qquad (17.4)$$

since the sum of the probabilities must equal 1.

Using equation (17.4) to solve for π_2 and substituting the result in equation (17.2), we obtain

$$\pi_1 = 0.9\pi_1 + 0.2(1 - \pi_1)$$
$$\pi_1 = 0.9\pi_1 + 0.2 - 0.2\pi_1$$
$$\pi_1 - 0.7\pi_1 = 0.2$$
$$0.3\pi_1 = 0.2$$
$$\pi_1 = \tfrac{2}{3}.$$

Then using equation (17.4), we can conclude that $\pi_2 = \tfrac{1}{3}$.

Thus we see that solving the simultaneous equations given by equations (17.2) and (17.4) allows us to solve for the steady-state probabilities directly. You can check for yourself that we could have obtained the same result using equations (17.3) and (17.4).[2] In our example, these steady-state probabilities represent the share of the market each store would receive in the long run regardless of its initial market share.

This market share information is often quite valuable in decision-making situations. For example, suppose Ashley's Supermarket is contemplating an advertising campaign to attract more of Murphy's customers to its store. Let us suppose further that Ashley's believes this promotional strategy will increase the probability of a Murphy's customer switching to Ashley's from 0.10 to 0.15. The new transition probabilities that would result are given in Table 17.4.

---

[2]Even though equations (17.2) and (17.3) provide us with two equations and two unknowns, we must include equation (17.4) when solving for π_1 and π_2 to ensure that the sum of steady-state probabilities will equal 1.

TABLE 17.4   **New Transition Probabilities for Murphy's and Ashley's Food Stores**

		Next Weekly Shopping Period	
		Murphy's Foodliner	Ashley's Supermarket
Current Weekly Shopping Period	Murphy's Foodliner	0.85	0.15
	Ashley's Supermarket	0.20	0.80

Given the new transition probabilities, we can solve for the new steady-state probabilities or market shares as we did before, using equations (17.2) and (17.4). Thus we obtain

$$\pi_1 = 0.85\pi_1 + 0.20\pi_2.$$

Substituting $\pi_2 = 1 - \pi_1$ from equation (17.4), we get

$$\pi_1 = 0.85\pi_1 + 0.20(1 - \pi_1)$$
$$\pi_1 = 0.85\pi_1 + 0.20 - 0.20\pi_1$$
$$\pi_1 - 0.65\pi_1 = 0.20$$
$$0.35\pi_1 = 0.20$$
$$\pi_1 = {}^4\!/_7 = 0.57$$

and

$$\pi_2 = 1 - 0.57 = 0.43.$$

Thus we see that the proposed promotional strategy will lead to approximately a 10 percent increase in Ashley's market share. Suppose that the total market consists of 6000 customers per week. The new promotional strategy will approximately increase the number of customers doing their weekly shopping at Ashley's from 2000 to 2580. If the average weekly profit per customer is $1.00, the proposed promotional strategy can be expected to increase Ashley's profits by $580 per week. Clearly, then, if the cost of the promotional campaign is less than $580 per week, Ashley should seriously consider such a strategy.

This is but one illustration of how a Markov analysis of a firm's market share can be useful in a decision-making situation. Suppose that instead of trying to attract customers away from Murphy's Foodliner, Ashley's directed a promotional effort at increasing the loyalty of its own customers. In this case p_{22} would increase and p_{21} would decrease. Once we knew the amount of the change, we could calculate new steady-state probabilities and compute the impact on profits.

17.2   Accounts Receivable Analysis

Another area in which Markov processes have produced useful results involves the estimation of the allowance for doubtful accounts. This allowance is an estimate of the amount of accounts receivable that will ultimately prove to be uncollectable (that is, bad debts).

Let us begin our analysis by considering the accounts receivable for Heidman's Department Store. Heidman's has two aging categories for its accounts receivable: (1) accounts that are classified as 0–30 days old and (2) accounts that are classified as 31–90 days old. If any portion of an account balance exceeds 90 days, that portion is written off as a bad debt. Heidman's follows the procedure of aging the total balance in any customer's account according to the oldest unpaid bill. For example, suppose one customer's account balance on September 30 is as follows:

Date of Purchase	Amount Charged
August 15	$25
September 18	10
September 28	50
Total	$85

An aging of accounts receivable on September 30 would assign the total balance of $85 to the 31–90 day old category because the oldest unpaid bill of August 15 is 46 days old. Let us assume that one week later, October 7, the customer pays the August 15 bill of $25. The remaining total balance of $60 would now be placed in the 0–30 day aging category, since the oldest unpaid amount, corresponding to the September 18 purchase, is less than 31 days old. This method of aging accounts receivable is called the *total balance method,* since the total account balance is placed in the age category corresponding to the oldest unpaid amount.

Note that under the total balances method of aging accounts receivable, dollars appearing in a 31–90 day age category at one point in time may appear in a 0–30 day age category at a later point in time. In the above example this was true for $60 of September billings which shifted from a 31–90 day to a 0–30 day aging category after the August bill had been paid.

Let us assume that on December 31 Heidman's shows a total of $3000 in its accounts receivable and that the firm's management would like an estimate of how much of the $3000 will eventually be collected and how much will eventually result in bad debts. The estimated amount of bad debts will appear as an allowance for doubtful accounts in the year-ending financial statements.

Let us see how we can view the accounts receivable operation as a Markov process. First, concentrate on what happens to *one* dollar currently in accounts receivable. As the firm continues to operate into the future, we can consider each week as a trial of a Markov process with a dollar existing in one of the following states of the system:

State 1:   Paid category,

State 2:   Bad debt category,

State 3:   0–30 day age category,

State 4:   31–90 day age category.

Thus we can track the week-by-week status of one dollar by using a Markov analysis to identify the state of the system at a particular week or time period in the future.

Using a Markov process model with the above states, we define our transition probabilities as follows:

p_{ij} = probability of a dollar in state i in one week moving to
state j in the next week.

Based on historical transitions of accounts receivable dollars, the following transition matrix P has been developed for Heidman's Department Store:

$$P = \begin{bmatrix} p_{11} & p_{12} & p_{13} & p_{14} \\ p_{21} & p_{22} & p_{23} & p_{24} \\ p_{31} & p_{32} & p_{33} & p_{34} \\ p_{41} & p_{42} & p_{43} & p_{44} \end{bmatrix} = \begin{bmatrix} 1 & 0 & 0 & 0 \\ 0 & 1 & 0 & 0 \\ 0.4 & 0 & 0.3 & 0.3 \\ 0.4 & 0.2 & 0.3 & 0.1 \end{bmatrix}.$$

From the transition matrix we see that the probability of a dollar in the 0–30 day age category (state 3) moving to the paid category (state 1) in the next period is 0.4. Also we see that there is a 0.3 probability that this dollar will remain in the 0–30 day category (state 3) one week later, while there is a 0.3 probability that it will be in the 31–90 day category (state 4) one week later. Note that a dollar in a 0–30 day account cannot make the transition to a bad debt (state 2) in one week.

An important property of the Markov process model for Heidman's accounts receivable is the presence of *absorbing states*. Note that once a dollar makes a transition to state 1, the paid state, the probability of making a transition to any other state is zero. Similarly, once a dollar is in state 2, the bad debt state, the probability of a transition to any other state is zero. Thus once a dollar reaches state 1 or state 2, the system will remain in this state indefinitely. This leads us to conclude that all accounts receivable dollars will eventually be absorbed into either the paid or the bad debt state, hence the name *absorbing state*.

When a Markov process has absorbing states present, we do not compute steady-state probabilities in the context of the previous section because the process will eventually end up in one of the absorbing states. However, we may be interested in knowing the probability that the dollar will end up in each of the absorbing states. To determine these probabilities, we need to develop the notion of a fundamental matrix.

The Fundamental Matrix and Associated Calculations

In the following discussion we present the appropriate formulas for determining the probability that a dollar starting in state 3 or 4 will end up in each of the absorbing states. The underlying concept in the analysis involves the notion of a *fundamental matrix*. We begin the development of this concept by partitioning the matrix of transition probabilities into four parts; that is, we let

$$
P = \left[\begin{array}{cc|cc}
1 & 0 & 0 & 0 \\
0 & 1 & 0 & 0 \\
\hline
0.4 & 0 & 0.3 & 0.3 \\
0.4 & 0.2 & 0.3 & 0.1
\end{array}\right] = \left[\begin{array}{c|c} I & O \\ \hline R & Q \end{array}\right],
$$

where

$$
I = \begin{bmatrix} 1 & 0 \\ 0 & 1 \end{bmatrix}, \qquad O = \begin{bmatrix} 0 & 0 \\ 0 & 0 \end{bmatrix},
$$

$$
R = \begin{bmatrix} 0.4 & 0 \\ 0.4 & 0.2 \end{bmatrix}, \qquad Q = \begin{bmatrix} 0.3 & 0.3 \\ 0.3 & 0.1 \end{bmatrix}.
$$

A matrix N, called a *fundamental matrix,* can be calculated using the following formula:

$$
N = (I - Q)^{-1}. \tag{17.5}
$$

The superscript -1 is used to indicate the inverse of the matrix $(I - Q)$. In Appendix E we present formulas for finding the inverse of a matrix with two rows and two columns. In our current problem,

$$
I - Q = \begin{bmatrix} 1 & 0 \\ 0 & 1 \end{bmatrix} - \begin{bmatrix} 0.3 & 0.3 \\ 0.3 & 0.1 \end{bmatrix}
$$

$$
= \begin{bmatrix} 0.7 & -0.3 \\ -0.3 & 0.9 \end{bmatrix}
$$

and (see Appendix E)

$$
N = (I - Q)^{-1} = \begin{bmatrix} 1.67 & 0.56 \\ 0.56 & 1.30 \end{bmatrix}.
$$

If we multiply the fundamental matrix N times the R portion of the P matrix, we obtain the probabilities that accounts receivable dollars initially in states 3 or 4 will eventually reach each of the absorbing states. The multiplication of N times R for the Heidmen's Department Store problem is shown below (see Appendix E for the steps of this matrix multiplication):

$$
NR = \begin{bmatrix} 1.67 & 0.56 \\ 0.56 & 1.30 \end{bmatrix}\begin{bmatrix} 0.4 & 0 \\ 0.4 & 0.2 \end{bmatrix} = \begin{bmatrix} 0.89 & 0.11 \\ 0.74 & 0.26 \end{bmatrix}.
$$

The first row of the product NR is the probability that a dollar in the 0–30 age category will end up in each of the absorbing states. Thus we see that there is a 0.89 probability that a dollar in the 0–30 day old category will eventually be paid and a 0.11 probability that it will become a bad debt. Similarly, the second row tells us the probabilities associated with a dollar in the 31–90 day category; that is, a dollar in the 31–90 day category has a 0.74 probability of eventually being paid and a 0.26 probability of proving to be uncollectible. Using this information we can predict the amount of money that will be paid and the amount that will be lost as bad debts.

Establishing the Allowance for Doubtful Accounts

Let B represent a two-element vector which contains the current accounts receivable balances in the 0–30 day and the 31–90 day age categories; that is,

$$B = [b_1 \quad b_2]$$

total dollars   total dollars
in the 0–30   in the 31–90
day category   day category

Suppose that the December 31 balance of accounts receivable for Heidman's shows $1000 in the 0–30 day category (state 3) and $2000 in the 31–90 day category (state 4).

$$B = [1000 \quad 2000]$$

We can multiply B times NR to determine how much of the $3000 will be collected and how much will be lost. In our example,

$$BNR = [1000 \quad 2000] \begin{bmatrix} 0.89 & 0.11 \\ 0.74 & 0.26 \end{bmatrix}$$

$$= [2370 \quad 630].$$

Thus we see that $2370 of the accounts receivable balances will be collected and $630 will have to be written off as a bad debt expense. Based on this analysis, the accounting department of the company would set up an allowance for doubtful accounts of $630.

The matrix multiplication of BNR is simply a convenient way of computing the eventual collections and bad debts of the accounts receivable. Recall that the NR matrix showed a 0.89 probability of collecting dollars in the 0–30 day category and a 0.74 probability of collecting dollars in the 31–90 day category. Thus as was shown by the BNR calculation, we expect to collect a total of $0.89(1000) + 0.74(2000) = 890 + 1480 = \$2370$.

Suppose that on the basis of the previous analysis Heidman's would like to investigate the possibility of reducing the amount of bad debts. Recall that our analysis indicated that a 0.11 probability or 11 percent of the dollars in the 0–30 day age category and 26 percent of the amount in the 31–90 day age category will prove to be uncollectible. Let us assume that Heidman's is considering instituting a new credit policy involving a discount for prompt payment.

Management believes that the policy under consideration will increase the probability of a transition from the 0–30 day age category to the paid category and decrease the probability of a transition from the 0–30 day to the 31–90 day age category. Let us assume that a careful study of the effects of this new policy leads management to conclude that the following transition matrix would be applicable:

$$
P = \begin{bmatrix} 1 & 0 & 0 & 0 \\ 0 & 1 & 0 & 0 \\ \hline 0.6 & 0 & 0.3 & 0.1 \\ 0.4 & 0.2 & 0.3 & 0.1 \end{bmatrix}
$$

We see that the probability of a dollar in the 0–30 day age category making a transition to the paid category in the next period has increased to 0.6 and that the probability of a dollar in the 0–30 day age category making a transition to the 31–90 day category has decreased to 0.1. To determine the effect of these changes on bad debt expense we must calculate N, NR, and BNR. We begin by using equation (17.5) to calculate the fundamental matrix N:

$$
\begin{aligned}
N = (I - Q)^{-1} &= \left\{ \begin{bmatrix} 1 & 0 \\ 0 & 1 \end{bmatrix} - \begin{bmatrix} 0.3 & 0.1 \\ 0.3 & 0.1 \end{bmatrix} \right\}^{-1} \\
&= \begin{bmatrix} 0.7 & -0.1 \\ -0.3 & 0.9 \end{bmatrix}^{-1} \\
&= \begin{bmatrix} 1.5 & 0.17 \\ 0.5 & 1.17 \end{bmatrix}.
\end{aligned}
$$

By multiplying N times R we obtain the new probabilities that the dollars in each age category will end up in the two absorbing states:

$$
\begin{aligned}
NR &= \begin{bmatrix} 1.5 & 0.17 \\ 0.5 & 1.17 \end{bmatrix} \begin{bmatrix} 0.6 & 0 \\ 0.4 & 0.2 \end{bmatrix} \\
&= \begin{bmatrix} 0.97 & 0.03 \\ 0.77 & 0.23 \end{bmatrix}.
\end{aligned}
$$

We see that with the new credit policy we would expect only 3 percent of the funds in the 0–30 day age category and 23 percent of the funds in the 31–90 day age category to prove to be uncollectible. If, as before, we assume that there is a current balance of $1000 in the 0–30 day age category and $2000 in the 31–90 day age category, we can calculate the total amount of accounts receivable that will end up in the two absorbing states by multiplying B times NR. We obtain

$$BNR = [1000 \quad 2000] \begin{bmatrix} 0.97 & 0.03 \\ 0.77 & 0.23 \end{bmatrix}$$

$$= [2510 \quad 490].$$

Under the previous credit policy we found the bad debt expense to be $630. Thus a savings of $630 − 490 = $140 could be expected as a result of the new credit policy. Given our total accounts receivable balance of $3000, this is a 4.7 percent reduction in bad debt expense. After considering the costs involved, management can evaluate the economics of adopting the new credit policy. If the cost, including discounts, is less than 4.7 percent of the accounts receivable balance, we would expect the new policy to lead to increased profits for Heidman's Department Store.

Summary

In this chapter we have presented Markov process models as well as examples of their application. We saw that a Markov analysis could provide helpful decision-making information about a process or situation which involved a sequence of repeated trials with a number of possible outcomes or states on each trial. A primary objective of our analysis was obtaining information about the probability of each state occurring a certain number of transitions or time periods in the future.

A market share analysis showed the computational procedure for determining the steady-state probabilities which could be interpreted as market shares for two competing supermarkets. In an accounts receivable application of Markov processes we introduced the notion of absorbing states. The two absorbing states were bad debt and paid categories, and we showed how to determine the percentage of accounts receivable balances that would be absorbed in each of these states.

Glossary

1. *Trials of the process*—The events that trigger transitions of the system from one state to another. In many applications successive time periods represent the trials of the process.
2. *State of the system*—The condition of the system at any particular trial or time period.
3. *Transition probability*—Given the system is in state i during one period, the transition probability p_{ij} is the probability that the system will be in state j during the next period.

4. *State probability*—The probability the system will be in any particular state. [$\pi_i(n)$ is the probability that the system will be in state i during period n.]

5. *Steady-state probability*—The probability that the system will be in any particular state after a large number of transitions. Once steady state has been reached, the state probabilities do not change from period to period.

6. *Absorbing state*—A state is said to be absorbing if the probability of making a transition out of that state is zero. Thus once the system has made a transition into an absorbing state, it will remain there forever.

7. *Fundamental matrix*—A matrix necessary for the computation of probabilities associated with absorbing states of a Markov process.

Problems

1. In the market share analysis of Section 17.1 suppose that we are considering the Markov process associated with the shopping trips of one customer but we do not know where the customer shopped during the last week. Thus we might make the assumption that there is a 0.5 probability that the customer shopped at Murphy's and a 0.5 probability that the customer shopped at Ashley's at time period 0; that is, $\pi_1(0) = 0.5$ and $\pi_2(0) = 0.5$. Given these initial state probabilities, develop a table similar to Table 17.2 showing the probability of each state in future periods. What do you observe about the long-run probabilities of each state?

2. Management of the New Fangled Softdrink Company believes that the probability of a customer purchasing Red-Rot Pop and the company's major competition, Super Cola, is based on the customer's most recent purchase. Suppose the following transition matrix is appropriate:

		To	
		Red-Rot Pop	Super Cola
From	Red-Rot Pop	0.9	0.1
	Super Cola	0.1	0.9

a. Show the two-period tree diagram for one customer who last purchased Red-Rot Pop. What is the probability that this customer purchases Red-Rot Pop on the second purchase?

b. What is the long-run market share for each of these two products?

c. A major advertising campaign is being planned to increase the probability of attracting Super Cola customers. Management believes that the new campaign will result in the probability of a customer switching from Super Cola to Red-Rot Pop to increase to 0.15. What is the projected effect of the advertising campaign on the market shares?

3. The computer center at Rockbottom University has been experiencing substantial periods of computer downtime. Let us assume that the trials of an associated Markov process are defined to be one-hour periods and that the probability of the

system being in a running state or a down state is based upon the state of the system in the previous period. Historical data show the following transition probabilities:

		To	
		Running	Down
From	Running	0.90	0.10
	Down	0.30	0.70

a. If the system is initially running, what is the probability of the system being down in the next hour of operation?
b. What are the steady-state probabilities of the system being in the running state and in the down state?

4. In Problem 3 one cause of the downtime problem was traced to a specific piece of computer hardware. Management believes that switching to a different hardware component will result in the following transition probability matrix:

		To	
		Running	Down
From	Running	0.95	0.05
	Down	0.60	0.40

a. What are the steady-state probabilities of the system being in the running and down states?
b. If the cost of the system being down for any period is estimated to be $500 (including lost profits for time down and maintenance), what is the breakeven cost for the new hardware component on a time-period basis?

5. A major traffic problem in the greater Cincinnati area involves traffic attempting to cross the Ohio River from Cincinnati to Kentucky using Interstate I-75. Let us assume that the probability of no traffic delay in one period, given no traffic delay in the preceding period, is 0.85 and that the probability of finding a traffic delay in one period, given a delay in the preceding period, is 0.75. Traffic will be classified as having either a delay or a no-delay state, and a time period will be considered to be 30 minutes.

a. Assuming you are a motorist entering the traffic system and receive a radio report of a traffic delay, what is the probability that for the next 60 minutes (two time periods) the system will be in the delay state? Note that this is the probability of being in the delay state for two consecutive periods. A tree diagram should be helpful.
b. What is the probability that in the long run the traffic will not be in the delayed state?
c. An important assumption of the Markov process models presented in this chapter has been the constant or stationary transition probabilities as the system operates in the future. Do you believe this assumption is appropriate in the above traffic problem? Explain.

6. The purchase patterns of two brands of toothpaste can be expressed as a Markov process with the following transition probabilities:

		To	
		Special B	MDA
From	Special B	0.90	0.10
	MDA	0.05	0.95

a. Which brand appears to have the most loyal customers? Explain.
b. What are the projected market shares for the two brands?

7. Suppose that in Problem 6 a new toothpaste brand enters the market such that the following transition probabilities exist:

			To	
		Special B	MDA	T-White
	Special B	0.80	0.10	0.10
From	MDA	0.05	0.75	0.20
	T-White	0.40	0.30	0.30

What are the new long-run market shares? Which brand will suffer most from the introduction of the new brand of toothpaste? Note that solving for the steady-state probabilities for this problem requires the solution of three equations and three unknowns.

8. Given the following transition matrix with states 1 and 2 as absorbing states, what is the probability that units in state 3 and state 4 end up in each of the absorbing states?

$$P = \begin{bmatrix} 1 & 0 & 0 & 0 \\ 0 & 1 & 0 & 0 \\ 0.2 & 0.1 & 0.4 & 0.3 \\ 0.2 & 0.2 & 0.1 & 0.5 \end{bmatrix}$$

9. In the Heidman's Department Store problem of Section 17.2, suppose the following transition matrix is appropriate:

$$P = \begin{bmatrix} 1 & 0 & 0 & 0 \\ 0 & 1 & 0 & 0 \\ 0.5 & 0 & 0.25 & 0.25 \\ 0.5 & 0.2 & 0.05 & 0.25 \end{bmatrix}$$

If Heidman's has $4000 in the 0–30 day age category and $5000 in the 31–90 day age category, what is your estimate of the amount of bad debts the company will experience?

10. The KLM Christmas Tree Farm owns a plot of land with 5000 evergreen trees. Each year KLM allows retailers of Christmas trees to select and cut trees for sale to individual customers. KLM protects small trees (usually less than four feet tall) so that they will grow and be available for sale in future years. Currently 1500 trees

are classified as protected trees, while the remaining 3500 are available for cutting. However, even though a tree is available for cutting in a given year, it may not be selected for cutting until future years. While most trees not cut in a given year live until the next year, some trees die during the year and are lost.

In viewing the KLM Christmas trees operation as a Markov process with yearly time periods, we define the following four states:

State 1:   Cut and sold,

State 2:   Lost to disease,

State 3:   Too small for cutting,

State 4:   Available for cutting but not cut and sold.

The following transition matrix is appropriate:

$$P = \begin{bmatrix} 1 & 0 & 0 & 0 \\ 0 & 1 & 0 & 0 \\ 0.1 & 0.2 & 0.5 & 0.2 \\ 0.4 & 0.1 & 0 & 0.5 \end{bmatrix}.$$

How many of the farm's 5000 trees will be sold eventually and how many will be lost?

Chapter 18

Calculus-Based Solution Procedures

In this chapter we consider mathematical models where the functions or mathematical relationships involved are not all linear. For example, in formulating a profit or cost function for a specific problem we may find that a linear function is inappropriate and that a curve or a nonlinear function is necessary. Recall that in our analysis of inventory models (see Section 12.1) we developed the following nonlinear function to show how total inventory cost could be expressed in terms of the order quantity Q:

$$\text{TC} = \frac{Q}{2} C_h + \frac{D}{Q} C_0.$$

The graph of a typical total cost curve is shown in Figure 18.1.

In order to determine the optimal values of the decision variables in nonlinear models, we will find calculus-based solution procedures quite valuable. In this chapter we show how differential calculus can be used to find maximum and minimum values for such models. We begin by using differential calculus to analyze nonlinear objective functions having only one decision variable. Then we discuss the procedures for handling nonlinear functions with two or more decision variables. Finally, we show how calculus-based solution procedures can be used to solve nonlinear models which have constraints.

This is the only chapter in this book where a working knowledge of calculus, specifically differential calculus, is a prerequisite. However, the reader with no calculus background may still find this chapter useful in terms of learning about nonlinear models and the role that calculus-based solution procedures play in analyzing these models.

18.1   Models With One Decision Variable

The Macon Psychiatric Institute, a nonprofit organization, is interested in redesigning its mental health care delivery system in such a fashion that the maximum number of people can benefit from its services. Based on some recent studies, the institute has learned that the average treatment time per patient is a function of the number of patients the clinic is simultaneously treating. With more patients simultaneously receiving treatment, the patients remain in residence longer; that is, with more patients in the system, the clinic's staff becomes overloaded and the patient's time in residence at the clinic increases. If the institute reduces the number of patients simultaneously being treated, the patients can receive more personal attention, and thus the treatment time can be shortened. Since the institute's goal is to maximize the number of people it can benefit, it first attempted to treat as many people as possible at any given time. However, because of the resulting inefficient operation and long recovery times, management is considering reducing the number of active patients so that the average recovery period will be shortened, thus enabling more patients to be treated over a specific time period. The institute's problem can be stated in terms of how many active or in-residence patients should be maintained by the clinic so that the total number of patients treated per year is maximized.

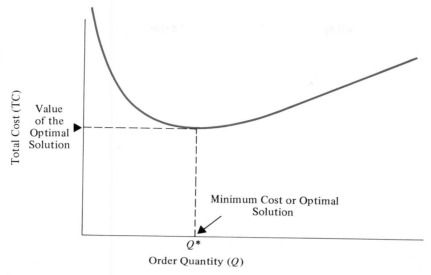

FIGURE 18.1   **Total Cost Curve for the Economic Order Quantity Inventory Model**

Based on patient records and recovery time estimates by the clinic's staff members, the following mathematical relationship can be used to describe how the number of in-residence patients affects the patient treatment or recovery time:

$$T = \frac{45}{180 - P} \qquad (18.1)$$

where

T = average patient treatment time in years,

P = number of in-residence patients.

This relationship is believed to be valid as long as the number of in-residence patients P remains between 45 and 135.

Using equation (18.1), we see that if the clinic operates with $P = 135$ patients, then $T = 45/(180 - 135) = 1$ year (that is, on the average a patient receives one year of treatment before being released). However, if the clinic reduces its number of in-residence patients to 60, then the average recovery period can be shortened to $T = 45/(180 - 60) = 0.375$ year, or 4.5 months. The relationship between the number of in-residence patients and the average treatment time is shown in Figure 18.2.

The institute wants to maximize the total number of people treated per year. Since T is the average treatment time per patient, you might conclude that they could treat $1/T$ patients per year. However, since the clinic treats P patients *simultaneously,* the total number of patients treated per year, N, is given by

$$N = (1/T)P = P/T \qquad (18.2)$$

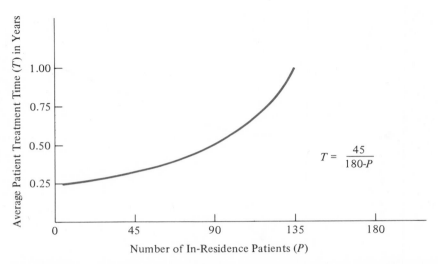

FIGURE 18.2   **Average Treatment Time** T **as a Function of the Number of In-Residence Patients** P

For $P = 135$ we saw earlier that $T = 1$ year; thus $N = P/T = 135/1 = 135$ patients per year. However, for $P = 60$, $T = 0.375$ and $N = 60/0.375 = 160$ patients per year. Therefore reducing the number of active patients to 60 does improve the effectiveness of the clinic; more patients can be treated over a specified time period. However, the question of what is the optimal number of in-residence patients still needs to be answered.

Since T is a function of P [equation (18.1)], we can substitute into equation (18.2) and write the mathematical model for our problem as a function of the one variable, P:

$$N = P/T = P/\left(\frac{45}{180 - P}\right) = \frac{(180 - P)P}{45} = 4P - \frac{1}{45}P^2 \quad (18.3)$$

We are interested in maximizing the number of patients treated per year, N. Thus the above model provides a nonlinear objective function for a maximization problem with one decision variable, P, and our problem becomes

$$\max N = 4P - \frac{1}{45}P^2. \quad (18.4)$$

With only one decision variable we can observe how the number of patients treated per year varies for different P values by drawing a graph of the relationship. This graph, shown in Figure 18.3, indicates that the maximum value of the objective function is 180, corresponding to an in-residence patient volume of 90. Since sketching the graph of a function may be time consuming, and since the determination of the optimal solution is dependent upon the accuracy of the graph, we will usually want to use a differential calculus procedure for solving such a problem.

Recall from calculus that the first derivative of an unconstrained function must be equal to zero at a *local maximum* or *local minimum*. The

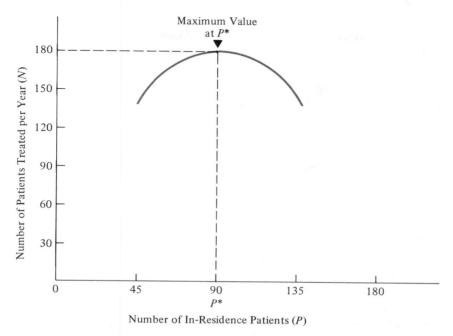

FIGURE 18.3   Number of Patients Treated per Year as a Function of the Number of Patients in Residence

reason for this is that the first derivative is the slope of the line tangent to the curve, and the slope of the tangent line is zero at any local maximum or local minimum value of the function. In the Macon Psychiatric Institute problem we see that the function relating the number of patients treated per year to the number of in-residence patients has one local maximum (Figure 18.3). Many functions, however, possess a number of local maxima and/or minima. For example, consider the graph of the function depicted in Figure 18.4, which has two local maxima and one local minimum. At each of the local maxima and at the local minimum the first derivatives, and hence the slope of the tangent lines, are equal to zero. Rule 1 below summarizes the above discussion in the form of a *necessary condition* for determining all the local maxima or minima of an unconstrained function of one variable:

Rule 1 (Necessary Condition). The first derivative of an unconstrained function of one variable must equal zero at its local maximum or local minimum points.

Let us now calculate the first derivative for the institute's problem[1]:

$$\text{First derivative} = \frac{dN}{dP} = 4 - \frac{2}{45} P.$$

[1]A short table of derivative formulas is provided in Appendix D.

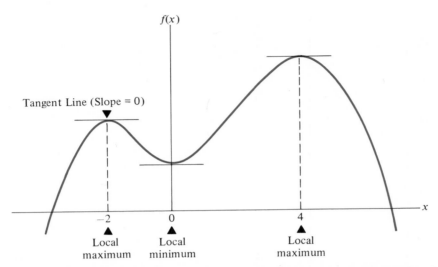

FIGURE 18.4   Graph of a Function $f(x)$ Having Two Local Maxima and One Local Minimum

Setting the first derivative equal to zero and solving, we obtain

$$\frac{dN}{dP} = 4 - \frac{2}{45} P = 0$$

$$\frac{2}{45} P = 4$$

$$P^* = \frac{(4)(45)}{2} = 90.$$

Thus we see that $P^* = 90$ is the value of P that sets the first derivative equal to zero. Figure 18.5 shows that the slope of the line tangent to the curve at this local maximum point is in fact zero.

Unfortunately, while it is a necessary condition that the first derivative equal zero at a local maximum point, this is not sufficient to guarantee that we have in fact located a local maximum. Actually, a point where the first derivative equals zero could be a local maximum, a local minimum, or an inflection point. Thus a second derivative test is needed to determine whether or not we have a local maximum. Rule 2 provides such a test and establishes a *sufficient condition* that guarantees that we have reached a local maximum (or a local minimum) solution.

Rule 2 (Sufficient Condition). If rule 1 is satisfied at a point, and

a. if the second derivative[2] is *greater than* zero, then the point is a local *minimum;*

---

[2] The second derivative is found simply by applying the differentiation rule to the first derivative function.

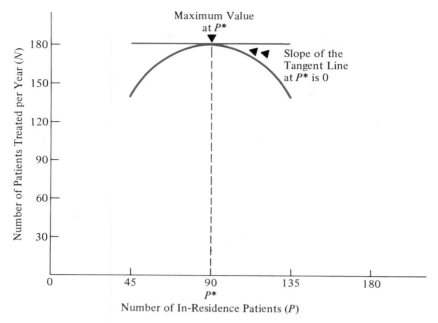

FIGURE 18.5   Number of Patients Treated per Year as a Function of the Number of In-Residence Patients

b.   if the second derivative is *less than* zero, then the point is a local *maximum*.

Let us apply this second derivative test to the Macon Psychiatric Institute problem. The second derivative is given by

$$\text{Second derivative} = \frac{d^2 N}{dP^2} = -\frac{2}{45} < 0.$$

Since the second derivative is less than zero, rule 2 tells us that $P^* = 90$ does indeed yield a local maximum of the objective function for our problem.

We call a point a *global maximum* if it yields the highest value for the function. Similarly, we call a point a *global minimum* if it yields the lowest value. In this case it is easy to verify that the local maximum, $P^* = 90$, is also a global maximum. Since the function has only one point at which rule 1 is satisfied, and since rule 2 says that this point is a local maximum, this local maximum must be the global maximum. In other words, the function has only one mode, and we have found it.

Assuming that the relationships we used in developing the mathematical model are accurate reflections of reality, the institute should admit 90 patients and maintain this many patients in residence all the time. This will maximize the number of patients the institute can treat per year at 180.

The problem we have just described provides a nice illustration of how calculus can assist in finding the optimum for an unconstrained function of one variable. However, in some situations we will find that it is of interest to consider finding the optimal value for a function over a specified interval. This situation may come about because of constraints placed on the decision maker or because the function of interest is defined only over a specified interval, and as a result we choose to limit ourselves to finding the best value for the function over that interval. In problems of this type the optimal solution could occur at the endpoints of the interval as well as at points where rules 1 and 2 hold.

As an illustration of the type of situation we are referring to, suppose we are trying to find the maximum of the function $f(x) = x^3 - 3x^2$ over the interval $-1 \leq x \leq 4$. A graph of the function over this interval is shown in Figure 18.6.

Clearly, the global maximum of the function over this interval occurs at $x = 4$. However, rule 1 is not satisfied at this point because the first derivative (the slope of the tangent line) is not equal to zero. When we are constrained to a specific interval in our search for the optimum of a function of one variable, we must extend our solution procedure beyond just checking points that satisfy rules 1 and 2. The general procedure for finding the global maximum or minimum of a function of one variable is as follows:

Step 1:   Find all the points that satisfy rules 1 and 2. These are candidates for yielding the optimal solution to the problem.

Step 2:   If the solution is restricted to a specified interval, evaluate the function at the endpoints of the interval.

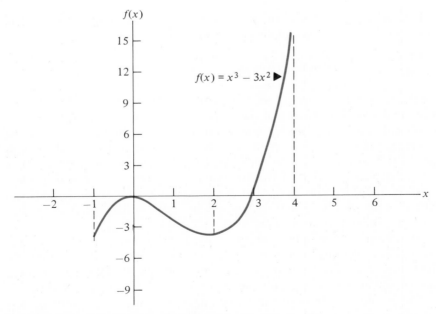

FIGURE 18.6   Graph of the Function $f(x) = x^3 - 3x^2$

Step 3: Compare the values of the function at all the points found in steps 1 and 2. The largest of these is the global maximum solution; the smallest is the global minimum solution.

Let us apply this procedure to the function in Figure 18.6. Following step 1 we first find all the points at which the first derivative equals zero:

$$\frac{df(x)}{dx} = 3x^2 - 6x = 0.$$

Therefore

$$x(3x - 6) = 0$$

and we see that both $x = 0$ and $x = 2$ satisfy rule 1. Checking rule 2, we find

$$\frac{d^2f(x)}{dx^2} = 6x - 6.$$

At $x = 0$,

$$\frac{d^2f(0)}{dx^2} = -6 < 0$$

and we have a local maximum of the function at $x = 0$. The value of the function at $x = 0$ is $f(0) = 0^3 - 3(0)^2 = 0$. Looking back to Figure 18.6 we see that this is indeed a local maximum and the slope of the tangent line is equal to zero at this point. At $x = 2$,

$$\frac{d^2f(2)}{dx^2} = 6(2) - 6 = 6 > 0.$$

Therefore by rule 2 we have a local minimum at $x = 2$. The value of the function $x = 2$ is $f(2) = (2)^3 - 3(2)^2 = -4$.

Proceeding to step 2 we evaluate the function at both of its endpoints:

$$f(-1) = (-1)^3 - 3(-1)^2 = -4$$
$$f(4) = (4)^3 - 3(4)^2 = 16.$$

At step 3 we compare the values at the points found in steps 1 and 2. The largest value occurs at $x = 4$ and yields a global maximum value of 16 over the specified interval. The smallest value occurs at both $x = -1$ and $x = 2$; that is, there is a tie for global minimum, and we say that both $x = -1$ and $x = 2$ are global minima. The minimum value is -4. Note that one of these candidates was found in step 1 and the other in step 2 of our solution procedure. Figure 18.6 illustrates graphically the conclusions we have reached.

Let us return for a moment to the Macon Psychiatric Institute problem. The objective function for this problem was believed to be applicable only over the interval $45 \leq P \leq 135$. It may be reasonable to assume that this means the institute will not consider letting the number of in-residence patients fall below 45 or exceed 135. If this were the case then, why did we not need to check the endpoints of this interval in our search for a maximum? The reason is that there was only one point ($P^* = 90$) which satisfied rule 1, and it was a local maximum. Since P^* is a local maximum, the value of the function decreases as we move away from it, and since no other points satisfy rule 1, we know that the function does not turn up again anywhere. Therefore no other point could yield a higher value than $P^* = 90$. Nevertheless, the three-step procedure we have specified for maximizing or minimizing a function of one variable would have led to the same conclusion. The value of the function is smaller at $P = 45$ and $P = 135$ than at the maximum, $P^* = 90$.

Before concluding this section, let us consider another numerical example to make sure that we know how to apply steps 1, 2, and 3.

Example.   Suppose we want to minimize the function

$$f(x) = x^3 - 6x^2 + 50 \qquad (18.5)$$

over the interval $0 \le x \le 5$.

Step 1:   Setting the first derivative equal to zero, we find

$$\frac{df(x)}{dx} = 3x^2 - 12x = 0$$

or

$$x(3x - 12) = 0.$$

This provides us with two possible values for x: either $x = 0$ or $3x - 12 = 0$ and $x = 4$. That is, $x = 0$ and $x = 4$ both set the first derivative equal to zero, satisfying rule 1. To see if either of these yields a local minimum, we must calculate the second derivative:

$$\frac{d^2f(x)}{dx^2} = 6x - 12.$$

At $x = 0$, we have

$$\frac{d^2f(0)}{dx^2} = 6(0) - 12 = -12 < 0.$$

Therefore by rule 2, $x = 0$ yields a local maximum for $f(x)$. At $x = 4$, we have

$$\frac{d^2f(4)}{dx^2} = 6(4) - 12 = 12 > 0.$$

Therefore by rule 2, $x = 4$ yields a local minimum for $f(x)$. The graph of $f(x)$ [equation (18.5)] is shown in Figure 18.7. Again note that the slopes of the lines tangent to the curve at these local minimum and local maximum points are both zero.

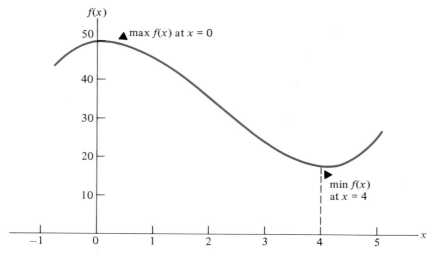

FIGURE 18.7 **Graph of the Function** $f(x) = x^3 - 6x^2 + 50$

Step 2: Evaluating the function at the endpoints, we obtain

$$f(0) = 50$$
$$f(5) = 25.$$

Step 3: Since we are searching for a minimum and $f(4) = 18 < f(5) = 25$, we conclude that $x^* = 4$ is the global minimum solution. We note also in this example that the local maximum found in step 1 corresponded to one of the endpoints. This is purely a coincidence where the first derivative of the function happens to be zero at an endpoint of the interval.

18.2 Unconstrained Models with More than One Decision Variable

As we have seen in the previous section and elsewhere in the text, there are a number of problem situations for which we can develop mathematical models involving only one decision variable. However, there are perhaps even more decision-making situations in which the decision maker must select the best values for two or more controllable inputs or decision variables. In this section we discuss a problem situation that leads to the formulation of a nonlinear mathematical model involving two decision variables. Then we show how first and second derivative tests similar to rules 1 and 2 can be developed for finding the local maximum and local minimum values of unconstrained functions of two variables. We do not attempt to extend the analysis to the case where each of the variables is restricted to an interval. This case is inherently more difficult than the situation for one variable, and its analysis would take us too far afield for an introductory text of this nature.[3] For completeness, we will discuss the extension to unconstrained models involving several decision variables.

In order to see how a mathematical model involving two decision variables might arise, let us suppose that Lawn King, Inc. manufactures two styles of lawn mower. One is a riding mower, and the other is a standard walking power mower. Lawn King is interested in establishing a pricing policy for the two mowers that will maximize the total profit for the product line. Sales for these two products are not independent. Over time, Lawn King has observed that an increase in the price of the riding mower is usually accompanied by a decrease in the number of riding mowers sold and an increase in the number of walking mowers sold. Similarly, increases in the price of the walking mower have been accompanied by a decrease in sales of the walking mower and an increase in sales of the riding mower. Economists would say that the two types of lawn mower are *substitutable products*. Because these two products are substitutable, we should expect that an appropriate mathematical model for maximizing total profit would involve the simultaneous consideration of prices for both products.

Suppose that after a study of the relationships between sales prices and quantities sold, Lawn King has established the following expressions:

$$q_1 = 95 - 2p_1 + 0.7p_2 \tag{18.6}$$

$$q_2 = 188 + 0.3p_1 - 0.5p_2 \tag{18.7}$$

where

q_1 = number of walking mowers sold in thousands

q_2 = number of riding mowers sold in thousands

p_1 = price of walking mower in dollars

p_2 = price of riding mower in dollars.

Further information, prepared by the accounting department, is available on the total cost of producing each type of mower:

$$c_1 = 100 + 90q_1 \tag{18.8}$$

$$c_2 = 50 + 250q_2 \tag{18.9}$$

where

c_1 = total cost of producing q_1 walking mowers in thousands of dollars

c_2 = total cost of producing q_2 riding mowers in thousands of dollars.

Note that the production costs are in thousands of dollars and the number of lawn mowers are being measured in thousands of units. The fixed cost of producing walking mowers (the part that is independent of the number of units produced) is thus $100,000, and the variable cost is $90,000

---

[3]The analysis of this case essentially involves treating each endpoint as a separate constraint. For a discussion, see Gottfried, B. S., and J. Weisman, *Introduction to Optimization Theory*, Englewood Cliffs, N.J., Prentice-Hall, 1973.

per 1000 walking mowers, or \$90 per mower. Similarly the fixed cost of production for riding mowers is \$50,000, and the variable cost is \$250,000 per 1000 mowers, or \$250 per mower.

We would like to develop a mathematical model of the relationship between the controllable inputs p_1 and p_2 and the output we would like to maximize, gross profit (GP). The appropriate relationship is established as follows:

$$GP = \text{total revenue} - \text{total cost}$$
$$= (p_1q_1 + p_2q_2) - (c_1 + c_2). \tag{18.10}$$

We can use equations (18.6) through (18.9) to eliminate q_1 and q_2 from the model, permitting us to write a mathematical model that is a function of only the two decision variables p_1 and p_2. Using equations (18.6) and (18.7) to substitute into equations (18.8) and (18.9), we obtain (in thousands of dollars)

$$c_1 = 100 + 90(95 - 2p_1 + 0.7p_2)$$
$$= 8650 - 180p_1 + 63p_2$$

and

$$c_2 = 50 + 250(188 + 0.3p_1 - 0.5p_2)$$
$$= 47,050 + 75p_1 - 125p_2.$$

Substituting these two expressions along with equations (18.6) and (18.7) into our gross profit expression (18.10) allows us to write the gross profit model as a function of p_1 and p_2 only:

$$GP = p_1(95 - 2p_1 + 0.7p_2) + p_2(188 + 0.3p_1 - 0.5p_2)$$
$$- (8650 - 180p_1 + 63p_2) - (47,050 + 75p_1 - 125p_2).$$

After multiplying and collecting terms we obtain

$$GP = -2p_1^2 - 0.5p_2^2 + p_1p_2 + 200p_1 + 250p_2 - 55,700. \tag{18.11}$$

This is the function we would like to maximize. The gross profit in this model is represented by an unconstrained nonlinear function of two variables. The rules for finding the local maximum and/or local minimum of functions of two variables are similar to the ones we developed in the previous section for functions of one variable. There is a first derivative test that serves as a necessary condition that must be satisifed by any local maximum or local minimum point. In addition, there is a second derivative test that can be applied to determine whether a point satisfying the necessary condition is a local maximum, a local minimum, or neither. This second derivative test is referred to as a sufficient condition. The first derivative test is stated as rule 3:

Rule 3 (Necessary Condition). Both partial derivatives of an unconstrained function of two variables must equal zero at any local maximum or local minimum point.

Let us apply the first derivative test to the gross profit function (18.11) in our Lawn King problem. Recall from calculus that when taking the partial derivative of a function of more than one variable, we treat all the variables except the one we are taking the partial derivative with respect to as if they were constants. Taking the two partial derivatives of the gross profit function yields

$$\frac{\partial GP}{\partial p_1} = -4p_1 + p_2 + 200 \qquad (18.12)$$

and

$$\frac{\partial GP}{\partial p_2} = -p_2 + p_1 + 250. \qquad (18.13)$$

Following rule 3 and setting both partial derivatives equal to zero, we obtain a system of two simultaneous equations in the two variables p_1 and p_2:

$$-4p_1 + p_2 + 200 = 0 \qquad (18.14)$$

$$p_1 - p_2 + 250 = 0. \qquad (18.15)$$

Adding equations (18.14) and (18.15) yields

$$-3p_1 + 450 = 0.$$

Thus we have

$$3p_1 = 450$$

or

$$p_1 = 150.$$

Substituting $p_1 = 150$ into equation (18.15) yields

$$p_2 = 400.$$

Hence the point $p_1 = 150$ and $p_2 = 400$ satisfies the necessary condition given by rule 3. Since $p_1 = 150$ and $p_2 = 400$ are the only values of p_1 and p_2 satisfying the necessary condition, we know that if this point is a local maximum, it must also be global maximum for our function. Just as in the single-variable case, when there is only one point satisfying the necessary condition, the function cannot have more than one local maximum or local minimum. In order to ensure that we have found a local maximum, and not perhaps a local minimum, a second derivative test is necessary.

The second derivative test requires that we know the values of all the second partial derivatives of the function. There are four second partial derivatives for a function of two variables; each of the two first partial derivatives has two partial derivatives itself. Let us calculate the second partial derivatives for our Lawn King problem.

In order to calculate the partial derivative of GP, first with respect to p_1 and then again with respect to p_1, we simply take the partial derivative of equation (18.12) with respect to p_1. Thus

$$\frac{\partial^2 GP}{\partial p_1^2} = -4.$$

The notation $\partial^2 GP/\partial p_1^2$ is used to indicate that the partial derivative of GP was taken first with respect to p_1 and then again with respect to p_1.

To calculate the second partial derivative denoted by $\partial^2 GP/\partial p_2 \partial p_1$ we first take the partial derivative of GP with respect to p_1 and then again with respect to p_2. Thus we can compute this partial derivative by taking the partial derivative of equation (18.12) with respect to p_2. Doing so, we obtain

$$\frac{\partial^2 GP}{\partial p_2 \partial p_1} = 1.$$

Similarly, the notation $\partial^2 GP/\partial p_1 \partial p_2$ is used to indicate that the partial derivative of GP was taken first with respect to p_2 and then with respect to p_1. Taking the partial derivative of equation (18.13) with respect to p_1, we obtain this second partial derivative:

$$\frac{\partial^2 GP}{\partial p_1 \partial p_2} = 1.$$

Finally, the notation $\partial^2 GP/\partial p_2^2$ is used to indicate that the partial derivative of GP was taken first with respect to p_2 and then again with respect to p_2. Hence we obtain this second partial derivative by taking the partial derivative of equation (18.13) with respect to p_2:

$$\frac{\partial^2 GP}{\partial p_2^2} = -1.$$

We can make one observation as a result of calculating these second partial derivatives. In our Lawn King problem the *mixed partials* (that is, with respect to one variable, then the other) are equal. This is always true except for certain rare cases. We shall not be interested in such cases and thus will assume that the second mixed partials are always equal. Rule 4 can now be stated as supplying sufficient conditions for a point (x_1, x_2) to give a local maximum, a local minimum, or a saddle point of an unconstrained function $f(x_1, x_2)$ of two variables:

Rule 4 (Sufficient Condition). If rule 3 is satisfied at the point (x_1, x_2) and

    a. if

$$\frac{\partial^2 f}{\partial x_1^2} > 0$$

and

$$\left(\frac{\partial^2 f}{\partial x_1^2}\right)\left(\frac{\partial^2 f}{\partial x_2^2}\right) - \left(\frac{\partial^2 f}{\partial x_1 \partial x_2}\right)^2 > 0$$

then the point is a local *minimum;*

b. if

$$\frac{\partial^2 f}{\partial x_1^2} < 0$$

and

$$\left(\frac{\partial^2 f}{\partial x_1^2}\right)\left(\frac{\partial^2 f}{\partial x_2^2}\right) - \left(\frac{\partial^2 f}{\partial x_1 \partial x_2}\right)^2 > 0$$

then the point is a local *maximum;*

c. if

$$\left(\frac{\partial^2 f}{\partial x_1^2}\right)\left(\frac{\partial^2 f}{\partial x_2^2}\right) - \left(\frac{\partial^2 f}{\partial x_1 \partial x_2}\right)^2 < 0$$

then the point is a *saddle point,* which is neither a local maximum nor a local minimum.

Condition (c) of rule 4 referring to a saddle point means that the point we have found attains a maximum with respect to one of the variables but a minimum with respect to the other. Hence the function indeed looks like a saddle at that point, and the solution is neither a local maximum nor a local minimum value of the function.

Cases in which

$$\left(\frac{\partial^2 f}{\partial x_1^2}\right)\left(\frac{\partial^2 f}{\partial x_2^2}\right) - \left(\frac{\partial^2 f}{\partial x_1 \partial x_2}\right)^2 = 0$$

have not been mentioned. In this situation the point could actually be a local minimum or a local maximum, but further analysis would be necessary to establish that fact. However, that further analysis is beyond the scope of this text.

Let us now apply rule 4 to our Lawn King problem to see if we have found a local maximum. We have

$$\frac{\partial^2 GP}{\partial p_1^2} = -4 < 0$$

and

$$\left(\frac{\partial^2 GP}{\partial p_1^2}\right)\left(\frac{\partial^2 GP}{\partial p_2^2}\right) - \left(\frac{\partial^2 GP}{\partial p_1 \partial p_2}\right)^2 = (-4)(-1) - (1)^2 = 3 > 0.$$

Therefore case b of rule 4 applies and we have indeed found a local maximum, which from our previous discussion we know to be a global maximum.

Our analysis of the Lawn King problem is now complete. We have determined that a pricing policy of $150 for the walking mower and $400 for the riding mower will maximize the company's gross profit. Using equation (18.11), the gross profit the company can anticipate if it employs this pricing policy is

$$GP = -2(150)^2 - 0.5(400)^2 + (150)(400) + 200(150)$$
$$+ 250(400) - 55,700 = 9300.$$

Since the model measures gross profit in thousands of dollars, Lawn King can anticipate a gross profit of $9,300,000 with this pricing policy. Of course, there are a number of other expenses that must yet be subtracted before we can determine the company's net profit.

At a price of $150 for the walking mower and $400 for the riding mower, we can now determine the number of mowers that will be sold by using equations (18.6) and (18.7). The number of walking mowers sold, q_1, is

$$q_1 = 95 - 2p_1 + 0.7p_2$$
$$= 95 - 2(150) + 0.7(400)$$
$$= 75 \text{ (thousand)}.$$

The number of riding mowers sold, q_2, is

$$q_2 = 188 + 0.3p_1 - 0.5p_2$$
$$= 188 + 0.3(150) - 0.5(400)$$
$$= 33 \text{ (thousand)}.$$

Thus if Lawn King produces 75,000 walking mowers at a price of $150 each and 33,000 riding mowers at a price of $400 each, the company will maximize gross profit at an anticipated level of $9,300,000. Note that the applicability of these results depends critically upon the confidence management has in the relationships established between sales prices and quantities sold and costs and quantities sold. That is, if management believes equations (18.6)–(18.9) are accurate representations of the true relationships between these factors, then the information developed using our calculus-based solution procedures can be valuable input to the decision-making process.

In our discussion of the Lawn King problem we concluded that the local maximum point $p_1 = 150$ and $p_2 = 400$ was also the global maximum, since $p_1 = 150$ and $p_2 = 400$ were the only values satisfying the necessary condition given by rule 3. Let us now discuss in general how we can determine the global optimal solution for any unconstrained function of two variables. We will state the procedure for a maximization problem in order to simplify the exposition. The modifications necessary to solve minimization problems should be apparent.

Step 1: Find all local maxima by applying rules 3 and 4.

Step 2: Select the largest of the local maxima as the global maximum (maxima).[4]

---

[4]For those unconstrained functions that go to infinity, a global maximum does not exist. Hence in such cases steps 1 and 2 will not yield a global maximum. However, such functions could never be realistic models of real-world optimization problems, and consequently we avoid a digression into such considerations in this text.

Note that a function can have more than one global maximum. Such situations are analogous to the case of alternate optima in a linear program.

To make sure that we understand the concepts involved in optimizing unconstrained mathematical models with two decision variables, let us consider the following numerical example:

Example   Suppose we want to find all the minimum and maximum points of the function below:

$$f(x_1, x_2) = 5x_1^2 + 10x_2^2 + 10x_1x_2 - 22x_1 - 26x_2 + 25. \quad (18.16)$$

Applying rule 3, we must set the partial derivatives with respect to x_1 and x_2 equal to zero and then solve the resulting equations for x_1 and x_2:

$$\frac{\partial f}{\partial x_1} = 10x_1 + 10x_2 - 22 = 0$$

$$\frac{\partial f}{\partial x_2} = 20x_2 + 10x_1 - 26 = 0.$$

Solving these equations, we obtain the solution $x_1 = \frac{9}{5}$, $x_2 = \frac{2}{5}$. To see if this is a local maximum or a local minimum, we must calculate the second partial derivates and apply rule 4. Calculating the second partial derivatives, we get

$$\frac{\partial^2 f}{\partial x_1^2} = 10, \qquad \frac{\partial^2 f}{\partial x_2^2} = 20, \qquad \frac{\partial^2 f}{\partial x_1 \partial x_2} = 10.$$

Since

$$\frac{\partial^2 f}{\partial x_1^2} = 10 > 0$$

and

$$\left(\frac{\partial^2 f}{\partial x_1^2}\right)\left(\frac{\partial^2 f}{\partial x_2^2}\right) - \left(\frac{\partial^2 f}{\partial x_1 \partial x_2}\right)^2 = (10)(20) - (10)^2 = 100 > 0,$$

case (a) of rule 4 applies, and the point $x_1 = \frac{9}{5}$, $x_2 = \frac{2}{5}$ yields a local minimum value for the function. Since this is the only point at which rule 3 applies, we can further conclude that this local minimum is the global minimum.

Let us pause for a moment to reflect on what we have learned in this section. Just as for unconstrained functions of a single variable, there is a first and second derivative test that must be applied in order to determine if a point is a local maximum or local minimum. The first derivative test, which must be satisfied by both local maximum and local minimum points, is called a necessary condition and is stated in rule 3. The second derivative test, just as with functions of a single variable, allows us to distinguish between a local maximum point, a local minimum point, and a point which may be neither a local maximum nor a local minimum. This is called a sufficient condition and is stated in rule 4.

We would like to comment, before closing this section, that for unconstrained functions of more than two variables the first and second derivative tests are given by extensions of rules 3 and 4. For an unconstrained function of n variables, $f(x_1, x_2, \ldots, x_n)$, the first derivative test for a local maximum or local minimum requires that all n of the partial derivatives equal zero. Since it is a simple extension of rule 3, we state it here as rule 5:

Rule 5 (Necessary Condition). All n partial derivatives of an unconstrained function of n variables, $f(x_1, x_2, \ldots, x_n)$, must equal zero at any local maximum or local minimum point.

For an unconstrained function of n variables, the second derivative test requires that all the second partial derivatives be calculated. Although this test is similar to rule 4, a simple statement of the test requires that we construct a matrix of second partial derivatives and perform some tests on the matrix. The tests require a knowledge of determinants of matrices which is not a prerequisite for the text. Thus we omit an extension of rule 4 to a second derivative test for functions of n variables. This extension is discussed in a number of more advanced texts on mathematical programming.[5]

18.3   Models with Equality Constraints—Lagrange Multipliers

In this section we discuss a problem situation that leads to the formulation of a nonlinear mathematical model involving two decision variables and one constraint equation. After we have seen how such a problem might arise, we present a solution procedure which once again involves a calculus-based first and second derivative test.

Green Lawns, Inc. provides a lawn fertilizer and weed control service. The company provides four treatments of fertilizer and weed control chemical to its subscribers each year. Green Lawns is adding a special aeration treatment as a low-cost extra service option which it hopes will help attract new customers. Management is planning on promoting this new service in two media: radio and direct-mail advertising. A budget of $2000 is to be used on this promotional campaign over the next quarter. Based on past experience in promoting its other services, Green Lawns has been able to obtain an estimate of the relationship between sales and the amount spent on promotion in these two media:

$$s = -2x_1^2 - 10x_2^2 - 8x_1x_2 + 18x_1 + 34x_2 \qquad (18.17)$$

where

s = total sales in thousands of dollars

x_1 = thousands of dollars spent on radio advertising

x_2 = thousands of dollars spent on direct-mail promotion.

---

[5]A good discussion of these tests is contained in Luenberger, D. G., *Introduction to Linear and Nonlinear Programming,* Reading, Mass., Addison-Wesley, 1973.

Green Lawns would like to develop a promotional strategy that will lead to maximum sales subject to the restriction provided by the promotional budget. Recognizing that the promotional budget is $2000, we may state Green Lawn's problem as the following constrained optimization problem:

$$\max \quad -2x_1^2 - 10x_2^2 - 8x_1x_2 + 18x_1 + 34x_2$$
$$\text{s.t.}$$
$$x_1 + x_2 = 2. \tag{18.18}$$

We note that the constraint is written as $x_1 + x_2 = 2$ because x_1 and x_2 are being measured in thousands of dollars. Also, the objective function calls for the maximization of sales in thousands of dollars.

In general, all problems involving the minimization or maximization of a function of two variables subject to an equality constraint can be written as follows:

$$\min \text{ or } \max \quad f(x_1, x_2)$$
$$\text{s.t.}$$
$$g(x_1, x_2) = b \tag{18.19}$$

The approach we shall follow to solve the above class of problems is to first introduce a new variable, called a *Lagrange multiplier,* and use this new variable to combine the constraint and objective function together into a single function. The new single function we shall form is called a *Lagrangian function* and is written below, where λ denotes the Lagrange multiplier:

Lagrangian function $= L(x_1, x_2, \lambda) = f(x_1, x_2) + \lambda[g(x_1, x_2) - b]$ (18.20)

The first derivative test that every local minimum or local maximum point of a constrained problem must satisfy[6] is stated in rule 6:

Rule 6 (Necessary Condition). For a function of two variables, x_1 and x_2, subject to one constraint to have a local minimum or a local maximum at a point, the partial derivatives of the Lagrangian function with respect to x_1, x_2, and λ must all equal zero at that point.

Thus once we have set up the Lagrangian function, this first derivative test for a constrained problem turns out to be very similar to the first derivative test for unconstrained functions. Let us now apply this test to the problem faced by Green Lawns, Inc.

Introducing a Lagrange multiplier as indicated by equations (18.19) and (18.20), we obtain the following Lagrangian function:

$$L(x_1, x_2, \lambda) = -2x_1^2 - 10x_2^2 - 8x_1x_2 + 18x_1 + 34x_2$$
$$+ \lambda(x_1 + x_2 - 2). \tag{18.21}$$

Following rule 6, we first determine the partial derivatives with respect to x_1, x_2, and λ, and then set them equal to zero:

$$\frac{\partial L}{\partial x_1} = -4x_1 - 8x_2 + 18 + \lambda = 0 \tag{18.22}$$

---

[6]There are certain examples that can be constructed for which the maximum or minimum does not satisfy rule 6, but these are exceptions that rarely occur in practice. Thus we shall not be concerned with them.

$$\frac{\partial L}{\partial x_2} = -20x_2 - 8x_1 + 34 + \lambda = 0 \qquad (18.23)$$

$$\frac{\partial L}{\partial \lambda} = x_1 + x_2 - 2 = 0. \qquad (18.24)$$

We are left with three equations in three unknowns: x_1, x_2, and λ. Solving these will give us a point satisfying rule 6 and thus a candidate for a maximum solution of the Green Lawns problem. Subtracting equation (18.22) from equation (18.23) allows us to form a new equation not including λ:

$$-4x_1 - 12x_2 + 16 = 0. \qquad (18.25)$$

Multiplying equation (18.24) by 4 and adding to equation (18.25) yields

$$-8x_2 + 8 = 0.$$

Hence

$$x_2 = 1.$$

Substituting $x_2 = 1$ into equation (18.24), we find that $x_1 = 1$. As a consequence, from equations (18.22) and (18.23) we find that $\lambda = -6$. Thus the necessary condition of rule 1 is satisfied with

$$x_1^* = 1$$
$$x_2^* = 1$$
$$\lambda^* = -6.$$

Since there is only one solution satisfying rule 6, we know that if it is a local maximum it is also a global maximum. It remains to be seen if this point truly yields a local maximum solution for the Green Lawns problem. We must develop a second derivative rule in order to make that determination. Rule 7 provides such a test and thus gives sufficient conditions for a local maximum or local minimum point.

Rule 7 (Sufficient Condition). If rule 6 is satisfied at a point $(x_1^*, x_2^*, \lambda^*)$, apply conditions a and b of rule 4 to the Lagrangian function with λ fixed at a value of λ^* in order to determine if the point (x_1^*, x_2^*) is a local maximum or a local minimum.

Rule 7 says to first fix λ at the value necessary to satisfy rule 6. Then the Lagrangian function is expressed as a function of the two variables x_1 and x_2 with λ fixed at the value λ^*. Conditions a and b of rule 4 may be applied to this new function in order to determine if we have a local maximum or a local minimum.[7]

Let us apply rule 7 to our Green Lawns problem to see if the solution we have found is a local maximum.

---

[7] Condition c of rule 4 is not used for equality constrained problems, since a saddle point of the Lagrangian function need not correspond to a saddle point of the equality constrained problem we want to solve.

The Lagrangian function [equation (18.21)] with λ fixed at $\lambda^* = -6$ is

$$L(x_1, x_2, \lambda = -6) = -2x_1^2 - 10x_2^2 - 8x_1x_2 + 18x_1 + 34x_2$$
$$- 6(x_1 + x_2 - 2).$$

We need to find the second partial derivatives of this function with respect to x_1 and x_2 to determine if the $x_1^* = 1$ and $x_2^* = 1$ solution yields a maximum. Taking the first partial derivatives with respect to x_1 and x_2, we obtain the same result we could have obtained by substituting $\lambda = -6$ into equations (18.22) and (18.23):

$$\frac{\partial L}{\partial x_1} = -4x_1 - 8x_2 + 18 - 6 = -4x_1 - 8x_2 + 12$$

$$\frac{\partial L}{\partial x_2} = -20x_2 - 8x_1 + 34 - 6 = -20x_2 - 8x_1 + 28.$$

The second partial derivatives of this function with respect to x_1 and x_2 are

$$\frac{\partial^2 L}{\partial x_1^2} = -4, \qquad \frac{\partial^2 L}{\partial x_2^2} = -20, \qquad \frac{\partial^2 L}{\partial x_1 \partial x_2} = -8.$$

To see if the Lagrangian function with λ fixed at $\lambda^* = -6$ has an unconstrained minimum at $x_1^* = 1$ and $x_2^* = 1$, we apply the second derivative test developed in rule 4 for unconstrained functions of two variables:

$$\frac{\partial^2 L}{\partial x_1^2} = -4 < 0$$

$$\left(\frac{\partial^2 L}{\partial x_1^2}\right)\left(\frac{\partial^2 L}{\partial x_2^2}\right) - \left(\frac{\partial^2 L}{\partial x_1 \partial x_2}\right)^2 = (-4)(-20) - (-8)^2 = 16 > 0$$

Case b of Rule 4 applies, and the point $x_1^* = 1$, $x_2^* = 1$ is an unconstrained maximum of the Lagrangian function with $\lambda = -6$. Thus we see that $x_1^* = 1$ and $x_2^* = 1$ is the optimal solution to the Green Lawns problem. The company should invest \$1000 in radio advertising and \$1000 in direct mail promotion. To determine the expected sales volume from this strategy we must evaluate the objective function, equation (18.17), with $x_1 = 1$ and $x_2 = 1$. Doing so, we obtain

$$\text{Sales} = -2(1)^2 - 10(1)^2 - 8(1)(1) + 18(1) + 34(1) = 32$$

Thus the expected sales volume resulting from this promotional strategy is \$32,000.

The following numerical example provides another illustration of the use of the Lagrange multiplier method for solving equality constrained optimization problems:

Example Suppose we have the following constrained optimization problem:

$$\min \quad x_1^2 + 2x_2^2 - 8x_1 - 12x_2 + 34$$
$$\text{s.t.}$$
$$x_1 + 2x_2 = 4.$$

Setting up the Lagrangian function for this problem, we obtain

$$L(x_1, x_2, \lambda) = x_1^2 + 2x_2^2 - 8x_1 - 12x_2 + 34 + \lambda(x_1 + 2x_2 - 4). \quad (18.26)$$

Applying rule 6 we set the partial derivatives of this Lagrangian function with respect to x_1, x_2, and λ equal to zero:

$$\frac{\partial L}{\partial x_1} = 2x_1 - 8 + \lambda = 0$$

$$\frac{\partial L}{\partial x_2} = 4x_2 - 12 + 2\lambda = 0$$

$$\frac{\partial L}{\partial \lambda} = x_1 + 2x_2 - 4 = 0.$$

Solving the resulting three equations for the three unknowns, we obtain

$$x_1^* = 2, \qquad x_2^* = 1, \qquad \lambda^* = 4.$$

Once again, there is only one solution satisfying rule 6. Thus if it is a local maximum or minimum, it must also be a global maximum or minimum.

We must now apply rule 7 to see if this is a local maximum or a minimum point. Setting $\lambda^* = 4$ in equation (18.26), the second partial derivatives of the Lagrangian function with respect to x_1 and x_2 are

$$\frac{\partial^2 L}{\partial x_1^2} = 2, \qquad \frac{\partial^2 L}{\partial x_2^2} = 4, \qquad \frac{\partial^2 L}{\partial x_1 \partial x_2} = 0.$$

Checking conditions (a) and (b) of the test procedures for rule 4, we have

$$\frac{\partial^2 L}{\partial x_1^2} = 2 > 0$$

and

$$\left(\frac{\partial^2 L}{\partial x_1^2}\right)\left(\frac{\partial^2 L}{\partial x_2^2}\right) - \left(\frac{\partial^2 L}{\partial x_1 \partial x_2}\right)^2 = (2)(4) - (0)^2 = 8 > 0.$$

Thus we have a local minimum of the Lagrangian function with λ fixed at 4, and in light of our previous discussion we have found a global minimum at $x_1 = 2$ and $x_2 = 1$.

The Green Lawns, Inc. problem and the above problem are examples of models having a nonlinear objective function and a linear equality constraint. In applying rules 6 and 7 we were able to develop the necessary and sufficient condition test relatively easily. However, for problems where the equality constraint is also nonlinear, you will find that the solution computations become somewhat more difficult. Problems 12 and 14 at the end of this chapter ask you to use rules 6 and 7 to solve a problem with a nonlinear objective function and a nonlinear equality constraint.

To complete our discussion we mention briefly how rule 6 can be extended to supply a necessary condition for minimizing or maximizing a function of n variables subject to m equality constraints. This extended problem may be stated in the following form:

$$\text{min or max} \quad f(x_1, x_2, \ldots, x_n)$$
$$\text{s.t.}$$

$$g_1(x_1, x_2, \ldots, x_n) = b_1$$
$$g_2(x_1, x_2, \ldots, x_n) = b_2$$
$$\vdots \qquad \qquad \vdots$$
$$g_m(x_1, x_2, \ldots, x_n) = b_m. \tag{18.28}$$

A Lagrangian function, combining the objective function and all the constraints into one function, can be formulated by introducing a separate Lagrange multiplier for each constraint:

$$L(x_1, x_2, \ldots, x_n, \lambda_1, \lambda_2, \ldots, \lambda_m)$$
$$= f(x_1, x_2, \ldots, x_n) + \lambda_1[g_1(x_1, x_2, \ldots, x_n) - b_1]$$
$$+ \lambda_2[g_2(x_1, x_2, \ldots, x_n) - b_2] + \cdots$$
$$+ \lambda_m[g_m(x_1, x_2, \ldots, x_n) - b_m]. \tag{18.28}$$

The extension of rule 6 to this problem can now be stated in terms of this new Lagrangian function:

Rule 8 (Necessary Condition). For a function of n variables, $f(x_1, x_2, \ldots, x_n)$, subject to m constraints to have a local minimum or a local maximum at a point, the partial derivatives of the Lagrangian function with respect to $x_1, x_2, \ldots, x_n$ and $\lambda_1, \lambda_2, \ldots, \lambda_m$ must all equal zero at that point.

The second derivative test for this problem is a natural extension to rule 7; that is, we would check for a local maximum or a local minimum of the Lagrangian function with $\lambda_1, \lambda_2, \ldots, \lambda_m$ fixed at the values found when applying rule 8. This would require that we have a second derivative test for an unconstrained function of n variables. A matrix of second partial derivatives provides the basis for this test; however, as we stated earlier, the methodology is beyond the scope of this text.

Before concluding this section, we comment briefly on its similarity to the previous two sections. Once again we had a first derivative test that any local maximum or local minimum point had to satisfy. Then we had a second derivative test that could be used to determine if a point satisfying the first derivative test was indeed a local maximum or a local minimum. The only conceptual difference in solving these constrained problems was that we had to formulate a Lagrangian function and then perform the first and second derivative tests on that function. Only conditions (a) and (b) of the second derivative test were applicable for constrained problems.

18.4   Interpretation of the Lagrange Multiplier

In the previous section we saw that it was necessary to introduce an additional variable called a Lagrange multiplier in order to solve constrained problems. This variable was used in setting up the Lagrangian function. In meeting the necessary condition (rule 6), we actually found a value for the Lagrange multiplier. The value of this Lagrange multiplier can often be used to provide valuable managerial information about the sensitivity of an optimal solution to changes in resource levels.

In order to be more specific, let us reconsider the Green Lawns problem, which is restated below:

$$\max \quad -2x_1^2 - 10x_2^2 - 8x_1x_2 + 18x_1 + 34x_2$$
$$\text{s.t.}$$
$$x_1 + x_2 = 2.$$

Here, x_1 represents the amount spent on radio advertising and x_2 the amount spent on direct-mail promotion. The constraint indicates that $2000 is to be used for the promotional campaign and that it is to be divided between the two media, x_1 and x_2. In the previous section we saw that the optimal allocation was to divide the budget equally between the two media: $x_1 = 1$ and $x_2 = 1$. Management might wonder what the effect on sales would be if a different amount, say $1000 or $3000, were budgeted for the promotional campaign. The value of the Lagrange multiplier provides an estimate of that effect. Let us see how.

Recall that the general model with two decision variables and one equality constraint was written as

$$\min \text{ or } \max \quad f(x_1, x_2)$$
$$\text{s.t.}$$
$$g(x_1, x_2) = b.$$

The interpretation of the Lagrange multiplier for this problem is stated as property 1.

Property 1 (Interpretation of the Lagrange Multiplier). The value of the Lagrange multiplier associated with the general model above is the negative of the rate of change of the objective function with respect to a change in b. More formally, it is the negative of the partial derivative of $f(x_1, x_2)$ with respect to b; that is, $\lambda = -\partial f/\partial b$ or

$$\frac{\partial f}{\partial b} = -\lambda. \tag{18.29}$$

In other words, this property means that if we were to increase b, the value of λ would indicate approximately how much the value of the optimal solution would decrease. Conversely, this propery means that if we were to decrease b, the value of λ would provide an approximation of how much the value of the optimal solution would increase. Let us return to the Green Lawns problem and see how this property applies in that situation.

The optimal solution to the Green Lawns problem has

$$x_1^* = 1, \qquad x_2^* = 1, \qquad \lambda^* = -6.$$

Since $\lambda^* = -6$, property 1 indicates that with $\partial f/\partial b = -\lambda = -(-6) = 6$, the objective function should increase by approximately 6 if b is increased by 1. For example, if the budget is increased from \$2000 to \$3000 in the Green Lawns problem, the objective function should increase by approximately \$6000. Let us change the budget to \$3000 and see what happens.

After increasing the budget to \$3000 the Green Lawns problem can be written as follows:

$$\max \quad -2x_1^2 - 10x_2^2 - 8x_1x_2 + 18x_1 + 34x_2$$

s.t.

$$x_1 + x_2 = 3 \tag{18.30}$$

Formulating the Lagrangian and setting the partial derivatives equal to zero yields

$$L(x_1, x_2, \lambda) = -2x_1^2 - 10x_2^2 - 8x_1x_2 + 18x_1 + 34x_2$$
$$+ \lambda(x_1 + x_2 - 3) \tag{18.31}$$

and

$$\frac{\partial L}{\partial x_1} = -4x_1 - 8x_2 + 18 + \lambda = 0$$

$$\frac{\partial L}{\partial x_2} = -20x_2 - 8x_1 + 34 + \lambda = 0$$

$$\frac{\partial L}{\partial \lambda} = x_1 + x_2 - 3 = 0.$$

Solving these three equations simultaneously for x_1, x_2, and λ yields

$$x_1^* = 2.5, \qquad x_2^* = 0.5, \qquad \lambda^* = -4.$$

To check to see if we have a maximum we must determine the second partial derivatives of the Lagrangian with λ fixed at $\lambda^* = -4$. Using equation (18.31) with $\lambda = -4$, these second partial derivatives are

$$\frac{\partial^2 L}{\partial x_1^2} = -4, \qquad \frac{\partial^2 L}{\partial x_2^2} = -20, \qquad \frac{\partial^2 L}{\partial x_1 \partial x_2} = -8.$$

Applying rule 4, we see that $x_1^* = 2.5$ and $x_2^* = 0.5$ does indeed yield an unconstrained maximum of the Lagrangian with λ fixed at $\lambda^* = -4$. According to rule 7 we have found the maximum for this new problem.

Now we would like to see how close the \$6000 increase in the objective function predicted by $\lambda^* = -6$ comes to the true increase. The value of the objective function for $x_1^* = 2.5$ and $x_2^* = 0.5$ is

$$f(x_1, x_2) = \text{sales} = -2(2.5)^2 - 10(0.5)^2 - 8(2.5)(0.5)$$
$$+ 18(2.5) + 34(0.5) = 37.$$

The maximum value of sales given a budget of \$3000 is thus \$37,000. Since the maximum value for a budget of \$2000 was found previously to be \$32,000 the increase in sales is \$5000 and not the \$6000 which the value of the Lagrange multiplier predicted. We should not be too surprised at this.

What we are observing is the law of diminishing returns in action. As the amount of resources available increases (advertising budget in this case), the per unit increase in the objective function decreases. Note that the value we obtained for the Lagrange multiplier when the budget was increased to $3000 was $\lambda^* = -4$. This would lead us to predict that sales would increase by another $4000 if the budget were further increased to $4000. The rate of return per unit increase in the budget has decreased from 6 to 4 as the budget has increased from 2 to 3.

Also, we should note that the Lagrange multiplier value associated with a budget of $3000, $\lambda^* = -4$, would lead us to predict that sales would decrease by $4000 if the budget were decreased to $2000. The actual change, as we now know, is 5000. Thus if we used the Lagrange multiplier associated with $b = 2000$, $\lambda^* = -6$, to predict the change in sales associated with a $1000 change in the budget, we would overestimate the change. On the other hand if we used the Lagrange multiplier associated with $b = 3000$, $\lambda^* = -4$, to predict the change in sales associated with changing the budget from 2000 to 3000 we would underestimate the change. The actual change, $5000, is halfway between.

The reason the Lagrange multiplier only provides an estimate of the change in the objective function and not the exact change is that it is a partial derivative of the objective function with respect to b. Thus for different values of b we get different values for the Lagrange multiplier. The estimate provided by λ^* will be very good as long as the change in b is small, but will be increasingly poor as the change in b gets larger.

In Table 18.1 we show the maximum sales levels for budget amounts varying between $1000 and $3000 in increments of $200 together with the maximum sales levels we would have predicted by using the property of the Lagrange multiplier.

TABLE 18.1 Maximum Sales Levels for Varying Budgets Compared with Estimates Based on the Lagrange Multiplier of $\lambda = -6$ for the Green Lawns Problem

Budget	Actual Maximum Sales $f(x_1^*, x_2^*)$	Estimated Maximum Sales $\lambda^* = -6$	Difference
$1000	$25,000	$26,000	−1000
1200	26,560	27,200	− 640
1400	28,040	28,400	− 360
1600	29,440	29,600	− 160
1800	30,760	30,800	− 40
2000	32,000	32,000	0
2200	33,160	33,200	+ 40
2400	34,240	34,400	+ 160
2600	35,240	35,600	+ 360
2800	36,160	36,800	+ 640
3000	37,000	38,000	+1000

Table 18.1 verifies that the estimates based on the Lagrange multiplier are good as long as the change in *b* is not large. For a $200 change in the budget the estimate based on the Lagrange multiplier is pretty good. There is only a $40 error in the sales estimate. Of course, as we get further away from a budget of $2000, the predictions continue to get worse. We can also see the effect of diminishing returns with respect to the advertising budget from studying the table. When the budget is set at $1000, a $200 increase causes an increase in sales of $1560. When the budget is set at $2800, a $200 increase causes an increase in sales of only $840.

From a managerial point of view we see that the value of the Lagrange multiplier can provide important information. It is an indication of the sensitivity of the optimal solution to changes in resource levels. In most real-world problems these resource levels are not some sacred number that cannot be changed. For example, in the Green Lawns situation management has initially budgeted $2000 for an advertising campaign. If the quantitative analyst can show the manager that an increase in the advertising budget of $1 can be expected to increase sales by $6, then the manager may want to consider expanding the budget. Of course, whether or not the manager chooses to expand it will depend on a number of other considerations as well. Can funds be freed from other uses for the campaign? How much confidence do we have that our model is representative of the real relationship between advertising in the two media and sales? Also, since the $6 increase in sales will cost us $1 of advertising, is the remaining $5 enough to offset all the other costs associated with the increased sales? Regardless of how this sensitivity information is eventually used by the manager, it is important to know what it means and that it can be made available as a by-product of the model solution.

The Lagrange multiplier analysis can be extended to problems with more variables and more constraints. However, because of the additional complexity involved, we leave a discussion of this extension to more advanced texts on mathematical programming.

18.5   Models Involving Inequality Constraints

In this section we study problems which lead to nonlinear mathematical models involving two decision variables and one inequality constraint. We will find that this type of problem can be solved using the approaches we have already learned in the previous sections of this chapter.

Suppose that instead of stating that a budget of $2000 had to be spent on an advertising campaign for the aeration service, management of Green Lawns, Inc. had stated that the amount spent had to be less than or equal to the $2000 budget. This is actually a more realistic interpretation of the budget constraint. Certainly if more sales could be realized by spending less on advertising, the company would be willing to do so. Given this less-than-or-equal-to interpretation of the constraint, the Green Lawns model would involve two decision variables and one inequality constraint as shown at the top of page 651.

$$\max \quad -2x_1^2 - 10x_2^2 - 8x_1x_2 + 18x_1 + 34x_2$$
$$\text{s.t.}$$
$$x_1 + x_2 \le 2.$$

In solving this problem we recognize that there are actually two possibilities with respect to the constraint. The first is that the constraint $x_1 + x_2 \le 2$ will be binding at the optimal solution. In this case we could assume that the constraint has the form $x_1 + x_2 = 2$ and solve just as we did in Section 18.3 for problems with equality constraints. The second possibility is that at the optimal solution the constraint is not binding, that is, $x_1^* + x_2^* < 2$. In this case we could simply ignore the constraint and solve as we did in Section 18.2 for unconstrained problems. The recognition that these are the only two possibilities is what motivates the solution procedure we are about to present.

We state the solution procedure for a maximization problem in order to simplify the exposition. The modifications necessary to solve minimization problems should be apparent.

Step 1:   Assume the constraint is not binding and apply the procedures of Section 18.2 to find the global maximum of the function, if it exists. (Functions that go to infinity do not have a global maximum.) If this global maximim satisfies the constraint, stop. This is the global maximum for the inequality constrained problem. If not, the constraint may be binding at the optimum. Record the value of any local maximum that satisfies the inequality constraint and go on to step 2.

Step 2:   Assume the constraint is binding and apply the procedures of Section 18.3 to find all the local maxima of the resulting equality constrained problem. Compare these values with any feasible local maxima found in step 1. The largest of these is the global maximum.

Let us apply this solution procedure to our new version of the Green Lawns problem. Applying step 1 and ignoring the constraint $x_1 + x_2 \le 2$ would lead us to solve the unconstrained problem

$$\max \quad -2x_1^2 - 10x_2^2 - 8x_1x_2 + 18x_1 + 34x_2.$$

Applying rule 3, we set the partial derivatives of the objective function equal to zero:

$$\frac{\partial f}{\partial x_1} = -4x_1 - 8x_2 + 18 = 0$$

$$\frac{\partial f}{\partial x_2} = -20x_2 - 8x_1 + 34 = 0.$$

Solving these two equations simultaneously, we obtain $x_1^* = 1\frac{1}{2}$ and

$x_2^* = -\frac{1}{2}$. Before checking the second derivatives for a local maximum or minimum, however, let us see if these values for x_1 and x_2 satisfy our constraint. Clearly, $x_1^* + x_2^* = 5\frac{1}{2} - \frac{1}{2} = 5$ is not less than or equal to 2, and therefore even if this solution did yield the global maximum to our unconstrained problem (which it does, by the way), it could not be optimal since it does not satisfy the inequality constraint. There are no other local maxima to record the values of; therefore we go on to step 2 and solve the following equality constrained optimization problem:

$$\max \quad -2x_1^2 - 10x_2^2 - 8x_1x_2 + 18x_1 + 34x_2$$

$$\text{s.t.}$$

$$x_1 + x_2 = 2.$$

The global maximum for this problem was found in Section 18.3 and is given by $x_1 = 1$ and $x_2 = 1$. Since there are no feasible local maxima from step 1, the optimal solution to our constrained optimization problem is also $x_1 = 1$, $x_2 = 1$, with an expected sales volume of \$32,000.

Let us now look at another example involving a minimization problem:

Example   Suppose we want to solve the following problem:

$$\min \quad f(x_1, x_2) = x_1^2 - 10x_1 + x_2^2 - 10x_2$$

$$\text{s.t.}$$

$$x_1 + 2x_2 \le 20.$$

Step 1 of the solution procedure says to ignore the constraint and solve the resulting unconstrained optimization problem. Applying rule 3, we set the partial derivatives of the objective functional equal to zero:

$$\frac{\partial f}{\partial x_1} = 2x_1 - 10 = 0$$

$$\frac{\partial f}{\partial x_2} = 2x_2 - 10 = 0.$$

Solving these two equations, we obtain $x_1^* = 5$ and $x_2^* = 5$. Since this point satisfies the constraint, we must check to see if it is a local minimum. Applying the second derivative test of rule 4, we obtain

$$\frac{\partial^2 f}{\partial x_1^2} = 2 > 0$$

and

$$\left(\frac{\partial^2 f}{\partial x_1^2}\right)\left(\frac{\partial^2 f}{\partial x_2^2}\right) - \left(\frac{\partial^2 f}{\partial x_2 \partial x_1}\right)^2 = (2)(2) - 0^2 = 4 > 0.$$

Therefore the point $x_1 = 5$, $x_2 = 5$ yields a local minimum for our function. Further, since no other values of x_1, x_2 satisfy rule 3, we can conclude that $x_1 = 5$, $x_2 = 5$ yields a global minimum for our unconstrained function. Thus it is unnecessary to go on to step 2, since no point on the constraint boundary could possibly be better than the global minimum. We can therefore conclude that $x_1 = 5$, $x_2 = 5$ is the global minimum for our inequality constrained problem.

We have seen how the solution procedure of this section can be applied both in the case where the constraint is satisfied as an equality at the optimum and when it is satisfied as a strict inequality. Unfortunately the solution procedure we have outlined here cannot be extended to problems with more than one inequality constraint nor to problems with both equality and inequality constraints. We will comment briefly on what to do in such cases.

In some applications the appropriate mathematical model may have a mixture of equality and inequality constraints. In these kinds of mathematical models, the solution approach invariably requires a computerized mathematical programming algorithm. There are many research papers and a number of mathematical programming textbooks devoted to these computerized algorithms. The approach taken by all these algorithms is iterative in nature. Initially a starting point, which is a guess at the optimal solution, is picked and then an improved solution is determined by the computer algorithm. Another improvement is made, and so on, until eventually the optimal solution is reached. The details of these solution algorithms are beyond the scope of this text.

Summary

The kinds of problems discussed in this chapter have been examples of decision-making situations in which the appropriate mathematical model of the problem involved nonlinear relationships. When these decision-making situations arise, the linear programming procedures of Chapters 2 through 5 are not applicable, and calculus-based solution procedures must be employed.

For both unconstrained and constrained problems we saw that a first and a second derivative test were required. In the unconstrained single-variable case these tests were made on the first and second derivatives of the objective function. In the unconstrained two-variable case these tests were made on the first and second partial derivatives of the objective function. Equality constrained problems with two decision variables and one constraint were solved by first introducing a new variable called a Lagrange multiplier. A Lagrangian function was then formed by combining the objective function and constraint into one function. Tests on the first and second partial derivatives of the Lagrangian function were then developed to find the optimal solution. The Lagrange multiplier was found to provide valuable managerial information about the sensitivity of the optimal solution to changes in the value of the right-hand side of the constraint (the resource level).

Glossary

1. *Necessary conditions*—Conditions, usually requiring first derivatives to be equal to zero, that must be satisfied at an optimal solution. They do not guarantee an optimal solution.
2. *Sufficient conditions*—Conditions, usually involving the sign of second derivatives, that determine whether a solution meeting the necessary conditions is a maximum solution, a minimum solution, or no solution.
3. *Saddle point*—A condition that occurs in models with more than one decision variable when one variable reaches it maximum value and another reaches its minimum value at the same point.
4. *Lagrange multiplier*—A new variable added to a constrained nonlinear model in order to obtain a solution. In sensitivity analysis this variable tells us what effect a change in the level of resources will have on the objective function.
5. *Lagrangian function*—The function formed by using the Lagrange multiplier to combine the objective function and the constraint(s) into one function. For example, the constrained problem

$$\text{min. } f(x_1, x_2)$$
$$\text{s.t.}$$
$$g(x_1, x_2) = b$$

has the following Lagrangian function:

$$L(x_1, x_2, \lambda) = f(x_1, x_2) + \lambda[g(x_1, x_2) - b]$$

where λ is the Lagrange multiplier.

6. *Local maximum (minimum)*—A point which gives at least as high (low) a value of the objective function as any nearby point.
7. *Global maximimum (minimum)*—The point, or points, at which a function takes on its greatest (lowest) value.

Problems

1. a. Maximize the function

$$f(x) = 12x - 6x^2 - 30.$$

    b. Maximize the above function over the interval

$$0 \leq x \leq 10.$$

    c. Maximize the above function over the interval

$$2 \leq x \leq 10.$$

2. a. Find the minimum of the function

$$f(x) = 3x^3 - 20x^2 + 60.$$

    b. Find the minimum of the above function over the interval

$$0 \leq x \leq 4.$$

3. A large grocery chain is interested in determining the best size for a new store that is being built at a particular site. The chain has made an extensive study of the sector within which the new store will be located. Based on such factors as sector population, weekly per capita food expenditures, and competition, the grocery chain has developed the following model that relates sales (in thousands of dollars) to the size of the store x (in units of 10,000 square feet):

$$\text{Sales} = 100x - 10x^2 - 150.$$

Determine the size of the store that will maximize sales. What are the maximum sales corresponding to the store size?

4. The manufacturer of King's Chunk Style Peanut Butter has determined that sales in any particular store are related to the amount of shelf space devoted to the peanut butter and the amount of traffic through the store. A detailed analysis led to the following equation relating the square feet on shelves and the number of store customers per week to the total weekly sales in dollars:

$$\text{Sales} = -20x^2 - 50C^2 - 60Cx + 220x - 340C + 610$$

where

$$x = \text{square feet of shelf space}$$
$$C = \text{thousands of customers.}$$

King uses the above formula to determine the optimal amount of shelf space for its product in any particular store.

Suppose a particular store averages a thousand customers per week. How many square feet of shelf space would be required to maximize sales?

5. Suppose that the total cost (TC) of producing x pounds of a certain cleaning fluid is given by

$$\text{TC} = \tfrac{4}{3}x^4 - 3x^3 + 2x^2 + 5x.$$

What batch size will lead to the minimum cost per pound?

6. A certain product sells for \$5 per unit. The total cost (C) of producing and selling this product is given by

$$C(x) = x^2 - 15x + 20.$$

a. What is the fixed cost of production? That is, what portion of the cost is independent of the number of units produced?

b. Develop a mathematical model that shows total profit as a function of the number of units produced.

c. What level of production will maximize profit?

7. The cost per batch of a certain production process is related to the setting of two control instruments. Suppose the total cost per batch is given by

$$f(x_1, x_2) = 4x_1^2 + 2x_2^2 + 4x_1x_2 - 8x_1 - 6x_2 + 35.$$

Determine the settings for the two instruments that will minimize this cost.

8. Consider the function $f(x_1, x_2) = 2x_1^4 - 12x_1^2 + 2x_1^2x_2 + x_2^2 - 4x_2 + 20$. Determine whether the points below yield local minima, local maxima, saddle points, or none of these.

$$\begin{pmatrix} x_1 = 0 \\ x_2 = 2 \end{pmatrix} \begin{pmatrix} x_1 = +2 \\ x_2 = -2 \end{pmatrix} \begin{pmatrix} x_1 = -2 \\ x_2 = -2 \end{pmatrix}$$

9. The prices for two products, denoted by p_1 and p_2, are related to the quantities sold of the two products, x_1 and x_2, by the expressions

$$x_1 = 32 - 2p_1$$
$$x_2 = 22 - p_2.$$

Further, the total cost (TC) of producing and selling the product is related to the quantities sold by the function

$$TC(x_1, x_2) = \tfrac{1}{2}x_1^2 + 2x_1x_2 + x_2^2 + 73.$$

a. Develop a mathematical model that shows profit as a function of the quantities produced.

b. Determine the prices and quantities that maximize profit.

10. A shoe store has determined that its earnings $E(x_1, x_2)$, in thousands of dollars, can be approximated by a function of x_1, its investment in inventory in thousands of dollars, and x_2, its expenditure on advertising in thousands of dollars:

$$E(x_1, x_2) = -3x_1^2 + 2x_1x_2 - 6x_2^2 + 30x_1 + 24x_2 - 86.$$

Find the maximum earnings, along with the amount of advertising expenditure and inventory investment that yields this maximum.

11. Consider the problem

$$\min \quad x_1^2 - 14x_1 + x_2^2 - 16x_2 + 113$$
$$\text{s.t.}$$
$$2x_1 + 3x_2 = 12$$

a. Find the minimum solution to this problem.

b. How much would you expect the value of the solution to change if the right-hand side of the constraint were increased from 12 to 13?

12. Consider the problem

$$\max \quad -x_1^2 - 4x_1x_2 + 20x_1 - 5x_2^2 + 82x_2 - 397$$
$$\text{s.t.}$$
$$2x_1^2 - 16x_1 + 9x_2^2 - 18x_2 + 5 = 0.$$

Determine whether or not the point $x_1 = 4$, $x_2 = 3$ provides an optimal solution.

13. Heller Manufacturing has two production facilities which manufacture baseball gloves. Production costs at the two facilities differ because of varying labor rates, local property taxes, type of equipment, capacity, and so on.

The Dayton plant has weekly production costs which can be expressed as a function of the number of gloves produced:

$$TC_1(x_1) = x_1^2 - x_1 + 5,$$

where x_1 is the weekly production volume in thousands of units and $TC_1(x_1)$ is the cost in thousands of dollars.

The Hamilton plant's weekly production costs are given by

$$TC_2(x_2) = x_2^2 + 2x_2 + 3,$$

where x_2 is the weekly production volume in thousands of units and $TC_2(x_2)$ is the cost, in thousands of dollars.

Heller manufacturing would like to produce 8000 gloves per week at the lowest possible cost.

a. Formulate a mathematical model which can be used to determine the number of gloves to produce each week at each facility.

b. Find the solution to your mathematical model to determine the optimal number of gloves to produce at each facility.

14. Solve the problem

$$\min \quad x_1^2 + 2x_2^2 - 8x_1 - 12x_2 + 34$$
$$\text{s.t.}$$
$$x_1^2 + 2x_2^2 = 5.$$

15. Consider the problem

$$\min \quad 2x_1^2 - 20x_1 + 2x_1x_2 + x_2^2 - 14x_2 + 58$$
$$\text{s.t.}$$
$$x_1 + 4x_2 \le 8.$$

   a. Find the minimum solution to this problem.
   b. If the right-hand side of the constraint is increased from 8 to 9, how much do you expect the objective function to change?

16. Jingle Bells, Inc. has received a rush order for as many of two types of Christmas bells as can be produced and shipped during a two-week period. Preliminary analysis by Jingle Bells indicates that the profit on this order is related to the number of each type of bell manufactured by the following function:

$$P = -x_1^2 - x_2^2 + 12x_1 + 10x_2 + 61$$

where

   P = profit in thousands of dollars

   x_1 = number of units of type 1 bells in thousands

   x_2 = number of units of type 2 bells in thousands.

Because of other commitments over the next two weeks, Jingle Bells has available only 60 hours in the shipping and packaging department to get the order out. It is estimated that every 1000 units of type 1 bells will require 20 hours in the shipping and packaging department and every 1000 units of type 2 bells will require 30 hours. Given the above information, how many of each type of bell should Jingle Bells produce in order to maximize profit?

17. Through regression analysis a firm has learned that total profit (P) as a function of the number of units of two products manufactured is given by the following function:

$$-x_1^2 - 4x_2^2 + 6x_1 + 16x_2 + 500$$

   where x_1 = thousands of units of product 1

             x_2 = thousands of units of product 2.

The number of units of each product that can be produced in the next planning period is constrained by the fact that there is only 12,000 pounds of an ingredient that is used in the production of both products available. Both products required 2 pounds of the ingredient per unit produced.

   a. Develop a mathematical model that can be used to determine how many units of each product to manufacture in the next planning period.
   b. Solve the mathematical model to determine how many units of x_1 and x_2 should be produced in order to maximize profit.
   c. How much would you expect profit to increase if one extra pound of the scarce ingredient became available?

Chapter 19

Management Science And Decision Support Systems

In previous chapters of this text we have emphasized how the mathematical models of management science can be used to aid or support the decision-making process. Computer-based information systems is a field that has grown and developed simultaneously with management science. People working in this area state that an objective of information systems is to support the decision-making process. Thus providing decision support capabilities is a common objective of the work of the management scientist and the information systems specialist. Jim Scott, a manager in Procter & Gamble's Management Systems Division, points to a combined role of management science and information systems by stating, "We in information systems are finding the application of management science skills vital to accomplishment of our jobs as they exist today, and the application of their approach is providing an important change for our work in the future."[1]

The purpose of this chapter is to briefly explore the area of overlap between management science and information systems. We begin by providing a brief overview of the types of computer-based information systems in use today. Then we focus our attention on the type of information system that has recently been receiving considerable publicity: a decision support system. This type of information system frequently makes use of the models developed in this text and as a result is a system that can require the joint efforts of management scientists and information systems specialists. An application of a decision support system for truck fleet scheduling is described at the end of the chapter.

19.1 Computer-Based Information Systems

In order to be effective, managers need accurate and timely information which can be used as a basis for decision making. Just as a production manager needs the latest and best possible product demand forecast information in order to prepare a production schedule, a stockbroker needs good up-to-date information on stock market behavior in order to make buy and sell decisions. Virtually any system designed to provide such information can be called an *information system*. Simply stated, an information system is any system designed to collect, organize, process, and/or analyze data to provide the information management needs to make decisions. Figure 19.1 shows the information system process of transforming data into decision-making information.

Figure 19.1 The Information Systems Process

[1]Scott, Jim, "The Management Science Opportunity: A Systems Development Management Viewpoint," at the Society for Management Information Systems Annual Conference, Washington, D.C., September 1978.

In any information system, it is essential that data be captured and transformed in a timely manner so that critical information can be available to managers when needed. There have been, and still are, information systems that do not make use of the computer. However, the time demands for information, coupled with the sheer volume of data and information needed, have tended to make the computer an essential feature of most information systems. When a computer is the primary mechanism for collecting, organizing, processing, and/or analyzing data, we have a *computer-based information system.*

A key component of any computer-based information system is the data base, an organized collection of all data that can be accessed by the information system. Thus we could describe the purpose of an information system as transforming the data contained in a data base into useful information.

Among professionals in the field, there is as yet no generally accepted classification scheme for computer-based information systems. However, three types of system have emerged as the focus of much discussion: the Transaction Processing System, the Management Information System, and the Decision Support System. Moore and Chang[2] describe these three systems as follows:

1. *Transaction Processing System* (TPS)—pure data-processing programs for gathering, updating, and posting information according to predefined procedures. Examples include a basic payroll system or an order processing system;

2. *Management Information System* (MIS)—a system with predefined aggregation and reporting capabilities, often built upon a TPS. Examples are a payroll system with managerial reports, such as a labor distribution summary;

3. *Decision Support System* (DSS)—an extensible system with intrinsic capability to support ad hoc data analysis and reduction, as well as decision modeling activities. For example, a general ledger based planning system with both preformated and user-defined reports (loosely interpreted as models).

Transaction processing systems were used for the first types of computer application in business. These data-processing systems are devoted to routine tasks encountered in daily business operations. An example of this kind of system would be one that processes sales transactions. Such a system might be *on line* (i.e., under direct control of the computer), so that when a sale is entered into the cash register the inventory level for the item sold is automatically reduced. Other transaction processing systems are used for updating accounts receivable, accounts payable, and so on. Generally,

[2]Moore, Jeffery H., and Michael G. Chang, "Design of Decision Support Systems," *Data Base,* September/November 1980, pp. 8–14.

transaction processing systems do not directly provide decision-making information. As a result, TPS's are often referred to as electronic data-processing (EDP) systems rather than management information systems.

A key distinction between a transaction processing system and a management information system (MIS) is that an MIS is an organizational information system that supports not only operations but also management processes.[3] Management information systems often are built with transaction processing systems as components. For example, periodically an inventory status file which is routinely updated by a TPS can be scanned and a report prepared listing items with low inventory levels. A report showing the low inventory items would keep management informed of inventory needs and provide information necessary to assist managers in making purchase/reordering decisions. Such a system would be a management information system.

Management information systems tend to be report-oriented. They may provide periodic and exception reports on such things as inventory status, accounts receivable status, cost variances, etc. Another common use of an MIS is to respond to queries. Two examples of this type of use are airline reservation systems and the QUOTRON system which provides timely information concerning stock prices, price–earnings ratios, etc. In both instances, the queries provide managers with current status information which is essential for effective management.

In the introduction to this chapter we cited Procter & Gamble's Jim Scott as stating that the approaches of management science are beginning to have more of an impact on information system development. Scott was referring to the role the methods of management science play in the development of decision support systems. In the next section we discuss decision support systems in more detail and examine the role of management science in their development.

19.2   Decision Support Systems

A decision support system is a computer-based information system designed to provide support to a decision process. According to Donovan, "Traditional intuitive methods of decision making are no longer adequate to deal with the complex problems faced by the modern policymaker. Thus systems must be developed to provide the information and analysis necessary for the decisions to be made. These systems are called decision support systems."[4] Alter[5] states that the principal tenets of the decision support systems approach are as follows:

---

[3]Davis, Gordon B., *Management Information Systems: Conceptual Foundations, Structure and Development,* New York, McGraw-Hill Book Co., 1974.
[4]Donovan, J.J., "Database System Approach to Management Decision Support," ACM Transactions on Database Systems, Vol. 1, No. 4, December 1976, pp. 344–369.
[5]Alter, Steven, *Decision Support Systems: Current Practice and Continuing Challenges,* Reading, Mass., Addison-Wesley, 1980.

These systems can be designed specifically to facilitate decision processes (as opposed to making clerical transaction processing more efficient);

These systems should support rather than automate decision making; and

These systems should be able to respond quickly to the changing needs of decision makers.

Alter points out that the focus of decision support systems is on improving individual effectiveness by improving personal efficiency, expediting problem solving, and improving organizational communications.

Key features often found in DSS's are

1. Interactive capability,
2. Continually evolving design as users discover new applications for the system, and
3. System is used for semistructured and unstructured problems.

A Classification of Decision Support Systems

The classification schemes that have been proposed for decision support systems parallel previous efforts from studies of decision making in general. The following are illustrative of the possible classifications:

1. By function area (we could refer to a DSS for marketing, a DSS for finance, and so on);
2. By level of management involvement (for example, a DSS for strategic planning, a DSS for operational control, and so on);
3. Type of problem (does the DSS support highly structured problems [as in simple inventory control systems] or unstructured types of problems [as in where to locate a new warehouse or plant])
4. Type of computer system (a large on-line, real-time system versus a network of small minicomputers or microprocessors);
5. Orientation of the system (is the DSS data-oriented or model-oriented?).

It is not surprising, then, that decision support systems take on a variety of forms. In some cases the DSS will contain a mathematical model that provides a decision maker with recommended courses of action—for example, a large-scale linear programming system designed to be used as a decision aid for production scheduling. In other cases, the decision support system may involve a sophisticated computer hardware/software system that simply provides easy and rapid access to decision-making information contained in the data base.

Many of the applications provided at the end of selected chapters of this text describe systems that can be called decision support systems. In particular, the application presented at the end of this chapter describes a decision support system used to schedule a fleet of trucks. The initial objective in this application was to develop a system for determining the optimal fleet size, the number of shifts required, and the number of drivers necessary. Although the system was used for these purposes, it is now being used by a dispatcher for making daily truck scheduling and routing decisions. We note that several of the key features previously mentioned are present in this DSS for truck scheduling. The design evolved as new uses were discovered for the system (from fleet sizing to routing trucks). The system has an interactive capability. The dispatcher usually makes modifications in the model solution and iterates through two or three model solutions before the daily schedule is finalized. The problem is semistructured. There is a minimum-cost performance criterion, but other considerations, such as balancing workload among drivers, assigning high priority loads to company trucks, and so on, cause the problem to lose some of its simple structure.

Keen and Morton[6] describe a DSS to assist portfolio managers. The system is called Portfolio Management System (PMS) and was initially designed by T.P. Gerrity.[7] PMS is a decision support system designed for use by investment managers in the trust departments of banks. It is an interactive system that is designed to provide decision-making support for managing portfolios.

A command language is provided with PMS to assist portfolio managers in interacting with the system. Some of the capabilities of the DSS are as follows:

1. The user can request a display of the contents of a portfolio.
2. Portfolio values and other information, such as price–earnings ratios, etc., can be requested.
3. Graphs and figures can be constructed.
4. Portfolios satisfying certain conditions can be identified.
5. Hypothetical portfolios can be created and evaluated.

The PMS is an example of a DSS for an unstructured problem. No recommended solutions (such as with the DSS for truck fleet scheduling) are presented. In fact, it isn't clear what problem the system is assisting in solving. In general, it is designed to help with the portfolio management process, but there are no specific criteria. Indeed, a variety of uses have been found for the system with different managers selecting different uses. Some found the system an aid in making cash management decisions, while others found it most helpful in providing a variety of information for interacting with customers.

Weak Versus Strong DSS Designs

Moore and Chang[8] describe a weak versus strong dimension for DSS design in terms of how much influence the system exerts on the decision process of the user:

[6]Keen, Peter G.W., and Michael S. Scott Morton, *Decision Support Systems: An Organizational Perspective,* Reading, Mass., Addison-Wesley, 1978.
[7]Gerrity, T.P., Jr., "The Design of Man-Machine Decision Systems: An Application to Portfolio Management," *Sloan Management Review,* Vol. 12, No. 2, 1971, pp. 59–75.
[8]Moore, Jeffrey H., Chang, Michael G., "Design of Decision Support Systems," *Data Base,* September/November 1980, pp. 8–14.

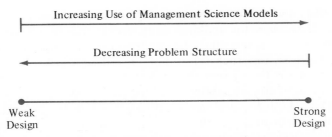

Figure 19.2   Interaction between Use of Management Science Models and Problem Structure on Weak-Strong Design Dimension

1. A stronger design is appropriate in a situation where more effective decision making is required but the user is passively resistant to changes in the decision-making process demanded by the client, . . .
2. A weak design is appropriate whenever the client elects not to influence the user's decision-making style. In such cases, the system design may either degenerate into an information-retrieval and -control system (higher efficiency), or else, in the case of a self-motivated user, may expand into a sophisticated support system for improved decision making (higher efficiency).

Clearly the DSS for truck fleet scheduling has the characteristics of a strong design. The dispatcher is required to choose from among solutions satisfying a minimum-cost criterion. Of course, the dispatcher does have some latitude for interacting and rerunning the model. The DSS for portfolio management, PMS, is at the weak end of the spectrum. Information is provided to support the manager's decision process, but the system does not suggest solutions to the user.

Decision support systems that make use of management science models tend to fall on the stronger end of this design dimension. While such systems do not replace the judgment of the decision maker, they do force more structure on the problem by the introduction of performance criteria. This is, of course, good if it is desired to influence the decision process so that better decisions can be made. On the other hand, one would prefer a weaker design in cases where performance criteria are not clear and problem definition is vague. All that we can hope for is to provide better support for the decision maker and rely on that person's judgment to develop alternatives and select solutions. Figure 19.2 shows the interaction between problem structure and use of management science models on the weak–strong design dimension. Several additional examples of decision support systems currently in use are shown in Table 19.1.

19.3   Management Science in Decision Support Systems

The purpose of this text is to provide students with a sound conceptual understanding of the role that management science plays in the decision-making process—specifically, that portion of management science dealing

TABLE 19.1   Examples of Current Decision Support Systems

Organization	Nature of Decision Support System
Goodyear Tire & Rubber Co.	Scheduling maintenance personnel
Equitable Life Assurance	Assist underwriters in calculating renewal rates on group life insurance policies
American Airlines	Analyzing performance trends from historical data
Kroger	Retail store performance model
Xerox	System for evaluating service technicians
Marathon Oil Company	Market planning model

with quantitative approaches to decision making. As you have seen, the emphasis has been on management science models and how they can be used to contribute to the decision-making process. In this regard, the most important purpose of management science is to support managerial decision making by improving the quality of the information made available to an organization's managers. Thus to a great extent the reason for using management science models and the objective of decision support systems are the same.

As we have seen, not all decision support systems make use of the mathematical models of management science. But many DSS's are based heavily on the mathematical models and solution procedures developed by management scientists. The DSS for truck fleet scheduling in the application at the end of this chapter makes extensive use of management science models. The same is true of the decision support system described in the application at the end of Chapter 8, which makes use of a mixed integer programming model to assign customer orders to sources of supply. DSS's which do make use of mathematical models are the ones with a stronger design in the sense of Moore and Chang. Thus we can expect them to have a significant influence on the user's decision process.

Decision support systems are showing promise of being a vehicle for integrating the efforts of management scientists and information system specialists. The potential exists for decision support systems to have a major impact on future managerial decision processes. We are enthusiastic about this potential and anticipate a larger combined role for management science and computer-based information systems in the organizations of the future.

Summary

In this chapter we discussed the relationship between management science and computer-based information systems. First, we presented a brief overview of the types of computer based information systems in use today. Then, we focused our attention on one information system that has received considerable recent attention: a decision support system. Finally, we discussed how a greater integration of management science and decision support systems concepts can offer the potential for an improved decision-making process.

Glossary

1. *Information system*—Any system designed to collect, organize, process, and/or analyze data to provide the information management needs to make decisions.
2. *Computer-based information system*—An information system making use of a computer for collecting, organizing, processing, and/or analyzing data.
3. *Data base*—An organized collection of data.
4. *Transaction processing system (TPS)*—A computer-based system utilizing data processing programs for gathering, updating, and posting information according to predefined procedures.
5. *Management information system (MIS)*—A computer-based information system with predefined aggregation and reporting capabilities, often built upon a TPS.
6. *Decision support system (DSS)*—An extensible computer-based information system with intrinsic capability to support ad hoc data analysis and reduction, as well as decision modeling activities.
7. *On line*—A component of a computer system is said to be on line if it is under the direct control of the computer. When the user has the ability to interact directly with the computer, we say the user is on line.

Optimal Decision Systems, Inc. *

Cincinnati, Ohio

Optimal Decision Systems, Inc. (ODS) is a management consulting firm which specializes in the development and implementation of decision support systems for manufacturing, transportation, and distribution applications. ODS was formed in 1978 and has a clientele which includes several Fortune 500 companies.

Systems developed by ODS use computerized models to provide managers with a menu of "good" alternatives from which the "best" alternative can be selected. Several examples of the types of problems for which ODS has developed decision support systems are listed below:

1. Locating manufacturing and distribution facilities;
2. Designing sales territories, including how various distribution centers should supply the territories;
3. Routing and scheduling of truck fleets;
4. Scheduling production systems to minimize inventory costs while maintaining desired service levels;
5. Allocating capital to various investment opportunities.

The majority of these decision support systems (80%) have involved the development and implementation of large-scale mathematical programming models (linear programming, network, or mixed integer linear programming models). Probability models and simulation have been the primary quantitative methodologies employed in the remaining applications. In addition, in almost every application, statistical analysis has played a heavy support role, particularly in the estimation of the parameters of the models.

Decision Support System for Truck Fleet Scheduling

A large food processing firm was faced with the problem of effectively utilizing its fleet of trucks. Management was particularly concerned that the

*The authors are indebted to Richard Murphy, president of Optimal Decision Systems, Inc., for providing this application.

ineffective utilization of the company fleet was causing the cost of using common carriers to be too high. The company wanted a system that could be used to determine the optimal size of the company fleet, the number of shifts and drivers necessary, and so on. ODS undertook to build such a system.

During the course of developing the fleet sizing system, it became clear that the system, properly modified, could be used by the dispatchers for scheduling trucks. The company's 13 plants were located within 4 hours' transit time of one another. Under a manual dispatching system, three dispatchers developed a daily schedule for the fleet of trucks. Loads or shipments not moved by the company's fleet were moved by one of several local common carrier trucking companies. Management was convinced that the inefficiencies of the manual dispatching system were a major factor in the excessive cost of common carriers.

ODS consultants met with the distribution manager of the food processing firm and discussed the issues involved with the scheduling of the fleet. This discussion revealed that management wanted a method for daily scheduling which would maximize the savings generated by an improved utilization of the company's fleet. The approach suggested by ODS involved the development of a network model of the trucking operation.

The network developed by ODS models the flow of trucks during each 8-hour shift. Each truck begins the shift at the central warehouse and is routed between the various plants making pickups and deliveries. Trucks are not permitted to pick up a load which cannot be delivered by the end of the 8-hour shift because all plant receiving docks close at the end of the eighth hour. If necessary, a truck may operate beyond the 8-hour shift in order to return to the central warehouse. In this case, the driver is paid an overtime rate.

The network model was implemented as part of an interactive decision support system. The scheduling process begins with the DSS generating a schedule and displaying it on a cathode ray tube (CRT). The schedule presented on the CRT shows the complete assignment of all drivers to all loads (at the various plants) for the day's operation. The dispatcher (system user) reviews this solution and then makes modifications to the daily model, based on a variety of factors. High priority loads that have been assigned to common carriers may be reassigned to company trucks. Loads may be switched to accommodate driver preferences. The dispatcher tries to balance driver workloads; if a driver has a difficult assignment one day, the dispatcher tries not to give that driver a heavy load the next day. The dispatcher might also, after consulting the plants, assign different pickup times in hopes of improving the schedule.

After the dispatcher has modified the network model to accommodate the above considerations, a new solution is generated by the DSS. The new solution is displayed on the CRT, and the dispatcher reviews it to see if any further modifications are necessary. When the dispatcher is satisfied, the process is terminated and the schedule implemented. Experience with the DSS has shown that usually two or three iterations are required before the dispatcher is satisfied with the schedule. Figure 1 depicts the use of this decision support system by the dispatcher.

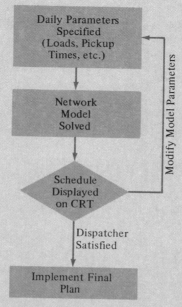

Figure 1   Decision Support System for Truck Fleet Scheduling

The decision support system developed by ODS is now being used by the company on a daily basis. This system is used to generate daily schedules for the truck fleet which provide an increase in the productivity of the fleet and a reduction in the need for common carriers. The improved schedules have increased the productivity of the fleet 28% in terms of the total number of loads transported during an 8-hour shift. The cost of using common carriers has been reduced by $1500 per day. At the same time, the new system can be managed by one rather than three dispatchers.

In addition to the sizable savings in the day-to-day operating cost for the firm, management was able to experiment with the model and project consequences in performance and cost for an enlarged company fleet. Information provided by the decision support system justified a significant expansion in the firm's trucking operation, which further reduced the need for the outside carriers.

The decision support systems developed by Optimal Decision Systems make extensive use of the management science models presented in this text. The models are an integral part of the decision support systems.

Appendices

Appendix A   Areas for the Standard Normal Distribution

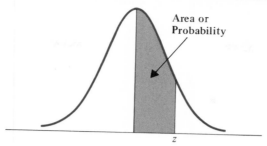

Entries in the table give the area under the curve between the mean and z standard deviations above the mean. For example, for $z = 1.25$ the area under the curve between the mean and z is 0.3944.

z	0.00	0.01	0.02	0.03	0.04	0.05	0.06	0.07	0.08	0.09
0.0	0.0000	0.0040	0.0080	0.0120	0.0160	0.0199	0.0239	0.0279	0.0319	0.0359
0.1	0.0398	0.0438	0.0478	0.0517	0.0557	0.0596	0.0636	0.0675	0.0714	0.0753
0.2	0.0793	0.0832	0.0871	0.0910	0.0948	0.0987	0.1026	0.1064	0.1103	0.1141
0.3	0.1179	0.1217	0.1255	0.1293	0.1331	0.1368	0.1406	0.1443	0.1480	0.1517
0.4	0.1554	0.1591	0.1628	0.1664	0.1700	0.1736	0.1772	0.1808	0.1844	0.1879
0.5	0.1915	0.1950	0.1985	0.2019	0.2054	0.2088	0.2123	0.2157	0.2190	0.2224
0.6	0.2257	0.2291	0.2324	0.2357	0.2389	0.2422	0.2454	0.2486	0.2518	0.2549
0.7	0.2580	0.2612	0.2642	0.2673	0.2704	0.2734	0.2764	0.2794	0.2823	0.2852
0.8	0.2881	0.2910	0.2939	0.2967	0.2995	0.3023	0.3051	0.3078	0.3106	0.3133
0.9	0.3159	0.3186	0.3212	0.3238	0.3264	0.3289	0.3315	0.3340	0.3365	0.3389
1.0	0.3413	0.3438	0.3461	0.3485	0.3508	0.3531	0.3554	0.3577	0.3599	0.3621
1.1	0.3643	0.3665	0.3686	0.3708	0.3729	0.3749	0.3770	0.3790	0.3810	0.3830
1.2	0.3849	0.3869	0.3888	0.3907	0.3925	0.3944	0.3962	0.3980	0.3997	0.4015
1.3	0.4032	0.4049	0.4066	0.4082	0.4099	0.4115	0.4131	0.4147	0.4162	0.4177
1.4	0.4192	0.4207	0.4222	0.4236	0.4251	0.4265	0.4279	0.4292	0.4306	0.4319
1.5	0.4332	0.4345	0.4357	0.4370	0.4382	0.4394	0.4406	0.4418	0.4429	0.4441
1.6	0.4452	0.4463	0.4474	0.4484	0.4495	0.4505	0.4515	0.4525	0.4535	0.4545
1.7	0.4554	0.4564	0.4573	0.4582	0.4591	0.4599	0.4608	0.4616	0.4625	0.4633
1.8	0.4641	0.4649	0.4656	0.4664	0.4671	0.4678	0.4686	0.4693	0.4699	0.4706
1.9	0.4713	0.4719	0.4726	0.4732	0.4738	0.4744	0.4750	0.4756	0.4761	0.4767
2.0	0.4772	0.4778	0.4783	0.4788	0.4793	0.4798	0.4803	0.4808	0.4812	0.4817
2.1	0.4821	0.4826	0.4830	0.4834	0.4838	0.4842	0.4846	0.4850	0.4854	0.4857
2.2	0.4861	0.4864	0.4868	0.4871	0.4875	0.4878	0.4881	0.4884	0.4887	0.4890
2.3	0.4893	0.4896	0.4898	0.4901	0.4904	0.4906	0.4909	0.4911	0.4913	0.4916
2.4	0.4918	0.4920	0.4922	0.4925	0.4927	0.4929	0.4931	0.4932	0.4934	0.4936
2.5	0.4938	0.4940	0.4941	0.4943	0.4945	0.4946	0.4948	0.4949	0.4951	0.4952
2.6	0.4953	0.4955	0.4956	0.4957	0.4959	0.4960	0.4961	0.4962	0.4963	0.4964
2.7	0.4965	0.4966	0.4967	0.4968	0.4969	0.4970	0.4971	0.4972	0.4973	0.4974
2.8	0.4974	0.4975	0.4976	0.4977	0.4977	0.4978	0.4979	0.4979	0.4980	0.4981
2.9	0.4981	0.4982	0.4982	0.4983	0.4984	0.4984	0.4985	0.4985	0.4986	0.4986
3.0	0.4986	0.4987	0.4987	0.4988	0.4988	0.4989	0.4989	0.4989	0.4990	0.4990

Appendix B   Random Digits

63271	59986	71744	51102	15141	80714	58683	93108	13554	79945
88547	09896	95436	79115	08303	01041	20030	63754	08459	28364
55957	57243	83865	09911	19761	66535	40102	26646	60147	15702
46276	87453	44790	67122	45573	84358	21625	16999	13385	22782
55363	07449	34835	15290	76616	67191	12777	21861	68689	03263
69393	92785	49902	58447	42048	30378	87618	26933	40640	16281
13186	29431	88190	04588	38733	81290	89541	70290	40113	08243
17726	28652	56836	78351	47327	18518	92222	55201	27340	10493
36520	64465	05550	30157	82242	29520	69753	72602	23756	54935
81628	36100	39254	56835	37636	02421	98063	89641	64953	99337
84649	48968	75215	75498	49539	74240	03466	49292	36401	45525
63291	11618	12613	75055	43915	26488	41116	64531	56827	30825
70502	53225	03655	05915	37140	57051	48393	91322	25653	06543
06426	24771	59935	49801	11082	66762	94477	02494	88215	27191
20711	55609	29430	70165	45406	78484	31639	52009	18873	96927
41990	70538	77191	25860	55204	73417	83920	69468	74972	38712
72452	36618	76298	26678	89334	33938	95567	29380	75906	91807
37042	40318	57099	10528	09925	89773	41335	96244	29002	46453
53766	52875	15987	46962	67342	77592	57651	95508	80033	69828
90585	58955	53122	16025	84299	53310	67380	84249	25348	04332
32001	96293	37203	64516	51530	37069	40261	61374	05815	06714
62606	64324	46354	72157	67248	20135	49804	09226	64419	29457
10078	28073	85389	50324	14500	15562	64165	06125	71353	77669
91561	46145	24177	15294	10061	98124	75732	00815	83452	97355
13091	98112	53959	79607	52244	63303	10413	63839	74762	50289
73864	83014	72457	22682	03033	61714	88173	90835	00634	85169
66668	25467	48894	51043	02365	91726	09365	63167	95264	45643
84745	41042	29493	01836	09044	51926	43630	63470	76508	14194
48068	26805	94595	47907	13357	38412	33318	26098	82782	42851
54310	96175	97594	88616	42035	38093	36745	56702	40644	83514
14877	33095	10924	58013	61439	21882	42059	24177	58739	60170
78295	23179	02771	43464	59061	71411	05697	67194	30495	21157
67524	02865	39593	54278	04237	92441	26602	63835	38032	94770
58268	57219	68124	73455	83236	08710	04284	55005	84171	42596
97158	28672	50685	01181	24262	19427	52106	34308	73685	74246
04230	16831	69085	30802	65559	09205	71829	06489	85650	38707
94879	56606	30401	02602	57658	70091	54986	41394	60437	03195
71446	15232	66715	26385	91518	70566	02888	79941	39684	54315
32886	05644	79316	09819	00813	88407	17461	73925	53037	91904
62048	33711	25290	21526	02223	75947	66466	06232	10913	75336

This table is reproduced with permission from The Rand Corporation, *A Million Random Digits,* The Free Press, New York, 1955.

Appendix C   Values of $e^{-\lambda}$

λ	$e^{-\lambda}$	λ	$e^{-\lambda}$
0.0	1.0000	3.3	0.0369
0.1	0.9048	3.4	0.0334
0.2	0.8187	3.5	0.0302
0.3	0.7408	3.6	0.0273
0.4	0.6703	3.7	0.0247
0.5	0.6065	3.8	0.0224
0.6	0.5488	3.9	0.0202
0.7	0.4966	4.0	0.0183
0.8	0.4493	4.1	0.0166
0.9	0.4066	4.2	0.0150
1.0	0.3679	4.3	0.0136
1.1	0.3329	4.4	0.0123
1.2	0.3012	4.5	0.0111
1.3	0.2725	4.6	0.0101
1.4	0.2466	4.7	0.0091
1.5	0.2231	4.8	0.0082
1.6	0.2019	4.9	0.0074
1.7	0.1827	5.0	0.0067
1.8	0.1653	5.1	0.0061
1.9	0.1496	5.2	0.0055
2.0	0.1353	5.3	0.0050
2.1	0.1225	5.4	0.0045
2.2	0.1108	5.5	0.0041
2.3	0.1003	5.6	0.0037
2.4	0.0907	5.7	0.0033
2.5	0.0821	5.8	0.0030
2.6	0.0743	5.9	0.0027
2.7	0.0672	6.0	0.0025
2.8	0.0608	7.0	0.0009
2.9	0.0550	8.0	0.000335
3.0	0.0498	9.0	0.000123
3.1	0.0450	10.0	0.000045
3.2	0.0408		

Appendix D   A Short Table of Derivatives

1. $\dfrac{d(c)}{dx} = 0$ (where c is a constant)

2. $\dfrac{d(x^n)}{dx} = nx^{n-1}$

3. $\dfrac{d(cu)}{dx} = c\dfrac{du}{dx}$

4. $\dfrac{d(u+v)}{dx} = \dfrac{du}{dx} + \dfrac{dv}{dx}$

5. $\dfrac{d(uv)}{dx} = u\dfrac{dv}{dx} + v\dfrac{du}{dx}$

6. $\dfrac{d(u^n)}{dx} = nu^{n-1}\dfrac{du}{dx}$

7. $\dfrac{d\left(\dfrac{u}{v}\right)}{dx} = \dfrac{v\dfrac{du}{dx} - u\dfrac{dv}{dx}}{v^2}$

8. $\dfrac{d(\ln x)}{dx} = \dfrac{1}{x}$

9. $\dfrac{d(e^x)}{dx} = e^x$

10. $\dfrac{d(\ln u)}{dx} = \dfrac{1}{u}\dfrac{du}{dx}$

11. $\dfrac{d(e^u)}{dx} = e^u\dfrac{du}{dx}$

Appendix E   Matrix Notation and Operations

Matrix Notation

We define a matrix to be a rectangular arrangement of numbers. For example, the following arrangement of numbers is a matrix D:

$$D = \begin{bmatrix} 1 & 3 & 2 \\ 0 & 4 & 5 \end{bmatrix}.$$

The matrix D is said to consist of six elements, where each element of D is a number. In order to identify a particular element of a matrix, we have to specify its precise location. To do this, we introduce the notion of rows and columns.

All elements across some horizontal line in a matrix are said to be in a row of the matrix. For example, elements 1, 3, and 2 in matrix D are in the first row of D, and elements 0, 4, and 5 are in the second row of D. Thus we see that D is a matrix that has two rows. By convention, we always refer to the top row as row 1, the second row from the top as row 2, and so on.

All elements along some vertical line are said to belong to a column of the matrix. Elements 1 and 0 in matrix D are elements in the first column of D, elements 3 and 4 are elements of the second column, and elements 2 and 5 are elements of the third column. Thus we see that matrix D has three columns. By convention, we always refer to the leftmost column as column 1, the next column to the right as column 2, and so on.

An easy way to identify a particular element in a matrix is to specify its row and column position. For example, the element in row 1 and column 2 of matrix D is the number 3. This is written as

$$d_{12} = 3$$

In general we use the following notation to refer to specific elements of the matrix D:

d_{ij} = element located in the ith row and jth column of D.

We always use capital letters for the names of matrices and the corresponding lowercase versions of the same letter with two subscripts to denote the elements.

The *size* of a matrix is defined to be the number of rows and columns in the matrix and is written as the number of rows $\times$ the number of columns. Thus the size of matrix D above is 2×3.

Frequently we will encounter matrices that have only one row or one column. For example,

$$G = \begin{bmatrix} 6 \\ 4 \\ 2 \\ 3 \end{bmatrix}$$

is a matrix that has only one column. Whenever we have a matrix that has only one column like G, we call the matrix a column vector. In a similar manner, any matrix that has only one row is called a row vector. Using our previous notation for elements of a matrix, we could refer to specific elements in G by writing g_{ij}. However, since G has only one column, the column position is unimportant, and we need only specify the row the element of interest is in. That is, instead of referring to elements in a vector using g_{ij}, we specify only one subscript which denotes the position of the element in the vector. For example,

$$g_1 = 6, \qquad g_2 = 4, \qquad g_3 = 2, \qquad g_4 = 3.$$

Matrix Operations

Matrix Transpose

Given any matrix, we can form the transpose of the matrix by making the rows in the original matrix the columns in the tranpose matrix, and by making the columns in the original matrix the rows in the transpose matrix. For example, if we take the transpose of the matrix

$$D = \begin{bmatrix} 1 & 3 & 2 \\ 0 & 4 & 5 \end{bmatrix},$$

we get

$$D^t = \begin{bmatrix} 1 & 0 \\ 3 & 4 \\ 2 & 5 \end{bmatrix}.$$

Note that we use the superscript t to denote the transpose of a matrix.

Matrix Multiplication

We will demonstrate how to perform two types of matrix multiplication: (1) how to multiply two vectors, and (2) how to multiply a matrix times a matrix.

The product of a row vector of size $1 \times n$ times a column vector of size $n \times 1$ is the number obtained by multiplying the first element in the row vector times the first element in the column vector, the second element in the row vector times the second element in the column vector, and continuing on through the last element in the row vector times the last element in the column vector, and then summing the products. Suppose, for example, that we wanted to multiply the row vector H times the column vector G, where

$$H = \begin{bmatrix} 2 & 1 & 5 & 0 \end{bmatrix} \quad \text{and} \quad G = \begin{bmatrix} 6 \\ 4 \\ 2 \\ 3 \end{bmatrix}.$$

The product HG is given by

$$HG = 2(6) + 1(4) + 5(2) + 0(3) = 26.$$

The product of a matrix of size $p \times n$ and a matrix of size $n \times m$ is a new matrix of size $p \times m$. The element in the ith row and jth column of the new matrix is given by the vector product of the ith row of the $p \times n$ matrix times the jth column of the $n \times m$ matrix. Suppose, for example, that we want to multiply D times A, where

$$D = \begin{bmatrix} 1 & 3 & 2 \\ 0 & 4 & 5 \end{bmatrix}, \qquad A = \begin{bmatrix} 1 & 3 & 5 \\ 2 & 0 & 4 \\ 1 & 5 & 2 \end{bmatrix}.$$

Let us denote by $C = DA$ the product of D times A. The element in row 1 and column 1 of C is given by the vector product of the first row of D times the first column of A. Thus we get

$$c_{11} = \begin{bmatrix} 1 & 3 & 2 \end{bmatrix} \begin{bmatrix} 1 \\ 2 \\ 1 \end{bmatrix} = 1(1) + 3(2) + 2(1) = 9.$$

The element in row 2 and column 1 of C is given by the vector product of the second row of D times the first column of A. Thus we get

$$c_{21} = \begin{bmatrix} 0 & 4 & 5 \end{bmatrix} \begin{bmatrix} 1 \\ 2 \\ 1 \end{bmatrix} = 0(1) + 4(2) + 5(1) = 13.$$

Calculating the remaining elements of C in a similar fashion, we obtain

$$C = \begin{bmatrix} 9 & 13 & 21 \\ 13 & 25 & 26 \end{bmatrix}$$

Clearly the product of a matrix and a vector is just a special case of multiplying a matrix times a matrix. For example, the product of a matrix of size $m \times n$ and a vector of size $n \times 1$ is a new vector of size $m \times 1$. The element in the ith position of the new vector is given by the vector product of the ith row of the $m \times n$ matrix times the $m \times 1$ column vector. Suppose, for example, that we want to multiply D times k, where

$$D = \begin{bmatrix} 1 & 3 & 2 \\ 0 & 4 & 5 \end{bmatrix}, \qquad k = \begin{bmatrix} 1 \\ 4 \\ 2 \end{bmatrix}.$$

The first element of Dk is given by the vector product of the first row of D times k. Thus we get

$$\begin{bmatrix} 1 & 3 & 2 \end{bmatrix} \begin{bmatrix} 1 \\ 4 \\ 2 \end{bmatrix} = 1(1) + 3(4) + 2(2) = 17.$$

The second element of Dk is given by the vector product of the second row of D and k. Thus we get

$$[0 \quad 4 \quad 5] \begin{bmatrix} 1 \\ 4 \\ 2 \end{bmatrix} = 0(1) + 4(4) + 5(2) = 26.$$

Hence we see that the product of the matrix D times the vector k is given by

$$Dk = \begin{bmatrix} 1 & 3 & 2 \\ 0 & 4 & 5 \end{bmatrix} \begin{bmatrix} 1 \\ 4 \\ 2 \end{bmatrix} = \begin{bmatrix} 17 \\ 26 \end{bmatrix}.$$

Can any two matrices be multiplied? The answer is no. In order to multiply two matrices, the number of the columns in the first matrix must equal the number of rows in the second. If this property is satisfied, the matrices are said to conform for multiplication. Thus in our example D and k could be multiplied because D had three columns and k had three rows.

Matrix Inverse

The inverse, denoted by A^{-1}, of any square matrix A consisting of two rows and two columns is computed as follows:

$$A = \begin{bmatrix} a_{11} & a_{12} \\ a_{21} & a_{22} \end{bmatrix}$$

$$A^{-1} = \begin{bmatrix} a_{22}/d & -a_{12}/d \\ -a_{21}/d & a_{11}/d \end{bmatrix}$$

where $d = a_{11}a_{22} - a_{21}a_{12}$ is the determinant of the 2×2 matrix A. For example, if

$$A = \begin{bmatrix} 0.7 & -0.3 \\ -0.3 & 0.9 \end{bmatrix}$$

then

$$d = (0.7)(0.9) - (-0.3)(-0.3) = 0.54$$

and

$$A^{-1} = \begin{bmatrix} 0.9/0.54 & 0.3/0.54 \\ 0.3/0.54 & 0.7/0.54 \end{bmatrix} = \begin{bmatrix} 1.67 & 0.56 \\ 0.56 & 1.30 \end{bmatrix}.$$

Answers
To
Even
Numbered
Problems

Chapter 1

2. See section 1.3
4. Problem definition; model development; data preparation; model solution; report generation
6. Models usually have time, cost, and risk advantages over experimenting with actual situations
8. Deterministic
10. a. Total units received $= x + y$
    b. Total cost $= 0.20x + 0.25y$
    c. $x + y = 5000$
    d. $x \leq 4000; y \leq 3000$
    e. min $0.20x + 0.25y$
       s.t.
$$\begin{aligned} x + \quad y &= 5000 \\ x \quad\quad &\leq 4000 \\ y &\leq 3000 \\ x, y &\geq 0 \end{aligned}$$
12. a. At \$20, $D = 600$
       At \$70, $D = 100$
    b. TR $= Dp = 800p - 10p^2$
    c. At \$30, TR $= 15,000$
       At \$40, TR $= 16,000$ (revenue max)
       At \$50, TR $= 15,000$
    d. $D = 400$ units, TR $= 16,000$
14. a. Total cost $= 1000 + 10x$
    b. $p = 5x - 1000$
    c. 200 units

Chapter 2

2. a. $(3, 1.5)$
    b. $(0, 3)$
    c. 4; $(0,0)$, $(4,0)$, $(3,1.5)$, and $(0,3)$
4. a. $(300,420)$, $z = \$10,560$
    b. $(708,0)$, $z = \$14,160$
    c. Sewing constraint is redundant; no change
6. a. 500 regular model; 150 catcher's model
    b. \$3700
    c. Cutting & Sewing, 725
       Finishing, 300
       Packaging & Shipping, 100
    d. Cutting & Sewing, 175
       Finishing, 0
       Packaging & Shipping, 0
8. a. 700, 500
    b. 500, 800
10. $\frac{7}{10}x_1 + 1x_2 = 630$
    $\frac{1}{10}x_1 + \frac{1}{4}x_2 = 135$
12. 15, $\frac{5}{2}$
14. 12, 3

16. b. $x_1 = {}^{18}/_7; x_2 = {}^{15}/_7$
  c. $s_1 = 0; s_2 = 0; s_3 = {}^4/_7$
18. b. $x_1 = 6; x_2 = 4$
  c. $s_1 = 4$ (surplus); $s_2 = 0; s_3 = 0$
20. b. $(4,1); (2^1/_4, {}^9/_4)$
  c. $x_1 = 4; x_2 = 1$
22. c. $(0,0), (300,0), (300,100), (225,150), (0,150)$
  d. $(300,100)$
26. Unbounded
28. b. Yes
  c. $(3,0)$
  d. No
30. a. Infeasible
  b. Alternate optimal solutions
  c. All three constraints would have to be removed from the model
32. a. $2.5 \le c_1 \le 10$
  b. $^3/_2 \le c_2 \le 6$
34. a. Dealer preparation and number of automobiles
  b. Yes, $166.67
  c. Yes, net $146.67 per hour
  d. Excess cannot be used because other constraints become binding
36. Sewing Dept., $0
  Finishing Dept., $6.9375
  Inspection and Packaging, $0

Chapter 3

2. $x_1 = 5, x_2 = 1, x_3 = 4$
4. b. 2
  c. $x_1 = 4, x_2 = 6, s_3 = 4$
  d. $x_2 = 4, s_1 = 4, s_2 = -6$
  e. Answer to part c only
6. $x_1 = 7, x_2 = 3$
8. $x_1 = 200, x_2 = {}^{400}/_3, s_1 = {}^{500}/_3$
10. $x_2 = 650, s_1 = 690, s_3 = 310$
12. 35
14. b. No, any $c_j - z_j > 0$ will work
16. x_1 = number of units of product A; x_2 = number of units of product B; x_3 = number of units of product C; $x_1 = 0, x_2 = 0, x_3 = 33^1/_3$
18. x_1 = Gal. Heid. Sweet, x_2 = Gal. Heid. Reg, x_3 = Gal Deut.
  a. $x_1 = 0, x_2 = 50, x_3 = 75$
  c. Grade B grapes and hours
22. $x_2 = 2, x_3 = {}^1/_2, x_1 = 9$
24. $x_1 = 20$ Gal., $x_2 = 30$ Gal., $x_3 = 33$ Gal;
  $x_1 = 0, x_2 = 0, x_3 = 2400$
26.

	Incentive	Temptation
John	480	0
Brenda	0	480
Red	0	800

28.   b. $x_1 = 300$, $x_2 = 420$, $s_3 = 100$, $s_4 = 128$

      c.   Extreme point 4; binding constraints are inspection & packaging and cutting & dyeing

30.   23,333.33 bags of the regular mix; 8,333.33 bags of deluxe mix; 833.33 bags of almonds

32.   Infeasible

34.   Unbounded

36.   Degenerate

38.   150 Ridge Runners and no Fat Wheels or Toads

Alternate optima:

$$x_1 = 50, x_2 = 0, x_3 = 100$$
$$x_1 = 0, x_2 = 50, x_3 = 100$$
$$x_1 = 37.5, x_2 = 37.5, x_3 = 75$$

40.   a.   No feasible solution

      b.   1000 All-Pro, 0 College, and 250 High School

Chapter 4

2.   a.   1.875

      b.   7.5

      c.   0

4.   a. $20/3 \le c_2 \le 300/21$

      b.   No change in product mix; however, profit drops to $7,164

      c. $6.67 to $14.29

      d. $x_1 = 300$, $x_2 = 420$

6.   a.   Feasible region gets bigger

      b.   For $b_1 = 650$, $x_2 = 289.5$, $s_2 = 101.25$, $x_1 = 515$, $s_4 = 11.125$

         For $b_1 = 550$, $x_2 = 102$, $s_2 = 195$, $x_1 = 640$, $s_4 = 45.5$

8.   b.   No. s_4 would become nonbasic and s_1 would become a basic variable

10.   a.   Value of the objective function increases.

      b.   No

12.   a. $40/9 \le b_1 < \infty$

      b. $-\infty < b_2 \le 160/3$

      c. $0 \le b_3 < \infty$

18.   b.   Primal (2,3); dual ($5/4$, $1/4$)

22.   b. $u_1 = 0$, $u_2 = 0$, $u_3 = 0$, $u_4 = 5/3$, $u_5 = 10/3$

      c. $x_1 = 25$, $x_2 = 100$

24.   a. $x_1 = 4$, $x_2 = 1/2$, $x_3 = 0$

      b.   75

      c.   Row 1 and row 2

      d.   Row 3; slack = 1.5

      e.   Row 1 $7.50, row 2 $15.00, row 3 $0

      f. $12.5 \le c_1$; $20 \le c_2 \le 60$; $c_3 \le 22.5$

      g. $0 \le b_1 \le 6$; $2 \le b_2 \le 6$

26.   a. $x_1 = 1000$, $x_2 = 200$, $x_3 = 0$

      b. $4000

      c.   Sewing

      d.   CD = 4000 min, IP = 5200 min

      e.   Yes

      f.   Up to 100 hours

g. Relaxing the All-Pro constraint will add a $2 profit for each unit reduced
h. Yes, $5 \leq c_2$
i. Alternate optimal solution exists

Chapter 5

2. 4 television advertisements, 20 radio, and 10 newspaper; total audience = 1,160,000
4. Industrial 480, discount 100, marine 0; profit $50,200
6. 400 households with children during the evening
    500 households without children during the day
    100 households without children during the evening; cost = $9800
8. 50 units of product 1
    0 units of product 2
    300 hours Dept. A, 600 hours Dept. B
10.

	Modern Line	Old Line	
1	500	0	
2	300	400	Cost = $3850

12. Bostock to Southwest; Miller to Northwest; total 185
14.

	Mfr.	Purchase	
Base	3750	1250	
Cartridge	5000	0	
Handle	3750	1250	Cost = $11,875

b. Depts. A and B; Add only to A
c. Only 25 hours can be used
16. x_i = number of 10-inch rolls processed by cutting alternative i
    a. $x_1 = 0$, $x_2 = 125$, $x_3 = 500$, $x_4 = 1500$, $x_5 = 0$, $x_6 = 0$, $x_7 = 0$; 2125 rolls with waste of 750 inches
    b. 2500 rolls with no waste; however, $1\frac{1}{2}$ inch size is overproduced by 3000 units
18. a. 5 super, 2 regular, and 3 econotankers
        Total cost $283,000; monthly operating cost $4650
    b. Order all supertankers
20. 20 Betsy Ross, 110 George Washington, profit = $240
22. b. $x_1 = 5$, $x_2 = 7$
24. a. 281.25 units product 1, 87.5 units product 2; profit = $1300
    b. 350 units product 1, 0 units product 2; profit = $1400

Chapter 6

2. a. Jackson—A; Smith—C; Burton—B
    b. 2 days
    c. Ellis
4. Toy—4; Auto parts—1; Housewares—3; Record—2
6. Washington—B; Benson—D; Fredricks—C; Hodson—A
8. Phyllis—C; Linda—A; Marlene—B
10. a. Banks—1; Minta—2; O'Donnel—3
    b. Banks—1; Nash—2; Minta—3
12. Lester to Rossville to Charleston to Madison to Lester

14. 1 to 4 to 3 to 2 to 1
     2 to 1 to 4 to 3 to 2
     3 to 2 to 1 to 4 to 3
     4 to 3 to 2 to 1 to 4
     All 15

Chapter 7

2. Corning–Fairport 100; Corning–Mendon 200; Corning–Penfield 300; Geneva–Fairport 200

4. a. Detroit–Boston 100; St. Louis–Boston 200; St. Louis–Atlanta 100; Denver–Atlanta 100; Denver–Houston 200
    b. Detroit–Boston 100; St. Louis–Atlanta 200; St. Louis–Houston 100; Denver–Atlanta 100; Denver–Boston 200; Denver–Atlanta 100; Denver–Houston 100
    c. Detroit–Atlanta 100; St. Louis–Atlanta 100; St. Louis–Houston 200; Denver–Atlanta 100; Denver–Boston 300

6. Detroit–Boston 100; St. Louis–Boston 200; St. Louis–Houston 100; Denver–Atlanta 200; Denver–Houston 100.

8. a. O_1–D_1 150; O_1–D_2 50; O_1–D_3 50; O_2–D_2 150; O_3–D_3 100
    b. O_1–D_1 50; O_1–D_2 50; O_1–D_3 150; O_2–D_2 150; O_3–D_1 100

10. Clifton Springs–D_2 4000; Clifton Springs–D_4 1000; Danville–D_1 2000; Danville–D_4 1000; dummy–D_2 1000; dummy–D_3 3000

12. a. I–A 300; I–C 1200; II–A 1200; II–dummy 300; III–A 500; III–B 500; 5 set-ups required
    b. I–A 1500; II–C 1200; II–dummy 300; III–A 500; III–B 500; 4 set-ups required

14. b. Denver–St. Paul 10; Denver–dummy 90; Atlanta–Boston 50; Atlanta–Dallas 50; Chicago–Dallas 20; Chicago–Los Angeles 60; Chicago–St. Paul 70
    c. **Prefer Vogel's method; northwest corner rule requires 6 iterations to reach optimality**

Chapter 8

2. b. $x_1 = 1.43, x_2 = 4.29$; its value is 41.47
        $x_1 = 1, x_2 = 4$; its value is 37
    c. $x_1 = 0, x_2 = 5$; its value is 40

4. a. $x_1 = 3, x_2 = 0$; its value is 30
        Lower bound = 30, upper bound is 36.7 (actually an upper bound of 36)
    b. $x_1 = 3, x_2 = 2$; its value is 30
    c. LP relaxation: $x_1 = 0, x_2 = 5.71$; its value is 34.26
        Rounding down: $x_1 = 0, x_2 = 5$ with value 30
        Upper bound = 34.26, lower bound = 30
        Optimal integer: $x_1 = 0, x_2 = 5$; its value is 30

6. b. $x_1 = 1.96, x_2 = 5.48$; its value is 7.44
        Upper bound = 7.44, lower bound = 6.96
    c. $x_1 = 1.29, x_2 = 6$; its value is 7.29

8. $x_1 = x_2 = x_3 = 1$ and $x_4 = 0$ with a value of $140,000

12. a. $x_4 \leq x_1$
        $x_4 \leq x_3$
    b. $x_4 \leq x_1$
        $x_4 \leq x_3$
        $x_4 \geq x_1 + x_3 - 1$

   c. $x_1 + x_3 + x_5 + x_6 = 2$
   d. $x_3 - x_5 = 0$
   e. $x_1 + x_4 = 1$

Chapter 9

6. a.

Activity	Expected Time	Variance
A	5.00	0.11
B	9.00	0.11
C	8.00	0.44
D	8.83	0.25
E	7.17	0.25
F	6.00	0.11

   b. Expected project completion time = 23.83, variance = 0.47

8. a. A–D–F–G
   b. 1.5 days
   c. Expected time = 29.5 days, variance = 2.36
   d. 0.6255

10. b. A–B–G–H–I; 15 weeks
    d. 17.38 ahead

12. b. 25 weeks: 0.3121
         30 weeks: 0.9756

16.

Activity	Cost /Week
A	15
B	8
C	1
D	20
E	2
F	1
G	20
H	5
I	2
J	1

18. b. 6% overrun; followup desired on activity D

20. Corrective action desired:
     Activity E—one week behind
     Activity F—$3000 cost overrun

Chapter 10

2.

Node	Shortest Route from Node 7
1	7–6–5–3–1
2	7–4–2
3	7–6–5–3
4	7–4
5	7–6–5
6	7–6

4. 1–4–5–6–8

6.

Node	Shortest Route from Node C
1	C–1
2	C–2
3	C–3
4	C–4
5	C–3–5
6	C–3–6
7	C–3–8–7
8	C–3–8
9	C–4–10–9
10	C–4–10

8.

Branch	Flow
1–2	3
1–3	5
1–4	3
2–5	4
3–4	3
3–6	2
4–2	1
4–5	2
5–6	6

10. Current max flow = 6000; 2000 units/hour for 3–4

12. 1–2, 2–5, 5–6, 6–3, 6–8, 3–4, 8–7; length = 29

Chapter 11

2. a. d_2 or d_3

b. d_1

c. d_2

4. Sell the rights; EVPI = 25

6. d_2

8. b. Purchase blade attachment

c. Same as (b)

d. 2150

10. Expected value criterion—d_1; however, d_2 may be preferred

12. b. d_3

c. EVPI = \$600

14. b. d_2–EMV(d_2) = 206.25

16. $P(s_1 | I) = 0.19, P(s_2 | I) = 0.24, P(s_3 | I) = 0.57$

18. a. $P(I_1) = 0.56, P(I_2) = 0.44$

b. 0.57, 0.43, 0.18, 0.82

c. If I_1–d_2, if I_2–d_1, EMV = 292

20. b. If I_1–d_1, if I_2–d_2, EMV = \$101.5

c. EVSI = \$1500, sell for \$100,000

22. If I–d_1, if $\bar{I}$–d_3

24. a. 0.355

b. If favorable–d_1, if unfavorable–d_2

c. \$3710

d. 41.2%

26. a. Do not fund
    b. Do not hire the consultants
28. a. $I_1-d_2, I_2-d_2, I_3-d_2$
    b. 0
    c. 0
30. a. $P(I|s_1) = 0.0000, P(I|s_2) = 0.048, P(I|s_3) = 0.092, P(I|s_4) = 0.133$
    b. 0.000, 0.159, 0.488, 0.353
    c. 100% inspect

Chapter 12

4. 240
6. a. 16
    b. $2106
    c. 15/year, every 3–4 weeks
8. 12; 5/year; $225,200
10. a. 1789
    b. 1333
    c. 894
    d. 827
        $Q^* = 800$
12. 4500, 9 days
14. 136
16. 67, 27
18. $Q = 144$
20. 3000, 1500, 500
22. 2000, 500, 0

Chapter 13

2. a. 14
    b. 18
    c. 2 ($10/year), 6 ($30/year)
4. a. 32
    b. $r = 21; 0.21$
    c. 15, $15
6. Yes, $Q = 1000$ ($5000)
8. 19
10. a. 398
    b. 0.70
    c. 489, 0.35
12. a. 475
    b. 0.60
    c. 604
    d. $15

Chapter 14

2. a. 0 – 0.12, 1 – 0.24, 2 – 0.37, 3 – 0.19, 4 – 0.08
4. a. 0 – 0.04, 1 – 0.10, 2 – 0.16, 3 – 0.44, 4 – 0.20, 5 – 0.06

6. Number served = 3, total profit = \$3.75, average profit = \$1.25, number lost = 0
14. Average costs: holding – 181.67, order – 12.50, shortage – 0, total – 185.83

Chapter 15

2. a. 6/hour
   b. 39.35%
   c. 63.21%
   d. 4.98%
4. a. 0.833
   b. 0.167
   c. ½ hour
   d. 4.167
6. a. ½ day
   b. ⅜ day
   c. Yes
8. a. 0.54
   b. 0.14
10. Two-channel system: $P_W = 0.644$
    Three-channel system: $P_W = 0.237$
12. Use the one-channel, two-person system
14. $P_0 = 0.4118$; $L = 1.01$; $W_q = 1.08$ min; it appears acceptable
16. a. ¹⁄₁₀
    b. 24 seconds
    c. ⁶⁄₁₀
    d. Excellent
18. 0.3410

Chapter 16

2. a. 1 – 4 – 6 – 9 – 10
   b. 4 – 6 – 9 – 10
4. a. Set up a stage for each possible length of the log
   b. Create a stage for every length
6. 200 – 3, 200 – 2, 100 – 1 (\$2900)
8. a. $d_1 = 200$, $d_2 = 300$, $d_3 = 500$
   b. Same as part a
10. 800°F catalyst C_2, separator S_1, weekly profit = \$4470

Chapter 17

2. b. $\pi_1 = 0.5$, $\pi_2 = 0.5$
   c. $\pi_1 = 0.6$, $\pi_2 = 0.4$
4. a. $\pi_1 = 0.92$, $\pi_2 = 0.08$
   b. \$85
6. a. MDA
   b. $\pi_1 = ⅓$, $\pi_2 = ⅔$
8. 3 – 1 (0.59), 4 – 1 (0.52)
10. 1420 will be lost

Chapter 18

2.   a. $^{40}/_9$
     b.   4
4.   4 ($540)
6.   a. $20
     b. $-x^2 + 20x - 20$
     c.   10
8. $x_1 = 0, x_2 = 2$ is a saddle point
     $x_1 = 2, x_2 = -2$ is a local minimum
     $x_1 = -2, x_2 = -2$ is a local minimum
10. $x_1 = 6, x_2 = 3$ ($40,000 earnings)
12.   Provides maximum solution
14. $x_1 = \dfrac{4}{\sqrt{34/5}}, \quad x_2 = \dfrac{3}{\sqrt{34/5}}$
16. $x_1 = {}^{36}/_{13}, x_2 = {}^2/_{13}$

References
and
Bibliography

The Role and Nature of Management Science (Chapter 1)

Churchman, C. W., R. L. Ackoff, and E. L. Arnoff, *Introduction to Operations Research,* New York, John Wiley & Sons, 1957.

Gaither, N., "The Adoption of Operations Research Techniques by Manufacturing Organizations," *Decision Sciences,* Vol. 6, No. 4, 1975, pp. 797–813.

Grayson, C. J., Jr., "Management Science and Business Practice," *Harvard Business Review,* Vol. 51, 1973, pp. 41–48.

Hillier, F., and G. J. Lieberman, *Introduction to Operations Research,* 3rd ed., San Francisco, Holden-Day, 1980.

Ledbetter, W. and J. Cox, "Are OR Techniques Being Used?," *Industrial Engineering,* Vol. 9, 1977, pp. 19–21.

Radnor, M., and R. D. Neal, "The Progress of Management Science Activities in Large U.S. Industrial Corporations," *Operations Research* 21 (1973): 427–450.

Shannon, R. E., Long, S. S., and B. P. Buckles, "Operations Research Methodologies in Industrial Engineering: A Survey," *AIIE Transactions,* Vol. 12, No. 4, 1980, pp. 364–367.

Turban, E., "A Sample Survey of Operations Research Activities at the Corporate Level," *Operations Research,* Vol. 20, 1972, pp. 708–721.

Linear Programming, Goal Programming, Transportation, and Assignment Problems (Chapters 2–7)

Anderson, D. R., D. J. Sweeney, and T. A. Williams, *Linear Programming for Decision Making,* St. Paul, West Publishing, 1974.

Bazarra, M. S., and J. J. Jarvis, *Linear Programming and Network Flows,* New York, John Wiley & Sons, 1977.

Charnes, A., and W. W. Cooper, *Management Models and Industrial Applications of Linear Programming,* New York, John Wiley & Sons, 1961.

Charnes, A., W. W. Cooper, J. K. DeVoe, D. B. Learner, and W. Remecke, "A Goal Programming Model for Media Planning," *Management Science,* Vol. 14, No. 8, April 1968, pp. B423–B430.

Daellenbach, Hans G., and J. Bell, *User's Guide to Linear Programming,* Englewood Cliffs, N.J., Prentice-Hall, 1970.

Dantzig, G. B., *Linear Programming and Extensions,* Princeton, N.J., Princeton University Press, 1963.

Gass, S., *Linear Programming,* 4th ed., New York, McGraw-Hill, 1975.

Hillier, F., and G. J. Lieberman, *Introduction to Operations Research,* 3rd ed., San Francisco, Holden-Day, 1980.

Ijiri, Y., *Management Goals and Accounting for Control,* Chicago, Rand-McNally, 1965.

Lee, S. M., *Goal Programming for Decision Analysis,* Philadelphia, Auerback, 1972.

Phillips, D. T., A. Ravindran, and J. J. Solberg, *Operations Research: Principles and Practice,* New York, John Wiley & Sons, 1976.

Wagner, H., *Principles of Operations Research with Applications to Managerial Decisions,* 2nd ed., Englewood Cliffs, N.J., Prentice-Hall, 1975.

Integer Linear Programming (Chapter 8)

Garfinkel, R. S., and G. L. Nemhauser, *Integer Programming,* New York, John Wiley & Sons, 1972.

Plane, D. R., and C. McMillan, *Discrete Optimization,* Englewood Cliffs, N.J., Prentice-Hall, 1971.

Salkin, H. M., *Integer Programming,* Reading, Mass., Addison-Wesley, 1975.

Zionts, Stanley, *Linear and Integer Programming,* Englewood Cliffs, N.J., Prentice-Hall, 1974.

PERT/CPM (Chapter 9)

Evarts, H. F., *Introduction to PERT,* Boston, Allyn & Bacon, 1964.

Moder, J. J., and C. R. Phillips, *Project Management with CPM and PERT,* 2nd ed., New York, Van Nostrand, 1970.

Wagner, H., *Principles of Operations Research with Applications to Managerial Decisions,* 2nd ed., Englewood Cliffs, N.J., Prentice-Hall, 1975.

Wiest, J., and F. Levy, *Management Guide to PERT-CPM,* 2nd ed., Englewood Cliffs, N.J., Prentice-Hall, 1977.

Network Models (Chapter 10)

Bazarra, M. S., and J. J. Jarvis, *Linear Programming and Network Flows,* New York, John Wiley & Sons, 1977.

Ford, L. R., and D. R. Fulkerson, *Flows and Networks,* Princeton, N.J., Princeton University Press, 1962.

Minieka, Edward, *Optimization Algorithms for Networks and Graphs,* New York, Marcel Dekker, 1978.

Decision Theory (Chapter 11)

Chernoff, H., and L. E. Moses, *Elementary Decision Theory,* New York, John Wiley & Sons, 1959.

Raiffa, H., *Decision Analysis,* Reading, Mass., Addison-Wesley, 1968.

Schlaifer, R., *Analysis of Decisions under Uncertainty,* New York, McGraw-Hill, 1969.

Winkler, R. L., *An Introduction to Bayesian Inference and Decision,* New York, Holt, Rinehart & Winston, 1972.

Winkler, R. L., and W. L. Hays, *Statistics: Probability, Inference and Decision,* 2nd ed., New York, Holt, Rinehart & Winston, 1975.

Inventory Models (Chapters 12 and 13)

Buffa, E. S. and W. Taubert, *Production-Inventory Systems: Planning and Control,* 3rd ed., Homewood, Ill., Richard D. Irwin, 1979.

Greene, J. H., *Production and Inventory Control Handbook,* New York, McGraw-Hill, 1970.

Hadley, G., and T. M. Whitin, *Analysis of Inventory Systems,* Englewood Cliffs, N.J., Prentice-Hall, 1963.

Hillier, F., and G. J. Lieberman, *Introduction to Operations Research,* 3rd ed., San Francisco, Holden-Day, 1980.

Naddor, E., *Inventory Systems,* New York, John Wiley & Sons, 1966.

Orlicky, J., *Material Requirements Planning,* New York, McGraw-Hill, 1975.

Plossl, G. W., *Manufacturing Control: The Last Frontier for Profits,* Reston, Va., Reston, 1973.

Starr, M., and D. Miller, *Inventory Control: Theory and Practice,* Englewood Cliffs, N.J., Prentice-Hall, 1962.

Stockton, R. S., *Basic Inventory Systems: Concepts and Analysis,* Boston, Allyn & Bacon, 1965.

Wagner, H., *Principles of Operations Research with Applications to Managerial Decisions,* 3rd ed., Englewood Cliffs, N.J., Prentice-Hall, 1975.

Wight, O. W., *Production and Inventory Management in the Computer Age,* Boston, Cahners Books, 1974.

Computer Simulation (Chapter 14)

Emshoff, J. R., and R. L. Sisson, *Design and Use of Computer Simulation Models,* New York, MacMillan, 1970.

Fishman, George S., *Principles of Discrete Event Simulation,* New York, John Wiley & Sons, 1978.

Greenberg, S., *GPSS Primer,* New York, John Wiley & Sons, 1972.

Maisel, H., and G. Gnugnoli, *Simulation of Discrete Stochastic Systems,* Chicago, SRA, 1972.

Naylor, T. H., *Computer Simulation Experiments with Models of Economic Systems,* New York, John Wiley & Sons, 1971.

Naylor, T. H., J. L. Balintfy, D. S. Burdick, and K. Chu, *Computer Simulation Techniques,* New York, John Wiley & Sons, 1968.

Schmidt, J. W., and R. E. Taylor, *Simulation and Analysis of Industrial Systems,* Homewood, Ill., Richard D. Irwin, 1970.

Schriber, T. J., *Simulation Using GPSS,* New York, John Wiley & Sons, 1974.

Waiting Lines (Chapter 15)

Bhat, U. N., *Elements of Applied Stochastic Processes,* New York, John Wiley & Sons, 1972.

Cooper, R. B., *Introduction to Queueing Theory,* New York, Macmillan, 1972.

Cox, D. R., and W. L. Smith, *Queues,* New York, John Wiley & Sons, 1965.

Gross, D., and C. M. Harris, *Fundamentals of Queueing Theory,* New York, John Wiley & Sons, 1974.

Hillier, F. and G. J. Lieberman, *Introduction to Operations Research,* 3rd ed., San Francisco, Holden-Day, 1980.

Newell, G. F., *Applications of Queueing Theory,* London, Chapman & Hall, Ltd., 1971.

Dynamic Programming (Chapter 16)

Bellman, R., *Dynamic Programming,* Princeton, N.J., Princeton University Press, 1957.

Dreyfus, S., *Dynamic Programming and the Calculus of Variations,* New York, Academic Press, 1965.

Dreyfus, S., and A. M. Law, *The Art and Theory of Dynamic Programming,* New York, Academic, 1977.

Hillier, F. and G. J. Lieberman, *Introduction to Operations Research,* 3rd ed., San Francisco, Holden-Day, 1980.

Nemhauser, G. L., *Introduction to Dynamic Programming*, New York, John Wiley & Sons, 1967.

Markov Processes (Chapter 17)

Derman, C., *Finite State Markovian Decision Processes*, New York, Academic Press, 1970.

Howard, R. A., *Dynamic Programming and Markov Processes*, Cambridge, Mass., M.I.T. Press, 1960.

Kemeny, J. G. and J. L. Snell, *Finite Markov Chains*, Englewood Cliffs, N.J., Prentice-Hall, 1960.

Phillips, D. T., A. Ravindran, and J. J. Solberg, *Operations Research: Principles and Practice*, New York, John Wiley & Sons, 1976.

Ross, S. M., *Applied Probability Models with Optimization Applications*, San Francisco, Holden-Day, 1970.

Calculus Based Solution Procedures (Chapter 18)

Beightler, C. S., D. T. Phillips, and D. Wilde, *Foundations of Optimization*, 2nd ed., Englewood Cliffs, N.J., Prentice-Hall, 1979.

Cooper, L., and D. Steinberg, *Introduction to Methods of Optimization*, Philadelphia, W. B. Saunders, 1970.

Gottfried, B. S., and J. Weisman, *Introduction to Optimization Theory*, Englewood Cliffs, N.J., Prentice-Hall, 1973.

Himmelblau, D. M., *Applied Nonlinear Programming*, New York, McGraw-Hill, 1972.

Luenberger, D. G., *Introduction to Linear and Nonlinear Programming*, Reading, Mass., Addison-Wesley, 1973.

Management Science and Decision Support Systems (Chapter 19)

Alter, Steven, *Decision Support Systems: Current Practice and Continuing Challenges*, Reading, Mass., Addison-Wesley, 1980.

Davis, Gordon B., *Management Information Systems: Conceptual Foundations, Structure and Development*, New York, McGraw-Hill, 1974.

Donovan, J. J., "Database System Approach to Management Decision Support," *ACM Transactions on Database Systems*, Vol. 1, No. 4, December 1976, pp. 344–369.

Gerrity, T. P., Jr., "The Design of Man-Machine Decision Systems: An Application to Portfolio Management," *Sloan Management Review*, Vol. 12, No. 2, 1971, pp. 59–75.

Keen, Peter G.W., and Scott Morton, Michael S., *Decision Support Systems: An Organizational Perspective,* Reading, Mass., Addison-Wesley, 1978.

Moore, Jeffery H., and Chang, Michael G., "Design of Decision Support Systems," *Data Base,* September/November 1980, pp. 8–14.

Scott, Jim, "The Management Science Opportunity: A Systems Development Management Viewpoint," presentation at the Society for Management Information Systems Annual Conference in Washington, D.C., September 1978.

Index